THE IDEA OF
SOCIAL STRUCTURE

Papers in Honor of
Robert K. Merton

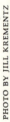

THE IDEA OF SOCIAL STRUCTURE

Papers in Honor of Robert K. Merton

EDITED BY

LEWIS A. COSER

STATE UNIVERSITY OF NEW YORK
AT STONY BROOK

HARCOURT BRACE JOVANOVICH
NEW YORK   CHICAGO   SAN FRANCISCO   ATLANTA

PREFACE

Editors are often tempted to write a wordy prologue in order to explain and justify their efforts. I shall resist that temptation and let the readers of this book make their own judgments. All that seems necessary are a few words to explain the way *The Idea of Social Structure* came into existence.

When a few of Robert K. Merton's friends and former students realized, hard as it was to believe, that he would reach the age of sixty-five in a few years, they thought about how to celebrate the event and honor the man. To publish a *Festschrift* seemed an appropriate way to express our gratitude and to register our indebtedness. I was pleased to be asked to become the editor. Our sampling of some earlier *Festschriften* indicated that those that had best withstood the test of time consisted of work written specifically for the occasion rather than of miscellaneous contributions. I resolved to ask all but a few of those whom I approached to relate their contributions, in any way they judged appropriate, to the work of the man we wished to honor. Most of the contributors agreed to take up a topic that I had suggested to them, and most of them, I am happy to report, stayed with that topic. If the contributions offered here range over a very large sociological territory, this is but a tribute to Robert K. Merton's own breadth of vision and thought.

I am most grateful to all those who have joined me in this venture. I speak for all of them when I say that whatever effort went into writing this volume discharges only a small fraction of the debt we owe, individually and as part of the sociological collectivity, to the work of Robert K. Merton. We hope that it will give pleasure to the man to be honored, but not to him alone.

LEWIS A. COSER

v

CONTENTS

CONTENTS

ON THE SHOULDERS OF MERTON

CONTENTS

THE IDEA OF
SOCIAL STRUCTURE

Papers in Honor of
Robert K. Merton

ROBERT K. MERTON
THE MAN
AND THE WORK

Merton and the Contemporary Mind

An Affectionate Dialogue

LEWIS A. COSER AND ROBERT NISBET

Robert Nisbet. Bob Merton's intellectual roots are in the Depression thirties. I've thought for some time now that before the century is out we're going to find that decade among the more vital and creative periods in American history. We can paraphrase Dickens and call it the best of times and the worst of times. What was bad about it needs no recapitulation here, nor the slightest nostalgia. What was good about the decade, at least as far as the sciences are concerned, seems to me to have sprung in the first instance from the great influence on American thought of European perspectives. In large degree, of course, these were brought directly by intellectual refugees from Hitler's Germany, though there were other, less direct and dramatic channels. Merton's mind is rooted in American soil—no question about that when one looks at the overall character of his work—but he was certainly one of the first social scientists in this country to begin to use European perspectives in his approach to problems.

Lewis A. Coser. I fully agree. Yet we may perhaps speculate why it was that this European perspective entered into Merton's way of thinking in a more "organic" way than was the case with most of his predecessors. A pilgrimage to Europe or attendance at European universities had, of course, been quite common for American academics long before Merton's days.

Lewis A. Coser is Distinguished Professor of Sociology at the State University
of New York at Stony Brook.
Robert Nisbet is Albert Schweitzer Professor in the Humanities
at Columbia University.

Men like W. l. Thomas and Robert Park in the preceding generation, and William Graham Sumner or William James somewhat earlier, had also been thoroughly acquainted with European thought. Yet one has the impression that in Merton's case there was a greater openness to this influence, that he assimilated European thought patterns more thoroughly than most of his predecessors. Could it be that Merton, having come from the slums of Philadelphia, and having done his undergraduate work at a city university, was less hampered by the genteel assumptions of American upper-class culture?

R.N. Do you mean that being a "stranger" in traditional American culture made him more open to outside influences?

L.C. Yes. When he came to Harvard he was, to be sure, not as much of a stranger to the academic proprieties as Veblen had been. But J. G. Crowther's description of him in those days gives the distinct impression of the outsider in academia. "He seemed to have a subtler cultural sense than Harvard men in general," wrote Crowther. "This was all the more conspicuous because he wore an old and rather bucolic suit, the air of which contrasted with the fineness of his mind." Could it be that in his fierce desire to make a mark in the academic world, and unhampered by some of the cultural baggage of many of his predecessors, he was more open to new winds of doctrine that blew in from the other side of the Atlantic? It seems to me that to be among the New Men who had crashed the gates of the academy in the thirties carried with it many burdens that had been spared the sons of clergymen and other genteel professionals of preceding generations. But it also allowed a receptivity to the lure of what was most exciting in the novel ideas of European thinkers, an openness of vision that was denied to the more settled denizens of the American cultural scene. Do you think that there is something to these speculations?

R.N. There's a great deal! It is impossible to miss in Merton's work from the very beginning—starting with his remarkable Ph.D. dissertation, *Science, Technology, and Puritanism in Seventeenth-Century England*—a knowledge of and sensitivity to European insights that were exceedingly uncommon in this country until the late 1940s. He once told me that if there had been nothing else to get from Sorokin's courses at Harvard (and, of course, there was much else) there were the massive reading lists, heavily oriented toward European works.

L.C. It goes without saying that Bob set himself to read everything on the lists.

R.N. Indeed! And it would be difficult for any young mind in sociology today to realize how separated this country was for a long time from the European sociologists, lasting until the middle of the 1930s. American isolationism was as much a fact in sociology as in foreign policy from about World War I until World War II. Merton had a great deal to do, as did Talcott Parsons, with counteracting this isolation. And just as Parsons made the Europeans relevant to a grand theory, Merton made them relevant to a middle-range theory and also to some impeccably empirical researches. It wouldn't have been enough simply to have written descriptively and analytically about Weber, Durkheim, and the other Europeans. What was necessary

4

was to show their ideas as vital, even indispensable elements of sociological research and theory. Merton did this superbly, starting, as I said, with his Ph.D. dissertation, working on through his theories of function, structure, anomie, bureaucracy, and so on.

L.C. This is where the influence of Sorokin may have been especially important. Sorokin, to be sure, had a propensity to large-scale theorizing, and his mind had an incurably speculative bent. Yet these tendencies were counterbalanced by an equally pronounced inclination toward empirical research and statistical inquiries. Most of his students seem to have molded themselves after either the one or the other side of Sorokin's stance. But Merton set himself the task of emulating both. Yet Sorokin was, of course, not his only model at Harvard. In fact, one has the impression that Harvard teachers in the thirties provided a very complex role-set for their eager students. At times, the student probably had to shield himself, to use Merton's later conceptualization, from observability by some of his professorial role partners in order fully to profit from intellectual intercourse with others. The winds of doctrine that converged at Harvard were many, and it required a good deal of mental agility to profit from all of them while not becoming entirely beholden to any.

R.N. I can't help thinking that a good deal that lies in Merton's work wouldn't exist, or would certainly be shaped very differently, if it hadn't been for the relation—a kind of counterpoint relation, wouldn't you say?—he's had with Talcott Parsons. The minds of the two are quite different, as is evident enough, and their characteristic kinds of work are assuredly different. Even so, I'm tempted to say that for both Merton and Parsons if the other hadn't existed he would probably have had to be created.

L.C. You are so right! When one compares their work, one is struck as much by the difference in their styles of thought as by the communality of many of their fundamental assumptions. There is a Calvinist earnestness to Parsons' frame of mind that is alien to Merton's playful intellect. Parsons is above all concerned to convey an urgent message engraved on rough-hewn tables. Merton, much like Simmel before him, delights in the elegant display of ideas. One has the impression that often, for Merton, systematization is undertaken for the sake of elegance; there is an esthetic quality to it that is utterly missing in Parsons.

R.N. Would you say, as Ortega y Gasset said of Simmel, that he plays with ideas, like a squirrel might play with nuts?

L.C. Not really. Simmel's was a studied disorderliness of method; Merton always strives to establish paradigms. Yet, while Parsons' world has a kind of unitary solidity that is to be fixed in the sociologist's mind, Merton's world is composed of multiple ambiguities, of conflicting and contradictory demands and requirements that need to be articulated and made accessible by the sociologist. For Parsons, disorder is only a special case of order; for Merton, the order that is achieved is always precarious, it is a fragile and unstable victory over the ever present threats of disorder. There is a great deal of basic affinity between Adam Smith's patterns of thought in this respect and those of Parsons, whereas Merton belongs more to the company of Lord Keynes.

5

Parsons *knows* that the sons of light will prevail against the forces of darkness; Merton only permits himself some hope that they will.

R.N. Yes! Somewhere, probably in a letter I had from you, you compared Parsons and Merton to Sir Isaiah Berlin's hedgehog and fox, with Parsons the hedgehog and Merton the fox. I liked that. Both types have been absolutely vital, of course, to Western social thought. I wish you would expand a little on the two likenesses.

L.C. The essential point, which I deal with at some length in another essay, seems to be, as a Greek poet whom Sir Isaiah quotes puts it, "The fox knows many things, but the hedgehog knows one big thing." Despite the great diversity of topics that Parsons has dealt with, they all seem to be related to one central message. Merton, in contrast, juggles with many diverse ideas, much as in his adolescence, as a semipro magician, he kept his youthful audience enthralled by virtuoso displays of the conjurer's art. In fact, might this have been a kind of unwitting anticipatory socialization?

R.N. Who knows! There certainly is continuity in Merton's development. Moreover, in this case the hedgehog and the fox are complementary, if I may be permitted to use Parsons' notion. Much the same thing can be said about Harvard and Columbia during the period especially of the 1940s and 1950s in American sociology. A kind of counterpoint, or symbiotic relation, seems to me, as I look back, to have existed there as well as with respect to Parsons and Merton personally. What we had, starting in the late 1930s in this country, was a distinct renaissance in sociology. I take nothing whatever away from earlier centers such as Chicago and Michigan when I say that Harvard and Columbia were in a sense the Venice and Florence of the sociological renaissance. I'm not sure which was Venice and which was Florence, but it doesn't matter. The point is, we had a couple of extremely creative centers, relatively small in size, that drew an impressive number of talented minds which, when they got there, achieved heights of excellence they just might not have achieved elsewhere.

L.C. Your Venice/Florence analogy is most apt. I am not sure either which was which. But if the art historians are right in stressing that Venetian painting excelled by its dazzling display of color whereas Florence was the home of austere structural arrangement and precise elaboration of perspective, then I would say that Columbia was Venice and Harvard Florence.

R.N. Probably so. I hadn't thought of it in quite that way. The parallels make sense to me in those terms. What fascinates me about Harvard sociology in the 1930s is the utter disproportion between reputation and breadth and depth of the department, on the one hand, and the extraordinary results, on the other. Harvard produced Merton and his contemporaries in a department that by all ordinary criteria was a weak department of sociology in the 1930s. After all, it had just been established when Merton went up.

L.C. There were Sorokin and Zimmerman, I believe. Parsons was then, if I heard it correctly, an assistant professor of economics, although his interest in Weber and in sociology had already taken shape.

R.N. Even so, by the standards of the day, Harvard was a weak department compared to, say, a Wisconsin, Michigan, Chicago, or North Carolina.

But what a stream of first-rate minds came forth from the Harvard department: Merton, Davis, Williams, Wilson, Blackwell, Moore, among others, all of whom made a lasting impact on sociology beginning almost from the moment of their dissertations. And from then until now Parsons and Merton have been, so to speak, the two poles of sociological theory. I suppose it was a case of unusually gifted minds coming to a historic and distinguished university from, in many of those instances, small, impoverished, or very distant origins.

L.C. Yes, they were strangers to each other but ready to become intellectually rooted, ready for intellectual communality.

R.N. They were stimulated by great scholars, irrespective of field, lifted by the very exposure to Harvard tradition and, after that, doing a lot of rubbing of shoulders among themselves. One of the group, I can't remember which one, once told me: "We did a lot of educating of each other just by being around each other while we were working." That makes sense whether one is talking about universities or great cities.

L.C. Much the same was, of course, true for Merton's Columbia students after he moved there in the forties. Yet there was a subtle difference between Harvard and Columbia. Most of Merton's students—Gouldner, the Blaus, Selznick, Lipset, the Rossis, the Cosers, Keller, and many others—tended to be more politically engaged than the Harvard students of the thirties. The New Deal "revolution" already belonged to the past, yet Merton had been profoundly influenced by it. These young, and predominantly Jewish, intellectuals dreamed of pushing the frontiers of American politics further toward the Left. Robert Lynd, and later C. Wright Mills, encouraged them in this respect. Merton on his part dazzled them with his profound knowledge of the Marxian canon, while attempting to defuse their ideological propensities by stressing that sociological ideas of very different ideological origins can fruitfully be combined in an effort to build systematic theories of the middle range, which in turn could inform policy-making. Theoretical gold, he often repeated, could be found in the most unlikely ideological quarries. And there was, of course, the close intellectual companionship of Lazarsfeld and Merton. At first blush this combination of European positivistic empiricism and American functionalist theory seemed most unlikely. Yet it worked. Merton's students tended to be held back from undue flights of fancy by Lazarsfeld's earthy and rigorous methodological style, and Lazarsfeld's students, in their turn, were reminded that the facts never speak for themselves.

R.N. I don't think many people realize that Bob had his due share of influence in the scene at Berkeley just after World War II as far as sociology was concerned. As you probably know, Berkeley had no sociology in the strict sense prior to about 1947, when three or four of us, all young, were trying to get something started. Bob was invited out to teach summer session in 1948. Why he accepted, I don't know; the climate, probably. Berkeley was not generally strong in the social sciences at that time—its big burst came in the next decade. Anyhow, as I remember vividly, Bob's two courses—one, his celebrated course on social structure; the other on the city, as I recall—drew many graduate students, most of them auditors, from the prestige departments

7

on the campus: economics and political science foremost, but also anthropology. And such were the stimulation and luster of those courses that our infant department's reputation was begun if not made during the year following. It was also during that summer, at a lunch I arranged, that Bob was able to get over the importance of a research center to a group of distinguished Berkeley faculty. That too bore fruit later.

L.C. It must have been a joy to have been alive in Berkeley in those days. As for myself, I first sat in Merton's classes at Columbia at roughly the same time. (You will recall that we too first met at Columbia at that time when I took a summer course with you there.) What impressed me most in Merton, even more than his writings, was his masterful lecturing. I had previously been exposed to a number of eminent sociologists at the Sorbonne. As you know, French academicians tend to be at least as "expressive" in their delivery as they are "instrumental," all the while maintaining what they proudly call "clarté française." Although I had been spoiled that way, I was utterly bowled over by Merton's lectures. He hardly ever consulted his notes, yet his sentences built into paragraphs and his paragraphs into blocks of ideas with a precision and logical clarity that amazed me no end. Each lecture seemed a publishable and finished work of art. He was a master at persuasion. Once caught in his systematically woven net of ideas, it was most difficult to escape from his logic.

R.N. Yes, Merton has a way of letting his students participate in his discoveries; he leads them on to "aha" experiences.

L.C. Indeed, he did not limit himself to the presentation of abstract conceptualizations. His lectures abounded in factual information, culled, as the case may be, from previous empirical investigations or ongoing research. But each datum was embedded in a conceptual framework, thus providing theoretical relevance, and frequently implicit value relevance as well. When Bob Lynd lectured next door, he used to submerge his listeners in an avalanche of factual information, which all seemed to him of equal importance; it was a kind of democracy of facts. With Merton, to the contrary, a fact passed muster only if and when it helped point to something beyond it. To him, there was a severely graded hierarchy of facts from the useless to the highly significant.

R.N. Somewhere—I think in the *New Yorker* profile that was done ten years ago on Bob—Kingsley Davis is quoted as saying of Bob that it is his knack for seeing the ordinary world through extraordinary eyes that is characteristic of him and also of good sociology generally. A marvelous example of that, as you have indicated in your essay on Merton's European sociological roots, is his treatment of anomie. The concept reached us through Durkheim, but what a world of difference between Merton's perceptions of the phenomenon and Durkheim's. I mean, whereas Durkheim had left anomie pretty much in descriptive terms, marking only its rise and fall with overall economic changes in the business cycle, Merton set himself to discovering what the actual *social* processes are that result in anomie. Without Durkheim, admittedly, no Typology of Modes of Individual Adaptation; but without Merton I'm inclined to think we would still be in the suburbs of the matter.

L.C. Yes, and an important aspect of this ability to build extraordinary insights from the common clay of the quotidian empirical world is Merton's ability to coin new sociological terms and categories. Naming is creating, the Word is the beginning of all things; hence, the sociological world assumed a different shape when Role-Set, Serendipity, Matthew Effect, the Self-Fulfilling Prophecy, and *tutti quanti* began to become familiar features of the furniture of the sociological mind. Herbert Butterfield, the eminent historian, once wrote that "of all forms of mental activity the most difficult to induce . . . is the art of handling the same bundle of data as before, but placing them in a new system of relations with one another and giving them a different framework, all of which virtually means putting on a different thinking-cap for the moment." This is what Merton has done over and over again. Empiricism uninformed by theory always gets stuck on the skin of things; Merton's conceptual naming allows one to penetrate beneath that skin. He is our foremost manufacturer of sociological thinking caps.

R.N. Very true, but also of sociological spectacles—including microscopes and telescopes! I mean only that Merton has never been in danger of forgetting that what is primary for the sociologist is what's *out there,* not what can be dredged up from internal consciousness or awareness of one's own awareness. Goethe says somewhere in his *Conversations with Eckermann:* "Epochs which are regressive and in the process of dissolution are always subjective, whereas the trend in all progressive epochs is objective." I find it reassuring that at a time when a great deal of American sociology was showing signs of the subjectivism that was to hit it like a tidal wave in the 1960s, Merton returned to the history and sociology of science with results which are by now historic. There has always been a strong element of objectivism in Merton's mind even when, as in an analysis of friendship he did with Lazarsfeld years ago, there was, as there had to be, a good deal of digging into the nature of personality. For all of his interest in ideas, feelings, and what you so well call the ambiguities of thought and action, Merton is much more the Baconian—modified, to be sure—than the Cartesian. I think Bob would be much more likely to say *Video: ergo sum* than *Cogito: ergo sum.* I have a feeling, though it may be my congenital optimism, that we are now shaking off our skins the consciousness-sociology of the 1960s, and it's nice to know that Merton's middle-range theories will be around, along with those of Weber and Durkheim and a few other classic minds, to provide good weather.

L.C. There are probably equally pronounced Cartesian and Baconian aspects to Bob's thought. His finely honed mind has a Cartesian rigor in logical deduction, but it also has a Baconian openness to all the multiple facets of objective phenomena "out there."

R.N. I don't think younger sociologists today have much if any appreciation of how very low on the American academic totem pole sociology ranked until just after World War II. Heaven knows, this country has had some first-rate sociologists from the beginning of the century on: Sumner, Small, Cooley, Thomas, among others, all creative minds in sociology, not to mention Mead in philosophy and social psychology. These minds notwith-

9

standing, I have a very vivid recollection to this moment of how generally disparaged sociology as a field was through the 1930s. A number of scholars just after the war did a lot, it seems to me, to change that situation profoundly. There was David Riesman's *Lonely Crowd,* which perhaps did most to get sociological insights over to the humanists. There was Parsons' work at Harvard. And, not to be forgotten, there was C. Wright Mills. I'm inclined to think that Merton did the most, though, to make the other social sciences and also history aware for the first time of the uses of sociology and thus to raise us up somewhat on the totem pole and to bring to sociology for a good while some of the brightest young minds that might otherwise have chosen one of the other social sciences.

L.C. Yes, indeed. It seems to me that what a truly great teacher manages to convey to students is excitement about the new world of ideas that he opens to them. This is what Robert Park managed to do at Chicago when he stimulated their sociological imagination by pointing to the exciting hypotheses that could be tested in that grand laboratory that was the city of Chicago. That was what Parsons did at Harvard when he kindled in the minds of his eager students the quest for fitting a welter of hitherto unconnected observations into the rigorous framework of systematic structural-functional theory. This is what Merton did when he taught his students the uses of middle-range theory as a way of avoiding the twin temptations of "raw empiricism" and grand theorizing. Middle-range theory was presented as a way of mapping the social world. What he conveyed may be somewhat comparable to the excitement of a geographer of old who had succeeded in filling in some of the blank spaces on the existing map, so that a precise outline emerged where earlier there was only a vague indication that "here dwelleth tigers."

As to the status judges of the intellect in the outside world, Merton helped immensely, as you say, to raise the intellectual standing of our discipline when he convinced them that it was more than mere head counting, grandiose speculation, or humanitarian busywork. By self-consciously placing his work in the wake of a great sociological tradition that he helped revive, he contributed mightily to making sociology a dignified member of the world of scholarship.

Merton's Theory of Social Structure

ARTHUR L. STINCHCOMBE

O F all contemporary theorists of social structure, Merton has had the greatest impact on empirical research. Investigators find it easy to understand how Merton's general ideas about social structure imply hypotheses about the pattern of behavior and the pattern of associations between variables in the setting in which their research is conducted. The argument of this essay is that this is due to the common logical and substantive character of all of Merton's theories of social structure. I would further argue, though I will not defend it in detail here, that this logical and substantive character of Merton's theories distinguishes him from almost all the other contemporary currents of social theory: Parsonian, symbolic interactionist, the Linton-Nadel kind of role theory, functionalism of the non-Mertonian kind. The main exceptions seem to me to be Homans and the exchange theory tradition, and to some degree the balance theory tradition, which have a similar logical structure and similar empirical fruitfulness.

What I will be trying to do, then, is to codify Merton's codifications, to outline the principles behind the choice of those elements in a theoretical tradition that he chose as central and worth codifying and those he ignored. The test case for the success of my effort is his approach to the social structure of science, where he was choosing freely what to pay attention to because there was not much to codify.

Arthur L. Stinchcombe is Professor of Sociology at the University of California at Berkeley.

11

Briefly, I will argue that the core process that Merton conceives as central to social structure is *the choice between socially structured alternatives*. This differs from the choice process of economic theory, in which the alternatives are conceived to have inherent utilities. It differs from the choice process of learning theory, in which the alternatives are conceived to emit reinforcing or extinguishing stimuli. It differs from both of these in that for Merton the utility or reinforcement of a particular alternative choice is thought of as socially established, as part of the institutional order.

For example, the choice of illegitimate means to socially established goals is *defined* in terms of the institutional definitions of legitimacy and of worthwhile goals. The choice between the alternative "innovation" and another alternative, say, of "ritualism" (legitimate means, lack of commitment to socially approved goals) is a choice between alternatives whose utilities or capacities for reinforcement are institutionally structured.[1] Because the alternatives are socially structured, the resulting choice behavior has institutional consequences.

But the focus of Merton's theory of these "choices with institutional consequence" is on variations in the rates of choice by people differently located in the social order. For example, when he discusses the choice of political loyalties between the machine that gives "help, not justice" and the reform parties that give formal justice, he wants to know which social groups (for example, new ethnic groups) will be structurally induced to prefer help to justice and which to prefer justice to help. That is, the core variable to be explained is different rates of choice in different social positions in a structure, or in different structures, between these institutionally consequential alternatives.[2]

The reason that I have chosen the term "core process" for rates of choice between structured alternatives, rather than independent or dependent variable, is that the causal chain goes both ways from this patterned choice. When scientists for example choose early publication as a method of claiming rights in a finding, rather than choosing secrecy, the high rate of early publication has the consequence of supporting the communism of science, supporting equal access of all scientists to past achievements regardless of intellectual property. This is using the rate of choice for early publication as an independent or causal variable to explain how an institutional pattern is maintained.[3] When Merton explains the difference in frequency of felt role conflict in a role-set by the degree of visibility (the degree of segregation of audiences to which the different roles connected to a status are played), he is explaining a difference in rates of types of solutions to role conflict by the structure of relations among audiences and between audiences and role performance.[4] That is, in the case of priority as a motivation for communism of knowledge, he is tracing the consequences of a high rate of choice of early publication. In the case of choice between segregation of audiences and other resolutions of role strain, he is asking the structural causes of different rates of choices.

The reason the causal chain goes forward from the rates of choice is that the alternatives are socially structured exactly because they are institutionally consequential. The reason the causal chain goes backward is that many details of structural position determine the exact nature of the structuring of those alternatives for particular people.

To this basic linking process which connects structural forces to institutionally consequential choices, and thence to institutional patterns, Merton adds two kinds of causal loops. The first is the one for which he is perhaps best known: namely, the recasting of the nature of functional analysis so that institutional consequences of action act back to shape the nature of the alternatives that people are posed with. The consequence of a group choosing help, not justice, is the viability of the political machine, which then provides alternative ways for businessmen to serve illegal but profitable markets, alternative career opportunities for lawyers to become judges when they are good at giving help and not so good at giving justice, and so on.[5]

The second kind of loop is in the historical development of a social character out of a systematic biographical patterning of choices. For example, a cosmopolitan is structurally induced to choose nonlocal patterns of information collection, and corresponding areas and styles of influence, which differ from the behavior patterns of locals. These styles become imprinted as basic character orientations toward information and influence which lead people to have consistent biographies as local and cosmopolitan influentials, so that the patterns of behavior do not change with each change in particular situational circumstances.[6] Thus, the second loop is a feedback through character formation which produces personal continuities in *the kind of link a given person is* between structural pressures and patterns of choice behavior. The figure below gives a schematic outline of the structure that I will argue is common to Merton's theorizing.

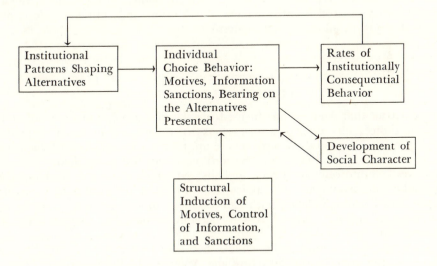

SCHEMATIC OUTLINE OF THE COMMON THEORETICAL STRUCTURE
OF MERTON'S ANALYSES

The remainder of this essay is directed at fleshing out this alleged common logical form of Merton's theorizing about social structure with illustrations chosen from many of his theoretical essays. I will try to suggest at the end why this pattern of theorizing has lent itself better than most others to the derivation of empirical hypotheses about social structures.

Before doing that, however, I would like to make a brief comment about the relation of this theoretical structure to the historical tradition of sociological theory. The striking thing about it is how many elements of different traditions there are in it, traditions that have thought themselves opposed. The core process of choice between socially structured alternatives owes a great deal (explicitly acknowledged) to the W. I. Thomas–G. H. Mead analysis of definitions of situations and self-conceptions. Where it differs from much contemporary work derived from that tradition is in *not* adding to it the hopeless proposition, "God only knows what definitions people will give to situations." The focus on institutional consequences of choices owes a great deal to the functionalist tradition, again thoroughly acknowledged. But Merton does not add the untrue proposition that institutions will always manage to get people to behave in the way required for their effective functioning. The analyses of character and biography clearly owe a good deal to Freud and the neo-Freudians, to Thomas' typology of character types, and many other sources. But Merton adds neither theories of the limited variety of characters that might be produced, nor theories of the indelibility of early experience, to the core perception of socially formed character structure.

What we find repeatedly is a free willingness to borrow and a free willingness to shear off from the borrowings the grandiosity and sectarianism of the originals, which made them fit uncomfortably with other processes in an overall theory. We will each be well served in the history of social theory if our successors consistently behave like Merton and refuse to adopt our dogmatisms while adopting our virtues.

1. INDIVIDUAL CHOICE OF STRUCTURALLY PATTERNED ALTERNATIVES

If it is true that Merton has focused his theories around processes of individual choice, why do his theories look so different from those of people who proclaim they study choice? There are four main traditions in the social sciences that make that proclamation: economic decision theory and its relatives;[7] reinforcement theory and its exchange extension in Homans;[8] symbolic interactionism with choice determined by definitions of the situation;[9] and Parsonian theory with choices about inherent value dilemmas determined by cultural values.[10] It will therefore be useful to contrast Merton's strategy with each of these.

Consider, for example, the choice between legitimate and illegitimate means in the essay "Social Structure and Anomie." In the first place, Merton is trying to explain different rates of crime, that is, different rates of choice to do behavior well known to land people in prison if they get caught. I

14

presume he would agree with what I take to be the main point of new criminology: if theft or running a numbers game or peddling heroin were not defined as crimes, people would not go to prison for them. But, of course, that is not the situation of choice that slum dwellers are confronted with. There are connections between the choice of a career running a numbers game and the likelihood of going to prison, the likelihood of social opprobrium, the likelihood of involvement in groups with other criminal enterprises. These connections are set up by "the society." That is, the character of the criminal alternative to a regular career is socially structured and, by virtue of that structuring, entails multiple simultaneous consequences for the individual.

In contrast to the basic postulates of microeconomic theory, the different aspects of this alternative are not separate commodities, so that a person can take the money but not the likelihood of a prison sentence, nor can he take as much of each as he most prefers within his budget constraints.

In reinforcement theory, the argument would be that people choose a pattern of socially structured flows of reward and punishment. No doubt, once in the numbers business, people avoid as far as possible those acts that lead to prison or to obloquy. But their own control over not "emitting" the behavior that brings prison, *but* emitting that which brings money, is preempted (as far as it can be) by the society.

Because the laws and sanctions of the larger society and its officials have a coercive power to define the situation, criminals cannot simply make up their minds that numbers games are O.K. People define situations, but do not define them as they please. I do not know which value dilemma policemen are resolving when they decide that numbers people are a bunch of crooks, nor the one resolved by a person who decides then to be a crook. But it is hard to imagine that value orientations at the most general level have much to do with choosing a criminal career.

That is, in each alternative theory of choice there is theoretical awkwardness about the society putting together bundles of predictable social reactions to acts, so that an innovative career outside the law is the choice of a social status, a choice of the schedule of reinforcements, a choice of a complex of determinate definitions of the situation, a choice of the values one will live by. This theoretical attention to bundling of choices is the distinctive feature of Merton's analysis.

To take another example, the essay on the intellectual in a public bureaucracy is principally organized around the choice by the intellectual between investigating all alternative policies and improving that policy that has already been decided upon. This choice comes in a socially structured form. Policy-makers tend to listen to intelligence about how to do what they want to do and tend not to listen to intelligence about why what they are doing is all wrong. The choice between having a broad and accurate assessment while being unheard in policy councils and having the right answer to the wrong problem while being heard is structured by the place of intellectual activity along the "continuum of decision."[11] Presumably, many intellectuals find both having the right problem *and* having their right

15

answer heard rewarding, or in keeping with their basic value premises. They would like to define their situation as involving both.

But they are not free to choose the combined alternative bundle of wide-ranging consideration of alternatives and of having the cabinet's ear. The eminently practical answer I once heard a college professor give to the question, "But how can we get out of Viet Nam?" "By getting on ships," is socially structured as woolly thinking, while the most fantastic theories of the effects of bombing or of the possibility of the South Vietnamese government becoming a revolutionary force in the countryside are socially structured as hardheaded realism. This is because the fantastic theories bear on the policy options in consideration by the cabinet, while the theory that one could come home on ships does not.

The point, then, is that the social process presents a socially structured choice between alternative cognitive styles. People do choose among cognitive styles in order to make history, but again they do not make history as they please.

Perhaps the most straightforward case of the social structuring of choice is in reference group theory. Out of the whole field of gestalt analysis of how frames of reference determine perception and evaluation, the most theoretically and methodologically intractable must be the process of comparison of oneself with abstract ideas about groups. We know a great deal about how judgments of oneself are shaped by motivated distortion. We know that sociologists themselves can hardly figure out what a given group's norms or status are. Out of all the choices of comparison processes to study, then, the choice of reference group psychology is the least likely to yield clean and powerful theories. But Merton insists, and correctly.

We take as an example of how he proceeds his analysis of the "completeness: ratio of actual to potential members" of a group.[12] He uses the example of the AMA ("about 65 percent of all licensed physicians") and the American Nurses' Association ("about 41 percent of all employed professional nurses"). The point of the analysis is the relation of completeness to "social standing and power." But social standing and power are important because in normative judgments about medical matters, or comparison of oneself as a medical student with the status of the physician one hopes to become, the social standing and power of a group socially structure the choice. It is much harder to choose to be another kind of physician than the AMA normatively defines than to be another kind of nurse from that which the ANA defines. Thus, the variable at the core of the analysis is the degree to which the choice of reference groups is socially structured.

This approach to society through individual choice between socially structured alternatives is the opposite of either psychological or sociological reductionism. There is, to be sure, consistent attention to the fact that people have to do all social actions. And there is close empirical analysis of norms, structures, collective representations, and so on. But Merton is engaged in understanding the world, not in drawing university departmental lines' projections onto the world. Externally constraining social facts have to get into people's minds in order to constrain them. But people are clever about getting what they want out of a constraining social structure. The whole question of whether social action is "really" psychological or "really" social appears as a fake problem.

2. STRUCTURAL CAUSES OF VARIATIONS IN PATTERNS OF CHOICE

THE PATTERNING OF ALTERNATIVES

The first strategic consideration in explaining patterns of choice between structured alternatives is of course that structuring itself. If quick publication of a scientific finding secures priority, while secrecy does not with any certainty do so, then quick publication becomes a more common pattern. The development of institutions (scientific journals, citation norms) which structure the choice so that priority can be reliably established by publication itself changes the motivational field of the choice. Before this development, publication would not reliably reach the relevant audience, each author could defend his own false claim to priority by mobilizing friends to use minor distinguishing features of his writing to claim priority (for example, using Newton's clumsy notation for the derivative rather than Leibnitz' elegant one was a symbol of loyalty to Newton's priority claims), people were not negatively sanctioned for failing to cite sources or parallel developments, and so on. Thus priority could better be established by attaching a finding to a "system" to make a major splash than by getting it published quickly.[13] The change from one system of structured alternatives ("system" publishing) to another (journal article publishing) increases the frequencies of the choice to publish quickly.

Or consider the explanation for the hypothesis that ritualistic adaptations to high success goals and limited means will be more common in the lower-middle-class. In this class ". . . parents typically exert continuous pressure upon children to abide by the moral mandates of the society . . . ."[14] The hypothesis is then that moral constraints structure the alternatives of the lower middle class into two of the possible five adaptations: success within the norms or failure within the norms. The possible alternatives of crime ("innovation") or vagrancy ("retreatism") are excluded by the moral environment of this class.[15] Thus, the rate of ritualism as a choice should increase in this class because the alternatives to ritualism are bundled together with dishonor, personal rejection, and nagging by lower-middle-class parents. This increase of the costs of the alternatives to ritualism leaves ritualism as the only likely reaction to lack of success for that class.

In both these cases we have the same pattern of explanation. The attachment of specified rewards (for example, priorities) or punishments (for example, parental disapproval) to the structured bundles among which people must choose, by specific social structures (modern scientific publication structures, lower-middle-class families), determines the motivational potential attached to the bundles. As these structurings of choice change (by institutional development of science, by moving from one class to another), the rates of choice change. They may change either by increasing the reward attached to one alternative or by increasing the punishments associated with the others.

STRUCTURALLY INDUCED MOTIVATION

In "Social Structure and Anomie," Merton talks about American social structure as inducing a high motivation for success in all parts of the class system. In the sociology of science, he talks about the special motivation induced by the social structure of science for prestige, especially prestige by publication. In the analysis of "Reference Group Theory and Social Mobility,"[16] motivation is treated in two different ways: on the one hand, attachments to nonmembership groups are structurally motivated by the prospect of social mobility; on the other, conformity to the norms of a nonmembership group is motivated by positive attachment to it.

In each of these cases, we have social influences on people's goals, which in turn affect their rates of social choice. These are exogenous to the formation of the alternatives themselves, in some sense. That is, the sources of motivation to succeed are not the same as the sources of the bundling together of innovation (crime) and prison by the criminal justice system. Promotion in universities based on publication, or the public validation of arduous scientific work by publication, is not the same as the institutionalization of priority rights through publication. Nor in fact is the induction of the goal of establishing priority among scientists directly due to the bundling of priority with publication. Let us discuss the distinction between social structuring of alternatives and structurally induced motivation further, because the distinction is subtle.

Exogenous variation in the different components of a social theory of choice is, as econometricians have pointed out much more sharply since these essays, an essential element in untangling causes that go around in circles. Since people making choices analyze the situation as a whole, the causes in theories of choice almost always go around in circles. This logical point about the structure of Merton's theories is therefore crucial, and needs further elaboration.

Consider the fact that in order for ordinary people to establish priority for a scientific discovery they would have to publish. Ordinary people do not publish, at least not very often, and do not worry about it. Scientists publish a great deal in journals that do not pay them—in fact, in some one may pay the costs. And they worry about it a good deal.

The systemic quality of the high rate of publication therefore incorporates two elements. In the first place, there is the institution of scientific journals, citation practices, and so on, which ties together priority and publication. Second, there is the passion for priority among scientists, which Merton's historical studies of science evoke so well.

The institution that bundles the alternatives varies over historical time. At any given point in time, the passion for priority (the structurally induced motivation) varies over individuals, with scientists being far more passionate than ordinary people, university scientists much more than industrial scientists, scientists in fields in which one can tell whether something has been discovered or not (for example, physics) much more than scientists in fields in which one cannot (for example, sociology). The leisurely pace of publication in sociology is not to be explained entirely by different publication institutions (though the preference for books about the system of sociology as a whole over articles reminds one of ancient times in the physical sciences). Rather, it is to be explained by the different induction of the goal of establishing priority in the social structure of sociology.

Thus, the distinction between the structural sources of motivation and the structuring of alternatives allows us to untangle the motivational aspect of the structured alternatives from the goals people are trying to reach by choosing those alternatives. The two forces cause variations over different sorts of observations: historical in one case and cross-sectional in the other. That rare quality in sociological writing, of wandering easily from history to survey research without giving the feeling that one is lost, is due to Merton's preeconometric instinct for the problem of identification in systems of interacting causal forces.

With the same logical structure, adopted from "Social Structure and Anomie," I tried to identify the interaction of motivation and structured alternatives in producing high school rebellion.[17] The argument took the form that young men were more exposed to success ideology than young women, and middle-class men more than working-class men. When the school tells some of *each* group that they will not get into the middle class by legitimate means (for example, tells them by giving them low grades), then the middle-class failed men should react with most rebellion, working-class failed men with somewhat less, and failed women with least. I am not as sure as when I wrote the book that the data support this. The point here, however, is that the logical structure of the theory permits a test of a complex interactive model of how motivation and constraints on alternatives produce differential rates of choices of those alternatives.

There are four main kinds of sources of variation in structurally induced motives in Merton's work: socialization into a culture, reward systems, self-affirmation in a social role, and structurally induced needs.

Thus, American children are taught (socialized) that people ought to succeed and that success is a measure of personal worth. There may be cultures that stress success but have alternative standards of personal worth as well. The first structural source of variable induction of motives, then, is differential socialization.[18]

Besides being socialized to value scientific discovery, university scientists in modern societies are involved in reward systems (status systems) which make money, power, freedom at work, and social honor all dependent on priority of scientific discovery. Such a status system cumulates motivations of diverse people around the same goal. Whether one wants to be rich, powerful, free, or honored, if one is a scientist in a university he or she satisfies his or her motives by establishing priority. Thus the dependence of all rewards on one performance criterion in a status system induces the cumulation of motives around that performance.[19]

In the social psychology of reference group behavior, the generalization from wanting to be an officer to wanting to be like an officer involves a motivational postulate of the kind now often discussed as "ego identity." Conforming attitudes in the military, and anticipatory socialization for becoming an officer, are partly motivated by affirming one's (potential) social role as an officer.[20] The intellectual in a public bureaucracy who wants to do as he thinks is right rather than as he is told does so partly because he wants to affirm his identity as an intellectual and as a person with an ideological commitment to effective public policy.[21]

A fourth source of differential motivation is illustrated by the special need of immigrant ethnic groups for help, not justice, from the political machine. Many motives in people's lives (jobs, getting out of difficulties with the law, special food for ritual occasions like Christmas) require manipulation of the social structure. When people are unskilled, legally disadvantaged, or poor, this manipulation poses special difficulties.[22] A set of structurally induced special problems in satisfying the motives of everyday life creates in turn in a person a special motive to have trusted friends in high places who can manipulate for him. That is, ordinary motives create special motives under conditions of need, under conditions in which those ordinary motives can only be satisfied through a single channel.

Thus, there are four main structural sources of goals or motives in Merton's theories: socialization, reward systems, affirmation of identities, and needs. As structures vary in the degree to which they induce relevant motives in individuals, they will vary in the rates of choice of alternatives to which those motives are relevant.

STRUCTURAL GOVERNANCE OF INFORMATION

Many of Merton's central concepts have to do with information. Among the distinguishing features of science is its communism, but this does not refer to salaries or research grants or monopolies over the teaching function. Instead it refers to information. A central concept in his role theory is visibility. Influentials are distinguished as cosmopolitans or locals in the first instance by their readership of newsmagazines. Self-fulfilling prophecies start on their spiral course by the communication to a public. Manifest functions and latent functions are distinguished by the information of the relevant public about them. Clearly, then, information is crucial to the whole of Merton's structural analysis.

There seem to be three major mechanisms by which information flows affect the pattern of structured choice behavior. First, sanctions depend on information. One person cannot sanction another for something he or she does not know the other has done. Second, information affects people's ideas about what choices they are confronted with. People do not choose alternatives they do not know about. Third, people use information in the concrete construction of successful activities, and success in an activity makes the activity more likely to continue. The collective competence of a science to solve scientific problems would be impossible if scientists could not find out the answers of other scientists to their questions. Most of what we teach or use in our research is the wisdom of others—our competence consists of others' wisdom.

INFORMATION AND SANCTIONS

. . . Social groups so differ in organization that some promote efficient 'feed-back' of 'information' to those who primarily regulate the behavior of members, while others provide little by way of efficient feed-back. The structural conditions which make for ready observability or visibility of role-performance will of course provide appropriate feed-back when role-performance departs from the patterned expectations of the group.[23]

The probability of rewards and punishments is, of course, a central feature of the motivational situation in structured choices, and this probability is centrally affected by information. For example, the rate of choice to speak frankly to physicians, lawyers, and priests is affected by the confidentiality of those communications. The rate of choice of a professor saying what he thinks, instead of what he thinks socially acceptable, is affected by the low observability of the college classroom.[24] The troublesomeness of an intellectual in a public bureaucracy is partly that he is likely to publish the arguments for a rejected alternative.[25] Although I do not find the argument explicitly, it is clear that one of the reasons the functions of a political machine for the rackets are latent rather than manifest is that if they were manifest the whole group would be in jail.

INFORMATION AND ALTERNATIVES

The core of the argument in "The Self-Fulfilling Prophecy" is that information about what collectively is likely to happen (whether it is a priori false or true) affects the rate of choice of individuals, which affects the probability of the collective outcome. Before depositors' insurance, runs on banks destroyed many banks. The "knowledge" that there was a run on the bank therefore caused depositors to want to get their money out. As more banks failed because of runs, it took less information on a run to start one. Thus, there was a cumulation *within* each bank of information on a run causing rates of choice that produced a run, and a cumulation of collective consequences producing still further information on runs *in the banking system as a whole,* so that there was an acceleration in the number of bank failures up to the banking reform of the New Deal.[26]

Information on what is going to happen puts a future-oriented animal such as man into a different choice situation. One behaves differently toward a bank that will be solvent than toward a bank that will not be. One behaves differently in providing educational opportunities for black people when he or she "knows" black people will fail than when he or she "knows" they will succeed. In general, what we mean by "reality" is what *will* happen, and what has already happened is of very little interest unless it influences the future.

In some ways, these observations are very closely related to the discussion of social structuring of alternatives above. That is, the social alternative with which a bank depositor is confronted "really" changes if he or she "knows" the bank will fail, in much the same way that the method of establishing priority really changes with the institution of scientific journals. But what differs is that the alternatives change with only an input of socially established information, instead of with changes in the true situation. Either type of change in the alternatives changes the rates of socially structured choice.

INFORMATION AND SUCCESS

Merton has spent much effort on the one institution in which collective success is almost purely determined by information, namely, science. In some ways, therefore, it is no sign of extraordinary acumen that he should notice that the flow of information determines the success of activities. The communism of information in science is vitally relevant to the success of each scientist in solving his or her own puzzles. The exponential growth of knowledge in physics had a sharp downturn during World War II, a downturn not made up by a spurt of accumulated creativity after the war.[27] Presumably, this is directly related to the destruction of the communism of physics by secrecy in the interests of national security (whether it is a good idea to preserve national security by maiming physics is, of course, an infinitely debatable question). No one with any experience in scientific work would be likely to doubt that upwards of nine-tenths of what he or she knows is due to the giants from whom he has learned. And Merton's central contributions to the sociology of science do not consist in repeating the obvious.

What is more relevant is that he has generalized this function of information to other structural processes. The cosmopolitan influential plays a different role in the local social system presumably because he or she can perform some leadership functions better than the local (and vice versa, of course). The central thing he or she can do is to mediate between the problems of the local system and the larger institutional and cultural system within which many local problems have their solution. The reason he or she can do this is that he or she routinely collects information from, and about, that larger system.[28] That is, the peculiar information of cosmopolitans makes them more successful at tasks that use that information.

Though the main subject of Merton's work on seventeenth-century science is the development of science itself, he was forced to construct a theory of the information needs of practical activity. The compass was only really useful when the error of measurement of direction at different points (due to the displacement of the magnetic poles from the geographical poles)

22

was known.[29] Clearly, knowing which direction is north contributes to one's success in arriving where one wants to arrive. And success in navigation was important to the social support of astronomical and magnetic investigations.

The social patterning of information flows thus influences rates of socially significant choices by influencing the sanctions attached to choices, by influencing the perceived alternatives between which people choose, and by influencing the rate of success of the alternative chosen.

STRUCTURAL PATTERNS OF SANCTIONING POWER

Besides knowing whom to reward and punish, a person or group has to be *able* to reward and punish in order to control behavior. The rate at which a person will choose to behave in a way that offends or helps another depends on whether the other can punish or reward that person. The two central mechanisms that Merton discusses are *power* and *usefulness*. These are not conceptually radically distinct, but their connotations are quite diverse. Roughly speaking, "power" connotes the capacity to get another person something (or to deny him or her something) from society at large. Thus, the capacity of a bureaucratic superior to allocate blame for mistakes to his or her subordinates rests on his or her special access to organizational blame-allocating centers. This is organizationally generated "power," which produces fearful ritualism in subordinates.[30] The cosmopolitan's "influence" is interpreted primarily in terms of his or her "usefulness" for, for example, managing the cultural life of Rovere.[31] The distinction could be described as a strategic place in the *social flow* of rewards and punishments ("power") versus a strategic place in the *social production* of rewards and punishments ("usefulness").

Aside from information determinants of this placement in the flow of rewards and punishments, discussed above, Merton has not systematically analyzed power systems and their implications. Consequently, I will leave the topic with the note that a systematic account of the implicit theories of power in the variety of Merton's structural essays would repay the effort.

3. STRUCTURAL OUTPUTS OF PATTERNED CHOICE

LATENT AND MANIFEST OUTPUTS

The output of one of these systems of patterned choice is socially organized behavior. But Merton's crucial interest is how such patterns fold back on themselves to maintain or undermine the pattern, or otherwise to affect the structure as a whole. As a rough scheme, not to be taken too seriously, I would distinguish five types of structural implication for this causal folding back: manifest and latent functions, manifest and latent structural locations of an output, and deviant "symptoms" of these four realities. This is all very abstract, so let me carry through an example.

When analyzing the place of publication in science, Merton talks about at least five different kinds of things. First, he speaks of the manifest function of speeding information. Since most research workers in a field read important results before they are published, and many volumes of journals are never checked out even in leading research libraries, this manifest function cannot be the whole story. Second, there are at least two latent functions of publication, namely, establishing priority for scientific discoveries and the validation to oneself that the discovery (and hence the life that went into making such a discovery) is important. This was analyzed above. Third, there is the structural place of the manifest function, in the norm of the communism of science. Publication is one of many institutional devices (university education is another) that manifest the norm of communism in science, that people ought not to be excluded from ideas for one's personal benefit. The latent structural place of the output is on the vita of the individual scientist, and consequently in the promotion system of universities and the interuniversity competition for prestige and resources. That is, the latent social processing of the output is processing in scientific status systems, and it is the fact that there is a firm social structure processing the latent output (priority claims) that makes the system hang together. This is what makes the latent function of establishing priority by publication a critical one—one that makes it likely that the latent function will maintain the practice even when the manifest function is hollow. The solid social location of the latent function then produces pressures for "deviant" behavior according to the manifest institution of communism, namely, bitter fights over priority, over "private property" rights in ideas. Fights over priority are *not* latent functions (perhaps latent dysfunctions), but rather symptoms that all is not as it seems. Sensitivity to socially patterned deviance is one of the skills Merton repeatedly uses to locate these systems of intertwined manifest and latent functions with their corresponding structural location.[32]

We see the same pattern in the analysis of the political machine. The diagnostic symptom is patterned behavior deviant from good government democratic norms (though obviously dependent on democratic norms). The latent functions include "help, not justice," service to illegitimate business, decision-making capacity in a system of decentralized formal powers, and so on. The manifest structural place of the output is the institution of democratically elected local government. The latent structural place is an organized system of ethnic groups, big businesses, illegitimate businesses and their markets, and so on, which turns the latent functions into a reliable supply of social capital for the machine. Just as the tenure decision has no formal structural place in the communism of science, so the whorehouse has no formal provision in the City Charter.[33]

The crucial point here is that latent functions are not merely outputs of a pattern of choice that happen to come about but *strategic inputs* for other structures in the system as a whole. This strategic quality in turn makes them into effective causes of the maintenance of the pattern. Happenstance outputs that some people happen to like and others not to like will not effectively fold back casually to maintain the pattern.

24

STRUCTURAL PATTERNS OF INDIVIDUAL RISKS

A second type of output of a patterned choice is a social distribution of life chances. The differential risk of different social classes for ending up in prison is an example. The point of the "Social Structure and Anomie" paper is that these differential risks are built into the structure of the society and are characteristics of the structural position rather than of the individual in it. The point to note, then, is that a subtle psychological mechanism of strain in people's reactions to ends and means produces a characteristic of a social position. Such subtle transformation of levels is a specialty of Merton's. It serves the latent function for a discipline unsure of its identity of allowing us to be psychologically subtle while proclaiming our nonpsychological character—nothing here but social class, the most eminently sociological of all ways to get psychology into the discipline.

Let us take, for an example, the most difficult case for this—the mapping of complex products of extended activities of the mind on social structure—the sociology of knowledge. In the midst of an astringent account of the massive confusion of the sociology of knowledge at the time (1945) comes a passage of Merton's own commitments:

> A basic concept which serves to differentiate generalizations about the thought and knowledge of an entire society or culture is that of the "audience" or "public," or what Znaniecki calls "the social circle." Men of knowledge do not orient themselves exclusively toward their data nor toward the entire society, but to special segments of that society with their special demands, criteria of validity, of significant knowledge, of pertinent problems, etc. It is through the anticipation of these demands and expectations of particular audiences, which can be effectively located in the social structure, that men of knowledge organize their own work, define their data, seize upon problems.[34]

Note how the structural position has been defined in terms of a subtle set of psychological considerations, of how to organize work, define data, seize upon problems. The audience becomes a force on the man of knowledge by his expectations about it, and these expectations are a complex mental construction on his part.

The example that follows is a contrast between the audience of newly established scientific societies ("plain, sober, empirical") and the universities ("speculative, unexperimental").[35] Of course, it is true that these audiences are mentioned as being located in different structures ("societies" versus "universities"), but it is not the structural position that explains the rate of choice of the individual (of experimental versus speculative science). Instead, it is the social psychological dynamics of that structural position. The degree of determinacy relating the structural characteristics to the social psychological processes can be left undecided (in fact, of course, experimental science took over the university structures a century or two after the example, which Merton dated in the seventeenth century). But the social mapping of these processes does two things. First, it allows sociologists to study complex psychological patterns without butchering the complex reality. Second, it produces a discriminating social map of rates of social choice, without having to

25

resort to residual categories like "false consciousness," or "degrees of autonomy from the substructure," or "ultimately always asserts itself," or petty bourgeois determination of thought because "in their minds they do not exceed the limits which [the petty bourgeoisie] do not exceed in their life activities" which clutter up the sociology of knowledge.

Thus, one set of outputs of patterns of choice between socially structured alternatives is different rates of different psychological outcomes mapped onto different structural positions in a social order. These range in social determinacy from inherent in the structure (social class and crime [innovation], for example, are inherently connected in American social structure) to "accidentally" connected with the structure (for example, empirical science and nonuniversity audiences).

SOCIALLY PATTERNED CHARACTER DEVELOPMENT

These different socially induced rates of patterned choice socialize people exposed to them. The timidity of a bureaucrat and the systematically narrowed view of the intellectual in a public bureaucracy are not merely situational adaptations. Repetitive situational adaptations form character. Thus, the timidity and narrow-mindedness of a bureaucracy are not only maintained because the situations that produce timidity and narrowness are continuously present. They are also maintained because over time the people in them become timid and narrow.[36]

Likewise, a person in a structural position in the flow of communication that makes him or her specialize in translating cosmopolitan information into local influence works out a pattern of life to do that translation regularly. He or she becomes a cosmopolitan, rather than happening to serve in the situation at hand as a cosmopolitan.[37]

The promotable person becomes a future noncom in many areas of life; the innovator becomes a professional criminal; the discoverer becomes a career scientist. Social patterns maintain themselves then not only because they shape the situations of people. The situations then shape characters which fit them and contribute added stability to the system.

4. WHY IT WORKS

Let me now suppose both that I have correctly identified the paradigm behind the paradigms in Merton's work on social structure and that I am right that his work has started more (and more penetrating) traditions of empirical research than that of other contemporary theorists. How might we explain this superiority?

First, I do not agree with Merton's implicit diagnosis that it is because he works on "theories of the middle range."[38] It seems to me that in the dialectic between Parsons and Merton, generality has been confused with woolliness. Merton, in taking up the correct position on woolliness, has tricked himself into taking up the incorrect position on general theory. The

26

true situation is precisely the opposite. It is because Merton has a better general theory than Parsons that his work has been more empirically fruitful. I will try to discuss this under the traditional general virtues of theories: elegance, power or fruitfulness, economy, and precision.

ELEGANCE

Making consensual esthetic judgments of theories is harder than making other kinds of judgments. In the first place, there are major differences in esthetic style: spare classical styles which use simple material to create complex effects—Merton or James S. Coleman are examples; emebellished rococo in which an immense variety of beautiful theoretical detail is more or less integrated by thematic means—Claude Lévi-Strauss provides an example; romantic in which concepts are evoked with incantations and words heavy in connotations—Edward Shils is a good example. Only a few people can make an esthetic impact in all three styles: Clifford Geertz maybe. My own taste is classical; in the extreme I like geometry with a complex theoretical structure made up of only points and lines.

But I think two aspects of esthetic experience in sociological theory would get wide assent. The most fundamental is the capacity of a theory to say with the same set of statements something complex and realistic about individual people and what they are up to and something complex and realistic about a social pattern. The impact of George Herbert Mead or Max Weber is partly explained by the fact that they make both people and structures real. Much of the sparely classical beauty of economics comes from the easy translation between market equilibria and striving individuals.

The central intractable problem for sociology has been the relation of individuals to the social order. The drive to "bring men back in,"[39] to develop a "naturalistic sociology,"[40] reflects dissatisfaction with the crude picture of individuals that structural explanations tend to give. And although the defense of professional monopoly has altogether too much to do with objections to explanations as being "too psychological," there is also a flat obvious quality to explanations of social behavior that come down to "they did it because they wanted to" or "they did it because of their thalamus."

Merton's theoretical structure provides multiple opportunities to move back and forth from striving or thalamic men to social structural outcomes. Sometimes the psychology is obvious, as when people do not react to what they do not know about. Sometimes, as in the case of audiences as central structural units in the sociology of knowledge, the connection between the behavior of individuals and the structure is extraordinarily complex.

Merton gains this esthetic effect principally by modifying the structural concepts so that people fit as natural parts of them. A role-set is a much easier thing into which to fit one's experience of trying to figure out what a professor is supposed to do than is a Linton role. A notion of deviance that says there is something wrong with ritualistic overconformity, that the rule-bound petty office tyrant was not what we had in mind when we passed the rules, rings truer to our experience of conformity and deviance.

27

If the kernel of esthetic experience in sociological theory is the unity of social and psychological statement, the outer covering is irony. Good comes from evil, complexity from simplicity, crime from morality; saints stink while whores smell good; trade unions and strikes lead to industrial peace under a rule of law and a collective contract; law and order candidates are fond of burglary. Merton clearly loves irony. He is most pleased to find motives of advancing knowledge creating priority conflicts among scientists, and hardly interested in the fact that such motives also advance knowledge. He likes to find political bosses helping people while good government types turn a cold shoulder. He likes to find Sorokin offering statistics on ideas to attack the empiricist bent of modern culture and to urge an idealistic logico-meaningful analysis of ideas. He likes to range Engels and functionalists down parallel columns to show them to be really the same. The immediate subjective feeling that one has learned something from reading Merton is probably mainly due to the taste for irony.

A third esthetic advantage is closely related to irony: the onion-like layers of the theories. That is, like Lévi-Strauss or Freud or Marx, the esthetic effects of Merton's theory have to do with the process of moving from a more superficial view of a matter to a deeper underlying view. The onion looks brown, then light tan, then white but coarse, then white but fine-grained. Just as some of the finest effects in novels consist of shifts in point of view, so in social theory a layered structure gives an impression of movement, of learning, of an active social scientist figuring things out. There is more feeling of motion in Merton's essays than in most social theorizing.

Esthetic qualities of theory make it more useful in two ways. First, it makes it easier to persuade yourself to work with it, makes it fun to read and fun to play with. There is nothing duller to think about than "Is social class really related to delinquency?" We would not have the right answer now (yes, but not strongly related) if we had not had something interesting to think about in the tedium of collecting the data.

The second is that esthetic experience encourages a shift in perspective, breaks up and re-forms the molds in the mind. I do not know a good analysis of the relation between esthetic experience and creativity, but I offer the empirical generalization that people who cannot experience a thrill at a beautiful idea hardly ever amount to anything in a science.

POWER OR FRUITFULNESS

In some ways, the body of this essay is directed at showing, first, that there is a general theory of social action in Merton's work and, second, that it is fruitful in many different empirical problems. I have commented about how, for example, the power of the theory allows diverse evidence from history to survey research to be brought to bear on the same empirical problem. The power has its most obvious (because easiest) manifestation in the apparent effortlessness of the destructive criticism of other theorists in his essays on functionalism and on the sociology of knowledge. If it were really as easy as it looks, brilliant minds like Malinowski or Sorokin could have done it.

But though the power of the general theory leads to quick perception of the holes in other theories, being one up on Malinowski or Sorokin is a trivial accomplishment. The crucial benefits in explanatory power come from two general characteristics of the theory. First, it combines attention to stability and maintenance of social patterns with attention to disruption of them. In the nature of things, if there is an equilibrium or self-maintaining state of a system, the state one is most likely to observe is that equilibrium state. If in a given setting a political machine is a self-maintaining state, then one common structure that will be found there is a machine. As in a Markov process with absorbing states, eventually everything ends up absorbed. This means that Merton's equilibrium theory has an inherent tendency to be about states of the system that are most commonly observed. But further, it focuses on the sources of variation and tension that explain deviations from these most commonly observed states. Whenever an equilibrium theory is something more than a vague notion that things will probably all work out for the best, it has an inherent advantage in explanatory power.

The second main explanatory power advantage of Merton's general theory is that it focuses attention on social magnification processes. For example, racketeers want to make money. But by being organized into a system together with legitimate business and with ethnic groups with precarious citizenship, both their capacity to make money is increased and the canalization of that impulse and the money by the machine produces a large impact on, for example, the judicial system. By canalizing the impulse to establish priority into early publication, scientific journals magnify the impulse to gain prestige from communicating results and maximize its impact on the speed of communication and on the norm of communism of knowledge. By monopolizing medical licensing and access to hospitals, and enrolling most of the profession, the AMA increases the power of consensual norms in the profession about what a physician should be and becomes a stronger reference group for aspiring physicians. Magnification and canalization of causes create discriminating impacts, thus increasing the information content of a theory of causes.

The crucial feature of the theorizing that does this job of focusing on magnification is the constant attention to the structural location of a given pattern of choice. It is the structural location of corruption in the machine that makes it more than random temptation of public officials. It is the institutionalization of priority in the communication process itself that magnifies the impulse to publish. It is the location of a reference group in the power system that makes it a crucial channel for transmitting ideals.

ECONOMY

There is one trivial kind of economy in social theorizing which many of us could learn with profit: the willingness to write about one thing at a time. The brunt of one version of "scholarly" norms in social theorizing is that one should always introduce distinctions that might be useful in some other situation, but do not bear on the problem at hand, in order to show awareness of the tradition of the discipline. The frequent experience of not quite knowing the subject of a theoretical essay is partly due to our penchant for writing books to be entitled "The Social System" or "Economy and Society," "The Rules of Sociological Method" or "Constructing Social Theories," which give a cover for introducing bright ideas in the order they occur to the author. A book with a pretentious title like "Social Theory and Social Structure" is much more palatable if made up of essays making one argument at a time. It is easy in Merton to figure out which idea is being talked about at which time and what is the relevance of a conceptual distinction to that idea. Besides being an epistemological principle, Occam's razor is also a principle of rhetoric—not to clutter an argument with multiplied conceptual entities.

But I have tried to show above that the great variety of Merton's empirical theories is generated from a small set of common elements, organized around a core theory of rates of choice among socially structured alternatives. A half dozen or so major elements, in two or three major varieties each, generate structurally similar theories in a wide variety of empirical situations.

PRECISION

Perhaps the main epistemological mistake of sociologists is to confuse generality with lack of specificity. Newton in generalizing the theory of gravitation did *not* say the Earth goes sort of around the Sun, and Mars goes sort of around slower and farther out, and this is the same general kind of thing as rolling balls down an inclined plane. The theory of gravitation is simultaneously very general and very specific about exactly what will happen under various exactly described circumstances. The sociological tradition that defines a theorist by the absence of exact empirical description and prediction is completely foreign to the tradition of theorizing in the mature sciences.

Merton's theory is set up to explain variations, specifically variations in rates of choice. It is a perfectly answerable empirical question whether the establishment of scientific journals decreased the time between major discoveries and the use of those discoveries in further scientific work. The generality of the notion of socially structured alternatives is no bar to precise predictions about the rate of scientific communication. The generality of latent functions is no bar to a precise prediction about which kinds of political structures will collect higher rates of contributions from rackets. The structural distribution of delinquency and hyperconformity is precisely predictable from the argument of social structure and anomie.

There are two main elements to this precision. The first is that Merton never loses sight of the fact that the only thing that can be explained is variation. This means that no scientific theory can ever be about less than four things: two states of the effect and two states of the cause. The frequency with which this elementary matter is left implicit in sociological theorizing is little short of astounding. Whatever, for example, causes role conformity, its absence has to cause something else. That something else is a phenomenon out in the world, which has to be described before one knows what role conformity is and, consequently, what has to be explained. An entirely fictional portrayal of a Hobbesian state of nature will not do for the other end of the variable of conformity. Merton puts various phenomena at the other end, depending on his purpose—concealment or role audience segregation, having a bad attitude toward the army, hyperconformity of a ritualistic kind, solving problems by political machine methods, and so on. Contextually, then, role conformity becomes a number of different things, resulting in greater conceptual precision. Further, a distance between two people or two structures along one of these conceptual scales becomes an intractable fact to be explained. Because it is conformity as opposed to ritualism, *or* as opposed to role segregation, *or* as opposed to something else, the distance between a more conforming and a less conforming person means something precise. Distances along different scales then have different explanations, but one is not reduced to "multiple causation" or "failure of a system to meet its functional requisites" to explain deviance.

Yet this precision is not lack of generality. Visibility occupies a stable place in the general conceptual scheme, bearing the same relation to other concepts in a wide variety of empirical circumstances. Hollow conformity likewise, at least ideally, occupies the same place when it is pretending to pursue a manifest function while really being after a latent one as it does when it is a kind of behavior especially characteristic of the lower-middle-class or of the bureaucratic personality.

CRITIQUE

This last example, however, illustrates the main difficulty of Merton's way of proceeding. Because the general theory is nowhere extracted and systematized, we are not quite sure that hollow conformity to a manifest function is exactly the same as hollow ritualism of the lower middle class, bearing the same relation to other major concepts in the system. The piecemeal presentation of the theory makes a primary virtue of its power, its extensibility into many empirical areas. Taken as a whole, the structure of the corpus of theoretical work does not forcefully communicate the elegance, economy, and precision of the theory. And this makes it hard to work on the lacunae.

NOTES

1. Robert K. Merton, "Social Structure and Anomie," in his *Social Theory and Social Structure,* enl. ed. (New York: Free Press, 1968), pp. 185–214. (Hereinafter referred to as *STSS.*)
2. Robert K. Merton, "Manifest and Latent Functions," in Merton, *STSS,* pp. 73–138.

3. Robert K. Merton, "Science and Democratic Social Structure," in Merton, *STSS*, pp. 604–15.
4. Robert K. Merton, "Continuities in the Theory of Reference Group Behavior," in Merton, *STSS*, pp. 428–31.
5. Merton, "Manifest and Latent Functions."
6. Robert K. Merton, "Patterns of Influence: Local and Cosmopolitan Influentials," in Merton, *STSS*, pp. 441–74.
7. Economic decision theory is outlined in any intermediate level text in microeconomic theory; for example, Alfred W. Stonier and Douglas C. Hague, *A Textbook of Economic Thory* (London: Longman, 1972).
8. For reinforcement theories of social choice, see George C. Homans, *Social Behavior: Its Elementary Forms* (New York: Harcourt Brace Jovanovich, 1961).
9. For the symbolic interactionist tradition, a fine outline is the first and last part of David Matza, *Becoming Deviant* (Englewood Cliffs, N.J.: Prentice-Hall, 1969).
10. The attribution to Parsons of a social choice theory is genetic in the sense that he has never renounced the orientation of *Structure of Social Action (1937)*, especially the introductory essay. People have become much less active choosers of what to value and what to do about those values as Parsonian theory has "matured." It would be hard to tell from recent Parsonian writings that this was a theory of socially conditioned choices of the meanings of actions. See Talcott Parsons. *The Structure of Social Action* (New York: Free Press, 1949; copyright Mc-Graw-Hill, 1937).
11. Robert K. Merton, "Role of the Intellectual in Public Bureaucracy," in Merton, *STSS*, p. 269.
12. Merton, "Continuities in the Theory of Reference Group Behavior," pp. 368–69.
13. Merton, "Science and Democratic Social Structure," pp. 610–12; Harriet Zuckerman and Robert K. Merton, "Patterns of Evaluation in Science: Institutionalization Structure and Functions of the Referee System," *Minerva* 9, no. 1 (January 1971): 66–100; and Robert K. Merton, "Behavior Patterns of Scientists," *American Scientist* 57, no. 1 (1969): 1–23.
14. Merton, "Social Structure and Anomie," p. 205.
15. Cf. *ibid.*, pp. 205–07.
16. Robert K. Merton, with Alice S. Rossi, "Contributions to the Theory of Reference Group Behavior," in Merton, *STSS*, pp. 316–25.
17. Arthur H. Stinchcombe, *Rebellion in a High School* (Chicago: Quadrangle Books, 1964), chap. 6.
18. Merton, "Social Structure and Anomie."
19. Merton, "Behavior Patterns of Scientists."
20. Merton and Rossi, "Contributions to the Theory of Reference Group Behavior," pp. 319–22.
21. Merton, "Role of the Intellectual in Public Bureaucracy."
22. Merton, "Manifest and Latent Functions."
23. Merton, "Continuities in the Theory of Reference Group Behavior," p. 374.
24. *Ibid.*, p. 427.
25. Merton, "Role of the Intellectual in Public Bureaucracy," p. 277, by implication.
26. Robert K. Merton, "The Self-Fulfilling Prophecy," in Merton, *STSS*, pp. 476–77.
27. Robert L. Hamblin, R. Brooke Jacobsen, Jerry L. L. Miller, *A Mathematical Theory of Social Change* (New York: John Wiley and Sons, 1973), Fig. 8.6, p. 143.
28. Merton, "Patterns of Influence," pp. 460–63.
29. Robert K. Merton, "Science and Economy of Seventeenth-Century England," in Merton, *STSS*, pp. 673–74.

30. Robert K. Merton, "Bureaucratic Structure and Personality," in Merton, *STSS,* pp. 249–60.
31. Merton, "Patterns of Influence," p. 461.
32. Zuckerman and Merton, "Patterns of Evaluation in Science"; Merton, "Behavior Patterns of Scientists" and "Science and Democratic Social Structure."
33. Merton, "Manifest and Latent Functions."
34. Robert K. Merton, "The Sociology of Knowledge," in Merton, *STSS,* p. 536.
35. *Ibid.,* p. 537.
36. Merton, "Bureaucratic Structure and Personality" and "Role of the Intellectual in Public Bureaucracy."
37. Merton, "Patterns of Influence."
38. Robert K. Merton, "On Sociological Theories of the Middle Range," in Merton, *STSS,* pp. 39–72.
39. Homans, *Social Behavior.*
40. Matza, *Becoming Deviant.*

Working with Merton

PAUL F. LAZARSFELD

1. SOCIOLOGY OF KNOWLEDGE AND KNOWLEDGE OF APPLIED SOCIOLOGY

IN January 1961 the journalist Morton M. Hunt published a "New Yorker" profile on Robert Merton that is still a very well documented source of information about his biography and his work up to the age of fifty. On numerous occasions, Hunt interviewed both Merton and me as to our collaboration. His description of how we met is essentially correct. I had been director of a Rockefeller Foundation project to study the social effects of radio. Originally, the headquarters were in Princeton; but in 1939 the funds were transferred to Columbia, where I had been given the nominal title of lecturer, without faculty status. A year later, a full professorship in sociology became vacant, but the department could not agree on a nomination. The issue was whether the appointment should go to someone who emphasized social theory or to someone primarily concerned with empirical research. Finally, the professorial line was divided into two lower faculty positions, which were filled, respectively, by Merton and by me. Hunt describes the complex situation in more detail and in a somewhat satirical tone. But he is correct in saying that, for quite a while, Merton and I had no personal contact. He then continues:

> . . . In November of 1941, Lazarsfeld felt that, as the older man, he ought to do the graceful thing and acknowledge the existence of his opposite number. He invited Merton to dinner, but on the afternoon of the engagement he got an

urgent call from the Office of Facts and Figures (the predecessor of the O.W.I.), requesting him to conduct an audience-reaction test that evening on a new radio program that had been devised as part of the agency's pre-war morale-building effort. When the Mertons arrived, Lazarsfeld met them at the door of his apartment and said, as the guests recall it, "How nice, how nice that you are here at last. But don't take off your coat, my dear Merton. I have a sociological surprise for you. We will have to leave the ladies to dine alone together, and we will return as soon as we can." Then he bustled off with Merton to a radio studio where a score of people were listening to a recorded broadcast of "This Is War". . . . After the program, when an assistant of Lazarsfeld's questioned the audience on the reasons for its recorded likes and dislikes, Merton perked up; he detected theoretical shortcomings in the way the questions were being put. He started passing scribbled notes to Lazarsfeld. . . . As a second batch of listeners entered the studio, Lazarsfeld asked Merton if he would do the post-program questioning. Merton did, and his errant host said afterward, "Marvellous job. We must talk it all over. Let's phone the ladies and let them know we're still tied up." . . . This they did, went down to the Russian Bear, and talked sociology until long after midnight.

As far as I am concerned, only the last sentence is not exactly correct. I did not "talk sociology"; instead, I tried to explain to Merton my efforts to build up at Columbia what was shortly thereafter officially called the Bureau of Applied Social Research. My purpose was to recruit Merton's collaboration. His side of the story is available in a letter he wrote to Kingsley Davis a few months later. The essential passages are as follows:

March 18, 1942. As for me, my trouble lies in not having learned to say "no". As a consequence, I've been spending six and eight hours a day on a "project" which has the advantage of being in some small measure a patriotic undertaking as well as an intrinsically interesting job. I accepted the invitation of the Office of Radio Research, here, to "test" the effectiveness of the morale-program, This Is War, which is broadcast over all four networks Saturday nights. We have a fairly elaborate setup at the NBC and CBS studios which enables us to check the spontaneous responses of samples of listeners on the spot. This is followed through with fairly detailed interviewing around the "peaks" of response to various parts of the program. My immediate interest lies in having run into a problem where preliminary analysis and hunches can be checked by direct observation of human beings in action. . . . But it does rip into my private program—I've been getting home at one and two a.m., times without end. . . . As you can gather from this scrambled paragraph, my chief interest lies in the rare opportunity of having more or less immediate checks on theoretically derived hypotheses (or, if you prefer, "bright ideas"). I hope we can refine our procedure to the point where some real progress will become evident.

This letter has several interesting features. The notion of an organized research project was so new to Merton—and probably to the majority of our colleagues—that he puts it in quotation marks. There is a tone of ambivalence: he feels trapped, but it is interesting. He is impressed by the setup but feels he has to justify his decision by referring to its patriotic implications. There is no doubt, however, as to the main source of his interest: he liked the opportunity to watch the interrelation between a practical problem and his main theoretical concerns.

Probably the most interesting aspect of the letter is its date—six months after our first encounter. He speaks of himself as being in charge of one specific study, while I thought of him by then as a co-director of the Bureau, a role he officially took on a few months later. And he mentions his presence at the office until late at night probably without knowing how that came about. Soon after he began to work at the Bureau, we arranged that he have an office there (we were then located in the abandoned building of the College of Physicians and Surgeons); this provided more space for him and me than was available in Fayerweather Hall. Both of us had our headquarters at the Bureau and went uptown only for lectures.

In the beginning, however, there was one difference. Merton worked conscientiously in his office from 9 to 5. At 5 o'clock he left, often without even saying good-bye. I, in turn, had to spend most of the day on administrative or public relations duties, because the existence of the Bureau was not yet assured. The situation was somewhat paradoxical. I badly wanted to discuss with Merton events of the day and plans for the next day, but only after 5 o'clock did I have the time for exchanging ideas. So I invented a special strategy. About 4:45 I would come to his office with a problem I thought would interest him. The ensuing discussions gradually lasted longer and longer until, finally, the time between, say, 5 and 8 o'clock was rather regularly devoted to the scheming sessions. This became almost proverbial, first among the staff of the Bureau and later among our faculty colleagues when the Bureau moved up to the main campus. While the subsequent expansion of the Bureau would have been impossible without Merton's administrative and "political" contribution, he was never an "organization man." But the problems of applied social research were always part of his overriding interest in the sociology of knowledge, and it is not difficult to trace the various ways in which the two were connected.

It begins with his famous dissertation on science in seventeenth-century England; it will, I am sure, be assessed by other contributors to this volume. The chapter headings alone talk of military techniques, transportation, and other technological developments of the period he studied.[1] But I think it fair to say that the core of Merton's analysis was how science developed as a social institution in its own right and with norms that did not require "justification by use." Defending science for science's sake remained, for a while, an important theme. As late as 1945 he wrote a paper on the role of the intellectual in public bureaucracy. It is a compendium of the difficulties an academician is likely to encounter when he tries to adjust his values to agencies responsible for public service.[2] Little sympathy is expressed for the poor bureaucrat who has to put up with the intellectual. The balanced approach of later papers is still absent.

In the meantime Merton obviously had discovered his tremendous talent for supervising and analyzing studies which grew out of contracts made by the

Bureau. I shall review many of them in part 2 of this memorandum, but first a word must be said about the policy of the Bureau in the 1940s. We were quite willing to accept virtually any contract that would give us financial support and so prolong our existence. There was no need to stipulate that the study should have scientific relevance, as we were sure that this would be the case. A simple division of labor existed between Merton and me: I abstracted a series of methodological publications, and he derived from each empirical report some new theoretical idea. The best examples are our two contributions to the *Continuities in Social Research,* a volume that was Merton's idea.[3]

In 1948 he formulated his general ideas on the bearing of empirical research on the development of sociological theory in a special paper.[4] I notice that in Merton's work in the 1940s, up to a certain time, he hardly ever asks whether all this—empirical social research or social theory—is of any use to those who commissioned the studies. This aloofness changes radically in a paper published in 1949, which deserves more detailed discussion.

During the Second World War the government had made increasing use of social research by organizing public opinion surveys, doing systematic content analysis of radio broadcasts and newspapers, applying anthropological ideas to its Far East strategy, and so on. The monumental four volumes of *The American Soldier* began to show that studies carried out for practical purposes could contribute to the fund of systematic sociological knowledge. It is not surprising, therefore, that in 1948 the Social Science Research Council (SSRC) called a conference to discuss the relation between applied and basic research. Nor is it surprising that Merton was asked to prepare the keynote document. Through his work at the Columbia Bureau, he had added to his earlier fame as a leading social theorist and also had earned a reputation as an expert in the practical application of social research.

Most of the papers read at the conference were published in a 1949 issue of the *Journal for the Philosophy of Science.* In the twenty-five years since then, the literature on the basic-applied issue has accumulated to almost unmanageable proportions; at the same time, the topic itself has acquired ever greater social significance, and the funds available for applied work have greatly increased. Rereading Merton's paper today, it is almost uncanny how he anticipated and organized the whole array of issues that discussion and experience have brought to the fore in recent years.

He sees himself commissioned to undertake an inquiry into the current status of the uses of social research and to propose a program for research. Four groups would be interested in such a review: the social scientist concerned with his professional role; foundations deliberating on the extent to which they should support work done for practical purposes; government and business who wish to know how much they could count on help from the social sciences; and, finally, the intelligent layman who wants to know about this new controversy and who might influence it by his vote or other forms of political action. The title of the essay is "The Role of Applied Social Science in the Formation of Policy: A Research Memorandum," [5] and it is divided into fourteen parts. The first three sections serve as an introduction, and to assure a clear organization Merton says he will "distinguish the two distinct though related types of problems attending the utilization of policy-oriented social research. . . ."

(1) interpersonal and organizational problems: stemming from the relations between the research worker and the "clientele" (operating agency, administrator, etc.).

(2) scientific problems involving the difficulty of developing scientific researches adequate to the practical demands of the situation.

In the first group of topics, he speaks of a cultural (section 4) and an organizational context (section 5). Under the former heading he assesses the factors likely to influence the esteem in which applied work will be held in the future. In section 5 he offers a detailed schema cross-tabulating the type of client and the type of research agency.[6]

Section 6 is called "situational context," but according to my reading it really introduces the discussion of what Merton calls "scientific problems." He attempts to classify the collaboration between policy-maker and social scientist according to who originates the issue to be dealt with. This section should be read together with section 10, specifically called "types of problems." Anyone who has tried to classify current publications of applied research reports, and has found how difficult the assignment is, will profit from Merton's examples. This effort is not just an exercise in classification. Merton stresses that it is important to find the right fit between what the policy-maker needs and what the social sciences can do, given the present stage of the art:

> . . . with the excessively large problem only failure can presently be reported and with the excessively limited problem, the results are often trivial. It would be important to identify the strategic, intermediate range of problems; namely, those which have generalized theoretical and practical significance, but which are not too large in scope to be subjected to disciplined research.

The entire discussion centers around an interesting idea: what is considered a practical problem requiring research is, because of that very fact, a sociological issue. (This idea, incidentally, has obviously remained on Merton's mind. In 1961, writing the Epilogue to the Merton/Nisbet collection on social problems, Merton lists a number of aspects a sociologist should bear in mind. One of the major themes is again that what is a social problem is a question that requires empirical sociological concern.[7])

Returning to the structure of the 1949 memorandum, we see emerging clearly the idea of utilization as a sequence of steps which must be investigated separately. After a practical problem has been properly identified, it must be translated into a research design. This step of translation must avoid a number of dangers. In section 7 Merton discusses what the sociologist can do if the policy-maker either overspecifies or overgeneralizes his problem. The somewhat hackneyed topic of values gains a fresh look because in section 8 it is related to the translation problem. There may be a tacit assumption on the part of the client that certain factors are unchangeable and, therefore, do not deserve to be studied; the sociologist, on the other hand, may have such strong preferences for certain research techniques that he overlooks others which might be more adequate to the policy problem on hand.

Once the problem is properly identified and translated into a research design, the utilization process faces what is probably the most difficult step of all: how to fill the gaps between research and policy. The memorandum devotes two sections (11 and 12) to this topic; I shall treat them together to bring out more sharply the notion of utilization as a process clearly implied in terms such as "the leap from research to practice." Any recommendation made by a sociologist explicitly or implicitly contains assumptions as to the future, and here the connection with Merton's work on unanticipated consequences is, of course, most pertinent.[8] He is also fully aware of the reverse side of the coin: the policy-maker must accept the risks involved in some of these implications. But men of private and public affairs vary according to the size of the risks they are willing to take. This comes close to the mode of a formalized decision theory, where action is guided by a set of alternatives to which one attaches subjective probabilities of future occurrences and to each of which cost benefits are attached, in case they do come about. The two sections link the gap problem with many other comments in the paper: for example, the way the original translation into a research design constrains the type of recommendation which can be justified in the end; or how the social or organizational relations between the researcher and the policy-maker may affect the chances that recommendations are implemented.

The memorandum ends with two short sections, one on the mutual relation betweent theory and applied social science (section 13) and one on methodology and applied social science (section 14). The former summarizes ideas taken from his two earlier papers on the mutual relation between theory and empirical research; no special notice is taken of the linguistic shift from "empirical" to "applied" research. The last section shows how practical demands often lead to research improvements and considers the proper balance of quantitative and qualitative procedures.

For a variety of reasons, I have analyzed this paper in special detail. Since I left the directorship of the Columbia Bureau, I have tried to codify the process of utilization of social research. The first visible result of this effort was the publication of *The Uses of Sociology*.[9] My two co-editors entrusted me with a first draft of the Introduction, I am quite sure that at that time I had not reread Merton's paper; nevertheless, the distinction between the organizational and "cognitive" aspects of applied social research appears there as a major editorial device. And the emphasis on the translation and the gap problems are as central in my Introduction as in Merton's paper. Some years later, James Coleman reflected on the history of his well-known survey on equality of opportunities.[10] He derived a number of principles, and I am sure he had not reread the Introduction to the "Uses" volume. Nevertheless, again, many of the same ideas reappear. We have learned from Merton that one need not apologize for time-lagged multiple discoveries; still, there ought to be occasions where priorities of this kind should be solemnly acknowledged.

(It would be interesting to explore whether the similarities of the three essays are due to the intrinsic nature of the problem or to the fact that the three of us worked so closely together during some crucial years.)

Merton's paper is a turning point in his own career. As I mentioned before, it represents his full acceptance of applied research as a legitimate domain for intellectual inquiry. As a matter of fact, he says at one point that there is need for more research on applied research. And the legitimacy of the topic seems to him so obvious that he accepts the basic-applied distinction without discussing any terminological issues. One might, therefore, have expected that Merton would now either do some major applied research and apply to it systematically the framework he had just developed or turn to collecting many more examples in order to develop a full-blown theory of application—a turn, incidentally, that Merton suggested and I took. But Merton chose neither of these two options.

For a while, nothing seems to have changed. From 1952 to 1958, Merton directed a large Bureau program on medical sociology reported by another contributor in this volume. About the same time, I worked with Wagner Thielens and other Bureau personnel on *The Academic Mind*. We both employed the tradition of Bureau seminars: regular meetings of graduate students working on separate but coordinated parts of the material, contributing to the final publications, and often writing dissertations on their part of the study. The directorship of the Bureau had been turned over to Charles Glock, an able leader who held together a fine generation of "Young Turks" and at the same time got help from Merton and myself, who had become associate directors.

I continued my interest in problems of specific application. With Robert Dahl and Mason Haire, I collaborated on a book on social science in business, commissioned by the Ford Foundation. And in 1959–60 I spent a year at the Harvard Business School on a visiting professorship created by the Ford Foundation to strengthen the role of the social sciences in the education of future business leaders.

Merton, however, took another turn by picking up the elements he, possibly with hesitation, had eliminated from his SSRC memorandum. In section 2 of his paper he stressed that, although all applied social science research involves advice (recommendation for policy), not all advice on social policy is based on research. For a full page, he analyzed the notion of advice, an analysis that still deserves careful attention. At the end of the page he said that "the role of the social science expert who proffers advice out of his general fund of knowledge will receive only secondary attention." His own inquiry "will be centered on research in applied social science." But soon thereafter he became increasingly interested, not in the work, but in the *social role* of the applied social scientist. The Bureau always had amicable relations with the research groups at AT&T. Merton obtained access to some of their files in order to see under which conditions they called on the help of social scientists. Together with Edward Devereux he analyzed this material. The resulting four volumes, which, unfortunately, are available only in mimeographed form, deserve to be brought to the attention of a broader public; only a brief summary was published.[11] He participated actively in a Columbia University seminar on the professions. In his Introduction to *The Student Physician,*[12] he made a detailed comparison of the different roles psychologists and sociologists are likely to play in medical education. He also participated in a series of discussions, organized by the late Lyman Bryson, on the function of the social science adviser in public affairs. I suppose, although I have no concrete evidence, that he also played a role in stimulating Zetterberg's monograph *Social Theory and Social Practice,*[13] which described the role of the sociological adviser in a Bureau study commissioned by a municipal museum. And he became a consultant to various professional and commercial organizations.

I avoid outlining a specific chronology because I had only distant contact with this turn of his interests. Once the organizational needs of the Bureau were no longer our main concern, our personal meetings became less habitual. The after-5 o'clock pattern gradually disappeared. The leads contained in this paragraph are intended mainly to encourage further research on this transitional period. But I can at least contribute some personal recollections.

Around 1950, both Merton and I felt that Columbia's Bureau of Applied Social Research should change its function. Many similar institutions had grown up at other universities, some of them under the directorship of our own students. It seemed incongruous that our Bureau should remain in competition with our progeny. Conversely, the rapid proliferation of these new centers required trained personnel, but such training was not available anywhere. I felt that the best turn for the Bureau would be that it become a training center for applied researchers. Merton agreed in principle with this idea, and we wrote a memorandum on the need for a professional school in social research.[14] The memorandum was widely circulated, but the plan which was submitted to the Columbia authorities got nowhere. The idea probably did not succeed at Columbia because Merton approved of it only in principle; he did not want to expend a second time all the effort required for a new institutional creation.

The 1949 paper, including its title, reads like an urgent appeal to carry out the program it so ably delineates. I cannot remember today whether the SSRC conference had implied such a possibility or if Merton just chose this type of rhetoric as a way of organizing his ideas. In fact, here, as well, nothing concrete happened.[15]

It took another fifteen years before the need for the systematic approach to applied social sciences was generally acknowledged. The signs of this awakening in the second half of the 1960s are numerous. The study groups established to clarify the nature of the social sciences, so interestingly reported by Gene Lyons,[16] increasingly stress the problem of applications. In 1968 the BASS report proposed a graduate school of applied social sciences in a chapter which takes up the ideas of the 1950 memorandum;[17] the Brim report is called "knowledge into Action."[18] Lasswell's idea of a policy science leads to a journal of the same name, which, however, does not satisfy the need for the systematic analysis of concrete cases. Specialized literature appears: Ikenberry shows how the universities have not been able to incorporate applied social sciences into their structure.[19] Orlans reviews how, as a result, the so-called nonprofit research organizations proliferate;[20] Biderman warns of the intrusion of avowedly commercial research agencies;[21] and A. D. Little applies to the Massachusetts Board of Education for a charter to give a Ph.D. in applied social research. In the end, the present chaos may prove to be creative, but it certainly shows little continuity with, or awareness of, what we might call the 1950 Columbia program.

Meanwhile, Merton slowly returned to his first love, the sociology of science. Still, one last time, he made a major contribution to the theory of applied social science; it is found in a paper which is a most interesting fusion of two topics: the sociology of science and the theory of applications.

An insurance company sponsored a special issue of the journal *American Behavioral Scientist* on research related to the general problem of life insurance. Merton contributed a paper in which the whole problem is stated in the very terms used in his dissertation.[22] Science is an institution in its own right, parallel to, say, the family, the economy, religion, or education. While these institutions are interdependent in various ways, each maintains a measure of independence. The relation between business firms and basic scientific research can now be seen as a special case of the relations between two connected but independent types of social institutions.

The relations between the two institutions are analyzed in terms of a principle he calls "potential of relevance." The idea is roughly as follows: science is divided into a number of substantive sectors, and so is business. It is in the interest of business to support basic research, but it is free to choose what sector of the research world to support.

> . . . Different sectors of the spectrum of basic research have differing probabilities of being germane to current and future functions of various types of organizations. Applied to the case of business organizations, the concept gives rise to the policy of supporting those lines of inquiry in basic research which, so far as can be judged, will have the greatest degree of relevance for the particular firm. (This is removed from the policy of supporting applied and developmental research directed toward the solution of specific problems.)

The sentence in parentheses implies that Merton considers this paper a supplement to his 1949 paper. He is confident that his principle is able "so far as possible to maintain simultaneously the integrity of basic research and the integrity of the business firm."

It is impossible to reproduce in a short space the subtlety of his analysis. He is aware that at a given time some basic sciences have little potential of relevance for any organization. It is then the task of private and public foundations to support these interstitial areas. He also reminds the reader that he is talking about business, because that is the topic of the symposium in which he participates. But, clearly, the principle applies to the relation between science and government, thus making sense of the somewhat paradoxical term "mission-oriented basic research."

After he has developed his general idea, he applies it to the specific relation between basic social research and the life insurance business. He sketches out a large number of relevant topics. In addition to the more obvious connection with population and family research, he mentions such ideas as the time perspectives of various classes of people and attitudes toward death.

One idea in this paper deserves special attention. He is now concerned with the distinction between basic and applied research. But he does not approach the matter by stringing out a number of sentences, as so many other writers have done.

> These dialogues seldom result in exact agreement on the meanings of the principal terms just as they seldom result in such full disagreement as to cut off further discussion. Rather than enter still another pair of definitions into the lists, we can identify the bases of agreement at the core and of the disagreement at the periphery of these concepts.

He suggests that any scientific activity has at least three components: the individual motivation by which a scientist chooses his work; the collective use made of his findings and of the social settings of his work; and the degree of autonomy and the difference in reference groups. This provides what one might call a "three-dimensional space" within which any concrete activity or organizational form can be located.

This kind of analysis was later applied with skill by Norman Storer to the nature of university departments.[23] It is perhaps no coincidence that Storer became the editor of Merton's most recent publication, the collection of his papers on the sociology of science.[24] Storer wrote an introductory history of Merton's work in this field and it contains an interesting sentence: "Following the 1942 paper on the norms of science there was a hiatus of about seven years in Merton's publications in the sociology of science strictly conceived."[25] In a way, the preceding section of my paper fills in this hiatus. But I still want to add a few guesses as to what accounts for the return of the native.

At the time of the SSRC paper Merton had begun to collect his earlier publications; in 1949 the first edition of *Social Theory and Social Structure* made its appearance. Out of fifteen chapters, five were assembled under the title "Sociology of Science." Two were studies related to our joint work at the Bureau. I would guess that the task of assembling this collection revived his earliest interest and he began to return to it seriously. In 1957 his Presidential Address before the American Sociological Association dealt with multiple discoveries[26] and started the series of related papers now included in section 4 of the volume edited by Storer. In 1957 the new and enlarged edition of *Social Theory and Social Structure* came out, containing the part he contributed to the continuities of *The American Soldier* but none of his other Bureau studies. Most of all, it did not include the SSRC paper on applied social science to which I attach so much importance. It is, however, included in the Storer volume, with a new title which avoids the term "applied social science." It is now called "Technical and Moral Dimensions of Policy Research."[27] Not included in the Storer volume is the paper on potentials of relevance which I have just reviewed.

Merton has assembled around his sociology of science program a group of very gifted young scholars. I am sure that some of them will shift their attention from the natural to the social sciences. Once so oriented, they will confront the problems of social science utilization, the controversies, the movement, and the organizational problems surrounding them. If they apply Mertonian analysis to all the evidence accumulated in recent years, they will make important contributions to a confusing but socially very important situation.

2.   THE EMPIRICAL STUDY OF AGGREGATED ACTIONS

The work of the Bureau is mainly identified with formal survey and panel analysis; but while Merton followed these studies with interest and wise counsel, they were not at the center of his activities. True to the purposes of this paper, I want to concentrate on a type of research which has always remained marginal and partially misunderstood in American sociology; for a while Merton made important contributions to it; my point is that his later writings can be read in such a way that a new kind of continuity can be derived from them. I am not sure whether he will accept my interpretation. Be that as it may, at this point I have not only come to praise Merton but also to resurrect a type of empirical research which I still consider important. I must temporarily desert him in order to build up a somewhat broader background for my story.

A HISTORICAL DIGRESSION

At the end of the nineteenth century and during the first quarter of the twentieth, a term was used by most German human scientists with an almost reverent connotation. It was the word *Handlung*—the chain of external behavior and inner experiences which began at some vaguely determined point with the vision of a goal and could be observed up to the point where a person's visible performance either had consequences for himself and others or could be used to understand his real intent. The English word "action" is a correct translation; but it does not reflect the broad sweep of the German word. Two disciplines were especially concerned with it. One was cultural, moral, and legal philosophy on matters closely related to problems of responsibility and causality, free will, and so on. Radbruch, the friend of Max Weber and the minister of justice in the first Weimar Republic, wrote a classic book on the history of the notion of *Handlung*.[28] The other discipline was experimental psychology, which fought the earlier mechanistic associationism. All the concepts of Kurt Lewin, for example, which in this country became known as "topological psychology," were originally published in a large series of papers entitled "Zur Theorie der Menschlichen Handlung."[29]

There was a third trend which, for a variety of reasons, was not located in a special discipline. It never had a definite name, but in retrospect I would call it the *empirical study of aggregated actions*. The actions were aggregated in the following sense: the studies dealt with groups of people who were in approximately the same situation—they had committed some theft, they were schoolboys facing their first occupational choices, or they had just come from the farm and had to adjust to industrial work. The "actors" were studied in their natural setting, not in the laboratory. The type of data collected covered a broad range, and the investigators used introspection unashamedly; one study dealt with people who had tried to commit suicide, were rescued, and then were interviewed as to the reasons for their suicide attempts. The locations of such work were diverse: centers for industrial training, schools of education, social work organizations, private reform groups, and so on. Academically, only a number of psychology departments undertook such work; the small group of academic sociologists were not involved in this trend. Susanne Schad has analyzed this strange situation.[30]

As an assistant at the Psychological Institute of the University of Vienna, I was in charge of the courses in social psychology and statistics. These subject matters made the empirical aggregated actions a natural focus of interest. But, in an academic context, mere description of findings would not have been accepted. Results had to be linked to a "Theorie der Handlung," the title of a book written by the chief of the Institute, Karl Buhler—a book which, incidentally, had great influence on the then incipient movement of formal linguistics.

The link between my empirical studies and the more systematic approach came about in a curious way. Quite a number of the publications I had to review at one time contained statistical reports of answers to the question: "Why did you choose this occupation?" The categories into which the replies were classified were quite arbitrary, and statistical results of comparable studies were quite contradictory. The conclusions I reached were an almost necessary outgrowth of the intellectual atmosphere in which we worked. The objects we were studying (choices, adjustments, effects) were segments of *Handlungen* extending over more or less long periods of time and were connected streams of inner experiences and outside influences: perceived characteristics of the actors' more permanent dispositions, their changing frames of references, and so on. *Handlung*, seen in this way, had no "natural" structure like a piece of furniture or a table of organization. Any structure assigned to a set of comparable actions had to be imposed by the investigator on the empirical elements. The structure so spelled out had no logical necessity; it depended instead on the purpose of the investigation. The question "Why did you do this?" was meaningless in the sense that it did not indicate to the respondent what aspect of an action he was supposed to report—even assuming that he could reconstruct in his memory the flow of the events. If in a study of voting we wanted to know what was decisive, the personality of the candidate or his position on issues, we had to conduct completely different interviews than would have been the case if we wanted to know to what extent he was influenced by friends or by a propaganda pamphlet. Out of all this a special technique, "The Art of Asking Why," developed. The technique consisted essentially of the following steps:

1. The fullest possible picture of the type of action under study had to be obtained.

46

2. A decision had to be made as to which elements in this continuing stream would be analyzed for the purpose of the study. In other words, the full *Handlung* had to be reduced to a finite skeleton, later labeled "accounting scheme."
3. The actual information needed to fill in this accounting scheme had to be ascertained by so-called specifying questions, the function of which was to come as close to the actual events as was possible by a collaboration between the actor and the investigator.
4. The statistical results of such a study could in no way be represented by a linear tabulation of so-called reasons. Each element in the accounting scheme showed considerable variations among the actors included in the aggregate empirical studies; the answers to "why" questions were a multidimensional phenomenon, and each dimension required its own statistical account; these dimensions, of course, could form clusters and patterns deserving careful study.

When I came to this country, empirical action studies[31] with or without theoretical foundations were rare. I was eager to explain to an American audience the Vienna experience, but only market research people were interested. Finally, the *Harvard Business Review* published an article showing how much would be gained if one were to look at purchases as a specific kind of action. The article appeared in 1934, the same year as Parsons' *Structure of Social Action*.

The difference in scope and in subsequent influence is, of course, beyond measure. (If I were to write for a European audience, I should add here: *Si licet parva componere magnis*.) On one issue, certainly unknown to both authors, there was a head-on contradiction. Parsons stated that an action "logically" has four elements. My own position was that an action consists of a practically infinite number of parts but that for research purposes any action has to be structured into a small number of elements. The ensuing divisions are not logically necessary but depend, instead, on the purpose of a study. (I called the research technique I advocated "reason analysis," a name I now find very unfortunate.) The Princeton Office of Radio Research, the predecessor of the Columbia Bureau, provided, from 1937 on, an opportunity to exhibit concrete cases of empirical action studies: Why do people like quiz programs? Why did they run away from the "Invasion from Mars"? In other studies, the starting point was reversed: the effect of radio on the farmer or the effect of serious music programs on American musical tastes. With the transfer to Columbia in 1937 the topics broadened: Why do people change their residences? Why do people volunteer for social service organizations? When we began to work on the *Language of Social Research* in 1952, we built section 5 around the title "The Empirical Analysis of Action," and in these hundred pages the reader can find excerpts from many of these studies.[32]

Before reintroducing Merton into this scene, one methodological point must be expounded. The idea of an accounting scheme is, in its core, not new; every student of migration, for example, distinguishes between "push" and "pull." The accounting scheme idea generalizes to all kind of actions this interplay between a priori analysis and inquiring procedures to get the necessary factual information. Penetrating discussion was given by Charles Kadushin in 1968. Here is a crucial passage:

> A model of action—that is, a list of the basic elements in terms of which human action can be described, together with some notion of how action proceeds—is essential to the development of an "accounting scheme." Such a scheme contains an organized list of all the factors that, for the specific purposes at hand, are said to produce or inhibit an action. An element of action is one in a broad category of factors that propel or repel. For example, a craving for ice cream may be a factor in an accounting scheme for studying ice cream purchases; being a six-year-old boy is an important characteristic of an actor that must be taken into account but is not in itself a propelling factor, even though a cross-sectional analysis might show high ice-cream consumption among six-year-olds as compared to sixty-year-olds.[33]

He discusses in detail reason analysis, "strategies for assessing causes," and problems of validity; his bibliography covers sixty entries. The general theory of accounting schemes appeared as early as 1947, in the first edition of Zeisel's *Say It with Figures*.[34] In later editions of this book, especially in the fifth, Zeisel's ideas are greatly extended because they include his own work on the way juries reach their decisions. To his many concrete examples he added material on the relation between reason statistics and conventional correlation analysis.[35] This is the topic Kadushin alluded to in the last sentence of the preceding quotation.

MERTON'S MANIFEST CONTRIBUTIONS TO EMPIRICAL ACTION ANALYSIS

At the age of twenty-six, Merton published his paper on the unanticipated consequences of purposive "social action."[36] The notion of unanticipated consequences has become enshrined in the conceptual treasure house of sociologists. But little attention has been given to the fact that this paper was clearly divided into two parts. In the second part, Merton does indeed deal with the problem of people not anticipating correctly. But less attention has been given to the first half of his paper addressed to the other element of the title—action. There he uses a language familiar to the reader of my preceding section. He stresses that he will deal with "isolated purposive acts rather than with their integration in a coherent system." More important for us, he then distinguishes two types of action: unorganized and formally organized. The former refers to "actions of individuals considered distributively." The examples he gives move freely between this aggregated level and what he later would call the "institutional" or "structural" level. He stresses that the notion of unanticipated consequences is part of a long history of philosophical and legal discussion; but "no systematic scientific analysis of it has as yet been effected." It is tantalizing to read in a footnote that because of "limitations of space I had to eliminate most of the concrete material upon which the discussion is based." But from the methodological discussion in his first part and the concrete examples in the second, it is easy to see that Merton was not on unknown territory when he joined the work of the Bureau four years later. I do not know in any detail what he was doing in this intermediate period; but from the bibliography attached to *STSS* (1949) one would gather that he was mainly concerned with the extensions of his original work on science in seventeenth-century England. The paper on unanticipated consequences is not reprinted in either *STSS* (1949 or 1957).

As mentioned before, Merton's first assignment at the Bureau was to supervise a series of studies for various governmental agencies and especially for the information branch of the U.S. Army, which had developed a number of films for enlisted men to justify America's entry into the war and to extol the merits of its allies. These films were subjected to detailed research, which is analyzed in volume three of *The American Soldier*. Carl Hovland was in charge of the whole operation, and he was mainly interested then, and later at Yale, in controlled experiments. He delegated to us what he called "The Audience's Evaluation of Films."[37] The procedure consisted of showing the films to small groups of soldiers and then discussing in detail with them their reactions to specific parts of the films. These were singled out in various ways, including very detailed content analysis. A sophisticated interviewing technique was needed to establish that a special element of a film affected in concrete ways the reactions of various viewers. These techniques were clearly relevant to point 2 (the accounting scheme) of my preceding list; but they were different from the technique of discerning, which was mainly directed toward locating the role of what we call "influences"—other people, external events, advertisements, and so on. The new technique was called the "focused interview" because it concentrated on the specific features of a broad stimulus, which seemed to be effective.

A group of gifted interviewers was especially trained for such "program analysis," but it remained a craftsman's art until Merton spelled it out in systematic detail. Together with two of his associates, he published a monograph under the title "The Focused Interview."[38] We used to call "codification" the careful description and consolidation of a specific field of research, a term to which, as we shall see, Merton later gave a much broader meaning.

Because problems of propaganda have recently received less attention, the technique of focused interviews is not part of contemporary sociological literature. But it can be predicted that it will come into prominence again, as our profession is forced to pay increasing attention to evaluation. To understand the nature of effective teaching in colleges, for instance, will require more than the testing of knowledge acquired by students. Also, as we develop more and more government programs that are centrally conceived but that must be implemented in the field, this problem of implementation will become more urgent. Whenever something happens between cup and lip, some variation of the focused interview—be it on an individual or an organizational level—will turn out to be of great methodological importance. (In the commercial field of advertising research, various forms of the focused interview technique are still very much in use, especially in the pretesting of television commercials.)

On one occasion, Merton carried out a full study in which the linkage between a public relations effort and the reaction of the audience was examined in detail and its general implications extrapolated. During the war, great efforts were made to sell war bonds. One of the more spectacular efforts was staged by CBS. The popular entertainer Kate Smith remained on the air for twenty-four hours and returned every fifteen minutes, urging people to buy war bonds. The episode seemed to me almost as bizarre as the "Invasion of Mars" five years earlier, and again I obtained from Frank Stanton the necessary funds to arrange for a hundred interviews with people who had pledged over the telephone to purchase war bonds. Why had they done so?

The whole study was carried out under Merton's direction and was very soon published under the title *Mass Persuasion*.[39] He analyzed the various techniques used by the managers of the "marathon" and matched them with detailed comments of the respondents. He noticed how the listeners were impressed with Kate Smith's sincerity. This struck him as significant because the whole affair was so obviously staged. After a detailed analysis, he concluded that people felt they lived in a world where deception threatened from all sides. The desire to find something that was genuinely sincere was so great that it created an irrational interpretation of this day's staged event. Merton distilled this idea from the general notion of people's search for sincerity in a world of mechanized mass communications. Thus, he carried the purpose of a typical empirical study of aggregated action one step further. Later literature showed the importance of his insight. The best study on the role of television in politics was done in 1969 in England.[40] The authors translated Merton's ideas into a set of clever statistical indicators and were able to show that what people wanted most from a political candidate was for him to be sincere and, paradoxically, that they were convinced they could judge a candidate's sincerity by watching him on television.

The Introduction to *Mass Persuasion* uses all the "right terms"; its task is "discerning the processes and elements of persuasion . . . which have gone largely unexamined or have been matters of speculation rather than research." This kind of study is able "to ferret out from the complexities of a concrete life situation the variables which appear to be decisive. . . ." But one point is striking on careful rereading: the report does not use the word "sociology." Merton consistently describes his study as "social psychology." The "social and cultural context" is, of course, emphasized, but not more than in, say, the "Invasion from Mars."

Having noticed this point only in writing this paper, I have never discussed it with Merton. Therefore, I have to attempt an interpretation. I take my cue from a term which, as we shall see, plays an increasing role in Merton's later writings: "ambivalence." As a student of Sorokin and a younger colleague of Parsons, he took part in an effort to develop a specific sociological vocabulary and conceptualization. Coming to the Bureau, he was asked to work on studies that certainly portrayed people as part of a social network and imbedded in a historical context; but this was, so to say, taken for granted. The emphasis was on the way such people made choices, formed opinions, or acted in emergencies. From Merton's earlier—we might say,

Durkheimian—background, this was interesting but sounded like the "enemy from within" psychology. Remembering our historical background, he was right. But knowing the fullness of his later publications, he thought of psychology and sociology as complementary and not antithetical. Still, at the time of *Mass Persuasion*, he wanted to keep the two separate until he had made up his mind as to how they—and the two environments he had lived in—were to be related.

Two of Merton's subsequent Bureau studies can be used to trace this hypothetical ambivalence and the way it was finally resolved. One is Merton's well-known distinction between cosmopolitan and local influentials. In an early election study, the Bureau had discussed what were then called "horizontal leaders." A new technique had been developed: a sample of people were asked how they made a recent decision, and the purpose of the interviews was to obtain the names and addresses of people who had influenced them; the people so designated were in turn interviewed, and it was found that they belonged to social strata very similar to those of the original respondents. The substantive result was interesting to the MacFadden magazine group, who had maintained that their readers were mainly "wage earners"; to show that wage earners could be influential was obviously important to them, and they subsidized a follow-up study in Decatur, Illinois. At the same time, the technique itself interested Time, Inc. Their research staff had always stressed that their readers were "opinion leaders" in the old sense of bankers, important merchants, top lawyers, and so on. They liked what looked like a new way of tracing big shots; they were confident that our technique would again corroborate that their magazine was read by all opinion leaders, a term made popular by public relations experts. So *Time* magazine commissioned a follow-up study in Dover, New Jersey.

I do not think that anyone was aware at first of the possible contradictions between the purposes of the two studies. Merton was put in charge of the Dover study. He changed the term "opinion leaders" to that of "influentials" but otherwise followed the standard procedure of interviewing first a random sample and then the people who had been named as influentials. When he began to analyze this latter group of reports (he had, of course, a staff of interviewers), he noticed considerable variations and tried to make sense of them. In his report he told of a first "sterile" effort at classification. Here is how he described this unsuccessful phase:

> [He tried] to distinguish influentials according to their dynamic position in the local influence-structure . . . the influentials occupying a supposedly stable position . . . the rising star—still upwardly mobile, the waning influential—now downwardly mobile, etc. . . . [41]

One does not need to be an analyst to see here an effort to apply classical sociological categories to material collected in a different world. As Merton tells it, the solution came when he looked at these influentials as aggregates of concrete actors pursuing a variety of goals. Some used mass communications for their private activities; others, for their public functions. Some were mainly interested in local affairs; others, in the larger outside world. I cannot even remotely summarize the subtlety with which he described how he came to the new classification: cosmopolitans and locals—two "orientations" derived from the influentials' activities, just as the Bureau had often distinguished types of news listeners who had different orientations to the world. I do not know whether Merton felt sad about the defeat of his first effort. Subsequent generations of sociologists have read with delight and used with profit the second effort, which described in great detail the roots, correlates, and consequences of the two orientations.

In *Mass Persuasion* Merton felt the lack of "sociology" in the empirical studies of aggregate action and expressed his uneasiness by referring to social psychology. In "Patterns of Influence" he called the purpose of the study "a problem in the sociology of mass communications" but ended with a typology, highly interesting but characteristic of the Bureau-type of empirical studies. It should be remembered that both studies were assigned to him as the senior staff member, and not by his own choice. He undoubtedly felt a discrepancy between this work and his ongoing concern with sociological theory.

The first sign of how he would solve his dilemma in his own terms becomes visible in a third (and, if I remember correctly, the last) task he performed during the period in which the work program of the Bureau was still basically determined by the traditions of the director. Some time in 1947 I gave a speech for a symposium organized by Lyman Bryson and published later.[42] My presentation was a combination of two earlier speeches which had been published by then and which were sequential summaries of the Bureau's work on the effect of mass media. The transcript of this new speech was, as usual, unprintable, and I asked Merton to make it suitable for publication. When I got the text back from him, my own ideas were put into fluent English and occasionally enriched by references to classical writers I probably had never heard of. But he had included a four-page section called "Some Social Functions of the Mass Media." It contained Merton's own analytical reflections, and therefore I felt the paper should be published jointly. With details still very interesting to read, he lists the following functions:

a. The status-conferral function. The idea is that just being mentioned in the newspaper in whatever context makes a person more important. His main examples are the advertisements "Men of Distinction." It makes the whisky more important because of the testimonial of a well-known man. It increases the status of the man because he has been asked to testify for the whisky.

b. The enforcement of social norms. Here the idea is that deviation from irksome social norms are generally tolerated as long as they are not exposed in a newspaper. Then the man in the street has to take a stand and for his own protection has to let public morality override his more tolerant private attitudes. Here again, incidentally, Merton stresses the circular, self-sustaining process. The successful crusade punishes the malefactor and at the same time increases the prestige of the newspaper.

c. The narcotizing dysfunction. The idea is that many educated people spend an increasing amount of time in reading and listening. As a result they have less time available for organized action. They mistake knowing about problems of the day for doing something about them—this is an interesting version of an example I had in my original paper. In France the critics of the mass media are not so much concerned with cultural values but are afraid that entertainment keeps workers from being active in the labor movement.

Each idea in this section was new at the time, but each reappeared and was elaborated on in Merton's subsequent writings: the privately tolerated deviations from public norms, the problem of visibility, the circularity of certain social processes, and so on. The section stands as a bloc in the paper not related to my parts of it. But it presages the solution of the ambivalence referred to before. He had found a way to relate his own sociological bent of mind to the empirical study of aggregated action, which he obviously found attractive but unsatisfactory. I shall call his solution the "sociological radiation"[43] of empirical action research. My next section will try to extract this notion from the papers he wrote after his full involvement in the Bureau's activities began to decline.

MERTON'S LATENT CONTRIBUTIONS TO EMPIRICAL ACTION ANALYSIS

It should be fairly obvious by now what direction my discussion will take. I shall assume the position that one who is interested in empirical action analysis can pluck from Merton's writings in the last twenty years endless ideas on how to enrich the accounting scheme for any concrete study and to trace out fruitful new connections.

1. I begin with two examples from a study on housing problems, which Merton started when he was an associate director of the Bureau. The final study was never published; there are only occasional references to it in Merton's other writings and some progress reports from his staff.

It is now a cliché in consumer research to say that specifying questions are needed to make sure what respondents really mean. If they say they buy their gasoline at the station nearest to their house, it is sometimes found that two other stations are actually closer but "they do not sell nationally advertised brands." In a new community (Craftown) Merton noticed that parents of young children found the baby-sitter problem alleviated because "there are so many more teenagers around here than where we used to live." On checking the data, he discovered that "the ratio of adolescents to children under ten years of age was 1:10 in Craftown, whereas in the new residents' communities of origin the ratio hovered around 1:15." Merton's explanation of this "social illusion" was that due to the social cohesion in this new town where people knew all the other residents they had more confidence in each other.[44]

It is also quite conventional in empirical studies of this kind to ask respondents how their actual experiences, say, with today's price structure, compare with their preceding expectations. But, again, in the housing study Merton gave this expectation "a broader founding." He divided people in a biracial housing project (Hilltown) into two groups; those who had previously lived in a "mixed neighborhood" and those who had not. Forty-three percent of the "inexperienced" whites said that the relations between the races in the new setting were better than they had expected, while only 17 percent of those with experience gave this answer.[45]

In both cases, a conventional study would have talked of "predispositions," meaning biographical data preceding the onset of the total process which the investigator singles out for more detailed analysis. But Merton's predispositions are likely to be elements that position the actors in a specific social environment.

2. With the appearance of the first two volumes of *The American Soldier*, Merton becomes interested in the reference group idea.[46] This shifts the social environment from a *pre*disposition to an element *within* the core process of action as a direct object of study. These two papers should be read as an inventory of all possible ways in which "others" can affect the behavior of people acting under similar conditions. At the same time, the intervening steps in this process multiply. We have groups to which people belong and more distant groups which they can only observe. In the latter case, what do they know about them? The notion of "visibility" briefly alluded to in the mass media paper is now extended into a major theme. The "insider" and the "outsider" have different information. How does this affect people who move from one position to the other? How in the process of accumulating decisions do people altogether "select" their reference groups?

Using our simile of "sociological radiation," we have now reached a wider circumference. The network of reference groups is more distant from the actor under observation than his immediate neighborhood. To get a very concrete idea of how this would shape the practice of empirical action analysis, we had better move our radius still further out.

3. Merton wrote a paper on "Bureaucratic Structure and Personality."[47] His main idea was that a bureaucratic organization requires careful attention to rules; this leads to a "trained incapacity" of its members to handle situations requiring unusual solutions. The chain of connections is carefully argued,[48] and as one of the consequences Merton mentions "conflict in the bureaucrats' contacts with the public or clientele."[49] Now, let us turn around and visualize an educational program designed to improve the client relations of a public agency. As part of the plan, the following study is contemplated: complaints will be collected and the accused functionaries will be interviewed as to why they behaved the way they did. It is easy to visualize how Merton's analysis would broaden the range of topics to be brought up with the respondents: Did they have similar difficulties before? Are they periodically overloaded with paper work? Have some superiors reprimanded them for not following regulations? What do they do to observe the rules? Such questions would be added to the more conventional reason analysis because from the beginning Mertonian analysis would introduce into the accounting scheme the possible role of the bureaucratic background. The questions suggested here are only meant to show how it could be tested with people unfamiliar with sociological ideas. Without the study having actually been made, one cannot tell in advance how many of these links between a person's position

in a specific bureaucracy and his behavior to outsiders can be traced, with what frequency they would exhibit various patterns, or how they might differ according to the position of the client. This, of course, is only one of many possible examples. Other studies could start with a set of officials who had to make decisions on comparable cases. Merton himself, in a final paragraph of his paper, calls for empirical studies and bemoans the limited accessibility of concrete data. But he seems to be thinking more of statistical studies relating personality tests to characteristics of organizations. The latent message of his analytical reflections, however, points much more to the need for retrospective analysis of concrete actions guided by an enriched technique of interviewing and multidimensional statistical analysis of the reports.

4. The scope of the sociological radiation in such studies can have ever larger perimeters. Let me discuss one last case. There is a rather extensive literature on the relation between age and creativity: When are people most productive? How late in their lives do they still work?[50] Merton, in collaboration with Harriet Zuckerman, has recently collected new information and reanalyzed preexisting material.[51] From the rich content of their paper, I want to focus on only one element. The authors introduce the notion of the "degree of codification" characteristic of a given discipline. In the natural sciences, that means whether a small number of theoretical ideas cover a large amount of empirical knowledge: physics is more codified than biology. In the social sciences, the difference is more whether certain subareas have been consolidated into coherent presentations: sociology is probably more codified than anthropology.

The authors make the observation that this " structural factor" of consolidation—probably very distant from the consciousness of the scholar—still affects many decisions he makes in his own career. In the less codified social sciences, individual experience is important, and so researchers can still be "original" at a late period in their lives. Lack of codification also leads to long-lasting competitive "schools," which force younger people to enter into allegiances which may constrain their own work later. Inversely, in the more codified sciences, younger people are less likely to keep on quoting the classics because there is agreement as to which part of the work in the field is, mostly anonymously, carried forward in textbooks.

The paper makes brilliant use of the limited data available, but it properly states how "little effort has been made to trace the consequences of the cognitive structure of the various sciences for their distinctive social structures." This task can have many meanings and thus may require a variety of methodological approaches. But one type of work will certainly require more attention: to take scholars at various decision points—choice of graduate school, of dissertation topic, of first job—and find out how one stage moves into the next. By comparing various disciplines, we shall certainly not ask: Were you influenced by the state of codification of the field in question? But the concept itself, as a sociological element in the flow of aggregated individual actions, together with the many possible links the paper suggests, would greatly affect such an inquiry and it would, I am confident, make new contributions to a general sociology of science.

I am, of course, perfectly aware that I turn these papers upside down. Merton wants to spell out all the implications of the theoretical notion of reference groups by "progressive clarification" and "reconceptualization." He shows that the concept of bureaucracy, properly analyzed, should lead one to expect constraints on and directives for the conduct of its members. He traces out the possible consequences of the age structure of a corps of scientists on all phases of their work.

My point is that this whole avalanche of ideas could also be read in reverse: they broaden immensely the range of sociological elements which can and should enter into empirical studies of aggregate action. The idea may be clarified somewhat further by translating it into the terminology of *impact analysis*. The animal psychologist studies the impact of a bell's sound on a dog's salivation. The social psychologist greatly broadens the notion of "stimulus" by studying the impact of a teacher on a pupil, or of a propaganda message on an audience. Some sociologists are interested in the impact of the family or the neighborhood—a set of various stimuli exercised over a long period of time. One could interpret Merton's several approaches to the "social structure" as an increasing widening of the "stimulus" idea—as to complexity, duration, and distance from the concrete situation within which concrete actions are performed.

There is no doubt that Merton is aware of this second possibility. I have in my files a memo written to me in 1963. The occasion was as follows. I had been asked to give a series of lectures on my own work; they were part of a yearly recurring event, and I was featured as the sociologist in the sequence. Not to mislead the audience, I decided that one of the lectures should be devoted to what difference it would make if a "real" sociologist were to speak, and had asked Merton to provide me with a list of possible examples. His memo is entitled "Specimens of Sociological Diagnosis—Candidate Items for the Sociological Perspective." The term "diagnosis" was obviously suggested as an appropriate title for the studies he knew I was reporting. And the cases he suggested are clearly the mirror image of his own thinking formulated for the benefit of my "party line." Here are three typical (abbreviated) specimens:

> The beliefs of others about individuals or groups lead these others . . . to act as others had prophesied.

> Look not only at how A happened to create works of science or art but also at interactive processes with others, evoking or suppressing talent.

> So seemingly trifling a factor as a direction in which the front door faces can be shown to affect the probability of making friends with people next door or across the street.

He signaled to me that it could be done this way. But there is no question of ambivalence. He preferred his way by taste, talent, and conviction as to the task of sociology.[52]

3. FURTHER RESEARCH NEEDED

Merton's contributions to the corpus of contemporary sociology and especially to social theory are discussed by many contributors to this volume. In part 2 I selected as my main example an approach to his work which is likely to be overlooked by others and with which I personally am much concerned. But many other observations grew out of my work with Merton and some of them I want to put on record for future work.

Soon Merton will become the subject of dissertations. Here is a list of suggestions compiled after just rereading most of his publications.

1. I begin where my last section ended. Perhaps some readers would like to try their own hand at the reinterpretation of other Merton papers in terms of further possible empirical action research; it would give them, at least, an additional avenue to appreciate the finely chiseled filigree of his deductions. I recommend especially three papers. Two choices are obvious. What would have been added to the Merton-Zuckerman paper on the referee system if they had carried out "focused interviews" with the referees as to how they came to make their decisions?[53] And the paper on the ambivalence of scientists directly raises the question of why scientists become involved in so many priority disputes and why they refuse to study, or even acknowledge, this fact.[54] Merton's answers are based on general considerations about the reward system of science and on an astute scrutiny of published documents. Would it be worthwhile to interview living scholars on such experiences? Certainly Merton's analysis would enrich the interview guide; in reverse, would such an empirical study add to his insights?

The third unfinished example in this series would be more complex.

In a paper titled "Sociological Ambivalence," not yet included in any of his collections, Merton and his co-author, Elinor Barber, begin by defining their topic as distinct from psychological ambivalence.[55] As a crucial example, they first mention that the well-known ambivalence of the apprentice to master would vary according to the degree to which the "table of organization" provides advancement opportunities for the younger man.[56] The main topic, however, is the ambivalence between clients and professionals (lawyers, doctors, and so on), which is first defined as "relational." But the bulk of the essay is devoted to asymmetric material: how the client reacts to the elements built into the norms of the profession. The section on "structural sources of ambivalence" comes as close as one would wish to a brilliant program for an empirical study: why do patients feel uneasy about their physicians?[57] Incidentally, I consider the whole paper one of the best examples of Merton's sociological bent of mind.

2. Another promising key would be certain word counts. In the crucial last ten pages of the article just mentioned, the term "patterned" occurs ten times. Throughout his writings, this is probably the technical term he uses most often. Sometimes it means that an event takes place with different frequencies in different social groups. At other points, the term refers to sequences that derive necessarily from each other. But it also refers to con-

duct which is generally expected by a group; and if acknowledged as differentially available to various statuses, it is again patterned. I would guess that the word is intended to approximate Durkheim's "social facts" and means to convey their main characteristics. One should ascertain how the frequency of the term varies with the topic at hand or with the phases of Merton's professional development. This undoubtedly would show how he tries to establish his own coherent vision within the confines of a fallible language.

I offer this suggestion very seriously because I think it would also reveal one aspect of Merton's success as a teacher. For many students, his sociology has an appeal that emanates from psychoanalysis. In the latter, people are pushed around *from within* by unconscious motives—and to discover them is fascinating. Now it turns out that people are also pushed around *from without,* and here too they do not know about it. To learn that the patterned social structure accomplishes it all is equally stunning—and deservedly so.

More difficult will be the interpretation of Merton's frequent use of the term "ambivalence." It appears in the title of at least three of his published papers, and I have the impression that it is used more from one decade to the next. Only by a detailed scrutiny could one determine whether he increasingly feels that various aspects of ambivalence are a central sociological topic or whether a patterned sequence of doubts—unavoidable in any social scientist today—is involved. In the pursuit of this topic, the help of an experienced analyst of style will be needed. After hearing a few bars of music, I can recognize that the composer is Brahms, even though I cannot explicate the criteria on which my impression is based. I have the same feeling in the case of Merton—I would recognize him after reading one paragraph, but I do not know how. I can only supply one observation which seems to me somehow connected with the "ambivalence" theme: the frequent use of double adjectives to characterize the same object. Some concepts are separate but related; some facts are generally believed but never documented; some ideas are provisional but definite; some issues are as complex as they are unexplored; and so on.

3. To turn to another topic for one of the imaginary dissertation candidates: perhaps he will want to defend Merton's confidence in social theory. He would do well to peruse his publications on the lookout for predictions—often hidden in off-stage places—which later on were vindicated. They are of various kinds, and I can give only a few examples.

His early interest in the sociology of science has by now made him a leading public figure in the movement toward technological assessment. Some conceptual conjectures have later become official disciplinary themes. Thus, for example, the first paper on reference groups introduces a problem "deserving attention which it has not yet received."[58] Any situation a person is involved in can be seen by him in "two types of evaluations, self-appraisals and appraisals of institutional arrangements." He first discusses an example from *The American Soldier,* and then wants to see the idea extended to strategic areas of study in the larger social system. He elaborates this in terms of basic political issues, culminating in the following quotation:

58

For example, the sociological factors which lead men to consider their own, relatively low, social position as legitimate, as well as those which lead them to construe their position as a result of defective and possibly unjustified social arrangements clearly comprise a problem area of paramount theoretical and political importance. When are relatively slim life-chances taken by men as a normal and expectable state of affairs which they attribute to their own personal inadequacies and when are they regarded as the results of an arbitrary social system of mobility, in which rewards are not proportioned to ability?[59]

This is, of course—writ large—a topic which recently has received extensive attention: attribution theory. But it should also be remembered that in the first part of his paper on unintended consequences he stresses that he will deal mainly with "isolated purposive acts" and that this involves "the problem of causal imputation"—although he chooses for the time being not to discuss this in further detail. The problem of such imputations is, of course, a major concern of attribution theory.[60]

Another example is an insertion of Merton's in our joint paper on mass communications.[61] He suggests, as a question for disciplined research (one of his favorite terms), "whether mass media have robbed the intellectual and artistic elite of the art forms which otherwise have been accessible to them." Ten years later a symposium was held at which social scientists, artists, and managers discussed the dilemma of "culture for the millions."[62] Probably the most interesting contribution was made by the musicologist Arthur Berger, who documented this point under the title "The Plight of the American Composer." Finally, regarding Merton as a futurist, a personal recollection is relevant. His pilot study on influentials originally appeared in one of a series of Bureau publications.[63] He wanted to include a long conceptual chapter which did not fit in with the general style so far developed for this series. We finally agreed on a sort of appendix, which he called "The Provisional Concept of Interpersonal Influence (Added Remarks)." Rereading it now, I see that he advocated distinctive clarification of related concepts such as "power" and "exchange," which, of course, have become increasingly popular topics in the sociological literature, often with special emphasis on problems of measurement.

4. Merton as a consultant would have to be studied by methods of oral history—involving himself and his clients. Sometimes it is found that clients keep matters confidential much longer than is necessary. Usually some persuasion or techniques of camouflage overcome this resistance, at least to the point where the sociologically relevant ideas can be brought out. But the prospective candidate for this especially challenging topic will at first be startled by Merton's seeming lack of memory; this is not feigned but can, I think, be explained. He keeps a daily diary of his activities and his readings, including clippings of additonal examples for topics on which he has previously published. I am convinced—although I do not quite understand the underlying mechanism—that in this way he "clears" the overload of his personal memory bank and leaves it free for new ideas and observations.

The task would be to read this material first, use it to reconstruct concrete episodes, and then ask Merton for the connections with his theoretical thinking at the time. While I have never seen his files, I can give two examples of which I have outside knowledge of the concrete situations. One is an episode in his consulting work for an organization of nurses. The problem was how to increase the professional prestige of this group. Merton had the idea that a large conference on medical problems, called jointly by a prestigious medical association and his clients' organization, would be more effective than detailed negotiations with individual hospitals, as had been orginally planned. I understand that the conference was a great success and finally led to federal legislation improving the status of nurses everywhere. This seems to me an effective application of what I earlier called "sociological radiation"—the detour through more complex structural levels.

My second example involves the utilization of Merton's sensitivity to latent factors. In the tax load of a corporation, it makes a difference whether an advertisement is intended to augment the sale of a product or increase the corporation's prestige. The latter—institutional advertising—has some tax advantages. Sometimes it is not easy to make the distinction. If a company stresses the care with which it selects its raw materials, to which type of advertising does such promotion belong? I understand that Merton redefined the problem in terms of latent messages. By combining quantitative content analysis, talks with copywriters (who were not aware of the legal implications), and, I believe, some interviews with consumers, he developed criteria acceptable to the tax authorities. I am convinced that the cumulation of such cases, covering twenty-five years of experience, would greatly contribute to codifying the nature of sociological advice.

There is one topic left to which on a future occasion I hope to turn myself in more detail. I have often heard Merton say that one must be serious about conceptual matters. He wants to discourage the frequent habit of authors of applying a tag to an idea and leaving things there. It is necessary to look at a notion, try out variations and implications, see how it is related to ideas developed in another context, and draw on empirical data which would illustrate the original notion. Watching him do this is like watching an expert examine a possibly precious stone by turning it over in his hand, studying all the facets from different angles and in different lights. I like to call this talent of his "conceptual ramification." Students should and could be trained to acquire such a skill. But it would be important to explicate it in more detail; sources come easily to mind. One is his relentless pursuit of a theme. The papers on anomie and on reference groups in the 1949 edition of *Social Theory and Social Structure* are followed up in the second edition by two papers, called "continuities" on the two topics. The concern with multiple discoveries began with his presidential address and was followed up by three more papers, all now juxtaposed as chapters 16, 17, and 18 in *The Sociology of Science*. It should not be too difficult to bring out what each phase of these continuities adds to the earlier ones.

But the idea of conceptual ramification can also be studied within one single paper. Consider, for example, the paper on what he calls the "Matthew effect."[64] It starts out with the well-known observation that in the collaboration of younger and older authors the more famous one gets more recognition. Merton then explores the consequences this has for the two partners, for the diffusion of information among scientists, and for the allocation of resources to various scientific pursuits. One could even try to be one's own Mertonian and see whether the notion cannot be extended to areas other than the sociology of science. Psychologists have noticed that good students receive more attention from teachers and so eventually become even better—the Pygmalion effect. Only educated people pay attention to educational broadcasts. Should such observations be considered variations of the Matthew effect? What is the optimal range of conceptual ramification?[65]

Sometimes one can make more explicit a technique used by Merton in the service of conceptual ramification. He starts with imaginary cross-tabulations and then follows where the ensuing typologies might lead. The famous anomie paper centers on a cross-classification of cultural goals and institutional means;[66] the first classification of reference groups is the combinatorial result between the relative status of the group to which an individual orients himself and whether he is himself a member or not.[67] More recently two kinds of recognition and two kinds of excellence lead to four types which clarify problems involved in the education of and rewards for elites.[68] Many other such derivations are implied, if not always explicitly stated, in several of Merton's papers.

If I have the courage I shall even take a Levi-Straussian turn and try to show that many of Merton's papers deal, on a deeper level, with the same theme, even when the titles and the apparent subject matter seem quite different. Take as an example an undeservedly less well-known book built around the aphorism that sitting (or standing) on the shoulders of giants is an advantage to people with minor gifts. By intention the essay is a stylistic *tour de grande force,* drawing upon an almost unbelievable store of historical and literary knowledge.[69] But in fact it discusses the relation between generations of scholars and how this relation has been looked upon at different historical periods. (Merton proposes, half ironically, to call it the OTSOG issue.)

But does this not really have the same mythological kernel as the Matthew effect—master and apprentice, predecessor and successor, the painful tension between genuine respect and nagging doubt? I would like to have a good dichotomous term. "The tried and true" could do, but it does not quite catch the idea. I might end with inventing "le cru et le cuit," and this would almost bring us back to conceptual ramification. Seriously, I think that such a theme could be found at many—often surprising—points in Merton's writings.

I began this memorandum with Merton's joining the Columbia Bureau of Applied Social Research, undoubtedly the most important event in its history. The publications of the Bureau have received wide attention, and many of its graduates are now among leading figures in American sociology.

And yet one should not forget that the Bureau also had an organizational purpose. It was meant to incorporate the rapid expansion of empirical social research into the structure of American universities, especially their social science faculties. It is not at all clear whether this goal has been achieved. In the last two hundred years the trend was for the universities to be the guardians of all teaching and research. The trend began at the turn of the nineteenth century in the German universities; the pattern was followed basically by all American universities. When in the middle of the nineteenth century the rapid expansion to the west created many social and technological difficulties, it was taken for granted (in the double sense of the word) that a network of new state colleges would provide solutions to those problems. When at the beginning of the twentieth century general medical practice did not live up to the rapidly developing scientific knowledge, the Flexner report, with one stroke, turned over all medical education to university administration.

For a variety of reasons, this practice has not been adopted in our day, when the machinery of empirical social research has become so complex; the universities have so far not been able to absorb the research. At the moment, probably the majority of such work is done outside of the campus. No one knows yet whether this is a temporary situation or a permanent trend; as a matter of fact, there is considerable debate as to which of the two outcomes is more desirable. I do not think that Merton and I are on the same side of the debate, but probably it will end with the two forms coexisting: on the one hand, research centers firmly incorporated into universities and, on the other, a number of independent programs—either major foundation grants built around leading scholars, or specialized institutes financed by public or private sources. If this is the outcome, Merton will have been a charismatic figure in the growth of both forms.

NOTES

1. Robert K. Merton, *Science, Technology and Society in Seventeenth-Century England* (New York: Fertig, 1970).
2. Robert K. Merton, *Social Theory and Social Structure* (Glencoe, Ill.: Free Press, 1949), chap. 6. Whenever possible, Merton's papers will be quoted from the 1949 edition or the 1957 revised edition of *Social Theory and Social Structure* and will be referred to as *STSS* (1949) or *STSS* (1957).
3. Robert K. Merton and Paul F. Lazarsfeld, eds., *Continuities in Social Research, Studies in the Scope and Method of the American Soldier* (Glencoe: Ill.: Free Press, 1950).
4. Merton, *STSS* (1949), chap. 3.
5. Robert K. Merton, "The Role of Applied Social Science in the Formation of Policy: A Research Memorandum," *Journal for the Philosophy of Science* 16 (July 1949): 161–81.
6. *Ibid.*, p. 168.
7. Robert K. Merton and Robert Nisbet, *Contemporary Social Problems*, 3rd ed. (New York: Harcourt Brace Jovanovich, 1971).
8. Robert K. Merton, "Unanticipated Consequences of Purposive Social Action," *American Sociological Review* 1 (1936): 176.

9. Paul Lazarsfeld, William Sewell, Harold Wilensky, eds., *The Uses of Sociology* (New York: Basic Books, 1968).

10. James S. Coleman, *Policy Research in the Social Sciences* (Morristown, N.J.: General Learning Press, 1972).

11. Robert K. Merton and Edward C. Devereux, Jr., "Practical Problems and the Uses of Social Science," *Transaction,* a publication of Washington University, St. Louis, Mo., 1964, pp. 18–21.

12. Robert K. Merton, George Reader, and Patricia L. Kendall, eds., *The Student Physician: Introductory Studies in the Sociology of Medical Education* (Cambridge, Mass.: Harvard University Press, 1957).

13. Hans L. Zetterberg, *Social Theory and Social Practice* (New York: Bedminster Press, 1962).

14. The memorandum is reprinted as Chapter 8 in Paul F. Lazarsfeld, *Qualitative Analysis* (Boston: Allyn & Bacon, 1972), a collection of some of my older papers, most of which come from the early period of the Bureau. Chapter 8 also briefly traces the relation of the memorandum to the subsequent foundation of the Ford Center for the Advanced Study of the Behavioral Sciences.

15. After this review was written, I inquired at the Social Science Research Council whether they had any material on file referring to this conference. I received the following information:

"The small conference to which you refer was held in the Council office on March 20, 1948, and the subject, according to our records, was 'The Expert and Applied Social Science.' We regret that our files do not contain a program, a letter of invitation, nor a list of participants in the conference. Pendleton Herring served as its chairman. In a very brief report made at the meeting of the Council's board of directors in April 1948, he noted that the conference was concerned with the possibility of clarifying the relations between the expert and those who use his knowledge in government and business. Robert Merton, because of his interest in research on this problem, had been asked to prepare the agenda for the conference. He had written and distributed to the participants a memorandum 'The Expert and Research in Applied Social Science: Topics for Discussion at a Conference under the Auspices of the Social Science Research Council,' as well as a longer outline (dated November 1947) of a study he was then proposing to undertake. Mr. Herring reported that the conference was much interested in the research aspects of the subject, and that there might be opportunity for aiding in the development of a project. However, nothing further appears in our records."

16. Gene M. Lyons, "The Social Science Study Groups" in Irving L. Horowitz, ed., *The Use and Abuse of Social Science* (New Brunswick, N.J.: Rutgers University Press, 1971).

17. (BASS) "Institutes and University Organizations for Research on Social Problems," *The Behavioral and Social Sciences Outlook and Needs* (Washington, D.C.: National Academy of Sciences, 1969), chap. 12.

18. Orville Brim, "Knowledge into Action," report of the special commission on the Social Sciences, National Science Foundation, 1969.

19. Stanley Ikenberry and Renee C. Friedman, *Beyond Academic Departments—The Story of Institutes and Centers* (San Francisco: Jossey-Bass, 1972).

20. Harold Orlans, "The Nonprofit Research Institute," Carnegie Foundation for the Advancement of Teaching, 1972.

21. Albert Biderman and Laure M. Sharp, *The Competitive Evaluation Research Industry* (Washington, D.C.: Bureau of Social Science Research, 1971).

22. Robert K. Merton, "Basic Research and Potentials of Relevance," *American Behavioral Scientist* 9 (May 1963): 86–90.
23. Norman W. Storer, "Relations Among Scientific Disciplines," in Saad Z. Nagi and Ronald G. Gorwin, eds., *The Social Contexts of Research* (New York: Wiley, 1972), chap. 8.
24. Robert K. Merton, *The Sociology of Science*, ed. Norman W. Storer (Chicago: University of Chicago Press, 1973). This volume will play an increasing role in the following pages.
25. *Ibid.*, p. 20.
26. Robert K. Merton, "Priorities in Scientific Discovery," Presidential Address delivered at the annual meeting of the American Sociological Association, August 1957; first published in *American Sociological Review* 22, no. 6 (December 1957): 635–59.
27. Robert K. Merton, "Technical and Moral Dimensions of Policy Research," in Storer, ed., *The Sociology of Science*, pp. 70–98.
28. Gustav Radbruch, *The Concept of Action in Its Importance for Legal Systematics* (Berlin, 1903). (Title translated.)
29. See Lazarsfeld, *Qualitative Analysis*, chap. 2.
30. Susanne P. Schad, *Empirical Social Research in Weimar-Germany* (Mouton, 1972).
31. I shall hereafter use this shorter expression as identical with, but more convenient than, the more correct term used so far.
32. Paul F. Lazarsfeld and Morris Rosenberg, eds., *The Language of Social Research* (New York: Free Press, 1955).
33. Charles Kadushin, "Reason Analysis," in *International Encyclopedia of the Social Sciences*, vol. 13 (New York: Macmillan, 1968).
34. Hans Zeisel, *Say It with Figures* 5th ed. (New York: Harper & Row, 1968; first published, 1947), chaps. 10, 11, and 12.
35. *Ibid.*, p. 195.
36. Merton, "Unanticipated Consequences of Purposive Social Action."
37. Carl I. Hovland, Arthur A. Lumsdaine, and Fred D. Sheffield, *Experiments in Mass Communication* (Princeton, N.J.: Princeton University Press, 1949), chap. 4.
38. For easy orientation, a shorter article, written with Patricia Kendall, is available under the same title; Robert K. Merton and Patricia Kendall, "The Focused Interview," *American Journal of Sociology* 51 (1946): 541–57.
39. Robert K. Merton, *Mass Persuasion* (New York: Harper & Bros., 1946).
40. "Television and the Credibility of Campaigning Politicians," in Jay G. Blumler and Denis McQuail, *Television in Politics* (Chicago: University of Chicago Press, 1969), chap. 5.
41. Merton, *STSS* (1957), chap. 10.
42. Paul F. Lazarsfeld and Robert K. Merton, "Mass Communication, Popular Taste and Organized Social Action," in Lyman Bryson, ed., *The Communication of Ideas* (New York: Harper & Bros., 1948).
43. For quick reference, slogans are needed; but they often evoke images in the reader not intended by the writer. As I hope the following examples will show, I mean a type of analysis that can move back and forth between individual actors and sociological constructs, becoming an element in the explanatory accounting scheme.
44. Merton, *STSS* (1949), chap. 3.
45. Marie Jahoda and Patricia Salter West, "Race Relations in Public Housing," *The Journal of Social Issues* 7 (1951): 132.
46. Merton, *STSS* (1957), chaps. 8 and 9.

47. Merton, *STSS* (1949), chap. 5.

48. *Ibid.*, pp. 197–204.

49. *Ibid.*, p. 204.

50. One of the earliest books on this topic partly based on biographical statistics is, unfortunately, still untranslated: Charlotte Bühler, *Die Psychologie des Menschlichen Lebenslaufes* (Hirzel, 1932).

51. Robert K. Merton, with Harriet Zuckerman, "Age, Aging, and Age Structure in Science," in Robert K. Merton, *The Sociology of Science,* ed. Norman W. Storer, chap. 22.

52. Why has empirical action analysis never reached great popularity in our profession? We read occasional recent studies as to why people became dentists or why they joined nudist camps; but such papers are not seen as part of a tradition, let alone as being an established field or specialization. Why is this so?

One answer might be that asking sets of people why they did something or how they are affected by exposure to comparable situations cannot lead to generalizations. But this is certainly not true, as Merton's own example shows. At one point during the work for the army, Merton wrote a paper, "Studies in Radio and Film Propaganda," for which he gave me joint credit (*STSS* [1947], chap. 10). The principles presented were based completely on audience interviews, just as so much of recent work in the sociology of science is based on statistics of publication and citation records.

A second possibility is the distaste for "psychologism." But this would be a misunderstanding. The persons interviewed in such studies are used as informants, as sources of data. The proportion of people who say they are influenced by (in addition to having listened to) a presidential speech is as much a "social fact" as the suicide rate. It could be argued, of course, that it is misleading information, because "people don't know why they act the way they do." My answer is well known: researchers have neglected the art of finding out. This is not the place to argue this point beyond the references I gave in my historical digression.

A third and very cogent argument would go like this: sociology should exploit as much as possible unobtrusive measures, data that can be derived from existing records and observation without direct questioning of actors. Still, this leaves the possibility open that empirical action analysis can add a great deal wherever it is feasible and may even be economical. (Kadushin has aptly described research problems where this is actually the case; "Reason Analysis," p. 338.)

There is today much talk of paradigms in the sciences, their generational shifts, and the role star performers play in all this. By showing Merton's actual and potential contribution to an older paradigm, some of its still viable merits might be saved from oblivion.

53. Merton, *The Sociology of Science,* chap. 21.

54. *Ibid.*, chap. 18.

55. Robert K. Merton and Elinor Barber, "Sociological Ambivalence," in Edward A. Tiryakian, ed., *Sociological Theory, Values and Sociocultural Change* (New York: Harper Torchbooks, 1967).

56. Evidence on this point can be found in Patricia L. Kendall, "The Learning Environments of Hospitals," in Eliot Freidson, ed., *The Hospital in Modern Society* (New York: Free Press, 1963).

57. Merton and Barber, "Sociological Ambivalence," pp. 109–15.

58. Robert K. Merton, with Alice S. Rossi, "Contributions to the Theory of Reference Group Behavior," *STSS* (1957), p. 240.

59. *Ibid.*

60. The literature on attribution theory has grown very large in recent years. In the present context, the most helpful paper is Edward Jones and Keith Davis, "From Acts to Dispositions," in Leonard Berkowitz, ed., *Advances in Social Psychology*, vol. 2 (New York: Academic Press, 1965).

61. Lazarsfeld and Merton, "Mass Communications, Popular Taste and Organized Social Action."

62. Norman Jacobs, ed., *Culture for the Millions* (Princeton, N.J.: Van Nostrand, 1959).

63. Paul F. Lazarsfeld and Frank N. Stanton, eds., *Communications Research 1948– 1949* (New York: Harper & Bros., 1949).

64. Robert K. Merton, "The Matthew Effect in Science," in Merton, *The Sociology of Science*, chap. 20.

65. It is indeed not clear how far one should go in subsuming facts and ideas under one conceptual notion. But certainly Merton has taught us where *not* to stop. Two years before I met him I had published data which showed the high positive correlation between the educational level of listeners and their interest in educational radio programs. The results were described under the subtitle "Giving to Those Who Have." I then turned directly to the question of how to raise poorly educated people to a higher level of intellectual aspiration. It never occurred to me to see in the findings and in the apercue the possible starting point of what I call in the text conceptual ramification.

66. Merton, *STSS* (1949), p. 133.

67. Merton, *STSS* (1957), p. 232.

68. Merton, *The Sociology of Science*, p. 425.

69. Robert K. Merton, *On the Shoulders of Giants* (New York: Free Press, 1965).

The Present Status of "Structural-Functional" Theory in Sociology

TALCOTT PARSONS

S INCE Robert Merton and the present author are generally labeled what might be called the "arch-functionalists" in contemporary sociology—among whom Marion Levy[1] would also often be included—it seems appropriate that in a volume honoring Merton on the occasion of his sixty-fifth birthday his old teacher and fellow functionalist should say something on the topic indicated by the title of this paper. After an interval of some years, I have reread Merton's seminal essay "Manifest and Latent Functions"[2] and tried to fit his thought and my own together. In that essay and in other writings,[3] he clearly made a major contribution to the understanding and clarification of the theoretical methodology of what he, I think quite appropriately, called "functional analysis"—what it was about, what its assumptions were, what some of its potentialities were, and the like.

I well remember at a meeting of the International Sociological Association, held in Washington, D.C., in 1961, Merton very cogently made the point of objecting to the phrase "structural-functionalism." He particularly did not like having it labeled an "ism" and suggested that the simple descriptive phrase "functional analysis" was more appropriate. I heartily concur in this judgment.

The hyphenated label "structural-functionalism" has seemed to me to be decreasingly appropriate. I might, therefore, begin with a statement of my grounds for this feeling. They consist essentially in the view that the two con-

Talcott Parsons is Professor Emeritus of Sociology at Harvard University.

cepts "structure" and "function" are not parallel. Both are entirely indispensable in sociology and any other theoretical enterprise that deals with living systems, but it is important to understand the relation in which they stand to each other. I will not, as Piaget[4] does, extend my consideration beyond the category of so-called living systems, which is common to the biological and the social sciences and indeed, in certain respects, the humanities as intellectual disciplines.[5]

System seems to me to be an indispensable master concept, the meaning of which is directly concerned with its relation to the concept "environment." The crucial point is that the state of affairs internal to a living system is always different from the state of affairs in its environment and is in general more stable. Merton,[6] following Walter B. Cannon,[7] has given an exposition of the nature of this system-environment relation with exemplary clarity in the paper on "Manifest and Latent Functions." The idea, in turn, was derived from the great French physiologist Claude Bernard,[8] but particularly developed by Cannon. The difference between system and environment has two especially important implications. One is the existence and importance of boundaries between the two. Thus, the individual living organism is bounded by something like a "skin" inside of which a different state prevails from that outside it; for example, in the so-called warm-blooded organisms the internal temperature is different from the environmental temperature and is maintained at a nearly constant level in the face of major variations in environmental temperature. There are many other examples of this, such as the level of sugar in the blood. Cannon[9] discusses both these cases at considerable length.

The second basic property of living systems is that in some sense they are self-regulating. The maintenance of relative stability, including stability of certain processes of change like the growth of an organism, in the face of substantially greater environmental variability, means that, again as Merton puts it, there must be "mechanisms" that adjust the state of the system relative to changes in its environment. Thus, a fall in environmental temperature, again for a warm-blooded organism, necessitates either some mechanism that has the effect of checking the rate of heat loss or some mechanism that has the effect of increasing the rate of heat production, or some combination of the two. It is in this kind of setting that the relevant meaning of the concept "function" for present purposes is to be understood.

It is taken as a matter of empirical fact, verified by observation, that certain kinds of living systems maintain certain kinds of constancies and boundaries relative to the environments in which they live. Given the empirical state of affairs, then, the question inevitably arises, "How is it maintained?" Or we might put it slightly differently in the phrase used by the eminent biologist Ernst Mayr,[10] in his paper "Teleological and Teleonomic," that in the study of living systems, three basic questions, not two, must always be asked. The first is, "What are the characteristics of the living system?" The second, "How do these characteristics develop and are they maintained?" And the third, as Mayr puts it, "Why?" "Why?" in Mayr's sense is a functional question. Thus, why do human beings outdoors on a very cold day jump up and down? Cannon's answer, with which Mayr would clearly agree, is that they are counteracting the loss of body heat in a cold environment by muscular activity, which is a way in which heat is produced in the body.

It is, of course, important in this connection that the functions of bodily or other events may be in Merton's sense latent rather than manifest. If we take the case not of jumping up and down but of shivering, which Cannon discusses, most of us are unaware that shivering is another form of muscular activity which increases the rate of heat production and is therefore functionally related to the problem of maintenance of constant body temperature. It is a mechanism in this context.

The examples I have been giving are drawn from biology, but the same principles are equally relevant to social systems or personality systems. Thus, fund raising activities, initiated by officers of a university administration, may be said to have the function of maintaining or enhancing the financial support on which the operation of the university as a social organization is dependent. Correspondingly, let us suggest that a living human person driving a motor vehicle will consult maps and road signs in order to make the directional decisions that will insure arriving at his planned destination. The function of observing the maps and/or the road signs, therefore, is to facilitate the regulation of the person's behavior in the interest of attainment of a postulated personal goal, that is, arrival in "good time" at a projected destination. Seen in this context, the concept "structure" does not stand at the same level as that of function, but at a lower analytical level. It is cognate with the concept "process," not function.[11]

We do not wish to hypostatize structure. It is any set of relations among parts of a living system which on empirical grounds can be assumed or shown to be stable over a time period and under a set of conditions relevant to a particular cognitive enterprise. Broadly speaking, the anatomical structure of an organism can be safely assumed to be constant over considerable periods of, we might say, maturity or adulthood. If, however, the concern is with the growth from fertilized ovum to mature organism, its structure is continually changing. Similarly, various kinds of disease lead to changes in the structure of the organism. If our concern is with social systems or personalities, the relevant considerations are entirely parallel.

Process, then, is the correlative concept designating the respects in which the state of a system or the relevant part or parts of it changes within the time span relevant and significant for the particular cognitive purpose in mind. A physiologist studying the process of digestion does not assume that the input of food substances from the environment will remain constant over a period of, let us say, several hours. In the stomach and intestines, food materials undergo a complicated set of changes, a major part eventually being absorbed into the bloodstream, other parts being rejected and eventually evacuated through defecation. Correspondingly, in a social organization, there are continual changes taking place: members of university faculties change their status by promotion, by its failure to materialize, by breaking their contracts, by retirement, or by resignation. Similarly, every academic year new cohorts of students are admitted and become members of the organization and old ones leave by graduation or some other process. Clearly, they are all processes, not structures, but they usually occur within a relatively stable and constant structure.

Thus, to make it as clear as possible, the concept "function," unlike that of structure and of process, is not a rubric in terms of which an immediately empirical description of a set of features of a living system can be stated. It is, rather, a concept that stands at a higher level of theoretical generality and is more analytical than either structure or process. Its reference is to the formulation of sets of conditions governing the states of living systems as "going concerns" in relation to their environments. These conditions concern the stability and/or instability, the survival and/or probable extinction, and, not least, the temporal duration of such systems. In the organic field, crucial distinctions must be made between different system references, for example, the individual organism and the species, and we will argue that parallel distinctions must be made for the analysis of human systems of action, including social systems.

The concept "function," then, is the rubric under which the larger theoretical problems involving the general character of a class of living systems, and its relation to one or more environments, can be effectively stated and their solution approached. It concerns, above all, the *consequences* of the existence and nature of certain empirically describable structures and processes in such systems. Included, of course, are considerations relevant to the conditions under which the structures and processes of reference can arise, or the probabilities that they will in fact develop, or persist.

All this seems very simple and straightforward. Perhaps the only serious issue concerns the question, following Ernst Mayr,[12] of "Why?" Certain types of "reductionists" and "positivists" allege that such questions do not need to be asked, whether they be about organisms, species, social systems, or human personalities. The next question, however, is in certain respects more difficult. Our use so far of the term "system" has referred to classes of objects "out there," in the sense that they are not to be identified with the seeker of knowledge about them. The seeker of knowledge or the investigator must, however, if he is to know something about these objects, form the equivalent of what E. C. Tolman has called "cognitive maps."[13] He must, that is to say, describe, conceptualize, and analyze the "data" available concerning the objects in which he is interested. But the cognitive products coming out of this process must not be identified with the objects themselves. They are entities of quite a different order.

The crucial point we must emphasize is that, although there is presumptively some kind of correspondence between the cognitive structures produced by investigators and the objects the nature of which they are investigating, literally *never* is the cognitive account of the object a complete and concrete reproduction of everything that can be known or "felt" about such an object. It is always and in the nature of the case in some sense abstract, in that it formulates and calls to attention certain structures and processes pertaining to the object but omits consideration of many others or plays them down. This point has become standard in the methodology of science, in my own experience, having been particularly clearly elucidated by Max Weber[14] and by A. N. Whitehead.[15] The illusion that a "conceptual scheme" reproduces the full reality of the concrete object is what Whitehead so illuminatingly analyzed as the "fallacy of misplaced concreteness."[16] When, therefore, we refer to living systems—whether it be a human organism, a human personality, a social system, or what not—the cognitive structure in which we attempt to describe and analyze it is *always* in some degree and in some senses abstract. I wish to emphasize the word "always." It therefore becomes extremely important for investigators to be as clearly aware as they possibly can of the nature and extent of the abstraction they are undertaking and the consequences of these cognitive processes for the solution of a very wide variety of problems involving the classes of objects with which they are concerned.

I may use an example of special concern to that category of investigators labeled "sociologists." From a common sense point of view, what we sociologists call a "society" is usually conceived to be a completely concrete entity, comparable, let us say, to a stone or a dog. For technical theoretical purposes, however, it is strictly impossible for any investigator to deal with an entity he calls "American society" in its full concreteness. He can fill vast encyclopedic volumes with statements about it, but he will never come anywhere near exhausting what can validly be said to be true of it.

Does this mean that the cognitive enterprise is inherently self-defeating or impossible? Of course not. But the investigator must quite self-consciously select the "aspects" or features or properties of what he calls a society with which he can deal feasibly in a cognitively meaningful way. This imperative goes to the point that his very concept of the society itself becomes an abstraction in a sense parallel to that in which in the theory of the solar system in classical mechanics the earth is a truly heroic abstraction. Its units are said to have only the properties of mass, location in space, and velocity and direction of motion. There is no mention in the theory of the solar system of the flora and fauna, societies and cultures on the planet Earth, or even of its geological features. Newtonian mechanics was not for this reason simply wrong or incompetent. Indeed, Einstein's versions are, from this point of view, even less concrete than Newton's. It is, indeed, one of the most difficult features of the role of scientific investigator to become and stay critically aware of the nature and extent and directions of abstraction with which he is working. One of the commonest sources of difficulty in intellectual discourse is that parties to such discourse "talk past each other" because they do not assume the same patterns of abstraction.

Coping with the implications of the above consideration has been a perennial source of difficulty in all sophisticated fields of cognitive endeavor, not least the social sciences. Presumably, it is inherently impossible to exhaust the possibilities of awareness of the relations between what is being selected for specific consideration and what is being left out. Nevertheless, in the course of the evolution of knowledge, certain extremely important steps have been taken along this line.

The most important of these steps which I have in mind is the gradual realization that what we call a "social system" in sociological terminology, including a society, is only *one* analytically distinguishable sector or subset of the much larger complex we call "human action." It has gradually become

71

theoretically imperative to make clear, first, a distinction between social and cultural systems. Beyond that, it has become evident that it is not legitimate—theoretically speaking, that is—to identify either a cultural or a social system with the psychological or personality system of an individual or class of them, any more than it is legitimate to identify a particular living organism with a species. Finally, it has also become clear that what is usually called "the personality system" is by no means the only major theoretical reference for consideration of "the individual." I have tended to deal with a fourth primary subsystem of what I would call the general system of action under the heading of the "behavioral organism."[17]

These considerations have very major implications for what sociologists ought to mean by societies or other categories of social system. The conceptual formulation of such systems, not only in the logical but also in the empirical-referential sense, abstracts from other considerations which bear on cultural, personality, and behavioral problem areas, but it implies that these analytically distinguishable systems function as environments to each other around the clock and across the board. It is a very difficult conception to grasp, for example, that the personality systems of individual "members" of a society should be treated as constituting an environment for purposes of analyzing the functioning of the society. Common sense will always tell us that since the personalities of its members are internal to the society they do not constitute an environment to it or vice versa. The society is alleged to be "composed" of individuals.

To my knowledge, Durkheim was the first social scientist to have a profound insight into this tremendous complexity of the analytical task of the social sciences when he spoke of the social environment from the point of view of the acting individual as being factually given to him.[18] His two basic concepts of "social facts" and the *milieu social* incorporate this insight. Once the purport of Durkheim's insight is understood, the action-system parallel to the physiological distinction between the external and the internal environment, stressed so strongly by Claude Bernard and by Cannon, becomes striking indeed.[19]

In Durkheim's work this view was first clearly suggested in his *Rules of Sociological Method* (1895), but its significance was difficult to "tease out" because of Durkheim's own confusing tendency to treat "society" as a concrete entity.[20] It comes out much more clearly in Durkheim's late work, *The Elementary Forms of the Religious Life,* essentially because by that time Durkheim had explicitly theorized at the level of the "general system of action," as I and several colleagues have called it. By discriminating subsystems, this made it possible to treat the "individual" as acting in relation to a "social environment" external to himself but still part of the system of action. This provides a new clarification of Durkheim's early conception of "social facts" as concerning, from the point of view of the individual actor, properties of a given set of objects in the external world. (Compare my article cited in note 19, p. 81.)

All of this has an exceedingly important bearing on problems of the nature and status of functional analysis. The most important single proposition is that attempts at functional analysis will become intolerably confusing if there is not the best possible clarification of "system references." This obviously has to be a problem concerning data about the objects of investigation "out there." At the same time, however, it must concern the theoretically defined cognitive system with which the investigator is working.[21]

We therefore cannot emphasize too strongly the importance of being clear about exactly what system is the frame of reference for raising and trying to answer functional questions. The problem is the more complicated and urgent because it has become so evident that the field of human action cannot be dealt with in terms of one system reference, such as "society," but must involve multiple system references; perhaps the problem of keeping these system references straight has been the most prolific single source of difficulty and confusion in theoretical analysis in this field.

Essentially, all of the above is in very close agreement with Merton's position, although it lacks his very careful and illuminating analysis of the many confusions which have appeared in sociological writings over functional analysis. I have differed from him mainly in my strong stress on the importance and centrality of the concept "system," on the inevitability of abstraction, and on the necessity for the self-conscious use of plural or multiple system references.

I also agree with him strongly on two further points, which I would like to mention now. The first is that the status of functional analysis is entirely independent of any ideological implications in the usual sense. In particular, it has nothing to do with political conservatism or a defense of the status quo. It has nothing essentially to do with judgments about the specific balances between elements of integration in social systems and elements of conflict and/or disorganization. The concept "dysfunction" is, of course, just as legitimate and important as that of function in the positive sense and is entirely central. We are, I think, entirely agreed in our repudiation of the Dahrendorf idea of "two theories," a consensus theory and a conflict theory.[22] This consideration again emphasizes continuity with biology. Biology does not have two basic theoretical schemes, a theory of healthy organisms and one of pathological phenomena in organisms, but health and pathological states are understandable in basically the same general theoretical terms. This proposition, of course, implies that "theory" in the present sense does not refer to empirical generalizations about certain classes of concrete phenomena but to an abstractly analytical "conceptual scheme."

A related polemical orientation is the claim frequently put forward that "functionalists" are incapable of accounting for social change; that is, their type of theory has a built-in "static" bias. This also is entirely untrue. If we have any claim to competence as social scientists, we must be fully aware that there are problems both of stability and of change, as there are problems of positive integration and malintegration.[23] The student's orientation to these problems is not a matter of the type of general theory he subscribes to but of his more empirical interests and his empirical judgments.

There is, however, one complicating consideration in this general area which needs to be made explicit. This derives from the very deep-seated human propensity to put forward what is perhaps best called "utopian" ideas—

73

a propensity very strongly expressed in many ideologies. By utopian I mean specifically assertions about the desirability or feasibility of social states of affairs, statements which do not take adequate and competent account of the conditions necessary if the state of affairs discussed is in actual fact to be brought into being and/or maintained. Functional analysis, however, like any other solid and competent scientific procedure, must make a special point of pushing the analysis of conditions as far as it can. Since in response to utopian ideas it often says, yes, that might be nice, but for such and such specific reasons we think it cannot be accomplished, the sociologist of the functional persuasion, as well as others, is likely to be felt to be intolerably conservative because he seems to be placing obstacles in the way of the realization of what is clearly considered to be desirable. The problem of planned or advocated social change is scientifically, of course, a very complicated one. The errors in such a field are by no means only those pointing in a utopian direction— belief in the possibility of the impossible—but frequently errors in the other direction—failure to see the possibilities of change. In this, as in so many other contexts, the only remedy is command of information, careful analysis, and balanced judgment. None of us, however, can expect perfection in such a complex combination, and both types of errors are certain to recur again and again.

FUNCTIONAL ANALYSIS IN THE BIOLOGICAL AND THE PSYCHOSOCIAL DISCIPLINES

Merton makes very competent and effective use of the theoretical models of Walter B. Cannon as they were developed for physiological study. At the same time, however, he states a negative polemical attitude toward the use of biological "analogies" by social scientists, citing the unfruitfulness of the use of many of them made by an earlier generation of sociologists such as Herbert Spencer, René Worms, and others.[24] I quite agree with his strictures on that set of uses, but I would like to raise certain further questions. First, it is interesting that in the biological sciences, as is also true of law, the term "analogy" does not have the pejorative connotations which have been so prominent in connection with its social science uses. For biologists, an analogy exists between two or more anatomical structures or physiological processes that are similar in function but differ from each other in mechanism. A classical example is the analogy between organs and processes of vision in the insects on the one hand, the vertebrates on the other.[25]

The existence of fruitful analogies between the phenomena of organic life and those of human personalities, societies, and cultures rests essentially on the common features and continuities of different types of living systems. To take one example, both sociologists and anthropologists went through a stage of violent objection to the use of evolutionary ideas with reference to human societies. Very often these objections have been based on misunderstanding of the biological theory of evolution and on its misapplication to human social phenomena. I, however, would subscribe firmly to the view that social science

74

cannot be complete without the careful study of dimensions that can properly be called "evolutionary."

Let us cite, however, certain other examples. The first of these is the analogy between the concept "society," as used by at least some sociologists, and the concept "species," as used by some biologists of high standing. I think particularly of Ernst Mayr in his notable book *Populations, Species, and Evolution.*[26] Mayr defines a species in a very careful statement as having three primary foci or aspects. First, it is a reproduction community; for the most part, only members of the same species interbreed with each other. Put in these terms, it is a bounded system with respect to the reproductive function. Second, it is a territorial community; it has a habitat, or a niche, that in most cases is shared with other species, but the distribution of organisms of the same species is never random in territorial location. In this respect also it is a bounded system. Third, it is a genetic community that shares a common gene pool which is distinctive relative to the gene pools of all other species.

A human society, of course, is not a species. All human biologists, to my knowledge, are agreed that there is only one human species. The analogy of the reproductive community is at the level of what biologists, including Mayr, call a "population," which is a subunit of a species; a society organizes a population, which is a subsector of the human species. It also does so with a territorial reference sometimes characterized by the phrase "politically organized." Finally, a society is also characterized by a common culture, although the sharing of this need not be absolutely uniform among its whole population, any more than every member of an organic species has the same genetic composition. Clearly, in all these respects the mechanisms by which a society functions as a bounded system differ from those by which organic species do, but the functions are clearly comparable.[27]

Another important analogy between the two classes of living systems lies in the applicability to both of the fundamental concepts *adaptation* and *integration.* Adaptation was, of course, one of the few key concepts of Darwin's theory of evolution[28] and is universally central to the conceptual armory of the biological sciences. It, of course, concerns the relations of a living system to its external environment, whether that system be an individual organism or a species.

Integration concerns the relations internal to the system of parts with each other. It is intimately related to the conception of the internal environment mentioned above. The integration of a system is in one primary aspect the adaptation of its parts to the internal environment. In our field, I, together with Neil Smelser, have conceived of the function of economic production as primarily an adaptive mechanism of the society in relation to several of its environments.[29] It will be remembered that we mean here not only the physical environment but also the personalities of individuals. Durkheim was probably the most seminal theorist in the field of studying the integration of social systems, notably in his conception of organic solidarity. As I have noted, this was also intimately connected with the sociological analogue of the biologists' conception of the internal environment.

Another way in which I differ from Merton is that, to my knowledge, he has never seriously attempted to achieve theoretical closure of the set of primary functions of a social system. I have attempted to do so in the four-function paradigm I have been using extensively for nearly twenty years. This paradigm developed out of the so-called pattern-variable scheme by emphasis on one specific set of relations among the four central pattern-variable pairs.[30]

I think it is now possible to say with confidence that this set as a whole is part of a highly generalized analogy between organic and sociocultural living systems. Unless the use of the terms "adaptation" and "integration" in the scheme is simply arbitrary labeling, those two concepts are central to it and are clearly of functional significance; that is to say, they designate aspects or phenomena of living systems that are of functional significance to the systems.

Besides adaptation and integration, a third consideration has to do with the concept goal attainment, or purposiveness, as it has so frequently been called. This has been extremely controversial among comparative psychologists for a long time, but I think we can say that the balance has now tipped in the direction of consensus about the fundamental importance of purposiveness in the behavior of living organisms. This goes across the line between psychology and biological science and is, for example, strongly endorsed by Mayr[31] in the paper referred to above, as it was by Tolman.[32] Of course, in the lower phylae of the evolutionary scale, goal directedness is relatively rudimentary, but when we come to virtually all of the higher species it is very central indeed. The concept is sometimes confused with that of adaptation because it has to do with relations between organism and external environment, but they should be analytically distinguished.

Finally, there is the concept that my associates and I have long called *pattern maintenance*. On the biological side, the analogy has been immensely strengthened by some of the most important advances of biological science in the last generation, especially those connected with molecular genetics.[33] I was first made aware of it by a statement made by an eminent biologist, Alfred Emerson,[34] at an interdisciplinary conference in which I participated. Emerson explicitly used the terminology in the technical biological sense, and his formula was that in the human action fields the *symbol* is analogous to the gene in the organic field. I think a better way of phrasing it would be to say that in the action sciences the patterns of culture are analogous to the genetic heritage of a species. This way of looking at it means drawing a careful distinction between the cultural and the social systems, which is parallel to that drawn by biologists between germ plasm on the one hand, somatoplasm on the other—or genotype and phenotype.

That there is an analogy from the functional point of view of control of the development of individual organisms or social units has been enormously strengthened by the dramatic development of the science of linguistics, again in about the last generation. Symbolic communication through speech utterances is, in the linguistic case, made possible through the operation of what some linguistic scientists call a "linguistic code" or Chomsky calls "deep structures."[35] Such codes are not themselves meaningful utterances at all but rather the symbolic frame of reference within which meaningful utterances can be formulated. The famous biochemical molecule DNA is looked at by microgeneticists from very much the same point of view as embodying the genetic code and a more detailed "program," which regulates the processes of synthesis of the biochemical components of the living cell, notably the proteins.[36]

The understanding of phenomena of this sort, extending all the way from the microbiology level through the theory of evolution and species formation to language and human society and culture, has been enormously furthered by another development in general science, the relevance of which extends even beyond the sciences dealing with living systems. I refer to cybernetics and information theory. What is common between the genetic code and the gene pool on the one hand, linguistic codes and other aspects of human culture on the other, is that they can function as cybernetic mechanisms which, in certain fundamental respects, control life processes. This perspective has dealt what will probably turn out to be a death blow to the older ideas of biological "mechanism" and to various kinds of biopsychological reductionism which have been so prevalent in the history of the social disciplines. If we can successfully adapt sociological and other action science data to cybernetic models —and vice versa—we have the possibility of greatly enhanced analytical power in our fields, and an enormous range of codification between these and the other relevant fields.

There is a further point about cybernetics which bears very directly on functional analysis. This is the fact that functionally specialized or differentiated sectors of living systems stand in some kind of an order of cybernetically hierarchical control relative to each other. This is quite a fundamental principle of ordering of such systems and, as such, is an enormous aid to the solution of a wide variety of theoretical problems.

There is one further analogy in the present series which in my opinion helps enormously to clarify a very difficult and controversial sociological problem area. This is the problem of understanding the processes by which what we call "institutionalization" takes place. The commonest reference is to the incorporation of normative elements of cultural origin into the structure of a social system. Certain patterns of legal ordering can serve as a convenient example. The problem, however, comes up whenever new elements that have not previously been incorporated into social structure in fact become so.

The organic analogy is with nothing less than the famous principle of natural selection. The mere fact of the presence of certain genes in the gene pool of a species is not a sufficient determinant of their role in the generation of phenotypical organisms. For this to occur, there must be integration of the genetically given patterning with a series of exigencies defined by the nature of the species' life in its environment. In the course of meeting such exigencies, some genetically given patterns arising as variations or mutations, or from new combinations, will be built into the actual structure of the species and its members, whereas others will be eliminated by the processes of natural selection. Similarly, in social subject matters some cultural values or norms arising in processes of social change do in fact become constitutive of concrete social structures, whereas others fail to do so. The problem of institutionalization is the problem of understanding the exigencies and mechanisms by which these differential outcomes occur. For codification of the analogy, it is a crucially important fact that the theory of natural selection has made very substantial advances[37] since Darwin's first epoch-making formulation of it.[38] Had this not occurred, I do not think a sociologist would have perceived that there was potentially a very fruitful analogy present in this area.[39]

Finally, there is one still further theoretical development in the action theory area which seems to me to be an integral part of functional analysis and to hold very great promise for the furtherance of the dynamic analysis of process in systems of action, not least social systems. There are certain elements of analogy here also to comparable phenomena in the organic world, but the analogies are not so highly developed or well known as in some of the other cases. I refer to the role in action processes of what I and some of my associates have come to call "generalized symbolic media of interchange." The proto-typical case is money, which has come to play such a very important role in highly developed and differentiated economic systems.[40] Indeed, some go so far as to say that the core of economic theory is to be found in the understanding of monetary phenomena. Money, however, is a paradigmatic case of a phenomenon that is high in information but very low in energy. This point was already understood by the classical economists as expressed in their formula that money has value in exchange but no value in use. It is essentially a phenomenon of symbolic communication. Money is anchored, institutionally speaking, in the property system; hence, its special relation to economic relations.

It has been widely assumed that money was an entirely unique phenomenon in social systems, but there has developed increasingly cogent reason to question this. In fact, we have identified three other generalized media that operate at the social system level, becoming visible, of course, only when the system's level of differentiation has advanced sufficiently far. These are, specifically, political power, influence, and value commitments. To fit them into the paradigm of generalized symbolic media, since their common sense meanings are not adequately specific or consistently clarified, they have to be redefined in technical senses. An attempt to do this has been made in three of my essays over a period of years.[41] More recently, it has proved possible to develop a comparable set of generalized media that are conceived to operate at the level of the general system of action, not the social system. We have defined these as intelligence, performance-capacity, affect, and definition of the situation—a list owing a great deal in different ways to W. I. Thomas, to Freud, and to Piaget.[42]

I will not take space in the present brief essay to attempt to explicate them, especially the latter set which operates at the general level of action. One publication[43] has made a beginning, but a full statement is yet to be made. However, they have been very much further developed in one recently published book and a second one in preparation, the title of which has not been finally settled upon yet but which will focus on the integrative problems of social systems.

When I said above that the media of interchange are integrally part of the functional context, one of the things I wished to convey was that their clarification and use as analytical tools would not have been thinkable had it not been possible to see them in a functional perspective. They operate essentially as mechanisms that regulate the flow of interactional transactions among the different unit components of social and other action systems. Again, as I noted, they fit very definitely into the cybernetic frame of reference because they are uniformly, predominantly mechanisms for the exchange of information, not of energy, and have functions of control, for example, of the allocation and combination of factors and outputs.

There are, presumably, many analogues at organic levels. One of the most prominent sets of them, significant for physiological process, is the hormones, knowledge of which was relatively new in Cannon's day and of which he made a great deal, for example, in presenting a rather detailed analysis of the nature and functions of insulin in the regulation of levels of blood sugar.[44] In recent years, the microbiologists have been paying intensified attention to another set—namely, the enzymes—which play an essential role in the synthesis of proteins.[45] Finally, there have been immense advances in the recent period in understanding the functioning of the central nervous systems of the higher animals, including, of course, man, and it would seem that neural process is essentially a communication process within the central nervous system and between it and other parts of the organism. With improved relations between the two sets of disciplines and further development within each set, a much fuller picture of these extremely important phenomena should gradually take shape.

CONCLUSION

In recent years there has been considerable talk about the decline of concern with "structural-functional" theory, or, as I prefer to call it, "functional analysis," in favor of other types of conceptualization and theoretical generalization. It is my considered opinion that, to paraphrase Mark Twain's famous remark about the rumors of his own death, these rumors are "slightly exaggerated." I think Kingsley Davis, in his Presidential Address to the American Sociological Association, was nearer the mark when he took the view that there was less talk about functional analysis because essentially all serious theory in the field had become functional and took this for granted.[46] Of course, there will be considerable difference of opinion on the point and there are, indeed, exceptions, particularly where what I would think of as theoretical considerations are subordinated to political movements and goal seeking and where generalization, insofar as it figures, tends to become mainly empirical generalization, as in many strictly quantitative studies.

I think the kind of developments I have sketched in this paper indicate a very lively intellectual ferment in this field, and it should not be forgotten that a quite substantial number of people are self-consciously working within a somewhat similar framework or others that bear sufficiently close relation to it so that it would be arbitrary to allocate them to radically different "schools." Not least important to note is the fact that I think the great development of economic theory on the one side, and of linguistics on the other, should definitely be judged to belong to the category of functional analysis.

I have in the present paper strongly stressed how the kinds of developments with which I have been concerned in the social field relate to those in the biological sciences and, to a lesser degree, in linguistics. One could say comparable things about a good deal of psychology, political science, and social anthropology. Within all this, however, the relation to the biological sciences seems particularly impressive because they cover such a wide range of the problems of living systems and some of them occur at such a high level of theoretical development and generality. Given more space, I could have included others, but I think the ones reviewed will suffice.

I think we can look forward to at least a strong possibility, if not a probability, that in coming years there will be a good many advances beyond analogy in anything like the usual sense to very fruitful interaction between the various disciplines involved, especially insofar as suggestions emanating from one of them turn out to be usable to develop theory in one or more others. I, for one, find the present reality and prospects very exciting and do not have in the least the feeling of being identified with a moribund theoretical perspective. Let us salute Robert Merton for his highly creative role in developing the foundations of this challenging intellectual situation.

NOTES

1. Marion J. Levy, Jr., *The Structure of Society* (Princeton, N.J.: Princeton University Press, 1952) and *Modernization and the Structure of Societies,* 2 vols. (Princeton, N.J.: Princeton University Press, 1966).
2. Robert K. Merton, "Manifest and Latent Functions," in his *Social Theory and Social Structure,* rev. ed. (New York: Free Press, 1957), pp. 19–84.
3. See Merton, *Social Theory and Social Structure.*
4. Jean Piaget, *Structuralism,* trans. and ed. Chaninah Maschler (New York: Basic Books, 1970).
5. See Talcott Parsons, "Theory in the Humanities and Sociology," *Daedalus* 99, no. 2 (Spring 1970): 495–523.
6. Merton, "Manifest and Latent Functions," op cit.
7. Walter B. Cannon, *Bodily Changes in Pain, Hunger, Fear and Rage* (New York: Appleton, 1929) and *The Wisdom of the Body* (New York: Norton, 1932).
8. Claude Bernard, *An Introduction to the Study of Experimental Medicine,* trans. Henry Copley Greene (New York: Dover, 1957; first published in French, 1865).
9. Cannon, *Bodily Changes in Pain, Hunger, Fear and Rage,* op cit.
10. Ernst Mayr, "Teleological and Teleonomic: A New Analysis," in Marx Wartovsky, ed., *Method and Metaphysics: Methodological and Historical Essays in the Natural and Social Sciences,* Proceedings of the Boston Colloquium for the Philosophy of Science, 1969–72 (Leiden, Holland: Brill, 1974), vol. 6, pp. 78–104.
11. Sometimes, the levels are consolidated or fused by reference not to functions but to functioni*ng.* From this point of view, the verb form may be considered to be a synonym for process.
12. Mayr, "Teleological and Teleonomic," op. cit.

13. Edward C. Tolman, "A Psychological Model," in Talcott Parsons and Edward A. Shils, eds., *Towards a General Theory of Action* (Cambridge, Mass.: Harvard University Press, 1951), part 3, pp. 279–361.

14. Edward A. Shils and Henry A. Finch, eds. and trans., *Max Weber on the Methodology of the Social Sciences* (Glencoe, Ill.: Free Press, 1949).

15. Alfred N. Whitehead, *Science and the Modern World* (New York: Macmillan, 1925).

16. *Ibid.*

17. I have, however, recently come to be convinced through a paper written by Victor and Charles Lidz that this particular designation of the fourth primary subsystem of "action" is not correct and should be replaced by what the Lidzes call the "behavioral system," which centers on what we sometimes call "cognitive functions." See Victor Lidz and Charles Lidz, "The Psychology of Intelligence of Jean Piaget and Its Place in the Theory of Action," in J. Loubser, R. Baum, A. Effrat, and V. Lidz, eds., *Explorations in General Theory in the Social Sciences* (New York: Free Press, forthcoming). The essential thesis of the paper is that what I, in a number of publications, most recently *The American University* (Cambridge, Mass.: Harvard University Press, 1973), have been calling the "behavioral organism," as one of four primary subsystems of action, should not be treated as part of the action system but as part of its environment. They propose substituting for it what they call the "behavioral" system, the nature of which they outline in a very ingenious analysis, which takes its departure from Piaget's well-known studies of intelligent human cognitive patterns and capacities, adapting Piaget's discussion to the framework of the general theory of action. I have been in general terms willing to accept this highly original theoretical innovation; indeed, this is the first occasion on which I have done so in print. The Lidz and Lidz paper is expected to be published in the volume referred to above in 1975.

18. Émile Durkheim, *The Elementary Forms of the Religious Life,* trans. J. W. Swain (London: George Allen & Unwin, 1915; first published in French, 1912), and *The Rules of Sociological Method,* trans. S. A. Solovay and J. H. Mueller (New York: Free Press, 1964; first published in French, 1895).

19. See Talcott Parsons, "Durkheim on Religion Revisited: Another Look at the Elementary Forms of the Religious Life," in Y. Glock and P. E. Hammond, eds., *The Scientific Study of Religion: Beyond the Classics?* (New York: Harper & Row, 1973), pp. 156–80.

20. Cf. Robert N. Bellah, ed., "Introduction," to *Émile Durkheim on Morality and Society* (Chicago: University of Chicago Press, 1973).

21. In the classical literature of the "functional point of view," this point is very sharply illustrated by the difference between the theoretical positions of the two most prominent so-called functionalists in the last generation of British social anthropology, namely, Radcliffe-Brown (see A. R. Radcliffe-Brown, *Taboo* [New York: Cambridge University Press, 1939] and *Structure and Function in Primitive Society* [New York: Free Press, 1952]) and Malinowski (see Bronislaw Malinowski, *Magic, Science and Religion* [Glencoe, Ill.: Free Press, 1948] and *A Scientific Theory of Culture and Other Essays* [Chapel Hill: University of North Carolina Press, 1944]). Radcliffe-Brown, taking his cues especially from Durkheim, adhered quite consistently to the consideration of social systems, notably societies, as his systems of reference. Malinowski, on the other hand, very conspicuously refused to do this and quite explicitly included the personality of the individual in his definition of systems of reference. It is not surprising that the two eminent anthropologists arrived at such very different empirical generalizations about

societies, or more correctly we should say human action systems, in their respective work. See Talcott Parsons, "Malinowski and the Theory of Social Systems," in Raymond Firth, ed., *Man and Culture* (London: Routledge & Kegan Paul, 1957).

22. Ralf Dahrendorf, *Class and Class Conflict in Industrial Society* (Palo Alto, Calif.: Stanford University Press, 1959), chap. 5, pp. 157–65.

23. See Francesca Cancian, "Functional Analysis of Change," *American Sociological Review* 25, no. 6 (December 1960): 818–27.

24. Herbert Spencer, *Essays,* 3 vols. (London: Longmans, 1858–76), and *A System of Synthetic Philosophy* (London: Appleton, 1862–96), vols. 9–10, *Principles of Sociology*; René Worms, *Organisme et Société* (Paris: Giard & Brière, 1896).

25. George Wald, "Molecular Basis of Visual Excitation," *Science* 162, no. 3850 (October 11, 1968): 230–39.

26. Ernst Mayr, *Populations, Species, and Evolution* (Cambridge, Mass.: Harvard University Press, 1970), esp. chap. 1.

27. For a sociological conception of a society, see Talcott Parsons, *Societies: Evolutionary and Comparative Perspectives* (Englewood Cliffs, N.J.: Prentice-Hall, 1966), chap. 2, and *The System of Modern Societies* (Englewood Cliffs, N.J.: Prentice-Hall, 1971), chap. 2.

28. Charles Darwin, *The Origin of Species by Means of Natural Selection,* ed. J. W. Burrow (Harmondworth, Eng.: Penguin Books; first published, 1859).

29. Talcott Parsons and Neil Smelser, *Economy and Society* (New York: Free Press, 1956).

30. Talcott Parsons, Robert F. Bales, and Edward A. Shils, *Working Papers in the Theory of Action* (New York: Free Press, 1953), esp. chaps. 2 and 4, and Talcott Parsons, "Some Problems of General Theory in Sociology," in John C. McKinney and Edward A. Tiryakian, eds., *Theoretical Sociology: Perspectives and Developments* (New York: Appleton-Century-Crofts, 1970).

31. Mayr, "Teleological and Teleonomic," op cit.

32. Edward C. Tolman, *Purposive Behavior in Animals and Men* (New York: Appleton-Century, 1932).

33. See Curt Stern, "The Continuity of Genetics," and Gunther S. Stent, "DNA," in Gerald Holton, ed., *The Twentieth-Century Sciences: Studies in the Biography of Ideas* (New York: Norton, 1972).

34. Alfred E. Emerson, "Homeostasis and the Comparison of Systems," in Roy R. Grinker, Sr., ed., *Towards a Unified Theory of Human Behavior: An Introduction to General Systems Theory* (New York: Basic Books, 1956). See also Talcott Parsons and Robert F. Bales, *Family, Socialization, and Interaction Process* (New York: Free Press, 1955), Appendix A.

35. Noam Chomsky, *Syntactic Structures* (The Hague: Mouton, 1957).

36. Cf. Stent, "DNA."

37. Mayr, *Populations, Species, and Evolution.*

38. Darwin, *The Origin of Species.*

39. Since submitting the manuscript of the present article, further investigation in the biological literature has convinced me that the analogy between institutionalization and natural selection can be extended also to the microbiological level. In this case the problem concerns the processes by which the patterns of DNA are, as the microbiologists themselves say, "transcribed" and "translated" through the mediation of RNA and the enzymes into the synthesis of proteins, which are the principal operative agents of the functioning of the cell. For further reference see Stent, "DNA," op. cit., and S. E. Luria, *Life: The Unfinished Experiment* (New York: Charles Scribner's Sons, 1973).

40. Cf. J. M. Keynes, *General Theory of Employment, Interest and Money* (New York: Harcourt Brace Jovanovich, 1936).
41. Talcott Parsons, "On the Concept of Political Power," "On the Concept of Influence," and "On the Concept of Value-Commitments," in *Politics and Social Structure* (New York: Free Press, 1969), chaps. 13, 14, and 16.
42. William I. Thomas, *The Unadjusted Girl* (Boston: Little, Brown, 1931); Sigmund Freud, *The Interpretation of Dreams*, vols. 4 and 5 of the *Standard Edition of the Complete Psychological Works of Sigmund Freud*, trans. James Strachey (London: Hogarth Press and Institute of Psycho-Analysis, 1953), esp. chap. 7 (first published, 1900); and Jean Piaget and Bärbel Inhelder, *The Growth of Logical Thinking from Childhood to Adolescence* (New York: Basic Books, 1958).
43. Parsons, "Some Problems of General Theory in Sociology." Also Talcott Parsons and Gerald M. Platt, *The American University* (Cambridge, Mass.: Harvard University Press, 1973).
44. W. B. Cannon, *Wisdom of the Body,* op cit.
45. Cf. Stent, "DNA."
46. Kingsley Davis, "The Myth of Functional Analysis as a Special Method in Sociology and Anthropology," *American Sociological Review* 24, no. 6 (December 1959): 757–72. Presidential Address read at the annual meeting of the American Sociological Association, Chicago, Ill., September 1959.

Merton's Uses of the European Sociological Tradition

LEWIS A. COSER

The sense of the past has usually
been linked in human consciousness
with a sense of the future.

J. H. PLUMB[1]

1

THIS volume celebrates the achievements of a modern master of sociological thought. Many of its chapters explicate in convincing detail the originality of Robert K. Merton's contributions to modern sociology. In what follows I shall use a strategy that is slightly at variance with that employed in most other chapters. By pointing to some of the European thinkers in whose lineage Merton self-consciously placed his own work, I shall attempt to highlight his capacity to draw from many sources and, in a grand synthesizing effort, to rise above all of them.

Pitrim Sorokin, one of Merton's teachers, once said about the work of his former student that it presented mainly "variations on the themes of earlier masters." He allowed that, "like Beethoven's variation on Mozartian themes or Brahms's variations on the themes of Paganini, Merton's variations are admirable in many ways...,"[2] but the context makes it clear that he did not think highly of such an enterprise. Yet it happens that what was meant to be an ungenerous and disparaging remark has had the unanticipated consequence of pointing to one of the most characteristic, distinctive, and admirable aspects of Merton's contributions to sociology. More than any native-born American social scientist, Merton has been preoccupied throughout his career with the continuity of sociological tradition and the cumulation of sociological knowledge. He has been intensely aware of sociology as a

Lewis A. Coser is Distinguished Professor of Sociology at the State University of New York at Stony Brook.

perennial enterprise. Although he has presumably been quite conscious of the originality of his own contributions, he has always been at some pains to put these contributions within the context of earlier work and to stress his indebtedness to the masters of the past.

Although Merton's delightful and whimsical book *On the Shoulders of Giants,*[3] an extended gloss on the theme of continuity in science, appeared relatively late in his career, it seems clear that his concern with cumulation antecedes this book by many years. A prepotent interest in continuity is not only part of his substantive contributions; it informs his long-time preoccupation with the transmission of ideas to subsequent generations of scholars. It is this concern that explains Merton's emphasis on the codification of sociological knowledge and his efforts to develop paradigms. As he himself has noted, "A major concern of [*Social Theory and Social Structure*] is the codification of substantive theory and of procedures of qualitative analysis in sociology."[4] Paradigms set forth "as a basis for codifying previous work in the field," Merton stressed, "have great propaedeutic value."[5]

If a scientific tradition is to be kept alive, its achievements must be put in such manner that they can be communicated and transmitted with clarity. It is hence of vital importance that irrelevant "noise," to use the language of communication theory for a moment, be excluded as much as possible so that the essential message can be clearly received. The codification of knowledge serves this purpose insofar as it "reduce[s] the inadvertent tendency to hide the hard core of analysis behind a veil of random, though possibly illuminating, comments and thoughts."[6] Codification allows a thorough winnowing out of the quotidian harvest of scientific investigation and research so that those elements can be discerned that might have larger significance as building blocks for theoretical structures yet to come. Such codification is especially important in relatively new sciences, such as sociology, which tend still to exhibit large-scale discontinuities between empirical research and systematic theorizing. Much of Merton's work, though by no means all of it, must be understood as a self-conscious effort to extract from the body of the work of his predecessors, and in particular from the diffuse, scintillating, but often confused and confusing heritage of European thought, the central core that needs to be transmitted to American students and practitioners alike if they are indeed to work within a living tradition. The German sociologist Helmuth Plessner once remarked, "Only those who are capable of developing the new out of the old fit into the framework of scholarship."[7] Merton would strongly endorse this statement.

In an age dominated in so many ways by a kind of antinomian neophilia in which only the "tradition of the new" still seems to be acceptable, and where a hectic preoccupation with the newest offerings on the market of ideas has tended to displace concern for the certified and coolly assessed value of intellectual products, Merton has stood firm in his concern for the continuity of tradition. In an age when so many lesser minds have thought it expedient to proclaim to the world at large that they are the fountainheads of Kuhnian "scientific revolutions," Merton has staked his reputation on the self-conscious assertion that he does indeed stand on the shoulders of giants. And this claim, which would seem to diminish his stature in the eyes of currently modish and fashionable thinkers, has in fact increased it. By standing in the line of great ancestors, and by acknowledging the shadow they cast, one enhances the chance that he, in his turn, will later be reckoned among the ancestors himself.

Merton's lifelong preoccupation with the sociology of knowledge must likewise be understood in the light of this concern for the continuity of the sociological enterprise. Ever since the Enlightenment, and still pronouncedly in the work of Marx, the sociology of knowledge has frequently been used as a means of debunking the thought of ideological adversaries. By pointing to the existential roots of an adversary's ideas, it was hoped to discredit them. Such uses of the sociology of knowledge are emphatically foreign to Merton. His effort, on the contrary, is to surgically remove those layers and tissues of a thinker's thought that show the mark of his time, his place, his milieu, so as to be able better to expose that vital core of his message which transcends the various existential limitations that might have entered into his perspective. By attempting to separate the "objective consequences [from] the intent of an inquiry,"[8] he wishes to salvage the usable intellectual products of a past thinker.

When Merton attempted to show, for example, the amazing parallelism between insights of such ideologically divergent thinkers as, say, Winston Churchill and Harold Laski, or of Marx and Engels and the fathers of functional analysis, he highlighted the fact that wide disagreements in the domain of values did not preclude agreement in cognitive procedures and substantive findings. In this respect Merton seems to believe that, despite the bewildering variety of languages and styles of thought on the modern intellectual scene, it is by no means a tower of Babel allowing only a dialogue of the deaf. By stripping evaluative dross and time-and-place-bound elements from the intellectual productions of the past, it becomes possible for Merton to incorporate past contributions into the body of current paradigms which can become springboards for future advances.

2

When Merton came to intellectual maturity in the thirties, the American sociological enterprise was in a most unsatisfactory state. Largely unaware of its intellectual roots in the European tradition, it threatened to succumb to simple-minded empiricism or to a parochial concern with immediate problems. In their avid quest for "facts," most sociologists failed to understand that facts do not speak for themselves and are hence likely to produce a miscellany of curiosa rather than the lineaments of a science.

The founding fathers of sociology, to be sure, often had a profound knowledge of their European ancestors and contemporaries. Ward and Sumner, for example, were steeped in European scholarship, and the founders of the Chicago school were by no means theoretical innocents abroad as they have been pictured. But even though Ward and Sumner were familiar with the work of Comte or of the Social Darwinists, and even though Small and Park had received major intellectual stimulation from Georg Simmel, they had not been able to salvage the European contributions in systematic ways so as truly to incorporate them in their own investigations or to transmit them to their students.

The earlier generation of the fathers of American sociology tended to construct grandiose systems which in their one-sided and somewhat monomaniacal single-mindedness soon turned into whitened sepulchers. A later generation, in partial reversion and revulsion from such overambitious projects, turned to a grubby and often mindless empiricism and apparently believed that a science of sociology could be built up in the same manner as botanists build a collection of butterflies by rummaging around with a large enough net.

It is the merit of Talcott Parsons to have helped overcome this deplorable state of affairs with his pathbreaking *The Structure of Social Action*,[9] a monumental effort at arriving at a synthesis of major contributors in the European tradition and at outlining the distinctive features of an integrated theoretical system. Merton's subsequent work was deeply marked by that book and by Parsons' teaching at Harvard. Yet, upon closer inspection, it becomes apparent that even in the thirties there were profound differences in their respective approaches. Parsons still aspired to build an integrated and all-encompassing system similar to those of some of the founding fathers. His selection of the European ancestors was hence highly selective. He focused attention on a few among them and dealt only with those European thinkers who seemed to him best fitted to assist in the building of his *summa*. Merton, in contrast, set himself a task that seemed considerably more modest but that, so I believe, paid greater intellectual dividends.

While Parsons neglected, or paid only peripheral attention to, seminal thinkers such as Simmel, Marx, or Mannheim, Merton seems to have been determined to inventory the whole storehouse of European sociological and social thought and to select a much greater array of ideas from a much wider variety of sources. Parsons was in Isaiah Berlin's terminology a "hedgehog [who] knows one big thing." Merton was like Berlin's fox who "knows many things." Parsons related everything "to a single central vision, one system less or more coherent or articulate . . . a single, universal organizing principle," while Merton was among those who "entertain ideas that are centrifugal rather than centripetal, [whose] thought is . .. moving on many levels, seizing upon the essence of a vast variety of experiences and objects for what they are in themselves, without consciously or unconsciously seeking to fit them into, or exclude them from, any one unchanging, all-embracing . . . . unitary inner vision."[10] Parsons is of the company of Plato, of Dante, or of Nietzsche; Merton of that of Aristotle, of Montaigne, or of Erasmus.

In a short (and unpublished) autobiographical essay Merton sheds more light on the pattern of his studies and indicates that a European sociologist, Émile Durkheim, became his consciously chosen role model. He writes,

... Almost from the beginning of my independent work ... , I was resolved to follow my intellectual interests as they developed, rather than to hold fast to a predetermined plan. That is to say, I chose to adopt the practice of a self-selected master-at-a-distance, Émile Durkheim, rather than the practice of my master-at-close-range, George Sarton. Durkheim had repeatedly changed the subjects which he investigated. Starting with studies of the division of labor, he examined methods of sociological inquiry and then turned successively to the subjects of suicide, religion, moral education and socialism, all the while evolving a theoretical orientation that, to his mind, could be most effectively developed by attending to these varied aspects of man's life in society. ... [This pattern] seemed ... suitable for me.[11]

It is precisely the wide-openness of Merton's mind that fitted him to be freshly receptive to an amazing array of divergent European (and of course American) ideas. Wishing to eschew what he considered to be a vain, or at least premature, quest for an all-embracing general theory, Merton embarked upon the task of creating a variety of "theories of the middle range," while always aware that "the search for them is coupled with a pervasive concern with consolidating special theories into more general sets of concepts and mutually consistent propositions."[12]

While Parsons, in tune with his general project, was mainly preoccupied with the overall theoretical or even metatheoretical contributions of a selected few among the Europeans, Merton could afford to embrace a much wider array of thinkers whom he could use as a stimulus or point of departure for his more detailed and more delimited analytical exercises. Parsons had commerce only with those Europeans whose pedigree he judged to be impeccable; Merton could afford to learn selectively from many thinkers whose overall lines of descent were less illustrious.

Merton's self-conscious effort to ransack the whole house of European erudition for the benefit of his American readers is nowhere more evident than in his abundant use of footnote references, often to thinkers of relatively minor stature. This abundance of reference footnotes, indeed a hallmark of his writings, has often been misunderstood as a misplaced endeavor to show off his great erudition. In fact, it represents his conscious effort to place American sociology, which up to then, with some honorable exceptions, was not exactly in the forefront of scholarly excellence, in the mainstream of worldwide scholarship. The common American variety of *homo sociologicus* was up to the thirties remarkably untouched by intellectual sophistication and scholarly range. Merton subverted this theoretical innocence by providing a steady diet of largely European scholarship. Even though the habit of abundant footnoting may at times have acquired a functional autonomy of its own in his work, its mainly heuristic thrust is readily apparent.

Parsons footnotes very sparingly, and his notes tend to refer in the main to the overall contributions of a selected few. This befits a sociological hedgehog. But what about Georg Simmel, the sociological fox par excellence, who used practically no footnotes at all? Simmel wrote within a long-established scholarly tradition. He largely addressed himself to an intellectual elite in which knowledge of the major scholarly contributions was, as it were, *de rigueur*. The apparatus of scholarship, he probably felt with a measure of coquetry, was to be taken for granted, much like true elegance in dress is inconspicuous. Merton wrote in an intellectual climate in which sophisticated scholarship could not be taken for granted; writing that aimed at providing models for a subsequent generation needed to impress on them the necessity of becoming aware of its heritage. Goethe's dictum, "What you have inherited from your fathers, acquire it in order to possess it," assumed salience in the American environment of the thirties. A *praeceptor sociologicus* had to stress again and again the heritage of European sociology even while he taught his contemporaries that in order truly to possess it they had to turn it to their peculiar uses. By Americanizing the heritage of European sociological theory, by grafting many sprigs of European origin onto the tree of American empirical tradition, Merton wished to lay the groundwork for a true flowering of a theoretically sophisticated American sociology.

3

Merton has written relatively little that deals directly with European sociological theories. Two papers on the sociology of knowledge and two early papers on Durkheim's *Division of Labor* and on French sociology are about all that he has devoted to such direct commentary. His more characteristic way of dealing with the European inheritance is through its incorporation into the texture of his own theories and research. He honors it chiefly by putting it to his own distinctive uses.

One of the ways in which past theories can be of major value to a contemporary scientist is through their power to identify problems that need investigation. In an illuminating essay on "Problem Finding in Sociology," Merton takes his point of departure from a statement by Darwin: "You would be surprised at the number of years it took me to see clearly what some of the problems were which had to be solved." Merton comments that "it is often more difficult to find and to formulate a problem than to solve it."[13] Though I do not have the privilege of being privy to the concrete workings of Merton's mind, I am under the strong impression that, at least in a number of cases, he derived the initial formulation of a problem he posed for himself from some aspects of the writings of one or the other of his European forebears. He would probably agree that an American sociologist of the twentieth century has an initial advantage over a Darwin, who was forced largely, though of course not wholly, to create *ab ovo*, in that he can draw continuously on the rich inheritance of European theory for the identification of what are crucial questions. The findings of significant problems, Merton has written, ". . . is not a matter of dull routine but a difficult task that taxes the trained imagination."[14] A sociological imagination that is indeed trained is powerfully aided in its tasks by continuing recourse to the tradition in which it is rooted.

Yet the uses of past theory are not limited to problem-finding. In attempting to specify one way in which a theory develops through successive approximations, Merton has written,

> A set of ideas serves, for a time, as a more or less useful guide for the investigation of an array of problems. As inquiry proceeds along these lines, it uncovers a gap in the theory: the set of ideas is found to be not discriminating enough to deal with aspects of phenomena to which it should in principle apply. In some cases, it is proposed to fill the gap by further differentiation of concepts and propositions that are consistent with the earlier theory. . . . In other cases, the new conceptions put in question some of the assumptions underlying the earlier theory which is then replaced rather than revised.[15]

Scholarly inquiry and research hence are never restricted to the routine task of verifying and testing theory, of confirming or falsifying hypotheses. "It *initiates,* it *reformulates,* it *deflects* and it *clarifies* theory,"[16] and in the process the concrete research effort leads continuously to new confrontations between empirical results and attempts to explain and clarify them through reference to previous theoretical findings.

What Merton has called the "interactive effect of developing new ideas by turning to older writings within the context of contemporary knowledge"[17] may involve assistance in the identification of crucial problems or in the formulation or reformulation of theoretical propositions. In yet other cases, current findings may be buttressed "through the satisfaction of independent confirmation of these ideas by a powerful mind."[18]

It may be of some utility to attempt to codify, even though in a most tentative and informal manner, the ways in which Merton, the codifier par excellence, related his work to the European tradition. When choosing a problem for investigation, Merton seems most of the time to have been stimulated by (1) a public issue that was salient at the time; or by (2) a theoretical formulation advanced by a previous thinker who may have been European or American (although only European thinkers will be considered here); or by (3) general scholarly interest in a particular area of inquiry. The execution of the project, in turn, led him to either (a) use previous scholarship to buttress his argument; or (b) use that scholarship in order to suggest formulations, refinements, and reformulations; or (c) use that scholarship to suggest new lines of inquiry. In all cases, Merton did not passively accept European theories but always reached out, actively appropriating and reconceptualizing them in tune with his own analytical needs.

4

Merton's characteristic relationship to the European tradition will be illustrated at the hand of a few examples.

His first major work, his dissertation *Science, Technology and Society in Seventeenth-Century England,*[19] already exemplifies one of his characteristic ways of putting the European heritage to his own uses. The original stimulus for Merton to undertake a study of the interplay of science, technology, and social structure in seventeenth-century England presumably came to him from a number of his teachers—Edwin Gay, George Sarton, and Pitrim A. Sorokin, in particular. It was also stimulated by Merton's familiarity with the works of Marx, to which, doubtlessly, he was drawn as a young radical. The first vague problem—concern with the interplay between the development of science and social and cultural conditions conducive to its growth—was present in Merton's mind when he embarked on his work. But, as he himself has recently explained,[20] only at a somewhat later point, when he was already immersed in a study of documentary material on seventeenth-century men of science and had been struck by the frequency of Puritan orientations among them, was he led to the intellectual tradition of Max Weber, Troeltsch, and Tawney centering on the relation of the Protestant ethic and the emergence of modern capitalism. A major part of the finished work ultimately developed into a self-conscious effort to extend Weber's thesis and to relate it in detail to the emergence of modern science. Even though Merton's earlier orientation had led him to the vague formulation of a general problem, only the later specification of the problem under the spur of Weberian theorizing allowed him to reformulate the problem so as to provide an answer specific enough to carry conviction.

As the work proceeded, Merton drew on other intellectual sources. A provocative essay by the Soviet scholar B. Hessen helped induce him to ferret out the stimulus to scientific development provided by the requirements of mining, navigation, and selected manufacturing industries. Werner Sombart's work led him to inquire about the relations of scientific development and the arts of war.

The last part of the book explores possible interrelations between increasing population densities and concomitantly increasing social interaction rates, and the efflorescence of scientific productivity. Surprisingly, there is no mention of Durkheim in this respect, but the abundant footnotes make it amply clear that here again Merton's queries were stimulated by a whole array of European thinkers.

In Merton's first book then, though an initial problem had been suggested by his general scholarly orientation, it became specified and made more precise and manageable after it was reformulated through the analyst's recourse to a number of European thinkers who, in addition, offered a series of hypotheses which directed the research into new and theoretically fruitful channels.

Merton's latest paper at the date of this writing, "Insiders and Outsiders: A Chapter in the Sociology of Knowledge,"[21] may serve as an instructive example of a different theoretical strategy. In this paper, written some thirty years after his book, the reader will also easily discern the influence of a wide array of European writers. The marvelously subtle analytical observations Merton brings to bear upon the problem of deciding whether the insider's position is especially conducive to providing "real knowledge," or whether the outsider occupies a privileged position in this respect, were stimulated, it is apparent, by his familiarity with the European sociology of knowledge. Yet one feels in this essay that Merton has by now so "internalized" this tradition that he draws upon it, as it were, without effort. There is no longer the sense of discovery on the part of the author that one feels in his earlier work. Merton does not discover any more in a territory that is by now well mapped for him.

The occasion for writing this essay, the immediate problem, is located in Merton's desire to oppose certain currently fashionable ideas as to the privileged position of the insider in the domain of knowledge. No reformulation of that problem occurs in the course of writing. Merton simply draws upon his impressive "internalized" knowledge in order to buttress his thesis and to follow various ramifications of the initial problem. His fine analytical exercises serve in this case mainly as rich embroidery around the central topic.

In the first instance, Merton seizes upon European theoretical ideas in order to refine and reformulate his empirical data through theoretical analysis and is led to new data, which in turn led him to ask questions that originated in the European theoretical tradition. In the second instance, Merton's supreme command of the tradition of the sociology of knowledge has allowed him to provide convincing answers to a problem first suggested to him by the twists of the *Zeitgeist*.

The examples that follow illustrate still a third and fourth use of the tradition of the European sociological past. In these cases Merton takes his point of departure, as in the above example, from current issues and confronts them with relevant European formulations. But here his formulations do not only serve to buttress his argumentation; they lead either to new lines of inquiry not envisaged by his European forebears or to formulations, reformulations, and refinements of previous European theorizing.

Merton wrote his essay on "Bureaucratic Structure and Personality" in the late thirties,[22] at a time when American society had just begun to emerge from its greatest crisis since the Civil War and when its established institutions had come under considerable scrutiny by critical observers both inside and outside the academy. Bureaucratic organization and centralization, especially in the federal administration, had made unprecedented strides in the New Deal days. Merton's overall concern with large-scale bureaucratization may hence have been largely initiated by its development on the American scene. In order to make sense of these developments, he turned for aid to his European predecessors.

The point of departure of the paper is located in Weber's ideal-typical depiction of the *modus operandi* of bureaucratic organizations with their high degrees of efficiency based, *inter alia,* on their exclusion of personal criteria, the constant recourse to well-specified rules, and the predictability of their operations. Weber, as is well known, was highly ambivalent about such bureaucratic organization; he felt that without it the achievements of the modern world, both with regard to the domination of nature and the gathering of social resources, would never have been possible. Yet he also feared that the further bureaucratization would lead to the death of freedom and spontaneity in the "iron cage" of a completely regulated and totally managed world.

Karl Mannheim, the second major European sociologist on whom Merton drew, did not go much beyond Weber in his overall characterization of bureaucracy but was more explicit in his emphasis on dysfunctional aspects of bureaucratic arrangements. It was indeed true, Mannheim asserted, that bureaucratic structures fostered the spirit of functional rationality, but this very increase of functional rationality tended, he argued, to lead to a decrease in substantial rationality, that is, in the ability of men to make choices on the basis of rational assessments of alternative courses of action. Functional rationality, it turned out, tends to subvert substantial rationality.

Sensitized in part by Mannheim's acerbic comments about the consequences for human freedom of an instrumentality that seemed to increase efficiency and rationality in human affairs, Merton chose to concentrate his analytic attention on the dysfunctional aspects of bureaucratic operations; the impersonality of the behavior of bureaucratic officeholders, which Weber had seen as a major aspect of their efficient functioning, became to Merton the source of dysfunctionality. Reliance on rules and regulations to the exclusion of other criteria, Merton reasoned, might well lead to ritualistic overconformity, to a displacement of goals whereby instrumental values become terminal values and mechanization takes command through structurally induced repression of innovating and adaptive responses to novel circumstances.

In this case Merton's theorizing, though it was presumably stimulated by somewhat ambivalent feelings about the proliferation of bureaucracies in his America, led to entirely fresh results only after he used the European heritage of Weber and Mannheim to help him specify some of the structural sources of the dysfunctional aspects of bureaucratic behavior. His delineation of the ritualistic elements in the bureaucratic personality led him in turn to depict a bureaucratic type that is not to be found in the work of either Weber or Mannheim.

"Social Structure and Anomie,"[23] perhaps Merton's most famous essay, reveals a somewhat different aspect of Merton's reliance upon the European tradition. The immediate impetus for its writing is surely to be found, as in the last case, in the circumstances and the social and cultural conditions of the thirties. America was undergoing during the years of the Depression a profound upheaval in its values and in its cherished moral predispositions. The center did not seem to hold any more. A profound disjunction between cultural expectations and actual behavior, especially among the disadvantaged, struck sensitive observers as a sign of moral breakdown and decay. As is customary in such situations, many of these observers deplored the demise of old-fashioned virtues and the decline of moral fiber among Americans. Not only a great many victims of the Depression,[24] but many scholarly observers also, attributed the predicaments of the times to the failing of individuals rather than to the sickness of the body social. The faulty operation of social structure was most often attributed "to failures of social control over man's imperious biological drives."[25] Much as in our day Edward Banfield[26] professes to find the root of our urban ills in the inability of slum dwellers to postpone instinctual gratifications, so it was widely attempted in the thirties to lay the causes for deviance and breakdown at the doorstep of insufficient control of wayward human impulses.

Attempting to counter such individualistic interpretations of social problems, Merton wished to provide a social structural, as distinct from a psychological, interpretation of the crisis. In the search for theoretical guidance, he turned to Émile Durkheim, the structural analyst par excellence. Durkheim's theory of anomie is the foundation stone upon which the Mertonian analytical scheme is built. Yet Merton did not mechanically apply a French theory of the late nineteenth century to the American scene of the thirties. He refined the theory in such a way that his version fitted the American experience while Durkheim's original insight did not.

In Durkheim's usage, and without following him in the intricacies of his thought, anomie essentially involved disruptions in the normative as well as in the relational aspects of society that lead to a social state in which the values and norms are no longer capable of exerting sufficient control over its component members. Under these circumstances, no meaningful limits are provided for the potentially insatiable desires of the human animal, and the individual is doomed to a life of constant search for satisfactions that cannot ever find genuine fulfillment. To Durkheim, anomie thus involves, first and foremost, a potentially deadly lack of control of human propensities. The way out of the predicament, he argued, was through a restructuring of society that would help build institutions that could effectively serve to reintegrate men into their community.

When Merton turned Durkheim's concept to his own uses, he was first of all concerned with divesting it of some of its conservative presuppositions. Merton was not concerned with philosophical questions about the real nature of human nature, and he was certainly not willing to commit himself to a philosophy resting on the alleged need to repress the ill effects of human nature in the raw. He was, however, much concerned in pinpointing the social structural aspects of the predicaments of his time. Thus he retained Durkheim's structural, and antipsychological, point of departure while reformulating the problem in terms of his concrete preoccupations with the American scene and his continued focus on class factors which had been stimulated by his immersion in Marxian thought. The Durkheimian interplay between biological propensity and societal regulation was transformed in Merton's work into the discrepancy between culturally prescribed goals and the socially available means of reaching these goals. In American society, he argued, there arose a disjunction between the prevalent emphasis on material success and the class system so that "social structures exert a definitive pressure upon certain persons in the society to engage in nonconforming rather than conforming conduct."[27]

The "typology of modes of individual adaptations" to the disjunction between cultural goals and structurally determined means of access to these goals could only be developed after Merton's thorough reformulation of Durkheim's original notion. Furthermore, and this is of the essence, while in Durkheim's formulation attention was focused on the effects of deregulation on the upper and middle classes (the poor being protected, in Durkheim's view, against inordinate desires by the very fact of poverty), Merton's formulation made it possible for him to deal with the problem of anomie among the lower middle and lower strata of the society. He sensitized the sociological analyst to problems of disjunction between goals and means among those strata that, for structural reasons, were shut off from channels of opportunity easily available to those in the higher reaches of the social structure. This thorough recasting of Durkheim's thought served Merton to make a contribution to the debates of his day, by showing that the types of disaffection and deviance, especially among lower strata, that current observers had seen and deplored were not amenable to change through moralistic exhortation or psychological counseling but were rooted in the social structure. They could be remedied only through structural change, that is, through a widening of the structure of opportunity. Merton retained Durkheim's emphasis while he recast his conceptualization so as to spell out the effects of the class structure on persons variously placed within it. Through Durkheim's theory of anomie as a point of departure, and with a powerful assist from Marxian class theory, Merton arrived at a theory of differential opportunity structures leading to systematic departures from normative expectations by persons variously placed in specific class situations.

Not only whole papers by Merton but particular analytical points within larger papers, as well as general theoretical orientations, reveal his creative appropriation of the European heritage.

In an ambitious attempt to clarify and elucidate the concept of *reference group* and to point to the major problematics associated with reference group theory, Merton developed a codification of the structural properties of a variety of groups.[28] In the process of setting down significant aspects of groups and group membership, Merton used his extended empirical knowledge as well as his immersion in the works of his predecessors and contemporaries. Though the sources of Merton's manifold observations clearly were diverse, he has said himself that in a number of cases "a point of departure is provided by Georg Simmel."[29]

Even though Merton has said that "beyond the teachers under whom I studied directly, I learned most from two sociologists, Georg Simmel and Émile Durkheim . . . ,"[30] Simmel's shadow does not loom very large in Merton's work prior to this essay. But when he turned to the analysis of group properties, he turned or returned to a close reading of this incomparable, though highly unsystematic, master. Thus, early in his essay, Merton reflects that the well-known notion of group membership is evidently related to the heretofore much neglected notion of nonmembership. Membership and nonmembership relate to each other like figures to their grounds. In order to further explicate the relationship, Merton then rediscovers a notion by Simmel largely buried in one of his pages, the notion of "completeness." Merton proceeds to so reformulate Simmel's notion that it could become part of systematic theory. For Merton, completeness "refers to a group property measured by the proportion of *potential members . . .* who are *actual members.*" This leads him to the important realization that there are in fact, "as Simmel apparently sensed, . . . distinct and structurally different *kinds of non-members* of a group,"[31] and to a classification of nonmembers into those eligible for membership and those judged to be ineligible, as well as to further considerations about open and closed groups. This seems clearly a case where Merton's general preoccupations with the structural properties of groups led him to reread Simmel and where Simmel's observations, now highlighted in Merton's mind because of his prior concern, serve an important function in the specification and refinement of his thought.

Simmel's acute insights into the importance of degrees of visibility or observability of group members served Merton in similar ways. For all I know, Merton may already have worked his way to the notion that whether role performances are visible to others, be they status-inferiors, peers, or status-superiors, may have highly important consequences. But he has himself indicated how he was powerfully stimulated in pursuing this notion by the work of Simmel.[32] The development of the concept shows Merton at his analytical best. It illustrates the marvelous alchemy through which he transformed incidental remarks by Simmel into the systematic proposition that what people are allowed to conceal from each other may be as important as what they are induced to reveal, and that the dialectic of revealing and concealing has deep roots in the structural properties of groups.

Merton's indebtedness to at least two general traditions of European theorizing, those of the sociology of knowledge and those of functional analysis, is so well known that it hardly needs extended commentary. He sometimes has remarked, semifacetiously to be sure, that European theorists seem often to be saying: "We do not know whether what we say is true, but it is at least significant." Americans, in contrast, seem to be saying: "This is demonstrably so, but we cannot indicate its significance." Merton's endeavor has been to overcome these contrasting emphases. In the attempt to do so, he has been led to eliminate from European theories weaknesses that were rooted in overgeneral or overconfident formulations and to recast, refine, and systematize these theories in tune with the empirical exigencies of his research in an American setting.

Merton's magisterial essay on "Manifest and Latent Functions" is an attempt to systematize a method of analysis through a critical evaluation of the methods of his predecessors. While registering his deep indebtedness to the tradition of functional analysis as originated by Durkheim, and as pursued by such British luminaries as Radcliffe-Brown and Malinowski, Merton pays them the type of homage that alone befits one's ancestors in the world of science: he shows how by profiting from their vision a later generation can, from its vantage point, afford to correct and extend it.

Merton's strictures against a global panfunctionalism, his crucial distinctions between latent and manifest functions, his highlighting of dysfunctional consequences, his insistence on the imperative necessity of specifying precisely what unit is subserved by what function, his distinction between motivation or purposes and objective consequences, his insistence on the search for functional alternatives—these and many other aspects of functional analysis that he codified in his "Paradigm for Functional Analysis in Sociology"[33] reveal his building upon the analytical strategies of his predecessors. By putting them to his own uses, he modifies them in the light of his analytical experience and immensely increases the opportunity to put them to creative uses.

Merton's discussion of the sociology of knowledge proceeds in a parallel manner. Here again, he pays homage to a tradition of which he is proud to be a part. And here again he shows how methodical reflection and immersion in concrete research have led him to modify what he feels are the overly general propositions of Mannheim, Scheler, Durkheim, and others by a more modulated, more modest, and altogether more defensible set of formulations about the relation between mental products and the location of their producers in the social structure. Warning against the variety of highly ambiguous terms that have served in the past to designate the relations between mental products and their societal basis, stressing the need to distinguish between different types and aspects of mental products, emphasizing the requirement clearly to demarcate what such notions as social or cultural basis specifically connote and denote, Merton developed a "Paradigm for the Sociology of Knowledge."[34] Just as in the case of functional analysis, he has helped modify previously overrigid or excessively elastic theories, concepts, and notions and has made them into more usable instruments for the concrete research tasks facing the American sociologist of knowledge.

5

Since other essays in this volume delve more deeply into the matter, a bare enumeration must suffice of some general characteristics that distinguish Merton's approach from most of his European predecessors (and also from Parsons'). While the latter think in more or less global categories, Merton's analytical strategies are characterized, *inter alia,* by his close attention to contradictions and conflicts within global structures, to ambivalences in the motivations of actors, and to ambiguities in the perceptual field to which they orient themselves. As befits a sociological fox, Merton is never content with establishing one overall vision, and he is at pains to show that what holds for himself is likely to also hold for the subjects of his analysis. Parsons' actor *knows* what are the role requirements that flow from the position he occupies, even though he may upon occasion be motivated to deviate from them. Merton's actors face role- and status-sets with often contradictory expectations and are continuously navigating between them. They attempt cautiously to avoid the Scylla of overconformity and the Charybdis of deviance, while often falling prey to the lures of the one or the other. His actors are not only part of a Durkheimian or Parsonian society with a capital S. They belong to conflicting, mutually repulsive, and yet mutually attractive, subgroups that contend for their members' loyalties and allegiance. The Mertonian world is a universe of warring gods, and matters are never at ease in his Zion.

In tune with this overall vision, Merton decided early in his career to hearken to many of the voices that spoke to him from the European past but never to pay homage at any shrine exclusively. He has attempted to arrive at a synthesis of many of the traditions in the shadow of which he stands and so to transcend every particular influence. Putting them to use, he rose above them all while remaining deeply in their debt.

Merton has succeeded in transmitting to us a multifaceted and many-colored fabric of ideas, both European and American, which he has managed to incorporate into the rich texture of his own lifework by harnessing them to his own creative purposes. Those of us who have followed him on the journey are grateful to him even as we now try in our own way to transform his heritage to our own uses.

NOTES

1. J. H. Plumb, *The Death of the Past* (New York: Macmillan, 1969), p. 11.
2. Pitrim A. Sorokin, *Sociological Theories of Today* (New York: Harper & Row, 1966), p. 455.
3. Robert K. Merton, *On the Shoulders of Giants: A Shandean Postscript* (New York: Free Press, 1965).
4. Robert K. Merton, *Social Theory and Social Structure,* enl. ed. (New York: Free Press, 1968), p. 69. (Hereinafter referred to as *STSS.*)
5. *Ibid.*
6. *Ibid.*
7. Helmuth Plessner, "Zur Soziologie der modernen Forschung," in Max Scheler, ed., *Versuche einer Soziologie des Wissens* (Munich: Dunker und Humblot, 1924), pp. 407–25.
8. Robert K. Merton, "Notes on Problem-Finding in Sociology," in Robert K. Merton, Leonard Broom, and Leonard S. Cottrell, Jr., eds., *Sociology Today* (New York: Basic Books, 1959), p. xxi.
9. Talcott Parsons, *The Structure of Social Action* (New York: Free Press, 1949; originally published, 1937).
10. Isaiah Berlin, *The Hedgehog and the Fox* (New York: Mentor Books, 1959).
11. Robert K. Merton, "Account of Studies and Research in the Past," mimeod., ca. 1962.
12. Merton, *STSS,* p. 53.
13. Merton, "Notes on Problem-Finding in Sociology," p. ix.
14. *Ibid.,* p. xi.
15. Robert K. Merton, "Social Conformity, Deviation and Opportunity Structures: A Comment on the Contributions of Dubin and Cloward," *American Sociological Review* 24, no. 2 (April 1959): 177.
16. Merton, *STSS,* p. 157.
17. *Ibid.,* pp. 37–38.
18. *Ibid.*
19. Robert K. Merton, *Science, Technology and Society in Seventeenth-Century England* (New York: Harper Torchbooks, 1970; originally published, 1938).
20. *Ibid.,* p. xvii.
21. Robert K. Merton, "Insiders and Outsiders: A Chapter in the Sociology of Knowledge," *American Journal of Sociology* 78, no. 2 (July 1972): 9–47.
22. Robert K. Merton, "Bureaucratic Structure and Personality," in Merton, *STSS,* pp. 249–60.

23. Robert K. Merton, "Social Structure and Anomie," in Merton, *STSS,* pp. 185–214.
24. Cf. E. W. Bakke, *The Unemployed Worker* (New Haven: Yale University Press, 1940).
25. Merton, *STSS,* p. 185.
26. Edward Banfield, *The Unheavenly City* (Boston: Little, Brown, 1970).
27. Merton, *STSS,* p. 186. See also Ephraim H. Mizruchi, *Success and Opportunity* (New York: Free Press, 1964).
28. Robert K. Merton, "Continuities in the Theory of Reference Groups and Social Structure," in Merton, *STSS,* pp. 335–440.
29. *Ibid.,* p. 346.
30. Merton, "Account of Studies and Research in the Past."
31. Merton, "Continuities in the Theory of Reference Groups and Social Structure," pp. 342–43.
32. *Ibid.,* pp. 373 ff.
33. Merton, *STSS,* pp. 104 ff.
34. *Ibid.,* pp. 514 ff.

ON THE SHOULDERS
OF MERTON

Toward a New View of the Sociology of Knowledge

BERNARD BARBER

IN this essay I should like to recommend the view that the sociology of knowledge—in regard to its theory, its research methods, and its data, all three—should be integrated into general or "mainstream" sociology. Such integration, a reciprocal process in which what is presently defined as the sociology of knowledge would have to conform to the standards of theory, method, and data of general sociology and in which general sociology would be improved and enriched by the contributions of the new sociology of knowledge, would obviously be beneficial to both. The sociology of knowledge, like all sociological specialties, can only flourish if it is an integral part of general sociology. The sociology of knowledge has languished for more than thirty years.

The isolation of what is presently viewed as the sociology of knowledge is not hard to see. Judging both from books and articles that call themselves works in the sociology of knowledge and from what graduate students in sociology who elect to take a course in this field expect to hear in lectures and read, the predominant present view of the sociology of knowledge is of a separate, "foreign," philosophical, ideological, speculative, and nonresearch field of study.[1] I have been perhaps especially impressed with the unsatisfactoriness of the predominant view of the sociology of knowledge by my experience with beginning graduate students. For more than twenty years now, in teaching a course in this field every other year, I have had to confront, counter, and correct this predominant view. Graduate students in social stratification

Bernard Barber is Professor of Sociology at Barnard College, Columbia University.

courses are different from one biennium to another: they seem to have heard of new theories, or new research methods, or new research studies. But sociology of knowledge students do not change.

It is not that previous efforts to counter the predominant present view of the sociology of knowledge do not exist—indeed, powerful and prestigious efforts. Twenty-five years ago Robert Merton, using numerous examples from the study of mass communications, pointed out that the research methods and standards of empirical data of the sociology of knowledge needed to be integrated with those of general sociology.[2] But in this instance Merton has not had the triumphant success he has had in several other sociological specialties. The old sociology of knowledge has gone its old way.

It is perhaps time again, then, to recommend a new view of the sociology of knowledge. That is my purpose here, and toward that end I shall, all too briefly, address five topics: the problem of philosophy; the problem of theory; the problem of the nature of the relationships among culture, social structure, and personality; the problem of the hierarchy of knowledge; and the problem of research methods and data. Finally, I want to say something about the future of the sociology of knowledge.

THE PROBLEM OF PHILOSOPHY

The predominant, traditional view of the sociology of knowledge is preoccupied, to a degree that is no longer the case in other sociological specialties, by the philosophical problems of knowledge. Graduate student novices are more concerned with problems of the possibility, relativity, and validity of sociological knowledge than with the concepts, hypotheses, propositions, methods, and data that constitute it. In short, it is ontology and epistemology they wish to discuss, not sociology.

The new view of the sociology of knowledge recognizes, indeed insists upon, the importance of the philosophical problems of knowledge. But the philosophical problems of science and other forms of knowledge have been attended to by an ancient, highly developed, and necessarily separate discipline—philosophy. These problems cannot be confused or merged with sociological problems of knowledge. Of course, as the newer sociology of knowledge further insists, sociological and philosophical aspects of knowledge are interconnected—that is, affect one another—at certain important points. But through considerable and important ranges of analysis, they are independent and separate from one another. Each has its own technical methods of analysis, its own findings, its own need for disciplinary specialists and courses of instruction, its own subspecialties. The sociologist who has aspirations to contribute to the philosophy of sociology will have to master not only his own discipline but the relevant parts of the discipline of philosophy as well. Until the necessity of this double mastery is acknowledged and surmounted, we shall continue to have what we now have in the philosophy of sociology: a few small successes and many failures. No one, sociologist or philosopher, has yet produced a philosophy of sociology in the grand manner.

104

Recognizing the importance of philosophy, then, the newer view of the sociology of knowledge recommends a philosophical position of pragmatism (note the small "p")[3] which assumes and then takes for granted that the social world can be known, and can be known to a desired degree of objectivity, validity, and usability by scholars conforming to scientific standards and methods that have produced such knowledge about the physical and biological aspects of the world. Such a philosophical position is obviously a prerequisite to the sociological enterprise. The mature scholar or novice who cannot accept it is better cut out for philosophy itself than for sociology.

THE PROBLEM OF THEORY

In this section I should like to present a broad sketch of how the sociology of knowledge fits into general sociological theory and therefore why it should be integrated into that theory. For this purpose I shall describe very succinctly a theoretical model for social system analysis that helps to locate the nature and tasks of the sociology of knowledge as part of general sociology.

The sociology of knowledge is but one of many sociological specialties devoted to the analysis of action in social systems. As Figure 1 (below) may help to make clear, we assume that "action" or "interaction" is the basic stuff of sociological analysis, as "matter" is for physics and "life" for biology. Figure 1 shows that we further assume that the endless process of action or interaction is usefully conceived, not necessarily ontologically but only for purposes of scientific analysis, to be broken up into separate, boundary-maintaining, dynamic, and changeful systems. One type of system that is useful for sociological analysis is the one we label "society," but the system assumption is useful also for those elements that are constituents of a society and for those that describe the interaction of two or more societies.

Figure 1. DIAGRAM OF RELATIONS AMONG ACTION, SOCIAL SYSTEM, AND SOCIETY

ACTION (INTERACTION)

SOCIAL SYSTEM

SOCIETY

SOCIAL STRUCTURE	CULTURE	PERSONALITY
BASIC UNIT = STRUCTURED AND PROBABLY INSTITUTIONALIZED "ROLE"	BASIC UNIT = STRUCTURED AND PROBABLY INSTITUTIONALIZED "IDEA"	BASIC UNIT = "?"

105

Figure 1 also illustrates the assumption of this model that all action in social systems has three analytic aspects: social structure, culture, and personality. That is to say, there is no unit of action in any social system, societal or larger or smaller, in which all three of these aspects of its structure and functioning cannot be discerned. As Figure 1 shows, the basic unit of analysis for social structure is "role" and for culture is "idea." Because of the paradigm differences among various schools of psychologists, who are the disciplinary experts with regard to personality, the basic unit of analysis for that aspect of action is left unspecified in this model. This merely signifies the lack of general theoretical commitment among sociologists to any one theory of personality. In practice, of course, sociologists doing research as social psychologists do make specific commitments in psychological theory. They are predominantly Freudians and Meadians, though there are a few Skinnerians among them.

All three aspects of action are conceived of as structured (or patterned, which is to be taken as a synonym for structured). That is to say, again for purposes of scientific analysis and not because of ontological assumptions, there are assumed to be discernible uniformities of regularity and recurrence in the process; these are defined as structures. It should be clear that structure and process are but two ways of conceiving the basic stuff of action.

Figure 1 also indicates that role and idea structures have to be analyzed as more or less "institutionalized," that is, as supported by more or less moral consensus among those who are engaged in those structures. Institutionalization is very much a matter of degree, with some structures having very little such moral consensus attached to them, many having a moderate amount, and some having a great deal. In his discussion of folkways and mores, Sumner was talking about this important matter of institutionalization. It is essential to see that structure and institutionalization are different and independently variable aspects of action in social systems. It should also be carefully noted that although sociologists tend to use the term "institution" vaguely and to mean different things that should be kept separate, they do tend on the whole to use the term only to refer to social structures. According to our definition of institutionalization, idea structures are as much subject to analysis in these terms as are role structures. Language, ideologies, science, and the several other types of idea-systems are analyzable not only in terms of their cognitive or logical structures but as the foci of sentiments of moral consensus and dissensus among those who use them.

Finally, Figure 1 is intended to show that all three aspects of action—social structure, culture, and personality—are independent of one another to some extent, as well as being interdependent to some degree. That is to say, in some ways their essential types of structure, dynamics, and change are different from one another. These differences are matters for empirical research as well as theoretical analysis. Later in this essay, in discussing what I call "the hierarchy of knowledge," I shall be giving an example of the different type of structuring which occurs in culture in comparison with social structure.

It is also an important assumption of the model presented in Figure 1 that social structure, culture, and personality are in principle all equally important aspects of action. Because we read from left to right in English and

106

because I have listed social structure, culture, and personality in that order from left to right, there may be a tendency to infer that this order is an order of theoretical importance or weight. Not so at all. In this system model, we might have listed the three aspects in any order as far as their generalized importance as analytic structures or variables is concerned. In concrete cases of analysis, of course, any one may be more important than the others, but that is something to be established empirically and by controlled or natural experiment.[4] The model of the social system illustrated in Figure 1 accepts none of the monofactorial theories—whether social structural, cultural, or personality—which are rife in the social sciences today.

It is now possible, using the condensed account we have given up to this point of a model for the analysis of action in social systems, to give some initial statements about the sociology of knowledge. It is clearly culture, or systems of structured ideas of various types, that is the central focus of concern of the sociology of knowledge, just as it is social structure that is central to other sociological specialties. But it is also clear that the sociology of knowledge will have to study the relationships between culture and social structure, and personality too, as well as sometimes limiting itself to analysis of the endogenous types of structure, process, and change within culture itself. Both of these kinds of study, of course, will be done best in reference to one another, since only with such reference can one establish what is endogenous and what is interrelationship. And it is clear that both kinds of study require the necessary expertise of the relevant knowledge of both culture and social structure. Sociologists of knowledge cannot be casual about social structure any more than social structuralists can be crude or rudimentary in their knowledge of culture. The stores of certified knowledge accumulated by disciplinary specialists in both areas are now too large to be ignored or treated lightly by any one specialist seeking to show connections between his own area and some other one. Difficulties of this kind seem to be one source of the controversy between certain historians of science, the "internalists," who stress the endogenous problems of scientific idea-systems and ignore their social structural connections, and certain sociologists of science, derided as "externalists" by the historians, who are more competent in discerning these social structural connections than they are in understanding the subtle substance of the idea-systems in question.[5]

So much for knowledge, or culture, and social structure and their relationships in general. For some more detailed understanding of the place of the sociology of knowledge in general sociological theory, let us now move on to Figure 2 (page 108). That figure shows that each of the three broad categories of social structure, culture, and personality is composed of several constituent subsystems. In finer perspective, then, the sociology of knowledge consists in relating any one or more of the cultural subsystems either to other subsystems in culture, or to subsystems in social structure, or to subsystems in personality. Because of the complexity of concrete reality, of course, it is likely that any given analysis will be multivariate and will relate several of these subsystems to one another. Thus, one might relate art to philosophy and economic structure. Or one might relate science to stratification and organizational structure. Or one might relate ideology to science and political structure.

107

SOCIALIZATION (EDUCATION) STRUCTURE	
ECONOMIC STRUCTURE	
POLITICAL STRUCTURE	
STRATIFICATION STRUCTURE	SOCIAL STRUCTURE
KINSHIP STRUCTURE	
COMMUNICATIONS STRUCTURE	
ORGANIZATION (GROUP) STRUCTURE	
IDEOLOGY (STRUCTURED OR PATTERNED)	
SCIENCE (STRUCTURED OR PATTERNED)	
RELIGION (STRUCTURED OR PATTERNED)	
VALUES (STRUCTURED OR PATTERNED)	CULTURE
PHILOSOPHY (STRUCTURED OR PATTERNED)	
LANGUAGE (STRUCTURED OR PATTERNED)	
ART (STRUCTURED OR PATTERNED)	
- -	PERSONALITY

SOCIETY

Figure 2.

The several social structural, cultural, and personality subsystems are not, of course, undifferentiated categories. Each of them has been shown, analytically and empirically, to have a limited number of structural subtypes. Ideally, then, the sociology of knowledge seeks to make statements of determinate relationships among these structural subtypes. Thus, it is a certain type of art that is related to a certain type of philosophy and a certain type of economic structure. And it is a certain type (degree of development) of science that is related to a certain type of stratification structure and a certain type of organizational structure. What holds for relationships among the subtypes of these subsystems considered as structures holds for them also in their processual and changeful aspects. Thus, the sociology of knowledge is interested in how change in type of ideology might lead to change in type of kinship structure.[6] Or it is interested in how changes in science relate to changes in philosophy, and the other way around.

It is perhaps somewhat clearer now, after looking at Figure 2, how the sociology of knowledge is a part of general sociological theory and work and why it needs to be integrated into them. Such integration would be profitable to sociology all around.

Though there is a great deal of at least latent consensus among sociologists on the list of subsystems that has been included in Figure 2, that list, both in the social structural and cultural categories, is merely provisional, as all such paradigmatic lists of analytic categories always have to be in science. At any given point in the development of a science, though it is helpful to have consensus on a comprehensive and systematic model or paradigm of this kind, that model and its list of conceptual subcategories is very much subject to revision, through either minor reform or major revolution.[7]

The provisional character of the list of subsystems given in Figure 2 is perhaps even greater for culture than it is for social structure. Certainly one of the key and long-persisting problems of the sociology of knowledge is the establishment of a systematic, comprehensive, agreed-upon list of the functional subsystems of culture.[8] In references to various types of idea-systems, not merely the lay public but scholars themselves use different terms for what seems to be a single type and the same term for different types of idea-systems. For example, terms like "belief," "myth," and "ideology" are used in ways so various and obscure that it is hard to come to grips with the analysis being offered. And the terminological variants for an idea-system type such as ideology include such terms as fables, doctrines, lore, dreams, mystiques, rhetoric, and so forth.[9]

In the absence of a theoretically systematic and comprehensive list of the cultural subsystems, these subsystems blur into one another and are hard to keep separate for purposes of analysis and research. Consider, for example, some of the discussions of what is "religion" and what "ideology" in Communist and non-Communist but secular modern societies. Such a list is an essential prerequisite for specifying what is the degree of independence of each of the cultural subsystems, that independence which we indicated above was an important assumption about culture in general and characterizes its several subsystems as well, and what is the degree and nature of that interdependence among the subsystems which sometimes seems more obvious than the independence. A list which precisely and analytically specified the independence of the several subsystems would help to obviate the tendencies to reductionism and monofactorial explanation which have existed in social science for a long time.

THE PROBLEM OF THE NATURE OF THE RELATIONSHIPS AMONG CULTURE, SOCIAL STRUCTURE, AND PERSONALITY

Mention of reductionism and monofactorial explanation provides us with an opportunity to confront directly the problem of the nature of the relationships among culture, social structure, and personality system types or variables. We have deliberately avoided this problem up to now by speaking generally and therefore somewhat vaguely about "relationships," but obviously this will not do and we need more specific statements about this problem.

In item number three of his paradigm for the sociology of knowledge, Robert Merton indicated the enormous confusion about this problem that existed thirty years ago, a confusion that still persists. Facing the almost infinite variety of terms used in the field for relationships between knowledge and social structure, he valiantly constructed a classification for them which included: "causal or functional relations," "symbolic or organismic or meaningful relations," and a necessary catchall category, "ambiguous terms to designate relations."[10]

The problem of the nature of relationships among system variables is, of course, far from settled even in general sociology. There is a certain amount of consensus around "causal" language and also around "functional" language, but much research settles for mere correlations and some still evades the problem by using a number of terminological alternatives for relationship. There is very little use now in professional sociology of what Merton categorized as the "symbolic or organismic or meaningful" terms for relationship, though such terms do persist in some other areas of social science.

Because of this somewhat unsettled state of the problem even in general sociology, the integration of the sociology of knowledge into general sociology would not wholly solve this problem for the sociology of knowledge, but it would somewhat reduce it. Work in the sociology of knowledge could face the problem in a more disciplined way and could profit from the considerable and useful discussion of the problem which is a continuing part of general sociology. In any case, it is important to establish as a working assumption that there is nothing unique to the sociology of knowledge with regard to this problem of the nature of the relationship among social system variables.

THE PROBLEM OF THE HIERARCHY OF KNOWLEDGE

If there is nothing unique in the nature of the relationships among cultural variables or between them and social structural and personality systems, is there anything special or different about the nature of the internal structuring

110

of idea systems? Some of the discussions about the nature of relationships among cultural systems or between them and others, such as discussions involving notions of "logico-meaningful" or "organismic" relations, seem to imply peculiarities and differences of some sort. With regard to culture or knowledge, are we in a wholly different realm from social structure as far as criteria and patterns of structuring are concerned?

Two things are clear. One is that we do not have a satisfactory answer to this question. The other is that we do not have such an answer because neither sociology in general nor the sociology of knowledge as a specialty has given sufficient analytic attention to the problem. Much more attention has been given to the structural problems of social structural systems than to the same problems in cultural systems.

To suggest, and certainly not to give, a complete or definitive solution of both the possibilities of a generalized analysis of structuring in the cultural realm and the sociological uses of such an analysis, I should like to give a brief account of what I have been calling for some time "the hierarchy of knowledge problem." We start from the fact that the structure of every one of the several types of idea-systems in culture may vary in the degree of its *abstractness* (or generalization, as it is alternatively called), its *systematization,* and its *comprehensiveness.* Abstractness refers to and provides a principle for measuring the fact that the units of any type of idea-system range from the very concrete to middling abstract to extremely abstract. The systematization principle refers to the extent to which any set of units from a given cultural system type are consistently and explicitly interrelated with one another. And, finally, comprehensiveness measures the degree to which a system of ideas of any cultural type confronts all the relevant analytic problems that can be seen to exist for that given cultural type. These three principles or dimensions of structuring for cultural systems are often thought to apply only to scientific ideas, but they apply as well to ideologies, religious ideas, values, philosophies, and idea-systems in the several arts.

From the fact of the structuring of idea-systems along these three dimensions, some important sociological problems and consequences emerge. For example, given the tendency for each of the types of idea-systems to move toward more abstract, systematic, and comprehensive formulations, and given the fact that indeed there has been an evolutionary tendency of this kind from earlier to modern societies, what are the sociological conditions favoring and resisting that tendency? Again, sometimes we have asked this question with regard to science, but what about the other types of idea-system, for example, ideology, or music? Or what about variations among different types of science, physical or biological or social? These are important problems for the sociology of knowledge to investigate.

In the modern world, as a result of the development of greater abstractness, systematization, and comprehensiveness in idea-systems of all types, the phenomenon of the hierarchy of knowledge comes to exist, attended by some interesting social and sociological problems. The phenomenon consists in the fact that there now coexist, for each and all of the types of idea-system, ideas that range from the most concrete, least systematic, and least comprehensive,

111

on the one hand, to those that are most abstract, systematic, and comprehensive, on the other, with intermediate-level ideas in between. To use the popular lingo, which does catch up the rudiments of the important phenomenon I have been describing but which needs to be made more analytic and more precise, we now have "high brows," "middle brows," and "low brows." Or, to use some other not-quite-satisfactory terms used by some high brows, we now have "intellectuals" and "men in the street," or "high culture" and "mass culture."

As Figures 1 and 2 imply, ideas do have consequences for each other and for social structural systems. And so also the hierarchy of knowledge has consequences. Among other things, it results in differences of prestige and power among those who can locate themselves differently in the hierarchy, and not infrequently such differences can lead to conflict. Further, the hierarchy of knowledge raises problems of communication among those located at different levels. Even those with basically the same idea may not understand one another if one speaks in slogans and the other delivers systematic disquisitions. And the hierarchy of knowledge, to mention just one more consequence, brings about the need for mechanisms of accommodation and consensus in social systems, small or large, where the divergencies of sophistication in ideas may diminish the possibilities for whatever is desired or required in the way of solidarity among the members of the system.

In modern society we live with the hierarchy of knowledge the way we live with hierarchies of power and prestige, though they are constructed along other dimensions. The hierarchy of knowledge ought as much to be an analytic focus of the sociology of knowledge as the social structural hierarchies are of their respective sociological specialties.[11]

THE PROBLEM OF METHODS AND DATA

We can, by now, be very brief on the problem of methods and data for the sociology of knowledge. The predominant present view, unfortunately, is that methods and data for the field can be unsystematic, untested, and intuitive, with a great deal of autonomy for the individual scholar in his modes of inquiry and in his supporting evidence. The newer view of the sociology of knowledge holds that there is nothing different in the necessary research methods and data of this field from any of the other special fields of general sociology. Its data can be qualitative or quantitative, its methods can involve participant observation, historical inquiry, controlled observation, or survey research. The whole developed armamentarium of modern sociological research is available for and usable by a sociology of knowledge that is satisfactorily integrated into general sociology.

THE FUTURE OF THE SOCIOLOGY OF KNOWLEDGE

What of the future of the sociology of knowledge? I hope it is clear that we should move toward full integration with general sociology in all the several respects that I have discussed. The substantive theoretical model that I have offered in Figure 2 is not, of course, the only possible basis for such integration. There may be alternatives to it and there certainly are necessary supplements to it even if it is used as the basic conceptual framework for research in this field. In the line of supplements, for example, Lewis Coser has used Znaniecki's concept of "the social circle" very effectively in his *Men of Ideas,*[12] an excellent work in the sociology of knowledge exemplifying some of the points I have made above. Similarly, Diana Crane has offered "the paradigm, the social circle, and the invisible college as unifying theoretical concepts" for what she calls, following influences shared with this essay, "the sociology of culture."[13] Such supplements are specifications of some parts of the model offered in Figure 2 or compatible with it. For the future of the sociology of knowledge, the particular substantive models and concepts that are to be used to integrate it with general sociology are perhaps less important than the sharp and continuing awareness that such integration is desirable all around.

Moreover, as we move toward the future recommended by the newer view of the sociology of knowledge, we already have more than just theoretical models and methodological precepts to help us. For as far as actual research is concerned—research of various kinds which could easily be integrated into general sociology by our newer view—some of the future is already here. There already exists a great deal of work which is not defined by either its authors, its readers, or any of the relevant professional social circles or invisible colleges as work in the sociology of knowledge. Yet in the newer view, in which the sociology of knowledge is integrated into general sociology with mutual benefit to both, that is definitely what it is and it ought to be recognized as such. In the Selected Bibliography given below, I have given a small but representative list of such work. When works such as these become the standard models for research in the sociology of knowledge, and when such models are seen as contributing to general sociology as well as the special field, the future of the new sociology of knowledge will have arrived.

NOTES

1. For lack of space in this essay and because only partial documentation from published works would be invidious, I trust my undocumented statements will be received tolerantly. In a future book I hope to remedy this fault with adequate references not only for my impressions of the present view of the sociology of knowledge but for my assertions about what that view should be.

2. See Robert K. Merton, Introduction to "The Sociology of Knowledge and Communications," in his *Social Theory and Social Structure,* 1st ed. (Glencoe, Ill.: Free Press, 1949), part 3, pp. 100–216. In part 3 of the essays, for valuable contributions to the theory and substance of what should be the new view of the sociology of knowledge, see also "The Sociology of Knowledge" and "Karl Mannheim and the Sociology of Knowledge." Finally, all of part 4, "Studies in the Sociology of Science," is a contribution to the sociology of science that is still of premier importance.

3. The small "p" on pragmatism is intended to indicate that this position may be acceptable to schools of method and philosophy other than Pragmatism.

4. For an earlier and more fully empirically illustrated statement of some of these points, see Bernard Barber, "On the Relations Between 'Culture' and 'Social Structure,'" *Transactions, New York Academy of Sciences* 17 (1955): 613–20. For a recent set of statements from the several social sciences on the nature of "culture," see Louis Schneider and Charles Bonjean, eds., *The Idea of Culture in the Social Sciences* (New York: Cambridge University Press, 1973).

5. For a sensible view of these matters by historians of science, see Steven Shapin and Arnold Thackray, "Prosopography as a Research Tool in History of Science," *History of Science,* forthcoming.

6. For an empirical treatment of just this kind of change, see the analysis and material from W. J. Goode, *World Revolution and Family Patterns* (New York: Free Press, 1963), pp. 19, 369, cited in Bernard Barber, "Function, Variability, and Change in Ideological Systems," in Bernard Barber and Alex Inkeles, eds., *Stability and Social Change* (Boston: Little, Brown, 1971).

7. On paradigms and revolutions in science, see T. S. Kuhn, *The Structure of Scientific Revolutions,* 2nd ed., enl. (Chicago: University of Chicago Press, 1970).

8. Twenty-five years ago, Robert Merton spoke of his paradigm for the sociology of knowledge, one part of which was a list of "mental productions," or what we have here called "culture," as "partial" and a "temporary classification." He expressed the hope that it would soon give way to "an improved and more exacting model" (Merton, *Social Theory and Social Structure,* p. 221). For a theoretically rigorous but only partial treatment of this problem, see Talcott Parsons, *The Social System* (Glencoe, Ill.: Free Press, 1951), chap. 8, "Belief Systems and the Social System: The Problem of the 'Role of Ideas.'"

9. For example, Richard Hofstadter, in *The Age of Reform* (New York: Knopf, 1955), chap. 1, "The Agrarian Myth and Commercial Realities," gives an excellent discussion of an important American ideology.

10. Merton, *Social Theory and Social Structure,* pp. 221–22.

11. For some earlier remarks on aspects of the hierarchy of knowledge phenomenon, see Parsons, *The Social System,* pp. 335, 337. Also Bernard Barber, "The Hierarchy of Ideas and the Functions of the Middle Brow," unpublished, 1958.

12. Lewis A. Coser, *Men of Ideas* (New York: Free Press, 1965).

13. Diana Crane, *Invisible Colleges: Diffusion of Knowledge in Scientific Communities* (Chicago: University of Chicago Press, 1972), chap. 8, "Toward a Sociology of Culture."

SELECTED BIBLIOGRAPHY

These works, not usually defined as sociology of knowledge, and coming from many different social science specialties, have been selected from among a much larger number of possibilities to illustrate the variety of findings, methods, and types of data available to and usable by the new sociology of knowledge. I have also included a few works sometimes recognized as bearing on the older sociology of knowledge which are important for the newer view as well and which have not been cited in the body of my essay.

Almond, Gabriel A. *The American People and Foreign Policy*. New York: Harcourt, Brace, 1950.

Apter, David E., ed. *Ideology and Discontent*. New York: The Free Press, 1964.

Bailyn, Bernard. *The Ideological Origins of the American Revolution*. Cambridge, Mass.: Harvard University Press, 1967.

Bauer, Raymond A. *The New Man in Soviet Psychology.* Cambridge, Mass.: Harvard University Press, 1952.

Ben-David, Joseph. *The Scientist's Role in Society.* Englewood Cliffs, N.J.: Prentice-Hall, 1971.

Benson, Lee. *Turner & Beard: American Historical Writing Reconsidered.* Glencoe, Ill.: The Free Press, 1960.

Brim, Orville G., Jr., David C. Glass, John Nuelinger, and Ira J. Finestone. *American Beliefs and Attitudes About Intelligence.* New York: Russell Sage Foundation, 1969.

Campbell, Angus, *et al. The American Voter.* New York: Wiley, 1964.

Caplow, Theodore, and Reece J. McGee. *The Academic Marketplace.* New York: Basic Books, 1968.

Cole, Jonathan R. and Stephen. *Social Stratification in Science.* Chicago: University of Chicago Press, 1974.

Duncan, H. D. *Language and Literature in Society.* Chicago: University of Chicago Press, 1953.

Gilpin, Robert, and Christopher Wright. *Scientists and National Policy Making.* New York: Columbia University Press, 1964.

Gusfield, Joseph R. *Symbolic Crusade: Status Politics and the American Temperance Movement.* Urbana, Ill.: University of Illinois Press, 1963.

Haberer, Joseph. *Politics and the Community of Science.* New York: Van Nostrand Reinhold, 1969.

Hagstrom, Warren O. *The Scientific Community.* New York: Basic Books, 1965.

Hofstadter, Richard. *Anti-Intellectualism in American Life.* New York: Alfred Knopf, 1963.

————. *Social Darwinism in American Thought, 1860–1915.* Philadelphia: University of Pennsylvania Press, 1945.

Hyman, Herbert H. *Political Socialization.* New York: The Free Press, 1959.

Inkeles, Alex. *Public Opinion in Soviet Russia.* Cambridge, Mass.: Harvard University Press, 1950.

Joravsky, David. *The Lysenko Affair.* Cambridge, Mass.: Harvard University Press, 1970.

Key, V. O., Jr. *Public Opinion and American Democracy.* New York: Alfred Knopf, 1961.

Kuhn, Thomas S. *The Structure of Scientific Revolutions,* 2nd ed., enl. Chicago: University of Chicago Press, 1970.

Lakatos, Imre, and Alan Musgrave. *Criticism and the Growth of Knowledge.* Cambridge, Eng.: Cambridge University Press, 1970.

Lazarsfeld, Paul F., and Wagner Thielens, Jr. *The Academic Mind.* Glencoe, Ill.: The Free Press, 1958.

Lipset, Seymour Martin, and Earl Raab. *The Politics of Unreason: Right-Wing Extremism in America, 1790–1970.* New York: Harper & Row, 1970.

Lowenthal, Leo. *Literature & the Image of Man: Sociological Studies of the European Drama and Novel, 1600–1900.* Boston: The Beacon Press, 1957.

McCaughey, Robert. "The Professionalization of the American Academic: The Case of Harvard," in Bernard Bailyn and Donald Fleming, eds. *Perspectives in American History, 1974.* Cambridge, Mass.: Harvard University Press, 1974.

Machlup, Fritz. *The Production and Distribution of Knowledge in the United States.* Princeton, N.J.: Princeton University Press, 1962.

Mayhew, Leon H. "Stability and Change in Legal Systems," in Bernard Barber and Alex Inkeles, eds. *Stability and Social Change.* Boston: Little, Brown, 1971.

115

Orlans, Harold, ed. *Science Policy and the University*. Washington, D.C.: The Brookings Institution, 1968.

Pelles, Geraldine. *Art, Artists & Society: Painting in England and France, 1750–1850*. Englewood Cliffs, N.J.: Prentice-Hall, 1963.

Pipes, Richard, ed. *The Russian Intelligentsia*. New York: Columbia University Press, 1961.

Price, Derek J. de Solla. *Little Science, Big Science*. New York: Columbia University Press, 1963.

Price, Don K. *The Scientific Estate*. Cambridge, Mass.: Harvard University Press, 1965.

Rieff, Philip, ed. *On Intellectuals*. Garden City, N.Y.: Doubleday, 1970.

Shils, Edward. *The Intellectuals and the Powers & Other Essays*. Chicago: University of Chicago Press, 1972.

Sutton, Francis X., Seymour E. Harris, Carl Kaysen, and James Tobin. *The American Business Creed*. Cambridge, Mass.: Harvard University Press, 1956.

White, Harrison C. and Cynthia A. *Canvases and Careers: Institutional Change in the French Painting World*. New York: Wiley, 1965.

White, Winston. *Beyond Conformity*. New York: The Free Press, 1961.

Wilensky, Harold L. *Intellectuals in Labor Unions*. New York: The Free Press, 1956.

Williams, Robin M., Jr. "Change and Stability in Values and Value Systems," in Bernard Barber and Alex Inkeles, eds., *Stability and Social Change*. Boston: Little, Brown, 1971.

Wilson, Logan. *The Academic Man*. New York: Oxford University Press, 1941.

Znaniecki, Florian. *The Social Role of the Man of Knowledge*. New York: Columbia University Press, 1940.

Structural Constraints of
Status Complements*

PETER M. BLAU

T HE most frequent label applied to Merton is that of a functional theorist. The reason is, of course, that his well-known functional paradigm greatly refined the theoretical framework for systematic functional analysis. Yet I think it is more appropriate to consider him a structural theorist, not in the special sense in which Lévi-Strauss's followers use the term, but in the distinctly sociological sense of structural analysis, in the tradition of Durkheim and Radcliffe-Brown.[1] Indeed, this has been noted by several commentators on Merton's work. Thus, Wallace classifies Merton as a structuralist, whose theory he contrasts on three basic dimensions of his typology of social theories with functionalism, which is represented by Parsons, although he distinguishes Merton's "functional structuralism" from two other kinds of structuralism.[2] Barbano goes one step further and contends that "the whole of Merton's work is directed toward the emancipation of structural analysis; it is directed, that is, to making structural analysis independent of functional analysis." [3]

The concept of structural constraints has been of central significance in Merton's theoretical analyses throughout, already before he developed the functional paradigm, in this paradigm itself, and in his subsequent work. The fundamental question he regularly poses, in Durkheimian fashion, is how external social constraints influence observable patterns of conduct, and

*I gratefully acknowledge helpful comments from Rebecca Z. Margulies and Judith R. Blau.

Peter M. Blau is Professor of Sociology at Columbia University.

117

he answers this question by analyzing the structures of role relations among persons that exert external and often unanticipated influences on their orientations and behavior. This structural focus is evident in the functional paradigm, and it is what Barbano means by saying that Merton has emancipated structural from functional analysis. To be sure, Merton emphasizes in his paradigm that the analysis of social patterns involves tracing their consequences and ascertaining which ones are functional and contribute to adjustment and which ones are dysfunctional and disturb adjustment. In contrast to classical functionalism, however, he does not *explain* the existence of these social patterns in terms of their consequences.

Having criticized the assumption that a pattern or institution that serves certain functions is therefore indispensable, he introduces the concept of functional substitutes to call attention to the fact that alternative patterns or institutions rather than the existing one could serve its functions. Moreover, he adds the concept of structural constraints to indicate that to explain why a given institution has developed, the social context in which it has emerged must be investigated.[4] Hence, the functional paradigm is in effect a structural paradigm, which accounts for observable social patterns in terms of the structural conditions that give rise to them, except that it supplements this analysis of antecedents by stressing the importance of tracing the functional and dysfunctional consequences of these patterns. The structural nature of Merton's explanatory principles is apparent in his substantive theoretical writings.

STRUCTURES OF ROLE RELATIONS

Merton's paper on locals and cosmopolitans serves as a convenient illustration of his structural focus,[5] since I shall here also examine conditions that promote an orientation to local ingroups rather than one to the wider national scene. Although this paper, "Patterns of Influence: Local and Cosmopolitan Influentials," was published in 1949, the same year the functional paradigm was, it does not present a functional but a structural explanation of why influential citizens in a community exhibit two contrasting orientations to issues. Merton starts by noting that the original formulation of the problem—Who are the influential persons in a community?—seemed to defy systematic explanation until a conceptual refinement was introduced, distinguishing influentials oriented to local community issues and those with a cosmopolitan orientation to national and international issues, which led to the reformulation of the initial problem. The question now became which persons are influential on local issues and which ones on broader issues beyond the community's boundaries, and Merton answers it by analyzing the structures of role relations of influentials with these contrasting orientations.

Thus, he finds that locals have deeper roots in the community than cosmopolitans, having been there longer and being more committed to remaining there. Furthermore, locals have a much wider network of interpersonal relations, associating with more people in the community in disregard of their specific status and role, whereas cosmopolitans tend to restrict their associations to others with whom they have things in common. Other differences reflect the same underlying contrast in social relations; for instance, cosmopolitans join voluntary associations because they are interested in their activities, while locals join in order to meet more people. As a result, the influence of locals, in contradistinction to that of cosmopolitans, *"rests not so much on what they know but on whom they know."*[6] Merton goes on to surmise what differences in the structural context among communities would lead to the preponderance of one or the other of these two types of influentials. In short, differences in orientations and in the kind of influence exerted are explained in terms of the structures of role relations in which individuals are involved and which exist in communities.

A simple but important paradigm for the analysis of structures of role relations has been developed by Merton in his paper "The Role-Set," originally published in 1957.[7] His starting point in this instance is Linton's distinction between the status persons occupy in a social system and the role they perform as incumbents of this status and Linton's observation that each person occupies multiple statuses and hence has multiple roles, one for each status.[8] He departs from Linton's conceptualization by emphasizing that a certain social status does not entail a single role

> but an array of associated roles. This is a basic characteristic of social structure. This fact of structure can be registered by a distinctive term, *role-set,* by which I mean that *complement of role relationships which persons have by virtue of occupying a particular social status.* As one example: the single status of medical student entails not only the role of a student in relation to his teachers, but also an array of other roles relating the occupant of that status to other students, nurses, physicians, social workers, medical technicians, etc.[9]

Role-set, so defined, clearly differs from the familiar concept of multiple roles, which refers to the various roles of an individual associated with *different* statuses he or she occupies, such as medical student, daughter, Catholic, and Bostonian, and for which Merton adopts the term *status-set.*

The concept of status-set appears merely to substitute a neologism for the conventional term of multiple roles, yet it thereby alters the conceptual focus of the inquiry from a concern with sociopsychological to one with structural problems. The concept of multiple roles directs attention to the ways individuals cope with the diverse and often conflicting demands made on them by the various statuses they occupy. The concept of status-set, in contrast, directs attention to the various parameters or dimensions in terms of which social positions are distinguished and the consequent multiplicity of partly overlapping and partly crosscutting statuses that characterize the social structure. For example, in a recent essay in the sociology of knowledge Merton employs the concept of status-set to go beyond the simplified issue of whether insiders or outsiders can understand social life better by emphasizing that in complex societies insiders in one respect are necessarily outsiders in others and by analyzing the implications of this point.[10]

The concept of role-set introduces a new, important analytical distinction that provides a similar structural focus. The significance of even a single social status cannot be clarified by analyzing a single role, because any one status comprises an entire set of different role relations. Teachers do not only associate with students, after all, but also, in their capacity as teachers, with colleagues, the principal, parents, the superintendent, and other groups, and a corresponding variety of role relations characterizes other social positions. Since the categories of persons in a teacher's (or other social position's) role-set occupy different statuses in the social structure, their role expectations of teachers often differ, creating conflicting social pressures, just as multiple roles often subject individuals to conflicting pressures. Merton's interest centers on the structural, not on the sociopsychological, problems this raises—that is, on how the varying statuses of the members of the teacher's role-set and the possible social relations between their incumbents affect the teacher. In short, he analyzes the structural constraints on status occupants mediated by their role-set. Thus, he examines the implications of differences among the members of the role-set in their power over status occupants and in their opportunity to observe the role behavior of status occupants. He goes on to disect how different role relations combine and are modified in the social structure, as illustrated by the formation of power coalitions among members of the role-set, or alternatively by the conflicts between them that may neutralize their power over status incumbents, or by the coalitions the various incumbents of the same status form to defend themselves against the diverse demands of those in their role-set.

Of special significance is the fact that the degree of role involvement of various members of the role-set with status occupants is not the same. The principal of a school is more involved with teachers than members of the school board are—for example, he or she interacts more frequently with them, has more occasions to observe them, and can influence them more directly. These differences in the intensity of the social relations between status occupants and their various role partners underlie some of the other differences in the role-set Merton discusses, and they imply that status occupants are more strongly enmeshed in certain parts of the social structure to which their role-set relates them than in others, and this would be expected to affect their orientations and conduct. As a matter of fact, Merton attributed the contrasting orientations of locals and cosmopolitans to the greater role involvement of locals with certain members of their role-set—other residents of their town— although he had not yet made explicit the concepts of role-set and role involvement when he carried out this analysis in 1949.

I want to introduce a further analytical distinction in Merton's conceptual scheme. In addition to distinguishing various statuses a person occupies, as Linton does, and various role relations associated with a given status, as Merton does, I want to distinguish various status complements that are associated with a given role relation. Take the status of faculty members in an academic institution as an illustration, and specifically their role relations with colleagues. But colleagues are not a uniform contingent of people all having the same status and the same role relation with one another. Faculty members have colleagues at their own college or university, and they also have colleagues in their discipline outside. This distinction should probably be considered merely a finer classification of the role-set: colleagues inside the academic institutions and -outside colleagues in the discipline are different members of a faculty member's role-set. Even among the colleagues in the same institution, however, there are great variations in status and role performance. They belong to different disciplines, vary in training and qualifications, differ in rank, live up to the role expectations of a scholar in varying degree, make more or less contribution to their discipline, are not all equally involved with teaching undergraduates, and devote different amounts of time and energy to research. In brief, the partners in a given role relation—colleagues at the same institution—differ in role attributes and role performances, because they not only have the status and role that defines their relation—faculty colleagues— but also a variety of other statuses and roles.

The concept of status complement is designed to take into account such differences in status, role attributes, and role performance among persons who stand in a specific role relation to ego. But why not treat these differences simply as further refinements of status- or role-set? The reason is that doing so would confound two analytical elements of social structure which have distinct implications for social inquiry. If we are interested in the differential significance for assistant professors of their relations with other assistant professors and of those with full professors, we must treat these two ranks as different partners in the role-set of assistant professors. Regardless of how fine we make the distinctions in the role-set (unless we refer to a particular relation between two individuals), however, we would still find that persons classified as standing in a specific role relation to given status occupants differ with respect to statuses and roles other than those considered in classifying them, and these other differences are likely to impinge on the specific role relation under investigation.[11] The question of how a father's role relation to his daughters differs from his relation to his sons is quite different from the question of how his role as father is influenced by his children's sex and age compositions.[12] Similarly, what variations there are in the colleague relations at an academic institution is an entirely different question from the one that asks how the composition and structure of the colleague group influences the way faculty members perform their role. Answering the first question in either sentence requires making finer distinctions in the role-set, but answering the second requires analyzing the status complement, that is, the composition of the colleague group and the structure of the role relations in it.

The structural constraints exerted by variations in role-sets and role involvements are not the same as those exerted by variations in status complements. The significance of this distinction will be illustrated by using it to explain a paradox posed by empirical data about the allegiance of academic faculties to their local college or university. First, differences in the intensity of role involvement with various role partners in the role-set of faculty members will be investigated by tracing the structural sources of these differences in the academic stratification system and noting their consequences for orientations to the local institution. Then, the analysis will turn to the characteristics of the status complement of colleagues at an academic institution. These characteristics describe the social context and academic climate within which particular colleague relations are established and maintained, and they have distinctive implications for the role performance, academic standing, and orientations of faculty members. Finally, the question is raised whether faculty members are affected not only by the role attributes that are most prevalent among their colleagues but also by the degree of variation in these attributes, for example, by the extent of the division of labor or by pronounced differences in academic reputations. Attention will center throughout the discussion on the connections between the statuses and roles of faculty members in the larger academic system and in the subsystem constituted by their own university or college.

ROLE INVOLVEMENT AND LOCAL ALLEGIANCE

Merton's distinction between cosmopolitans and locals has been applied by Gouldner to college faculty members.[13] Cosmopolitans are academics who are oriented to outside reference groups in their wider discipline and who have little allegiance to the ingroup at their institution. Locals tend to confine their interest to their own college, are often much involved in teaching and sometimes in administration, and exhibit strong allegiance to their institution. A recent study of a sample of faculty members from 114 four-year institutions of higher education supports Gouldner's conclusions about these contrasting orientations of academics.[14] Superior academic qualifications and involvement in research promote a cosmopolitan orientation and reduce a faculty member's allegiance to his or her own university or college, whereas involvement in teaching and frequent contacts with undergraduates strengthen local allegiance. One would expect that in an academic community that has many members who express firm local allegiance, social pressures arise that further enhance allegiance to the local institution. For example, a prevailing involvement in teaching among colleagues, since such involvement is typically accompanied by local allegiance, would be expected to strengthen a person's local allegiance. Actually, however, the very opposite is the case. Although a faculty member's own involvement in teaching *increases* his or her local allegiance, the prevalence of teaching involvement among colleagues *decreases* it. The individual's own and his or her colleagues' academic qualifications also have opposite consequences for the orientation to the local institution.

Paradoxically, therefore, the larger the number of faculty members in an academic institution whose role attributes predispose them to have strong commitments to the local institution, the weaker are the commitments of the faculty to the local institution. In this blunt form, the statement seems to be a contradiction in terms. How can the same attributes of persons have opposite effects on them? They cannot, of course, as long as we are merely thinking of individuals, but once we think in terms of collectivities rather than isolated individuals, this is possible, because a given role attribute of some members of a collectivity tends to affect not only those who possess it but also others who associate with them or whose reference group they are. While these two effects are sometimes parallel, at other times they are opposite. Such opposite effects have their roots in the stratification system, and so does the paradox of faculty allegiance that is a manifestation of them. To explain these contrasting social influences of the academic stratification system for faculty orientations, those mediated by role-sets and role involvements will be disected first and those mediated by status complements in the next section.

The academic reputation of faculty members depends on their scholarly qualifications and performances. However, a person's potential or actual accomplishments must be socially recognized for them to govern his or her reputation. Unknown achievements do not affect the respect a person commands, of course, nor do role performances that are not acknowledged as significant achievements by relevant others, who are, in academia, primarily the fellow specialists in a person's discipline. There are a number of reasons why the quality of a scholar's work may not be adequately recognized, and why, therefore, scholarly accomplishments and academic reputations are not perfectly correlated. First, it is difficult to judge truly original contributions in science, and it is still more difficult in other fields. Individuals may only receive post-mortem recognition for their contributions, which means that their academic standing during their lifetime fails to reflect their accomplishments. Second, disagreements about scholarly standards in nonparadigmatic fields and preparadigmatic stages of sciences limit the recognition an academic can attain, since only colleagues of the same school of thought who apply the same standards will recognize his or her accomplishments. Ethnomethodologists and mathematical sociologists, for example, apply such different standards that they do not appreciate each other's work, which restricts the respect accomplishments in these specialties commands among sociologists generally. Third, the work of scientists or scholars who have an established reputation is more likely to be recognized as making important contributions and to further raise their reputation than that of others of lesser academic standing. This "Matthew effect," as Merton calls it, "consists in the accruing of greater increments of recognition for particular scientific contributions to scientists of considerable repute and the withholding of such recognition from scientists who have not yet made their mark."[15]

Finally, the visibility of the role performance of a faculty member has a distorting effect on the recognition he or she receives for it, as has been implicit in some of the foregoing.[16] The Matthew effect indicates that persons whose earlier work has made them visible receive greater recognition for later work than others. Similarly, a position in a major university makes individuals more visible and increases the chances that their work comes to the attention of others and enhances their academic standing. Most important is the fact that different kinds of academic work differ in visibility. Specifically, the role performance of the teacher in the classroom has very little visibility among colleagues in the discipline, whereas the role performance of the researcher who succeeds in publishing his or her results has much greater colleague visibility. Excellent teaching is therefore less likely to result in a wide reputation than research that is merely competent without being outstanding. Since research has greater visibility among significant others and earns higher social rewards than teaching, faculty members with sufficient qualifications have incentives to channel a good part of their energies into research and not to devote all or most of their time to teaching.

The best qualified faculty members tend to engage in research, which is the main avenue for acquiring academic recognition, and their recognized research accomplishments govern their academic standing. A superior academic reputation means, by definition, that a person is widely acknowledged to be capable of making significant contributions and that his or her participation in scholarly and scientific endeavors is consequently in wide demand. Owing to the greater demand for academics with research reputations, they are frequently drawn into scientific meetings and scholarly conferences and sometimes consulted by government and industry, which is rarely the case for teachers, whose lower visibility restricts the recognition they receive even if they have great talents. Hence, the involvement in their role-set as faculty members is not the same for those concentrating on teaching and those much involved in research. Researchers associate extensively with colleagues in their discipline outside their own institution, and, if they have high academic standing, also with renowned scholars in other disciplines and with political and business leaders, and they derive major gratifications from the respect they command in these outside associations. Teachers associate mostly with students and other teachers at their own institution, and these inside associations are their main source of professional recognition and satisfaction. The local orientation of teachers, just as that of the locals in the community Merton studied, is grounded in their greater role involvement with associates in a particular place.

The wide demand for academics with superior research reputations increases their opportunities for mobility to better positions. Major universities compete for faculty members with superior reputations, because their reputations depend on those of their faculties. To be sure, a university's high academic standing rests primarily on the recognized scholarly contributions of its past faculty, not of its present one, but to maintain or improve their academic standing universities must recruit faculty members with reputations for making substantial contributions to science and scholarship. The alternative job opportunities of faculty members with research reputations resulting from the demand for them in many places orient them to additional outside reference groups—other academic institutions—and further diminish their exclusive commitment to the place where they currently are. By the same token, the fewer alternative opportunities of teachers, who usually lack the reputations that would make them in demand in other places, fortify their local commitments.

Opportunity for mobility strengthens a person's bargaining power, and the greater bargaining power of researchers enables them to attain higher positions in their academic institution than teachers can. Universities and departments seek to protect their academic standing and to forestall the exodus of faculty members whose research reputation makes them in demand elsewhere by providing them with incentives to stay, in the form of higher

124

ranks, better salaries, and greater authority. These responses to the bargaining power of researchers are an institutional source of status crystallization. Researchers who are rewarded for their accomplishments by commanding superior academic prestige achieve bargaining power that enables them to command also higher incomes and greater authority. Rewards of one kind become resources for obtaining more rewards of other kinds, which may be considered another manifestation of the Matthew effect. As a result, individuals experience greater status consistency, with their hierarchical standing on one dimension being similar to their standing on others, but this also means, looking at it from another perspective, that inequalities are more pronounced and that status disadvantages in some respects are not mitigated by status advantages in others. In particular, it means that the low visibility of undergraduate teachers creates multiple disadvantages for them. Granting senior positions, which entail job security, higher salaries, and greater authority, is intended to strengthen the institutional allegiance of faculty members who might otherwise be tempted to leave, and it actually serves this manifest function, as indicated by the greater local commitments of faculty members in senior positions.[17]

Renowned researchers help raise the reputation of the academic community, which benefits its other members, and they receive superior status within it in exchange. The exchange does not seem equitable, however, owing to the Matthew effect, which enables famous scientists and scholars, and to a lesser extent researchers generally, to reap excess profits for their contributions. Research reputations may be considered social resources that can be used for obtaining positions in better universities and for obtaining better positions in a given university, but these resources are not inexhaustible, and their utilization for one purpose depletes those remaining for another. If persons with a certain academic reputation attain on its basis a position in a major university with a faculty whose academic standing is high, their academic standing relative to that of the rest of the faculty is not so high as it would be had they accepted a position in a less highly recognized academic community. Hence, reputable researchers are confronted in their career decisions by the choice of whether to be a big fish in a little pond or a little fish in a big pond. Given their reputation, the better the university and its faculty to which they move, the lower will be their bargaining power and status within the university. This dilemma is not confined to academic faculties but inherent in hierarchical status structures, and we shall encounter other indications of it.

Better academic positions bring extra rewards that can be assumed to increase the commitments of faculty members to the institution. Since qualified researchers are more likely than others to achieve positions in superior universities and to achieve superior positions in their university, though only the most highly recognized among them achieve both, research qualifications should indirectly—by improving academic positions—strengthen allegiance to the local institution. However, the role involvement of qualified researchers with outside reference groups outweighs these advantages of their academic positions, with the result that superior qualifications and active participation in research lessen a faculty member's allegiance to the local institution.[18] This

125

empirical result reveals two factors Merton has emphasized in his writings: the great significance role involvement with some rather than other partners in the role-set has for a person's orientations, and the dominant significance recognition from peers has in academic life, which can overcome the influence of the greater material rewards superior positions offer.

STATUS COMPLEMENT AND LOCAL ALLEGIANCE

The concept of status complement, to reiterate, refers to the composition of alters who stand in a specific role relation to egos. Egos are all incumbents of a given status. Although their role-set comprises persons who occupy different statuses, a given role relation refers to alters who occupy the same status. But these alters are identical in status only on the dimension employed to classify their role relation with ego. They naturally differ with respect to other status dimensions—or "structural parameters," as I have called such dimensions. In the case used for illustration, the egos are faculty members, and the alters who have a certain role relation with them are colleagues at their own institutions. These colleagues differ, of course, in their statuses and roles other than being faculty members at ego's college or university as well as in their role performance as faculty member. They differ, for example, in training, qualification, research performance, reputation, orientation to teaching, and involvement with students. Concern is now with the influences the attributes of the complement of the colleague ingroup have on a faculty member's role. The term "status complement" refers to the contingent of different statuses and roles of all the alters who share one status that defines their role relation with ego and that may be the same as ego's (for instance, colleague) or a different one (such as student).

The research qualifications and accomplishments of the status complement of colleagues at a faculty member's university or college enhance his or her academic reputation, and they do so partly independently of his or her academic performance and partly by affecting this performance. Recognized research accomplishments of colleagues in a university have a Matthew effect that combines with an institutional halo effect to raise the reputation of individual faculty members beyond the respect that their own research performance would command. Scientists and scholars of renown receive excess recognition for their work, and a few of them, or even one of them, can give a department a substantial academic reputation.[19] A position in a well-known department contributes to a faculty member's reputation, and so does a position in a university with high academic standing and numerous renowned scientists and scholars. Such a position creates the presumption that the work of an academic is worthy of recognition, making it more likely for it to be read, cited, and acknowledged as a significant contribution than its quality would warrant.[20] Thus, the halo of the prestige of some scientists and scholars resulting from their achievements reinforced by the Matthew effect, casts a reflection on the reputation of their colleagues at the institution and increases these reputations. Similarly, a position in a college or university with inferior academic standing and few if any faculty members whose work is widely recognized reflects adversely on the reputation of an individual and depresses it below the level his or her accomplishments might deserve.

The status complement of colleagues affects the reputation of faculty members not only spuriously, in disregard of their academic role performance, as just noted, but also genuinely, by influencing their performance. Superior academic training and qualifications promote active involvement in research. The larger the proportion of colleagues at a university with superior qualifications, most of whom are engaged in research, the greater is the likelihood that a faculty member will also engage in research, independent of his or her own qualifications, of the weight of research in the institution's appointments, and of other conditions influencing research involvement.[21] Whether a faculty member's research potential is activated or suppressed depends to a considerable extent on the research climate in his or her colleague group. To be sure, some academic institutions encourage research more than others through personnel selection, financial and other rewards, good facilities, and light teaching loads. Yet even when most of these differences are controlled, the research climate produced by the colleague group exerts a substantial influence on a faculty member's involvement in research.

The research interests of colleagues stimulate one's own, to be able to participate in their discussions about research problems and thus become a full-fledged member of the departmental colleague group. Besides, their research skills make them readily accessible consultants, facilitating one's research. Colleagues committed to research also create social pressures to engage in research, lest one lose their respect, since commitment to research as an important element in the faculty role makes respect contingent on research performance. Conversely, if most colleagues are not oriented to and experienced in research, their discussions do not arouse latent research interests, they are not an available source of helpful advice with research problems, and their normative expectations tend to discourage research by ridiculing scholarly endeavors with such slogans as "publish or perish." This difference in academic orientation in the colleague complement is much influenced by variations in administrative practices among institutions, notably in personnel selection procedures and teaching obligations. But the prevailing orientations among colleagues at an institution become independent forces that exert social influences in their own right, fostering the research involvement of faculty members and increasing their chances of making contributions to science and scholarship. In sum, the research performance of the status complement of institutional colleagues produces increments in the reputation of individual faculty members by increasing their research performance as well as additional increments independent of their performance.

Recognized research accomplishments of the faculty complement at an academic institution make positions there in great demand, owing to the benefits derived from these positions, just as recognized research accomplishments of individuals make them in great demand to occupy faculty positions, owing to the benefits derived from their occupancy. The wide demand for positions in a given institution improves its personnel recruitment and selection by making a large pool of applicants available, just as the wide demand for persons with certain role attributes improves their job opportunities by making many jobs available. These parallels must not be permitted to obscure the asymmetric role relations implicit in them, however. If the attributes of the faculty complement make positions in a particular place especially attractive, it implies that faculty members will exhibit strong *role involvement with the colleague ingroup* at the institution and have firm local commitments. But if the academic role attributes of individuals make them especially attractive to others in many different places, it implies that these individuals will exhibit extensive *role involvements with outsiders,* which limit their role involvement with colleagues at their own institution and reduce their local commitments. The paradox of faculty allegiance can be explained in terms of these contrasting implications for role involvement of the recognized academic performance of faculty members and that of their status complements.

What produces the paradox of faculty allegiance is that superior reputations of faculty members strengthen their local colleagues' but weaken their own commitment to their institution. The reason is that high academic standing of persons makes role relations with them attractive to both inside colleagues, whose local role involvement and allegiance is consequently enhanced by their presence, and to others outside, who draw them into role relations with wider circles that diminish their local role involvement and allegiance. Local commitments depend on a person's relative academic standing—his or her reputation relative to that of his or her status complement of colleagues. In these terms, high status of alters and low status of ego are equivalent, both depressing ego's standing relative to that of alters, and this equivalence finds expression in the parallel effects of the two (high status of alters and low status of ego) on strong local allegiance. The observed influences of academic role qualifications and performances on loyalty to the institution are assumed to be mediated by and hence reflect this significance of academic standing for institutional loyalty. Superior research qualifications tend to raise academic standing, and the prevalence of superior qualifications among colleagues strengthens the institutional allegiance of faculty members, although their own superior qualifications weaken their institutional allegiance. Similarly, predominant involvement in teaching rather than research reduces the chances of academic recognition, and a prevailing involvement with teaching among their colleagues weakens the local commitment of faculty members, although their own involvement with teaching strengthens their local commitment.[22] These findings provide an indirect indication of the pervasive significance of research in academia, inasmuch as even academics whose role is largely that of teacher seem to be more attracted to colleague groups that include many researchers than to those consisting mostly of teachers like themselves.

Firm commitments of faculty members to their institution fortify the social integration of the academic community. Local allegiance entails much role involvement with inside colleagues and with students and extensive social interaction with both, which create the social bonds among the faculty and between students and faculty that integrate them into a cohesive academic community. Concern with college teaching fosters such integrative communication with students and with colleagues in other disciplines to discuss common problems about the curriculum. Academic communities would be even more fragmented than they often are were it not for these contributions to social integration made by teachers, since the orientations to and role involvements with outside reference groups of researchers undermine social integration in the university or college. (To be sure, most faculty members represent various mixtures of these polar types of teacher and researcher.)

Social exchange among the faculty in an academic institution assumes at least two forms. Faculty members whose research accomplishments are widely recognized raise the reputation of their colleagues not only by increasing the prestige that inheres in a position at the institution, whatever an individual's role performance, but also by providing an academic climate that improves research performance. In exchange, they are accorded higher status within the institution—more respect, superior rank, better salaries, greater authority. Crosscutting this exchange between more and less highly recognized scholars, which was mentioned before, there is another exchange between teachers and researchers. The local role involvements of teachers sustain the integrated university community without which researchers would have no base for carrying out their scientific and scholarly pursuits. Teachers, in return, partake of the academic standing of the university that is largely maintained by these pursuits of researchers and, specifically, by their role involvements with outside reference groups in their disciplines, which enable them to contribute to the academic development of the institution by importing new ideas and initiating institutional innovations.[23] These exchange transactions make faculty members whose different roles benefit one another interdependent and thereby further social integration, but they simultaneously intensify differences in hierarchical status, which may become so large that they impede social exchange and undermine the integration of the academic community, as will be noted presently.

The preceding discussion has indicated that a role attribute of a faculty member and the same role attribute of his status complement of colleagues exert some parallel and some opposite influences on him or her. Superior qualifications of faculty members themselves encourage their active involvement in research, and so do superior qualifications of their colleagues. Here the influence of ego's role attribute on ego's performance is reinforced by the same role attributes of alters. By contrast, superior qualifications and research performance of faculty members themselves *decrease* their local role involvement and allegiance, whereas the same characteristics of colleagues *increase* them. In this case, ego's characteristics and the same characteristics of alters have opposite influences on ego. Why do the effects on a faculty member of his own and of his colleagues' role attributes sometimes reinforce and sometimes counteract each other? The answer is that which one of the two patterns occurs depends on whether the effects are mediated by normative role expectations or by relative standing.

Internalized norms and obligations find expression in one's own conduct and in one's expectations of the conduct of others. Thus, faculty members who consider working on research to be a basic role obligation of academics are likely to engage in research themselves and to expect their colleagues to do so, thereby creating normative pressures on colleagues to become involved in research. In this manner, normative role expectations exert parallel influences on those who have internalized them and on their associates who are subject to their social pressures. Hierarchical status in a collectivity, however, is relative to the status of its other members, so that the superior role attributes of persons and those of their associates have opposite significance for them. As already pointed out, the allegiance of faculty members to their institution is affected by their relative standing, which is raised by their own research accomplishments but which is lowered by those of their colleagues, with the result that own and colleagues' research performance exert opposite influences on local allegiance. Generally, orientations that depend on relative standing in a collectivity are affected in opposite ways by relevant role attributes of the persons exhibiting the orientations and by the same attributes of the rest of the collectivity. Two illustrations of this principle from different contexts may be mentioned.

The first is Stouffer's well-known analysis of the attitudes of soldiers to the army's promotion system. While noncommissioned officers are more satisfied with promotion opportunities than privates, a large proportion of noncommissioned officers in an outfit reduces its members' satisfaction with promotion opportunities.[24] The superior rank of a soldier raises but the superior rank of many members of his status complement lowers his relative standing and the attitudes affected by it. The second illustration is what Davis calls the "frog-pond effect" on college students. Whereas college students with superior abilities are more likely than others to plan to go to graduate school, the larger the proportion of superior students in a college, the less likely are those with given abilities to make plans to attend graduate school.[25] The estimation of undergraduates of their chances in pursuing advanced degrees depends on their relative standing among fellow students with whom they compare themselves—not only on how big frogs they are but also on how big the other frogs in their pond are. Since their own abilities raise but those of their status complement of fellow students lower their relative standing, the two have opposite effects on the rank of undergraduates among classmates, their grades, their academic self-confidence, and consequently their educational aspirations. The status structure among students poses the same dilemma as that among the faculty—whether to be a big fish (or frog) in a small pond or a small one in a big pond.

Although effects of the status complement's attributes that reinforce and those that counteract effects of the same role attributes of individuals have been discussed separately, they often actually occur together, because a given role attribute governs both normative expectations and relative standing. The research qualifications and interests of faculty members influence their normative definition of the proper role of faculty members and thus their own research performance and their colleagues', through social stimulation and pressures, in parallel, reinforcing ways. But by influencing research performance, qualifications indirectly influence relative standing and consequently have opposite, counteracting effects on ego's and on alters' role involvements and orientations that are affected by relative standing, as exemplified by the effects of qualifications on local involvement and allegiance. Similarly, superior abilities of the students in a school raise their own scholastic performance and, through social stimulation and pressures, that of their fellow students, with the two effects reinforcing each other. Scholastic performance, in turn, affects educational aspirations as well as relative standing or rank among classmates, which also influences aspirations. The abilities and performance of fellow students, therefore, in addition to reinforcing the positive effect of own abilities and performance on aspirations, counteract the effect of own abilities on aspirations, for they lower, while own abilities raise, the relative academic standing on which educational aspirations depend.[26]

DEGREE OF VARIATION IN STATUS COMPLEMENTS

A social structure, in the narrow sense of the term, may be defined as the differentiated social positions or statuses in a collectivity and the role relations of people as influenced by their statuses. It must be immediately added, however, that a social structure is delineated by numerous parameters that differentiate social status along various lines, lest the analysis of status differences and role relations confounds distinct concepts. To speak of the status of male, black, faculty member, and female as if these were comparable categories can only lead to confusion, since male and female are mutually exclusive positions defined by a single parameter, whereas black, faculty member, and female are statuses defined by different parameters and the same individual may occupy all three. The concept of status complement has been introduced to refer to all alters who, by virtue of occupying the same status on a given parameter, have a specific role relation with ego occupying a certain status on the same parameter, such as being ego's faculty colleagues at the same institution. But the statuses and roles other than being a faculty colleague of these alters naturally differ, and these differences in the status complement with respect to other parameters affect their role relation in terms of the parameter under consideration—in the case under discussion, their role relation with colleagues.

Concern so far has been with the influences the *prevalent* characteristics of the status complement exert on the role relations of colleagues and on the role performance and orientation of faculty members. Specifically, the significance of the training and qualifications of the colleague complement has been discussed, of the emphasis on research and teaching in it, and of the academic reputation of its members. Now we shall look at the significance of the degree of *variation* in such role attributes among colleagues. The implications for a person of many colleagues with high academic reputations are not the same as those of the extent of variation or differentiation in reputation among colleagues. Variation may entail horizontal differentiation or vertical differentiation—social heterogeneity or status inequality—depending on the parameter in terms of which the variation in the colleague complement is defined. Both are examined, heterogeneity being illustrated with the academic division of labor and status inequality with the degree of variation in academic reputation.[27]

The academic division of labor in a university or college is the source of the influence of faculty role orientation and performance on role involvement and allegiance. Given the division of labor, concern with scholarly work constrains faculty members to limit their local role involvement in favor of greater role involvement with colleagues in their discipline elsewhere, since there are so few colleagues in one's own specialty, if any, at one's own institutions. Most insiders according to one parameter—institutional affiliation—are outsiders according to another parameter—disciplinary affiliation. People generally prefer to associate with members of their ingroup, yet this observation leaves open the question which one or ones of their various ingroups primarily govern their choice of associates. While for teachers the institutional ingroup has most salience, for researchers the disciplinary ingroup does, which finds expression in the difference in the role involvements and local commitments between teachers and researchers.

The more pronounced the academic division of labor and specialization at an academic institution, the greater are the obstacles to communication about scholarly matters among its members, which encourages role involvement with outside colleagues who share one's specialized academic interests. Processes of social selection play an important part here. An extensive division of labor with specialized departments in an academic institution attracts faculty members with superior training and qualifications, who tend to prefer specialized academic work and to be oriented to reference groups in their specialty outside their own institution. By attracting better qualified researchers, institutionalized specialization improves the academic reputation of a university or college and attracts better students, even though specialization reduces the attention undergraduates receive from the faculty. Thus, institutional specialization facilitates recruitment of qualified researchers, who usually have a cosmopolitan orientation, and such faculty role involvement with a variety of disciplines outside further enhances institutional specialization, because it induces faculty members, aware of developments in their fields, to take the initiative in establishing new specialties at the institution.[28]

Whereas role involvement with local colleagues fortifies the internal social integration of the academic community, role involvements with outside colleagues at many different institutions fortify the integration of the institution in the larger academic system. Faculty members primarily oriented to teaching contribute to the internal and those primarily oriented to research contribute to the external integration of their university or college, inasmuch as the former are more involved with their colleagues at the institution and the latter with colleagues in their discipline outside. At major universities, which are large and have an extensive division of labor, faculties are more oriented to research and less to local colleagues than those at small colleges, where academic work is not highly specialized. This difference finds expression in the better internal integration of small colleges and better integration in the larger academic system of major universities. There is a tendency for such differences among academic institutions to give rise to a division of labor among them, with some concentrating on research and graduate training and others on undergraduate education. The continuation of this trend would be detrimental for academic work, since there are good reasons to assume that both research and undergraduate education benefit from being in the same institution.[29]

Having examined horizontal differentiation in universities or colleges— the extent of the division of academic labor—let us now look at vertical differentiation—the degree of inequality in hierarchical status. What significance does the status inequality in an academic community have for the role relations of its members? To answer this question, two forms of status inequality must be analytically distinguished. Great diversity in reputations implies that few persons have exactly the same reputation but that all have many colleagues whose reputation is not very different from their own. This situation contrasts with one in which there is a small elite whose academic status is far superior to most of the other members of an institution, with a relatively small "middle class" whose status is intermediate. More individuals are roughly equal in status in the second case than in the first, but inequality in the sense of great social distances and concentration of power and rewards is also more pronounced in the second than in the first case.[30]

Diversity in hierarchical status that accompanies differences in role performance is closely connected with social exchange. Accomplished researchers are motivated to give advice on research problems to less experienced colleagues, since being asked for advice is a welcome sign of respect for superior competence. They can talk about their research, the discoveries that excite them and the questions that puzzle them, to junior colleagues, whose research interests are stimulated by these discussions, and whose attentive listening and admiring comments furnish gratifying social rewards. Junior colleagues constitute a pool of potential collaborators for seniors, and collaboration between the two contributes to the research accomplishments of the seniors, of course, and usually also advances the careers of the juniors, unless seniors use their authority to exploit their collaborators.[31] Finally, differences in reputation have the result that widely recognized researchers raise the institution's academic standing, from which the rest of the faculty benefits, and that less widely known faculty members largely restrict their academic role involvement to local colleagues, and the contribution to an integrated academic community they thereby make benefits the recognized researchers by providing them with a stable base of operations. Without such diversity in reputation, that of locals would suffer, since it would not benefit from the increments resulting from affiliation with more widely recognized scholars, and that of renowned cosmopolitans would suffer too, since they would have to divert more time and energy from their research to teaching and to maintaining an integrated academic enterprise.

Great social distances between an elite and most of the faculty, however, disrupt these processes of social exchange from which all parties profit, albeit not equally. If most faculty members at an institution of higher education have little qualification and time for research and are preoccupied with their teaching responsibilities, they cannot benefit from the research experience and advice of one or a few famous scientists and scholars in their field at their institution. Poor qualifications and heavy teaching obligations stifle interest in research, and group norms are apt to develop under such conditions disparaging research endeavors, further discouraging an orientation to research. Besides, an outstanding researcher who has won wide recognition is no longer concerned with earning the respect of colleagues with low academic standing, which robs him or her of incentives to discuss research with them, particularly since their weak research qualifications and interest make it likely that they would not understand complex research problems. Neither does the academic reputation of a largely undistinguished faculty gain from the appointment of a few famous scholars, because the latter do not suffice to raise the academic standing of the institution, which remains known as one that has a poor faculty except for a few stars. Most of the faculty thus continue to depend for professional gratification on rewards from teaching and interaction with students. If excessive teaching loads and uninterested students make teaching an unrewarding experience too, the only rewards left are higher salaries and administrative authority, which are necessarily restricted to a minority. In such a situation, the majority of faculty members are likely to be alienated from the institution, and all that keeps them there is not their allegiance to it but their lack of alternative opportunities. Hence, the teaching faculty contributes little to the social integration of the academic community, and the few research stars contribute little to its academic standing.

In sum, great status differences in a faculty between a small elite and most of the rest inhibit the exchange transactions that underlie the interdependence among faculty members performing different roles, further the integration of the academic community, and enhance the reputation of most faculty members beyond the recognition their own accomplishments alone would achieve. Status diversity is essential for these processes of social exchange and the profits they yield. To be sure, much diversity of hierarchical status does not preclude the possibility of great social distances between those in the highest and those in the lowest positions, and these social distances will also create obstacles to communication and social exchange. The important fact for the academic community, however, is that diversity means that many faculty members occupy a range of intermediate statuses. This creates the condition for every faculty member to have a sufficient number of colleagues whose status differs some but not very much from his or hers and thus for all to participate extensively in exchange transactions with colleagues.

The significance in the degree of variation in academic standing *among institutions* in a society depends similarly on whether this hierarchical differentiation assumes the form of great diversity of institutional reputations or great differences between a few superior universities that dominate the academic prestige system and all others of much lesser reputations. Many academic institutions with diverse academic standing promote processes of social mobility of faculty members among them, as recognized academic accomplishments create new opportunities for superior positions, and as failure to realize earlier promise creates constraints to move to institutions of lower repute. The competition among diverse academic institutions for scientists strengthens their bargaining power, makes it easier for those in new specialties to obtain academic positions, reduces the conservative influence of academic administrators, fosters the institutionalization of new specialties, and is for these reasons an essential factor in a country's scientific progress, according to Ben-David.[32] The overshadowing reputation of one or a few universities in a society—for example, the Sorbonne's—impedes such competition and the advantages accruing from it by depriving the best scientists and scholars of viable alternative opportunities. It insulates the top university or universities from other academic institutions, which discourages cosmopolitan role involvements of faculty members there with those elsewhere, and which thus encourages local role involvements in the top as well as in other academic institutions. The predominant local orientations and role involvements interfere with the development of an integrated academic system in the society. These conditions resulting from the overpowering standing of a single or very few universities are detrimental for change in academic institutions and for advances in science and scholarship.

CONCLUSIONS

The concept of status complement suggested in this paper combines elements of Merton's concepts of status-set and role-set to extend his scheme. By status-set Merton refers to the fact that every individual occupies several social positions, and by role-set he refers to the fact that in each status he or she has several roles in relation to others who occupy different statuses. Although a given role relation—say, father-child—pertains to a single status of ego and a single status of alters by definition, this is so only with respect to the parameter that defines the role relation. The concept of status-set reminds us that these alters also have different statuses and roles, in terms of various other parameters; thus, a father's children are not only his offspring but also have sex roles, age roles, and perform different other roles, all of which probably influence the father's role. To take into account these influences on a person's role, the concept of status complement has been introduced, which refers to the different status and role attributes of alters who have in common that they occupy one identical status that places them in a specific role relation to ego. In the case discussed for illustrative purposes, the role relation was that between faculty members and their colleagues at their institution, and the status complement described other statuses and role performances of these colleagues. The analysis presented examined the influences of the characteristics of a faculty member's status complement at the academic institution on his or her role involvement, performance, and orientation.

The attributes of the status complement of persons sometimes reinforce and sometimes counteract the effects of their own corresponding role attributes on their performance and orientation. Whether these effects are reinforcing or counteracting depends on whether they are mediated by normative expectations or by relative standing. Thus, faculty members with superior qualifications are more likely than others to consider research a normative requirement of the faculty role, which influences their own role performance and their role expectations of colleagues. Consequently, superior qualifications of the colleague complement create normative pressures that reinforce the influence of faculty members' own superior qualifications, both increasing their participation in research. On the other hand, the research accomplishments of faculty members raise their relative standing, while the research accomplishments of their colleagues lower their own relative standing by comparison. Since relative standing influences the allegiance of faculty members to the local institution, their own research performance and that of their colleague complement, by having opposite implications for their relative standing, have counteracting effects on their local allegiance.

The degree of variation in the status complement as well as its prevailing attributes may affect role relations. Much diversity in status promotes processes of social exchange that contribute to scholarly performance, create interdependence among faculty members performing different roles, and strengthen the social integration in the academic community. Great social distances between a small elite and the majority of the faculty, by contrast, inhibit these exchange relations that further scholarship, and they endanger the integration of the academic enterprise. Great social distances between elite universities in a society and its other academic institutions of far lower standing also have deleterious consequences for the integration of the academic system and for the development of science and scholarship.

In conclusion, I want to mention two metatheoretical points underlying the foregoing analysis. One of these accords with current tendencies in social theorizing, while the other dissents from them. First, I consider an understanding of quantitative methods essential for systematic theorizing. I have not presented any mathematical formulations in this paper, of which I am in fact incapable, nor have I presented statistical analysis of quantitative data. However, my limited knowledge of path analysis and quantitative procedures generally has informed my thinking and helped me in tracing complex relationships. (I am, of course, not referring to the empirical findings I cited, which are based on quantitative procedures, but to the theoretical conjectures that went beyond these findings.) Second, we are underestimating the theoretical importance of conceptual analysis and refinement in our present emphasis on propositional and deductive theories. Merton in an early paper called attention to the distinctive significance of theories consisting of a system of logically interrelated propositions,[33] and I myself have been much concerned with deductive theorizing. However, Merton's own work illustrates the great contributions to theoretical understanding that can be made by introducing new concepts, refining old ones, devising simple conceptual schemes, and constructing complex paradigms. Although I am firmly convinced that developing deductive theories that explain society and thus help improve it is the ultimate goal of sociology, I do want to stress that the contributions to this goal that conceptual refinements and schemes can make should not be gainsaid.

NOTES

1. The sociological conception of social structure is compared with Lévi-Strauss's structuralism by Raymond Boudon, who is critical of the former and favors the latter; *The Uses of Structuralism* (London: Heinemann, 1971).

2. Walter Wallace, *Sociological Theory* (Chicago: Aldine, 1969), pp. 13–17, 24–34.

3. Filippo Barbano, "Social Structures and Social Functions," *Inquiry* 11 (1968): 58.

4. Robert K. Merton, *Social Theory and Social Structure*, enl. ed. (New York: Free Press, 1968), pp. 73–138, esp. pp. 86–91, 106–08. (Hereinafter referred to as *STSS*.)

5. *Ibid.*, pp. 441–74.

6. *Ibid.*, p. 454.

7. *Ibid.*, pp. 422–38; this revised version differs somewhat from the original paper.

8. Ralph Linton, *The Study of Man* (New York: Appleton-Century, 1936), pp. 113–15, 126–28.

9. Merton, *STSS*, p. 423.

10. Robert K. Merton, "Insiders and Outsiders," *American Journal of Sociology* 78 (1972): 21–29.

11. The concept of role impingement is used for the first time, I believe, in Elihu Katz and S. N. Eisenstadt, "Some Sociological Observations on the Response of Israeli Organizations to New Immigrants," *Administrative Science Quarterly* 5 (1960): 113–33.

12. Exactly where to draw such analytical distinctions is sometimes difficult to determine. Thus, Merton uses as illustrations of roles "associated, not with a single social status, but with various statuses ... teacher, wife, mother ..." (*STSS*, p. 423). According to my understanding of Merton's concepts, the line should be drawn differently. While teacher and wife are different statuses, wife and mother are not but are different roles associated with the single status an adult woman occupies in her conjugal family.

13. Alvin W. Gouldner, "Cosmopolitans and Locals," *Administrative Science Quarterly* 2 (1957–58): 281–306, 444–80.

14. Peter M. Blau, *The Organization of Academic Work* (New York: Wiley, 1973), pp. 123–28. (I am grateful to Talcott Parsons and Gerald M. Platt for making their data on individual faculty members available to me.)

15. Robert K. Merton, "The Matthew Effect in Science," *Science* 159 (January 1968): 58. For empirical data indicating the Matthew effect, see Jonathan R. Cole and Stephen Cole, *Social Stratification in Science* (Chicago: University of Chicago Press, 1973), pp. 191–215.

16. Merton discusses the significance of visibility and observability in social structures in *STSS*, pp. 373–76, 390–411, 428–31.

17. Blau, *The Organization of Academic Work*, p. 125.

18. The theoretical assumptions in this section posit a long chain of intervening factors between faculty qualifications and local commitments. Most of these intervening factors are theoretical terms for which no empirical measures were available in the research cited. Long chains of causal relations are known to attenuate the association between initial antecedent and ultimate consequence. It is the more surprising that the empirical data reveal a significant inverse association between a person's academic qualifications and his or her local commitment, although the association is weak, undoubtedly because there is a long chain of intervening links.

19. For two empirical studies of sociology departments supporting this point, see Norval D. Glenn and Wayne Villemez, "The Productivity of Sociologists at 45 American Universities," *American Sociologist* 5 (1970): 249; and Richard B. Sturgis and Frank Clemente, "The Productivity of Graduates of 50 Sociology Departments," *American Sociologist* 8 (1973): 174–75.

20. Data on physicists indicating this are presented in Cole and Cole, *Social Stratification in Science*, p. 197.

21. Blau, *The Organization of Academic Work*, pp. 112–14.

22. *Ibid.*, pp. 126–27.
23. An important institutional innovation essential for keeping up with scientific and scholarly developments is the establishment of new departments, which appears to be inhibited by predominantly local commitments of the faculty; see *ibid.*, pp. 209–10.
24. Samuel A. Stouffer *et al., The American Soldier* (Princeton, N.J.: Princeton University Press, 1949), vol. 1, 250–54.
25. James A. Davis, "The Campus as a Frog Pond," *American Journal of Sociology* 72 (1966): 17–31.
26. Two studies of college aspirations of high school students and one of graduate-school aspirations of college students provide empirical indications of both reinforcing and counteracting effects of the attributes of the status complement in a school; John W. Meyer, "High School Effects on College Intentions," *American Journal of Sociology* 76 (1970): 59–70; Joel I. Nelson, "High School Context and College Plans," *American Sociological Review* 37 (1972): 143–48; David E. Drew and Alexander W. Astin, "Undergraduate Aspirations," *American Journal of Sociology* 77 (1972): 1151–64.
27. The distinction made between influences of prevailing characteristics and those of variations in them applies only to continuous variables, such as reputation, for which the former is indicated by measures of central tendency and the latter by measures of dispersion. It does not apply to nominal variables, such as disciplinary affiliation, for which one can only ascertain heterogeneity and not a prevailing or average characteristic in a collectivity.
28. Empirical data in support of the statements in the last three sentences are presented in Blau, *The Organization of Academic Work*, pp. 83–84, 88, 148, 209–11, 257. On the significance of orientations to outside reference groups of faculty members for the institutionalization of new specialties within universities and scientific progress, see Joseph Ben-David, "The Universities and the Growth of Science in Germany and the United States," *Minerva* 7, no. 2 (1968–69): 1–35, esp. 24–25.
29. See Blau, *The Organization of Academic Work*, pp. 215–16, 221–23.
30. Georg Simmel implies this distinction when he observes that great concentration of power in the hands of rulers is more compatible with widespread equality among subjects than with diversity in status; *The Sociology of Georg Simmel* (Glencoe, Ill.: Free Press, 1950), pp. 197–200. Empirical measures of inequality, like the Gini index, tend to refer mostly to elite concentration rather than diversity.
31. On both the advantages and the problems of collaboration between junior and senior scientists, see Harriet Zuckerman, *Scientific Elite* (in press).
32. Joseph Ben-David, "Scientific Productivity and Academic Organization in Nineteenth-Century Medicine," *American Sociological Review* 25 (1960): 828–43.
33. Merton, *STSS*, pp. 139–55 (originally published, 1945).

The Emergence of
A Scientific Specialty:
The Self-Exemplifying Case
of the Sociology of Science*

JONATHAN R. COLE and
HARRIET ZUCKERMAN

O VER the course of their careers, all working scientists have the opportunity to observe the growth of new fields of inquiry and the demise of
old ones. Yet the emergence of new scientific specialties as cognitive and
social entities seems to be a fact of the modern scientific life that is little understood. Physical and biological scientists have understandably been impatient
to get on with their own work and few have paused to examine the emergence of one or another special field.[1] Sociologists of knowledge have also not
shown much interest in questions about the growth of scientific knowledge.
They have occupied themselves primarily with inquiries into the social and
existential bases of knowledge. It was not until a few sociologists began to
study science as a social institution that more serious inquiry into the growth
and differentiation of specialties began. In short, the emergence of scientific specialties became interesting only when a new scientific specialty came into being.

The sociology of science is curiously self-exemplifying. As a scientific
specialty, it exhibits many of the social patterns its own practitioners study in
other contexts, making it a convenient site for sociological study of emerging

*Research for this study was supported by a grant from the National Science Foundation GS
33359X1 to the Columbia Program in the Sociology of Science and by the Center for Advanced
Study in the Behavioral Sciences, where the second author was a Fellow in 1973–74. Bernard
Barber, Stephen Cole, Yehuda Elkana, Joshua Lederberg and Arnold Thackray were kind
enough to read and comment on early drafts of this paper.

*Jonathan R. Cole and Harriet Zuckerman are Associate Professors
of Sociology at Columbia University.*

139

specialties. It is evolving its own system of stratification, its own arrangements for formal and informal communication, its own politics and its own lines of cognitive and social conflict just as these have become major foci of attention in research by sociologists of science. As participants and observers of these developments, we are in a strategic position to examine how the growth of knowledge in a special field is related to the emergence of its organizational infrastructure.

Tracing the emergence of the sociology of science also provides us with an occasion for examining Robert Merton's contributions to these developments. Since he has shown an almost obsessive fascination with scientific paternity—assiduously cataloguing the fathers of numerous sciences in his analysis of priority and eponymy in science[2] and more recently focusing on George Sarton's efforts to institutionalize the study of the history of science[3]— it seems fitting that he himself now become a subject of inquiry as a father of the sociology of science.[4]

THE SOCIOLOGY OF SCIENTIFIC SPECIALTIES

After a long and desultory incubation, the sociology of science now seems to have acquired its own cognitive and professional identity. In the last decade or so, sociological investigations of science have focused primarily on its social organization, in particular, on its reward-and-evaluation-systems, its system of communication and its ethos. Mapping these organizational features of science seemed to many investigators a necessary and congenial set of first steps toward understanding how scientific knowledge grows, becomes codified and institutionalized. By contrast, comparatively little attention has been given to studying the interplay of science and other social institutions.[5]

The research attention of sociologists of science may now be shifting. In the last few years, there has been increasing discussion of the connections between cognitive structures of the sciences and their social structures and some efforts to study them empirically.[6] Sociologists of science are now turning to such problems as the extent to which there is consensus among scientists in different disciplines on theory, method and substance, and whether there are systematic differences in social organization between sciences which can be linked to their differential degrees of theoretical codification. These studies derive in part from Thomas Kuhn's work on scientific revolutions,[7] Derek Price's studies of the parameters of scientific growth[8] and from the work of philosophers of science such as Karl Popper and Imré Lakatos.[9] It is in this intellectual context that recent studies of growth and institutionalization of scientific specialties can be located.

Kuhn's model of revolutionary change in the sciences has been especially influential in studies of scientific specialties. He focuses of course on the birth of new theoretical perspectives, or paradigms, on the recruitment of adherents to the new viewpoint and on the cognitive conflict attendant on the revolution. By working through the implications of the new paradigm and gaining intellectual and social dominance, new recruits ultimately revolutionize the discipline. Even though Kuhn's analysis of paradigms and their role in scientific change has been widely criticized by historians and philosophers of science,[10] sociologists of science have continued to find it useful. As a consequence, sociological studies of the emergence of specialties in the Kuhnian mode have focused especially on cases representing major breaks with disciplinary tradition.[11]

Working from another perspective, Derek Price re-introduced the seventeenth century term, "invisible college"—originally used to describe the pioneer members of the group which later became the Royal Society of London—to characterize the informal network of investigators he takes to be the core of any specialty.[12] He links this emphasis on patterns of communication to his other work on rates of growth in scientific manpower and the scientific literature. The impact of both Kuhn and Price is easily discerned in sociological studies of the emergence of specialties.[13] But there are still no agreed-upon problematics for studying the institutionalization of specialties.

Most sociologists of science have assumed that patterns of growth and institutionalization are much the same in different specialties. This assumption ignores the variegated processes that characterize the birth of new specialties. The first step in understanding institutionalization of specialties is more precise description of their cognitive and social development with more systematic attention being given to *variability* in specialty differentiation and its sources. Griffith and Mullins[14] have hinted that the emergence of "elite" specialty groups may differ in important ways from what they call "revolutionary" groups but the implications of this distinction are not explored.

The cognitive orientation of new specialty groups should be a strong determinant of its rate of institutionalization and its successful establishment. "Cognitively radical" specialty groups which reject the legitimacy of established theoretical and methodological orientations should encounter more intellectual resistance, more difficulty in obtaining resources and recruits and engender more conflict in the process of their development than "cognitively conforming" specialties. The latter base their claims to specialty status on inquiry into new and previously unexamined phenomena or on the use of new research technologies and thus do not challenge prevailing views. The distinction between cognitively radical and cognitively conforming specialties seems central to understanding how scientific specialties emerge. It suggests why the sociology of science for example—as a specialty with a new subject matter— has encountered relatively little resistance albeit no great enthusiasm from sociological colleagues. We shall take up this matter again when we consider Merton's role in the development of the specialty.

The cognitive standing of a new specialty is only one element affecting its reception. Its goodness of fit with the prevailing structure of the academy should also affect its chances for survival and, if it survives, its pace of institutionalization. Those that grow up in the interstices between disciplines, such as biochemistry, astrophysics or social psychology, are thwarted by the lack of

141

ready-made academic niches; handicapped by the poor meshing of their intellectual interests with those of deans, journal editors, grant givers and reviewers, and other gate-keepers of resources.[15] These specialties are, in short, structurally atypical regardless of their cognitive content and should encounter different and more challenging functional problems than those, such as nuclear physics or the sociology of science, which have been firmly located within the bounds of established disciplines from their beginnings.

There is, then, some reason to suppose that the development of scientific specialties is highly variable. A paradigm in the early, Mertonian sense is needed that provides for systematic and comparative examination of the cognitive development of specialties and their institutionalization. Such a program would focus attention on at least three sets of problems and processes.

1. *Parameters of growth in personnel and in production of a literature, as they change over time.* Do they grow simultaneously? Do they exhibit patterns of lead and lag? To what extent are they independent of one another or causally connected? How are they linked to the cognitive state of specialties?

2. *Processes of Cognitive Development of Specialties.* To what extent is there consensus or conflict on problematics, methods of inquiry, and on principal contributors at various stages in specialty development? Are ongoing developments built upon a common base or diverse intellectual foundations? How rapidly are new contributions exploited and built upon? How are theory and empirical research linked, if at all, and how do these linkages change over time? When does theoretical codification begin, if ever, and what are its indicators? How do foci of attention in the specialty shift and are these shifts related to changes in the intellectual orientations of leading authors or influentials? What are the distinctive contributions of the founders to the cognitive development of the specialty? How long do their contributions continue to be used and in what ways?

3. *The Development of Organizational Infrastructures.* How rapidly is the specialty incorporated into the educational curriculum and how much resistance does it encounter? In what respects do the social and historical contexts of institutionalization affect its pace and success? How rapidly and from what sources are funds and facilities acquired and with what consequences for cognitive development? What provisions are made for routinizing communication between specialists? In what ways, if at all, is the system of communication among specialists connected to the *general scientific* communication system? How effective have its intellectual founders been as institution builders? Are the tasks of organizing the specialty assumed by its intellectual leaders or is there a division of labor in these activities? And finally, when do specialists develop a sense of professional identity such that they consider themselves, and are considered by others, to be working at a common task?

Having repeatedly referred to cognitive elements in science, we note that the concept of cognitive structure has not yet been defined. In fact, its precise

142

meaning for sociologists of science is still evolving. At present, sociologists of science, cognitive psychologists, and philosophers of science focus on different aspects of cognitive structures. Sociologists regard these structures as multi-dimensional; they include:

1. scientific knowledge as it is reported in theoretical and experimental investigations;
2. the standards by which scientists judge methods, instruments, techniques, and evidence to be acceptable;
3. theoretical orientations which provide criteria for assessing the significance of new problems, new data, and proposed solutions;[16]
4. commonly accepted problematics for further inquiry; and
5. responses to new contributions, particularly the extent and forms of consensus and dissensus.

The cognitive structures of the separate sciences and specialties differ from one another and vary over time.

Analysis of cognitives structures of the sciences from a sociological perspective attempts, for example, to identify their basic theoretical orientations and to determine whether one predominates or whether several compete for scientists' attention. It attempts to determine whether fields or specialties are intellectually fragmented or cohesive; the extent to which theories are interconnected; how intellectual work is organized in terms of substantive problems and theoretical schools; and how theory and experiments are related.

Development and elaboration of the cognitive structure of new specialties appear to depend in part on correlative development of their social structures —on the routinization of an evaluation and reward system, procedures of communication, acquisition of resources and the socialization of new recruits. In short, the tandem development of both cognitive and social structures of specialties seems central to their institutionalization and establishment as legitimate areas of inquiry. Since institutionalization is more usefully considered as a process than as a product, studies of the decline of specialties[17] should be on the agenda for sociologists of science along with studies of their development.

We turn now to the sociology of science as a case study in the emergence of a specialty. Laying claim to the institution of science as a legitimate subject for sociological inquiry, the specialty is cognitively conforming and located firmly within the established disciplinary structure of sociology although it has increasingly elaborate connections to other fields, principally the philosophy and history of science. These cognitive and structural attributes suggest that its growth and institutionalization should be comparatively untraumatic, uncontested and more rapid than specialties which are cognitively or structurally radical. Had we studied the emergence of platetectonics or numerical taxonomy, two cognitively radical specialties, quite different patterns of growth might well have been found. Still, as we shall see, the sociological study of science despite its benign character was not enthusiastically embraced by sociologists when it was first introduced.

PARAMETERS OF GROWTH

Although Robert Merton believed that sociological analysis of science was a promising line of inquiry in the mid-1930s, few shared his enthusiasm. He recruited his student and friend Bernard Barber to work on social aspects of science, but their efforts to convert others mostly failed. By 1949, just one percent of the members of what was then the American Sociological Society counted the sociology of knowledge among their three fields of competence;[18] no separate tabulation was even made for the sociology of science. A decade later, sociologists had not changed their minds. The *Directory* for 1959 shows that just one percent of the membership reported competence in the sociology of knowledge. Again in 1970, things were much the same: 1.4 percent of the American Sociological Association's membership who answered the questionnaire on areas of competence—about two-thirds of the total of 13,000—selected the category newly rechristened as the "sociology of knowledge and science" as one of two principal areas of competence.[19] But by 1973, the figure had risen to 2.2 percent, or 301 out of a total of 13,700.

These figures need to be seen in context. First, the most frequently mentioned specialty in 1970 was selected by 9 percent of all sociologists and only four of the thirty-three specialties were selected by more than 5 percent. Second, between 1970 and 1973, the overall membership of the association increased by 5.4 percent, but the numbers reporting competence in the sociology of knowledge rose by a half, suggesting that interest in the composite field grew considerably even though the small numbers involved produce rather high rates of change.

More intriguing than data on increasing numbers are differences between age groups in declarations of competence in the sociology of knowledge and science. Stehr and Larsen find that the specialty is mentioned most often as an area of competence by the youngest members of the American Sociological Association. For sociologists in their 20s, it ranked 17th out of the 33 mentioned, 22nd for those in their 30s, 26th for those in their 40s and 28th for the oldest cohorts who were in their 50s and 60s.[20] These figures imply a growing interest in the field among the young and no marked pattern of conversion among the old.

Information on the changing subject matter of doctoral dissertations is consistent with this interpretation. Drawing upon listings in *Dissertation Abstracts* and the new *Comprehensive Dissertation Index, 1861–1972*, we took inventory of dissertations on science and technology written by students in sociology departments in American universities.[21] In all, we identified 105 titles, 65 in the sociology of science, 28 in the sociology of sociology and 12 in the sociology of engineers, engineering, and technology. The two earliest, both submitted in 1929, were sociological studies of sociology.[22] Seven years went by before S. C. Gilfillan, then a student at Columbia, finished his study of the sociology of invention for his sponsor, W. F. Ogburn. The same year, Robert Merton submitted his study of sociological aspects of scientific development in seventeenth century England to his doctoral committee at Harvard. That committee included the dean of historians of science, George Sarton, the distinguished physiologist and Pareto scholar L. J. Henderson, and the sociologists P. A. Sorokin and Talcott Parsons.

Despite these auspicious beginnings, few graduate students tried their hands at dissertations on the social aspects of science for some time. Just 25 dissertations were completed in the thirty years between 1937 and 1967. But things changed markedly after that. In the five years that followed, 40 dissertations were turned in, suggesting a sudden increase in interest in the specialty. This number is about 1.4 times as large as would be expected if dissertations in the sociology of science were multiplying at the same rate as they did in sociology as a whole.[23] Students writing dissertations in the sociology of science have been clustered at a few departments: Columbia, Cornell, Chicago, Purdue, and Michigan State, in that order, account for almost half of all dissertations in this specialty. The same universities produced only 28 percent of all Ph.D.'s in sociology in roughly the same period.[24] It would seem that a critical mass of students may be developing at a small number of research centers.

Such data only hint at the social processes of specialty growth. Consider the following questions: Do all specialties require an equal number of students to get moving? How rapidly must their numbers grow? What is the ratio between masters and apprentices required for sustained growth? Do new specialties require a higher density of talented newcomers than established ones? What constitutes a "critical mass" of students and practitioners needed for the development of a cognitive and professional identity? How important for the recruitment of students and the forging of a group identity are the personal characteristics of leaders in the field? How much proselytizing is needed? And what form does missionary work take before the specialty gains legitimacy among potential recruits, young and old?

While a growing number who claim an interest and competence in a specialty would seem to signal its developing professional identity, a growing literature indicates an authentic commitment on the part of practitioners to work in a field. Price and others[25] who work on parameters of scientific growth report almost without exception that the literature of scientific disciplines and scientific specialties first grows slowly and erratically and then exponentially, with a doubling time of ten to fifteen years.[26] In order to examine the growth and texture chiefly of the American literature in the sociology of science, we compiled a bibliography and citation index for publications appearing in nine scholarly journals since 1950.[27] In all, 195 papers published over 24 years were identified.[28] In its early years, the specialty had no clear intellectual identity, no shared problematics or techniques of investigation. Early papers were often vague and speculative. It is not surprising that it was far more difficult to decide whether papers published in the nineteen fifties belonged in the bibliography than those published later on.

As in the literature of disciplines and specialties previously examined, the number of papers in the sociology of science published since 1950[29] has grown exponentially with a doubling time of five to eight years. Taking all 195 publications into account, a third or so (37 percent) were published between 1958 and 1965 and almost half (48 percent) since 1966.[30] In all then, 85 percent of all papers we identified appeared after 1957, the year of Merton's influential paper on priorities in scientific discovery.[31] We also find a marked increase in the relative number of papers reporting quantitative studies in the sociology of science, with 38 percent of the papers published in the 1950s being quantitative in one or another respect, 52 percent of publications in the 1960s and 56 percent of those appearing in the 1970s. There is little doubt that these data represent an authentic change in the character of research in the sociology of science in recent years, but they clearly do not tell the whole story. Content analysis of books and monographs is needed before firm conclusions can be drawn about changes in the extent of quantification and its relation to other aspects of cognitive development.

Although a growing literature may indicate increased scholarly effort, it is not necessarily evidence for a shared intellectual focus among those at work in the specialty. There are however other reasons to think that such a focus was emerging: among them a growing consensus on the usefulness of particular publications, a consolidating research front in which new papers built directly upon those just published, and increased rates of collaborative publication. We want now to consider these and other indications of a developing cognitive structure in the specialty.

SELECTED ASPECTS OF COGNITIVE DEVELOPMENT

COGNITIVE CONSENSUS

A growing consensus among specialists on the usefulness of certain publications is a prime indicator that a specialty is developing distinctive problematics and thus a cognitive identity. The extent of convergence of citations to particular papers and to the work of particular authors is a rough measure of such consensus. If there were no common orientation in the specialty, citations would be widely dispersed among cited authors. The emergence of a common orientation however should be reflected in increasingly large proportions of citations going to the work of a small group of influential authors whose work is judged useful.[32] Converging citations do not mean that all agree on the significance of cited research or that all highly cited authors have a common orientation but only that the cited work is influential in some respect.

Three measures of convergence of citations or consensus are employed here: the proportion of cited authors receiving two or more citations, the proportion of citations going to the top 10 percent of cited authors, and the overall concentration of citations as measured by Gini-coefficients. The first is a rough gauge of the extent of dispersion of citations among cited authors while the latter two are more sensitive measures of the same variable. Drawing upon references in the 195 papers, these three measures were computed for five successive time periods and the results are presented in Tables 1A through 1C.

Consider first the findings for the sociology of science reported in Columns 2 and 3 of Table 1A. (Comparisons with the sociology of deviance will be made presently.) Only 18 percent of all authors cited in the early 1950s were cited more than once. By the early 1960s, that proportion had increased

146

slightly to 26 percent. A substantial increase in focusing can, however, be observed by the late 1960s. Nearly half of all cited authors were cited two or more times, suggesting growing agreement about the usefulness of work by particular authors. The data reported in Columns 2 and 3 of Table 1B for the sociology of science show an increasing reliance on the work of a few authors. In the early 1950s, there was little consensus in the sociology of science about whose research was useful. The top 10 percent of all cited authors received approximately one-quarter of all citations. Twenty years later, the top 10 percent received 44 percent of all citations. The Gini-concentration ratios reported in Column 2 of Table 1C tell a similar story. In the early years, there is considerable dispersion in the distribution of citations. Later on, in the 1960s and 1970s, the data show increasing concentration in the distribution of citations, suggesting the emergence of a cadre of recognized intellectual leaders and convergence in judgments of usefulness among those publishing in the journals examined.[33]

Table 1A. COMPARISON OF LEVELS OF COGNITIVE CONSENSUS FROM 1950–1973 IN SOCIOLOGY OF SCIENCE AND SOCIOLOGY OF DEVIANCE

Percent of Cited Authors Receiving Two or More Citations

| | Sociology of Science | | Sociology of Deviance | |
Period	Percent	Total Authors Cited	Percent	Total Authors Cited
1950–54	18	(148)	44	(242)
1955–59	24	(323)	50	(538)
1960–64	26	(571)	53	(884)
1965–69	44	(775)	52	(1347)
1970–73	45	(899)	45	(723)*

*The literature in the sociology of deviance covers the period 1950–72 inclusive.

Table 1B. PERCENT OF CITATIONS RECEIVED BY TOP 10 PERCENT OF CITED AUTHORS

Specialty

| | Sociology of Science | | Sociology of Deviance | |
Period	Percent	Total Citations	Percent	Total Citations
1950–54	24	(198)	36	(1178)
1955–59	28	(444)	38	(2753)
1960–64	35	(931)	49	(5560)
1965–69	43	(1698)	46	(7469)
1970–73	44	(2145)	36	(3514)*

*The literature in the sociology of deviance covers the period 1950–72 inclusive.

Table 1C. GINI-COEFFICIENTS FOR DISTRIBUTION OF CITATIONS
IN FIVE TIME PERIODS*

Period	Sociology of Science	Sociology of Deviance
1950–54	.22	.23
1955–59	.23	.29
1960–64	.33	.40
1965–69	.42	.48
1970–73	.47	.30

*We are indebted to Stephen Cole for providing us with these data for the sociology of deviance. Extended discussion of these and other measures of intellectual structures can be found in his paper in this volume. See O. D. Duncan, "The Measurement of Population Distribution," *Population Studies* 11 (July 1957): 27, for discussion of the Gini-coefficient.

As we noted earlier, the sociology of science derives its claim to specialty status from its focus on phenomena not previously studied by sociologists. In the early fifties, there was no relevant literature to cite, to respond to critically, to correct, or to elaborate. Each author who published in those early years brought his own highly individualized apperceptive mass to bear on his research. Only as the intellectual identity of the field became fixed did a pattern of increasing consensus on influential authors appear. Once a specialty becomes a recognizable entity, however, the extent of consensus on influential authors need not continue to grow. It may even decline, if rival theoretical or methodological orientations develop. Such is apparently the case in the recent history of the sociology of deviance. (See Stephen Cole's essay in this volume, pages 175–220.)

As Tables 1A and 1C suggest, the larger literature on deviance contains more citations. More authors are cited even though the data are drawn from just four journals, as compared with the nine sampled for the sociology of science. Since "deviance" was the fifth most "popular" on the list of thirty-three areas of sociological competence selected by members of the ASA in 1970 and the sociology of science and knowledge, twenty-fifth, the differences in the size of their journal literatures are not surprising. The significant fact however is that these literatures also contain differences of dispersion of citations over time. The sociology of deviance shows a curvilinear pattern while a linear increase is observed for the sociology of science. Table 1A shows that nearly half (44%) of all authors cited in the deviance literature between 1950 and 1954 received multiple citations. Ten years later that proportion increased to a high of 53 percent. In the next ten years the rate of multiple citation began to taper off, reaching 45 percent for the current period.

Consider now the more sensitive indicators of consensus. The sociology of deviance shows some convergence in judgments about its most influential authors in the early 1950s: the top 10 percent of authors cited in the journals received 36 percent of all citations in this period. Cognitive consensus in the deviance literature by this measure increased and peaked in the years 1960–

148

1964, when the top 10 percent received almost half of all citations, the same level as has been observed in physics.[34] The Gini-coefficients indicate the same pattern. These years were the high point in the functional analytic study of deviant behavior, as Stephen Cole's essay in this volume reports (pp. 188–205). Toward the end of the 1960s, however, the functional orientation came under attack by ethnomethodologists and symbolic interactionists. The development of these rival perspectives appears to be reflected in the citation data.

Similar developments are not yet discernible in the referencing behavior of sociologists of science. Although in recent years some young English and European sociologists of science have proposed what they consider to be an alternative to the perspective exemplified in Merton's work, their papers are still largely programmatic and critical. They continue to cite Merton and those pursuing similar inquiries and to use their research.[35] Thus the global citation measures of consensus presented here are not an early warning system for cognitive conflict but only provide cues to the emergence of alternative and competing orientations after such orientations are embodied in new self-contained research literature.

THE CONSOLIDATION OF A RESEARCH FRONT

We have observed increasing convergence in citations in the sociology of science and have suggested that this is a signal of developing intellectual coherence and consensus. Such a convergence may indicate a consolidation of new work or mere reiteration of older inquiries. In order to determine whether current work is built on comparatively new contributions rather than on older ones— that is, whether a research front has developed and when—we need to examine the age of cited papers. Derek Price has observed that active research fields rely heavily on recent publications. Citations in active research areas are relatively younger than would be expected on the basis of sheer growth in the literature. This he calls "immediacy."[36] It has also been suggested that rates of citation to recently published work are correlated with the extent of theoretical codification in a science such that the more codified sciences exhibit higher proportions of citations to newly published work. This should be so because codification of theoretical and empirical knowledge makes it possible to identify the connections between new work and old; to gauge the significance of new contributions; and to facilitate their rapid incorporation into ongoing work.[37] Thus, if a specialty were becoming increasingly codified, the age of publications being cited in its literature should decline and "immediacy" measures should rise.

This is precisely what we observe in the literature of the sociology of science. In the first half of the 1960s, when the specialty appeared to "take off" and move toward a high growth rate and institutionalization, cited papers were an average of twelve years old, 48 percent of citations went to papers published in the preceding five years. Between 1965 and 1969, the average age of cited papers dropped to nine years and 56 percent of the references were to papers published no more than five years before. These data on citation of

149

recent publications can be better understood when juxtaposed with figures on production of journal literature in the sociology of science. Although 48 percent of citations in papers published between 1960 and 1964 went to literature published in the same five years, over half the literature (57 percent) then in print appeared during this period. This makes for an immediacy score of −9 percent, a figure that would surely have been larger if literature published before 1950 had been surveyed. Thus in the years when the sociology of science began to grow rapidly, recent research was not used as quickly as it was produced. In the following five years, things changed markedly. Thirty-six percent of the total literature was published, but 56 percent of citations went to recent work, making for an immediacy score of + 20 percent, a figure comparable to rapidly growing specialties in the physical sciences and much higher than that for sociology as a whole.[38]

Although this trend toward citing new publications may be related to the influx of young people into the field and their characteristic interest in new work, it is not confined to their publications. References in Merton's own work reflect this increasing reliance on new research. An avid student of the history of science and obsessed with documenting the filiation of ideas, Merton punctuated his early papers with references to works several centuries old. His recent papers, however, reveal that his perspective has shifted along with those of other sociologists of science. References in his own most cited papers in the sociology of science, the "Priorities" paper published in 1957 and "The Matthew Effect" published in 1968,[39] exemplify this trend, with the median age of references in the "Priorities" paper being 18 years and in "The Matthew Effect," 8 years. Not surprisingly, references in the same papers also reveal Merton's increased reliance on very recent work: 29 percent of the references in the "Priorities" paper were to publications no more than five years old as against half of the references in "The Matthew Effect." This does not, we think, reflect a conviction that pertinent older references are already well established in the bibliography of the specialty and thus no longer require citation even though they are used. Rather it is testimony to a genuine shift of attention to newer publications.

THE AGE STRUCTURE OF INFLUENTIALS

Turning from the age of citations to the ages of authors being cited, we see one of the important consequences of the pattern of recruitment among the young that we noted earlier. Not only is the sociology of science more popular among young sociologists, but their intellectual influence on the field has also increased dramatically. Although there are reasons for supposing that the age of contributors of important work to a science declines as that science becomes more codified,[40] there is no reason to think that youthful investigators are primarily responsible for increasing the extent of codification; rather it enables them to deal with important problems in the field. Keeping this observation in mind, we note the decline in average age of the thirty most-cited authors in successive five-year periods. It drops from 53 for the years 1950–64 to 46 for the

150

years 1965–72. The principal shift occurs between two five-year periods: 1960–64 when the mean age of influentials was 54, and 1965–69 when it fell to 44.[41] These data also reveal a slight increase in the age of influentials in the 1970s, a finding easily understood when we note that the young people who first became influential in the late 1960s continue to be so in the 1970s. In fact, the lists of the thirty most influential authors in the late sixties and early seventies overlap by 60 percent. Since each author on both lists was growing older, their average ages increased. New entrants among the influentials in the seventies were not young enough to make up for this trend.

COLLABORATIVE PUBLICATION

As specialties become organized around a set of problems, the extent of collaboration between specialists increases. This is one outcome of greater numbers simultaneously at work in research centers, increased requirements for specialized skills, and greater agreement on the nature of researchable problems. There is a marked increase in collaborative publication over the twenty-four years covered by our bibliography. In the first eight years, not one of the 29 papers abstracted had more than one author, but in the second 14 percent, or 10 out of 72, were multi-authored; and in the third, 31 percent or 29 out of 94 papers were collaborative. Altogether, only 3 percent of the 195 papers had three authors and none more than that. The figures for the last period are slightly lower than that for the journal literature in sociology as a whole.[42]

THE STRUCTURE OF INFLUENCE IN THE SOCIOLOGY OF SCIENCE

Thus far three points emerge from citation analysis of the journal literature of the sociology of science: (1) consensus on the work of particular contributors has been growing; (2) younger authors are increasingly represented among contributors cited most frequently; and (3) recent publications are more often cited now than in earlier years. Nonetheless Robert Merton has had greater influence on the evolving cognitive identity of the field from its beginnings than any other author. His impact on his colleagues' research is signaled by the extent of citation to his work. With a total of 154 citations in the journal literature surveyed here, his work is used roughly twice as often as that of the second most cited author in our list.[43] But apart from Merton and several others, the social and intellectual composition of the most influential group of authors has changed greatly. These changes are cues to marked shifts in foci of attention in the field and in types of work being published. (Given the high correlation in science between intellectual influence and authority, we suspect that they are also cues of changes in the intellectual composition of those occupying gate-keeping positions.) We increase the resolution of our citation analysis to the micro level by turning now to the question of continuity and change in the influence structure in the sociology of science.

Table 2 presents rank-ordered lists of the authors most often cited in the journal literature of the sociology of science in five time periods.[44] We have

Table 2.   MOST CITED AUTHORS IN THE SOCIOLOGY OF SCIENCE, 1950–1973
(SELF-CITATIONS EXCLUDED)

Period and Rank Order

1950–54	1955–59	1960–64	1965–69	1970–73
Gilfillan, S. C.	Merton, R. K.	Merton, R. K.	Merton, R. K.	Merton, R. K.
Lundberg, G.	Lazarsfeld, P. F.	Crombie, A. C.	Price, Derek	Price, Derek
Dewey, J.	Gaudet, H.	Barber, B.	Garfield, E.	Hagstrom, W. O.
Hart, H.	Wilkening, E. A.	Gillispie, C. C.	Hagstrom, W. O.	Cole, J. R.
Parsons, T.	Wilson, L.	Lazarsfeld, P. F.	Zuckerman, H.	Ben-David, J.
Merton, R. K.	Stimson, D. L.	Kornhauser, W.	Gordon, G.	Cole, S.
Weber, M.	Compton, A. H.	Flexner, A.	Glaser, B.	Zuckerman, H.
Shils, E.	Kellner, A.	Goodrich, H. B.	Garvey, W. D.	Gaston, J. C.
Conant, J. B.	Robertson, T.	Kuhn, T. S.	Kessler, M. M.	Kuhn, T. S.
Leighton, A. H.	Parsons, T.	Caplow, T.	Cartter, A. M.	Crane, D.
Isard, W.	Richards, I. A.	Shepard, H. A.	Ben-David, J.	Barber, B.
Kautsky, K.	Sarton, G.	Shryock, R. H.	Barber, B.	Cartter, A. M.
Lerner, D.	Ryan, B.	Wilson, L.	Pelz, D.	Glaser, B.
Lasswell, H. D.	Kluckhohn, C.	Glaser, B.	Cole, S.	Ogburn, W. F.
Kuhn, T. S.	Gross, N. C.	Gilfillan, S.	Cole, J. R.	McGee, R.
Chase, S.	Berelson, B.	Holland, J. L.	Gamson, W.	Parsons, T.
Durkheim, E.	Shepard, H. A.	Marcson, S.	Kaplan, N.	Polanyi, M.
Corey, L.		McGee, R.	Storer, N. W.	Shils, E.
Goren, G.		Pelz, D.	Lazarsfeld, P. F.	Storer, N. W.
Ogburn, W. F.		Parsons, T.	Kuhn, T. S.	Gouldner, A. W.
Gold, H.		Knapp, R. H.	Berelson, B.	Gordon, G.
Gee, W.		Price, Derek		Caplow, T.
Myrdal, G.				Watson, J. D.
Usher, A. P.				Pelz, D. C.
Sibley, E.				Hirsch, W.
Whitney, V.				Hargens, L. L.
				Berelson, B.

Number of Citations:

| Range 8–2 | Range 12–3 | Range 32–5 | Range 39–9 | Range 67–9 |

focused on the approximately twenty most-cited authors in each period because patterns are difficult to discern in longer lists. Our more extended enumerations show many of the same attributes as the shorter ones, and in no way contradict our general observations.

The list of most-cited authors in the first decade is striking in several respects. Major figures in the wider discipline of sociology—both historical and contemporary—seem to have dominated the literature. Since the sociology of science had not yet developed its own intellectual identity in the form of subject-specific ideas and techniques, specialists applied what they could from the prevailing theoretical and methodological corpus. Thus, Paul Lazarsfeld is among the most highly cited authors in the 1950s. Closer inspection of citations to Lazarsfeld's work reveals that it is his logic of multivariate analysis that is most often used, not his work in the history of quantification in sociology, which he had not even begun to publish at this time. We can detect no clusters of researchers on the list who worked on related problems and no identifiable similarities in the problems they addressed—in short, no signs of a shared intellectual orientation.

Table 2 also shows that few authors frequently cited in the early 1950s are included among those often cited in the later 1950s. In order to convey the extent of continuity from one period to the next, we constructed the transition matrix—or partial "turnover table"—that appears as Table 3. Two estimates of continuity are presented here. The first, located *above* the main diagonal, shows the proportion of authors in the most-cited decile in one period also in the most-cited decile in subsequent periods. Since the number comprising the most-cited decile grows as the number of cited authors grows, this measure of continuity is less demanding than the second measure, presented *below* the diagonal in Table 3. This second set of data reports the proportion of the thirty most-cited authors for each period who also appear in subsequent periods. Over time, the top thirty make up smaller and smaller proportions of all cited authors and thus represent an increasingly elite group.

Table 3. CONTINUITY AMONG INFLUENTIAL CONTRIBUTORS
TO THE SOCIOLOGY OF SCIENCE

(THE MOST CITED 10 PERCENT ARE PRESENTED ABOVE THE DIAGONAL;
THE THIRTY MOST-CITED INDIVIDUALS, BELOW THE DIAGONAL.)

Percent Carried Over Between Periods
Period

Period	1950–54*	1955–59	1960–64	1965–69	1970–73
1950–54	—	13	33	27	40
1955–59	8	—	19	22	19
1960–64	15	20	—	40	37
1965–69	12	17	27	—	47
1970–73	19	13	30	60	—

*The base figure for continuity for the period 1950–54 was 26, since there were only 26 of the 148 cited authors whose work was cited two or more times.

153

Confining ourselves to the extent of continuity of influentials in adjacent periods, we note a sharp increase in continuity in the most-cited decile in the late 1960s, as the data above the main diagonal show. The extent of continuity in the top decile approximately doubled from nineteen to forty percent in the 1960s and then increased slightly to forty-seven percent in the early 1970s. Data reported below the main diagonal show the same pattern even more sharply. Only two of the thirty authors (Parsons and Merton) whose work was most often used in the early 1950s also appear among those most often cited in the later 1950s. The extent of continuity increases somewhat in the 1960s but it is not until the early 1970s that a major shift in continuity is discernible. As many as eighteen out of the top thirty, or 60 percent, of the most-cited authors appear on both lists. Work in the sociology of science finally was focused on an identifiable set of problems, formally presented in the publications of a limited number of authors. Further, these same authors continued to work in the field and to produce research that was useful to their colleagues instead of moving on to other areas of substantive concern. This marked increase in continuity of influentials between the late 1960s and early 1970s is also reflected in the aging of influentials in these years reported earlier.

For those familiar with the literature of the sociology of science, a glance at the names of the most-cited authors listed in Table 2 will immediately convey the extent of change in the intellectual interests of the influentials. The lists are dominated after 1965 by sociologists of science and a handful of historians and philosophers of science. Distinguished figures from the physical, biological, and other behavioral sciences disappear from the list of most-cited authors.[45] The sociologists of science whose work is frequently cited are, with notable exceptions, quantitative empirical researchers. Given the increasing number of quantitative studies published and the tendency for authors of such studies to cite prior work of the same kind, this finding is not surprising. It does suggest that citation analysis of journal articles may overestimate the impact of quantitative empirical research and underestimate the role of authors who do not fit this mould. T. S. Kuhn is of course the most conspicuous example of this group.

These lists contain cues to a second kind of continuity among influentials: not simply across adjacent time periods but through more extended periods of time. Although Merton alone turns up in each of the five lists covering twenty-three years of literature, Thomas Kuhn, Derek Price, Bernard Barber, and Donald Pelz, all appear on the last three lists.[46] Thus, at least a small number of leaders have been working at the research front for some time. Mullins' contention that leaders of research specialties often turn to new problems before their specialty is fully institutionalized is not borne out in this case.[47] There are no signs that Merton, Price, or Kuhn, among the other leading influentials, are turning away from their interest in the sociology of science.

Thus we return once again to the question we raised earlier in other contexts: How much variability is there in the emergence of new specialties? Under what conditions do research leaders lose interest in specialties they helped to establish? Are founders of "cognitively radical" specialties, and those

154

which are structurally atypical more apt to move on to entirely new problems than leaders of conforming-specialties? Or does the exodus of founders depend on the extent to which the specialty remains fertile ground for studying fundamental issues.

"Insiders" in the sociology of science will also notice a third kind of continuity among the most cited authors listed in the fourth and fifth columns in Table 2. For the first time, a significant number of students of influentials appear along with those who trained them. Of the thirty-three different authors who were cited most between 1965–73, seven are Merton's former students.[48] Insiders will also note that a four-generation chain of masters and apprentices appears here, a chain much like those observed in the physical and biological sciences.[49] Starting with Talcott Parsons, one of Robert Merton's teachers at Harvard, we can trace an intellectual lineage through Norman Kaplan, who studied with Merton at Columbia and went on to supervise Norman Storer's doctoral work at Cornell. Had we set our cutoff point in citations just one step lower, the 1970–72 list would also have included Nicholas Mullins, who did his doctoral work with Storer at Harvard. These master-apprentice chains reflect the twin processes of self-selection and selective recruitment among different generations of influentials. By providing structural supports for continuing social relations between members of the same intellectual family, they make for a degree of cohesion between academic generations.

The next steps in citation analysis of specialty formation are clear. First, analysis of citations in books must be undertaken. Second, these lists of most-cited authors contain names of the most influential scholars in the specialty, but the intellectual linkages between them is not explored. Quantitative and qualitative analysis of such linkages between papers and influentials is needed. This will enable us to learn whether some authors are influential for all their colleagues, whether schools actually exist or are in formation, how the cognitive texture of the specialty has changed, and the extent to which the boundaries of groups identified are permeable. This analysis is in process.[50]

ROBERT K. MERTON: TEACHER, FOUNDER AND INFLUENTIAL

So much for the intellectual concerns and social composition of leading authors in the sociology of science. We turn now to Merton's impact on the specialty.

Unlike his own teacher, George Sarton, Merton has had some success in recruiting students to the discipline. In his concern to establish the history of science as a respectable scholarly enterprise, Sarton made demands on students so severe as to be self defeating. Not many learned the classical and oriental languages whose mastery, along with five or six major modern languages, Sarton deemed necessary. And still fewer obtained the equivalent of advanced degrees in both the physical and the biological sciences he also considered necessary for historians of science. He also failed to develop a coherent formulation of principal problems in the field and a set of usable research techniques. Although Sarton developed a distinctive perspective on the history of science it was not one that could be readily adopted by potential recruits. It is not surprising then that few historians of science count themselves among Sarton's students.[51] Although Merton shares some of Sartons' perfectionism in his demands on students (a characteristic not all of them find endearing), his work has brought many students into the specialty. It lays out a series of problems in the sociology of science and provides an orientation to sociological work in general. This becomes evident when we look closely at the uses made of Merton's work by different intellectual constituencies.

Although Merton continued his studies in the sociology of science and published more than twenty papers in this area in the two decades after he completed his dissertation, these efforts were not immediately recognized by sociologists, historians of science, or, for that matter, anyone else. This was so in spite of the considerable attention paid his theoretical work and his studies in the sociology of organizations, professions, and mass communications.[52] It now seems obvious that Merton's early papers (and, we think, those of any founder) had limited initial impact because they had no audience specifically attuned to publications on this subject. Merton's "Priorities in Scientific Discovery,"[53] his presidential address to the American Sociological Society, was warmly received. Sociologists clearly knew about this paper and may even have read it. Yet it had little immediate impact even in the literature of the sociology of science. Of all the citations the "Priorities" paper has received—which are more numerous than for any other paper in the literature —fewer than a third came in the eight years following its publication and only half in the first ten. This is most unusual considering the general pattern of intensive citation immediately following publication and a gradual tailing off afterward.[54] It also turns out that the average time elapsed—mean and median—between the publication of this paper and its use is ten years. Increasing citation of the "Priorities" paper in recent years no doubt reflects growth in the literature of the sociology of science. But over and above this artifactual element, the pattern of use observed here suggests how little influence ideas will have until a core of professional researchers with a common orientation are around to use them.

Although Merton's work overall has been increasingly influential in recent years, this is not uniformly true of all his papers. His recent publications, those appearing since 1959, seem to have had disproportionately great impact on the specialty. Comprising fewer than half of the papers he has published on science, they have received sixty-five percent of all citations to his work. With the exception of his studies of the normative structure of science, his early papers on the compatibility of Puritanism and the scientific ethos, on the sociology of knowledge, and on science and totalitarian politics are far less often used by sociologists of science than his later inquiries into competition for priority,[55] multiple discovery,[56] the Matthew Effect,[57] the evaluation-system in science,[58] and Insiders and Outsiders.[59] Thus the active interest taken in his later papers does not appear to have triggered renewed interest in his earlier ones.

The reasons for the differential influence of these earlier and later papers are more complex than it would first appear. As we noted, new publications are more apt to be cited in growing literatures than older ones. In no small part, this is so because older publications are "dated" or their content has already been incorporated into the cognitive structure of the field. Neither of these explanations appears to fit here. Instead, sociologists of science found in Merton's later work on priorities, stratification in science and its reward-system greater "potential for elaboration"[60] and a reasonably clear program of research. It focused attention on the operation of the evaluation and reward-systems, their efficacy in extending scientific knowledge, and the role of recognition in scientists' motivations to continue their work. Close inspection of the papers by newcomers to the field who appear on the list of most cited authors in the 1960s and 1970s shows that much of their empirical work begins with a problem posed in one or another of Merton's later papers.

Moreover the "potential for elaboration" of Merton's recent work has been much enhanced by three developments beyond the confines of the sociology of science: establishment of the Science Citation Index, publication of the American Council of Education's appraisals of graduate education, and growing interest in empirical studies of social stratification.

Developments in quantitative analysis of social stratification fed concurrent studies of stratification in science and, it would appear, gave research in the esoteric specialty a more general appeal. At the same time, sociologists have made little progress in studying structures of norms and values or the relations between social institutions, the most important issues Merton addressed in his earlier work in the sociology of science. Their potentials for elaboration are largely untested by sociologists of science.[61]

Historians of science have had different concerns. Had our bibliographic search and citation index been extended to recent publications in the history of science, greater interest in Merton's studies of Puritanism and the rise of science would have been registered. This would be particularly so among younger historians of science working on the social contexts of scientific development.[62] The influence of Merton's work on seventeenth-century science was invisible for some time, as Henry Guerlac tells us, since it ran counter to the dominant trend toward "internalist" or "idealist" history of science.[63] Merton's influence on historians of science has surfaced in the last decade or so. Although we find only one other sociologist even mentioned in papers dealing with the history of science in *Past and Present* and in *History of Science,* references to the Merton thesis have multiplied considerably in recent years. And such established "internalist" historians of science as I. Bernard Cohen,[64] A. Rupert Hall,[65] Charles Gillispie,[66] and Guerlac appear to be increasingly sympathetic to considerations of the social and ideological contexts of science, Guerlac calling Merton's dissertation a "landmark" in the literature of the history of science,[67] and Gillispie remarking, "Not many a thesis furnishes fuel for a controversy lasting as long as its author's career, much less bidding (as this one is beginning to do) for immortality."[68]

There are however a few signs that Merton's sociological perspective was being incorporated into the history of science. Charles Gillispie reports that on first reading the "Priorities" paper it appeared "a bit trivial. I don't believe I also said 'unworthy' but recollect that such a dark thought was in my mind."

He goes on to say that he and his colleagues in the history of science did not really understand what it was all about: "Only a few years later, when I began to study and teach materials in the social and institutional as well as the more traditional internal and intellectual history of science, did I come to take the full thrust of what he [Merton] had in fact said, and said clearly and convincingly."[69] Nevertheless, of the entire corpus of Merton's writings in the sociology of science it is the Puritan roots of English science which still preoccupy most historians of science. Merton's recent work that sociologists of science have found so "puzzle–producing" has not yet found its way into the thinking of the historians. But, nonetheless, he is an intellectual presence for them. Commenting in a book review on an error in indexing, John Murdoch writes, "Robert Merton... has been classified under 'Merton College.' (This kind of transformation of Merton into an institution is presumably a bit premature!)"[70]

Returning to the impact of Merton's work on sociologists of science, we note that citation analysis can not take us very far toward understanding how authors are influenced by publications they cite even though it does tell us how often they do so in our limited sample of journals. Procedures for analyzing types of citations and their frequency are not well developed. In fact, sociologists of science have not even settled on a standardized classification of citations.[71] Our own efforts at a content analysis of citations to Merton's work are, as a consequence, rather tentative. Altogether fifty-eight different authors writing in the nine journals sampled have used thirty-four of Merton's papers. Although his later publications have been disproportionately cited in recent research in the sociology of science, the kinds of citations these papers receive are not much different from those given his earlier publications at comparable times in their own life histories. By and large, Merton's work is cited for two purposes: to confer authority on statements authors make and to identify the source of problems. There are few ceremonial or perfunctory citations, and a few citations which are disparaging. In the absence of statistical norms on the relative frequency of different kinds of citations in the sociological literature it is not possible to interpret the distribution observed here. Authors who draw on Merton's work as a point of departure for their own research typically do so by developing ideas he originated or crystallized rather than using it as a source for specific hypotheses along the same lines as Stephen Cole's study of the "Matthew Effect."[72] Clearly sociologists of science are now taking the first steps toward understanding the ways in which knowledge develops, and how research by different generations of scholars is linked together as these are reflected in citations.

Thus, citation analysis at its present stage of development can only take us so far toward understanding the character of intellectual influence. Serious content analysis of manuscripts is required to fill out the skeletal facts provided by citations. The same is true when we attempt an account of networks of influence. The gross connections between publications can of course be mapped. But citations do not even hint at the decisive if only partly visible effects scholars have on one another via informal discussions and critical readings of manuscripts and grant applications. Painstaking documentary research and interviewing are needed to get at these informal linkages and their diverse consequences. Not only would studies of authors' acknowledgments be germane here, but also notes on seminars, research memoranda, letters, diaries, and commentaries on texts. Consider this fragmentary exchange in which Merton serves as facilitator and reference individual. In June, 1959, while at the Center for Advanced Study in the Behavioral Sciences, Thomas Kuhn wrote to Merton thanking him for his close reading of the paper Kuhn had sent him on measurement in science. He added:

> I am sending you ... a much-revised draft of my first chapter on "Scientific Revolutions." If you have a chance to look at it, I shall be very grateful for your reactions. Meanwhile, or at least until you call me off, I shall continue to pester you with pieces in this vein as they become available.[73]

Merton was deeply impressed by the manuscript. When Kuhn was ready to send *The Structure of Scientific Revolutions* to the University of Chicago Press, he wrote to Merton asking that Merton intercede with the Press if it proved reluctant to publish the volume independently of the Encyclopedia of Unified Science. Merton replied:

> Of course, I'll be glad to write to the Chicago Press along the lines you suggest. After all, I've read the earlier draft and this alone is enough to justify a strong recommendation to the Press that they proceed as you would have them do.[74]

Kuhn's apprehensions proved groundless. The Press agreed to publish the book as Kuhn requested and it appeared at the end of 1962. Merton wrote to Kuhn:

> I have just this day received a copy of your new book ... Having read this version in its entirety, I must say that it is merely brilliant. More than any other historian of science I know, you combine a penetrating sense of scientists at work, of patterns of historical development, and of sociological processes in that development.[75]

Kuhn replied:

> I think you know how much your good opinion of the sort of work I have tried to do in the book means to me. ... Of course I'll inscribe your copy. ... I always hate that particular task, but it will be a small price to pay for the chance to talk the whole area over with you.[76]

Bernard Barber, in his essay on L. J. Henderson, and Nicholas Mullins in his analysis of specialty formation, both conclude that the people who fill the role of the "trusted assessor" critically affect scientific development not only by setting standards but also by providing social and psychological support for those working in new areas.[77] The physicist and knowledgeable observer of science John Ziman goes even farther and asserts that "the creation of a group of reliable experts who can be trusted to give fair consideration to all new work ... [is] one of the difficulties in the establishment of an entirely new science."[78]

And, finally, crude quantitative analysis of citations is not fine-grained enough to detect the subtle and often unacknowledged influences of general theoretical and methodological orientations. In the process of "obliteration by incorporation,"[79] which is especially marked in the case of general ideas, original sources are lost to view. We want now to consider how some of Merton's generic sociological concepts have found their way into the sociology of science and, in doing so, to illustrate the interplay between the cognitive structures of specialties and those of the larger disciplines.

Merton's analysis of science and scientists did not develop independently of his other theoretical efforts. On the contrary, the problems he has selected and the mode of attack he has used are clearly related to his general interest in applying structural and functional analysis to social patterns in various institutional spheres. Four theoretical themes will serve the purpose:

1. Anomie and deviant behavior
2. Multiple consequences, manifest and latent functions
3. Over-conformity and maladaptation
4. Self-reinforcing social processes.

Anomie and deviant behavior. Merton's analysis of competition for priority in science closely parallels his widely known work on deviant behavior. The origins of deviant behavior in science and in the larger culture are located in a disjunction between goals and normatively prescribed means. And its incidence depends in large part on the structure of opportunities to conform to the norms.[80] He suggests that the strong emphasis in science on the extension of certified knowledge and thus on original discovery has much the same effect as the comparably strong emphasis in American culture on financial success. Although scientists are enjoined to humility and to disinterestedness, they are, at the same time, driven to seek recognition of their originality, since that is the only way they can be sure they have truly made contributions to science. As a consequence, they are under great pressure to stake claims to what they take to be their scientific property, to assert their priority of discovery, and, however uncontentious they might be personally, to engage in priority disputes. Rarely however do these efforts shade over into thoroughly deviant acts including plagiary, data manipulation, and slander of competitors for priority. Merton's analysis of competition for priority is formally similar to his treatment of other kinds of patterned nonconformity in two important respects: he is unwilling to accept psychological accounts of what he takes to be socially structured behavior and he looks for explanations of its origins and frequency in particular in normative ambivalence (norms and counter norms), in cultural inconsistencies, and in socially structured opportunities. Storer,[81] Gaston,[82] and Hagstrom,[83] among others, have used this analysis in studies of the sources of competition in science, its incidence, and the forms it assumes in various social contexts.

Multiple consequences, manifest and latent functions. Merton's analysis of the Matthew Effect in science[84] draws upon the perspective laid out in his "Para-

160

digm for Functional Analysis."[85] He begins with the observation that scientific recognition tends to accrue to those who already have it. Without deliberate intent, the Matthew Effect[86] penalizes the young and the unknown and, in the process, reinforces the already unequal distribution of rewards. But this is not all. Merton characteristically takes a step back from the phenomenon he has been examining from the perspective of individuals and asks how things look for the system as a whole and finds multiple and diverse consequences. He argues that the misallocation of credit which results from the Matthew Effect is unjust and exacts a high emotional cost from individuals. But at the same time it has the surprising effect of making the communication system more efficient; it thus contributes to the extension of certified scientific knowledge. For one thing, the Matthew Effect calls attention to the work of proven scientists and thereby increases the probability that work of value will get noticed and read. It also calls attention to different parts of the output of distinguished scientists, increasing the visibility of reappearing themes in their work that might otherwise go unnoticed. Merton's technique of shifting the angle of theoretical vision from social consequences for individuals to those for systems and from manifest to latent outcomes has been fruitfully used by sociologists of science. Two diverse examples are Menzel's[87] analysis of the functions of scientific communication and our own studies on the intended and unintended effects of rewards on scientists' subsequent productivity.[88]

Overconformity and maladaptive behavior. The notion that the same social pattern is likely to have multiple consequences for different units of a system is closely allied to the view that the same social patterns have different consequences over time and in diverse circumstances. For more than thirty years, Merton has been concerned with the idea that conforming behavior that is adaptive in some circumstances readily becomes maladaptive when circumstances change. One aspect of the analysis of "Bureaucratic Structure and Personality" illustrates this idea. For their effective operation, bureaucracies require their members to be punctual and methodical. However, characteristics which have positive consequences under one set of conditions can have negative consequences under other conditions. When temporal and procedural flexibility are required, excessive concern with temporal and formal rules makes for bureaucratic obsessiveness, red tape, and the development of bureaucratic virtuosity. Merton continually reminds us of the troubles created by too much of a good thing. In science, he observes, an excess of commitment to the norm of disinterestedness—to science for its own sake—has social consequences that make for public alienation from science. Similarly, overconformity to the norms requiring recognition of all participants in scientific research has made for increasingly large author-sets and, in some fields, great difficulty in identifying those responsible for the research who should be credited or tarred for it.

Self-reinforcing social processes. Among the self-reinforcing processes Merton has examined,[89] the accumulation of advantage has special interest for sociologists of science. Introduced in his 1942 essay on normative structure, the idea suggests that even evaluation which is impersonal and universalistic and perceived as fair can lead to the accumulation of differential advantage among certain segments of a population.[90] This idea has been taken up and elaborated by Crane,[91] the Coles, Zuckerman, and by Merton himself in the Matthew Effect. The process begins with an initial definition of some individuals as promising. These individuals are then given more resources and facilities for their work than those who are initially defined as less talented. Assuming that those who are thus advantaged are sufficiently competent to use the tools placed at their disposal effectively, it is hardly surprising that they often produce better research than others who are less advantaged. Once in operation, differences in performance between the "haves" and the "have nots" increase as the "haves" are, on universalistic grounds, consistently given more resources for their research and more recognition for it. This process and its components are difficult to study empirically because it is not evident how the performance effects of differential access to resources can be distinguished from effects attributable to differences in capacity. It is clear, however, that systems of evaluation operating in this fashion tend to be self-confirming. However effective they may in fact be in allocating resources to those who can best use them, their effectiveness cannot be judged by simple comparisons of performance between the advantaged and disadvantaged.

This brief review suggests how the sociology of science has drawn upon generic sociological ideas and how they have been adapted to its distinctive purposes. As special fields of inquiry develop, they typically elaborate ideas and techniques that are subject-specific. At the same time, the problems they take to be central as well as the concepts and procedures used to study these problems are often drawn from the larger discipline of which they are a part. How the relative proportions of these two aspects of cognitive structure, generic ideas and procedures, and those that are subject-specific, vary among types of specialties and over time is still another unanswered question in the cognitive and social evolution of science.

THE DEVELOPMENT
OF AN ORGANIZATIONAL INFRASTRUCTURE

New specialties, radical and conforming, require more than a developing cognitive identity for institutionalization. We do not yet know the extent to which cognitive development in special fields and the development of their organizational infrastructures are interdependent or how this interdependence varies at different stages of specialty development. It is clear, however, that mundane problems such as training students, arranging for jobs, obtaining funds for research, and finding outlets for publication have to be dealt with in routinized ways for specialties to develop.

Specialties can grow without provision for regular training if there are new recruits sufficiently interested and willing to teach themselves. However, chances for recruitment are greatly improved if undergraduate and graduate students have access to systematic course work in the special field. On this assumption, we surveyed the catalogues of the twenty-one departments of sociology receiving the highest rank in the 1969 American Council on Education study of the quality of graduate faculties[92] for courses being offered in the sociology of science in each of three academic years: 1960–61, 1964–65, and 1973–74. At the beginning of the sixties, Norman Kaplan, then at Cornell, offered the only course in the sociology of science in the United States. Four years later, six courses were offered by four departments. At the last reading, fourteen of the twenty-one ranking departments offered eighteen courses in the sociology of science.

Some implications of these data are obvious. Not only are there more students but there are also faculty members of leading departments willing to teach and presumably qualified by work in the field to do so. These signal that the specialty has acquired a certain legitimacy among sociologists—a legitimacy related to its compatibility with the fundamental theoretical and methodological commitments of most American sociologists. The same developments are also related to the historical fact that the take-off points in interest in the sociology of science coincided with a period of expansion and affluence in American science and in universities. The increased funds available in the 1960s led to substantial increases in the size of university faculties. Consequently, sociology departments were willing to hire people trained in new specialties such as the sociology of science. Growing interest among sociologists in science and increasing resources for it coincided. Both seem to be outcomes of the same underlying fact. Scientific development had become both a great national asset and a global problem.

Nonetheless, there still is little undergraduate teaching of the sociology of science. No general textbook has been published, Joseph Ben-David's *The Scientist's Role in Society*[93] being more monographic than didactic. In fact, few general introductory texts deal systematically with science.

RESEARCH SUPPORT

One of the distinctive features of American science is pluralism in funding. Consequently, information about who has gotten research money, how much, and for what purpose is scattered. The records of the National Science Foundation,[94] the principal source of support for work in sociology of science, indicate that a steady increase in funding paralleled growth in publications, dissertations, and recruitment. Less than one percent of NSF expenditures in sociology went to the sociology of science between 1957 and fiscal year 1964–65, 2.3 percent between 1965–66 and 1969–70, and 5.7 percent between 1970–71 and 1971–72. In this sixteen-year period, NSF grants to the sociology of science increased seven times compared to an increase of 1.75 times for sociology as a whole. Since sociological research is supported by multiple government agencies and by a variety of private foundations, NSF figures for the discipline underestimate total expenditures on sociological research. Nonetheless, whatever share of funds the sociology of science has received, it has been supported with increasing generosity. Since the NSF employs the procedure of peer review in allocating its resources, the increase in funds registers growing confidence among sociologists (and government administrators) that research in the sociology of science is worth doing.

FORMAL COMMUNICATION AND FORMAL ORGANIZATION

There is other evidence that the specialty was becoming interesting to sociologists and gaining a measure of legitimacy among them. An increasing number of the papers in the sociology of science appearing in sociology journals were published in the two principal journals in the field, the *American Sociological Review* and the *American Journal of Sociology*. Before 1957, too few papers were published to permit meaningful comparisons, but afterward things changed markedly. The number of papers published in the *ASR* and the *AJS* more than doubled from the 10 appearing between 1957 and 1965 to the 22 appearing between 1965 and 1972. During the same period, the average number of articles published in these journals remained roughly constant. Since the prime journals have by far the greatest circulation among sociologists, the specialty was clearly gaining visibility. This is of no small importance to young people interested in working in the specialty who want their papers to be read by sociological colleagues. That one could publish in one of the important journals in the field (and, as we have seen, have a position in a leading department) means that doing the sociology of science could now be a career as well as a labor of love.

Unlike other new and growing specialties, the sociology of science has not yet acquired its own journal. The willingness of the principal sociological journals to publish papers in the sociology of science, the limited size of the specialty, and the presence of functional alternatives in the form of other journals addressed to the wider audience of historians, philosophers, political scientists, and sociologists of science—*Minerva* (founded in 1962) and *Science Studies* (founded in 1970)—probably mean that a specialty journal will not be needed for some time to come.

Still another sign of its growing legitimacy among sociologists is the appearance of sociologists of science on the programs of the various national, regional and international meetings. Since the early 1960s almost every national meeting of the American Sociological Association has had a session devoted to the specialty and since 1966, there has been a Research Committee in the Sociology of Science in the International Sociological Association. Robert Merton's influence and efforts to build an organizational infrastructure are highly visible in this domain. Merton encouraged the scheduling of sessions at ASA meetings in the early 1960s by agreeing to chair them or to prepare papers, and was one of the chief organizers of the ISA Committee. But he does not find these activities congenial. He does not like to organize things or to run them. Unlike his teacher, George Sarton, who avidly devoted himself to establishing an elaborate organizational infrastructure for the history of science, Merton has set about most of these tasks reluctantly and has been far less effective than Sarton. But among physical and biological scientists his standing has helped him to call attention to the sociology of science in quarters such as the National Academy of Sciences and the National Science Foundation.

PROFESSIONAL IDENTITY

Patterns of consensus in citation practices noted so far are outcomes of un-self-conscious behavior of sociologists of science. For the specialty to develop a full-fledged cognitive and social identity, however, specialists, particularly influential ones, must self-consciously define themselves as having a common task. We use the citation data once again to see if a growing proportion of influentials specifically identify themselves as sociologists of science. Limiting our survey to two overlapping groups of cited authors, the thirty most often cited and the top ten percent of cited authors in successive five-year periods, we tabulated their self-described areas of specialization as they appeared in standard directories of the ASA and *American Men (and Women) of Science*.[95] Table 4 shows the sharp increase in the proportion of the thirty most influential authors who consider themselves sociologists of science. It rose from 10 percent in the early 1960s to 36 percent in the late sixties and to 40 percent in the seventies. While there are also significant increases in the extent of identification with the specialty among the top decile of influentials, the figures suggest that the major shift has occurred among the thirty most-cited authors. Such changes in self-definitions among influentials register a growing consolidation of the specialty and new commitment to it. This heightens its visibility and helps accord it legitimacy.

Table 4. SELF-DEFINITIONS OF INFLUENTIAL CONTRIBUTORS
TO THE SOCIOLOGY OF SCIENCE 1950–1972

Percentage Who Define Themselves as Sociologists of Science

Period	Top Thirty Authors			Top 10 Percent of All Cited Authors*		
	1st choice	1st and 2nd choice	(N)	1st choice	1st and 2nd choice	(N)
1950–54	7**	7**	(15)**	7	7	(15)
1955–59	7	10	(30)	7	9	(32)
1960–64	10	17	(30)	7	11	(57)
1965–69	36	40	(30)	16	18	(78)
1970–72	40	47	(30)	18	22	(90)

*The specialties of two authors on the 1955–59 list could not be identified along with one on the 1960–64 list, four on the 1965–69 list, and five on the 1970–72 list. For totals, see Table 1A.
**Only fifteen authors had more than a single citation in this period.

More than twenty years ago, in his Foreword to Bernard Barber's *Science and the Social Order*, Merton asked why "the sociology of science is still a largely unfulfilled promise rather than a highly developed special field of knowledge, cultivated jointly by social, physical and biological scientists?"[96] His inventory of neglect was dismaying indeed. Few courses were offered in the sociology of science and no standard textbook took notice of it; little empirical research was in process and what was being done was divorced from theory; publications were speculative, relying more on historical examples than on systematic historical evidence. Merton's own content analysis of Barber's bibliography of the field showed that half of all the referenced works were by "practicing physical and life scientists or by scientists who have turned to administration; more than a quarter by historians and philosophers of science and only the remaining fraction by sociologists."[97] In short, the field showed no signs then of impending institutionalization.

Things have changed. Taken together, the evidence we have examined suggests that the sociology of science is emerging as a special field of interest with a distinctive cognitive and professional identity. Having passed through an initial takeoff point in the middle 1960s, the field is still growing. It is too soon yet to tell how damaging hard times will be to further consolidation of the field. But it is not too soon to report that the sociological analysis of science is no longer the province of amateurs.

The next steps in studying the development of research specialties are reasonably clear. Continuing work will have to take account of the larger context of the growth of scientific knowledge and the relations between cognitive and social structures of science. Merton himself has now shifted his attention to developing an historical sociology of scientific knowledge. The growing emphasis among sociologists of science on the interplay of substantive and social aspects of science signals the beginnings of a new phase in the specialty.

NOTES

1. See Cornelis B. Van Niel, "The Microbe as a Whole," in S. A. Waksman, ed., *Perspectives in Microbiology* (New Brunswick, N.J.: Rutgers University Press, 1955), pp. 3–12; Gerald Holton, "Models for Understanding the Growth and Excellence of Scientific Research," in S. R. Graubard and G. Holton, eds., *Excellence and Leadership in a Democracy* (New York: Columbia University Press, 1962), pp. 94–131; D. R. Stoddart, "Growth and Structure of Geography," transactions and papers, Institute of British Geographers, 1967, no. 41, pp. 1–19; and J. S. Hey, *The Evolution of Radio Astronomy* (London: Paul Elek, 1973).

2. Robert K. Merton, "Priorities in Scientific Discovery," (1957) reprinted in *The Sociology of Science: Theoretical and Empirical Investigations,* ed. by Norman Storer (Chicago: University of Chicago Press, 1973), pp. 286–324. First published in 1957.

3. Arnold Thackray and Robert K. Merton, "On Discipline Building: The Paradoxes of George Sarton," *ISIS* 63 (1972): 473–95.

4. This is not to say, of course, that Merton was the first sociologist to study science and invention. Durkheim, Marx, Mannheim, Scheler, Znaniecki, Sorokin and others had addressed questions about the social determination of scientific knowledge long

before him as did W. F. Ogburn and Dorothy Thomas in their studies of the role of cultural accumulation in scientific and technical innovation. See their "Are Inventions Inevitable? A Note on Social Evolution," *Political Science Quarterly* 37 (1922): 83–98. Rather Merton took the lead in the systematic study of science as a social institution and provided models for how this might be extended. Sociologists of science generally agree that Merton established the field as an intellectual and social activity. For examples see Michael Mulkay, "Some Aspects of Cultural Growth in the Natural Sciences," *Social Research* 36 (1969): 22–53; Kenneth Downey, "Sociology and the Modern Scientific Revolution," *Sociological Quarterly* 8 (1967): 239–54; and Barry Barnes, ed., *Sociology of Science: Selected Readings* (Harmondsworth, Eng.: Penguin Books, 1972).

5. Joseph Ben-David, "Scientific Productivity and Academic Organization in Nine-teenth-Century Medicine," *American Sociological Review* 25 (1960): 828–43, and Joseph Ben-David and Awraham Zloczower, "Universities and Academic Systems in Modern Societies," *European Journal of Sociology* 3 (1962): 45–84; and Joseph Ben-David, *The Scientist's Role in Society: A Comparative Study* (Englewood Cliffs, N.J.: Prentice-Hall, 1971).

6. For examples of Merton's early interest in cognitive as well as social aspects of scientific knowledge, see his collaborative papers with Sorokin in Pitirim A. Sorokin, *Social and Cultural Dynamics,* 4 vols. (New York: American Book Co., 1937) II, pp. 125–80, 439–76; Chapters 7–11 of his *Science, Technology and Society in Seventeenth-Century England* (Bruges, Belgium: St. Catherine Press, 1938); reprinted with new Introduction (New York: Howard Fertig and Harper & Row, 1970). For recent examples of empirical and theoretical sociological studies of cognitive aspects of science, see Stephen Cole's paper in this volume (pp. 175–200) and John Law, "The Development of Specialties in Science: The Case of X-ray Protein Crystallography," *Science Studies* 3 (July 1973): 275–303; Michael J. Mulkay and David O. Edge, "Cognitive, Technical and Social Factors in the Growth of Radio Astronomy," *Social Science Information* 13 (1974): 25–61.

7. Thomas S. Kuhn, *The Structure of Scientific Revolutions* (Chicago: University of Chicago Press, 1962; new, enlarged edition, 1972).

8. Derek J. deS. Price, *Science Since Babylon* (New Haven: Yale University Press, 1961); *Little Science, Big Science* (New York: Columbia University Press, 1963); "Networks of Scientific Papers," *Science* 149 (1965): 510–15; and "Citation Measures of Hard Science and Soft Science, Technology and Non-Science," in Carnot E. Nelson and Donald K. Pollak, eds., *Communication Among Scientists and Engineers* (Lexington, Mass.: Heath, 1970); and Derek J. deS. Price and Donald Beaver, "Collaboration in an Invisible College," *American Psychologist* 21 (November 1966): 1011–18.

9. See for example, Karl R. Popper, *Logic of Scientific Discovery* (New York: Basic Books, 1959), a translation of *Logik der Forschung* (1935); *Conjectures and Refutations* (London: Routledge and Kegan Paul, 1963); *Objective Knowledge* (Oxford: Clarendon Press, 1972). Much of Imre Lakatos' seminal work is now being prepared for posthumous publication. His influential publications include "History of Science and Its Rational Reconstructs," in R. C. Buck and R. S. Cohen, eds., *Boston Studies in the Philosophy of Science* 8 (1971): 91–136, 174–82; "Falsification and the Methodology of Scientific Research Programmes," in I. Lakatos and A. Musgrave, eds., *Criticism and the Growth of Knowledge* (Cambridge: Cambridge University Press, 1970), pp. 91–195; "Popper on Demarcation and Induction" in the two-volume collection of critical essays on the Popperian tradition, P. A. Schilpp, ed., *The Philosophy of Karl Popper* (LaSalle, Ill.: Open Court,

1974), I, pp. 241–73; and the paper which he earmarked as best epitomizing his concept of "research programme," Imre Lakatos and Elie Zahar, "Why Did Copernicus's Programme Supersede Ptolemy's?" Presented at the Quincentenary Symposium on Copernicus of the British Society for the History of Science. London: January 5, 1973. Mimeod.

10. See in addition to Lakatos and Musgrave, *op. cit.*, Israel Scheffler, *Science and Subjectivity* (Minneapolis: Bobbs-Merrill, 1967) and Dudley Shapere, "The Structure of Scientific Revolutions," *Philosophical Review* 73 (1964): 383–94.

11. See Nicholas C. Mullins, "The Development of a Scientific Specialty," *Minerva* 10 (January 1972): 51–82, and "The Development of Specialties in Social Science: The Case of Ethnomethodology," *Science Studies* 3 (1973): 245–73; and Belver C. Griffith and Nicholas C. Mullins, "Coherent Social Groups in Scientific Change," *Science* 177 (September 15, 1972): 959–64.

12. Price, *Little Science, Big Science,* Chapter 3, "Invisible Colleges . . ."

13. Among those who have discussed the growth and change of scientific specialties are: Warren Hagstrom, *The Scientific Community* (New York: Basic Books, 1965); Joseph Ben-David and Randall Collins, "Social Factors in the Origins of a New Science: The Case of Psychology," *American Sociological Review* 31 (August 1966): 451–65; Charles S. Fisher, "The Death of a Mathematical Theory: A Study in the Sociology of Knowledge," *Archive for the History of Exact Sciences* 3 (1966): 137–59; Terry N. Clark, "Émile Durkheim and the Institutionalization of Sociology in the French University System," *European Journal of Sociology* 9 (1968): 37–91; Diana Crane, "Social Structure in a Group of Scientists: A Test of the 'Invisible College' Hypothesis," *American Sociological Review* 34 (1969): 335–52; Diana Crane, *Invisible Colleges* (Chicago: University of Chicago Press, 1972); Nicholas C. Mullins, "The Development of a Scientific Specialty," "The Development of Specialties in Social Science," and *Theories and Theory Groups in Contemporary American Sociology* (New York: Harper & Row, 1973); Griffith and Mullins, "Coherent Social Groups in Scientific Change"; M. J. Mulkay and D. O. Edge, "Cognitive, Technical and Social Factors"; John Law, "The Development of Specialties in Science"; Thackray and Merton, "On Discipline Building"; Griffith and Mullins, "Coherent Social Groups in Scientific Change," p. 960; Michael J. Apter, "Cybernetics: A Case Study of a Scientific Subject-Complex," in P. Halmos, ed., *The Sociological Review Monograph,* No. 18 (September 1972): 93–115.

14. Mullins, whose work *Theories and Theory Groups in Contemporary American Sociology, op. cit.,* is the most ambitious to date, proposes a four-stage model of specialty development. It emphasizes the structure of communication between specialty group members rather than the content of scientific innovations. The principal components are the roles of intellectual and social leaders, the role of programatic statements, the diffusion of group members from centers of activity to the periphery, and the thickening of communication nets with growth. The model involves problems of defining boundaries of groups and their orientations and requires revision to apply to cognitively dissident specialties. Further investigation is needed to specify the structural and intellectual conditions of movement from the "normal" to the "network" to the "cluster" and finally to the "specialty" stages of development. See also Paul D. Allison, "Social Aspects of Scientific Innovation: The Cases of Parapsychology," (Master's Thesis, University of Wisconsin, 1973).

15. For two pertinent case studies, see Aaron J. Ihde, "An Inquiry into the Origins of Hybrid Sciences: Astrophysics and Biochemistry," *Journal of Chemical Education*

46 (April 1969): 193–96, and Robert E. Kohler, "The Enzyme Theory and the Origin of Biochemistry," *ISIS* 64 (1973): 181–96.

16. Harriet Zuckerman and Robert K. Merton, "Age, Aging and Age Structure in Science," reprinted in Merton *The Sociology of Science*, pp. 497–559.

17. Charles S. Fisher, "The Death of a Mathematical Theory: A Study in the Sociology of Knowledge."

18. Matilda W. Riley, "Membership of the American Sociological Association, 1950–1959," *American Sociological Review* 25 (1960): 914–26.

19. Nico Stehr and Lyle E. Larson, "The Rise and Decline of Areas of Specialization," *American Sociologist* 7 (August 1972): 5.

20. *Ibid.*, p. 6.

21. Five colleagues in the sociology of science, Warren Hagstrom, Walter Hirsch, Norman Kaplan, Janice Lodahl, and Norman Storer, reviewed entries in the inventory, suggested additional titles, and identified sponsors of dissertations.

22. See Theodore F. Abel, "Analysis of Attempts to Establish Sociology as an Independent Science," doctoral dissertation, Columbia University, 1929; and Wilfred Binnewies, "A History and Evaluation of the Quantitative Trend in Sociological Analysis," doctoral dissertation, University of Nebraska, 1929.

23. Tabulated from *Doctoral Dissertations Accepted by American Universities* (Washington, D.C.: U.S. Office of Education), and *Earned Degrees Conferred* and *Doctoral Records File* (Washington, D.C.: National Research Council, National Academy of Sciences).

24. Calculated from Lindsey R. Harmon and Herbert Soldz, comps., *Doctorate Production in United States Universities, 1920–1962* (Washington, D.C.: National Research Council, National Academy of Sciences, 1963), no. 1142, Appendix 3, pp. 74–85.

25. Price, *Little Science, Big Science;* Crane, *Invisible Colleges;* Henry Menard, *Science, Growth and Change* (Cambridge, Mass.: Harvard University Press, 1971); and David L. Krantz, "Research Activity in 'Normal' and 'Anomalous' Areas," *Journal of the History of the Behavioral Sciences* 1 (January 1965): 39–41.

26. Holton has proposed several models for interpreting comparable data. See Chapter 12 in Gerald Holton, *Thematic Origins of Scientific Thought: Kepler to Einstein* (Cambridge, Mass.: Harvard University Press, 1973).

27. Six of these nine journals are wholly sociological: *American Sociological Review, American Journal of Sociology, Social Forces, Social Problems, Sociology of Education,* and the *British Journal of Sociology.* The others include *Minerva,* first published in 1962, which focuses on various aspects of the history, politics, philosophy, and sociology of science, the *American Behavioral Scientist,* which has devoted issues to problems in the sociology of science, and *Science,* the official publication of the American Association for the Advancement of Science, which has included papers on the sociology of science. A preliminary check of the very small number of papers published in other books or journals shows that their age and references do not differ systematically from those we have analyzed. Nevertheless, this sample underestimates growth in the literature since 1971, since it does not include newer journals such as *Science Studies* and *Research Policy.*

There is *prima facie* evidence that few papers were published before 1950. Bibliographies of work in the field compiled by sociologists show few entries before that date. Bernard Barber and Robert K. Merton, "Brief Bibliography for the Sociology of Science," *Proceedings,* American Academy of Arts and Sciences 80 (1952): 140–54; Norman Kaplan, "Science and Society: An Introduction," in Norman Kaplan, ed., *Science and Society* (Chicago: Rand-McNally and Co., 1965), pp. 1–8; and Bernard Barber and Walter Hirsch, eds., *The Sociology of Science* (New York: Free Press, 1962).

28. Of the total 195 papers, 165 were published in journals in print for the full twenty-four-year period under examination. Analysis of trends in publication is confined to these 165 papers. All papers were included that considered scientists and the institution of science from the sociological perspective. Papers on science were excluded if they were wholly historical or philosophical or if they focused on questions of science policy. Two lists of candidate papers were compiled independently and discrepancies between them resolved by two judges.

The citation index was constructed by compiling information on the citing authors, place and year of publication, and authors and dates of publications cited. Since citations and pairs of citations are the unit of analysis, multiauthored papers produced a multiplication of citations. When a publication is cited by collaborating authors, every author is counted as having been influenced by the cited publication. This gives extra weight to papers cited in empirical studies, since they are more often multiauthored. Self-citations were excluded. An additional procedure was used when Robert Merton was cited. In addition to registering his name and the year of the publication, its title and page number were recorded. This permitted a detailed content analysis of citations to Merton's work and enabled us to identify precisely which of his ideas had been influential.

29. The two journals established in the 1960s were excluded to avoid the biasing effects of increased publication outlets.

30. The slope of a scatterplot of publications over time approximates an exponential curve. We have not included the figure in the text, since it looks similar to other exponential growth curves. We suggest that in the future authors consider presenting temporal data on productivity in the form of a log-normal transformation. For illustrations of growth curves in science, see D. J. deS. Price, *Little Science, Big Science;* Diana Crane, *Invisible Colleges.*

31. Reprinted in Merton, *The Sociology of Science,* pp. 286–324. For observations on the significance of this paper, see Norman W. Storer, "Prefatory Note: The Reward-System of Science," *Ibid.,* pp. 281–85; and Joseph Ben-David, "The Sociology of Science," *New York Times Book Review,* November 11, 1973, p. 32.

The "Priorities" paper does not constitute a formal paradigm in the Mertonian or Kuhnian sense or a research program in the Lakatos sense. It does propose a general orientation for the sociological study of science and directs attention to certain central problems.

32. On the use of citations to measure scientific influence and significance, see M. M. Kessler, "The M.I.T. Technical Information Project," *Physics Today* 18 (March 1965): 28–36; Eugene Garfield, "Citation Indexing for Studying Science," *Nature* 227 (1970): 669–71; and "Citation Indexing Historico-Bibliography and the Sociology of Science," E. Davis and W. D. Sweeny, eds., *Proceedings of the Third International Congress of Medical Librarianship* (Amsterdam: Exerpta Medica, 1970), pp. 187–204; Jonathan R. Cole and Stephen Cole, "Measuring the Quality of Sociological Research: Problems in the Use of the Science Citation Index," *American Sociologist* 6 (February 1971): 23–29, and *Social Stratification in Science* (Chicago: University of Chicago Press, 1973).

33. For other examples, see S. Cole, "Scientific Reward Systems."

34. Cole and Cole, *Social Stratification in Science.*

35. For a recent collection of papers adopting this point of view, see Richard D. Whitley, ed., *Social Processes of Scientific Development* (London: Routledge & Kegan Paul, 1974), pp. 69–95; Mulkay, "Some Aspects of Cultural Growth in the

Natural Sciences"; S. B. Barnes and R. G. A. Dolby, "The Scientific Ethos: A Deviant Viewpoint," *European Journal of Sociology* 11, no. 1 (1970): 3–25; and Barnes, ed., *Sociology of Science.*

Since journal articles are subjected to refereeing, they may be less polemical than books. Content analysis of citations drawn exclusively from journals may underestimate "critical" and overestimate adulatory comments. In order to determine whether this is so, we examined citations to Merton and other authors in the indexes of several books recently published by Merton's critics. Using B. Barnes, ed., *Sociology of Science,* Leslie Sklair, *Organized Knowledge* (London: Hart-Davis, MacGibbon, 1973), and R. D. Whitley, *Social Processes of Scientific Development* as a crude sample, we found evidence consistent with our hypothesis. We also found fewer references to empirical literature.

36. Price, "Citation Measures of Hard Science and Soft Science, Technology and Non-Science"; see also Price, "Networks of Scientific Papers," and J. Margolis, "Citation Indexing and the Evaluation of Scientific Papers," *Science* 185 (March 1967): 1213–19.

37. See Zuckerman and Merton, "Age, Aging and Age Structure in Science," pp. 506 ff.

38. Stephen Cole, Jonathan R. Cole, and Lorraine Dietrich, "Measuring Consensus in Scientific Research Areas," in Y. Elkana, J. Lederberg, R. K. Merton, A. Thackray, and H. Zuckerman, eds., *Toward a Metric of Science: Thoughts Occasioned by the Advent of 'Science Indicators'* (New York: Wiley-Interscience, in press). For comparable data, see also Price, "Citation Measures of Hard and Soft Science."

39. Both reprinted in Merton, *The Sociology of Science.*

40. Zuckerman and Merton, "Age, Aging and Age Structure in Science," pp. 510–19.

41. Average ages for the extended periods 1950–64 and 1965–72 were calculated from the ages of the thirty most-cited authors at the midpoint of each of five periods.

42. For changing rates of collaboration in sociology, see Narsi Patel, "Quantitative and Collaborative Trends in American Sociological Research," *The American Sociologist* 7 (1972): 5–6.

43. Merton is, of course, heavily cited in the literature of general sociology and in its neighboring disciplines of anthropology and psychology. Recent studies of the impact of leading sociologists' work show that he is the most cited author in the current literature and is cited more often than all authors but Durkheim in current textbooks. Mark Oromaner, "The Most Cited Sociologists," *The American Sociologist* 3 (May 1968): 124–26; "The Structure of Influence in Contemporary Academic Sociology," *The American Sociologist* 7 (May 1970): 11–13; "Comparison of Influentials in Contemporary American and British Sociology," *British Journal of Sociology* 13 (1970): 324–32; Frank R. Westie, "Academic Expectations for Professional Immortality: A Study of Legitimation," *The American Sociologist* 8 (February 1973): 19–32. See also Howard M. Bahr, T. J. Johnson, and M. R. Seitz, "Influential Scholars and Works in the Sociology of Race and Minority Relations, 1944–68," *The American Sociologist* 8 (November 1971): 296–98; and William H. Swatos, Jr., and Priscilla L. Swatos, "Name Citations in Introductory Sociology Texts," *The American Sociologist* 9 (November 1974): 225–28.

44. Citation counts for individuals are omitted because the addition of journals other than those surveyed here would have changed the absolute numbers, if not the approximate relative positions. Moreover, we are less concerned with individual scores than with changing patterns of citation over time.

45. We note that just two authors (Barber and Merton) in the recent lists have also worked in the sociology of knowledge. To some extent, the sociology of science and of knowledge have developed independently. By way of illustration, a com-

pendium of recent work in the sociology of knowledge includes just one paper in the sociology of science and one in the sociology of sociology. The remaining twenty-five papers, classified as "Later Perspectives," contain no reference to any work in the sociology of science except the several in Merton's "Paradigm for the Sociology of Knowledge." See James E. Curtis and John W. Petras, eds., *The Sociology of Knowledge: A Reader* (New York: Praeger, 1970).

46. Kuhn's work on revolutions in science, Price's studies of patterns of scientific growth, Barber's comprehensive analysis of the institution of science, and Pelz's investigation of organizational climates of research have continued to be widely used since their publication.

47. Mullins, *Theories and Theory Groups in Contemporary American Sociology.*

48. The seven are: Bernard Barber, Stephen Cole, Barney Glaser, Alvin Gouldner, Norman Kaplan, Jonathan Cole, and Harriet Zuckerman. An eighth, Diana Crane, studied with Merton but did not do her doctoral work under his supervision.

49. For master-apprentice links among psychologists, see Joseph Ben-David and Randall Collins, "Social Factors in the Origins of a New Science: The Case of Psychology," *American Sociological Review* 31 (1966): 451–65; and among Nobel laureates, see Harriet Zuckerman, "Nobel Laureates in Science: Patterns of Productivity, Collaboration and Authorship," *American Sociological Review* 32 (1967): 391–403, and *Scientific Elites: Nobel Laureates in the United States* (Chicago: University of Chicago Press, 1975).

50. The Institute for Scientific Information, the organizational home of the Science Citation Index, is now undertaking different but related cluster analyses in order to identify groups of linked and frequently cited papers believed to presage the development of specialties. See Eugene Garfield, Morton V. Malin, and Henry Small, "Citation Data as Indicators of Scientific Activity" in Elkana *et al.,* *Toward a Metric of Science.*

51. Thackray and Merton, "On Discipline Building."

52. Oromaner, "The Structure of Influence in Contemporary Academic Sociology."

53. Merton, "Priorities in Scientific Discovery."

54. See P. E. Burton and R. W. Keebler, "'Half-life' of Some Scientific and Technical Literature," *American Documentation* 11 (1960): 18–22.

55. Merton, "Priorities in Scientific Discovery."

56. Robert K. Merton, "Singletons and Multiples in Scientific Discovery," in *Proceedings,* American Philosophical Society 105 (October 1961): 470–86; also in *The Sociology of Science,* pp. 343–70.

57. Merton, "The Matthew Effect," reprinted in *The Sociology of Science,* pp. 439–59.

58. Harriet Zuckerman and Robert K. Merton, "Patterns of Evaluation in Science: Institutionalization, Structure and Function of the Referee System," *Minerva* 9 (January 1971): 66–100; also in Merton, *The Sociology of Science,* pp. 460–96.

59. Robert K. Merton, "Insiders and Outsiders, A Chapter in the Sociology of Knowledge," *American Journal of Sociology* 78 (July 1972): 9–47. Reprinted in *The Sociology of Science,* pp. 99–136.

60. Allison, "Social Aspects of Scientific Innovation: The Case of Parapsychology."

61. Robert K. Merton, "The Normative Structure of Science," (1942) reprinted in *The Sociology of Science,* pp. 267–78. Ben-David has argued that Merton's analysis of the normative structure of science "gave a static and idealized picture of science as a social system and did not reveal how the system actually worked" ("The Sociology of Science," *New York Times Book Review,* p. 32). We would add that the later discussion of ambivalence in the norms ("The Ambivalence of Scientists,"

[1963] reprinted in *The Sociology of Science,* pp. 383–412) is not only sociologically instructive but also the point of departure for intriguing empirical studies of ambivalence by Ian Mitroff ("Norms and Counter-Norms in a Select Group of Apollo Moon Scientists: A Case Study of the Ambivalence of Scientists," *American Sociological Review* 38 [June 1974]: 579–95; and *The Subjective Side of Science: A Philosophical Inquiry into the Psychology of the Apollo Moon Scientists* [Amsterdam and San Francisco: Elsevier and Jossey-Bass, 1974]). The time has surely come for thorough empirical investigation of the distribution of norms among members of the scientific community and their conformity to them (see Marlan Blissett, *Politics in Science* [Boston: Little, Brown, 1972], for one effort) and for an end to speculation about whether scientists actually are conforming or deviant.

62. Until recently, the "Merton Thesis" has had greater influence on historians of science than any other part of his work. But the fact that Thomas Kuhn devotes practically one-third of his review of the "History of Science" in the *International Encyclopedia of the Social Sciences* (1968, 14: 74–83) to that thesis may say as much about what Kuhn finds interesting as about actual foci of attention in the field itself. Not surprisingly, Marxist historians of science find Merton's sociological analysis of science more congenial than do their colleagues doing traditional internalist history of science. The Marxists argue, however, that Merton does not confront the central issue of scientific knowledge as being "objective or value neutral." See Robert Young, "The Historiographic and Ideological Contexts of the Nineteenth-Century Debate on Man's Place in Nature," in M. Teich and R. Young, eds., *Changing Perspectives in the History of Science: Essays in Honour of Joseph Needham* (London: Heinemann, 1973), pp. 69–95.

63. Henry Guerlac, "History of Science: The Landmarks of the Literature," *The Times Literary Supplement,* April 26, 1974, p. 450.

64. I. Bernard Cohen, "Science, Technology and Society in Seventeenth-Century England," review, *Scientific American* 228 (1974): 117–20.

65. A. Rupert Hall, "History of Science: Microscopic Analyses and the General Picture," *The Times Literary Supplement,* April 26, 1974, pp. 437–38.

66. Charles C. Gillispie, "Mertonian Theses," *Science* 184 (May 10, 1974): 656–60.

67. Guerlac, "History of Science," p. 450. In the last fifteen years, a parallel concern with the history and the sociology of science has developed among some philosophers of science, especially Lakatos and Feyerabend. See R. N. Griere, "History and Philosophy of Science: Intimate Relationship or Marriage of Convenience," *British Journal for the Philosophy of Science* 24 (September 1973): 282–97.

68. Gillispie, "Mertonian Theses," p. 658.

69. *Ibid.,* p. 656.

70. John Murdoch, "Review of M. Witrow, *ISIS Cumulative Bibliography,*" *The British Journal for the Philosophy of Science* 25 (March 1974): 89–91.

71. Norman Kaplan, "The Norms of Citation Behavior: Prolegomenona to the Footnote," *American Documentation* 16 (July 1962): 179–84.

72. Stephen Cole, "Professional Standing and the Reception of Scientific Discoveries," *American Journal of Sociology* 76 (September 1970): 286–306.

73. Professor Kuhn has kindly given us permission to quote from his letters. Letter, June 1959.

74. Professor Merton has kindly given us access to his files of manuscripts and correspondence dealing with the sociology of science. Letter, 4 May 1961.

75. Letter, 13 December 1962.

76. Letter, 21 January 1963.

77. "Introduction" in Bernard Barber, ed., *L. J. Henderson, On the Social System*

173

(Chicago: University of Chicago Press, 1970), pp. 42–43; Mullins, *Theory and Theory Groups in Contemporary American Sociology.*

78. John Ziman, "Science Is Social," *The Listener* (August 18, 1960), p. 251.
79. On the process of obliteration by incorporation, see Robert K. Merton, *On Theoretical Sociology* (New York: Free Press, 1967), pp. 27–35.
80. Merton, "Social Structure and Anomie," in *STSS*, pp. 185–214.
81. Norman Storer, *The Social System of Science* (New York: Holt, Rinehart & Winston, 1966).
82. Jerry C. Gaston, *Originality and Competition in Science* (Chicago: University of Chicago Press, 1973).
83. Warren Hagstrom, *The Scientific Community* (New York: Basic Books, 1965), and "Competition in Science," *American Sociological Review* 39 (February 1974): 1–18.
84. Merton, "The Matthew Effect," in *The Sociology of Science.*
85. Robert K. Merton, "Manifest and Latent Functions," (1949) in *STSS*, pp. 73–138.
86. In the words of St. Matthew, "For unto everyone that hath shall be given, and he shall have abundance: but from him that hath not shall be taken away even that which he hath."
87. Herbert Menzel, "Scientific Communication: Five Themes from Social Research," *American Psychologist* 21 (1966): 999–1004.
88. Cole and Cole, *Social Stratification in Science,* pp. 113–15; and Zuckerman, "Nobel Laureates in Science," pp. 398–403.
89. Briefly introduced in Merton's 1942 paper on the ethos of science, the notion of "accumulation of advantage" and of disadvantage in systems of social stratification, which relates to the notions of the self-fulfilling prophecy and the Matthew Effect, has been developed in a series of investigations: Merton, *The Sociology of Science,* pp. 273, 416, 439–59, 497–559; Harriet Zuckerman, "Stratification in American Science," *Sociological Inquiry* 40 (Spring 1970): 235–57; Zuckerman and Merton, "Age, Aging and Age Structure in Science"; Cole and Cole, *Social Stratification in Science,* pp. 237–47; Paul D. Allison and John A. Stewart, "Productivity Differences Among Scientists: Evidence for Accumulative Advantage," *American Sociological Review* 39 (August 1974): 596–606; Zuckerman, *Scientific Elites,* Chapter 3.
90. Merton, "The Normative Structure of Science," in *The Sociology of Science.*
91. Diana Crane, "The Academic Marketplace Revisited: A Study of Faculty Mobility Using Cartter Ratings," *American Journal of Sociology* 75 (May 1970): 953–64.
92. K. D. Roose and Charles J. Andersen, *A Rating of Graduate Programs* (Washington, D.C.: American Council of Education, 1970). Although the ranks of some departments change slightly, the intercorrelations between readings taken in 1957, 1964, and 1969 are above 0.95. The twenty-one departments receiving the highest ratings granted 77 percent of all doctorates in sociology in 1968–69.
93. Ben-David, *The Scientist's Role in Society.*
94. These data were drawn from National Science Foundation, *Annual Reports,* fiscal years 1950–51 to 1971–72, and from its *Grants and Awards* series, first published in fiscal year 1963–64. Information for 1972–73 was generously provided by Dr. Donald Ploch of the National Science Foundation.
95. The self-designations of sociologists were tabulated but not those of information scientists, historians, or philosophers of science. These data refer only to the increasing tendency for sociologists to identify themselves as sociologists of science.
96. Robert K. Merton, "Foreword," in Bernard Barber, *Science and the Social Order* (Glencoe, Ill.: Free Press, 1952); also in *The Sociology of Science,* pp. 210–20.
97. *Ibid.,* p. 212.

174

The Growth of Scientific Knowledge

Theories of Deviance as a Case Study*

STEPHEN COLE

Robert K. Merton, in whose honor this essay is written, is probably best known for his theory of social structure and anomie (SS&A).[1] First published when Merton was twenty-eight years old, this theory has probably been more frequently cited and reprinted than any other paper in sociology. In undergraduate sociology courses it is still used as one of the finest examples of a sociological theory.

Until the late 1960s, SS&A was probably the dominant theory in the area of deviance. Recently, many sociologists have turned their attention to the symbolic interactionist-labeling perspective on deviance. The aim of this essay is not to criticize or analyze SS&A and the work that it generated but rather to understand its fate. What has been the role of the theory in the growth of knowledge in the field of deviance? How has the theory been used by both theoreticians and empirical researchers? Finally, has the theory been abandoned

* This essay represents the first report of an ongoing research program. Many people have helped in the formulation of the problem and the conducting of the research. I thank Lorraine Dietrich who has done all the programming and contributed many ideas to the analysis. Others who have contributed are Kenneth Bryson, Jonathan Cole, John Gagnon, Elizabeth Garber, Mark Sakitt, Hanan Selvin, Gerald Suttles, and Judith Tanur. This research was supported by a National Science Foundation grant to the Columbia Program in the Sociology of Science, NSF GS 33359 X1.

Stephen Cole is Professor of Sociology at the State University of New York at Stony Brook.

by sociologists doing deviance research, and if so, why? This essay is not primarily concerned with the substance of theories of deviance but with the sociology of science. The deviance literature is being used as a research site to explore the social processes through which knowledge grows and ideas change.

Until now, social scientists studying the development of science have been divided into two camps.[2] In one camp can be found historians of science who have conducted internal analyses of the filiation of ideas. In the work of the most eminent historians of science such as Sarton, Butterfield, and Koyré, little emphasis has been placed on the social organization of science and how such organization affected the growth of science. In the other camp are the sociologists of science who have concentrated on external analysis of the societies in which science has been conducted or the social organization of science itself. But the work of outstanding sociologists, such as Merton, Ben-David, Barber, and Hagstrom, has dealt only peripherally with the content of scientific ideas themselves. It was believed that sociological investigation could specify the conditions affecting the rate of scientific discovery and perhaps the foci of scientific attention but could tell us little about how the content of scientific ideas changed.[3] The sociologists seemed to agree with the historians that idea systems had their own internal dynamic and were ultimately guided by nature itself.

It is only in the last few years that sociologists have made a serious attempt to put the study of scientists and their institutions together with the study of their ideas. The first attempts to understand the growth of scientific knowledge from a sociological point of view were made by historians and scientists themselves.[4] The most important of these attempts has been Thomas Kuhn's book *The Structure of Scientific Revolutions.*[5] Kuhn has concluded that, ultimately, the process through which ideas change and develop can be understood only through sociological analysis. In this essay I shall outline some of the problems raised by Kuhn and then, using the field of deviance research as an example, illustrate how we might go about empirically investigating a few of these problems.[6]

PROBLEMS RAISED BY KUHN

PROGRESS IN SCIENCE

Prior to the 1950s most historians and philosophers of science described science as a body of knowledge approaching ever more closely "objective truth." There is one truth, one reality in nature, and the scientist aims to learn this truth. Science progresses because at each moment in time the currently held scientific theories are a better approximation to truth than past scientific theories. This does not mean that the past theories were necessarily wrong, but that they were incomplete or misstated in some detail. According to this view, it is unnecessary to conclude that Newton was wrong if you accept Einstein as being right. Newtonian theory was merely a special case of the new theory of relativity. In this view of scientific development, how is it determined whether one theory is superior to another? Both theories are compared with the known facts; the one that provides a closer fit with the data (nature) is clearly the better one.

Kuhn decisively rejects this view of science. Although he does not deny that a theory at T_2 is "better" than a theory at T_1, he does not use approximation to "truth" as a criterion in evaluating theories or paradigms.[7] In fact, the concept of "objective truth" plays no role in Kuhn's analysis. For Kuhn a new theory is a different rather than a better way of looking at reality. He points out that at the time when new theories are adopted they are usually inferior to the one they replace in ability to explain a wide range of empirical phenomena. In rejecting one theory for a new one, "there are losses as well as gains."[8] By this he means that there are some phenomena that the new theory will never explain as well as the old one. There are also some problems that can be more easily solved using an old theory than a new one. Thus, engineers find the assumptions of Newtonian mechanics more useful than those of quantum mechanics in solving some problems.

Kuhn also rejects the notion that science is cumulative in the sense that a new theory is an improvement on the one it replaces. "Einstein's theory can be accepted only with the recognition that Newton's was wrong."[9] Switches in theory or scientific revolutions lead scientists to research that is "not only incompatible but often actually incommensurable with that which has gone before."[10] The first respect, then, in which Kuhn's view of science breaks with what Suppe has called "The Received View" is that he rejects the notions that science is a body of knowledge increasingly approximating truth and that science is continuous in the sense that ideas at T_2 are merely improvements of ideas at T_1.[11]

RELATIONSHIP BETWEEN THEORY AND RESEARCH

The second respect in which Kuhn's view of science sharply differs from "The Received View" is in the perceived relationship between theory and research. Science was seen as being different from other idea systems in its dependence on empirical verification. Whereas which art style or philosophical theory was superior depended on values, which scientific theory was better could and should be determined by empirical evidence. The data will tell us which scientific theory is right. When negative evidence was discovered, the scientists had to abandon the theory. Until Polanyi and Kuhn, most philosophers and historians of science saw the decisions made by scientists on whether to accept or reject scientific theories as being primarily dependent on empirical evidence.[12]

Kuhn sees science as going through successive phases, which he calls "normal" and "revolutionary" science. Most of the time scientists are doing normal science. During this phase they accept, almost without question (or, as Popper calls it, "criticism"), the dominant scientific theories in their research area. *During normal science scientists will not reject theories because there is empirical evidence that the theory is unable to explain or that even suggests that the theory is wrong.* There is now substantial historical evidence to support this contention.

Kuhn gives several examples of theories maintained in the face of much counter-evidence or anomalies. Even the most important theories cannot explain all the known facts:

> During the sixty years after Newton's original computation, the predicted motion of the moon's perigee remained only half of that observed. As Europe's best mathematical physicists continued to wrestle unsuccessfully with the well known discrepancy, there were occasional proposals for a modification of Newton's inverse square law. But no one took these proposals very seriously, and in practice this patience with a major anomaly proved justified.[13]

In a work published prior to Kuhn's book, Polanyi gives many examples of how consensus is maintained by ignoring anomalies. For example, chemists continued to accept a theory after the discovery of facts that cast serious doubt on the theory's validity:

> The theory of electrolytic dissociation proposed in 1887 by Arrhenius assumed a chemical equilibrium between the dissociated and the undissociated forms of an electrolyte in solution. From the very start, the measurements showed that this was true only for weak electrolytes like acetic acid, but not for the very prominent group of strong electrolytes, like common salt or sulphuric acid. For more than thirty years the discrepancies were carefully measured and tabulated in textbooks, yet no one thought of calling in question the theory which they so flagrantly contradicted. Scientists were satisfied with speaking of the "anomalies of strong electrolytes," without doubting for a moment that their behavior was in fact governed by the law that they failed to obey.[14]

In a brilliant essay the historian of science Imre Lakatos sets out to criticize Kuhn and support the ideas of Popper. However, although he differs from Kuhn in some important respects, Lakatos' view of the relationship between theory and research seems to be at least as radical as Kuhn's. Lakatos too believes that theories are often not rejected in the face of negative evidence. He gives a hypothetical example illustrating this point:

> The story is about an imaginary case of planetary misbehaviour. A physicist of the pre-Einsteinian era takes Newton's mechanics and his law of gravitation (N), the accepted initial conditions, I, and calculates, with their help, the path of a newly discovered small planet, p. But the planet deviates from the calculated path. Does our Newtonian physicist consider that the deviation was forbidden by Newton's theory and therefore that, once established, it refutes the theory N? No. He suggests that there must be a hitherto unknown planet p' which perturbs the path of p. He calculates the mass, orbit, etc., of this hypothetical planet and then asks an experimental astronomer to test his hypothesis. The planet p' is so small that even the biggest available telescopes cannot possibly observe it: the experimental astronomer applies for a research grant to build yet a bigger one. In three years'

time the new telescope is ready. Were the unknown planet p' to be discovered, it would be hailed as a new victory of Newtonian science. But it is not. Does our scientist abandon Newton's theory and his idea of the perturbing planet? No. He suggests that a cloud of cosmic dust hides the planet from us. He calculates the location and properties of this cloud and asks for a research grant to send up a satellite to test his calculations. Were the satellite's instruments (possibly new ones, based on a little-tested theory) to record the existence of the conjectural cloud, the result would be hailed as an outstanding victory for Newtonian science. But the cloud is not found. Does our scientist abandon Newton's theory, together with the idea of the perturbing planet and the idea of the cloud which hides it? No. He suggests that there is some magnetic field in that region of the universe which disturbed the instruments of the satellite. A new satellite is sent up. Were the magnetic field to be found, Newtonians would celebrate a sensational victory. But it is not. Is this regarded as a refutation of Newtonian science? No. Either yet another ingenious auxiliary hypothesis is proposed or . . . the whole story is buried in the dusty volumes of periodicals and the story never mentioned again.*

* At least not until a new research programme supersedes Newton's programme which happens to explain this previously recalcitrant phenomenon. In this case, the phenomenon will be unearthed and enthroned as a "crucial experiment."[15]

Lakatos implies at the end of his hypothetical example that when evidence cannot be explained by the existing theory, the evidence is usually forgotten or ignored. Kuhn points out that during periods of normal science "fundamental novelties" are often suppressed because they are "necessarily subversive" of the commitments of scientists to the theory. When experiments fail to corroborate theory, scientists are supposed to abandon the theory, but what the scientists actually do is question their experimental methods and their abilities as scientists. Under most circumstances, they do not think that the theory may be wrong. It would be easy to misinterpret this position. Kuhn and Lakatos are, of course, not suggesting that a theory with *no* empirical support will be considered or maintained. No theory will be long maintained if there is little empirical support for it. There are, however, many theories that have some degree of empirical support. They are suggesting that, in choosing among two or more theories that have some empirical support, variables other than empirical evidence may become significant.

If scientists do not abandon theories when anomalous results are observed, how does science change and progress? Kuhn and Lakatos both agree that scientists will not abandon one theory until an alternate theory exists to take its place. But how and under what conditions will new theories emerge, given that scientists are committed to maintaining belief in the existing theory? To this crucial question, neither Kuhn nor Lakatos has a particularly convincing answer. Kuhn says that when an existing theory or paradigm is persistently unable to solve crucial problems or "puzzles" a crisis of confidence develops and scientists begin to look for new theories. When a crisis develops, "the profession can no longer evade anomalies that subvert the existing tradition of scientific practice—then begin the extraordinary investigations that lead the profession at last to a new set of commitments, a new basis for the practice of science."[16] The difficulty here is that it is unclear under what conditions anomalies will be ignored and when they will lead to a crisis. The answer Lakatos gives to this crucial question is not much better. He sees scientists as adhering to a theory or a research program as long as it is in a progressive phase, that is, leads to the discovery of new facts. When a research program loses its ability to produce new facts, it goes into a "degenerative" phase. Again, however, it is unclear as to the conditions under which scientists define failures in their research programs as temporary setbacks to be ignored or as the onset of a degenerative phase.

Kuhn and Lakatos agree that when a new theory does emerge it is not adopted on empirical grounds. Lakatos points out that it is not unusual for a theory to be abandoned for a new one, even when there is no empirical evidence at odds with the first theory. Kuhn concludes that "the competition between paradigms is not the sort of battle that can be resolved by proofs."[17] And later:

> Paradigm debates are not really about relative problem-solving ability, though for good reasons they are usually couched in those terms. Instead, the issue is which paradigm should in the future guide research on problems many of which neither competitor can yet claim to resolve completely. A decision between alternate ways of practicing science is called for, and in the circumstances that decision must be based less on past achievement than on future promise. The man who embraces a new paradigm at an early stage must often do so in defiance of the evidence provided by problem-solving.[18]

There are a large number of questions raised by the views of Kuhn and the recent work of many other historians and philosophers. Most of the data we have to help us answer these questions comes from analyses conducted by historians who have often reconstructed what happened in order to make it fit their preconceived view of how science should develop.[19] Clearly, we need a good deal more research, both of the qualitative case-study type conducted by Kuhn and Lakatos and of the systematic quantitative type done by sociologists. Below I shall outline some of the most important questions that must be answered.

1. *Science: Revolutionary or Evolutionary?* Kuhn hypothesizes that scientific development is continuous and cumulative only during periods of normal science. The change that occurs in a revolution from one paradigm to another, however, is discontinuous. This view has been challenged by Stephen Toulmin, who suggests that there are many more small revolutions than Kuhn's analysis would allow.[20] The gap between succeeding paradigms is not as great as described by Kuhn.

Because science leaves better records of its past than perhaps any other institution, we have the available data to examine the validity of Kuhn's theory. We are currently developing research techniques to systematically and quantitatively study change in scientific ideas over time. Suppose that we were to examine all the literature (or a good sample) published in a particular research area over a long period of time, say, forty years. To conduct this examination, we construct a historical citation index in which we list all the references made in all the papers in the population. After computerizing the index, we can produce a list of the most frequently cited works in each of the forty years.

In order to proceed further, we must make the assumption that the references listed in papers indicate roughly the intellectual influences on the author. We have some evidence to support this assumption. The most frequently cited scientists are also the ones most frequently mentioned by samples of scientists as having influenced their work.[21] Diana Crane compared citations made by samples of scientists with their statements of who had influenced their work. Both indicators yielded substantially the same results.[22]

With the aid of a knowledgeable historian of science, we can determine which of the most frequently cited works on our list were empirical pieces and which theoretical. The most frequently cited theoretical pieces represent the dominant theory in the research area at that point in time.[23] Now we can test the assumption of Kuhn that at any given time during normal science there is only one dominant theoretical orientation. By performing various types of cluster analysis, we can discover whether there is only one distinct theoretical orientation influencing scientists publishing papers in the area. If there is more than one, we can analyze the interrelations among them. Do adherents of any one orientation cite people working with others? Are these citations critical? Have we made an error and classified papers as being in one research area that in fact fall into another?[24] Assuming that we have not made any serious classification errors in selecting the population of papers and that Kuhn is correct, then we should find a heavy concentration of citations to the papers of the leading representatives of the dominant theory.

From one year to the next, we should find the same names appearing on the list of most-cited theoreticians. When a new name appears, by examining the citations in the new paper we should be able to trace its intellectual connection with the existing theoretical tradition. If we find this pattern occurring throughout the forty-year period, we conclude that no revolutions occur and that growth was cumulative and evolutionary. But what would we observe if a Kuhnian-type revolution were to occur? First, we should observe a crisis in which consensus breaks down. The proportion of citations received by the most frequently cited theoreticians should decline. More new names should appear on the list and the intellectual connections between the new papers and the tradition should be less clear. From this, a new consensus should emerge dominated by a new set of intellectual leaders. Furthermore, if there are frequent citations in the work of the new theoretical leaders to the work of the old tradition, we should be able to show that these are either critical or comparative in nature.

If we are able to identify a Kuhnian revolution, then we can also find out the characteristics of those scientists who are the originators of new theoretical orientations and what happens to adherents to the old tradition. Do some scientists switch their theoretical orientations or, as Planck suggested, do new theories triumph only through the aging of the adherents of the old theory? By examining historical citation networks, we can determine exactly when new theories emerge and the relationship between old and new theoretical traditions.

2. *The Role of Theory and Research.* If determining the extent to which science evolves through a revolutionary or an evolutionary process is the most important descriptive problem we face, understanding the relationship between theory and research is the most important analytic problem we face. A better understanding of the relationship between these two components of the scientific enterprise should lead us to the central problem: How do ideas change?

To study the relationship between theory and research, we are combining two analytic techniques, content analysis and in-depth interviewing. As an example, I shall briefly describe a case study I am currently doing in collaboration with a historian of science, Elizabeth Garber. We are studying the theory of superconductivity in solid-state physics for which Bardeen, Cooper, and Schrieffer were recently awarded the Nobel prize. The first part of our research consists of a content analysis of citations to the 1957 Bardeen, Cooper, Schrieffer (BCS) paper for which the Nobel prize was awarded. How is theory actually utilized by both theoreticians and experimentalists? For example, the traditional role of experiment is the testing of theory. The experimentalist compares the predictions of theory with nature. Is this what experimentalists actually do? We shall next do a content analysis of the citations appearing in the work of the theoreticians. How do they react to experimental evidence? What happens if the data do not support the predictions of their theory?

After tracing the interrelations between theory and experiment over a twenty-year period, we plan to interview some of the key participants in the field. Interviews are necessary because it is often difficult to determine what really happened by reading a scientific article. For example, if an experimentalist compares his findings with theoretical predictions, did he design the experiment to test the theory or is he using the theory as an explanatory device to interpret his data? And if experimentalists don't design studies to test theory, how do they decide what to do? What types of experimental evidence under what conditions lead theoreticians to modify their theory?

A sociological analysis of how intellectual work is actually done in science might show that here, as in other areas of human activity, there are differences between the manifest and latent functions served by various activities. For example, one of the manifest functions of theory is to explain, understand, and predict empirical phenomena. There can be no doubt that to some extent theory does serve this function. But *if Kuhn is right,* then we cannot explain the replacement of one theory by another simply by reference to the currently available empirical evidence.

Perhaps theories serve latent sociological functions, and when a particular theory no longer fulfills them there is pressure to replace it. This notion is implicit in the work of Kuhn when he describes the paradigm as presenting a series of puzzles for scientists to work on.[25] In their everyday activities scientists, both theoreticians and experimentalists, work on puzzles or problems suggested by current theory. When the scientific community has exhausted most of the puzzles provided by a given theory, there will be a necessity either to turn to new areas or to develop new theories. This may explain why some theories are abandoned even though little empirical evidence has put them in question. If a latent function of theory is to provide puzzles for scientists, then an important criterion to be employed in evaluating theories is the extent to which they stimulate additional scientific work.

One of the manifest functions of empirical investigation is to test the validity of theories (comparing the theory with empirical evidence). If Kuhn and Lakatos are correct, then we would have to conclude that much experimental work does not serve this function. What functions empirical research actually serves remain to be explicated. If it should turn out that indeed Kuhn and Lakatos are correct and that much empirical research is not done for the purpose of testing theory, we can then ask why working scientists have continued to believe that the primary function of experiment is to test theory. Perhaps such a belief is necessary for scientists to function.

To avoid oversimplification, it should be stated that there is already enough evidence to know that there are substantial differences in the ways in which different research areas have grown and changed. We may find that in some areas at some time theories *are* abandoned as a result of the accumulation of contrary empirical evidence and that in some areas most empirical research *is* designed to test theory.

Why do some specialties or fields seem to make more intellectual progress than others? Part of the answer to this question surely lies in the internal dynamics of ideas; but another part probably has to do with differences in the social organization of the various fields and specialties—differences that affect the relationship between theory and research. As an example, let us compare two specialties in physics: high-energy physics and solid-state physics. Impressionistically, it appears from discussions I have had with physicists and historians of physics that there is a closer relationship between theory and research in high-energy than in solid-state physics.[26] By this I mean simply that the experimental work in high-energy is more likely to be directed at significant theoretical problems than that done in solid-state.[27]

It would be easy to see the difference between these two specialties as a result of their respective intellectual states or of various differences between their respective practitioners. There are also, however, structural differences between the two fields which could explain the difference. There are only about five accelerators in the United States on which most high-energy experiments can be conducted. In order to get access to any of these, a scientist has to write a proposal that is then reviewed by a committee of his established colleagues. There is intense competition for access to the machine and many proposals are rejected. In order to increase the chances of having the proposal approved, the experimentalists try to show that their experiments will be theoretically relevant. Proposals that do not tie in the experiment directly with theory are not likely to be funded. Thus, it is not surprising that a high proportion of experimental work is theoretically relevant.

Solid-state physics does not generally require as expensive equipment and can be done at many more places than high-energy experiments. Money for this type of research can be obtained from many different sources. This means that the evaluation of proposals for research in solid-state physics is less centralized than it is in high-energy physics. Some agencies funding research in solid-state physics may employ referees who are not primarily concerned with theoretical questions. Also, in solid-state physics, once equipment is purchased and set up it can be used at will for any purpose the researcher desires. It is tempting to design experiments for which equipment is available rather than those that would be most theoretically relevant. For high-energy experiments, of course, equipment is never freely available in the same sense.

The general point is that the way in which funds are distributed and research proposals reviewed influences the intellectual development of the field. If this is true, we should be able to make some predictions about the type of research done in fields like sociology. In sociology, the nearest equivalent we have to the type of evaluation of proposals done in high-energy physics is the sociology section of the National Science Foundation. Proposals submitted by sociologists to NSF are evaluated by a committee of established sociologists who are concerned with the relevance of the research for general intellectual problems in the discipline. Contrast the NSF procedure with that employed, for example, by the National Institute of Mental Health. The NIMH is organized by substantive problems rather than by discipline. For example, a proposal from a sociologist to study the use of drugs will not be evaluated by a panel of sociologists but by an interdisciplinary panel of scientists interested in drug research. The panel might be made up of psychologists, pharmacologists, psychiatrists, and social workers. A sociologist may or may not be on the review panel. An interdisciplinary panel like this is not likely to be primarily concerned with the relevance of the proposed research for sociological theory. I would therefore hypothesize that research funded by the NSF will have a closer relationship to sociological theory than research funded by NIMH. In general, the way in which proposals are evaluated will influence the type of research done. Those fields in which evaluation is done by a central group of authorities will have more theoretically relevant research done than those fields where evaluation is de-centralized and done by people who are not authorities in the discipline.

THE CASE OF DEVIANCE RESEARCH

In order to carry out the research program outlined above, it is necessary to have at least an elementary familiarity with the substance of the scientific discipline being studied. I therefore decided to make the initial case study in an area that I have some substantive knowledge of—deviance research in sociology. In particular, I was interested in applying the techniques I am developing to study change in scientific ideas to an analysis of the fate of Merton's theory of social structure and anomie (SS&A).

It would be an error to see the theory of SS&A as a single paper. The theory is in fact a research program which Merton developed over a thirty-year period. If one compares the initial 1938 paper with a more recent statement such as the Merton essay in the Clinard collection, one can easily see that the theory has been added to and modified.[28] It has been a dynamic rather than a static theory, developing in response to its environment. A short summary of SS&A will serve my purpose.

Merton distinguishes between culture, the goals and values we are taught, and social structure, norms that regulate our behavior. In America there has long been a heavy emphasis on the goal of economic success. We are taught that everyone should strive for economic success, the sons and daughters of poor people as well as the sons and daughters of rich people. There is considerably less emphasis on the norms that regulate what types of behavior are legitimate in our attempts to achieve success. In any situation in which there is a heavy emphasis on the desired goal and much less emphasis on the norms regulating the means, these norms will tend to lose their regulating power. A state of anomie (normlessness) will develop. In America anomie exists because the norms regulating economic activity have lost their regulating power.

Merton uses the discrepancy between the goals and the norms regulating means in explaining deviant behavior. The majority of Americans are *conformists* who accept the dominant success goal and the institutionally prescribed means for attaining it. *Innovators* accept the goal but reject the means; they are most likely to come from the lower classes, where there is less access to legitimate means. *Ritualists* reject the goal, abandoning hope of success, but continue to adhere to the legitimate means. *Retreatists* reject both the goal and the means. Finally, *rebels* reject both goal and means while substituting new ones. Merton specifies the type of social conditions predisposing individuals to make one or another of these different adaptations. In summary, Merton is specifying how a certain type of society and location within that society generates motivation to commit deviant behavior. The theory posits that such motivation is generated by the disjunction between culturally prescribed aspirations and socially structured avenues for reaching these aspirations. Differential rates of deviance can be explained by location in a particular opportunity structure.

It is not my purpose in this essay to evaluate the theory of SS&A or to make evaluative statements about the way in which research and theory are conducted by sociologists. It is my purpose to describe and analyze what happened to the theory. The questions the research aims at answering are the following:

1) Have sociologists studying deviant behavior been divided up into distinctive theoretical schools of thought? My knowledge of the field led me to believe that we would find the following orientations: psychological-biological theories, differential association theories, symbolic interactionist-labeling theories, cultural theories, and structural theories. There can be no question that these theories exist, but are the sociologists doing research drawing predominantly from one orientation or are they eclectic?

185

2) Is the field organized more in terms of subject matter than theoretical orientation? There are several variables that we can use to characterize the work of people in the field of deviance. They are theoretical orientation, subject matter, qualitative-quantitative, theoretical-empirical. Theoretical orientation and subject matter would seem to be the two most important. There are two ideal-type models that would describe the intellectual organization of the field. The field might be organized into groups of people working with the same theoretical orientation but with different subject matters. Or the field might be organized into groups of people working on the same subject matter but employing a mix of theoretical orientations. Clearly, the "reality" is somewhere between these two ideal types. One purpose of the research was to discover the intellectual structure of deviance research over time.

3) At what points in time were which theoretical orientations dominant? I hypothesized that in the time period under consideration, 1950–73, psychological-biological theories and cultural theories were never very important. At the beginning of the period, differential association was probably the most influential orientation. The structural-functional theory, of which SS&A was the keystone, increased in popularity throughout the fifties and was the dominant orientation in the early sixties. In the mid-sixties, labeling theory (the symbolic interactionist approach to deviance) began to become more important and became the dominant orientation in the early seventies. To what extent is this impression of the intellectual orientation of the field correct?

4) What have been the intellectual connections among the adherents of the various theoretical orientations? Here we are concerned with the extent to which members of one school utilize work produced by members of other schools. If so, how do they utilize it—as a source of ideas for their own work or as a critical foil?

5) Finally, what is the relationship between theory and empirical research in the growth of knowledge in the field of deviance? In particular, how has the theory of SS&A been utilized by sociologists doing deviance research and how has the theory responded to its utilizers?

Before discussing the procedures I employed in analyzing the deviance literature, I shall discuss several generic problems in conducting quantitative analyses of the history of science.[29]

1. USING CITATIONS AS AN INDICATOR OF INFLUENCE

Although the use of citations to indicate the intellectual influences on an author will make it feasible to perform large scale quantitative analyses of the history of science, there are some serious drawbacks that must be considered. The drawbacks can be grouped into two categories: citation of works that have had little or no real influence on the author and failure to cite works which have had a significant influence on the author. The first drawback, over citation, creates primarily technical problems. It means that there will be a lot of "noise" in the data; included with the truly significant citations will be a mass of trivial or irrelevant citations. The researcher must be able to distinguish between these. Currently I am doing this by discarding from the data set all citations to authors who are not cited a minimum number of times during the period under consideration. This procedure is based upon the assumption that truly influential ideas will be more cited than relatively insignificant ideas.[30]

The second drawback, under citation, creates primarily conceptual problems. If one's data source is limited to citations, it is impossible to technically handle the problem of under citation. We must, however, consider how the type of data used may limit or even negate the conclusions drawn. First we must consider the difference between under citation and resistance to new ideas.[31] An idea that ultimately turns out to be important but is currently ignored is one which is being resisted or experiencing delayed recognition. If we are using citations to measure influence, we need not be concerned with resistance since a resisted idea has not yet had its influence. Under citation refers to ideas which have in fact already had an influence but are either not cited at all or are cited fewer times than their significance might merit.

Sometimes very well known work is implicitly cited in the text rather than explicitly cited in a reference. Thus, physicists might feel it unnecessary to give a precise reference to one of Einstein's papers when they are referring to an idea that he introduced. An example closer to home can be found in Merton's papers on SS&A. Perhaps the most significant influence on Merton's work was Durkheim's development of the concept of anomie. Yet in the 1957 version of SS&A, published in *Social Theory and Social Structure*, one will not find a reference to Durkheim in the footnotes. Durkheim is mentioned in the text. In the original version of SS&A (1938) there is one footnote to Durkheim; but it is to his *Rules of Sociological Method* rather than *Suicide*, where the concept of anomie was most fully developed. Thus some very significant work is not formally cited. This point is made well by Eugene Garfield, the founder of the *Science Citation Index:*

> ... an uncitedness *par excellence* [is] the uncitedness of distinction that comes to those whose work has become so well known (and presumably been previously so heavily cited) that one finds it at first tedious, then unnecessary, and finally actually gauche to cite such men at all.[32]

Another type of under citation occurs through what Merton has called "obliteration by incorporation."[33] Due to the cumulation of knowledge in science, important ideas are usually extended, improved, or in some way altered. Frequently, explicit reference is only made to the descendents rather than the parent. Sometimes an author will be unaware that his own ideas are heavily dependent upon a precursor. Looking only at explicit citations will cause us to ignore the significant influence of work that has been obliterated through incorporation. In our conclusions we must remember that the technique we have adopted causes us to ignore significant influences that are not formally cited. The extent to which this limitation of the technique distorts or invalidates results is a serious question for research.

2. SAMPLING

If we want to study the intellectual development of a research area over a period of time, it becomes virtually impossible to include all the literature in that area and related areas. We are, therefore, forced to sample. The procedure I have used is to include in the sample all articles in the research area published in several leading journals. This procedure automatically excludes from the analysis the great bulk of relevant literature. It excludes all references made in books, journals published in the United States other than the few most prestigious, all journals published in countries other than the United States, all small specialty journals, all applied journals, and so on. It is probable that if the literature appearing in these various sources were included, we would find patterns that differ in some ways and to some extent from that observed in the leading journals. Consider only the potential problems involved in excluding books from an analysis of the fate of SS&A. One of our concerns is the extent to which SS&A has been empirically tested. There can be little doubt that at least several major attempts at such a test have been published in books without the prior publication of papers in the journals included in our sample.[34] The extent to which citation patterns differ in various parts of the relevant literature must be studied.

3. DEFINING THE AREA OF ANALYSIS

The decision to limit the analysis to one research area undoubtedly will influence the results. Many important ideas have influence on many different research areas. If we were to trace the influence of a theory over time, it might lead us into many research areas and several scientific fields. Such a research design will substantially increase our knowledge of what happens to theories as they age. Certainly SS&A is a theory that has been utilized in many areas of sociology and in several other fields. It should be kept in mind that our research design will tell us nothing about the theory's influence in these other areas. In evaluating the results obtained in the research reported on below, we must consider the extent to which the actual procedures employed differ from the requirements of an ideal design.

EMPIRICAL ANALYSIS OF THE DEVIANCE LITERATURE

To study intellectual change in deviance research, we had to be able to define a sample of research published in the area. We decided to use as the sample all articles dealing with deviance that were published in the four leading sociology journals, *American Sociological Review, American Journal of Sociology, Social Forces,* and *Social Problems.* Articles in these journals were classified as to whether they dealt with deviance. Articles dealing with juvenile delinquency, criminology, white-collar crime, illegal use of drugs, sexual deviance, suicide, prisons and parole, mental illness, and the general topic of deviance were included. It was sometimes difficult to decide whether deviance

188

was the main concern of an author. For example, an article about prisons could sometimes be relevant for both the specialties of deviance and organizations. Where there was some doubt, we decided to include the article. The sample included a total of 533 articles: 51 published between 1950–54; 82 between 1955–59; 128 between 1960–64; 152 between 1965–69; and 120 between 1970–73.[35]

There can be no doubt that other analysts coding the articles in question might decide that we excluded some articles that should have been included and that we included others that should have been excluded. Given the size of the data set, however, it is unlikely that such errors have had much influence on the results obtained. Another criticism of this procedure might be that we excluded books and significant articles published in other journals. If the citation patterns in books and excluded articles were to diverge sharply from those in the sample, the results might be distorted. However, if they accurately reflect the work that was at the time most influential, then exclusion will not be a serious problem. For example, A. K. Cohen's *Delinquent Boys* was one of the most significant works produced in the period under consideration. This work was excluded from the sample, but the many citations to it were not.

The unit of analysis was the pair of citing author and cited author. Over 20,000 such pairs were examined. For the analysis presented in this essay, we excluded all citations made by authors other than the first author. Thus, if Smith and Jones wrote a paper in which they cited Merton, we counted this citation only once. This is to prevent more weight being given to citations made by authors of quantitative papers, which tend to be co-authored. Also, since the citation patterns of co-authors are exactly the same, it produces artificial homogeneity of citation patterns. We also obviously excluded self-citations. In addition, if one author cited another author more than once we counted this only as one citation. This is to prevent a few authors who might heavily cite a particular person from tipping the results. Thus, if we report that an author received ten citations, this means that he was cited by ten different people.[36]

We first examined the lists of the most frequently cited sociologists for each of the five periods (see Table 1). Merton was either the first or second most frequently cited author in all but the last period. The relative prominence of Merton declined slightly in the last period, 1970–73. A content analysis of all the citations made to Merton's work revealed that, although many different articles of his were cited, throughout the period under consideration two-thirds or more of the references to Merton were to some part of his work on social structure and anomie. [37]

Table 1. NUMBER OF CITATIONS RECEIVED BY
MOST FREQUENTLY CITED AUTHORS IN FIVE PERIODS

1950–54

Burgess EW	14	Dunham HW	7	Faris REL	5
Merton RK	8	Glueck S	6	Bronner AF	5
Sutherland EH	7	Glueck E	6	Healy W	5

189

Table 1. (continued)

Lindesmith AR	5	Clinard MB	4	Park RE	3
McKay HD	4	Harris DB	3	Shaw CR	3
Sellin T	4	Kallmann FJ	3	Sumner WG	3
Wirth L	4	Jenkins RL	3	Stouffer SA	3
Warner WL	4	Hughes EC	3	Sorokin P	3
Tappan PW	4	Duncan OD	3	Monachesi ED	3
Ohlin LE	4	Banay RS	3	Znaniecki F	3
Hollingshead AB	4	Redlich FC	3		
Hartung FE	4	Reckless WC	3		

1955–59

Parsons T	15	Lindesmith AR	6	Myers JK	4
Merton RK	15	Stouffer SA	6	Reckless WC	4
Cohen AK	14	Witmer HL	6	Porterfield AL	4
Dunham HW	13	Weinberg SK	6	Ohlin LE	4
Redlich FC	13	Lemert EM	6	Nye FI	4
Sutherland EH	13	Cavan RS	6	Sellin T	4
Hollingshead AB	13	Bales RF	6	Wirth L	4
Cressey DR	11	Adler LM	5	Wineman D	4
Faris REL	10	Burgess EW	5	Tappan PW	4
Glueck S	8	Srole L	5	Lazarsfeld PF	4
Durkheim E	8	Schuessler K	5	Korn R	4
Glueck E	7	Rose AM	5	Kluckhohn C	4
Short JF	7	Redl F	4	Henry AF	4
Shaw CR	7	Reiss AJ	4	Clinard MB	4
McKay HD	7	Riley JW	4	Clausen JA	4
McCorkle LW	7	Mannheim H	4	Bacon SD	4
Mills CW	6	Malzberg B	4	Davis K	4

1960–64

Merton RK	43	Lindesmith AR	12	Lemert EM	8
Cloward RA	35	Glaser D	11	Lazarsfeld PF	8
Cohen AK	32	Durkheim E	11	Kohn ML	8
Ohlin LE	29	Dunham HW	11	Bales RF	7
Hollingshead AB	25	Cumming E	10	Meier DL	7
Goffman E	23	Clausen JA	10	Williams RM	7
Cressey DR	22	Reiss AJ	10	Whyte WF	7
Short JF	22	Messinger SL	10	Bordua DJ	7
Redlich FC	21	McKay HD	9	Mead GH	7
Parsons T	19	Schrag C	9	Seeman M	7
Sutherland EH	17	Clemmer D	9	Rhodes AL	7
Nye FI	16	Cumming J	9	Porterfield AL	7
Sykes GM	15	Becker HS	9	Matza D	7
Reckless WC	13	Bell W	8	Dinitz S	7
Miller WB	13	Wheeler S	8	Hyman H	7
Shaw CR	13	Toby J	8	Glueck S	7
Srole L	12	Yablonsky L	8	Gurin G	7

1965–69

Merton RK	48	Reckless WC	14	Lipset SM	9
Cloward RA	39	Rhodes AL	14	Langner TS	9
Cohen AK	39	Dunham HW	14	Kleiner RJ	9
Short JF	39	Messinger SL	13	Kohn ML	9
Parsons T	30	Kitsuse JI	13	Clemmer D	9
Cressey DR	29	Homans GC	13	Dentler RA	9
Lemert EM	28	Strodtbeck FL	13	Glueck S	9
Ohlin LE	28	Wheeler S	12	Glueck E	9
Becker HS	26	Henry AF	12	Gold M	9
Hollingshead AB	24	Shaw CR	12	Goodman LA	8
Goffman E	24	Scheff TJ	12	Quinney R	8
Sutherland EH	24	Clark JP	12	Porterfield AL	8
Reiss AJ	23	Dinitz S	11	Korn R	8
Matza D	22	McKay HD	11	Lazarsfeld PF	8
Durkheim E	21	Lander B	10	Duncan OD	8
Sykes GM	21	Lindesmith AR	10	Blau PM	8
Nye FI	20	Blalock HM	10	Murray E	8
Clinard MB	18	Bordua DJ	10	Cavan RS	8
Miller WB	16	Ball JC	10	McCorkle LW	8
Redlich FC	16	Sellin T	10	Martin WT	8
Erikson KT	16	Wenninger EP	10	Skolnick JH	8
Glaser D	16	Wolfgang ME	10	Schuessler K	8
Srole L	15	Schrag C	9	Vinter RD	8
Gibbs JP	14	Faris REL	9	Yablonsky L	8
				Whyte WF	8

1970–73

Becker HS	26	Cloward RA	11	Langner TS	8
Lemert EM	24	Matza D	11	Skolnick JH	8
Gibbs JP	22	Cressey DR	11	Redlich FC	8
Scheff TJ	20	Rushing WA	11	Rosenberg M	8
Reiss AJ	19	Gove W	11	Scott RA	8
Piliavin T	18	Wheeler S	11	Chambliss WT	8
Cohen AK	16	Reckless WC	10	Davis K	8
Schur EM	16	Merton RK	10	Michael ST	7
Briar S	16	Clinard MB	10	Akers RL	7
Goffman E	16	Bell W	10	Hirschi T	7
Short JF	15	Bittner E	10	Blalock HM	7
Erikson KT	15	Duncan OD	10	Pasamanick B	7
Wolfgang ME	15	Szasz TS	9	Messinger SL	7
Kitsuse JI	15	Dinitz S	9	Simmons JL	7
Ohlin LE	14	Black DJ	9	Tannenbaum F	7
Parsons T	14	Empey LT	8	Toby J	7
Srole L	13	Clark JP	8	Blau PM	7
Hollingshead AB	13	Sellin T	8	Ball JC	7
Durkheim E	12	Strodtbeck FL	8	Douglas JD	7
Sutherland EH	12	Nye FI	8	Lofland J	7
				Hyman H	7
				Schuessler K	7

Our main concern was depicting the intellectual structure of the field of deviance during each time period. We are currently developing a set of techniques to analyze change in cognitive structure. These will include adaptations of numerical taxonomy, multidimensional scaling, and computer programs used by biologists to study evolution. Since none of these techniques has been developed to the point where they may be utilized, we decided to use factor analysis to empirically identify groups of authors who are cited by the same people. We used the most frequently cited authors in each period as the variables and the citing authors as the cases. Thus, for the first period, we asked whether each citing author cited Burgess, Merton, Sutherland, and so on. If they did, we scored that variable 1; if they did not cite the author, that variable was scored 0. We then computed a correlation matrix which showed the extent to which articles that cited each sociologist were likely to cite any of the others. A correlation of 1.0 between Merton and Burgess, for example, would mean that every author who cited Merton cited Burgess and every author who did not cite Merton also failed to cite Burgess.[38] This correlation matrix was used to conduct the factor analysis.

One of the major problems in conducting factor analysis is deciding how many factors to extract. Frequently, an arbitrary procedure is used whereby the analyst extracts additional factors until the proportion of additional variance explained by each new factor declines below some arbitrary point. We did not use this arbitrary technique. We began by rotating ten factors and then reduced the number rotated until we had the smallest number of factors that seemed to make substantive sense. This, of course, required substantive knowledge of the field.

Table 2. FACTORS ROTATED IN FIVE PERIODS

1950–54

Criminology Differential Association		Empirical Study of Delinquents		Social Class, Urbanism, Mental Illness	
Factor 1		Factor 2		Factor 3	
Merton RK	.57	Glueck S ⎱ Glueck E ⎰	.56	Faris REL	.68
Sutherland EH	.61			Wirth L	.54
Dunham HW	.44	Healy W	.63	Warner WL	.62
Lindesmith AR	.47	Bronner AF ⎱ McKay HD ⎰	.73	Hollingshead AB	.62
Sellin T	.69			Redlich FC	.44
Tappan PW	.79	Wirth L	.55	Park RE	.59
Clinard MB	.44	Harris DB	.55	Sorokin P	.64
Thomas WI ⎱ Znaniecki F ⎰	.48	Jenkins RL	.43		
		Shaw CR	.52		
		Thomas WI ⎱ Znaniecki F ⎰	.44		

192

1955–59

Correctional Institutions		Mental Illness		Anomie		Delinquency Differential Association	
Factor 1		Factor 2		Factor 3		Factor 4	
Parsons T	.58	Dunham HW	.55	Parsons T	.44	Dunham HW	.43
Glueck S ⎫	.44	Redlich FC ⎫		Merton RK	.51	Sutherland EH	.62
Glueck E ⎭		Hollingshead AB ⎭	.68	Durkheim E	.74	Cressey DR	.64
McCorkle LW	.73	Faris REL	.46	Short JF	.70	Shaw CR ⎫	.40
Weinberg SK	.58	Malzberg B	.50	Mills CW	.43	McKay HD ⎭	
Redl F	.62			Porterfield AL	.50	Lindesmith AR	.58
Mannheim H	.45			Lazarsfeld PF	.57	Lemert EM	.45
Ohlin LE	.67			Henry AF	.75	Cavan RS	.50
Wineman D	.62					Redl F	.56
Korn R	.78					Reiss AJ	.63
						Reckless WC	.71
						Wineman D	.56
						Clinard MB	.53

1960–64

Juvenile Delinquency		Correctional Institutions		Mental Illness		Anomie	
Factor 1		Factor 2		Factor 3		Factor 4	
Cloward RA	.53	Goffman E	.56	Hollingshead AB	.72	Merton RK	.55
Cohen AK	.63	Cressey DR	.56	Redlich FC	.77	Srole L	.65
Ohlin LE	.58	Sutherland EH	.48	Cumming E	.77	Durkheim E	.47
Short JF	.59	Sykes GM	.45	Clausen JA	.74	Bell W ⎫	.83
Nye FI	.67	Messinger SL	.72	Cumming J	.71	Meier DL ⎭	
Reckless WC	.45	Schrag C	.78	Kohn ML	.61	Williams RM	.59
Miller WB	.67	Clemmer D	.72	Gurin G	.49		
Reiss AJ	.55	Becker HS	.60				
Yablonsky L	.42	Wheeler S	.72				
Rhodes AL	.60						
Porterfield AL	.53						
Matza D	.55						
Dinitz S	.40						
Glueck S ⎫	.46						
Glueck E ⎭							

1965–69

Juvenile Delinquency		Correctional Institutions		Mental Illness	
Factor 1		Factor 2		Factor 3	
Cloward RA	.46	Cloward RA	.43	Hollingshead AB	.71
Cohen AK	.59	Cressey DR	.43	Redlich FC	.70
Short JF	.48	Sykes GM	.67	Srole L	.74
Ohlin LE	.58	Messinger SL	.52	Dunham HW	.58
Reiss AJ	.65	Wheeler S	.57	Faris REL	.54

Table 2. (continued)

Matza D	.41	Schrag C	.68	Langner TS	.75
Nye FI	.55	Clemmer D	.83	Kleiner RJ	.51
Miller WB	.62	Korn R	.63	Kohn ML	.61
Reckless WC	.50	McCorkle LW	.74		
Rhodes AL	.62	Vinter RD	.77		
Strodtbeck FL	.50				
Shaw CR	.71				
Clark JP	.56				
McKay HD	.74				
Lander B	.63				
Sellin T	.44				
Wenninger EP	.65				
Glueck S } Glueck E }	.41				

Anomie		*Symbolic* *Interaction Labeling*	
Factor 4		*Factor 5*	
Short JF	.46	Cressey DR	.42
Durkheim E	.52	Lemert EM	.59
Gibbs JP	.58	Becker HS	.68
Reckless WC	.41	Sutherland EH	.47
Henry AF	.61	Matza D	.45
Gold M	.51	Clinard MB	.45
Porterfield AL	.61	Erikson KT	.70
Martin WT	.63	Kitsuse JI	.51
		Lindesmith AR	.43
		Quinney R	.42

1970–73

Symbolic *Interaction* *Labeling*		*Juvenile* *Delinquency*		*Mental* *Illness*	
Factor 1		*Factor 2*		*Factor 3*	
Becker HS	.70	Cohen AK	.59	Hollingshead AB	.59
Lemert EM	.85	Short JF	.56	Redlich FC	.63
Gibbs JP	.44	Ohlin LE	.72	Langner TS	.60
Scheff TJ	.64	Sutherland EH	.47	Pasamanick B	.45
Schur EM	.66	Cloward RA	.78	Michael ST	.60
Goffman E	.48	Cressey DR	.62		
Erikson KT	.58	Matza D	.72		
Kitsuse JI	.72	Strodtbeck FL	.60		
Parsons T	.40	Nye FI	.47		
Gove W	.40	Empey LT	.43		
Bittner E	.44	Akers RL	.50		
Douglas JD	.42	Hirschi T	.50		
Lofland J	.55				
Simmons JL	.58				
Tannenbaum F	.53				

In Table 2 we present all of the sociologists (variables) in each of the factors rotated for each period. In determining whether a particular sociologist was part of a particular factor, we included every sociologist who had a loading of greater than .4. The higher the loading, the more likely the sociologist was to have a very distinctive group of citers. Sociologists cited by a wide range of people would probably not have a high loading on any particular factor.

INTELLECTUAL STRUCTURE IN EACH TIME PERIOD

1950–54. For this time period, the factor analysis was performed on the thirty-four sociologists who were cited in three or more papers. We rotated three factors for this period.[39] Factor 1 we have called "criminology differential association." This approach to criminology was dominated by E. H. Sutherland, who developed the theory of differential association. Sutherland made four significant contributions to the area. The first and the one for which he is best known was the theory of differential association. The second was the research he conducted and sponsored on white-collar crime. This was the main concern of his student Cressey. His third contribution was an early emphasis on the symbolic interactionist approach to deviance which he made in early versions of his famous text, *Principles of Criminology*. Finally, he devoted a good deal of time to combating psychologistic approaches to deviance, such as those utilized by several people in Factor 2. Also included in Factor 1 are Lindesmith, a colleague of Sutherland's at Indiana and an early symbolic interactionist. Lindesmith and Dunham co-authored papers on psychological influences on crime. Clinard (who was influenced by Sutherland) as well as the classical criminologists Sellin and Tappan also appear in this factor. Thomas and Znaniecki appear here, as their book *The Polish Peasant* was frequently cited for exemplary material.

How do we explain the fact that Merton appears in Factor 1 with a group of people with whom he had intellectually very little in common? If we look at the list of most-cited people in the first period (Table 1), we can see that during this period Merton was an intellectual isolate in the field of deviance as it was then constituted. There are virtually no other structural-functional analysts in the group. This is not surprising, as structural-functional analysis did not come into its own as an orientation until the 1950s.[40]

We must also realize that the procedure we are employing reflects what was intellectually dominant at least several years prior to the period under consideration. This is because we are not looking at the publication dates of important contributions but at the dates when they are cited. Before this can happen, an important piece must be published, diffused, utilized, and the works in which it is utilized must be put in print. Thus, the factors in the first period represent the type of orientation that was dominant in deviance in the 1940s.

Thus, although Merton was the second most frequently cited sociologist in the period, his work had not yet made a major impact on the field. He was cited by people who were still primarily doing the type of work done by Sutherland and Sellin. The content analysis of the citations to Merton's work enables us to specify the ways in which it was utilized in this first period. In four of the articles citing Merton, his work was cited as supporting the author's own idea or as a legitimation of the author's own ideas or interpretations. In two of these four articles, work other than SS&A was cited. One cited Merton's paper on unanticipated consequences of purposive social action and another his chapter on the bearing of theory on research. In one other article Merton's ideas on reference groups were casually referred to as part of the relevant literature. In an article about a nineteenth-century Polish community, SS&A is used as an interpretative device in an ex post facto fashion.[41] In another article S. Kobrin utilizes SS&A in developing his own theory, and in another article SS&A is used in formulating the research problem.[42] Thus, although by this time Merton had established himself as a prestigious theoretician, the theory of SS&A had had very little impact on deviance research being published in the four leading sociology journals. If we had merely looked at the total number of times Merton was cited without having conducted both the factor analysis and the content analysis, we might have been misled as to the significance of SS&A during this period.

Factor 2 in the first period contains sociologists who conducted empirical studies of juvenile delinquents. Typical was W. Healy, whose detailed quantitative analyses led him to list 170 different causes of delinquency. These researchers were interested in psychological, physiological, and ecological influences on delinquency.[43] What they have in common is the empirical investigation of groups of individual delinquents. Sociologists in Factor 1 were more theoretically concerned and more interested in adult criminal behavior. The sociologists in this factor were more psychologistic in their orientation.

Factor 3 contains sociologists who studied the role of both social class and urbanism in influencing mental illness and other forms of deviance. The major influence here was the work of Hollingshead and Redlich on social class and mental illness. Work coming out of this tradition continued to be a major influence throughout the period under consideration.[44]

Before completing the analysis of the first period, we should note that E. W. Burgess, the man who received the most citations, does not appear in any of the factors. This means that the work of Burgess was no more likely to be cited by one group than another; to put it more positively, that people throughout the field were equally likely to find his work useful. When we rotated four factors instead of three, Burgess appeared in a factor with Ohlin and Duncan, who had co-authored an article entitled "The Efficiency of Prediction in Criminology."[45] Burgess was also concerned with prediction. When five factors were rotated, Burgess, Ohlin, and Duncan appear in Factor 2 with the other sociologists doing empirical analysis.

1955–59. For this time period, the factor analysis was performed on fifty-one sociologists cited in four or more papers. Four factors were rotated. Factor 2 is the easiest to interpret. It contains sociologists who studied mental illness and is dominated by the collaborative efforts of Hollingshead and Redlich,

Faris and Dunham. Malzberg also wrote on mental illness.[46] Most of the people in the first factor wrote on penal institutions and correctional facilities for juveniles. McCorkle and Korn co-authored a book entitled *Criminology and Penology;* Redl and Wineman co-authored a book entitled *Children Who Hate,* based on their analysis of boys in a correctional institution; Mannheim studied British correctional institutions; and Ohlin wrote on parole. The work of Parsons was apparently utilized by some of the same authors who cited people in this "correctional institution" factor. A content analysis of the citations to Parsons would have been useful in gaining greater insight into this group. Do they cluster together merely because of interest in a common topic or were there common theoretical concerns among the authors citing the sociologists in Factor 1?

Factor 4 is an intellectual descendant of the criminology differential association factor in the first period. It is still dominated by sociologists influenced by the theoretical orientation of Sutherland, but the emphasis is beginning to switch from adult criminal behavior to juvenile delinquency. Shaw, McKay, Cavan, Redl, Wineman, Reiss, and Reckless all studied juvenile delinquents. It also contains some people working out of the symbolic interactionist orientation (Lemert and Lindesmith).

Merton appears in Factor 3 along with Parsons, Durkheim, and Short and Henry—all of whom employed the concept of anomie in their work.[47] Lazarsfeld was cited for his methodological contributions to the work that employed anomie theory. Again, an analysis of the ways in which Merton was cited during this period is useful in understanding the role that SS&A was playing. Five of the fifteen articles in which Merton was cited referred to work other than SS&A. It is a tribute to the wide influence of Merton that each of the five cited different contributions of Merton. The other ten articles cited various versions of SS&A. Three articles use SS&A to legitimate and support the ideas of the authors, and two others simply refer to it as part of the relevant literature. But two articles, those by Cloward and by Dubin, employ the theory in either developing further theory or extending the theory of SS&A.[48] The empirical article by Glaser and Rice uses SS&A as a major interpretative device, and articles by Powell and by Dohrenwend define and develop the concept of anomie.[49]

In the second period anomie theory had emerged as a distinctive orientation to the study of deviance. The theory of SS&A was further developed and extended, but at least in the four major journals there still were relatively few empirical studies aimed at testing it or in which it was utilized as an interpretative device.

It was during this period that A. K. Cohen published *Delinquent Boys.* Although Cohen has expressed disagreement with parts of anomie theory, he drew extensively on SS&A in developing his own theory. Cohen is the third most frequently cited author in this period, and was cited by the same people who cited the sociologists in factors 1, 3, and 4. It was also during this period that Richard Cloward published his major extension of SS&A by introducing the notion that access to illegitimate means as well as legitimate means were socially structured.[50]

1960–64. For this period, the factor analysis was performed on fifty-one sociologists who were cited in seven or more papers. Four factors were rotated. Once again we find a factor (3) made up of people who wrote on mental illness. To Hollingshead and Redlich were added work by E. and J. Cumming, J. Clausen, M. Kohn, and G. Gurin. Factor 1 is an eclectic group doing work on juvenile delinquency. Everyone in the factor published significant work on juvenile delinquency, but there is no coherent intellectual orientation. Thus, the factor contains Cohen and Cloward-Ohlin who made extensive use of SS&A, Miller who employed a cultural theory of delinquency, Matza who had a "normative drift" theory, the Gluecks who had a physiological theory of delinquency, and several people who did empirical research employing an eclectic group of theories (for example, Short, Nye, Reiss, and Rhodes). Although Merton did not receive a high enough loading to be included in this factor, he is cited by some of the same people who cite the sociologists listed in Factor 1.

Factor 2 is made up predominantly of people who studied prisons. These include Sykes, Messinger, Schrag, Clemmer, and Wheeler. Theoretically, this work was influenced by Sutherland, Goffman, and Becker. Goffman and Becker have been leading proponents of the symbolic interactionist–labeling orientation to deviance. It is not surprising that they appear in the same factor with Sutherland and Cressey. As we pointed out above, Sutherland was one of the first sociologists to employ the symbolic interactionist perspective in analyzing deviant behavior. The location of these people in the same group also indicates that the same types of sociologists who were sympathetic to the theory of differential association were beginning to utilize theory developed by symbolic interactionists. This may in part be a result of the fact that both theories had strongholds in the same institutions in the Midwest and West.

The anomie factor, which emerged in the second period, continues here. Besides Merton and Durkheim, the work of Srole, Bell-Meier, and Williams falls into this group. At the same time that deviance itself was becoming a more popular specialty, the ideas of Merton were increasing in significance. Not only did Merton receive the largest number of citations, but next on the list was the work of Cloward-Ohlin and Cohen, all of whom made extensive use of SS&A in their own work.

In what ways was the work of Merton being utilized during this period? Thirteen of the 43 articles citing Merton referred to work other than SS&A. Twenty-five of the 43 articles were quantitative. In 7 articles, Merton's work was cited to legitimate or support the ideas of the author, and in 9 articles Merton's work was cited as part of the relevant literature. However, in 7 articles SS&A was used in interpreting the results of the study; in 7 articles it was used in formulating the research problem; 6 articles employed concepts from SS&A; and 3 articles reported attempts to test either SS&A or a derivative theory. One article was critical of SS&A. We may conclude that during this period SS&A and derivative theories developed by Cloward-Ohlin and Cohen began to play a major role in guiding empirical research. At the same time, it is clear that subject matter was more important than theoretical orientation in determining the intellectual structure of the field. Juvenile delinquency, prisons, and mental illness were the main topics studied. Especially for the most popular topic, juvenile delinquency, it is evident that authors drew on work from several different theoretical orientations. Theoretical eclecticism prevailed.

1965–69. For this period, the factor analysis was performed on seventy-three sociologists who were cited in eight or more papers. Five factors were rotated. There is direct continuity between the third period and this period. Four of the five factors are essentially similar to the four factors rotated in the last period. Again, we find a separate group of people who have done work on mental illness. In addition to Hollingshead-Redlich and Dunham-Faris, this group contains Srole, Langner, Kleiner, and Kohn. Whereas in the last period Srole was being cited predominantly for his development of the "anomia" scale, here he is being cited for his work on the study of mental health in midtown Manhattan.[51]

Factor 1 for this period contains almost all the same people who were in Factor 1 in the previous period. Again, this is an eclectic juvenile delinquency group dominated by Cloward-Ohlin, Cohen, and Short. Many of these sociologists are now being cited for empirical studies that depended heavily on guidance from SS&A and the derivative theories. These would include Short, Nye, Reiss, Rhodes, Strodtbeck, Clark, Lander, and Wenninger. Factor 2 consists of a group of sociologists who studied prisons. Here Cloward is being cited for his doctoral work on prisons. McCorkle and Vinter also published works dealing with prisons.

The anomie factor (4) is still present, but this time contains Gibbs and Martin, who are being cited for their book *Status Integration and Suicide.* Merton is no longer included in this factor nor in any other. During this period Merton's work was so widely cited that he did not fall into any distinctive cluster. Of the 48 articles in which Merton was cited, 12 referred to work other than SS&A. Thirty-two of the articles in which Merton was cited contained quantitative data. In 3 articles Merton's work was used to legitimate the ideas of the author, and in 14 his work was cited as part of the relevant literature. Two articles attempted to develop or extend the theory, 10 used the theory in interpreting the results of the study, 8 used the theory in formulating the research problem, 3 employed concepts developed by Merton, and 3 presented data from studies designed to test derivative theories. This time 5 articles were critical of SS&A, indicating that the theory was beginning to be questioned at the same time as it was of central importance in many empirical studies.

In Factor 5 we have for the first time a group that can be identified as clearly having a symbolic interactionist orientation. Becker and Lemert, who along with Goffman have been the theoretical leaders of this orientation, appear here. Goffman received a loading of .34 on this factor. Included in this group also are the leaders of the differential association approach: Sutherland, Cressey, Clinard, and Lindesmith. When ten factors were rotated, these four along with Matza and Glaser formed their own group. The mixture of differential association criminologists along with symbolic interactionists confirms our earlier hypothesis that the same people who had utilized the work of the former were now utilizing the work of the latter.

There can be little doubt that in this period the theory of SS&A played a major role in deviance research. Not only was Merton the most frequently cited sociologist during this period, but books by Cloward-Ohlin and Cohen that drew heavily from SS&A were the most important works cited by the large group of delinquency researchers. To the extent that there was any dominant theoretical orientation it would have to be that represented by SS&A and derivative theories.

1970–73. For these last four years, we performed the factor analysis on 62 sociologists cited in seven or more papers. Three factors were rotated. The distribution of citations (see Table 1) shows two symbolic interactionists, Becker and Lemert, receiving the most citations. The factor analysis offers supporting evidence for the hypothesis that this has now become the dominant orientation in the deviance research being published by the four leading American journals.

The first factor is dominated by labeling theoreticians. This grouping is in fact the one which comes the closest to being organized around a theoretical perspective rather than subject matter. Most of the sociologists appearing in this factor employ the same perspective, although they apply it to different subject matters. Thus, for example, Becker has written on drug use, Scheff and Goffman on mental illness, and Kitsuse on juvenile delinquency.

It is of interest to note that Parsons appears in the symbolic interactionist group. This is probably because in *The Social System* Parsons considered the significance of the reactions of others in the development of deviance. Merton also received a relatively high loading on this factor. This is not primarily because some labeling theorists refer to SS&A as a contrasting approach; rather, it is because Merton's article "The Self-Fulfilling Prophecy" lays out a set of ideas that is substantially similar to those employed by many labeling theorists and has been so recognized by them.

Factor 2 is still an eclectic group of people who studied juvenile delinquency. Again, there is no common theoretical orientation among the members. If they have anything in common, it is that they have conducted quantitative empirical research on delinquency or have put forth theories that were utilized in such research. Factor 3 is the mental illness group, which has been stable throughout the period under consideration. This time, in addition to Hollingshead, it contains Langner, who co-authored a book with Michael on mental illness, and Pasamanick, who published articles on mental illness.

There are several pieces of evidence for the decline in significance of the anomie approach to deviance. The least significant of these is the decline in citation to Merton himself. Although Merton is no longer the first or second most cited author, he is still frequently cited. There is, however, no longer a distinctive anomie factor. Even when we rotated more than three factors we did not find a distinctive anomie group. Also, when we examine the make-up of the juvenile delinquency factor we can see that it is no longer as dominated by anomie theoreticians as it was in the two preceding periods.

One advantage of doing a case study of a research area that one has some substantive knowledge of is that you can spot points where data systematically collected generate questionable conclusions. The procedures that we have followed have led to the conclusion that SS&A has declined in significance in the last period. Yet there is a good deal of evidence that SS&A remains a very important theory. As I have several times pointed out, I have included in the sample only articles published in four leading American journals. In the last period SS&A was cited in these journals less than was the work of leading labeling theorists. Yet when, for example, we look up citations to Merton's work on deviance in the 1973 volume of the *Social Science Citation Index* (SSCI), we see that in this one year it has been cited approximately sixty times.[52] This is just about the same number of citations that the deviance work of Becker and Lemert received. Thus, although Merton is cited less frequently than Becker and Lemert in the four leading journals, his deviance work is cited as frequently as theirs when we consider all the journals included in the SSCI.

Consider some additional evidence on the continued interest in SS&A. This article has been reprinted many times and the rate at which it has been reprinted has increased in recent years rather than declined. The theory has been discussed in scores of introductory textbooks and continues to be discussed in virtually all the introductory textbooks published in the last few years. The theory is frequently discussed in both American and European symposiums on deviance. In short, the theory has anything but disappeared.

How can we explain the decline in citation to SS&A in the four leading journals at the same time that the theory continues to receive heavy attention in other places? Perhaps we must think of the various stages that a theory goes through from the time that it is presented until the time it is either abandoned or obliterated through incorporation. When SS&A was first published it may have experienced delayed utilization; later, it became the leading theory guiding work at the research front in deviance. Now its significance at the research front of deviance is perhaps declining. But its significance at the research front of other areas may be increasing, and as an exemplar or paradigm of sociological theory it may continue to be reprinted in anthologies and cited in introductory texts for years to come. In short, we must not assume that the life of a theory is unidimensional. A full understanding of the roles played by a theory would consider the full range of uses a theory is put to and the stages through which it progresses.[53]

COGNITIVE STRUCTURE OF DEVIANCE RESEARCH

In Figure 1 we present a schematic overview of the intellectual structure of the field of deviance between 1950 and 1973. In the early period differential association appears to have been the dominant theoretical orientation. In the 1960s

Figure 1. INTELLECTUAL STRUCTURE OF DEVIANCE, 1950–1973*

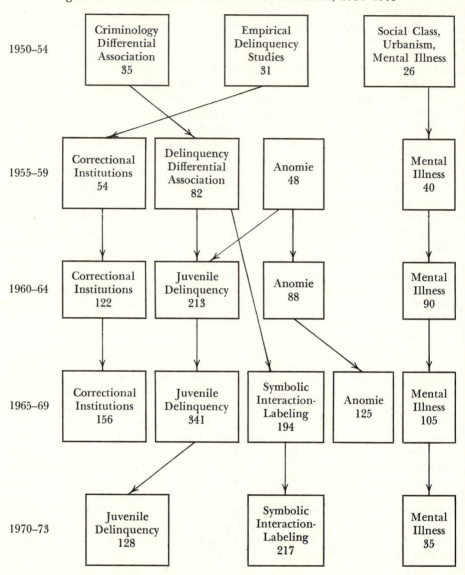

* Numbers in the boxes equal the total number of citations received by sociologists in each factor. The arrows indicate hypothesized direct influences of groups of researchers on their successors.

anomie theory became dominant, although differential association remained important. And, finally, in the last few years the symbolic interactionist approach has become increasingly important.

In general, subject matter seems to have been a more significant differentiator than theoretical orientation. Throughout the period there was a distinctive group studying mental illness with a special emphasis on the influence of social class and urban living on mental health. Hollingshead appeared in the mental illness group in all five periods. In three of the five periods, there were groups of sociologists who studied prisons and other correctional institutions. This group contained many who might be considered "old-fashioned" criminologists but was more held together by a common research site than by common theoretical interests. In all five periods there was an eclectic group of sociologists who studied juvenile delinquency. In fact, juvenile delinquency was the major research topic in the twenty-three-year period.

There can be no question that there were distinctive theories of delinquency. There was the theory of SS&A, Cohen's theory that depended heavily on SS&A, Cloward-Ohlin's theory that attempted to integrate SS&A with differential association, the cultural theory of Miller, and the normative drift theory of Matza. But sociologists doing research on juvenile delinquency drew ideas from all these theories. Rather than the field being organized into a group of researchers who, being primarily interested in a theory, attempted to apply and test the theory on different research sites, it was organized into groups of researchers with similar substantive interests. Throughout the period the number of sociologists appearing in the anomie factor was small—Merton, Durkheim, Srole, and a few others. Sociologists doing research employing the anomie theory were more likely to be cited by others studying juvenile delinquency than by colleagues using anomie theory to study other subjects. It is typical that in the fourth period Cloward, who employed anomie theory in both his work on juvenile delinquency and his work on prisons, appears in two different factors. The closest group we have that is organized around a theoretical orientation is the symbolic interactionist group in the last period. Although these sociologists have written on several different substantive areas, they all employ a similar theoretical orientation.

To what extent have sociologists doing research on deviance been a coherent group? What has been the level of consensus among researchers in this field? There is a wide range of techniques currently being developed to measure intellectual consensus.[54] We began by looking at the distribution of citations in each period. The more citations are concentrated on a small number of people, the more consensus there is on who is doing significant work. We used the Gini coefficient as a measure of concentration. The results are presented in Table 3. As the field grew in size and the popularity of deviance as a research subject increased, so did consensus. However, in the last period there was a decline in consensus. This can probably be explained by a decline in the significance of anomie theory, a relative decline in interest in delinquency research, and the emergence of symbolic interactionism as a major theoretical orientation.[55]

Table 3. COEFFICIENTS FOR DISTRIBUTION OF CITATIONS
IN FIVE TIME PERIODS

Number of Citations	Number of Authors				
	1950–54	1955–59	1960–64	1965–69	1970–73
30+	—	—	3	5	—
29–20	—	—	6	12	4
19–11	1	8	12	21	22
10–9	—	1	9	19	9
8	1	2	7	16	12
7	2	4	14	27	15
6	2	9	18	19	12
5	4	5	32	47	25
4	9	22	41	56	42
3	15	42	82	138	135
2	57	125	169	246	382
1	409	763	1120	1667	1216
	500	981	1513	2273	1874
Gini Coefficient	.23	.29	.40	.48	.37

The difficulty in using citation distributions as a measure of consensus is that there may be only minimum consensus among the scientists who are most frequently cited. It is possible of course, for leaders of several different and competing orientations to all be highly cited by different researchers. The factor analysis offers us a way of measuring the extent to which the field is divided into distinctive and nonoverlapping groups. The factor analysis tells us how much variance on the correlation matrix or patterns of citations can be explained by each factor.[56] The more distinctive and unique are the separate factors, the higher the proportion of variance will be explained by any given number of factors. In order to use proportion of variance explained as an indicator of the intellectual state of the field, we extracted ten factors for each time period. The results are presented in Table 4.[57]

Table 4. CUMULATIVE PERCENT OF VARIANCE EXPLAINED BY TEN FACTORS IN
EACH TIME PERIOD

Period	Percent Variance Explained
1950–54	73
1955–59	64
1960–64	55
1965–69	50
1970–73	59

Using this measure of consensus, the results parallel those obtained from the analysis of the Gini coefficients. In the first two periods and the last period, the ten factors were relatively distinctive and therefore explained more variance. In the first two periods the field was most sharply divided into distinctive groups. Consensus increased in the third period and reached a peak in the fourth. The factor analysis, as did the Gini coefficients, shows a decline in consensus in the last period. Before we can know more about the significance of these figures, we must perform similar analyses on other specialties and other disciplines. For example, if we performed similar analysis on the field of high-energy physics, what would we find? If, as we would expect, there is more consensus in high-energy physics, then we should find a higher Gini coefficient and the factor analysis should explain a lower proportion of variance. In the deviance literature there were not large differences in the amount of variance explained by the various factors. If we found a group of distinctive factors in high-energy physics, we would expect them to be based on theoretical rather than substantive problems.

When the deviance data were first collected, we included only articles published through 1972. Later we added data from 1973. If we compare the results of the analysis of papers published between 1970 and 1972 with the results for the full four-year period, we find several interesting differences. Before including the last year the total proportion of variance explained by ten factors was 72 percent (almost exactly what we found for the 1950–54 period); with the last year included, the proportion of explained variance dropped to 59 percent. Similarly, without the last year included the Gini coefficient is .30; with the last year it is .37. Without the last year we could identify four factors, one being an anomie factor. With the last year included the anomie factor simply disappears. Finally, with the inclusion of the last year the labeling factor moved from second to first place in proportion of variance explained. These findings might indicate that we are observing a mini-revolution in process. As labeling replaced anomie as the dominant orientation, consensus declined; and now, with the change completed, consensus is again increasing. These are, of course, merely speculations, and much more data collection and analysis would be necessary to confirm them.

THE PLACE OF SS&A IN DEVIANCE RESEARCH

One of the major aims of this research has been to trace the influence of the theory of SS&A on deviance research throughout the period under consideration. Both the factor analysis and the content analysis indicate that SS&A had a relatively minor influence on the field of deviance until the late 1950s. Yet the original paper was published in 1938. Why did the theory experience delayed utilization?

Part of the answer may lie within the development of the theory itself. There is a considerable difference between the paper published by the twenty-eight-year-old Merton and the new version of it published in 1949 by the thirty-nine-year-old Merton. The latter version is not only more well developed but much more clearly written—with many of the ambiguities in the early version eliminated. The early paper is like a rough draft when compared with the later version.[58] It could be that many sociologists found the later version more convincing and exciting than its predecessor.

Probably a more important reason for the delayed utilization of the theory was the position of structural-functional analysis. The development of this orientation, conceived at Harvard in the late 1930s, was interrupted by World War II. Although in the late 1940s and early 1950s structural-functional analysis was of major significance at a few leading graduate centers, it was not until Ph.D.'s trained at these centers went out into the field in the late fifties that it became the dominant theoretical orientation. Thus, the times were not intellectually ripe for the widespread utilization of the theory until the late 1950s.

One conclusion emerging from the factor analysis of citation patterns was that subject matter was a more important organizing principle than was theoretical orientation. The field consisted of groups of people doing research on criminology, juvenile delinquency, prisons, and mental illness. The aim of most researchers was not so much to develop theory as to investigate currently significant social problems. An increase in interest in topics like juvenile delinquency may have been in part responsible for the increased utilization of the theory. In the 1950s juvenile delinquency was seen as a pressing problem. The federal government demanded that the delinquency action programs it funded have a research component and be guided by some theoretical orientation. The theory of SS&A was utilized by many social scientists involved in such projects.[59]

The data that we have collected from the four leading sociology journals show a decline in the significance of anomie theory in the seventies. Just as the increased utilization of SS&A may have been in part attributable to a rise in importance of structural-functional analysis, the relative decline in its utilization may be partly a result of the end of the dominance of this orientation. Although structural-functional analysis is still one of the most significant orientations, impressionistically it no longer seems to occupy the dominant position it did in the late fifties and the sixties.

There has also been a relative decline in interest in both crime and delinquency and an increase in interest in other types of deviance. In fact, the predominance of interest in crime, delinquency, and prisons in the early periods leads us to question whether it would even be correct to call the field "deviance." Perhaps "crime and delinquency" would be a better label. In the latter period there has been an increase in interest in other forms of deviant behavior.

For example, if we look at the proportion of articles dealing with drugs, sex, and "miscellaneous" other forms of deviance, we find the first period having 10 percent, the second period 11 percent, the third 11 percent, the fourth 23 percent, and the last period 30 percent.[60] In the seventies, although more research is being conducted on crime and delinquency than on other subjects, there has been a sharp rise of interest in other forms of deviance.

206

Researchers studying so-called crimes without victims may find the labeling perspective more useful than SS&A; just as researchers on juvenile delinquency, for example, may have found SS&A more useful than other theories. Again, it is possible that the subject matter under consideration may be more important than theory in determining the direction of sociology.

Finally, in explaining the decline in citation of SS&A in the four leading journals, we must consider the theory itself and its relationship to empirical research. Many sociologists probably believe that the theory is less utilized now than in the past because it has been "proven to be incorrect." Most sociologists, like other scientists, believe that a theory is maintained as long as it is supported by empirical evidence and discarded when it is falsified by empirical evidence. The function of theory is to explain, understand, and predict empirical phenomenon. The function of empirical research is to test theory. To see how SS&A has actually been utilized and the ways in which it has been empirically tested, let us take a further look at the results of the content analysis of citations to Merton's work. Before, in tracing the development of ideas in deviance, I briefly discussed the ways in which Merton's work had been utilized. Here I shall treat the entire twenty-two-year period as a whole.[61] I have classified the citations into ten categories. The categories and frequency distribution are listed in Table 5.

Table 5. WAYS IN WHICH MERTON'S WORK HAS BEEN UTILIZED
IN DEVIANCE LITERATURE, 1950–1972*

Type of Use	Number of Articles	Percentage
1. Part of relevant literature, serves no explicit role in the analysis	29	24
2. Supports idea of author, legitimates author's ideas and interpretations	22	18
3. Uses concept developed by Merton	9	7
4. Extends or modifies the theory or used as part of author's own theory	9	7
5. Used in interpreting results of study	21	17
6. Used in formulating research problem	15	12
7. Attempt to test a derivative theory	5	4
8. Attempt to test part of SS&A	4	3
9. Critical of SS&A	7	6
10. Other	2	2
Total	123	100

* Where Merton's work was utilized in more than one way, I classified the article by the form of utilization that played the largest role in the article.

In about one quarter of the articles citing Merton, his work was referred to as part of the relevant literature and played no explicit role in the analysis.[62] In this type of reference Merton's work is frequently referred to in a lengthy footnote along with other relevant references. In the twenty-nine articles classified in this category, no additional reference is made to the work nor is the work utilized in any way in the analysis. But for the norm that we should cite other relevant literature (reviewing the literature) at the beginning of our articles, these twenty-nine articles could easily have deleted the reference to Merton's work. In another 18 percent of the articles, Merton's work was used to legitimate the author's own ideas or interpretations. Typically the author would make a statement and then say that Merton had reached a similar conclusion. In all twenty-two of the articles citing Merton in this way, only a sentence or two is devoted to Merton's work and his ideas play a noncrucial part in the research reported.

If we combine categories 1 and 2, we find that 42 percent of the articles citing Merton cite his work in a "ceremonial" fashion. *One function that theory serves is the legitimation of the work of the utilizer.* In fact, it is the theoretician as an authority that is being utilized rather than substantive theory. This should not be interpreted as a criticism of theory or of theoreticians. A particular theorist gets to be a legitimator by publishing work that is highly valued. It is not surprising that the most prestigious scientists, those who have contributed the most important theoretical ideas, are also the most likely to be utilized as legitimating authorities. Thus, if Merton, an intellectual authority, agrees with the author or has said something similar, it adds legitimacy to the author's own work. Although I currently have no comparative figures, it is my guess that 42 percent will turn out to be a relatively low proportion of ceremonial citations when compared to the proportion of such citations received by other theoreticians.

It is sometimes asserted that citations are not an adequate measure of quality of work because many citations may be critical in nature.[63] The content analysis of citations to Merton's work indicates that seven of the one hundred twenty-three articles in which Merton was cited were critical of his work. These critical citations are distributed fairly evenly throughout the twenty-two-year period. Although Merton's work is frequently cited by adherents of other theoretical orientations, rarely are such citations critical. In fact, I could only find two critical citations to Merton by adherents of the labeling perspective. In both cases Merton is criticized for employing an incorrect causal order in his theory. Thus, for example, Gould says "perceived opportunity [is] more likely to be a consequence of delinquency than a cause of it."[64] In the same article, Gould makes a positive reference to Merton's analysis of the self-fulfilling prophecy. The fact that Merton is cited frequently by adherents of other theoretical orientations and that few of these citations are critical adds support to our conclusion that deviance researchers are theoretically eclectic. They draw ideas from different orientations. It should be remembered that this content analysis only includes references to Merton made in the four leading journals. To anyone familiar with the field of deviance it will be obvious that there has been a great deal of criticism of SS&A. What remains problematic is the *proportion* of critical references in the total population of citations to the theory.

Nine articles cite Merton's development of concepts. Many of these articles refer to concepts other than anomie, such as "reference group," "role-set," "latent functions." In these articles the concept is employed meaningfully in the analysis and thus the theoretician's ideas have played a significant role in providing organizing or interpretative devices that other scientists find useful. But these nine articles do not try to test the validity of any of Merton's theories.

Lakatos has suggested that scientific theory has its own internal dynamic—one theory leads to an extension or modification independent of experimental research. He sees empirical research as playing only a minor role in the development of theoretical orientations. I find some support for this contention in the analysis of the deviance literature. There were nine theoretical articles in which SS&A was extended, modified, or employed in another theory. Some of the most important of these, such as those written by Cloward and Dubin and the book by Cohen (which, of course, is not included in the sample of journal articles) were published in the 1950s, before a great deal of empirical research had been conducted. In fact, it appears as if all the major extensions of the theory, such as Cloward and Ohlin's merging of SS&A with differential association theory, occurred independently of empirical investigations. Sometimes empirical researchers would suggest an ad hoc modification; but these were rarely developed or followed up empirically.

To extend this line of analysis, it would be desirable to conduct a content analysis of citations made in the work of theoreticians. (I have done the opposite, looking at how theory is used by others.) How do theoreticians utilize empirical work? How do they respond, if at all, to negative evidence turned up by empirical researchers? Does theory indeed develop, as Lakatos suggests, independently of empirical investigation?

The distinction that we make between attempts to test empirically a theory (categories 7 and 8), on the one hand, and utilizing a theory to set up a research problem (category 6) or to interpret the results of an empirical study (category 5), on the other, is crucial in understanding the role that theory actually plays in sociological research. As the figures in Table 5 indicate, throughout the entire twenty-two-year period in the four journals I examined, I found only nine articles reporting research designed to empirically test a part of SS&A or a derivative theory. Yet there were twenty-one articles that utilized SS&A in interpreting the results of an empirical study.

What is the difference between testing a theory and utilizing it as an interpretative device? In the first case, the research is designed to verify or falsify the theory. Do the data support the theory? In the latter case, a study is done for some other purpose, generally intrinsic interest in the subject matter or easy access to available data. After the study is completed, the sociologist attempts to interpret the results. Frequently, after a study is completed we are asked, "What is its theoretical significance?" We will then look around for some theory to make our research "significant." Research done in this manner cannot have the function of comparing a theory with empirical evidence. There would be no way that the theory could lose. Only theories that seem to offer insight into the collected data are selected as interpretative devices.

It might seem on the surface difficult to distinguish between these two uses of theory. How can we tell if a scientist collected data to test a theory or used a theory to interpret some data? Indeed, in the case study I am currently conducting of the theory of superconductivity in solid-state physics, it is difficult to answer this question. Natural scientists write up their articles in such a way as to make it difficult to follow the time order of their thought. In sociology it is considerably easier. When scientists set out to test a theory, they attempt to choose a research site that is suitable for such a test. In the case of SS&A, I would expect someone who is interested in testing the theory to study criminal or delinquent behavior committed by people variously distributed through the class structure. When SS&A is used to interpret a study of a nineteenth-century community of Polish Jews, the class structure in eighteenth-century France, or behavior of Eskimos, we can be relatively sure that the primary purpose of the study was *not* to test the theory. It should, of course, be clear that SS&A could have been, and in fact was, useful in interpreting data in these studies.

Frequently, even when a more appropriate research site for testing SS&A is used, it is easy to tell that the theory was utilized as an interpretative device. A typical article would be one by Glaser and Rice.[65] In this quantitative study of the relationship between age, employment, and crime rates, the theory of SS&A is not mentioned until the discussion section. It is clear that the theory is being used as an ex post facto interpretative device. The authors conclude that both SS&A and differential association theory are compatible with the data. We may conclude that one function of theory is to aid researchers in interpreting data collected for nontheoretical purposes. We may also conclude that at least in deviance research most empirical research is not done primarily to test theory.

Kuhn suggests that one of the functions served by theory is to provide puzzles or problems for scientists to work on. In sixteen articles in which Merton was cited, SS&A was utilized in formulating the research problem. For example, Simpson and Miller note that Merton suggests that there are class differences in prevalence of anomie.[66] But anomie is not equally distributed within a single social class. How can we explain within-class differences in anomie? The problem is clearly suggested by Merton's work, but the results can in no sense be seen as useful in determining the validity of SS&A. In another article, Killian and Grigg are interested in finding out whether social class or urban-rural location has a greater influence on anomia.[67] Again, without Merton's theory and work that it gave rise to, the problem might not have been thought of. But the results of the study are not relevant for a test of Merton's theory.

An example of a case that was difficult to classify is the research note by Clark and Wenninger, in which they begin by reporting contradictory findings on the correlation between social class and delinquent behavior. They then suggest that these contradictions might be explained "if one hypothesizes that the rates of illegal conduct among the social classes vary with the type of community in which they are found."[68] This study was classified as using SS&A and derivative theories in formulating the hypothesis; it could also have been classified as being an attempt to test the theories. Even in sociology it is sometimes difficult to make this decision.

Before examining those articles that did report attempts to test SS&A or derivative theories, I should point out that there were, of course, other attempts to make such tests which were not included in the sample. One of the best known perhaps is Hyman's analysis of the value system of different classes, in which he found that lower-class people were less likely to internalize the success goal than were middle-class people.[69] Indeed, most of the empirically based criticisms of SS&A challenge Merton's hypotheses that lower-class people as well as middle-class people internalize the success goal, that lower-class people are more likely to be exposed to anomie, and are more likely to engage in deviant behavior. Some of the most significant empirical work bearing on SS&A was included in the sample but not in the content analysis. This is because the authors cited only derivative theories and not SS&A.[70] Examples are the work of Short and Nye and of Dentler and Monroe, in which they found no significant differences in rates of some types of deviant behavior among the classes.[71]

Let us now examine those studies that attempted to test SS&A or derivative theories.

1. Mizruchi reports a study designed to find out if anomia is correlated with social class and finds that it is.[72]
2. Reiss and Rhodes design a study to find out if lower-class boys are more likely than middle-class boys to commit delinquent acts. They conclude that they are but that the causal chain is complex and offers support for Miller's cultural explanation as well as the structural one.[73]
3. Spergel designed a study to test Cloward and Ohlin and finds support for their theory.[74]
4. Rhodes does a study that shows lower-class boys are more likely to suffer from anomia than middle-class boys. There are some discrepancies between the data and predictions from the theory, for which Rhodes offers some ad hoc explanations.[75]
5. Landis and Scarpitti attempt to test both Cloward-Ohlin and Cohen and find support for both.[76]
6. Short, Rivera, and Tennyson report a study designed to test Cloward-Ohlin's theory. Although their data basically support most predictions made from the theory, they suggest that to fully understand delinquent behavior it is necessary to employ "personality level variables" and "group success" considerations.[77]
7. Voss attempts to test Cohen's theory and concludes that the data support neither Cohen's theory nor the differential association theory.[78]
8. Wilson reports a study designed to replicate Lander, who made one of the first attempts to operationalize empirically the concept of

211

anomie. He concludes that Lander was correct in his conclusion that "anomie is primarily a function of community stability, independent of poverty." This is seen as contradicting an assumption of SS&A.[79]

9. Rushing reports a direct test of SS&A and concludes that his results "are consistent with Merton's theory." He suggests that "cultural interpretation is a significant intervening variable in the relationship between aspirations and blocked perceived opportunity."[80]

I began this section of the paper by asking why there has been a decline in citation of SS&A in the four leading journals. Is it because the theory has been "falsified"? Let us first consider this question within the framework of the pre–1950s philosophy and history of science.

What can we conclude from the studies that have actively attempted to test the theory? There was certainly as much evidence in support of SS&A and derivative theories as in opposition. The strongest negative evidence confronting SS&A are the several studies finding no differences in rates of deviant behavior between lower-class and middle-class people.[81] By the time the 1949 version of SS&A was published, Merton was aware that actual rates of deviant behavior may be considerably higher in the middle classes than official crime statistics indicated. He cites an article by Wallerstein and Wyle entitled "Our Law-Abiding Law Breakers," which reports a study indicating that a large majority of respectable middle-class people have committed felonies.[82] At this point, Merton had to decide whether he should see anomie as characterizing the entire society and thus creating high rates of deviance in the society as a whole or as being unevenly distributed, with the lower class being more exposed than the middle class. He opted for the latter choice. If he had chosen the other alternative, most of the criticism of the theory would have been avoided.

The theory of SS&A does posit that exposure to anomie varies by class. The empirical evidence would at most lead us to restrict the applicability of the theory to specific types of deviant behavior. For even if it were true that overall rates of deviance do not differ from class to class, there are certainly some forms of deviant behavior more prevalent in the lower class than in the middle class, just as there may be other forms of deviance more prevalent in the middle class than in the lower. Thus, even within the framework of "The Received View," we could not say that there is enough negative empirical evidence to discard the theory.

It is easier to explain the decline of utilization of SS&A from what I should like to call the "sociological framework." From this point of view, the acceptance or rejection of a theory is not primarily dependent on empirical evidence. It is dependent on the way the theory fits in with the other interests of the community of scientists and the ability of the theory to fulfill what might be called its "functional requirements." First, what evidence is there in this case that the acceptance or rejection of a theory is not dependent on empirical evidence? I have shown that at least in the four major journals there were few attempts to directly test the theory and that there were even fewer studies that claimed to find evidence contradicting the theory. Even in articles reporting data seeming to contradict the theory, the authors usually fail to conclude that the theory is "wrong." The best example may be found in an article by Palmore and Hammond, in which they compare data with predictions generated by the theory of Cloward-Ohlin. The data are not of a kind appropriate for the theoretical predictions, but the authors make a point of not questioning the theory:

> These results should not be construed as a test of Cloward and Ohlin's theory. The latter is chiefly concerned with the nature of the content of delinquent subcultures, rather than rates of delinquent acts; in addition, the relation between the measures used here and the *concepts* of legitimate and illegitimate opportunity is tenuous. . . . [They go on to give several ad hoc interpretations of why the results didn't match the theoretical predictions.] To explain away unconfirmed predictions by claiming they have been tested with impure measures is to admit that the propositions that *were* upheld are open to question. Certainly no deception is warranted or intended, given these conditions. Our data, however, convincingly suggest that interaction affects of legitimate and illegitimate opportunity structures are worth looking for; either variable taken singly might leave out a significant portion of the story.[83]

This failure of the authors to accept evidence seeming to be out of line with predictions from the theory as grounds for discarding a theory is not an isolated case in the deviance literature. Furthermore, it is very similar to the patterns Elizabeth Garber and I have found in the analysis of empirical papers using the theory of superconductivity. It is not infrequent that physicists utilizing the theory would find experimental results that did not match the predictions of the theory; but in not one case did a physicist suggest that the theory might be incorrect. Although much more work must be done, it appears to us that the purpose of most experimental work utilizing the theory of superconductivity is *not* to test the validity of the theory. Likewise, it is evident that the purpose of most empirical work utilizing SS&A is *not* to test the validity of this theory. This is not to say that scientists never attempt to test the validity of any theories but that most of the time most scientists use theory to formulate their research problems and interpret their results. One functional requirement of theory is that it must be useful in these tasks.

The major latent function of theory is to provide puzzles for scientists to work on. From this point of view, Merton's decision to treat anomie as differentially distributed within the class structure turned out to be strategic. Although choosing the other alternative would have avoided much of the criticism the theory has faced, the theory would have been less useful in providing puzzles for sociologists to work on. There was much greater opportunity to study and greater interest in differential rates of deviance within the United States than there was in differential rates of deviance among societies.

Before I began this research, I believed that SS&A had been difficult to test because it had not been put forth in a precise enough manner to operationalize the key components. I believed that it would be possible to state the theory in a more precise way and that a definitive empirical test would then be possible. I, of course, no longer believe this would be either possible or desirable. SS&A is an approach to studying a wide range of behavior that stimulated much theoretical thought and a good deal of empirical research. The range of empirical phenomena for which SS&A is relevant is too wide for *a* definitive test to have been performed. Besides, theories that provide puzzles are not rejected in the face of negative empirical evidence unless an alternate theory is present and deemed superior. And, in fact, the utilization of SS&A may be declining, not because it has been empirically proven false but because we have exhausted most of the puzzles that it provided. Labeling theory is currently the major source of puzzles for deviance researchers and is providing them in substantive areas currently more fashionable than those in which SS&A provided puzzles.

At this point the crucial question that we face is the extent to which the intellectual organization of deviance is an isolated case, typical of work only in sociology or in other fields having a low level of codification, or is typical of science in general. There are two temptations that must be avoided.[84] The first is to make evaluative statements about the behavior of our colleagues. One might say, "All right, it is true that little research is done that attempts to test theory, and it is also true that theories are frequently maintained in the face of negative empirical evidence. But this is terrible; this is not the way scientists are supposed to conduct their work." Such a stance might be legitimate for a philosopher to take; but as sociologists we must be more concerned with how and why things actually work than with offering prescriptions for how they should work.

The second temptation we must avoid is to assume *without empirical evidence* that, in respect to the relationship between theory and research, sociology differs from the more advanced natural sciences. It would be easy to say "Well, this sorry state of affairs is true for sociology; but this merely reflects how undeveloped and 'unscientific' a field sociology is. Things are different in the natural sciences." They may be; but we should not assume this until the evidence is in. Our study of solid-state physics, although in a preliminary stage, thus far shows the relationship between theory and research to be not greatly dissimilar to that I have found for sociology. Although this is only a hypothesis, I currently believe that the intellectual organization of deviance research in sociology is not atypical and that the social sciences are not as different from the natural sciences as many of us are inclined to believe.

In conclusion I should like to list seven interrelated propositions that are suggested by the sociological view of scientific development and which are deserving of our attention.

1) *A theory is not rejected when negative empirical evidence is discovered unless there is a "better" theory available to take its place.* This proposition suggests that scientists do not like to operate in a theoretical vacuum. What remain to be discovered are the conditions leading scientists to turn their attention to new theories.

2) *A function of theory is to provide puzzles for research; when the puzzles are exhausted, scientists turn their attention to other theories.* This is a possible reason why scientists will turn to new theories.

3) *During periods of normal science, empirical studies that cast doubt*

upon accepted theories will be either ignored or misinterpreted. This is a corollary to my first proposition. If this proposition is correct, we could predict, for example, that if some sociologist were to come up with strong evidence that the theory utilized by Durkheim to explain rates of suicide was incorrect without offering an alternative *sociological* theory, most sociologists would continue to believe Durkheim's theory and perhaps misinterpret the empirical study to see it as not contradicting Durkheim's conclusions. It is crucial that if a new theory were to be offered it would have to be sociological in nature. Sociologists are committed to the assumption that sociological conditions explain human behavior. We are, therefore, resistant to explanations of human behavior employing nonsociological variables.

4) *One function of theory is to legitimate the work of its utilizer.* Citations to eminent theoreticians are often made in order to give credence to the author's work.

5) *One function of theory is to interpret the results of empirical research.* Rather than research being done to test theory, in most cases theory is utilized to make sense out of empirical results.

6) *The growth of theory has its own internal dynamic and often proceeds independently of empirical investigation.* If this is true, we would expect to find new theoretical developments being primarily influenced by past theoretical work rather than empirical work.

7) *The extent to which empirical research is aimed at testing and developing theory is dependent upon the social organization of the research area as well as the internal development of the ideas themselves.* In the past we have believed that, for example, there is a closer relationship between theory and research in a field like physics than in one like sociology because the former field is more intellectually developed. Although this may be true, I am proposing that even specialties within the same field may differ in the extent to which research is linked to theory depending on how the specialty is organized. For example in fields where resources necessary to do experiments are tightly controlled by a group of scientists who will evaluate proposals for research according to their theoretical relevance, there will be a closer integration of theory and research than in fields where control of resources needed to do research is more decentralized.

NOTES

1. Robert K. Merton, "Social Structure and Anomie," *American Sociological Review* 3 (1938): 672–82; revised version published in Robert K. Merton, *Social Theory and Social Structure* (Glencoe, Ill.: Free Press, 1949), hereafter referred to as *STSS*.
2. For an overview of the sociology of science and a discussion of the split between internalists and externalists, see Jonathan R. Cole and Stephen Cole, *Social Stratification in Science* (Chicago, Ill.: University of Chicago Press, 1973).
3. For an early example of this type of research, see Robert K. Merton, *Science, Technology and Society in Seventeenth-Century England,* repr. ed. (New York: Fertig, 1970; originally published in 1938).
4. Most often such attempts were not conscious efforts.

5. Thomas S. Kuhn, *The Structure of Scientific Revolutions* (Chicago, Ill.: University of Chicago Press, 1962). Two other very important books are Michael Polanyi, *Personal Knowledge* (London: Routledge & Kegan Paul, 1958); and John Ziman, *Public Knowledge* (Cambridge, England: Cambridge University Press, 1968).
6. Unfortunately, academic deadlines do not always coincide with the natural evolution of a research project. The research reported here is in progress and should be read more as a progress report than as a final statement.
7. Kuhn uses the term "paradigm" in many different ways. See Margaret Masterman, "The Nature of a Paradigm," in Imre Lakatos and Alan Musgrave, eds., *Criticism and the Growth of Knowledge* (Cambridge, England: Cambridge University Press, 1970). Since there is a good deal of confusion as to what a paradigm actually is, I prefer to refer to "theory" used loosely. I do not mean to imply that Kuhn means nothing more by "paradigm" than theory. Only further empirical research will tell us the utility in distinguishing between different levels of theory and paradigms.
8. Kuhn, *The Structure of Scientific Revolutions,* p. 167.
9. *Ibid.,* p. 98.
10. *Ibid.,* p. 103.
11. Frederick Suppe, ed., *The Structure of Scientific Theories* (Urbana: The University of Illinois Press, 1974).
12. As pointed out by Stephen G. Brush in "Should the History of Science Be Rated X?" *Science* 183 (March 1974): 1164–72, Koyré was one of the first historians to question the traditional view of the relationship between progress in science and empirical research. See A. Koyré, *Etudes Galiléennes* (Paris: Hermann, 1966), which is a reprint of three articles published separately, 1935–39.
13. Kuhn, *The Structure of Scientific Revolutions,* p. 81.
14. Michael Polanyi, *Personal Knowledge,* p. 292.
15. Imre Lakatos, "Falsification and the Methodology of Scientific Research Programmes," in Lakatos and Musgrave, eds., *Criticism and the Growth of Knowledge,* pp. 100–01.
16. Kuhn, *The Structure of Scientific Revolutions,* p. 6.
17. *Ibid.,* p. 14. It should be pointed out that "science" is not uniform either cognitively or socially. The role of theory and research and the ways in which they are related undoubtedly vary from one research area to another and within the same research area over time.
18. *Ibid.,* p. 157.
19. For examples, see the essay by Lakatos, "Falsification and the Methodology of Scientific Research Programmes."
20. Stephen E. Toulmin, "Does the Distinction Between Normal and Revolutionary Science Hold Water?" in Lakatos and Musgrave, *Criticism and the Growth of Knowledge.*
21. Jonathan R. Cole, research in progress, Columbia University, New York.
22. Diana Crane, *Invisible Colleges* (Chicago: University of Chicago Press, 1972), p. 46.
23. For the purpose of illustration, we are clearly oversimplifying the problems we face in this type of research. There are many problems in specifying the level of theories we encounter. The most frequently cited papers at any point in time may not represent the theoretical orientation that gave rise to them. They may be what Lakatos calls part of the "protective belt." An evolutionary approach should allow us to relate derivative theories to parent theories or theoretical orientations.
24. To do all this, it is obvious that we must collaborate with someone who is familiar with and capable of understanding the substance of the scientific ideas being studied.

25. For an anticipation of this idea see the first edition of Merton, *STSS* (1949), pp. 14–15.
26. It would obviously be desirable and possible to empirically verify this impression.
27. No hypothesis is made about the extent to which theoreticians depend on experimental work.
28. Robert K. Merton, "Anomie, Anomia, and Social Interaction: Contexts of Deviant Behavior," in Marshall B. Clinard, ed., *Anomie and Deviant Behavior* (New York: Free Press, 1964). This book also contains several informative critical essays and an inventory of empirical and theoretical studies of anomie prepared by Stephen Cole and Harriet Zuckerman.
29. For a more complete discussion of these problems see Stephen Cole, Jonathan R. Cole, and Lorraine Dietrich, "Measuring Consensus in Scientific Research Areas," in Y. Elkhana et al., eds., *The Metric of Science* (New York: Wiley, forthcoming).
30. See Cole and Cole, *Social Stratification in Science*, Ch. 2.
31. See Bernard Barber, "Resistance by Scientists to Scientific Discoveries," *Science* 134 (September 1961), pp. 596–602; and Ch. 8 of Cole and Cole, *Social Stratification in Science*.
32. Eugene Garfield, "Uncitedness III—The Importance of *Not* Being Cited," *Current Contents* 8 (February 21, 1973), pp. 5–6.
33. Robert K. Merton, *On Theoretical Sociology* (New York: The Free Press, 1967), pp. 26–37.
34. For one example see Richard Jesser et al., *Society, Personality, and Deviant Behavior: A Study of a Tri-Ethnic Community* (New York: Holt, Rinehart & Winston, 1968).
35. In a study of the effects of funding agencies on juvenile delinquency research, John F. Galliher and James L. McCartney ("The Influence of Funding Agencies on Juvenile Delinquency Research," *Social Problems* [Summer 1973], pp. 77–90) used the same four journals to analyze delinquency research. The number of articles on delinquency that they found in the same five periods were 12, 19, 35, 45. We found 15, 20, 36, 44. The small discrepancies between their count and ours may be accounted for either by error or the fact that they excluded research on juvenile courts and correctional institutions.
36. It should be noted that this procedure does differ from that normally employed in which each distinct reference to an author's work would count as a citation. For example, when we looked at the distribution of citations done in the typical fashion, Short rather than Merton received the most citations for this period. This is because Short was frequently cited for four or more articles within a single article, whereas Merton was usually cited for one or two contributions.
37. We included in the analysis all references to Merton's work, even those on topics other than SS&A. Many references were to Merton's well-known book, *Social Theory and Social Structure*. Using the page numbers or chapter numbers we classified these as to whether they were to SS&A (which appears in the book) or other topics.
38. Clearly, a correlation of 1.0 between Merton and Burgess would be impossible as they had different numbers of citations. Thus, *at least* six authors must have cited Burgess and *not* cited Merton. Using a matrix of product moment correlation coefficients in conducting the factor analysis may not be a satisfactory procedure. Given the unequal totals of citations received by different authors, all the correlation coefficients are artificially reduced in size. Thus if A has a total of 6 citations and B a total of 40, even if all 6 people who cite A also cite B the correlation between A and B will be positive but low. If Yules Q was used as the measure

of association, the correlation would be 1.0. We are currently experimenting with different measures of association.

39. We used the Data Text factor analysis program that employs a Varimax rotation procedure. In computing the factor analysis, we excluded all citers who didn't cite any of the most frequently cited sociologists (who were scored 0 on all variables).

40. The first systematic statement of the orientation was published by Merton in 1949 in *STSS*.

41. Celia Stopnicka Rosenthal, "Deviation and Social Change in the Jewish Community of a Small Polish Town," *American Journal of Sociology* 60 (1954): 177–81.

42. Solomon Kobrin, "The Conflict of Values in Delinquency Areas," *American Sociological Review* 16 (1950): 653–61.

43. In identifying the work of some of the sociologists I was not familiar with, I depended on the following texts: Edwin H. Sutherland and Donald R. Cressey, *Principles of Criminology*, 8th ed. (Philadelphia: Lippincott, 1970); Richard D. Knudten, *Crime in a Complex Society* (Homewood, Ill.: Dorsey Press, 1970); Marshall B. Clinard, *Sociology of Deviant Behavior*, 3rd ed. (New York: Holt, Rinehart & Winston, 1968).

44. Robert E. L. Faris and H. Warren Dunham co-authored a well-known book in this area, *Mental Disorders in Urban Areas* (Chicago: University of Chicago Press, 1939). Wirth and Park are probably being cited for their work on urbanism. Sorokin's work was cited for statistics on the effect of urbanism on crime rates; Pitirm A. Sorokin, *Social and Cultural Dynamics* (New York: American Book, 1937).

45. Lloyd E. Ohlin and Otis Dudley Duncan, "The Efficiency of Prediction in Criminology," *American Journal of Sociology* 54 (1949): 441–52.

46. Benjamin Malzberg, "The Prevalence of Mental Disease Among the Urban and Rural Population of New York State," *Psychiatric Quarterly* 9 (1935): 55–88.

47. Further analysis is needed to understand why Mills and Porterfield also appear in this factor.

48. Richard A. Cloward, "Illegitimate Means, Anomie, and Deviant Behavior," *American Sociological Review* 24 (1959): 164–76; Robert Dubin, "Deviant Behavior and Social Structure: Continuities in Social Theory," *American Sociological Review* 4 (1959): 147–64.

49. Daniel Glaser and Kent Rice, "Crime, Age, and Unemployment," *American Sociological Review* 24 (1959): 679–88; Elwin H. Powell, "Occupation, Status, and Suicide: Towards a Redefinition of Anomie," *American Sociological Review* 23 (1958): 131–39; Bruce P. Dohrenwend, "Egoism, Altruism, Anomie, and Fatalism: A Conceptual Analysis of Durkheim's Types," *American Sociological Review* 24 (1959): 466–73.

50. Cloward, "Illegitimate Means, Anomie, and Deviant Behavior."

51. Leo Srole et al., *Mental Health in the Metropolis: The Midtown Manhattan Study* (New York: McGraw-Hill, 1962).

52. It is difficult to determine the exact number of citations to that part of Merton's work which is on deviance. Many of these citations are to the various editions of *STSS*. Classification was made by the page cited. Of course, all of Merton's work received considerably more than 60 citations.

53. An interesting hypothesis that deserves examination is that some theories may be continually utilized by one age cohort of scientists. As the cohort ages and does different types of work, the ways in which the theory is utilized might change.

54. See Stephen Cole et al., "Measuring Consensus in Scientific Research Areas."

218

55. It should be noted that even in the last period juvenile delinquency is still the most frequently written-on topic. There has been, however, a relative decline in interest in this area.

56. In Table 2 we do not report the proportion of variance explained by each factor for two reasons: (1) there were not large differences between most of the factors; (2) which factor explained the most variance differed depending on how many factors were rotated.

57. The results are essentially the same when we examine the total proportion of variance explained by five factors. Given some of the problems in using correlation matrices as input for the factor analysis of these data (see note 38), the interpretation given to the results presented in Table 4 should be taken as suggestions for future analysis rather than as definitive.

58. I have frequently assigned SS&A to undergraduate classes and was always dismayed when some students said they had a hard time understanding the article. Now I realize why. The students were reading the Bobbs-Merrill reprint which is the 1938 version; I was reading the version in *Social Theory and Social Structure*.

59. Cloward and Ohlin's theory, a derivative of SS&A, was the intellectual base of Mobilization for Youth, one of the largest poverty program delinquency projects. Some believe that Cloward and Ohlin's theory gave rise to the program, but actually the action program was developed prior to their work. The original proposal was not funded because it did not contain a research component. It was only then that Cloward and Ohlin joined the MFY team.

60. Articles published in 1973 have been excluded from this analysis.

61. The references made in 1973 to Merton's work were not included in the content analysis.

62. It should be kept in mind that this analysis includes references to work other than SS&A. Slightly more than two thirds of the references were to SS&A. Also, since I was the only coder, it is not known whether other coders would classify the citations in the same way. An independent classification by another coder would be desirable.

63. As we have pointed out before (Cole and Cole, *Social Stratification in Science*, p. 25), the significance of an idea may not depend on whether it is "right" or "wrong." An idea that has been important enough to be heavily criticized is probably an important contribution.

64. Leroy Gould, "Juvenile Entrepreneurs," *American Journal of Sociology* 74 (1969): 710–19.

65. Glaser and Rice, "Crime, Age, and Unemployment."

66. Richard L. Simpson and N. Max Miller, "Social Status and Anomia," *Social Problems* 10 (1962): 256–64.

67. Lewis M. Killian and Charles M. Grigg, "Urbanism, Race and Anomia," *American Journal of Sociology* 67 (1962): 661–65.

68. John P. Clark and Eugene P. Wenninger, "Socio-Economic Class and Area as Correlates of Illegal Behavior Among Juveniles," *American Sociological Review* 27 (1962): 826–34.

69. Herbert H. Hyman, "The Value Systems of Different Classes," in R. Bendix and S. M. Lipset, *Class, Status and Power* (Glencoe, Ill.: Free Press, 1953), pp. 426–42.

70. This is a good example of the importance of considering what might be called "second generation citations" in tracing intellectual influences. One paper may have a group of important offspring; in later years the offspring but not the parent are cited.

71. See, for example, James F. Short, "Differential Association and Delinquency," *Social Problems* 4 (January 1957): 233–39; James F. Short and F. Ivan Nye, "Reported Behavior as a Criterion of Deviant Behavior," *Social Problems* 5 (Winter 1957–58): 207–13; F. Ivan Nye, James F. Short, and Virgil J. Olson, "Socio-Economic Status and Delinquent Behavior," *American Journal of Sociology* 63 (January 1958): 381–89; Robert A. Dentler and Lawrence J. Monroe, "Early Adolescent Theft," *American Sociological Review* 26 (October 1961): 733–43. The procedures we are currently developing employing evolutionary programs will eliminate this problem of not being able to connect work citing derivative theory with an original theory through citation analysis.

72. Ephraim H. Mizruchi, "Social Structure and Anomie in a Small City," *American Sociological Review* 25 (1960): 645–54.

73. Albert J. Reiss, Jr., and Albert Lewis Rhodes, "The Distribution of Juvenile Delinquency in the Social Class Structure," *American Sociological Review* 26 (1961): 720–32.

74. Irving Spergel, "Male Young Adult Criminality, Deviant Values, and Differential Opportunities in Two Lower-Class Negro Neighborhoods," *Social Problems* 10 (1963): 237–50.

75. Albert Lewis Rhodes, "Anomia, Aspiration and Status," *Social Forces* 42 (1964): 434–40.

76. J. R. Landis and F. R. Scarpitti, "Perception Regarding Value Orientation and Legitimate Opportunity: Delinquents and Non-Delinquents," *Social Forces* 44 (1965): 83–91.

77. James F. Short, Jr., Ramon Rivera, and Ray A. Tennyson, "Perceived Opportunities, Gang Membership, and Delinquency," *American Sociological Review* 20 (1965): 411–28.

78. Harwin L. Voss, "Socio-Economic Status and Reported Delinquent Behavior," *Social Problems* 13 (1966): 314–24.

79. Robert A. Wilson, "Anomie in the Ghetto: A Study of Neighborhood Type, Race, and Anomie," *American Journal of Sociology* 76 (1971): 66–88.

80. William A. Rushing, "Class, Culture and 'Social Structure and Anomie,'" *American Journal of Sociology* 76 (1971): 857.

81. See note 71.

82. James S. Wallerstein and Clement J. Wyle, "Our Law-Abiding Law Breakers," *Probation* 25 (March–April 1947): 107–12.

83. Erdman B. Palmore and Phillip E. Hammond, "Interacting Factors in Juvenile Delinquency," *American Sociological Review* 29 (1964): 848–54.

84. For a development of the concept of codification, see Harriet A. Zuckerman and Robert K. Merton, "Age, Aging and Age Structure in Science," in Matilda White Riley et al., eds., *A Sociology of Age Stratification* (New York: Russell Sage, 1972).

Legitimate and Illegitimate Use of Power

JAMES S. COLEMAN

NEGOTIATIONS, promises, inducements, threats, and bargains constitute the major mechanisms through which social choices are resolved and through which actors with differing interests manage to make mutual gains when it first appears that one of them must necessarily lose.

Yet in systems of collective choice, such as committees and legislative bodies, the use of these devices is often regarded with suspicion or disfavor, sometimes extending as far as legal constraints. Similarly, in other actions, which involve no public choice, certain negotiations and deals are similarly illegal: a policeman's acceptance of bribery for not enforcing the law, collusion leading to price-fixing by business firms, under-the-counter payments by contractors.

Why are these actions either illegal or illegitimate? And why, on the other hand, are certain of these actions, or actions very like them, seen by some social scientists and by some politicians as the principal means for resolving issues of social choice? It would be easy, but only a partial truth, to say that the citizen's view of legislative deals is distorted by the fact that they are often made secretly and by the suspicion that the parties to them are profiting unduly. It would also be easy to say that both sides are correct: that some such deals and negotiations are beneficial to the system, while others

James S. Coleman is Professor of Sociology at the University of Chicago.

are not. Common sense suggests that this is true; but common sense fails to suggest exactly which activities are beneficial to the system and which are not; and common sense does not specify for what "system" they might be beneficial.

Robert Merton's discussion of manifest and latent functions focuses on some of these same processes. He says:

> Since moral evaluations in a society tend to be largely in terms of the manifest consequences of a practice or code, we should be prepared to find that analysis in terms of latent functions at times runs counter to prevailing moral evaluations. For it does not follow that the latent functions will operate in the same fashion as the manifest consequences which are ordinarily the basis of these judgments. Thus, in large sectors of the American population, the political machine or the "political racket" are judged as unequivocally "bad" and "undesirable." The grounds for such moral judgment vary somewhat, but they consist substantially in pointing out that political machines violate moral codes: political patronage violates the code of selecting personnel on the basis of impersonal qualifications rather than on grounds of party loyalty or contributions to the war-chest; bossism violates the code that votes should be based on individual appraisal of the qualifications of candidates and of political issues, and not on abiding loyalty to a feudal leader; bribery and "honest graft" obviously offend the proprieties of property; "protection" for crime clearly violates the law and the mores; and so on.[1]

Merton goes on to discuss in detail the latent functions of the political machine. Merton's aim is to show how demands for certain kinds of activities, from voters in the ward, from businessmen with money, and from racketeers with money, are fulfilled by the political machine, through deals and arrangements that are morally proscribed.[2]

My interest here is to extend this examination to the study of a somewhat different question: certain of these transactions that occur in politics (and elsewhere) are regarded as legitimate, and others are illegitimate or illegal—and through this exploration to gain insight into certain elements of social structure that are not immediately apparent.

It is clear that not only citizens but also the legal system define as corrupt or illegal some deals, while they do not so define others. For example, it is illegal in many countries for a policeman to take a bribe from a motorist he has stopped for speeding, or a legislator to take a monetary bribe for casting his vote in a given way. But it is not illegal for a policeman to overlook a violation of a motorist who buys a ticket to the policeman's ball, or for a legislator to agree to reconsider his vote on a bill in response to a union leader's promise of support at his next election. Nor is it illegal for a legislator to propound in legislative debate the view of a businessman who has contributed to his campaign. It is seen as even less illegitimate for him to agree with another legislator to engage in logrolling: to agree on mutual support of two issues, one of which is of great importance to each of them. But this is seen as less "statesmanlike" than the activity of attempting to convince the other, with no inducements, that he should act in a given way because it is in the public interest.

What is it that makes some political deals illegal, others merely improper, and still others wholly proper? It is useful to begin by looking at different kinds of political deals and attempting to relate their characteristics to the degree of distaste they excite in persons not party to them. I will examine only deals made by legislators. From this examination, it may become possible to gain greater insight into the interests of various parties and the processes by which these interests are implemented or frustrated. In all these examples, the commodity the legislator is selling is his vote and support of legislation, for this is the principal commodity he has to sell. He may sell merely his vote, or his vote together with other political credits and similar resources that he can use to aid or defeat the legislation.

Commodity sold: Support for or opposition to legislation

1. Buyer: An interest group with economic resources, represented by a lobbyist

    Payment: a. money for his personal use

    b. promise of profitable business for firms in which legislator has a personal interest

    c. private information about lucrative investments

    d. personal favors or benefits: entertainment, women, jobs for friends and relatives

    e. money paid to his campaign fund

2. Buyer: An interest group with resources consisting of influence over a group of voters (a mass-based interest group, such as a labor union, a professional society, a veterans' organization)

    Payment: a. use of influence to give voter support in next election

3. Buyer: A government official with control over other government actions (for example, head of a government department who can decide where a new medical facility will be built, who has control over post office jobs, or who contracts for business with government)

    Payment: a. control or partial control over these other political actions

    (i) to benefit self, relative, or friends

    (ii) to benefit his constituents in general

4. Buyer: A party leader, with control over committee memberships and chairmanships, that is, over positions of special power in the legislature

    Payment: a. assignment to positions of special legislative power

5. Buyer: A party leader, with control over campaign support in next election

    Payment: a. campaign finances

    b. use of personal support to gain votes (for example, presidential appearance in campaign)

6. Buyer: Constituents unorganized or partially organized with control over own votes

    Payment: a. votes and campaign aid in next election

7. Buyer: Another legislator

    Payment: a. resources gained through his other transactions as listed in 1–6, such as information about investments (1c), or use of legislative power gained via 4a

   b. explicit promise to vote on another bill (logrolling)
   c. political credit: a vague indebtedness that will be paid later by a vote in committee or on the floor of the legislature

This list of transactions is neither analytically precise nor complete. It is intended merely as a description of some of the transactions entered into by legislators, transactions which constitute the essence of democratic government. Some exchanges involve two or more of the types of transactions listed here, for some "buyers" of political power have more than one kind of resource to give in return. For example, a labor union has both economic and voter-influence resources, and can thus engage in payments listed under both 1 and 2 above.

An examination of these transactions indicates that some are ordinarily seen as wholly legitimate, while others are not. Legitimacy as well may differ among different social systems. For example, in the early days of the United States, and in many homogeneous organizations in which political parties have sprung up, the use of party support in campaigns to maintain party regularity in legislative voting (transaction 5 above), and even the existence of parties, was looked upon as harmful to the society.[3] Yet parties depend on this kind of transaction; and in parliamentary systems party discipline is so strongly imposed that serious deviations from it are unusual. Today, at least in large diverse countries, these political exchanges in which parties constitute one member and a legislator another are viewed as part of the normal functioning of the system.

But in part the variations in legitimacy are independent of the particular social system. For example, in the above list certain of the payments benefit the legislator as a person, others benefit persons with a special relationship to him as a person, others benefit his constituents, while others benefit him in his capacity as legislator. Those transactions that are seen as most illegitimate, and are indeed often made illegal, are those that involve benefits to him as a person, apart from his actions as legislator.

Yet this dichotomy is not perfectly clear-cut. Consider the fundamental exchange on which the theory of political representation is based: constituents demand that the legislator act in their interest in the legislature; in payment, they give him their continued votes and support (transaction 6 in the list). This payment is a payment of political power, that is, extension of the tenure of the individual legislator. It is a payment to the person, but it is a payment in goods that he can use only in the political arena, that is, in his actions as legislator. (It is true that he may in turn exchange this power for goods usable in other activities, through subsequent transactions; but the resources as he receives them are directly usable only in political decisions, and if he exchanges them in later transactions for goods that benefit him as a person it is these later exchanges that are illegal.)

It appears that as a first approximation a useful way of looking at these payments is one that separates them into resources that can be used in his actions as legislator and those that cannot. In the list, 3a(ii), 4a, 6a, 7b, and

7c appear to give the legislator resources that can only be used in his actions as legislator: partial control over legislative actions that bring gains to his constituents, positions of power in the legislature, electoral support from constituents.

A second class of resources consists of those that are not directly resources for his legislative actions but can only be used to gain resources for those actions. This class includes money, but only money that is contributed to a campaign fund and restricted to campaign use; it includes as well all other resources that can be used in a political campaign (1e, 2a, 5a, 5b, 6a).

A third class of payments consists of all those that are not for use in his legislative capacity, nor for use in gaining resources for legislative activities, but for use by him in any other activity in which he engages.

It is obviously the last of these classes of payments that are seen as most illegitimate and are legally forbidden in some cases. The usual description of such transactions is "the use of public office for personal gain." Yet this description is not wholly accurate, because most of the payments in the first two classes give personal gain as well, though personal gain *through* the activities of a legislator: a special position of power in the legislature, election to office, and so on. Thus, it is not the personal gain that is morally proscribed, but rather the diversion of resources to uses that cannot benefit constituents.

In this case, the legitimate transactions are those that exchange a resource (a vote in the legislature) that results from an investment of sovereignty by constituents for something that also constitutes a resource valuable to those constituents. The illegitimate or illegal ones are those that use the resource to obtain something that does not bring valuable resources to constituents.

The illegitimate actions are regarded very much like theft, and I believe it is this similarity that provides the clue to their appropriate conceptualization. Theft ordinarily involves two persons, one who steals and the other from whom a good is stolen. Yet here there is only one tangible person, the legislator. The legislator is the one who steals, but who is the person from whom he steals? In some sense, it is his constituency. But if we are to accept this way of looking at things, then we must follow the implications of doing so and regard the constituency as a corporate person. The law has found it necessary to recognize such corporate persons, which have been variously termed "juristic persons" or "fictional persons" in legal writings, to enable corporate bodies to be parties to a contract, and to enable suits to be brought in law by corporations or against corporations.[4]

Such a corporate person can employ agents, just as can a natural person. Thus, the constituency itself may be regarded as a corporate person, or a "corporate actor" as I shall term it, and the legislator as its agent. If we do so, then the conceptual difficulties vanish. There are two actors, the legislator and the constituency, and the illegal actions are those that consist of a theft from the latter by the former.

The constituency is a corporate actor of a rather unusual kind. Its resources are concentrated in its only agent, the legislator. Its status as an actor, however, is made clear by the illegality of certain actions. That illegality implies the existence of resources that are the property of this corporate actor, and also implies at least a loose definition of the interests of the constituency as a corporate actor.

This conceptual framework indicates why it is that the use of constituency resources for personal gain is proscribed. If we think of the "constitutional intent" of the distribution of power in society, it is clearly the constitutional intent that the constituents hold political sovereignty and vest that sovereignty in the members of the legislature as their agents. The legislature, then, should function in the interests of those who by electing legislators invest their sovereignty—with the legislators as merely conveniences for the system, agents who are used to translate the resources of their constituents into social action beneficial to those constituents. If, instead of acting as such a disinterested agent, the legislator drains off a portion of these resources for his own use, then the benefits that would otherwise have gone to his constituents go instead to him in his activities outside the legislature.

Thus, whatever the distribution of sovereignty as given in the constitution, when representatives use the power given them by constituents' investment of sovereignty to pursue interests other than those of constituents, this is incompatible with constitutional intent, and makes the actual distribution of power different from constitutional intent. This is little more than stating the obvious, because both the laws and the norms of society recognize that positions of public power must be carefully hedged with protective devices (such as an elected official's divesting himself of securities of companies that do business with the government) which guard the interests of corporate actors —constituencies—that otherwise have no protection against their elected agent until the next election.[5] Similar hedges are, of course, built in economic organizations, such as the precautions taken with men who handle the money of a firm or rules in organizations against acceptance of gifts by purchasing agents.

Yet despite the fact that these points are obvious and generally recognized, their implications for a theory of social systems have not been drawn. First of all, they accord with a conceptual framework in which the power of resources or sovereignty in the system are a kind of quantity which is transmitted from one actor to another, invested by those with whom it originates in others who are in a position to use it more effectively. The perspective is similar, whether the sovereignty of the corporate actor originates with one person, as in a one-owner business firm (a "corporation sole," to use the English legal term), or with many persons, as in a trade union or a democratic society. In the former case investments of resources would be made from the one owner to the many agents, and in the latter case investments of resources are made from the many members or citizens to the few representatives and officials.

In the case in which the return to the corporate actor from the investments is monetary (for example, in a business firm, the returns to which are measured as profits), then the resources invested can, ideally, be measured in monetary terms. Where the resources invested are not wholly monetary (such as a trade union, where members invest in the union, giving up sovereignty over wage and working conditions negotiations and getting returns that are partly monetary and partly in other matters, such as satisfaction of grievances or improvement of certain working conditions), the investments cannot be measured only in monetary terms.

In examining the legitimacy of the various uses of power, such as those discussed above, it is useful to carry matters somewhat farther. Political power, or power within any well-defined authority system, differs from money in that there is only a narrow range of events for which it is usable.[6] Power in an authority system is power over, or control of, a specified set of events. The specific events over which it has control intrinsically have consequences for a given set of other actors. The use of money, in contrast, in an economic system is to purchase control over private goods, that is, control over activities that have direct consequences for the actor alone. Whether the private goods are consumed to provide direct benefits or processed and exchanged for money or other goods, the disposition of them has direct consequences only for the parties to the transaction.

The trading of money for goods is seen as the proper use of money. The trading of votes by a legislator, however, is an activity not accorded the full legitimacy of economic transactions, because the use of that vote has potential consequences for many other actors. Some constituents are likely to be helped by the transaction, but others are likely to be hurt by it. Thus, all those constituents with a direct interest in the use of the vote may try to exercise a claim to some restrictions upon its use. The vote, or any other kind of power in an authority system, is in effect a public good, whose domain extends to those actors who are directly affected by its use.

When such power is used to benefit some of those who experience direct consequences from it, and thus have a stake in its use (such as constituents who have an interest in having a government facility located in their district, in a case when a legislator gives up a vote to gain support for that facility), then those who lose by this transaction cannot restrain that transaction, unless they are more powerful than those who benefit. However, when the power is used in such a way that as a resource the potential benefits it could bring to those directly affected by its use are lost to them (as in a transaction that brings to the legislator resources for his personal use), then all, or nearly all, those with whom that power originated have lost by this use. These constituents can, without internal opposition, act to constrain such use, either by making it illegal or by applying moral constraints against it. If the resource derived from their investment of sovereignty—as with a legislative vote, where the legislator is their representative acting with their delegated resource—then they may act to withdraw the delegation of that resource.

The power of a legislator through his vote in the legislature has consequences for two corporate actors: his constituency whose members have invested their sovereignty to him through electing him, and other members of the larger corporate body served by the legislature as a whole. These two corporate actors have similar amounts of interest in his use of the vote, but only the former has a direct claim over its use. Thus, as long as he exchanges his vote resources for resources of equal or greater interest to his constituents, that use of the resource is regarded as *legitimate* by them. Some legislators, in fact, trade their votes on national issues principally to bring direct private benefits to their constituents—gaining government contracts or government agency sites or other direct economic benefits for them.[7] This is the most direct employment of the invested resource, wholly legitimate from the point of view of the constituency as corporate actor, despite the fact that it totally disregards the interests of others outside the constituency affected by this use of it. It is employed to benefit those who originally possessed the sovereignty—the constituents in that district. In fact, as legislators are aware, if he does not employ in this fashion *some* of the resources invested in him, his constituents are likely to conclude that he uses his resources too fully in the interests of the larger political body and not enough in the constituency's interests. In such use, the resources are not sequestered for the legislator's private use, but the action is nevertheless regarded with disfavor by many constituents. The legislator is taking resources belonging principally to one corporate actor and employing them for the benefit of the larger corporate actor of which the constituency is a part. Some constituents, on the other hand, ordinarily those outside his district who benefit as the system as a whole benefits from his actions, but also some inside his district, regard such actions as the highest statesmanship. Estes Kefauver was probably the prototype of this kind of legislator.

Another kind of political exchange that some legislators make distinguishes two kinds of issues: those on which the constituents feel strongly (ordinarily those that affect the local district most directly) and those on which they feel less strongly. He will vote in accordance with the constituency interests on the former issues, thus building up political credit, and against their interest but in accordance with his perception of national interests on the latter. He loses political credit by doing so, but because these issues are of lesser interest to constituents he loses only a portion of the credit he has gained. William Fulbright, voting in accord with Southern conservative interests on domestic issues concerning race relations but using his power on foreign policy issues in a direction he perceives to be the national interest (and against his constituents' opinions), provides an example of this kind of strategy.

These examples indicate the structural complexity of political representation. A constituent of the legislator can be conceived as a member of two corporate actors: the constituency and the political body as a whole. Sometimes the interests of these two corporate actors are alike; sometimes they are opposed. The interests are alike, for example, in their opposition to use of the political resources for private gain of the legislator. Thus, laws to prevent private use of these resources by the legislator will have the support of both corporate actors (though less fully the support of the legislators, against whose private interests such laws are directed).[8] The interests of these two corporate actors are opposed, however, concerning use of the resources to further national ends. Because a citizen is a member of both corporate actors, he may favor actions, that he sees as benefiting the constituency or actions that he sees as benefiting the nation. He may be conceived as having made, at a given time, a psychic investment of self in each of the corporate actors to a given degree. His own wishes in legislative action will depend on the relative sizes of those psychic investments. His investment of *resources* is in one concrete agent, the legislator. But his investment of *interests,* that is, of self, is in two corporate actors. Thus, the legislator can be regarded as the agent of two corporate actors simultaneously, the constituency and the nation-state.

This can be an anomalous position, because in any action where their interests are opposed the agent must implement the interests of one at the expense of the other. Such an anomalous position raises the question of what benefits to the constituents (in the sense of their expanded self) might accrue from a different mechanism for implementing constituency and national interests—possibly through the election of two representatives to represent the two corporate actors, with some device which allowed him to adjust his distribution of resources between the representatives.

Another way of expressing the illegitimacy of certain actions is by reference to the constitution—which may be implicit or explicit—of the corporate actor. That constitution indicates the locus of sovereignty and the mechanisms by which this sovereignty is vested in those agents who have direct control over corporate actions, such as legislators, judges, and executives in a nation-state, or managers in a bureaucracy. The illegitimate or illegal use of power by the agent is the use of this vested sovereignty to pursue interests of another actor, often the agent himself. A frequent way this is done is through an exchange between an agent of the corporate actor of some of the power vested in him, with another actor who has an interest in control over certain of the corporate actor's actions. In illegitimate legislative exchanges, this other actor may be a business firm or trade association represented by a lobbyist; in illegitimate exchanges in a business organization, the other actor may be a firm that is a vendor to the organization, represented by a salesman. In both cases the exchange is made for some resource, such as money, of personal interest to the corporate actor's agent (the legislator or the purchasing agent). From the point of view of the corporate actor, the loss is the loss of a portion of control over its actions to another actor outside the corporate actor.

What effect does the use of invested political sovereignty for the "private gain" of the constituents in each representative's district have upon the larger political body's functioning as a collectivity? Clearly, if constituents have made a psychic investment of self in the constituency and are interested only in such constituency gain, then the representative's employment of their political resources for gains of this sort is exactly what they want. The collectivity as a whole may suffer through this attention to district interests, but in such circumstances there is no reason for the collectivity as a whole not to suffer. By assumption, constituents' interests are only in constituency gain, and their sovereignty should be employed in that way.

It is here that the investment of self in the collectivity as a whole is important for the functioning of that collectivity. If each constituent has invested a large portion of himself in the collectivity, then the use of his political resources that will bring him most benefit is a use that is principally for the benefit of the whole collectivity.[9] In times of war, it is not seen as legitimate for a legislator to use his delegated political resources for the private gain of his district when issues of national importance are at stake. This is a complete about-face from the situation that often obtains in peacetime when he is expected to use resources to benefit his district. The difference in the two situations can perhaps best be described as a difference in the degree of investment that citizens have in the nation as a whole, a high degree during wartime and a lower degree during times of peace.

Thus, actions that are legitimate at one time are not at another, although the sovereignty ultimately belongs to, and is invested by, the same persons. The difference lies in the fact that the object of benefits may either be the constituency or the nation as a whole; and at different times the citizen as an actor in the system has different proportions of his self invested in the constituency and in the nation. When the proportion invested in the nation is large, he regards it as illegitimate for his representative to attend to constituency at the expense of the nation. When that proportion is small, he regards it as illegitimate for his representative not to do so.[10]

Although the process is well illustrated by nations and their legislative assemblies, it is a process that operates in all collective bodies. Each actor has a certain proportion of himself invested in the collectivity, and the legitimacy—as defined by members of the corporate body—of use of his sovereign resources, such as a vote in a collective decision for the benefit of the corporate body as a whole, depends on the size of the proportion of self that each member has invested. Regardless of this proportion, of course, the use of the resource to bring gain to another corporate actor is seen as illegitimate, unless that actor's benefit is only intermediate to longer run benefits for the individual or the corporate actor in which the vote is taken and in which he has investment of self.[11] The discussion above is specific to representative bodies, which introduce the constituency as a corporate actor. In a collective body that operates by direct democracy, in which the sovereigns directly cast votes, there are two actors in whose interests it is potentially legitimate for the sovereign to act: himself and the corporate actor, which is the collective body. At different times and under different circumstances of self-investment, votes will be cast more nearly in the interests of one or the other, toward private or collective goals.

The general principle which can be abstracted from these different structures of action is a straightforward one. When a unit of power that is delegated by a sovereign for use in a corporate body is ultimately employed to benefit those actors, including the sovereign himself, in which the sovereigns have invested large proportions of themselves, then that use is regarded as legitimate. All other uses are regarded as illegitimate, and the sovereigns may use their power to proscribe those uses. As psychic investments of self fluctuate over time, the legitimacy of particular uses will fluctuate over time, though some uses will never become legitimate because few of the sovereigns who have delegated their power have made investments in the actor that benefits.

A general principle of "preservation of power" within a corporate actor can be stated, following the above considerations. The principle is that the members of a corporate actor will establish rules or laws or norms to make illegitimate any use of the power that inheres in the corporate body (through the initial constitutional agreement by the members, by which they give up sovereignty to the corporate actor) to serve the interests of another actor.

Such use of power to serve the interests of another actor in effect removes, for the particular actions covered, that power from the corporate actor and places it in the hands of another actor. There are several ways in which such transfer of power can occur, as suggested above. Two will be explored in more detail below. One involves a special case in which power in two corporate actors is exchanged to serve the interests of two or more actors who are members of each, at the expense of actors who are members of only one. The other is the exchange of power in a corporate actor for a generalized resource—money— from another actor. Both of these occur with some frequency in corporate bodies.

POWER EXCHANGES ACROSS CORPORATE BOUNDARIES

When two actors, say, c and d, are agents of two different corporate actors, say, C and D, a special kind of transaction becomes possible. This is the theft of resources of one corporate actor, C, by actor c, used through exchange to serve the interests of one of the two parties to the exchange (actor d). Resources of the other corporate actor, D, are stolen by d for use in exchange to serve the interests of the other party to the exchange, c. The transaction is well illustrated in a fictional case of a conflict in a novel by C. P. Snow, *The Masters*.[12] The conflict surrounds the election of a new master of a College at Cambridge by the thirteen Fellows. One Fellow, Nightingale, appears at one point in the conflict to hold the deciding vote. He desires to become a Fellow of the Royal Society, and a College Fellow on one side of the conflict, a chemist, is a Fellow of the Royal Society. Nightingale attempts to use his power in the College election to induce this other Fellow to bring about his election to the Royal Society. The specific offer was an offer to change his vote in the College election. The other Fellow does not accept the offer, and the offer is not seen as legitimate by the other Fellows of the College. Similarly, it would not have been regarded as legitimate by the Fellows of the Royal Society.

In this example, the Fellows of the Royal Society had reason, corporately, to be against the action, because a decision intended to be made in the interests of the Royal Society would instead be made in the interests of another set of persons: the College Fellows to whom Nightingale intended to sell his vote for Master. Or, described differently, a resource of the Royal Society, a fellowship, would be used not to advance the interests of the Royal Society, but stolen and used to advance the interests of persons outside the Royal Society. To examine the point of view of the College Fellows, it is necessary to distinguish between the two sides of the conflict. Those Fellows who were on the same side as the member of the Royal Society, considered corporately, had interests in the conflict that would be aided by the proposed exchange. One of their members held a resource (Fellowship in the Royal Society) that he might be willing to add to their corporate resources to gain the vote. Those Fellows on the other side of the conflict, considered corporately, had interests that would be harmed by Nightingale's proposed action. Neither of these two parties, these two corporate actors within the College, however, had constitutional claims upon Nightingale's vote, and thus could not regard the action as theft of a resource. But the same Fellows, as Fellows of the College considered as a corporate actor, could (and did) regard this action as theft of a resource. Nightingale's vote was a resource constitutionally given him as a Fellow of the College, to be used to further the corporate interests of the College as he saw them. To use this resource for private gain in effect deprived the College, as a corporate body, of that resource. Those College Fellows who were on the side that would be harmed by Nightingale's action pressed the claim of illegitimacy most fully, but even members of the other side recognized the claim, and some were not happy with gaining Nightingale's vote in this way.

This example indicates that the corporate body in which the position of Mastership inheres, and which constitutionally distributes control of that position to its Fellows through votes, would be the victim of theft in this case. There were four relevant actors in this potential action: two potential thieves and two victims of theft. The thieves would have been persons, Nightingale and the College Fellow who was a Royal Society Fellow. They would have stolen a resource from the College and one from the Royal Society, using them to pursue private interests rather than the interests of the respective corporate bodies.

A second example shows a somewhat different structure but again involving exchanges across corporate boundaries to serve private ends. The case was France at the time when it, as governed by De Gaulle, was pressing for a revaluation of gold against the dollar (after having bought up large amounts of gold). De Gaulle attempted to negotiate the following exchange, involving the Common Market (EEC) and the International Monetary Fund (IMF): a consideration of Britain for membership in EEC by withholding France's use of veto in return for support by other EEC members for revaluation of gold against the dollar. Again, the exchange did not take place. In this case, the EEC members were all members of IMF, but not all members of IMF were members of EEC. The other members of EEC favored Britain's entry; consequently, although the corporate interests of EEC were opposed to the use of an EEC resource (a vote by France for or against Britain's membership), there were no member interests opposed to this use. On the other side, some of the members of IMF were not members of EEC, and they regarded as illegitimate the proposed exchange, for it involved the use of IMF resources (votes by members of EEC who were also members of IMF) to further interests outside IMF. Consequently, the exchange was not only possibly against the private interests but also definitely subversive to IMF, by withdrawing resources from IMF for the use of actors who were members of another corporate body.

These examples raise a more fundamental question, transcending the question of legitimacy within a corporate actor. This is the question of whether such transgressions, using resources of one corporate actor to serve ends outside the corporate actor, are necessarily harmful to broader social welfare. In these examples, votes were being offered to other actors in return for resources that lay outside the constitutional scope of the corporate actor, and thus could not replenish the corporate actor's resources. But votes are in another sense the property of the individual members, to be used in a way that will be beneficial to them. From this point of view, it should not be illegitimate or illegal for a member of a corporate actor, who retains in his vote the residue from the sovereignty he has given up to the corporate actor, to use that vote to serve whatever private ends he desires. The matter is, of course, different for a representative, who has received the resource from constituents. His use of the vote to serve his own private ends is clearly illegitimate and is regarded as such by law, which expresses the interests of the ultimate sovereign, his constituents. But for a member of a corporate actor who has a sovereign right embodied in his vote, is he not entitled to use it in any way he sees will best satisfy his interests, whether they are interests as a member of the corporate body or not? The answer is not clear, and I will only pose it as a problem for further theoretical study. The problems are in fact two. Does the free transfer of resources across corporate bodies by a subset of their members increase the overall social welfare or decrease it? Is the vote held by a member of a corporate actor best conceptualized as his property to be used for any ends whatsoever, or as the property of the corporate actor to be used by him only in pursuit of that segment of his interests that he realizes through the corporate actor?

EXCHANGES NOT INVOLVING VOTES

A frequent type of exchange of resources across corporate boundaries involves a generalized resource, money. This is well exemplified by the relation between salesman of one corporate body and purchasing agent for another. The purchasing agent has control over a corporate action, control vested in him by virtue of his position. This is control over certain economic resources of the corporate body, and the purchasing agent must use that control to obtain goods for the corporation. Ordinarily, there are certain auxiliary controls over these actions, such as the necessity to keep accounts subject to inspection by other agents of the corporate body. Nevertheless, the purchasing agent's control of the decision as to which vendor to buy from places great power in his hands for a single reason: the corporation's interests often can be equally well satisfied by, or at least be seen to be equally well satisfied by, any one of several vendors. Yet each vendor has a strong interest in making the sale. Under such circumstances, the purchasing agent has a resource that is valuable to the various vendors, a resource for which they (or sometimes the salesman himself, using a portion of his commission) are willing to pay. This gives rise to many ways of recompensing the purchasing agent for a favorable decision: presents, direct payments of money, entertainment, and others. The transaction is one in which the purchasing agent has, in effect, stolen a resource of the corporation, the purchase decision, using it to exchange for resources going to him rather than to the corporation.

It is useful also to ask which societies are those in which bribery, graft, and other forms of corruption on the part of public officials flourish most.

Generally, it is underdeveloped countries, in which the principal corporate actor of importance is, traditionally, the family and into which a modern bureaucratic form of organization has been transplanted. In such societies, there is little history of resources belonging to corporate actors of a bureaucratic form and little experience in the separation of corporate resources and personal resources. For the family, as a corporate actor whose members are permanent and whose size is small, such separation of personal and corporate resources is less important than for the modern bureaucratic corporate actor. Thus, we would expect such use of corporate resources for personal ends to be most fully pronounced in those societies that have least experience with bureaucratic corporate bodies.[13]

CONCLUSION

At the beginning of this paper, I asked why many of these political transactions I have been describing are illegal, or at least seen as illegitimate, while similar actions are regarded by social scientists and politicians as the principal mechanisms for resolving social issues.

I think the answer is now clear. It becomes clear by recognizing that the vote or other resource being sold by the legislator has an owner, and that a legislator's action is illegal or illegitimate when he employs the resource to the benefit of himself or another person not the owner.

But who is the owner? It is here that the necessity for introducing the concept of a corporate person as an actor in the social system arises. The constituency as a corporate actor, with the legislator as its agent, is the owner of the resources held by the legislator.

Thus, we begin to find ourselves forced to introduce into a framework for social theory an abstract concept that has no tangible concrete representation. We are in the same position, as social theorists, as the law found itself in the thirteenth through fifteenth centuries, when it was confronted with corporate bodies acting as single persons in market transactions and ended by inventing the concept of "corporate person" with many of the same rights and obligations as a natural person.[14]

To introduce the concept of corporate actor into a framework for social theory is only a small step toward building the theory itself. While it provides a principle by which the legitimacy or illegitimacy of certain actions can be accounted for in simple terms such as ownership and theft, it does not solve certain other problems. What becomes necessary is not merely to introduce the concept of corporate actor and from that point on to treat the corporate actor as a unitary actor. For a corporate actor draws its resources from natural persons, concentrates them, and then deploys them through natural persons acting as its agents. Thus, to be able to describe properly the behavior of a corporate actor requires more than to endow it with purposes, goals, or interests, and the resources to pursue those interests. It requires a derivation of those interests from the interests of persons whose resources are invested in it, and from its structure, and derivation of its actions in pursuit of those interests from the structure of agents through which it acts. But all this goes beyond the intent of the present paper and must be treated elsewhere.

NOTES

1. Robert K. Merton, *Social Theory and Social Structure,* enl. ed. (New York: Free Press, 1968), p. 125.
2. Ostrogorski, in his analysis of the machine, shows how the machine operates as a middleman in a three-way transaction that could not otherwise take place: businessmen with money who want certain legislation passed, citizens with votes who need jobs and money, and legislators with the power to pass legislation who need votes for reelection; M. Ostrogorski, *Democracy and the Organization of Political Parties,* vol. 2, *The United States* (Chicago: Quadrangle Books, 1964).
3. For example, the International Typographical Union (ITU), as discussed in S. M. Lipset, M. A. Trow, and J. S. Coleman, *Union Democracy* (New York: Free Press, 1956). In the early days of the ITU, parties were illegal under union laws, yet they developed and flourished into healthy organizations. See also Ostrogorski, *The United States,* who describes the suspicion with which party formation was viewed when Samuel Adams founded the Caucus Club in Boston at the time of the founding of the Republic.
4. See Frederick Pollock and F. W. Maitland, *The History of English Law,* vol. 1, book 2 (1898), for a discussion of the emergence of corporate persons in English law. I have discussed elsewhere (James S. Coleman, *Power and the Structure of Society* [New York: Norton, 1973]) the emergence of the concept of free corporate persons with the decline of feudal law in Europe.
5. Legal thought should be given to means of further protection of constituents, either by the law or by creating other agents of the constituency to safeguard its interests. The possibility of class actions by groups of constituents is one possibility, although probably feasible only in extreme cases of malfeasance, for which other legal protections are also available. In part because the resources of the constituency are only loosely conceived, it is difficult to show misuse of these resources (for example, attention or time of the legislator). Some of the safeguards developed to protect interests of owners against actions by managers, such as disclosure and audit, would be usefully applied in legislatures.
6. For a discussion of the properties of money and of political power, see James S. Coleman, "Political Money," *American Political Science Review* 64, no. 4 (December 1970): 1074–87.
7. One senator is reported to have said of Senator Mendel Rivers' actions in gaining government installations for his constituency of Charleston, South Carolina: "If he got any more military bases built around Charleston, it would have just sunk into the bay."
8. Thus, it is very difficult to obtain passage of laws requiring legislators to make full disclosure of their personal finances.
9. See Coleman, "Political Money."
10. Certain gains to "the constituency" are not at all or not solely gains to the constituency as a corporate actor but to constituents as individuals. For example, a new government installation is often seen as bringing individual private benefits and thus does not depend on a psychic investment of self in the constituency as corporate actor. I will not distinguish these cases in the present discussion, but

235

only note that the distinction is necessary in any specific case. I have discussed this variation in psychic investment in James S. Coleman, "Individual Interests and Collective Action," in Gordon Tullock, ed., *Papers on Non-Market Decision-Making* (Charlottesville, Va.: Thomas Jefferson Center for Political Economy, University of Virginia, Summer 1966).

11. An example of this is the use by a legislator of his political resources to gain a more powerful position in the legislature, a use generally approved by constituents since it increases their political resources through him.

12. C. P. Snow, *The Masters* (Garden City, N.Y.: Doubleday Anchor Books, 1951).

13. In Muslim law there is nothing comparable to the "corporate person" in Western law, but only individuals as persons. In contrast, in Japanese law the family had a corporate status not unlike that of modern corporations. It has been argued that the ease with which Japan adopted the modern corporate form was a result of the legal corporativeness of the family, which provided a conceptual model for the society. In Israel the confrontation between the bureaucratic organization of the society as established by Western Jews and the familistic organization of Eastern Jews has led to serious difficulties in the functioning of the society. See E. Katz and S. Eisenstadt, "Some Sociological Observations on the Response of Israeli Organizations to New Immigrants," *Administrative Science Quarterly* 5 (1960): 113–33, and Brenda Danet and Harriet Hartman, "On 'Proteksia': Orientations Toward the Use of Personal Influence on Israeli Bureaucracy," *Journal of Comparative Administration* 3 (1972): 405–34.

14. See Frederick W. Maitland, "Moral Personality and Legal Personality," in H. D. Haseltine, G. Lapsley, and P. H. Winfield, eds., *Maitland: Selected Essays* (Cambridge: Cambridge University Press, 1936).

The Complexity of Roles as a Seedbed of Individual Autonomy*

ROSE LAUB COSER

It is clear that the real intellectual
wealth of the individual depends
entirely on the wealth of his real
relationships.†

M ERTON'S work offers a conceptual framework for understanding the
social-structural elements that favor modern individualism. His theory
of role-set,[1] in particular, specifies social-structural variables that, in
combination with the findings and conceptualizations of Jean Piaget,[2]
Lawrence Kohlberg,[3] Melvin Kohn,[4] and Basil Bernstein,[5] can provide the
basis for a theory of individualism in modern society.

The differentiation among institutions in modern society—the family, the
place of work, the school—require that individuals segment their activities so
that they behave differently at different places and at different times, when
they interact with different people who themselves occupy different positions,
and that they show themselves in a different light by adjusting behavior to
circumstance. They behave differently at home than at work and relate differently to associates than to family members. To the extent that associates

* I am indebted to Beverly Birns for a critical reading of an earlier version of this paper,
especially in regard to the sections dealing with child psychology. My profound thanks go to
Melvin Kohn, from whose comments and general critique I have much profited during ex-
tended conferences. discussions, and correspondence while this paper was being written.
† *Writings of the Young Marx on Philosophy and Science,* translated and edited by Lloyd
D. Easton and Kurt H. Guddat (New York: Doubleday & Co., Inc., 1967), p. 429. Author's

*Rose Laub Coser is Professor of Sociology and Medical Social Science at the
State University of New York at Stony Brook.*

occupy different positions and hence have different perceptions and expectations, individuals must differentiate their behavior not only according to requirements of time and place but also according to the interests of those with whom they interact.

These perceptions and expectations may not only be different, they may be incompatible or contradictory. Modern society is characterized by conflict, contradiction, and incompatibility arising from the manifoldness of institutions, of positions within them, and of the patterned activities and expectations associated with these positions. It is precisely the contradictions and incompatibilities in social life that have been the focus of Merton's work.

Merton stands in a long tradition, from Vico to Hegel and Marx, that stresses conflict and contradiction in society. But he has gone further in the building of a theory because he has attempted to *specify* and *locate* disjunctions, contradictions, and conflicts within the social structure.

Most sociological theorists, from Durkheim in the past to Parsons in the present, have addressed themselves to the question of social order. In contrast, Merton's aim has been to identify the sources of disorder. He has addressed the problem of how people in specified social positions are likely to respond to the contradictions embedded in the social structure. Already, at age twenty-eight, when he first published his by now classic paper "Social Structure and Anomie,"[6] he selected the problem of how people in specified positions in the social structure adapt to conditions in which the values concerning culturally patterned means are not integrated with the opportunities for attaining culturally patterned goals. In his work on bureaucracy,[7] he focused on the contradiction between the efficiency of bureaucratic forms of organization and the conflicts that bureaucratic structures produce both within the organization and in relation to the public. In "The Self-Fulfilling Prophecy"[8]—a term that has found its way into everyday language—Merton highlighted the notion, repeatedly found in his later work, of norms and counternorms when he showed that the same behavior that is positively valued in the ingroup is often negatively valued when it is seen as an attribute of the outgroup, as when Abe Lincoln is congratulated for being *thrifty* while Abe Cohen is censored for being *miserly*.[9]

From this systematization and refinement of functional analysis, the concept of dysfunction has become so much a part of speech that its source[10] has been forgotten. The concept sensitizes the analyst to the differences, incompatibilities, and conflicts between subgroups; its coinage is part of Merton's early attempt to obtain conceptual clarification of the plural aspects rather than of the uniformity of social life. Finally, in his theory of role-set, which is part of his theory of reference group behavior, Merton's aim is not mainly to explore the patterns of rights and obligations associated with social roles but

comment: The translation reads: "...real connections." It seems, however, that the word "relationships" renders better the German word "Beziehungen." Cf.: "Dass das wirkliche geistige Reichtum des Individuums ganz von dem Reichtum seiner wirklichen Beziehungen abhaengt, ist...klar." Marx, *Deutsche Ideologie*, in *Karl Marx, Friedrich Engels* (Berlin: Dietz Verlag, 1958), Vol. 3, p. 37.

to identify the sources of contradictory expectations regarding such obligations, as well as the social mechanisms available for dealing with them more or less successfully.[11]

Merton's theory of role-set offers the tools for developing a theory of individual autonomy in modern society. I shall argue that the multiplicity of expectations faced by the modern individual, incompatible or contradictory as they may be, or rather precisely because they are, makes role articulation possible in a more self-conscious manner than if there were no such multiplicity. Rather than automatically engaging in behavior that is expected, the modern individual has choices and makes choices consciously and rationally. By this it is not meant that everybody always makes conscious and rational choices, but that there is a greater possibility for doing so than there would be in the absence of such multiple expectations.[12]

Role-set theory aims at explaining behavior from the vantage point of an individual's relationships with others, and from the vantage points of the relationships that these others maintain among themselves in their common interests in that individual. Merton has stood Durkheim on his head; rather than having the individual confronted with ready-made social norms that are external, coming down in toto, so to speak, for Merton individuals have to find their own orientations among multiple, incompatible, and contradictory norms.

The individual solutions are not arbitrary, to be sure; they are available in the social structure. Truly, in Merton's mind people *make their own history, but they do not make it just as they please . . . but under circumstances directly found, given and transmitted.*[13] Yet, rather than being satisfied with talking about "circumstances" in general terms, he seeks to identify the elements of social structure that put pressure on individuals to behave in specified patterned ways. And rather than only concerning himself with aggregates or categories of individuals, he frequently focuses on the individual as a status-occupant. From this derives his definition of social structure as being comprised of "the patterned arrangements of *role-sets, status-sets,* and *status-sequence."*[14] By *role-set* is meant that complement of role relationships that persons have by virtue of occupying a particular social status. As one example: "The single status of medical student entails not only the role of student in relation to his teachers, but also an array of other roles relating the occupants of that status to other students, nurses, physicians, social workers, medical technicians,"[15] and, one should add, patients.

The term "role-set" refers to all the role partners who relate to one single status-occupant, the medical student in Merton's example. This differs from the *status-set,* which refers to a person's multiple statuses and their associated roles, as when the person who is a medical student is also a daughter to her parents, and perhaps already a wife and mother.

In each status position, a person has a different role-set, and these sets may conflict in their demands for allegiance, as when the family claims priority from the professional woman, and her professional associates expect not to be disturbed by her family obligations. In addition, the expectations emanating from role partners within each role-set can also be incompatible.

The same woman, if she is a teacher, may face different demands from the principal and the children's parents; and as a mother she may have to take account of the expectations of neighbors and those of her children's teachers as well. The effort needed to conform depends in large part on the number of the partners she interacts with; and on whether those partners do or do not share similar expectations.[16]

It should be evident that Merton's model of social structure sensitizes the analyst to the presence of conflicts and contradictions. At the outset of his analysis, Merton asks these crucial questions: "Which social processes tend to ·make for disturbance or disruption of the role-set, creating conditions of structural instability? Through which social mechanisms do the roles in the role-set become articulated so that conflict among them becomes less than it would otherwise be?"[17] It is to be noted in this last formulation that Merton does not assume that conflict can be resolved or "eliminated"; he merely asks: Why do people hold their own in complex networks that are replete with traps of contradiction and disturbance?

The concepts of *role-set, status-set,* and *status-sequence* (the latter referring to the changes in status position over time) help operationalize a notion such as that of *plurality of life worlds.*[18] They make it possible to bring conceptual order into what otherwise leaves us with a sense of diffuse chaos. By specifying how individuals learn to differentiate as well as synchronize their relations with others, and the relationships of others among themselves, it will be possible to account for the large array of variability in the social behavior of the modern individual. It will help explain what Goffman has called the *multiplicity of selves,*[19] through which individuals are able to alter behavior according to the situational context, and with a repertoire of alternatives that have been learned through what the Bergers and Keller have termed *multi-relational synchronization.*[20] It will turn out that the mechanisms that Merton has specified as helping individuals articulate their roles in the face of multiple contradictions serve as spurs for individuation and free choice.

ALIENATION AND COMPLEXITY OF SOCIAL RELATIONS

The "plurality" of social relations, or, as it is mostly called, the "segmentation of roles," has often been seen as a source of alienation.[21] In the imprecise terminology currently in use, the term is supposed to mean a generalized feeling of frustration that overcomes a person who is expected to behave in a way that is not "meaningful." In this view, the several roles an individual has to play at different times and in different places do not express the "true self," do not reveal the "true" personality, prevent the development of an "inner" self. The source of this general uneasiness is often seen as lying in the separation between different activity systems. Nostalgically, the "unalienated" man is remembered who used to be farmer and father and head of household and entrepreneur all at once.

The popular notion of *alienation* has its origin in Marx's use of the term. But Marx did not apply the concept to modern life in general; he linked it to the condition of the working class. In Marx's reasoning, the alienation of

240

workers derives from the circumstance that they are deprived of the means of production, of the product, and of knowledge about the process of production. They work side by side, not understanding this process and not expecting to derive satisfaction from the product of their labors. They do not relate meaningfully to one another through their work, nor can they relate to themselves in this most important human activity. The condition of alienation arises because of the workers' exploitation and their subjugation to routine and meaningless tasks. This is a consequence, according to Marx, of the division of labor, in which "the worker . . . feels at ease only outside work, and during work he is outside himself. He is at home when he is not working and when he is working he is not at home. . . ."[22]

This allusion to the separation in time and place between productive and private life, together with the importance Marx attaches to the division of labor, seems to make the drudgery of meaningless work linked in his thought to the segmentation of roles. Yet these two variables ought to be distinguished. Separation between two activity systems is not necessarily associated with drudgery; the two can exist independently. Professionals, for example, may work away from home and yet have control over the process and end product of their work. Conversely, people who work in their place of residence can be engaged in drudgery, as the fate of live-in domestic workers of yesteryear or the fate of many a housewife today amply testifies.

What accounts for alienation is not the fact that the worker "is not at home when he is working" in the literal sense, but rather the nature of the relationships he is embedded in at the workplace. It is not the division of labor per se, nor the separation of the home from the place of work, that accounts for what Marx has seen as alienating. To the proposition that the worker is deprived of the means of production and the product of his labor must be added the proposition that the worker is deprived, when at work, of some vital social-structural prerequisites for the development of his individuality, not because of division of labor as such but because of the division of labor in the factory as we know it.

In contrast to the view that sees the segmentation of roles as a source of alienation is the view expressed by Georg Simmel, who sees in such segmentation a structural basis for modern individualism.[23] Not focusing on conditions of exploitation but rather attuned to the way of life of the middle class, Simmel sees a person's participation in multiple activity systems as a source of individual freedom. In Simmel's view, the fact that an individual can live up to expectations of several others in different places and at different times makes it possible to preserve an inner core, to withhold inner attitudes while conforming to various expectations. Moreover, in modern society a person partakes of several identities, some ascribed, others achieved. The combination of multiple identifications makes the person unique. For example, being at once a Jew, an American, a sociologist, a Democrat, having been born, let's say, in another country, worked for a decade or two in the West and residing in the East—such a combination of attributes, each of which has left an imprint and in regard to at least some of which a person has developed loyalties, is unique, since no other person can have the same combination of attributes.

241

Furthermore, the matter does not rest with the unique combination of an individual's historical and demographic properties. More importantly, a distinct identity is acquired by the unique way in which each person relates to others in the present.

> Today someone may belong, aside from his occupational position, to a scientific association, he may sit on a board of directors of a corporation and occupy an honorific position in the city government. In this way, the objective structure of a society provides a framework within which an individual's non-interchangeable and singular characteristics may develop and find expression, depending on the greater or lesser possibilities which that structure allows, [and] the individual may add affiliations with new groups to the single affiliation which has hitherto influenced him in a pervasive and one-sided manner. The mere fact that he does so is sufficient, quite apart from the nature of the groups involved, to give him a stronger awareness of individuality in general, and at least to counteract the tendency of taking his initial group's affiliations for granted. . . .[24]

Although Simmel's notion of the individualistic consequences of multiple relationships helps in understanding some important aspects of modern life, it does not come to grips with the notion of *alienation* that is currently in use. Indeed, it may be objected that individualism and alienation are part of the same phenomenon, a view taken by the Bergers and Keller.[25] In the sense they give to the term, alienation stems from the loss of *Gemeinschaft*—the loss of embeddedness of the person in a secure unchanging group with which one is thoroughly familiar and in which a person's cognitive and emotional mastery is not challenged. This is not the sense given here to the notion of alienation. It will be remembered that I am referring to the core sense of the term in Marx's use, where alienation stems from the workers' loss of control over the means of production, the product, and the process of production and leads to self-estrangement—a "mode of experience in which the person experiences himself as an alien . . . ," where "he becomes . . . estranged from himself."[26]

In this sense alienation means lack of control over one's creativity and deprivation of a sense that one's own activity belongs to oneself and is part of the self.[27] Alienation is likely to occur in the absence of individualism, where a strong sense of self in relation to others is lacking. Persons who are or feel alienated from their activities and relationships are those who are not in a position to articulate their roles in relation to others.

It should now be apparent why equating lack of alienation with the presence of *Gemeinschaft* relationships is likely to be seriously misleading. Persons deeply enmeshed in a *Gemeinschaft* may never become aware of the fact that their lives do not actually depend on what happens within the group but on forces far beyond their perception and hence beyond their control. The *Gemeinschaft* may prevent individuals from articulating their roles in relation to the complexities of the outside world.

Indeed, there may be a distinct *weakness in strong ties,* a phrase suggested by Mark S. Granovetter,[28] who analyzes the apparent contradiction between the closeness of relations in the Italian community of Boston's West End and the fact that this community was not strong enough to form an organization

242

to fight against the urban renewal which ultimately destroyed it.[29] In contrast, another working-class community in the same city of Boston successfully organized against the urban renewal plan.[30] In the first community, social ties were so close that the community's members were hardly encouraged to form other outside connections; in the second community, in contrast, there was a rich organizational life. That is, in the second community there was segmentation of interests and hence segmentation of roles. Here people were better able to understand the outside forces that had an immediate impact on their lives.

The notion of segmented as opposed to nonsegmented roles suggests an important typology: that between complex and simple role-sets. A *simple* (or *restricted*) *role-set*[31] is (a) one in which role partners do not differ much in status position among themselves and, insofar as they do, they are few in number; or (b) one in which the role partners are hardly ever changing and are thoroughly familiar, as in a family (as the root of the word implies) or in a *Gemeinschaft*. In contrast, a *complex role-set* is similar to the one described by Merton, in which at least several role partners are differently located in the social structure and are subject to change.

The distinction is important because a complex role-set—one that includes role partners who occupy different positions from one another—offers, at the same time as it may make incompatible demands, the structural opportunities for role articulation that are absent or inoperative in simple role-sets. Although the potential incompatibilities of expectations emanating from different positional points in the structure can be a "basic source of disturbance," as Merton points out,[32] it can also be argued that a threat of disturbance presents a challenge for its prevention and thus encourages the members of the role-set to make use of mechanisms that help diminish the disorderly effects of contradictory expectations.

Merton specifies some of these mechanisms. He notes that the status-occupant's adaptation to conflicting expectations from members of his role-set is facilitated by different degrees of *interest* of the various role partners in the behavior of the status-occupant—that is, by the fact that they are not all equally involved with him; that not all role partners are equally *powerful* in shaping the behavior of occupants of a particular status; that not all role partners are equally in a position directly to *observe* the behavior of the status-occupant. Moreover, "confronted with contradictory demands by the members of his role-set, each of whom assures that the legitimacy of his demands is beyond dispute, the occupant of a status can act to make these contradictions manifest. . . . This redirects the conflict so that it is one between the members of the role-set rather than, as was at first the case, between them and the occupant of the status. . . ."[33]

This last mechanism calls attention to the fact that the individual status-occupant can make a deliberate effort to make it operate.[34] But this also applies to the other mechanisms. That is, insulation from observability, or the limitation of the authority of powerholders, or simply the limited interest they have in him, affords a status-occupant some measure of leeway for making decisions as to what expectations he is going to live up to. The professor who closes his office door for the day in order to finish writing a paper and the teacher who invokes a chairman's announcement of a meeting against a student's request for an interview are examples in point. The mechanism of culturally established priorities, mentioned by Merton in another context, can also be used, as when a resident physician is late at a staff meeting "because the patient comes first" or when a committee member cannot come to the meeting because another one was scheduled previously. These are legitimate *excuses* that make it possible either to select among one's multiple obligations or even to withdraw from some of them while one reflects about the differential nature of the commitments to several role partners variously located in the structure.

Yet, persons in different social positions are not equally able to make such choices. The mechanisms for role articulation are more readily available to people of relatively high than of low social status. At the upper levels in the hierarchy, whether at the university, in government, or in industry—for example, in the relations between management and staff—people are forced to negotiate and compromise with others of diverse interests, rank, and outlook and hence must take many factors into account, reflecting upon various alternatives of action in relation to others.

The opportunity structure is such that there is an unequal distribution of available social mechanisms that permit or challenge people to articulate their roles. For factory workers at the assembly line, there are hardly any such mechanisms because workers are part of a narrow hierarchy, where they relate to few people in the structure who are in different positions than they are themselves.[35] Hence, they are not challenged to articulate their roles in relation to others. Alienation in the sense used here is more likely to occur in a *simple* than in a *complex* type of structure, that is, one in which the ties of solidarity that are formed are more likely to be the result of sameness than of interdependence.[36]

There is some evidence available that supports the hypothesis that the availability of only a restricted number of role partners in different positions fails to develop in workers the ability to relate to their work in unalienated and individualized fashion. William F. Whyte observed that "long, narrow hierarchies . . . are relatively low in economic efficiency and in employees' morale" and that in such organizations people are prevented from "discovering what their strengths and weaknesses are" and from "feeling that they themselves have really mastered their jobs."[37]

In my own research, a comparison between types of hospital wards of different complexity yielded results that are comparable with Whyte's observation. In one type of ward (here called Sunnydale) which was defined as dealing with "terminal illness," there were very few nurses, and there hardly ever was a physician, let alone any other health personnel. Although an intern was assigned to the ward, there was a tacit understanding that he need not be present. An intern explained that he found the nurses "outstanding [since they are] ultra-conservative in calling the doctor," and a nurse explained why she did not have conflicts with physicians: "I have nothing but pleasant experiences. They know I'm only trying to help them, keep them from coming

244

over here." In contrast, in another ward (here called Center) which was designed for rehabilitation, nurses had to deal with at least four physicians, several occupational and physical therapists, two psychologists, and psychiatrists as well. The nurses who had these diverse role-partners cited instances of how different physicians prescribed different courses of treatment or of how a physical therapist expected a different scheduling for a patient than the physician's prescription had led them to expect. "It puts the burden on me. I have to make the decision." The measure of autonomy that is thus forced on these nurses seemed to produce in them also a different image of themselves in relation to their work. At the Center, nurses developed what Everett C. Hughes has called a "social identity,"[38] which seemed to be lacking at Sunnydale. When asked what was the most important thing they did, Center nurses were more likely to use nouns than verbs; they described their tasks as being a "teacher," an "organizer," a "politician." This contrasted with Sunnydale nurses, who mentioned as their most important task routine activities such as "keeping patients clean."

This different conception of their tasks seemed to be associated with a different image of themselves in relation to patients, if we can infer from a projective test. Respondents were asked to draw a picture of "a nurse at work." Nine out of the ten Center nurses drew a patient next to the nurse; but only four out of the twelve Sunnydale nurses who responded to the request added to their picture of the nurse that of a patient. Significantly, also, contrary to the Center nurses who all responded to the request, at Sunnydale five of the seventeen nurses refused to draw the picture even after being prodded.

Everett Hughes has called attention to the importance of a person's work for his experience of self: "A man's work is one of the more important parts of his social identity, of his self; indeed, of his fate in the one life he has to live, for there is something almost as irrevocable about the choice of occupation as there is about the choice of a mate." So much is this the case, Hughes suggests, that when you ask people what work they do, they are likely to answer in terms of "who they are"; that is, they attempt to establish and validate their own identity by referring to the identity of their work in a publicly recognized and preferably esteemed occupational or professional category.[39] The interviews with nurses at this research site, however, suggest that not all of them gave such self-enhancing descriptions of "who they are." Nine of the ten Center nurses did so, compared with only two of the seventeen nurses from Sunnydale. Moreover, it seems that those who saw themselves in their professional roles were more likely to see themselves as relating to patients than those who mentioned routine tasks. Of the eleven nurses who mentioned their professional roles, ten drew the picture of the nurse together with a patient, indicating the likelihood that their self-image included their relation to a significant role partner; of the fourteen nurses who answered the question of the importance of their task by mentioning a routine activity, only three included a patient in the picture. One-half of these nurses (seven out of fourteen) did not include a patient in their drawings, and four refused to draw a picture at all. These responses seem to suggest that for the latter nurses the relationship with a patient was not part of their self-image.[40]

Center nurses continuously had to articulate their roles in the face of inconsistent, incompatible, and conflicting expectations on the part of the various members of the staff, each of whom had different interests and outlooks—the physical and occupational therapists, psychologists, social workers, and psychiatrists, in addition to physicians and nurses of different rank, and patients. Indeed, assuming that projective tests are good indicators, it seems that these nurses were better able to articulate their roles in relation to patients as well.

In a complex role-set, individuals are more likely to be confronted with incompatible expectations. Where this is the case, they are required to *reflect* upon an appropriate course of action in relation to their status position. They must decide whether to abide strictly by the rules or to reinterpret or even defy them, and weigh each decision in relation to their own purposes of action and the purposes of others. This calls for *innovation,* sometimes in the form of violation of custom and hierarchical modes, as when Center nurses repeatedly stated that "here we have to teach the doctors." It also forces a certain measure of *flexibility,* as differences are "ironed out," through negotiation and compromise, through a social process that forces each participant to take into account the vantage point of the other person. The attempt to integrate preferences, innovations, and compromises with what is socially legitimate is one of *reflection* and *self-direction.* The traits of *innovation, flexibility, reflection,* and *self-direction,* which will be scrutinized further in connection with Melvin Kohn's research bearing on these problems, are important factors in individualism.[41]

To these traits must be added another important ingredient of this type of interaction, namely *empathy.* Merton shows that this psychological trait is fostered by arrangements in the social structure.

> The extent to which empathy obtains among members of a society is in part a function of the underlying social structure. For those who are in the role-sets of the individual subjected to conflicting status-obligations are in turn occupants of multiple statuses, formerly or presently, actually or potentially, [and therefore] subject to similar stress. This structural circumstance at least facilitates the development of empathy.[42]

If reflection, flexibility, and empathy have, at least in part, their roots in the social structure, it raises an important question about the relation between social structure and mental activities. It implies that not only behavior but the thinking process itself would seem to be related to the nature of social relationships.

DIFFERENTIATION, SOCIAL COMPLEXITY, AND INTELLECTUAL FLEXIBILITY

The development of mental abilities takes place together with the progressive grasp of the complexity of social relations. That intellectual comprehension should be in large measure an attribute of the social structure seems at first to be a daring assertion. Yet it should not be surprising that people who have to deal with many others, each of whom may have a different perspective from the vantage point of a different position, are forced to reflect upon and take account of these other perspectives when making decisions about their own actions or, should they be in decision-making positions, about the behavior of others. The various intentions of others have to be gauged, and one's own actions have to be adapted to one's expectations of the different ways in which these others are going to behave.

The assertion that a person's thinking is related to the structure of the social context finds its support in everyday language, as when we call someone "parochial," implying that a person's limited mental capacity is grounded in restricted social relations. The assumption underlying the imputation of "parochialism" is that a simple social context, that is, one in which one interacts with people who have a similar outlook, makes for a limited perspective.[43] Such a social environment seems to require less mental effort than an environment that is differentiated by statuses, roles, and attendant opinions and attitudes, in which behavior of others cannot be predicted without reflection.

Socialization in modern middle-class society consists largely in helping develop the ability to make this mental effort. It differs from socialization in simpler societies in that it pushes further the requirements for increased differentiation of thought and action. If understanding others, that is, putting oneself in imagination in the position of others, is the essence of social interaction, to do so successfully means that one is able to differentiate between self and others and, more importantly, between the others who stand in mutual relationships. Increasing differentiation is the process by which the mind develops through childhood and adolescence to what is loosely called maturity. From the point at which, generally between six and eight months, the baby discovers the difference between itself and mother, becoming aware of the threat of abandonment,[44] and when it discovers the difference between the rattle and its arm, gaining a sense of mastery as it now picks up the object and drops it deliberately and repeatedly and causes it to make the familiar noise, all the while chuckling with pleasure at the discovery of its own power, to the development of the sense of "I" in the modern individual and the later ability to deal with advanced mathematics, there is one steady increase in a person's mental ability to differentiate between the self and others first, and between an increasing number of variables, symbols, and persons as they relate to one another.

The small child showing a picture to a person facing it keeps the picture turned toward itself because it does not know the difference between its own position and that of its partner. Once it knows that the picture has to be turned around so as to be seen from the other side, the child has made a big step in social development. Socialization consists largely in acquiring the ability to put oneself in the position of others while keeping one's own position in mind. Lawrence Kohlberg and Carol Gilligan quote a child who describes this process: "You have to like dream that your mind leaves your body and goes into the other person, then it comes back into you and you see it like he does and you act like the way you saw it from there."[45]

The image of the ball game used by George Herbert Mead is useful here. The individual "must be ready to take the attitude of everyone else involved in the game" and relate the players to one another; the individual "must know what everyone else is going to do in order to carry out his play" and "organize into a sort of unit the attitudes of the other players."[46] The decision as to what behavior to select for effective action will be made in relation to the *different positions* of the players in relation to one another. That is, not only must the child take the attitude of everyone else involved in the game in relation to his or her self, but he or she must be able to take the attitude of all others in relation to one another. The child must not only learn to *reverse* the roles but also to *relate* them. Reversibility is a necessary but not sufficient condition for acquiring a sense of relativity.

The ability should not be taken for granted, nor should its importance be underestimated. We are all familiar with the small child who, for example, invites the mailman into the house to "come have some of the cookies mummy baked today." We laugh and find this "cute," but would react quite differently if an older child, who *should know better,* behaved in this way. Knowing better means knowing that the mailman relates differently to the family than its own members.

Everyone who has children or younger siblings knows that a small child has quite some difficulty understanding that mother is not father's mother as well. Not before the age of seven or eight, and sometimes even later, is a child fully able to understand that someone relates in a *particular* way. The child universalizes its own relationships because it cannot yet differentiate them from others outside of itself. Motherhood is absolute, pertaining to the person, not to the relationship. The child cannot yet conceive of the relationship between mother and father as being independent of itself. Similarly, at this age children are not able to understand why a boat does not sink because they are not yet able to relate to each other two variables outside of themselves, in this case volume and weight.

Seeing things in perspective depends on that same ability. The small child's drawing of a table is a rectangle and four perpendicular lines. This is not the table *as we see it,* because in the young imagination the table is related to the self rather than to the framework of walls in the room. The table cannot be drawn in perspective before the child has reached the stage of mental development at which the outlines can be related to the surrounding walls.

To see things in perspective is to see things *relatively.* The ability to relate two variables to each other rather than to oneself develops at the same time as the ability to understand how two people relate to each other irrespective of oneself. The child who is ready to understand that mother is not also father's mother is also likely to understand the relation of weight to volume in keeping the boat afloat. Once the child has understood that what mother "is" is relative to her relation to the other person, the child will no longer offer hospitality to the mailman.

This sense of relativity contrasts with the earlier stage, when the child's world is ruled by absolutes. We are familiar with Piaget's demonstration that the rules are *attached* to the game in the mind of the child at that early stage.

Nor is this a peculiar, culture-bound phenomenon. For if the children in Piaget's Switzerland believe that the rules were made by William Tell or the Founding Fathers,[47] American children of the same age believe that the rules were made by George Washington or the pilgrims.[48]

Once a sense of relativity is achieved, the child will become more flexible in its adaptation. The following story illustrates the change from dependency on absolutes to the acquisition of such flexibility. At age seven and one-half, my daughter Ellen, who was in a class with nine-year-olds, explained why she did not like to play soccer with the other children during recess: "It's like this. I like to play soccer at gym because the teacher makes us play by the rules. At recess the kids don't play by the rules." The point here is not merely what is known since the appearance of Piaget's classic work—namely, that at that age rules are seen as absolutes—but that at that age the child is *not able to engage in the required interaction unless the rules are presented as absolute*. Ellen was not able to relate to other children under conditions of relativity of rules because she had not yet acquired the intellectual flexibility necessary for such accomplishment. One does not need to put oneself in the position of everyone else in the game, as Mead describes it, if one plays by absolute rules rather than by flexible rules; in the latter case, one must be able to relate the rules to the people who are engaged in interaction among themselves. It took Ellen another year, at which time she had reversed her liking of the game in the two situations. She said that she "hated gym" because "all they do is play soccer"; probed, she stated that she did like to play the game at recess because "the teacher wants us to play by the rules but [with considerable pride] *we* make *our own* rules."

The development of this flexibility, that is, of the understanding that rules can be changed because they are rooted in the relationships among people, takes place about the time when children begin to understand that their father is not also their mother's father. At this stage the child is able to understand how all others in the game relate to one another, and this is accompanied by a sense of power, as Ellen's pride about making "our own rules" illustrates. The understanding of some basic principle of mathematics follows the same process. Here, my son Steven took his turn at age eight. He came home from school with an abacus, exclaiming enthusiastically that "this is the best toy I've ever had," and proceeded to demonstrate multiplication with three figures. "Now let me test you," he said, "you do it." Pointing to successive rows of beads, I said: "It seems that first I must remember that these are the tens, and these the hundreds, and these the thousands. . . ." Here I was interrupted. "Wrong already," he said, "these beads are nothing, they have no value of their own." Then, lifting his head proudly and with a glimmer in his eyes: "They only have the value that *I* give them."

The discovery of relativity is an important landmark in the development of individualism. In Freudian terms, it is accompanied by an aggrandizement of the ego, as children become aware that they can make their "own" rules or that beads only have "the value that *I* give them." This is how children discover their own power, little by little, and one is reminded of the earlier happy chuckle of the baby who discovered its power in picking up the rattle or throwing it on the floor repeatedly and having it returned or, a little later, in the ability to hide an object and find it again. Growing up consists of successive discoveries of how things that have seemed "just to happen" can actually be brought about deliberately, changed and manipulated by one's own power. In this way, the understanding of relations outside the self helps develop in the young child the self-awareness that is the harbinger of adult individualism.

At the same time as children learn to differentiate between the game and its rules, between the particular role of "mother" and the person, they also learn to differentiate between motivation and behavior. Once they are able to understand that the rules are to serve the intended purposes of the players and therefore can be changed through agreement, they also learn that an act is to be judged according to the intention of the actor. In the earlier stage, to repeat one of Piaget's classical stories, Johnnie, who in helping mother with the dishes drops a tray and breaks twelve cups, is judged to be "naughtier" than Jimmie, who breaks one cup when he tries to steal a cookie.[49] Here the act is judged "good or bad" according to its external consequences. The act is part of the person. And the person is what the immediate consequences of behavior indicate.

It is only later, at the age of eight or nine at the earliest, that children learn to distinguish behavior according to the intention of the actor and that behavior is judged to be relative. The time at which this moral judgment develops is also about the time when the relativity of rules and the use of perspective in drawing objects have been learned.

Actually, moral and cognitive development continues up to age sixteen or later, according to Kohlberg and Gilligan.[50] They distinguish between an earlier stage, which they call "concrete-operational" (which they say takes place, in the average, between ten and thirteen), and a more mature stage, called "formal-operational" (between thirteen and sixteen). They illustrate these stages with this example. Children were asked what they thought about the following event: "Only brave pilots are allowed to fly over high mountains. A fighter pilot flying over the Alps collided with an aerial cableway, and cut a main cable causing some cars to fall to the glacier below. Several people were killed." A child at the concrete-operational level answered: "I think that the pilot was not very good at flying. He would have been better off if he went on fighting." A formal-operational child responded: "He was either not informed of the mountain railway en route or he was flying too low; also his flying compass may have been affected by something before or after take-off, this setting him off course causing collision with the cable."[51] This last answer shows the willingness to consider alternatives, to figure out various possibilities; it is a trait that can be called "intellectual flexibility" in that it makes judgment variable in accordance with the position of the actor and the circumstances surrounding the act.

It is important to note that modern legal thought is in large part based on the same principle. An investigating team that would have the task of establishing the guilt or innocence of the pilot in the above story would go about it in the same way as the youngster who considered the various alter-

250

natives. Yet a large part of the lay population is likely to argue that the law is the law no matter what the circumstances. While this could be called a more "primitive" type of legal approach, it is certainly one that corresponds to the mental orientation and sense of justice of many people. Kohlberg and Gilligan have empirical evidence to support the hypothesis that "almost 50 per cent of American adults never achieve formal-operational thinking." (And they found that in simpler cultures, for example, in villages in Turkey, "full formal operations never seem to be reached at all, though it is reached by urbanized, educated Turks.")[52]

The examples of children's reflections on the circumstances surrounding the plane crash show that "operational thinking" is related to moral judgment. The second child, who was ready for multivariate analysis, so to speak, was ready to suspend moral judgment until various possible circumstances could be considered. He put himself in the position of the pilot, reflecting on the various ways in which the accident could have happened.

The structure of thought and of moral judgment differs under different social conditions, not simply as a reflection of culture but as a result of inter-personal experience. The extent to which intentions are taken into consideration may be the result of material circumstance rather than dictated by a sense of what is deemed to be "desirable." If in a poor family a child accidentally breaks twelve cups, the parent will most likely let out a scream even though the accident happened while the child was trying to be helpful. In contrast, if middle-class Johnnie takes a clock apart, his mother may well be able to afford to be flexible in her judgment about his "scientific mind," a privilege which lower-class Johnnie will be deprived of if he has just put to pieces the only clock in the house.

However, material circumstances would seem to be one but not necessarily the main source of differential judgmental behavior. Following Piaget and Kohlberg, and some supporting empirical evidence to be presented below, intellectual flexibility and complex mental operations seem to be related in some important way, yet to be empirically measured, to the complexity of social relations. Kohlberg and Gilligan demonstrate that "stages are not direct reflections of the child's culture and external world, though they depend upon experience for their formation. Stages are rather the products of interactional experience between the child and the world, experience which leads to a re-structuring of the culture's pattern upon the child."[53]

If mental processes are, at least in part, the result of "interactional experience," it would seem useful to look at the social structure as a source of class differences in moral values and conceptualization. Otherwise put, the question arises whether the social structure exerts pressure on people in some strata to develop "formal operational thought" or "intellectual flexibility," and to deprive people in other strata of the opportunities for such development.

MENTAL PROCESSES, COMPLEXITY OF ROLE-SET,
AND SOCIAL CLASS

Social structures differ in the extent to which they encourage or discourage in their various status-occupants the use of intellectual flexibility. Generally, such encouragement, or even expectation, is directly associated with status position. Those who occupy high status positions are likely to have leeway in their behavior; they are expected to use their judgment, to weigh alternatives, and to be guided in their actions by moral principles, cognitive assessments, and commitments to goals. Those who occupy low positions in the hierarchy have much less leeway and fewer options among alternatives; for them, specific activities are more frequently prescribed in detail, and their relation to a goal is not always clear.

The question arises whether these class differences in expectations are related to the development of *formal-operational thought* and *intellectual flexibility*. It will be remembered that this mental development consists, in Piaget's terms, in the differentiation between behavior and the intention that motivates it. This psychological distinction is paralleled in sociology by Merton's distinction between behavior and attitude,[54] the latter referring to internal dispositions or values, and between behavioral and attitudinal conformity.[55]

Merton speaks of behavioral conformity when, whatever the individuals' dispositions, they act according to normative prescriptions; and of attitudinal conformity when individuals grant legitimacy to institutional values and norms. Behavioral conformity that is not backed up by involvement of internal dispositions is not conceived here as synonymous with "putting on an act" to placate a role partner. Rather, selection between these types of conformity is often socially prescribed. Some status-holders are expected to show mainly attitudinal conformity ("It's not that I mind the way he acts, it's his attitude I don't like"); others are expected to show only behavioral conformity ("Why doesn't he just do his job; who cares about what he thinks?"). It is important to realize that such varied expectations are by no means happenstances but emanate from the structural positions that particular role partners occupy.[56] In some positions, it is expected that people conform mainly behaviorally, without involvement of internal dispositions. For example, such involvement might do more harm than good to the expected precision and swiftness at the assembly line. In contrast, physicians in a hospital are expected to use their judgment and to adapt behavior to the needs and conditions of individual patients. To do this, they must call on internalized values and on their commitment as well as on their intellectual resources; yet the specific details of behavior are not prescribed.

Just as the expectation of intellectual flexibility is associated with status, so the measure of internal involvement occupations claim from their members is directly related to prestige in the stratification system.[57] In routinized occupations, performance requires mainly behavioral conformity to detailed prescriptions and little involvement of internal dispositions. In contrast, professionals are to be guided by attitudes and internal dispositions, and there exist alternatives concerning behavioral details.[58] Individual decisions regarding courses of action are to be made; and if these are to conform to standards they must be informed by internalized values on which to rest individual judgment. In this case, "sanctions do not attach to particular acts but only to very general principles and attitudes."[59] Between the two extreme expectations of almost exclusive behavioral and exclusive attitudinal conformity there is a continuum of relative emphasis on either type, determined by the measure of routinization or the measure of individualization of judgment and control that allegedly is involved in the practice of a particular occupation.

Where the emphasis is on behavioral conformity, as is usually the case at the lower levels of the hierarchy, authority-holders observe the behavior of their subordinates closely because it is assumed that the latter's conformity is contingent on direct supervision. This situation helps preclude the use of flexibility and reflection on the part of subordinates. It should be noted parenthetically that the concern for discipline characterizing such otherwise different authority-holders as foremen, hospital attendants, or some types of grade school teachers or nurses has its main roots in the structural position they hold in relation to their subordinates.[60]

A social structure that offers leeway in behavioral conformity and that relies on internal dispositions as guides to action is more complex than one in which emphasis is on behavior and its external consequences. The complexity consists in the fact that there are differences in expectations, as well as differences in observability, in types of authority, and in types of interest in the relationships as defined. That is, the very mechanisms that Merton has singled out as operating more or less successfully to help status-occupants resolve contradictions in expectations also add complexity to the structure. In contrast, in closely supervised situations the subordinates are "equalized"—a condition Karl Mannheim has called "negative democratization."[61] They tend to be oriented toward one type of supervisor who is in a position to observe practically at all times the details of their behavior. This is a simple type of relationship, in that it does not subject the subordinates to contradictory expectations, differential interest, authority, and observability by different status-occupants. In other words, according to a definition offered earlier, the degree to which internal dispositions are called on to guide behavior seems to be associated with *complexity of role-set.*

This hypothesis receives some support from Melvin Kohn's research. He finds that *substantive complexity of the job* is specifically pertinent for explaining flexibility in dealing with ideational problems.[62] Although *job complexity* is not synonymous with *complexity of role-set,* there is good reason to believe that the two notions are fairly similar.[63]

Not only is there a relation between complexity of relationships and the development of intellectual flexibility. In addition, Kohn has argued that the occupational experience has a determining effect on the formation of values.[64] This should not be surprising, since we would expect that the value system is integrated with the stratification system. He shows that just as self-direction and flexibility are highly valued traits in middle-class occupations generally, they are also emphasized in the socialization process in the middle class. When asked what traits they encourage in their children, middle-class mothers and fathers tend to "give higher priority to values that reflect internal dynamics—the child's own and his empathic concern for other people." In contrast, just as "working-class occupations require, in larger measure, that one follow explicit rules set down by someone in authority," in the working class both mothers and fathers are likely to "give higher priority to values that reflect behavioral conformity—obedience and neatness."[65]

The association between parental values and expectations on the job as well as the association between the latter and structural complexity do not yet tell us the causal direction, and no doubt there may be some mutual reinforcement. People who are brought up to emphasize behavioral conformity might be more likely to seek out work situations in which this is rewarded as well as social situations on the job that are less complex; and, in turn, social relations on the job may influence people's mental abilities regarding self-direction and intellectual flexibility.

Kohn has tackled this problem in his latest work with Carmi Schooler. They demonstrate that, with education controlled, effects of the occupational experience of job complexity are at least as strong as are the reciprocal effects of occupational self-selection and of job-molding processes, perhaps even twice as strong.[66]

Social structures differ in the extent to which they make demands·on an individual's effort at differentiation. Complexity of role-set, it will be remembered, means that status-occupants have role partners differently located in the social structure, who, mainly for this reason, have different and often incompatible expectations. They make demands on the status-occupants to negotiate, exercise judgment, reconcile, compromise, and take account of the intentions, purposes, motivations, and perspectives of these role partners. The mental operations that have to take place are much more demanding of reflection under these conditions than in a group of peers or in a *Gemeinschaft* type of society. If the role-set consists mostly of role partners in the same status position, or in firmly established ones where everyone knows what to expect at any time, motivations and internal attitudes can be taken for granted. One does not have to make as much effort to put oneself in the position of the other person if behavior is based more nearly on absolute rules as when norms are more fluid and are being interpreted in interaction with people whom, in addition, one knows only partially. In a *Gemeinschaft* everyone knows fairly well why people behave in a certain way. Little effort has to be made to gauge the intention of the other person, nor is much reflection needed to determine one's own response.

If this reasoning is correct, it would follow as a consequence that the manner of communication will tend to be different in a *Gesellschaft*. Hence, the type of speech people use should differ in these two types of structures. Evidence for this comes from the research of Basil Bernstein, who concludes that in relationships in which "the intent of the other person can be taken for granted as the speech is played out against a back-drop of common assumptions, common history, common interests," such speech does not have to be explicitly articulated. "Often in these encounters the speech cannot be understood apart from the context."[67]

This explains the peculiar charm one or the other dialect is said to have, and which often is said not to be translatable into official and codified language. This is because the richness in meaning of some shortcut expressions can hardly be rendered in a language that is used to address a far larger public which does not share the common assumptions of those who speak the local dialect. For the latter, "there is less need to raise the meanings to the level of explicitness or elaboration."[68]

The linguist Vigotsky notes that between people in close psychological contact words acquire special meanings understood only by the initiated. He calls this "inner" speech, that is, one in which a single word can be "so saturated with sense that many words would be required to explain it"[69] to the less initiated.

Parsons' distinction between *particularism* and *universalism* is useful here. In particularistic relationships, that is, where role partners relate to one another in a unique manner, like in a family,[70] there often exists a private language; sentences, for example, don't have to be finished. "When the thoughts of the speakers are the same the role of speech is reduced to a minimum."[71] A fine example is provided by Tolstoy in *Anna Karenina:*

> Now Levin was used to expressing his thought fully without troubling to put it into exact words: He knew that his wife, in such moments filled with love, as this one, would understand what he wanted to say from a mere hint, and she did.[72]

In contrast to such restricted speech among people who are close, speech in which people do not depend on intimacy and may not even know one another has to be more elaborate in universalistic relationships. "Universalistic meanings are those in which principles and operations are made linguistically explicit . . . , [in which] meanings are less tied to a given context. Where meanings are universalistic, they are in principle available to all because the principles and operations have been made explicit."[73]

Hence, we can distinguish with Bernstein between *restricted* and *elaborate* speech. The first is simpler and is typically used in particularistic relationships. It is more dependent on others, while elaborate speech can be understood by everybody. Particularistic meanings are "more context-bound, that is, tied to a local relationship and to a local social structure. . . ."[74]

Children who first learn to speak provide examples of the extreme restriction in language that can be afforded among intimates and that is dependent on the latter to be understood. It is a familiar fact that the small child who is learning to speak has an amazing ability to get a point across with very few words, provided they are addressed to mother or father or sibling. For example, for one fourteen-month-old the word "nomore" meant: "This is the end of the meal." But it also meant, when pointing to an empty glass, "I want orange juice." And a musical record on the shelf was also called "nomore," since it meant "no more music." With such a vocabulary, however, the child could hardly have survived outside the immediate family. There comes to mind the familiar scene of a mother called to the rescue in order to interpret the meaning of her child's speech. The baby who uses one word to mean many things is, clearly, most dependent on very few others.

It will be remembered that intellectual development proceeds through increasing differentiation, first between the self and others and then between the others as well. When others are understood to be different from oneself, a thought must be more clearly articulated into speech. And when the others are known to differ among themselves, the speech, to be understood by all, must be even more carefully elaborated. With less social support, more thought and reflection have to go into one's formulations.

> In written speech, lacking situational and expressive supports, communication must be achieved only through words and their combinations; this requires the speech activity to take complicated forms—hence the use of first drafts. The evolution from the draft to the final copy reflects our mental process. Planning has an important part in written speech, even when we do not actually write out a draft. Usually we say to ourselves what we are going to write; this is also a draft, though in thought only.[75]

One might add that the larger and more heterogeneous the audience, the closer the speech is to the written word; this is why it is safer, in order to be clearly understood, to read a paper that has been carefully formulated in advance than to rely on an oral performance without notes.

Elaborate speech is a result of reflection, and the need for this is greater when there is more difference between those to whom the speech is addressed. This should not lead, of course, to the fallacious conclusion that the more numerous the listeners, the more intelligent the speech that addresses them. A crowd is precisely undifferentiated; that is, its members do not occupy different positions in relation to the speaker. And since they have very little in common, it is only this small part that must be addressed.[76] This is why the crowd exercises pressure for mediocrity. Yet popular speeches are usually mediocre not because the speaker is unintelligent but because one has to be intelligent to gauge the low intellectual level of a crowd's common expectations.

A complex role-set differs from a crowd in that it consists of a finite number of individuals in different positions, who relate to one another each in a different way. Unlike a crowd, whose homogeneity is arrived at through the lowest common denominator, a role-set encompasses people whose different interests are salient from the point of view of the position they occupy. This imposes on the role partners the burden or the privilege, as the case may be, of reflection. They can then make use of the mechanisms available in the structure for articulating their roles—the mechanisms, it will be remembered, of differences in observability among the role-partners, their difference in authority over and interest in the status-occupant, as well as the latter's differential involvement with them. These mechanisms not only serve as protection in and of themselves, so that, for example, a role partner who is not supposed to be much interested (such as a school janitor in relation to a teacher's teaching methods) will not develop strong expectations. In such complex role-sets mutual expectations are subject to change, and small changes in positional relations are part of a process of change that results from repeated role-articulation.

In a simple role-set, in contrast, one can take one's role partners for granted. Less reflection is needed to communicate with them because one knows what they have on their mind; and one also knows that they know what one has on one's own mind. Such knowledge cannot be taken for granted in a complex role-set, where intentions and attitudes have to be mutually gauged for mutual understanding. This has its expression in the type of speech that is used. "Inasmuch as difference is part of the expectation, there is less reliance or dependency on the listener" and "difference lies at the basis of the social relationship, and is made verbally active, whereas in the other context it is consensus."[77] Consequently, in elaborate speech there is a relatively high level of individualism, for it results from the ability to put oneself in imagination in the position of each role partner in relation to all others, including oneself. In addition to fostering independence and individual ability, this conveys uniqueness, because in a complex role-set these "others" are hardly ever the same for two persons.

To operate in a complex role-set, one must gain perspective on the various attitudes of the diverse role partners by putting oneself in the position of each of them as they relate to one another. One must keep in mind that they are different from oneself and from one another and that this difference imposes certain adjustments in one's own stance. It is, therefore, the more individualistic rather than the less individualistic person who can adapt to the expectations of others. "As we move from communalized to individualized roles, so speech takes on an increasingly reflexive function. The unique selves of others become palpable through speech and enter into our own self; the grounds of our experience are made verbally explicit; the security of the condensed symbol is gone. It has been replaced by rationality."[78]

This helps explain Kohn and Schooler's findings that intellectual flexibility is associated with complexity on the job. And since complexity of role-sets, it will be remembered, is associated with hierarchical status position, it follows that some status-occupants have more access than do others to the social resources that facilitate the development of this trait.

The lower class is not only deprived of material means; another important deprivation is that of *structural* resources. Bernstein provides the evidence that "one of the effects of the class system is to limit the access to elaborated codes."[79] He finds that, controlled for IQ, lower-class children are more likely to use restricted speech, whereas middle-class children tend to use elaborate speech. The following example of his will make this clear.

Middle- and working-class children were given four pictures. The first showed some boys playing football; in the second the ball goes through the window of a house; the third shows a woman looking out of the window and a man making an ominous gesture; and in the fourth the children are moving away.[80] The children were asked to tell the story. The first is an example of how a middle-class child told it:

> Three boys are playing football and one boy kicks the ball and it goes through the window the ball breaks the window and the boys are looking at it and a man comes out and shouts at them because they've broken the window so they run away and then that lady looks out of her window and she tells the boys off.

The next was told by a working-class child:

> They're playing football and he kicks it and it goes through there it breaks the window and they're looking at it and he comes out and shouts at them because they've broken it so they run away and then she looks out and she tells them off.

Bernstein goes on to explain that with the first story the reader does not need to have the pictures to understand, whereas to understand the second story the reader would need them because the story is much more closely tied to its context. He continues: "It is not that the working-class children do not have . . . the vocabulary used by the middle-class children. Nor is it the case that the children differ in their tacit understanding of the linguistic rule system. . . . What we have here are differences in the use of language arising out of a specific context. . . ."[81] Middle-class children learn not to take their partners that much for granted. This is related to the concern with internal dynamics because middle-class parents are likely to accompany their "do's and don't's" with elaborate explanations, making things explicit in terms of relations between means and ends, between things, or between people. Working-class children are more likely to take their relations with others for granted. This means, in the light of Kohn's research, that where the emphasis is on obedience, it does not really matter what the reason is or who issues the order; the meaning of the order is implicit, rather than explicit, and speech does not need to be elaborate.

In summary, a social structure that is more complex seems to be associated with the development of intellectual flexibility and self-direction; this is accompanied by a speech pattern that is more universalistic, that is, one that addresses itself to people differently positioned in the structure; and this value is transmitted in the socialization process to the next generation. In contrast, a social structure that is simple seems to be associated with values emphasizing behavior and its external consequences; this is accompanied by a speech pattern that is particularistic, that is context-bound, in which reasons and motivations are not spelled out.

Some people in the social structure have more access to the conditions that favor development of elaborate speech patterns, intellectual flexibility, and self-direction. "As the division of labor changes from simple to complex, this changes the social and knowledge characteristics of occupational roles. In this process there is an extension of access, but access is controlled by the class system."[82] Virginia Woolf is dramatically right when she says that "a poor child in England"—and she might have added in America as well—"has little more hope than had the son of an Athenian slave to be emancipated into that intellectual freedom of which great writings are born."[83] It is the exceptional lower-class child who manages to leave the social-structural restrictiveness of his milieu through whatever minimal opportunity there exists in our educational or social systems to achieve the individualism and creativity that are born from the seeds of social distance and role segmentation.

It is in a differentiated social structure, where individuals are segmentally involved, where they are encouraged to take distance and to articulate their roles and their thoughts, that people are able to develop that degree of individuation that goes together with rationality and flexibility. This is not to say that all people in a differentiated social structure develop these traits, *but that more people develop them than would be the case in nondifferentiated structures.* Complex role-sets and differentiated roles are not alienating restrictions on individuality; they are its basic structural precondition. The many contradictions of modern life that have been analyzed in Merton's masterful writings are not a disaster, they are an opportunity.

NOTES

1. Robert K. Merton, "Continuities in the Theory of Reference Group Behavior," in Robert K. Merton, *Social Theory and Social Structure,* enl. ed. (New York: Free Press, 1968), pp. 422–40. (Hereinafter referred to as "Reference Group Behavior" and *STSS,* respectively.)
2. See especially Jean Piaget, *The Moral Judgment of the Child* (New York: Free Press, 1948).
3. See especially Lawrence Kohlberg and Carol Gilligan, "The Adolescent as a Philosopher: The Discovery of the Self in a Post-Conventional World," in Jerome Kagan and Robert Coles, eds., *Twelve to Sixteen: Early Adolescence* (New York: Norton, 1972), pp. 144–79.
4. Among others, Melvin Kohn, *Class and Conformity: A Study in Values* (Homewood, Ill.: Dorsey Press, 1969).
5. Among others, Basil Bernstein, *Class, Codes and Control,* vol. 1 (London: Routledge & Kegan Paul, 1971).
6. Robert K. Merton, "Social Structure and Anomie," first published in the *American Sociological Review* 3 (1938): 672–82; subsequently revised and extended in Ruth Anshen, ed., *The Family: Its Function and Destiny* (New York: Harper & Bros., 1949), pp. 226–57. This has now been reprinted and followed by "Continuities in the Theory of Social Structure and Anomie," in Merton, *STSS,* pp. 185–248.
7. Robert K. Merton, "Bureaucratic Structure and Personality" and "Role of the Intellectual in Public Bureaucracy," in Merton, *STSS,* pp. 249–78.
8. Robert K. Merton, "The Self-Fulfilling Prophecy," in Merton, *STSS,* pp. 475–90.
9. *Ibid.,* pp. 482 ff.
10. Robert K. Merton, "Manifest and Latent Functions," in Merton, *STSS,* pp. 73–138.
11. Merton, "Reference Group Behavior," pp. 422–38.
12. The phrasing of the last sentence is modeled after a much favored formulation by RKM. It should be permitted, in a book of this kind, to pause for a moment in order to reflect about some of RKM's teachings. Time and again he cautions his readers about the limited applicability of the generalizations he ventures. For example, writing about some mechanism that is at work to protect teachers from

conflicting expectations: "This is not to say, of course, that teachers are not vulnerable to these expectations which are at odds with their professional commitments. It is only to say that *they are less vulnerable than they would otherwise be* ..." (*ibid.*, p. 426; emphasis added); or again, speaking about mechanisms that prevent role partners from using sanctions if expectations are not met: "This does not mean, of course, that the status-occupant subject to conflicting expectations among members of his role-set is in fact immune to control by them. It is only to say that the power-structure of role-sets is often such that the status-occupant *more nearly has autonomy than would be the case if this structure of competing powers did not obtain*" (*ibid.*, p. 428; emphasis added). And he asks the question: "Through which social mechanisms do the roles in the role-sets become articulated so that conflict among them *becomes less than it would otherwise be?*" (emphasis added). It is to be noted that Merton insists that no social arrangement can work perfectly, without tensions or conflicts, and that stability of a system can never be complete or assumed. When he sets himself the task "of identifying the social mechanisms through which some reasonable degree of articulation among the roles in the role-sets is secured," he adds: "or, correlatively, the social mechanisms which *break down* so that structurally established role-sets do not remain relatively stabilized" (*ibid.*, p. 424; emphasis added). These are not mere caveats; and it is not mere caution. Rather, it is part of his general philosophy concerning the ever-presence of contradictions and conflicts in social life, and of his concern with the dynamics of social processes rather than with the conditions of social order.

13. We recognize here Karl Marx's familiar phrase from *The Eighteenth Brumaire* (New York: International Publishers, n.d.), p. 13.

14. Merton, "Reference Group Behavior," p. 423.

15. *Ibid.*, p. 424.

16. Cf., "There is a certain endemic potentiality of role conflict inherent in the fact that any actor has a plurality of roles, which involve differences of pattern, thus of relations to alters whose interests and orientations mesh with egos in different ways. . . . There are thus always a variety of activities which have their appropriate partners, which would not be appropriate with other partners . . ." (Talcott Parsons, *The Social System* [New York: Free Press, 1951], pp. 280–81).

17. *Ibid.*, p. 424.

18. The term was coined by Peter L. Berger, Brigitte Berger, and Hansfried Keller, in *The Homeless Mind* (New York: Random House, 1973), chap. 3 and *passim*.

19. Erving Goffman, "Role Distance," in Goffman, *Encounters* (Indianapolis: Bobbs-Merrill, 1961), pp. 85–152.

20. Berger *et al.*, *The Homeless Mind*.

21. For a fruitful systematization of the concept of "alienation," see Melvin Seeman, "On the Meaning of Alienation," *American Sociological Review* 24 (1959): 783–97.

22. Karl Marx, *Writings of the Young Marx on Philosophy and Society,* trans. and ed. Lloyd D. Easton and Kurt H. Guddat (Garden City, N.Y.: Doubleday, 1967), p. 292.

23. Georg Simmel, "The Web of Group Affiliations," in his *Conflict and the Web of Group Affiliations,* trans. Kurt H. Wolff and Reinhard Bendix (New York: Free Press, 1955).

24. *Ibid.*, pp. 150–51.

25. Berger *et al.*, *The Homeless Mind*, esp. chap. 8.

26. Erich Fromm, *The Sane Society* (New York: Rinehart, 1955), p. 120, as quoted by Seeman, "On the Meaning of Alienation."

27. Seeman, in "On the Meaning of Alienation," distinguishes five meanings of the word, of which "powerlessness" and "self-estrangement" come closest to my definition, which differs somewhat from his but does not contradict it.

28. Mark S. Granovetter, "The Strength of Weak Ties," *American Journal of Sociology* 78 (May 1973): 1360–80. The examples that follow are taken from this paper.

29. Herbert Gans, *The Urban Villagers* (New York: Free Press, 1962).

30. L. C. Keyes, *The Rehabilitation Planning Game* (Cambridge, Mass.: M.I.T. Press, 1969). ,

31. The notion of *restricted role-set* with its dysfunctional implications was first coined by Ingrid Galtung at a seminar at the Institute for Social Research, Oslo, Norway, in the spring of 1961.

32. Merton, "Reference Group Behavior," p. 424; cf. also J. Diedrick Snoek, "Role Strain in Diversified Role Sets," *American Journal of Sociology* 71 (January 1966): 363–72.

33. *Ibid.*, pp. 425 ff.

34. Cf. William J. Goode, "A Theory of Role Strain," *American Sociological Review* 25 (1960): 483–96.

35. Under conditions of "sameness," there is one mechanism available, which Merton also mentions as a means of dealing with conflicts of role expectations, that can be used for dealing with other problems as well, especially with problems concerning conflicts between workers and their employers. This is "the mechanism of social support by others in similar social statuses with similar difficulties coping.... The individual need not meet [the problems] as wholly private [ones] which must be handled in a wholly private fashion..." (Merton, "Reference Group Behavior," pp. 431–32). This mechanism, in contrast to the others, is more readily available under conditions where most role partners have largely the same social status; it is less usable in a complex role-set because the very difference among the members of the role-set makes the contradictions and incompatibilities hardly ever the same for many individuals. Workers have been making use of the mechanism of becoming aware of their similar fate; this is, indeed, the structural basis for class consciousness as understood by Marx. However, the very fact of *sameness*, that is, of lack of differentiation, minimizes the opportunities for self-direction in favor of opportunities for collective action.

36. This distinction is, of course, akin to Durkheim's distinction between mechanical and organic solidarity.

37. William F. Whyte, "Small Groups and Large Organizations," in J. Rohrer and M. Sherif, eds., *Social Psychology at the Crossroads* (New York: Harper & Bros., 1951), pp. 297–312.

38. Everett C. Hughes, *Men and Their Work* (New York: Free Press, 1958), p. 43. The findings reported here are consistent with those obtained by Larry L. Cummings and Aly M. ElSalmi in their study of managerial satisfaction. In their statistical study they found a relation, statistically significant at $p < 10$, between role-set diversity and possibility of fulfillment. That is, managers who have highly diversified role-sets are less likely to perceive "fulfillment deficiency," and more likely to perceive "need fulfillment." This relation "seems to be most prominent in the areas of self-actualization, information and autonomy." See "The Impact of Role Diversity, Job Level, and Organizational Size on Managerial Satisfaction," *Administrative Science Quarterly* 15 (March 1970): 1–10.

39. Hughes, *Men and Their Work*, p. 43.

40. For a more complete report of this research, see Rose Laub Coser, "Alienation and

the Social Structure," in Eliot Freidson, ed., *The Hospital in Modern Society* (New York: Free Press, 1963), pp. 231–65.

41. Cf. Melvin Kohn's work, among others *Class and Conformity, passim*. After this paper went to press, there appeared Sam D. Sieber's "Toward a Theory of Role Accumulation," which is based on a perspective similar to the one developed in this paper. Particularly relevant to the point made here is the following statement: "Role accumulation may enrich the personality and enhance one's self-conception. Tolerance of discrepant viewpoints, exposure to many sources of information, flexibility in adjusting to the demands of diverse role-partners . . . all of these benefits may accrue to the person who enjoys wide and varied contacts with his fellow men. . . ." (*American Sociological Review* 39 [August 1974]: 567–578).

42. Merton, "Reference Group Behavior," p. 436.

43. "Parochial" is defined by Webster as "restricted to a small area or scope; narrow; limited; provincial."

44. René A. Spitz, with Katherine M. Wolf, "Anaclitic Depression: An Inquiry into the Genesis of the Psychiatric Conditions in Early Childhood," *Psychoanalytic Study of the Child* (New York: International Universities Press, 1946), vol. 2, pp. 313–42.

45. Kohlberg and Gilligan, "The Adolescent as a Philosopher," p. 155.

46. George Herbert Mead, *Mind, Self and Society* (Chicago: University of Chicago Press, 1934), pp. 151–54.

47. Piaget, *The Moral Judgment of the Child*.

48. At least this was the opinion of my daughter Ellen when she was eight. The object here is not to pinpoint exactly the age at which each stage develops. For a good summary of the development of these stages, as well as further elaboration, see Kohlberg and Gilligan, "The Adolescent as a Philosopher." The authors state: "All movement is forward in sequence and does not skip steps. Children may move through these stages at varying speeds, of course, and may be found half in and half out of a particular stage. An individual may stop at any given stage and at any age, but if he continues to move, he must move in accord with these steps. . . . No adult in Stage 4 has gone through Stage 6, but all Stage 6 adults have gone at least through 4" (p. 162).

49. Piaget, *The Moral Judgment of the Child*.

50. Kohlberg and Gilligan, "The Adolescent as a Philosopher."

51. This illustration is quoted from E. A. Peel, *The Psychological Basis of Education* (Edinburgh and London: Oliver & Boyd, 1967), in *ibid.*, pp. 154–55.

52. *Ibid.*, pp. 158–59.

53. *Ibid.*, p. 152. Also, "while hereditary components of IQ, of the child's rate of information processing, have some influence on the rate at which the child moves through invariant cognitive sequences, experiential factors heavily influence the rate of cognitive-structural development."

54. Cf. Robert K. Merton, "Discrimination and the American Creed," in R. M. MacIver, ed., *Discrimination and National Welfare* (New York: Harper & Bros., 1949), pp. 99–126.

55. Robert K. Merton, "Conformity, Deviation and Opportunity Structures," *American Sociological Review* 24 (April 1959): 177–88.

56. Cf. Rose Laub Coser, "Insulation from Observability and Types of Social Conformity," *American Sociological Review* 26 (February 1961): 28–39.

57. Cf. Rose Laub Coser and Gerald Rokoff, "Women in the Occupational World: Social Disruption and Conflict," *Social Problems* 18 (Spring 1971): 535–54.

58. Cf. Rose Laub Coser, "Role Distance, Sociological Ambivalence, and Transitional Status System," *American Journal of Sociology* 72 (September 1966): 173–87.

59. Talcott Parsons, *The Structure of Social Action* (New York: Free Press, 1937), p. 323.

60. Coser, "Insulation from Observability and Types of Social Conformity."

61. Karl Mannheim, *Man and Society in an Age of Reconstruction* (London: Routledge & Kegan Paul, 1940).

62. Kohn finds that contrary to the popular stereotype (with education statistically controlled) "bureaucrats are found to value self-direction more highly than do non-bureaucrats, to have more personally demanding moral standards, to be more receptive to change, to be intellectually more flexible (especially in dealing with ideational problems), and to spend their leisure time in more intellectually demanding activities" (Melvin Kohn, "Bureaucratic Man: A Portrait and an Interpretation," *American Sociological Review* 36 [June 1971], pp. 461–74).

63. "Substantive complexity" is an overall measure, based on a factor analysis of information obtained about complexity of work with data, complexity of work with things, and complexity of work with people. The correlation between the "substantive complexity of the job" as a whole and the complexity of work with people is .82.

64. Melvin L. Kohn, "Social Class and Parent-Child Relationships: An Interpretation," *American Journal of Sociology* 68 (1963): 471–80; also in Rose Laub Coser, ed., *Life Cycle and Achievement in America* (New York: Harper Torchbooks, 1969), pp. 21–42. See also Kohn, *Class and Conformity*, chap. 11.

65. Kohn, *Class and Conformity*, p. 21 and *passim*.

66. Melvin Kohn and Carmi Schooler, in "Occupational Experience and Psychological Functioning: An Assessment of Reciprocal Effects," *American Sociological Review* 38 (February 1973), pp. 97–118, include the detailed methodological and statistical information.

67. Bernstein, *Class, Codes and Control*, p. 177.

68. *Ibid.*

69. L. S. Vigotsky, *Thought and Language* (Cambridge, Mass.: M.I.T. Press, 1962), p. 148.

70. See Parsons, *The Social System*, pp. 61–63.

71. Vigotsky, *Thought and Language*, p. 141.

72. *Ibid.*

73. Bernstein, *Class, Codes and Control*, pp. 175–76.

74. *Ibid.*

75. Vigotsky, *Thought and Language*, p. 144.

76. Cf. "Large masses can always be animated and guided by *simple* ideas: what is common to many must be accessible even to the lowest and most primitive among them" (Georg Simmel, *Sociology of Georg Simmel*, trans. and ed Kurt H. Wolff [New York: Free Press, 1950], p. 93).

77. Bernstein, *Class, Codes and Control*, pp. 112 and 178.

78. *Ibid.*, p. 186.

79. *Ibid.*, p. 176.

80. The test was designed by Peter Hawkins and quoted in *ibid.*, p. 194.

81. *Ibid.*, pp. 194–95.

82. *Ibid.*, p. 186.

83. Virginia Woolf (quoting from Sir Arthur Quiller-Couch, "The Art of Writing"), *A Room of One's Own* (New York: Harcourt Brace Jovanovich, 1929), pp. 111–12.

Reference Individuals
and Reference Idols

HERBERT H. HYMAN

Long ago, at mid-century to be exact, Merton presented to us all the "Contributions to the Theory of Reference Group Behavior."[1] For some of the very young who are inclined to neglect the past, it may seem to stem from ancient times. Victor Hugo should be their guide: "Let us, while waiting for new monuments, preserve ancient monuments." Indeed it is a monument, and one that has not crumbled in the quarter-century now passed since it was built. For some of the old who had played with the concept when they were very young, it is the elegant embodiment of ideas that have a long past but that are still vital. For the many, there is no need to urge special measures to preserve the monument. Its figure shines through their theorizing and research. It looms large enough for scholars in distant India or Israel, even as far away as Australia, to see it and take inspiration from it. It has, as Turner put it, a "meteoric prominence" for those working in all corners of the field: on studies of farmers, scientists, newspapermen, and drunkards; on problems of mental illness, formal organization, marketing and public relations, mass communication, opinion formation, consumer behavior, political behavior, acculturation, race relations, labor relations, juvenile delinquency, and jokes.

The original monument, however impressive it was to others, seemed incomplete to Merton. In 1957, he enlarged it with the "Continuities in the Theory of Reference Groups and Social Structure,"[2] so as "to bring out some

Herbert H. Hyman is Professor of Sociology at Wesleyan University.

of the specifically sociological, as distinct from the socio-psychological implications of current inquiries into reference group behavior." Thus extended, the modern monument has inspired and guided diverse investigators. Reference group theory and research continue to flourish, as does Merton. I personally rejoice. His sixty-fifth birthday is an occasion for us all to celebrate. What better way than by attempts at further theorizing and research.

Although reference group theory has flowered, not all its branches have flourished. Looking back in the "Continuities," Merton observed that "research and theory have tended to focus on reference *groups* to the relative neglect of reference *individuals*."[3] The discontinuity is strange and persistent. In the "Contributions," Merton had incorporated both concepts in his general formulation. In my own research, both concepts had been stressed, since over half of the subjects reported that they used particular other individuals, rather than larger categories or groups of people, as points of comparison for appraising their status. Newcomb's remark that a membership group may be a potent point of reference " (particularly as symbolized by leaders . . .)" suggested the role of the reference individual as the carrier of the reference group's norms. Sherif had described the glorified variety of reference individual with a term so vivid, the reference "idol," that it should have captured our attention. In the "Continuities" Merton not only noted the neglect, but he presented a string of intriguing questions about reference individuals that should have mobilized research especially on reference idols, on the "culture heroes," on the "public figures who are serving as role models for many."[4] In 1960, in some "Reflections on Reference Groups,"[5] I, too, lamented the neglect of the reference individual and reference idol, pointing out their fine lineage back to E. A. Ross who had described the hierarchy of public figures who act as "radiant points of conventionality" to guide us lesser lights, thus organizing "the anatomy of collective opinion" into an "intellectual feudal system," and further back to William James who had formulated the moral struggle toward an "ideal social self" in terms of our "thought . . . of a self that is at least *worthy* of approving recognition by the highest possible judging companion. . . ."

In the face of the continuing stimuli, the discontinuity in the study of reference individuals seems a mystery. Merton may have solved it. Perhaps it is simply that "the very terminology itself," reference group, although implying "behavior oriented both to groups *and* to particular individuals," is not sufficiently explicit and "has tended to fix the definition of problems by social scientists. . . ."[6] Perhaps the reference individual seems too heretical an object of study for scholars insecure in their relations to their own reference groups, sociologists and social-psychologists. It may seem too microscopic, too psychologistic, not a proper agenda item, despite Merton's assurance that "the selection of reference individuals is presumably no more idiosyncratic than the selection of reference groups." The evidence we shall soon present should reassure those who rejected the problem out of such fears.

Whatever the reasons, this major branch of the theory surely has remained dormant for many years, needing nourishment from some stream of research before it too can bloom. If we wait for a new, specially directed stream of research, still another period of dormancy lies ahead. If, however, we explore the many streams of survey research, already oceanic in extent, we may locate some little stream that fortunately is flowing in the general direction of a theory of reference individuals and can be tapped to nourish this branch.

IDOLS OF THE PEOPLE REVEALED BY SECONDARY ANALYSIS

The results of the Gallup poll's annual "Admiration Derby," in which the notabilities of the world have been raced every Christmas since 1946 to see who wins the admiration of the public, provide nourishment for a theory of reference *idols* that can be extracted by secondary analysis. This is an efficient strategy for adding to the theory, and it is symbolically appropriate to the occasion. After all, the "Contributions to the Theory of Reference Group Behavior" was based upon the reexamination of the survey data in *The American Soldier,* in which, as Merton noted, "the *term* 'reference group' is not employed," and *The American Soldier* itself is surely a monument to secondary analysis. The "Contributions" is almost a unique example of secondary analysis elevated to the second power. What better way to join in the celebration than by another, although smaller, secondary analysis.

Since 1948 the annual Gallup Derby has involved two races. National samples have been asked: "What man that you have heard or read about living today in any part of the WORLD do you admire the MOST?" "What woman that you have heard or read about living today in any part of the WORLD do you admire the MOST?" It is ironic in light of the times that women are always raced separately, and only were allowed to compete with men for public admiration way back in 1946 and 1947. Thus, there is no way to determine whether they can become reference idols in open competition in modern times and what the long-term trend in this respect is, but within the two segregated races the respective patterns of idolatry can be established. For its historic interest, we simply note the fact that in the 1946 open race one woman, Eleanor Roosevelt, placed in the first ten, and in the 1947 race Sister Kenny joined her, with Mrs. Roosevelt tying for fifth place and Sister Kenny finishing in a three-way tie for sixth place.

As we can see, under the special rules of this Derby, ordinary contestants are severely handicapped. Indeed, the very reference in the questions to a person one has "heard or read about" should operate to *exclude* ordinary people —a father, a mother, a neighbor—whom one knows and does not have to hear or read about. The surprising fact that ordinary people often place or show despite the odds against them is compelling evidence of the importance of reference *individuals* as well as reference idols and contributes to the more general theory.

As we should also be able to see, in Gallup's Derby as in life's race, all potential idols do not have an equal or fair chance to win. Admiration, to be sure, is in the eyes of the beholder, but those on the distant horizon must be magnified for us, given notability. However admirable they might be, they cannot be admired until they have been "heard or read about." The amount of publicity conferred on all potential reference idols is far from equal in quantity or quality. Some are made famous, others made infamous, still others never spotlighted. Admittedly, notability is a complex phenomenon, and its neglect by sociologists and social-psychologists makes it all the more confusing.[7] Despite publicity, some potential reference idols may not be noticed or all too quickly revert to obscurity. But surely those who become reference idols, winners of the Derby, may have had unfair advantage from the publicity conferred upon them.

As secondary analysts, we may regret the lack of auxiliary instruments to measure and control precisely the variable of notability in analyzing the reference idols chosen, but we must accept what we have and make the best of it, never forgetting to weigh the variable in interpreting the findings. If we often choose false or unworthy reference idols, to take poetic license, the fault *is* in the stars presented to us, not only in ourselves.

The instrument may not dissect, but it does describe the complex social and psychological pattern of reference idol selection. By now, the changes and uniformities in the pattern year by year can be examined over a span of almost thirty years. It is one of the longest, nationwide time series at our disposal, which makes it all the more surprising how few social scientists have analyzed these data.[8] Mueller[9] has exploited the full time series on *male* idols in connection with his thorough analyses of the ebb and flow and determinants of presidential popularity, the instrument revealing the idolatry toward presidents. They consistently win the Derby by a big margin, being chosen by about 25 percent of the sample. The admiration generally persists long after they leave the presidency (Hoover's showing through the fifties and as late as 1962 being the most dramatic example), although their *pre*eminence declines rapidly. Even presidential aspirants—Stevenson or Goldwater, for example—rank high. The record of presidents is only matched or *surpassed* by such wartime military, but also political, heroes as General MacArthur and Eisenhower prior to 1952, and approached by Winston Churchill, toward whom the admiration of Americans persisted for an unusually long period. He is the most dramatic departure from a strikingly ethnocentric pattern of choice, although, as Mueller remarks wryly, this may reflect Churchill's "wisdom in always stressing before American audiences the American lineage of his mother."[10] As Mueller notes, "the only men besides Churchill persistently able to overcome the disadvantage of foreignness have been Albert Schweitzer and the popes."[11] Two other religious figures rank relatively high, Billy Graham and Bishop Fulton Sheen, commanding the admiration of about 7 percent of American adults in several years. That male reference idols are chosen from this limited set of institutional spheres is partly determined by the greater publicity and notability conferred on figures in certain spheres and locations. We surely exhibit ethnocentric choices, but this reflects in part our ignorance about those in foreign places.

Yet our values must be shaping the selections. No star from the entertainment world ever shines in the admiration of the public. Stars of the athletic world, the great labor leaders, the titans of industry—the "idols of consumption" and the "idols of production," apt terms Lowenthal[12] employed in his content analysis of "Popular Biographies" in magazines—are never eminent reference idols. They do not lack notability. Serious artists, intellectuals, scientists never place with the exception of Dr. Salk, who tied for sixth place in two years, commanding the admiration of 2 percent of the national sample, and with the possible exception of Einstein, who was selected by a very few at one time in the fifties. Artists and intellectuals, to be sure, are seriously handicapped. As we shall document, they are only known in small, educated, and knowledgeable circles. But, surely, such great scientists as Einstein and Salk have not so lacked for publicity that their followings should be so minuscule.

In the pantheon of reference idols revealed by the question over the years, all sorts of other figures do appear, but these are the gods of minor sects, each compelling the greatest admiration only from some tiny minority of less than one percent of the sample. The major conclusions from Mueller's long-term analysis relate only to those idols who rank within the top ten in the pantheon, being worshiped by no less than 2 percent but never more than 29 percent of American adults.

There is, however, one other kind of figure revealed as a major normative point of reference for Americans. As Mueller notes, "usually about 5 percent nominate their father or husband." When one recalls the rules of the race, the emphasis of the question on a person living "in any part of the WORLD" that the respondent has "heard or read about," the frequency of such choices must be regarded as unusually high. In light of the fact that the only notabilities who ever command wider admiration than that are the presidents and the other political, military, and religious personages enumerated earlier, the magnitude is extraordinary. The potency of reference individuals within the immediate milieu is conveyed by this serendipitous finding, and reference idols are put down in their proper place.

John Reed, perhaps the only other secondary analyst to exploit these data, has also examined the tendency to select reference individuals from the immediate milieu in the course of studying the distinctive subculture of *white* Southerners.[13] The selection of kinfolk and other folks at home is used as one indicator of Southern parochialism or "localism." His data are derived from three of the annual surveys taken between 1958 and 1965, and he documents the consistent and substantial tendency among Americans, especially Southerners, to select reference individuals rather than reference idols. In the 1963 survey, for example, 9 percent of Southerners chose a male member of the family and 4 percent of Northerners. In addition, 19 percent of Southerners and 10 percent of Northerners selected a *local* man other than a family member as the most admired individual. All told, about 17 percent of the national white sample fly in the face of the instructions and choose a reference individual rather than a reference idol.

Reed, in contrast with Mueller, also examined the choice of *female* reference individuals and idols, exploiting the data from the corresponding question Gallup had asked in the annual surveys. The differential between South and North is again evident, as is a striking tendency (of about the same magnitude) for substantial numbers to select female reference individuals rather than reference idols. The findings from the 1963 survey are presented in Table 1.

Table 1. THE CHOICE OF REFERENCE INDIVIDUALS BY SOUTHERN AND NORTHERN
WHITE ADULTS IN RESPONSE TO A QUESTION ABOUT REFERENCE IDOLS*

	Percent of Respective White Groups in 1963 National Survey	
	South	Non-South
Man most admired is		
Member of family	9	4
Other local individual	19	10
Total percent	28	14
	N = 720	N = 2242
Woman most admired is		
Member of family	11	4
Other local individual	12	4
Total percent	23	8
	N = 697	N = 2242

* Adapted from Reed, *The Enduring South,* p. 36.

We should not draw the inference from these data that a substantial number, 15–25 percent, guide themselves through life without recourse to any reference idols at all. It is simply that reference *individuals* are foremost in their thoughts and take precedence over the idols they might *also* hold in mind as points of normative reference. There is, however, another dramatic finding which suggests that a considerable number of American adults do not have any *positive* reference idols at all. The true magnitude of the pattern and its full meaning are difficult to determine by secondary analysis. On this one point, the data leave much to be desired. Here again we must make the best of it. At least, we gain some tentative understanding of a most enigmatic and fascinating phenomenon revealed throughout these surveys and learn how to approach the problem better in the future.

About 20 percent of the sample usually answer "don't know" to the question on the most admired *male* reference idol or are recorded as a "no answer." Occasionally, the percentage approaches a third of the national sample. The magnitude of this datum is even higher for the question on the most admired *female* reference idol. It should be stressed immediately that this substantial group cannot be construed as having no reference *individuals*. They may well have complied with the instructions and regarded it as inappropriate to mention ordinary individuals in the local milieu in answer to such a question.

The true magnitude of the tendency to have no positive reference idols, of course, cannot be taken to be 20 percent or higher. The gross amount must be discounted, first, by two or three percentage points for the outright errors interviewers occasionally make in forgetting to ask questions or record answers, they, like all workers, being imperfect in the performance of their duties. Of the remainder, some unknown number are saying they "don't know" which particular public figure is their *most* admired one. They may have several idols they worship equally and simply be unable to decide among them in answer to the question. Unfortunately, the codes do not distinguish among the varieties of don't know answers, and no probes are available to make this refined distinction.

Surely, the substantial portion of the gross percentage are telling us that they truly have *no* reference idol at all, for one of two reasons. When Mueller weighs the fact that so many "seem unable to conjure up the name of even one admirable man," he proposes that we "should not credit much of the respondent reticence to *cynicism*."[14] Indeed, one finding in our secondary analysis suggests that his judgment is sound. But conservatism requires us to accept the fact that some of these individuals are very knowledgeable about the great figures in the world but regard none of them as worthy of admiration. A small number may be so erudite that they know a flaw in every contemporary idol which remains secret to those who are less knowledgeable, or they may be so learned that no living idol can compare with the towering figures they know out of the past. However, they may have *negative* reference idols, who, as Newcomb pointed out, can function as normative guides just as positive reference points can.[15]

No doubt, the largest portion of this gross number have no reference idols at all, neither positive nor negative, simply because of their general ignorance. They might like very much to guide themselves by some star, but they simply do not know enough notabilities in this world to find such a point of reference. They must drift, or anchor themselves to a reference individual from the immediate milieu. Table 2 shows that the group most prone to say "don't know" or "no answer" is the least educated, thus supporting the argument just advanced. We have chosen the 1950 survey where the codes and the interviewing seem, in our judgment, not to have distorted the magnitude of the pattern, in contrast with some of the other surveys at our disposal where obscurities are present. We present the findings on the lack of *female* reference idols as well, since they not only support the general argument but lead to certain interesting speculations.

Table 2. THE LACK OF A SPECIFIC REFERENCE IDOL
AS RELATED TO FORMAL EDUCATION

	Percent "Don't Know" or "None" or "No Answer" in 1950*	
	Male idol	*Female idol*
Grade school (361)	21	41
Some high school (287)	15	35
High school graduate (380)	13	30
Some college (135)	10	22
College (143)	4	26

* Gallup Poll, 469–K, December 30, 1950.

The number reporting no positive *male* reference idol declines with each step up in education and has reached almost the vanishing point among the college graduates. The drop cannot be construed as reflecting excessive leniency among the better educated about the performance of public figures or their freedom from obsessive hair-splitting about the track records of those racing in the Derby. What seems obvious is that the educated know a great many notabilities and have ample basis for a choice. But strange as it may seem, most of the shining figures in the world are seen only dimly or known not at all by the least educated. From the endless other survey evidence available, a few examples of the ignorance found among those with only grade school education in surveys around 1950 will prove the point. About 50 percent of the group could not name the Vice-President; less than 15 percent could identify Adlai Stevenson; about 25 percent had never heard of J. Edgar Hoover; less than a third knew who Chiang Kai-shek was; and about a quarter knew Tito. Among the college graduates, around 90 percent knew all these figures with the exception of Stevenson, who was known by about half. How ironic—although ignorance protects the uneducated from choosing some false idols, it also denies them of worthy gods.

Some might entertain the hypothesis that ignorance of the many notabilities of the world should make it easier for large masses to adopt a reference idol. True, there are so few contenders known to the ordinary man that each can attract a larger following. That, as implied earlier, is why the presidents do so well in these races. But this should be seen as an auxiliary, not an alternative, hypothesis. Among the crowds who decide to follow the Derby, ignorance increases the likelihood that they will choose the favorite.[16] But ignorance does not compel them to join in the sport. Indeed, as our evidence suggests, it turns many of them away.

The findings in Table 2 on *female* idols again reveal that lack of any reference idol is most characteristic of the less educated. But the slope of the line is much flatter. Among the highly educated, about a quarter report no idol at all. At each level of education, the number reporting no female idol is about double the number with no male idol. There is an apparent rejection of female reference idols, leading some to see a strange kind of double standard operative in the sphere of reference group processes, to argue that we demand more perfection from female notabilities before we will elevate them to the status of an idol who guides our thoughts and conduct. The fact that women and men are about equally likely to report no female reference idol—30 percent and 35 percent are the respective figures—is at least suggestive evidence against the hypothesis.

The parsimonious hypothesis is that women have been more likely to be deprived of notability—rarely being elevated to high and prominent status in the first place, and even when they reach high positions being denied publicity. Among those female idols chosen, the patterns differ in certain striking ways from those found for male idols and do suggest that their lack of notability has been a central variable in the process of selection.

Note first that Eleanor Roosevelt, who placed in the classic open competition in 1946, was the preeminent reference idol for a period of ten years out of eleven years up to the mid-fifties and remained within the pantheon until 1961. During the early period, she was a great goddess, towering above all others. In 1950 about 29 percent selected her as most admirable, whereas other so-called reference idols attracted no more than 2 percent of admirers, with the exception of Sister Kenny, who was regarded as most admirable by 4 percent.

Eleanor Roosevelt indeed was admirable, and Americans accordingly idolized her. But we should not credit all of it to our good judgment and good values. Why were other worthy reference idols ignored, and why the incredible ratio of choices toward her versus other idols? No male idol ever had such a near monopoly of worship. As the wife of a president she must have had a great advantage in notability which functioned to focus the choices of the public. Why else would women of such different and varied character as Patricia Nixon, Jackie Kennedy, Lady Bird Johnson, Bess Truman, and Mamie Eisenhower, during their husbands' presidencies and—for the latter quartet—for long periods thereafter, become eminent reference idols of their times? Admittedly, their followers, with the exception of Mamie Eisenhower, were relatively few compared to Eleanor Roosevelt, suggesting her singular appeal and the special values shaping that choice. Nevertheless, any president's wife has the marked advantage of notability, whatever her character may be.

Recall also that Sister Kenny, the Australian nurse and pioneer in the treatment of polio, had placed in the open competition of 1947. In 1951, the year before her death, she won *more* admirers than Mrs. Roosevelt. This might be taken hastily as the female exception (the parallel to Winston Churchill) that proves the rule of ethnocentrism in the choice of reference idols. Not so. Mme. Chiang and Queen Elizabeth became and remained reference idols for long periods; Princess Margaret of England, Princess Grace of Monaco, and Prime Ministers Indira Ghandi and Golda Meir entered the pantheon and remained there for extended periods; Mme. Ngo Diem Nhu even placed among the top ten idols in 1965–66. Are Americans less ethnocentric than had seemed to be the case, but only in the special respect that they idolize foreign women, not men?

The more one examines the differences between gods and goddesses chosen by the public in the aggregate, the more fascinated and confused one becomes. One could try to bring order out of the confusion by the principle that the attributes traditionally valued in any woman—gentleness, humaneness, and so on—are *different* from those valued in any man, and that these contrasted values also underlie the respective processes of reference idol selection. It is hard to make the principle fit the choice of female idols. What a strange conglomerate of values is implied by the choices made in the aggregate and over time. Our values are royalist and democratic, local and cosmopolitan, socialist and fascist. We may value the humane, kindly, or maternal type of goddess as implied in the choices of Eleanor Roosevelt and Sister Kenny or Kate Smith, who joined the pantheon, but we also opt for the esthetic or libidinal by our inclusion of Marilyn Monroe in 1955 and for the political in the long-enduring choices of Senator Margaret Chase Smith and Clare Boothe Luce.

We seem to value the popular entertainer not only by our choices of Kate Smith and Marilyn Monroe but by the selection in particular years of Irene

Dunne and Dinah Shore; we also idolized for a long period a serious artist like Marian Anderson. (Neither level of artistry was represented among the top male idols.) How can we derive a principle from the traditional role definition for women that can govern the selection of such a diversity of idols or that will apply to the instance of Helen Keller, who held a place among the top ten idols for about fifteen years, or to the case of Colonel Oveta Culp Hobby, who commanded the Woman's Army Corps and was among the ten most admired, if only for one year.

The findings seem truly serendipitous. They deserve and need further primary research to probe for the deeper meanings implicit in the process, so as to resolve the confusion and to uncover the true principles that account for the selection of female idols who function as points of normative reference. Some of the apparent confusion, however, may reflect the simple statistical treatment thus far applied to the data, the presentation of discrete findings on each of the *major* idols for the national sample in the aggregate. In a later phase of this secondary analysis, the idols will be combined in a conceptual scheme and the types of choices made by more homogeneous subgroups examined, for example, by men and women.

Tentatively advanced, the general principle of notability may once again lead to some clarification. All of the female reference idols, whatever their sphere of activity or accomplishments or traits, had to have become distinguished, made highly visible to the public eye. The distinctiveness of the figures is all the more marked because of their unusualness. They create a shock of recognition. *She* reigns alone over a nation, or governs it, or married a foreign prince, or commanded an army, or made U.S. senator, or overcame the twin handicaps of deafness and blindness. Some are admired because they are admirable; some not because they fulfill the usual female role but because they have dramatically departed from it.

In the selection of male reference idols, the public easily can indulge its ethnocentrism. People do not have to look far from home to find a notability to idolize, and visibility, other things being equal, is some function of distance. By contrast, there are few female notables close by, and the distinctiveness of some foreign figures makes them shine over long distances and heightens their visibility.

We have already learned something about the selection of reference idols, and there is more to come, despite the fact that the instrument itself does not probe deeply. Some may think too quickly of one apparent limitation. In the study of reference group processes, many people have been found to employ *multiple* reference groups and multiple reference individuals, and Gallup's question forces the respondent to mention only *one* individual, the most admired idol. Beginning in 1969, however, Gallup asked the supplementary question: "Who is your second choice?" for both male and female idols. About 50 percent answer no one or give no definite answer. A substantial minority have no reference idol at all, and, consistently, something close to the majority do not employ multiple reference idols.

The Gallup findings only apply to adults, but those secondary analysts interested in the developmental processes underlying the selection of reference individuals and reference idols could reexamine a series of old studies of children. Beginning around the turn of the century and spread over fifty years, some variant of the basic question was asked periodically of samples of children. Although the sampling procedures may not satisfy a modern statistician, the studies involve thousands of children at various age stages and in different countries, the investigators examining the formation and developmental changes in the ego-ideal, or what they sometimes called the "personification of ideals."

An adventurous secondary analyst might even attempt to trace further developmental changes from childhood into maturity by juxtaposing some of the subgroup findings from these old studies and from the Gallup surveys. For example, the ten-year-olds in Hill's 1910 study in Nashville became the fifty-year-olds in Gallup's 1950 survey, and those who were ten in his 1928 study in Alabama were in their thirties in Gallup's 1950 survey. The cohorts might be traced, although matching up the geographical and social locations of the respective samples would be critical. In some instances, the instrument employed is even better suited to the comprehensive study of reference individuals and reference idols than the Gallup question, permitting open competition among figures of both sexes within the immediate milieu and the remote environment, both living and dead, sharpening the dimension of identification with the idol, and probing the reasons for the choice. For example, a 1910 version was: "Which person (among those you have seen, or thought of, or heard of, or read about) would you most like to resemble? Why?"

With the passage of time, the studies had become buried, but I had excavated a number of these truly ancient monuments and reported in 1959 some findings relevant to reference group theory. Girls were more likely in that early, sheltered era to choose reference individuals from the immediate milieu and boys to pick idols from the remote environment. With age and the enlargement of knowledge, children of both sexes were more likely to select remote figures as reference idols. But between a quarter and almost a half of the samples, many of them in their teens, still chose reference individuals over idols.

Greenstein had been ingenious enough to exploit the spread of the studies over fifty years for a secondary analysis of social change in children's choices of reference individuals and idols.[17] He documents a dramatic increase over time in the selection of popular entertainers as reference idols; the absence of idols of production or individuals from business and industry throughout the long period; a marked decline with time in the selection of historic national figures, for example, Washington, as reference idols.

Some of these findings agree with the findings Gallup obtained from adults, and some provide a lovely complement to the adult data. A strange discontinuity between the early studies of children and the recent studies of adults is that the incumbent president in that era was almost never chosen by the child. This remains a mystery to be reexamined in *current* inquiry on samples of children. In explaining the historic growth of idols from the sphere of the popular arts, Greenstein emphasizes the variable of publicity, remarking on "the enormously greater availability of these figures for identification, resulting from the rise of a mass entertainment industry and new technologies of communication."[18] This is a sound conclusion, but why these idols then disappear from the pantheon of *adults* is another enigma to be solved by future research. For sure, it is not that they have faded into obscurity. Gallup's national surveys of adults establish that the stars of the entertainment and sport world are indeed famous. How ironic, for example, that Betty Grable, Bob Hope, Joe Louis, Jack Dempsey, Babe Ruth, Clark Gable, and Jack Benny were far, far better known to the public in 1945 than were General De Gaulle, Anthony Eden, or Henry Wallace, who had just helped win World War II.

Other large studies and national surveys provide missing pieces of the puzzle of reference idol selection. We shall only mention them here to suggest the fine targets for future secondary analysts. The Gallup affiliates in other countries have asked the same question periodically of their adult populations, establishing that the lack of any reference idol at all and the primacy of a reference individual from the local milieu over an idol among substantial numbers of adults, and the widespread ethnocentrism among those who do choose idols, are not American peculiarities but highly generalizable phenomena.

The Institute of Demoscopy has studied over the years the knowledge the German adult population has of the "eminent persons" of the world[19] and the sources of such knowledge. In 1958, for example, when Richard Nixon was Vice-President, he was an unknown to about two-thirds of all German adults, whereas Eisenhower, then the President, and Lyndon Johnson during his presidency were known by close to 90 percent of Germans. The supplementary questions establish that the image of the most famous world figures has been projected via television, movies, and pictures in newspapers—Queen Elizabeth's picture, for example, having been seen by over 80 percent of German adults. That the *persona* is in some way relevant to the selection of a female idol is conveyed by the findings that what is so likable about the Queen are such *visually* transmitted traits as "her manner," her "royal bearing," "her charm," "clothes, jewelry," "her friendly smile."

Almond and Verba asked the question about reference idols (excluding by the wording ordinary reference individuals but allowing open competition between gods and goddesses) in their 1960 surveys of the "civic culture" of five nations, making it an especially fine target for comparative analysis.[20] Some preliminary analysis of their American data confirms Gallup's finding that idols are drawn predominantly from the political sphere. They are almost never from the sphere of sports, only the very young adults making such selections, and almost never from the cultural sphere, only the highly educated being inclined in this direction. Their 1960 data show a considerable number of idols from the sphere of entertainment, this pattern much more characteristic of women respondents. This one finding presents a contradiction with the persistent Gallup finding over the years. One hypothesis may tentatively resolve the contradiction and suggest an interesting line of research. Almond and Verba allowed the respondent to mention *multiple* idols. Perhaps entertainers do function as *secondary* idols but are excluded from the Gallup surveys prior to 1968 which pressed the respondent to report only the single fore-most idol.

In the classic study of "the authoritarian personality," conducted in 1945–46, the investigators had included the question: "What great people do you admire most?" Given the elaborate set of measures in the original inquiry, the syndrome of personality and ideological characteristics that accompany the selection of particular reference idols could be determined by secondary analysis for the special universe and sampling involved. The original investigators did report a striking difference between the pantheon of false idols chosen by their ethnocentric respondents and the worthies chosen by their nonethno-centric subjects. But what was painfully evident to Sheatsley and myself[21] in a critique of the study was that, since education was not controlled in the comparison, the fault could not be blamed on the ethnocentric self. Such a person surely had not had the opportunities the educated had to have to learn about such worthy but esoteric idols as Whitman, Pushkin, Voltaire, Bertrand Russell, Comte, Herbert Spencer, Maimonides, Confucius, Sir William Osler, and Pestalozzi. These data dramatize once again the relevance of the variable of notability and its institutional determinants.

PATTERNS OF SELECTION AND SUBGROUP DIFFERENCES

There is an egregious and persistent omission from the pantheon of major idols of the people: only two black reference idols place among the top ten in the years 1946 to 1970. Ralph Bunche is admired by 2 percent of the total sample, finishing in a three-way tie for eighth place once in 1950, the year he was awarded the Nobel peace prize. Martin Luther King took fourth place in 1964, fifth place in 1965, and ended up in a three-way tie for sixth place in 1963, garnering between 2 and 3 percent of admirers in the nation as a whole. In 1964 he won the Nobel peace prize, but he had become famous in 1955–56 for leading the Montgomery Boycott. In the pantheon of female idols over those same years, Marian Anderson is the only high-ranking black idol, placing in six of the annual races. (Shirley Chisholm joined the pantheon in 1971.)

Examining the data at this discrete level for the aggregate sample may just possibly mislead us, and this gross finding deserves more refined analysis. There may be no *single* black god who attracts many admirers, despite the towering achievements of the two Nobel laureates, and the same situation may apply to black goddesses. Combining all the black reference idols, each of whom attracts very few admirers, may show some consolidated pattern, and cross-tabulation by the race of the respondent may help to reveal a pattern. The 2 percent of admirers in the aggregate sample might conceivably turn out to be 20 percent among black respondents; their putative choice of a black refer-ence idol as a point of normative reference is diluted in the aggregate statis-tics since they are so small a minority.

In connection with any theory that the selection of reference idols is deter-mined at an early stage of development, most of the adults in the 1950 survey

277

had completed their *early childhood* long before 1930, back in a period when publicity and notability were being conferred on few black individuals. That black respondents in considerable numbers will turn to black reference idols even when presented to them first in their adult years is suggested by findings from the 1950 survey. Among blacks, 18 percent selected Ralph Bunche, while less than 2 percent of whites chose him. Nevertheless, surveys from a more recent period may provide a more compelling test. Restricting ourselves to the more recent surveys also insures that the sampling and interviewing of black respondents are of better quality.

Table 3 presents data from two of the later surveys, 1961 and 1970. By 1970, the sampling can net many respondents who were young children in 1950, at which stage some black idols—Ralph Bunche, for example—might have been placed before them as personages worthy of admiration, no matter whether they themselves were white or black. Since the bond between a respondent and an idol may depend not only on race but on sex, the data are simultaneously broken down by both sex and race. As a result, any differences in the sex ratios because of the way the black and white stratums were sampled cannot affect the comparisons.

Table 3. THE CHOICE OF A BLACK REFERENCE IDOL
AS RELATED TO THE RACE OF THE RESPONDENT

	Percent Who Choose Any Black Male Person as the "Most Admired"	
	1961[a]	1970[b]
White male respondents	Under half of 1	0
White female respondents	Under half of 1	0
Black male respondents	11	6
Black female respondents	9	3

	Percent Who Choose Any Black Female Person as the "Most Admired"	
	1961[c]	1970[d]
White male respondents	0	1
White female respondents	Under half of 1	Under half of 1
Black male respondents	4	10
Black female respondents	5	19

[a] Reference idols mentioned are Ralph Bunche, Martin Luther King, Archie Moore, and Jackie Robinson. The Ns for the white cells are about 1300 and for the black cells about 150. Gallup Poll, 653-K.

[b] Reference idols mentioned are Ralph Bunche, Eldridge Cleaver, and Jesse Jackson. The Ns for the white cells are about 700 and for the black cells about 70. Gallup Poll, 820-K.

[c] Reference idols mentioned are Marian Anderson, Mahalia Jackson, Lena Horne, and Althea Gibson.

[d] Reference idols mentioned are Mahalia Jackson, Coretta (Mrs. Martin Luther) King, and Angela Davis.

In the two surveys examined, which begin and end the decade of the sixties, any pattern of selection of black reference idols by white adults is virtually nonexistent, suggesting a second variety of ethnocentrism. Among black respondents, there is a substantial tendency to choose black reference idols, most characteristic of black women in 1970 when almost all of the 19 percent involved chose Coretta King. Other years, before 1970, of course, should be examined before venturing a generalization, and those who grew up recently should be traced in the annual surveys Gallup will conduct in the future. Tentatively, one might conclude that even among black adults the prevalent pattern of the past has been for them to choose *white* reference idols, reflecting the institutional forces accentuating white notability and/or the internalization of the majority's values. Compared to their white counterparts, however, one must note that black respondents have been far freer of ethnocentrism in their selection of reference idols.[22]

We have searched these data for other, subtle patterns that might be magnified by combining discrete reference idols into *types* and that might be observed in other subgroups who were submerged within the aggregate. It is a laborious undertaking, and we have confined the search to the 1961 and 1970 surveys. Patterns that were more than fleeting, more than passing fancies of the public, should appear in these two surveys spanning a decade, and any systematic changes over time ought to be highlighted.

Apart from one possible find, the search has been unrewarding. Perhaps a more thorough search of a larger number and longer sequence of surveys will reward future secondary analysts who need not operate by labor-saving strategies, but the solution to the puzzle will also require more subtle modes of abstraction. Recall the clue Merton left us long ago when he was involved in a similar search for the hidden sources of "patterns of influence."[23] The parallel is rather eerie. He had located the fifty-seven "influentials," the preeminent opinion leaders selected by the people of Rovere, and he then remarks: "In what we now know to be the relatively sterile first phase of our analysis . . . distinctions were drawn between the currently influential . . . the potentially influential . . . the waning influential . . . the dormant influential. . . . This classification proved to be logically impeccable, empirically applicable, and virtually sterile." As we all remember, *finally* he arrived at the fruitful distinction between "the local and the cosmopolitan," but we should not forget his urging others to give accounts of such experiences in trying to catch a concept.

Our experience in combining the discrete, minor reference idols into categories so as to locate some *types* that are frequently selected by the general population, or common, at least within a subgroup of the population, has been frustrating. The patterning of reference idol selection is elusive, perhaps because we require not one but two subtle sets of concepts: one for classifying idols and the other for classifying people into the separate sects that seek and need particular kinds of gods. The data available for the latter classification are limited by the routine background characteristics available in the surveys, although we can also draw upon the questions in the body of the inquiry for a more psychological classification.

Staring at the data, rearranging them mentally more than once, breaking them down by the age, sex, race, education, religion, even military service—this process has produced only one possible fruitful distinction. Oddly enough, it might well be labeled the local versus the cosmopolitan idol, selected respectively by the less and the better educated. I stress that this did not come about because the memory of Merton prejudiced the search. Consider the gods and see for yourself.

In 1961, among those with grade school education, 3 percent chose Churchill, less than one percent Nehru, 2 percent Pope John, and one percent Schweitzer. Among those who had gone to college, the respective percents were 14, 4, 2, and 16. In 1970, *not a single* grade school respondent admired Dr. Christian Barnard, Moshe Dayan, Pierre Trudeau, U Thant, or Cesar Chavez. These figures had very few admirers among the college-educated, but they did have some. In 1961, *not a single* grade school respondent chose Adenauer, Pablo Casals, Khrushchev, De Gaulle, Willy Brandt, Bertrand Russell, Chiang Kai-shek, or Nasser, but each of these figures drew admirers, although few, from among the college-educated. These gods do not share a common ideology, or institutional sphere, a style more or less contemplative or active, violent or peaceful. The better educated themselves, being more cosmopolitan, have more of the universe to choose from. Their minor gods are highly variable, depending on factors unknown, but clearly there is no single factor and no single type of minor god. What about the goddesses? As noted earlier, they are most mysterious. Cosmopolitanism is surely at work, the *highly* educated choosing more frequently Golda Meir and Indira Ghandi, even Queen Elizabeth and Mme. Chiang. But among respondents of only modest education, there are admirers—few, but some and not less than among the best educated—of Margaret Mead and Pearl Buck. These may not be foreign goddesses, but they are exotic. The basis for the choice of minor and major female reference idols surely is manifold and complex.

My concern has been to emphasize a neglected aspect of reference group theory, to embark once again on a description of the reference individuals and reference idols people select and on an exploration of the factors shaping the selection process. I have not even looked at the other general aspect of reference group theory: the *consequences* of selecting particular reference idols. What the varied consequences are for individuals who have chosen *different* idols as points of normative guidance might conceivably be illuminated by additional secondary analysis. But there is another consequence that is brought to our attention for research by the moment in time at which this is being written—just before the three-quarter mark in the century—and which is underscored by the persistent major finding that the president is the one major idol of very large numbers. Indeed, the 1970 survey even unearthed a small but not insubstantial sect who worshiped Spiro Agnew. What happens when the idols are shattered?

NOTES

1. Robert K. Merton and Alice S. Kitt, "Contributions to the Theory of Reference Group Behavior," in Robert K. Merton and P. F. Lazarsfeld, eds., *Continuities in Social Research: Studies in the Scope and Method of the American Soldier* (New York: Free Press, 1950), pp. 40–105.
2. Robert K. Merton, "Continuities in the Theory of Reference Groups and Social Structure," in Robert K. Merton, *Social Theory and Social Structure*, rev. ed. (New York: Free Press, 1957), pp. 281–386.
3. *Ibid.*, p. 302.
4. *Ibid.*, pp. 303–04.
5. Herbert H. Hyman, "Reflections on Reference Groups," *Public Opinion Quarterly* 24 (1960): 383–96.
6. Merton, "Continuities," p. 302.
7. Although Lazarsfeld and Merton implicitly raised the problem of notability by their reference to the "status-conferral" function of mass communication, occasional Southern sociologists seem to be the only direct investigators of the problem, perhaps because of their observations of the differentially low production and retention of national notabilities by the region. (P. F. Lazarsfeld and Robert K. Merton, "Mass Communication, Popular Taste, and Organized Social Action," in L. Bryson, ed., *The Communication of Ideas* [New York: Harper & Row, 1948], pp. 95–118.) See, for example, Harry Moore or Austin Porterfield, whose hypothesis that a great body of population in the old South was "in non-notability congealed" should have stimulated, by its exquisite phrasing alone, further research. Some of their analyses may be helpful in understanding the findings presented later on the relative lack of reference idols among Southerners.
8. For conclusions about the *general* pattern over time that required only examination of the marginals for the aggregate samples, we drew upon all the surveys from 1946 to 1971. For more refined analyses that required special tabulations and breakdowns of the aggregate samples, it would have been too laborious and costly for us to use all or many surveys. We followed the essential principle in secondary analysis of "no peeking." We selected three surveys, from 1950, 1961, and 1970, *prior to inspecting the findings,* in order to obtain some replication of the tests and evidence on changes over a twenty-year period and to control any subtle tendencies to choose surveys that would confirm our preconceptions. Where a particular conclusion is based on only one or two of the three surveys, the choice is not on arbitrary or prejudiced grounds but for the explicit methodological or theoretical reason stated in the text.
9. John E. Mueller, *War, Presidents and Public Opinion* (New York: Wiley, 1973).
10. *Ibid.*, p. 184.
11. *Ibid.*, p. 186.
12. Leo Lowenthal, "Biographies in Popular Magazines," in P. F. Lazarsfeld and Frank Stanton, eds., *Radio Research, 1942–43* (New York: Duell, Sloan & Pearce, 1943), pp. 507–48.
13. John S. Reed, *The Enduring South: Subcultural Persistence in Mass Society* (Lexington, Mass.: Heath, 1972).
14. Mueller, *War, Presidents and Public Opinion*, p. 184. (Italics added.)
15. The prevalence of negative idols generally—which specific public figures are cast exclusively in this role, which function as positive idols for some and negative idols for others—would require a companion question on the "least admired." A brief news report of an exotic survey, although lacking in scientific stature, suggests the potentialities of such additional inquiry: "U.S. President Richard Nixon leads in the London Wax-Figure Room of Madame Tussaud. He is the most hated and

most frightening [*meistgefürchtete*]' man, as an inquiry among visitors established. Placing next: Adolf Hitler and Jack the Ripper" (*Der Spiegel* [January 21, 1974], p. 138).

16. Restricting ourselves to those who indicated by a specific choice that they were betting in the 1950 Derby, 13 percent of such grade school respondents chose President Truman but less than half of one percent of the college-educated chose the President. Among the corresponding groups in the 1961 race, 41 percent of grade school respondents chose President Kennedy and 17 percent of college-educated chose the President.

17. Fred I. Greenstein, *Children and Politics* (New Haven: Yale University Press, 1965).

18. *Ibid.*, p. 147.

19. Elisabeth Noelle and E. Neumann, *The Germans: Public Opinion Polls 1947–1966* (Allensbach, Germany: Verlag für Demoskopie, 1967).

20. Gabriel Almond and Sidney Verba, *The Civic Culture* (Princeton, N.J.: Princeton University Press, 1963).

21. Herbert H. Hyman and P. B. Sheatsley, "The Authoritarian Personality—A Methodological Critique," in R. Christie and M. Jahoda, eds., *Studies in the Scope and Method of the Authoritarian Personality* (New York: Free Press, 1954), pp. 50–122.

22. It should be noted that we have computed these percentages on the basis of the *total* sub-samples, rather than on the base of only those who chose a specific reference idol. It seems a fairer test of the prevalence of the pattern to include those who had a chance to select a black idol but who opted out and reported that they had no reference idol at all or only a reference individual from the immediate milieu. Obviously, the percents choosing black idols would be higher among those who chose any specific idol. But for white respondents, the entries that are "zero" must remain unchanged, and for only one entry—choice of a black female idol in 1970—does the recomputed, rounded figure reach 2 percent. Among black respondents, the only recomputed entries that reach a high figure are again for a black female idol in 1970, but even here the large majority of those who did select a specific idol chose a white person. It should also be realized that the complements of the present entries in the table are not simply those who chose white idols but include those who chose no idol or chose a reference individual.

23. Robert K. Merton, "Patterns of Influence: Local and Cosmopolitan Influentials," in *Social Theory and Social Structure* (New York: The Free Press, 1957), pp. 390–91.

The Planning of Communities: Anticipations and Hindsights

SUZANNE KELLER

THE writings of Robert K. Merton, the sociologist of the wingéd word, have become famous both for their substance and their felicity. "The Unanticipated Consequences of Purposive Social Action,"[1] the title of his first published paper in volume 1 of the *American Sociological Review*, lingers as much for its title as for the problem it explores.

After establishing, in his clear and unmistakable way, the main terms of the inquiry, including operational definitions of key concepts, Merton notes that the chief culprits in our long-standing inability to preview the future correctly are ignorance, both subjective (when one does not know what is known) and objective (when little is known), errors (of assessment and inference), and neglect of the ramifications of actions. There is also the problem, peculiar to the behavioral disciplines, of human volition interfering with heralded predictions by altering the conditions under which these are to hold true. This last observation led to another famous paper on the "self-fulfilling prophecy" and its obverse, suicidal or self-destructive belief.[2]

Then, as later,[3] Merton considered the "study of the unintended consequences of social practices" the locus of the "distinctive intellectual contributions of the sociologist." [4]

Suzanne Keller is Professor of Sociology at Princeton University with a part-time appointment in the School of Architecture and Urban Planning.

In this paper I would like to return to this primary and basic question by examining some of the more common errors in one kind of anticipatory behavior—the planning of human environments in fact and fantasy. My examples will be drawn from experiments in community and educational planning as well as from selected utopian proposals.

NEW COMMUNITIES

The planning of new communities offers a host of examples of unanticipated consequences both positive, as regards gloomy prophecies that did not come to pass, and negative, as high hopes turned to ashes. Their examination should prove useful at any time, but especially so when we consider that the future will see many more such social experiments at ever larger scales. Judging from our seeming inability to learn either from past failures or successes, we cannot enter the planning era opening before us with anything but trepidation.

When Golda Meir was once asked what had disappointed her in Israel's development, she replied:

Well...I believe none of us dreamers realized in the beginning what difficulties would arise.... Moreover—you'll think me silly, naive—I thought that a Jewish state would be free of the evils afflicting other societies: theft, murder, prostitution. I was encouraged to believe it because we had started so well. But now we have them all.[5]

Her sentiments would find an echo in many other instances of planning, though rarely admitted with such candor, for in truth the tendency to gloss over difficulties in prospective undertakings is striking.

This may be why Pitrim A. Sorokin, in the very same volume of the *American Sociological Review*, expressed his doubts and fears about planners being carried away by their often ill-fated projects. Noting that planning is both unavoidable and bound to fail in a rapidly changing world, he offered this "humble" plea to all overenthusiastic planners: "Please, go on with your game; but better underdo rather than overdo your gambling. Still better, if you can, study carefully the phenomena you are going to engineer before engineering them: still better, if you can, try your plan experimentally, on a small scale and in earnest." [6] Few seem to have heeded his warning.

THE NEW TOWNS MOVEMENT

In the next thirty years, thousands of new towns will be built throughout the world in preindustrial as well as in industrial countries. Whatever the social context within which they will take shape, planners share the task of translating collective requirements for shelter, transportation, services, and open spaces into tangible physical form, possessing texture, scale, and esthetic-cultural meaning. In other words, they must devise more or less enduring ways to satisfy human needs for food, work, shelter, health, sleep, amusement, security, and privacy. In a sense, it is no exaggeration to say that the future of human societies—as was their past—will in considerable part be a chronicle of ascendant and abandoned places and settings.

New towns go back a long way. There is Piraeus, planned by Hippodamus around 450 B.C., followed by Greek colonies, Roman military sites, Spanish cities in the New World, and religious settlements throughout the ages. In this century, the New Towns movement, inspired by the work of Patrick Geddes, Ebenezer Howard, Clarence Perry, and Clarence Stein, among others, led to the creation of garden cities on both sides of the Atlantic and from there spread throughout the world.

The goals of new towns are everywhere rather similar. They include the desire to:

1. redirect and channel population growth
2. manage urban development
3. provide satisfactory living-working-recreational environments, and a higher quality of life
4. integrate facilities, services, spaces, and people in balanced fashion
5. experiment and innovate with social and physical design

One big difference between old and new planned communities, however, concerns the accelerated rates of change confronting contemporary planners. In the past, when practices changed more slowly, inhabitants could modify the planned design through time, thus becoming partly responsible for the creation of their communities. Today, however, the intensified demand for large-scale, instant planning, at high costs, makes this sort of generational mending less possible and throws long-standing defects in physical-social planning into sharp relief. These defects, to be discussed below, impede the correct anticipation of human behavior in the planned environment. It is true, of course, as Merton cautioned, that unanticipated consequences need not be undesirable, but many are, and it is to these that this paper is largely addressed.

COMMON DEFECTS IN THE PLANNING OF NEW COMMUNITIES

It is by now generally recognized, though not often acted upon, that social and physical planning are interrelated and that one is not likely to be effective without the other. The success of national development plans, for example, ultimately depends on sound local-spatial planning, for in addition to setting national targets for housing, jobs, or education one must also spell out their geographic distribution. Nonetheless, fragmentary and piecemeal planning remains the rule rather than the exception. But if most national plans formulate their objectives too abstractly and without specifying the spatial distribution of their objectives, plans for new communities tend to fall into the opposite error. They often remain unintegrated with the larger national or even regional picture. This lack of coordination between the two levels then results in such well-known disasters as roads that stop in the middle of nowhere, mass facilities without parking places, and tourist hotels cut off from ways to get to or away from them.

Lack of teamwork among disciplines is part of the problem. As is well known, the elephant varies with the discipline examining it, and this partial view limits a full comprehension of its nature.

Selective perception also affects the paradigm of information and explanation utilized. Planners are not typically attuned to the significance of culture pattern and social structure and thus underestimate cultural and structural factors without dispelling their influence. The ensuing gap between intention and result is often filled in by ad hoc and arbitrary decisions.

Examples of the imposition of alien, hence arbitrary, standards and design criteria on groups they are unsuited for are endless. Planners and other experts frequently do not share either the experiences or the aspirations of those they are planning for and substitute the perspectives they are familiar with—that of middle-class professionals—for those required. This is true not only within but between cultures, as solutions relevant in one setting are automatically transferred to a different one without much regard for whether they will work there. An example is the Neighborhood Unit Idea exported from Britain throughout the world without checking on its viability under different cultural conditions. Both class and cross-cultural paternalism reflect the common, if erroneous, belief that expertise transcends culture and that properly trained outsiders can diagnose and design for insiders.[7]

This is not unrelated to the paternalism that continues to pervade the professions generally. The idea that one can plan *for* people, or that one class or group has a unique claim to truth, or that experts know best is still far from dead, though the results should give us pause. How many new housing projects, for example, are defaced or distorted, partly out of injured pride and partly out of sheer unfamiliarity with a design not suited to the ways of *these* people in *this* place and time? This may be one reason why the ghettoes, shantytowns, and favellas that the new projects are designed to displace keep reemerging. The failure to make the design fit different concepts of privacy, neighborliness, or amenity quickly results in its being perceived as an obstacle to be removed or circumvented. Residents then renounce responsibility for maintenance, illegal services may spring up in the gap left by poorly designed or placed facilities, and residents may practice passive resistance against management.[8]

Despite the accumulated evidence of the past century, planners continue to be reluctant to accept the existence, depth, and power of culture patterns to shape human conduct and desires. They still tend to consider human beings as basically alike and to reduce human needs and wishes to a common biological or economic denominator.

Nowhere is this more evident than in the dubious assumptions made about people's spatial responsiveness and behavior. Here, part of the blame must be placed on the indifference of social scientists to the significance of the spatial dimension for social conduct. Well-known exceptions notwithstanding,[9] there is too much that we do not know about the saliency of space in individual and collective life. Hence, planners fill in the missing information with prejudice or wish. One of their favorite articles of faith concerns the determinant role of physico-spatial factors in social life. Another attributes far greater rationality to human behavior than experience would seem to warrant.

This may be why so little effort is devoted to instruct people in the use of maps, signs, clover leafs, exits, and entrances. Somehow, they are just expected to know what to do in different behavioral settings or to infer the expected responses. One wonders, in this connection, how many highway accidents might be avoided if it were not taken for granted that everyone can read a given language and follow directions while driving.[10] Or, consider human behavior in disasters such as fires. Fire laws ostensibly exist to protect people, but once again the rules and the people do not necessarily and certainly not automatically connect. In high-rise buildings, it has been found that, instead of using fireproof stairs for their escape, people seem to head straight for the elevators at the first signs of smoke. Ordinarily the quickest means to reach the street, elevators would seem to be obvious escape routes. But in case of fire, elevators often turn into death traps.[11]

All too often, the laborious problem of translating designer intentions into behavioral prescriptions is bypassed. Directional signals, for example, may tell us where to go but not where we are. Little attention is paid to such routine human anxieties, in a world of increasing mobility, as the fear of getting lost. Perhaps this is a superfluous worry for healthy natives, but it is not insignificant for the elderly, the handicapped, children, or foreigners.

Then, there are the many specific deficiencies, too numerous to itemize here, turning up in project after project. The windows that do not open or close, roofs that leak, elevators that can carry only a fraction of those needing them, ill-defined rules of property maintenance that sour interpersonal relations, inadequate lighting, neglect of exits, inadequate parking facilities—we meet with them over and over again. Other familiar neglects concern the failure to anticipate seasonal variations in multiseasonal climates, as roads perfect in summer become impossible in rain and sleet or as outdoor recreational facilities become unusable, leaving a gap in leisure-time activities.[12]

Finally, an oft-recurring shortcoming concerns the aftermath of planning. Even when design and construction are performed with care and caution, there may be little or no follow-up. Designers tend to ignore or forget that buildings, parks, communities, and playgrounds must be operated, serviced, and maintained—and these too must be part of the plan. This links up with a kindred neglect, namely, a curious reluctance to plan for misuse or decay, as if the process of building up were not paralleled by the process of tearing down. Planners rarely consider that things wear out or break down eventually, which is why there is no room in most plans for the debris that accumulates in time.

This reluctance is not confined to physical planning but extends to social planning as well, as when family life is considered mainly in its formative phases and divorce or the empty nest are thus typically unprovided for. This

287

is yet another instance of what I think of as the incomplete gesture, the lack of follow-up and follow-through.

Columbia, Maryland, provides an instructive case of what can go wrong with the best-laid plans, drawing on the best of available skills under the leadership of an admired practical idealist.[13] To the dismay and disappointment of those whose painstaking efforts helped lay the community's foundation, a number of unforeseen problems have come to plague this carefully designed community. The most serious of these are crime, disaffected youth, and racial tensions. These are of course widespread social ills, and their presence in Columbia only attests to the not always acknowledged fact that new communities are part of an older society and cannot isolate themselves or be exempt from its problems. However, there are also more mundane problems concerning how people react to a new community, their houses, and their neighbors that comprise a ready list of the complicated interplay between users and environments which may alter the plan for good or ill.

Here, too, we meet with the familiar tendency alluded to earlier not to anticipate serious difficulties. While no one expects perfection, few are very explicit about what imperfections may arise. Hence, later interviews with some who had been centrally involved in the planning of Columbia led to the admission, "We really didn't anticipate . . . and it continues to amaze us—the infinite problems that can arise in building a city at such a rapid pace."[14]

Among their surprises were the multiple uses to which residents wanted to put their property, reflected in endless queries such as: "Will I be allowed to keep a horse? A dog? A bird? How many?" "May I practice medicine? Take in sewing? Have a dark room?" "What alteration can I make on my house?" Who, asked one informant later, would ever have believed the number of signs people would want to put up? Those in the know did not know the answers to most of these questions and had to entrust them to special committees set up to deal with the implementation of the plan.[15]

Specific and costly miscalculations involved traffic planning—in particular, the underestimation of traffic volume—and the phasing of new facilities and services that plagues all new communities. For example, Columbia's unique medical care plan needed 20,000 to 30,000 members to break even, but since only 3,000 members had enrolled during the first six months the plan could not survive without outside financial aid.

Then there are such problematic staples of planning theory as the ideal that all facilities be at walking distance or that work and residence be integrated. These had to be revised almost at once as the car and the work commute moved in right from the start. One wonders whether this will have any impact on future planning proposals.

CONCEPTUALIZATION OF PROSPECTIVE COMMUNITIES

Part of the difficulty in planning communities stems from the inadequate conceptual base supporting such efforts. Many of the concepts, it turns out, are based on highly oversimplified models of human association derived from some defunct or never tried utopian vision.

Utopian proposals for ideal communities are instructive even when they are not put into practice.[16] At the least, they indicate the complexities in store for those who would plan for collective life. Lacking more than a rudimentary theory of society, these always provocative and sometimes brilliant schemes for human betterment reflect a number of by-now-familiar shortcomings. Among these are an underestimation of the difficulties involved in constructing blueprints for living and ignorance of social structure and human psychology.

UNQUESTIONED ASSUMPTIONS

Every utopia is shot through with unexamined premises regarding values and social problems. Indeed, one trait common to many of these ideal societies is the degree to which they reflect the unsolved social problems with which the inventor of a given utopia happened to be familiar or concerned about—despotism, poverty, hunger, or crime. This partiality very much affects the kind of utopia the visionary is likely to propose.

Among the assumptions common to utopias of various stripes is the belief that if subsistence needs are satisfied, hitherto neglected artistic and spiritual talents can come to the fore. A somewhat related belief is that crime and other displays of antisocial sentiments will disappear once people have enough of the basics, such as the right kind of work and attractive opportunities for living and learning. Both of these are as yet undemonstrated, which does not mean that they have no measure of truth but only that it should not be assumed as self-evident.

Most utopias are immaculately conceived, thereby avoiding the knotty problem of how one gets from *here* to *there*. Often discovered in transit—in earlier writings by ship, more recently through space travel—they are already ongoing societies when we are introduced to them. No utopia I know of describes the process of going from the present into the future with the same people and institutions. The new order is always a fresh start, perhaps after a lucky escape from some devastation that destroyed the previous order. Therein lies one of the disutilities of utopias for contemporary planning—in neglecting the very question of mechanisms and process which ought to be central to the planning enterprise.

The selectivity and partiality of utopian visions would result in highly imbalanced communities in real life, imbalances that would probably be aligned via some sort of authoritarian solution. Social scientists could both learn from these flawed efforts at synthesis as well as contribute to their improvement.

Unfortunately, with few exceptions, Skinner's Walden Two being one, the social sciences play at best a minimal role in the design of these ideal societies. Information about elites and power, work and rewards, the family and settlement patterns is typically ignored, hence the simplistic and reductionist character of most utopias. Where social science information is utilized, it is highly selective. Economics and politics and, more recently, a narrow branch

289

of psychology (behaviorism, reenforcement theory), watered down to be sure, have found their way into one or another utopian scheme. Other branches of knowledge, such as criminology, developmental psychology, ethics, social theory, or architecture, are drawn on very little or very selectively. Above all, and this is also true for planned communities that are actually built, a systems approach is the exception rather than the rule, and this robs many utopias of complexity and comprehensiveness.

Another big omission is the absence of conflict, destructiveness, and hostility, as if selected improvements in social and economic arrangements would automatically do away with disagreement and nonconformity in the social order. Planned communities suffer from a similar pollyana-ish bias. Here, too, information on conflict, factionalism, and social envy would be most instructive. In part, these assumptions stem from differing strategies favored by those who seek to change human nature and the social order. One strategy opts for concentrating on improvements in the social order assuming that human nature will follow suit. The other opts for improving human nature and expects that the good society will then follow. Rarely are the two shown in dynamic interplay.

In sum, the weaknesses of the concepts used in devising these imaginary communities may be traced to ignorance, prejudice, and bias, defects also at work in the planning of actual communities. Both lack a comprehensive system model to guide the process of their construction. Both have a rather one-sided conception of human nature and are reluctant to accept human propensities to crime, conflict, illness, and antagonism.

Since many existing, large-scale social experiments rest on theories and beliefs held by utopian thinkers in times past, the substantive bases for these beliefs warrant critical scrutiny. This is not to say that information about social life and behavior is at all adequate to such a task, but the refusal to use it is indefensible. Surely, there is something to be gained from even a partial test of cherished articles of faith before devising plans and committing millions of people to them.[17]

WHAT IS THE LOCAL COMMUNITY?

Planning for a world in flux demands a huge effort of the imagination as well as the capacity to invoke new guiding images of what the future may be like. Such images are in short supply in current plans for new communities, most of which bear the imprint of nostalgia rather than anticipation.

A main source of the unanticipated developments in such communities stems from adherence to ideals no longer appropriate to emergent realities. For example, the desire to create comprehensive, self-contained, intimate, face-to-face communities akin to the cozy villages of yesteryear is an illusory quest, I fear, because it misreads the scale of life which is to characterize the twenty-first century. Just as one cannot reduce the scale of an adult by cutting off his legs—at most one impedes his locomotion—so one cannot keep the world of telemobility away from conceptions of modern communities. Still, the pretense persists that these settlements of technicians and professionals of more than average education and income, in constant contact with the wider world through televiewing, working, vacationing, and visiting, are small, comprehensive, territorially bound villages contentedly turned in upon themselves. In other words, the notion of the local community needs to be reexamined and overhauled.

In Merton's famous essay on influentials in local communities, the definition of what is meant by local was not as yet in doubt.[18] Indeed, Merton distinguished between locals and cosmopolitans in fairly clear-cut terms: locals were more likely to have lived in the community in question for a long period of time—how long was not specified—and did not wish to move from the town.[19] They were ardent local patriots, wedded to the community in which they had been born and tied to it sentimentally and economically. Locals became influential by virtue of their long-term association with the community, their concentration on it, and by their networks of local relationships.

Merton noted that local and cosmopolitan influentials may coexist in varying proportions in communities that have experienced change. And while he called for research on the characteristics of the social structure that makes for differential prevalence of "permanent" versus "transient" types, he speculated only slightly about the nature of the communities in which each was likely to prevail. Merton could leave unanalyzed what was meant by local community because its characteristics were widely agreed upon.

Using the indexes of localism Merton employed, it would seem that most communities would have become less local in the decades since the paper was written. Currently, people move rather than stay put to pursue jobs, education, romance, adventure. In new towns, in particular, none of the traditional indexes of localism would seem to apply since they tend to be inhabited by transients and strangers, ever in contact with wider and different worlds. Television, that ubiquitous boarder in modern homes, makes sure of that. Both in planning and in sociology, therefore, we need to reconceptualize current notions of community, territoriality, and permanence, as boundaries and distances recede and the world enters our living rooms at the flick of a dial.

It has, of course, long been noted that communities are being transformed in scale and function, but as yet the insufficient operationalization of these notions makes them of little use to planners and builders. In one sense, we are simply witnessing a further extension of a historic process, described by Toennies and other nineteenth-century thinkers, as a movement from *Gemeinschaft* to *Gesellschaft*. *Gesellschaft* referred to the diversified, large-scale, dynamic, social, political, and economic relations of macrosystems called "societies." *Gemeinschaft*, on the other hand, emphasized antithetical traits of local, territorially defined, closed systems and relations marked by common traditions and destinies.[20]

But what was dichotomy, idealized to be sure, in the nineteenth century has become continuum in the twentieth. Today, increasingly, the local com-

291

munity mirrors the very forces with which it was originally contrasted, as diversification and specialization break through its physical form and destroy the unity and uniformity that were its trademark. Accordingly, we must cease to look at community in holistic and dichotomous terms. This is as true of its spatial as of its social characteristics.

The traditional idea of community stressed the notion of place, whereas in modern communities accessibility would seem to be more crucial.[21] As accessibility becomes dissociated from physical proximity, communities are freed from their dependencies on territory. Melvin Webber has described this change as a contrast between communities of place and communities of interest that transcend place. The crucial determinant of membership in such communities is not spatial proximity but spiritual affinity. Increasingly, he suggests, people become part of varied interest communities that are not territorially defined.[22] Thus, place becomes the *locus for* rather than the *focus of* action and commitment. Accordingly, Webber proposes the notion of "urban realm"—a fluid symphony of contacts of heterogeneous groups of people communicating with each other through space.[23]

Place is no longer a comprehensive node of converging forces but a point in a farflung network of activities and people. Hence, a disjunction develops between spatial contiguity and the sense of community, between the form of a settlement and its saliency. In the effort to understand and grasp these new patterns of association and service, the study of communication patterns should supplement the study of settlement patterns.

Old-style communities, rooted in a common past, were created by memories and anticipations of solidarity. New communities cohere by means of orientations and current interests within a shared, though shifting, frame of reference.

As mobility and diversity increase in the decades ahead, the mobility long characteristic of sailors, traveling salesmen, students, and the jet set will spread to ever wider sectors of the public. New patterns of domesticity, friendship, and vocation will then compel us to rethink the very idea of settled living and the assumption, still widespread, that human beings require a fixed territorial base for their round of daily life. Permanent residence in a fixed location may eventually become characteristic of particular groups or stages in the life cycle and be but one among several acceptable modes of habitation. One need only to watch the mass exodus of vacationers each summer and their improvised communities along seashore and highway to know that the nomadic era is already (and again) upon us.

As Luther once said that he was in the world but not of it, so human beings will live in a given area but not necessarily and certainly not exclusively be of it. The impact of this socially condoned rootlessness on social solidarity, territorial loyalty, and patterns of association and service, still largely unexplored, is bound to be considerable.

The territorial imperative is so entrenched in our perceptions and mind sets, however, that we find it difficult to absorb, not to say plan for, that dramatic possibility. Hence, community planning is not yet geared to non-territoriality as an emerging concept. This is one reason why this sort of planning is often inadequate and why unanticipated consequences—for good or ill—defeat the loftiest of aims for community cohesion and commitment. This gap between intention and result will not be lessened by more money or time or good will. Needed are new assumptions and better concepts of community, concepts that are closer to the reality and humanity which are after all the ostensible targets and purposes of planning.

AN EXPERIMENT IN INNOVATION

My final example of failures to anticipate correctly comes from an effort to create a new university as described by the social scientist Warren Bennis, one of the principals involved in the endeavor.[24]

The setting was an old established university that needed a lift. Money was no object, spirits were high, and for once it was possible to follow one's heart's desires. The new president, full of hopes and dreams, could bring his considerable prestige to bear on recruiting an outstanding faculty capable of carrying out the innovative program.

In looking back at the 1,000 days between the start and finish of the venture, Bennis concludes "with all the unsettling clarity of hindsight" that they "undermined many of their own best aspirations for the university" of their dreams. Asking himself how he would proceed were he given a second chance, he selected a number of do's and don't's to heed in the future.

For one thing, he would no longer minimize the difficulties and drawbacks of the endeavor either to himself or to others whose efforts he wished to enlist. This tendency, which we noted in other planning efforts as well, has the double drawback of both setting the stage for later disillusionment and militating against mustering the energies needed for the hard work ahead. Soon, but not soon enough, it became apparent that it is easier "to break down barriers than to build bridges," a sentiment that finds its echo in many recent events the world over.

Bennis also cautions against succumbing to the temptation to recruit but a single type, namely, one who shares one's "omnipotent fantasies" and thus deprives one of the sobering sting of dissonance and disagreement. This is an all-too-common failing among leaders and prophets.

In addition, by presenting an overly bright picture of the situation to those already converted, oversell becomes inevitable and with it overexpectation and eventual disappointment amounting almost to a feeling of betrayal. As is true of many new town ventures as well, by sweetening the package in the hope of arousing support, one also encourages magical fantasies in which the day-to-day problems miraculously fade away.

In actual fact, day-to-day problems have a tendency to proliferate as reality intrudes. Such mundane questions as where to live and how long to wait for certain amenities can ground the loftiest visionary. In this case, the state legislature which controlled the purse strings turned against the experiment and funds suddenly dried up, an eventuality that had not been considered earlier when hopes were stated as pledges. The resulting disillusionment quickly soured the courtship mood of the early days.

Bennis warns in particular against proceeding without due regard for past traditions, thereby ignoring the fact that there are "no clean slates in established organizations." This is not unlike the aforementioned utopias that also bypass the past and spring to life full-grown without having to confront the baffling problems of generation and birth. Those who represent the older regime will oppose change if they perceive it as threatening to their existence. By neglecting their self-respect and needs for security, one creates the very opposition one had hoped to avoid.

Interestingly, here too the indifference of social scientists to physical-environmental factors created unforeseen obstacles. For example, instead of being able to move the new faculty into the futuristic offices displayed in the architectural models, they had to house them in existing quarters, which added overcrowding to the strains already engendered. As so often happens, moreover, target dates for the completion of facilities and buildings had been underestimated and a provisional campus had to be. set up away from the main campus. This makeshift arrangement increased the isolation of the new from the old and added to the general sense of frustration. Clearly, the erosion of favorable environmental conditions played no small part in the course of events. This is yet another illustration of the importance of ordinarily taken-for-granted physical comforts and settings for the fate of great undertakings.

Bennis' final comments echo my own concern for better conceptual and procedural models. "A statement of goals," he warns, "is not a program," and to be effective such statements must be translated into concrete specifications for change.

Once again we learn—how often shall we have to learn it—that change is most successful when those affected have a say in it. People will resist and reject proposed changes if these are imposed even if they are in basic agreement with them. Furthermore, it must be kept in mind that acceptance takes time, time for reflection, adaptation, and for coming to terms with the new. This is why Bennis now feels that a "clumsier, slower, but more egalitarian approach . . . would have resulted in more permanent reform."[25]

This candid assessment, which took courage considering the writer's stakes in the experiment in question, is as rare as it is instructive. It shows once again how difficult, arduous, and perilous a venture is planning for the future and the translation of the castles of our. minds into enduring earthly structures.

SUMMARY AND CONCLUSION

These, then, are the more common errors or failures in planning for change. In the concluding pages of this paper I will suggest steps we might take to prevent them in the future.

COMMON ERRORS IN PLANNING

1. Piecemeal, noncontextual planning
2. Ignorance of different cultures and subcultures, including people's spatial habits and attachments
3. The often inadvertent imposition of particular class or group codes onto others for whom they may be unsuitable
4. Lack of instruction to users of how to operate in the planned environment
5. Indifference to the aftermath of planning, including maintenance and morale
6. A general tendency toward reduction of human behavior to its biological or economic underpinnings; or of individuals to some kind of average; or of social structure to family structure
7. Poor conceptualization of basic terms—privacy, territoriality, community, and others

These shortcomings boil down to three:

1. Inadequate concepts
2. Inadequate information
3. Inadequate execution

These errors, common enough in routine planning ventures, become magnified in nonroutine situations that proliferate in a world in flux. If we are to minimize or eliminate these common cognitive and procedural failings, we must improve our capacity to anticipate consequences at two levels: methodological and conceptual. Let me briefly deal with these.

The plea for more holistic, integrative thinking is being voiced in many areas, practical as well as theoretical. The economist Oskar Morgenstern recently warned of what he perceived as a crisis in current economics, seemingly the most successful of the social sciences, for its failure to "come to grips with social and political reality." He deplored the lack of concepts with which economists could look at the economy as "a living and changing organism" comprising "human beings in conflict and cooperation."[26] Similar thoughts have been voiced in a variety of fields of late as interdependency displaces linearity as a guiding cultural metaphor.

As mechanistic and deterministic notions give way to ecological thinking, a concern with process becomes increasingly evident. So does the need to integrate human goals with the technical knowhow we possess. Such integration is still more hope than fact. For example, the warnings and extrapolations contained in the recently published book *The Limits to Growth*, which received worldwide attention, virtually ignored politics and social structure.[27] The authors, admitting that they found it "difficult to imagine what new forms of human societal behavior might emerge...," ignored them altogether.[28]

Similarly as regards the continuing indifference of social scientists to the physical-spatial ramifications of social behavior. This seriously affects the efficacy of planning since everything that human beings do occurs in some kind of spatial setting. A new system of health care, coeducation, new housing policies, price control—all have physical-spatial connotations along with their behavioral ones. They should therefore be considered jointly.

A second recommendation emerging from this review of past errors is the need for social indicators without which it is impossible to assess collective conditions. A considerable literature has developed on these questions[29] highlighting the need for performance standards now largely missing from much of social planning. Above all, if we are to improve upon past efforts, it is clear that we must follow up and evaluate what we have created, built, and planned.

SUBSTANTIVE LESSONS

Certain developments during the past several decades have shaken our faith in the myths that inspired and sustained the nineteenth century. Among these are the myths that science can save us, that growth means progress, that natural resources are unlimited, and that innovation is necessarily good.[30] These not entirely welcome lessons, combined with the decline of other old verities regarding work, sex, politics, and family, have created a crisis of conscience and values which many ajudge to be the most serious problems of the modern age.

High on the list of baffling questions is that of objectives and priorities as alternatives multiply. We need to find ways to order necessities and preferences so as to balance technical possibility with political feasibility and personal desirability. Despite the growing diversity and relativity of values, devising such a set of priorities is not impossible. According to Wilbert Moore, some universal goals are still possible. Among these are:

the preference of health over sickness
for longevity over early death
for material wellbeing over poverty
for orderly ways of dealing with conflict over solutions by bloodshed[31]

If we take seriously the need for comprehensive rather than piecemeal planning, moreover, legislators and politicians will have to become more cognizant of the fact that their programs have multiple consequences, direct and indirect. Though they may see themselves as "simply building highways, guaranteeing mortgages, advancing agriculture or whatever," they are "simultaneously distributing employment opportunities, segregating neighborhoods and desegregating them, depopulating the countryside or filling up the slums, etc.," all of these being "second-and-third-order consequences of nominally related programs."[32]

Finally, we have learned something, though not nearly enough, about the nature of human needs. First and foremost is the need for different disciplines to accept the fact, established during the past century, that human nature and culture interpenetrate in such a way that the one cannot be considered apart from the other. To plan for human beings, therefore, demands a respect for and knowledge of the cultures and subcultures in which they live. Second, no matter how right or desirable certain programs appear to the experts or the politicians, it can be shown that little is accomplished if this fundamental lesson is ignored and "correct" solutions are imposed rather than created jointly. People have innumerable ways to get even, usually by abusing and misusing what has been so laboriously built for them. If planners seek to affect human behavior, they can, as Gans has suggested, do one of two things: (1) develop plans suited to people's dispositions and desires, or (2) change people's dispositions in the direction of the plans by persuading people of their soundness. What planners cannot do is to change people's dispositions by their plans.[33]

Even if we try to heed the admonition not to impose values on people, this is easier said than done. For it demands not only an inventory of human needs now lacking but some way of classifying these according to level, intensity, and priority for different individuals and groups. We need also, at this stage, to find some way to incorporate what Karl Menninger has called the negative or destructive propensities of human beings into our plans.[34] If not, we will continue to underestimate, hence fail to provide for, such recurrent realities in human settlements as conflict, divorce, crime, ill-health, vandalism, and the impulse to disorder.

All in all, then, there is much we must do to improve our capacity for anticipating the consequences of our actions, a skill of increasing importance in a changing world. The ability to look toward a future different from the present is the final indispensable ingredient in planning for change. As Bury advised a century ago:

> The dark imminence of this unknown future in front of us, like a vague wall of mist, every instant receding, with all its indiscernible contents of world-wide change, soundless revolutions, silent reformations, undreamed ideas, new religions, must not be neglected, if we would grasp the unity of history in its highest sense. ... The unapparent future has a claim to make itself felt as an idea controlling our perspective.[35]

NOTES

1. Robert K. Merton, "The Unanticipated Consequences of Purposive Social Action," *American Sociological Review* 1, no. 5 (October 1936): 894–904.
2. Robert K. Merton, "The Self-Fulfilling Prophecy," in Robert K. Merton, *Social Theory and Social Structure,* rev. ed. (Glencoe, Ill.: Free Press, 1957), pp. 421–36.
3. Robert K. Merton, "Manifest and Latent Functions," in Merton, *Social Theory and Social Structure,* pp. 18–84.
4. *Ibid.,* p. 66.
5. Oriana Fallaci, "Golda Talks to Oriana Fallaci," *Ms.* (April 1973), pp. 73–75, 100–04.
6. Pitrim A. Sorokin, "Is Accurate Social Planning Possible?" *American Sociological Review* 1, no. 1 (February 1936): 25.
7. Robert K. Merton, "Insiders and Outsiders: A Chapter in the Sociology of Knowledge," *American Journal of Sociology* 78 (July 1971): 9–47.

8. Helen Icken Safa, "Puerto Rican Adaptations to the Urban Milieu," reprint no. 5, Latin American Institute, Rutger's University, New Brunswick, N.J., p. 172.

9. See, for example, Herbert J. Gans, *People and Plans* (New York: Basic Books, 1968); Edward T. Hall, *The Hidden Dimension* (Garden City, N.Y.: Doubleday, 1966); Robert Gutman, ed., *People and Buildings* (New York: Basic Books, 1972); Leo Kuper, ed., *Living in Towns* (London: Cresset, 1953); William H. Michaelson, *Man and His Urban Environment* (Reading, Mass.: Addison Wesley, 1970); Harold M. Proshansky *et al.*, eds., *Environmental Psychology: Man and His Physical Setting* (New York: Holt, Rinehart & Winston, 1970) ; and Robert Sommer, *Personal Space, the Behavioral Basis of Design* (Englewood Cliffs, N.J.: Prentice-Hall, 1969) .

10. Harry A. Grace, "Behavioral Science Adequacy for Purposes of Design," VYOUPOINT Grace Association, Calif.; mimeod. 1971.

11. Richard Roth, "New Laws Needed to Fight Fires in High Rise Buildings," *New York Times*, July 4, 1971.

12. Even technical calculations, long hailed as relatively clearcut and presumably easy to predict, are not immune to miscalculations, as in the recent example of a Boston skyscraper having to substitute plywood windows for the thermopane ones unexpectedly destroyed by the wind. John Kifner, "Boarding Up Boston Skyscraper," *International Herald Tribune*, July 27, 1973, p. 16.

13. Gurney Breckenfeld, *Columbia and the New Cities* (New York: Ives Washburn, 1971).

14. *Ibid.*, p. 289.

15. *Ibid.*

16. Examples of utopian writings are Plato, *The Republic;* Sir Thomas More, *Utopia,* 1551; Edward Bellamy, *Looking Backward* (Boston: Ticknor, 1888); H. G. Wells, *A Modern Utopia* (London: Chapman & Hall, 1905); Aldous Huxley, *Brave New World* (New York: Bantam Books, 1946); Arthur C. Clarke, *Childhood's End* (New York: Ballantine Books, 1953); B. F. Skinner, *Walden Two* (1948) (New York: Macmillan, 1962); and Olaf Stapleton, *Last and First Men* (New York: Dover, 1968).

17. For an important discussion of how a "live" communal experiment fared in translating principle into practice, see Kathleen Kinkade, *A Walden Two Experiment* (New York: Morrow, 1973).

18. Robert K. Merton, "Patterns of Influence: Local and Cosmopolitan Influentials," in Merton, *Social Theory and Social Structure,* pp. 387–420.

19. *Ibid.*, p. 394.

20. Ferdinand Toennies, *Community and Society,* ed. Charles F. Loomis (New York: Harper & Row, 1963).

21. Melvin M. Webber, "The Urban Place and the Nonplace Realm," in Melvin M. Webber *et al.*, eds., *Explorations in Urban Structure* (Philadelphia: University of Pennsylvania Press, 1964), pp. 79–153.

22. *Ibid.*, p. 111.

23. *Ibid.*, p. 116.

24. Warren Bennis, "Who Sank the Yellow Submarine?" *Psychology Today* (November 1972), pp. 112–20.

25. *Ibid.*, p. 120.

26. Leonard Silk, "Professor Sees a Crisis in Economics," *New York Times*, May 16, 1973, pp. 65, 73.

27. Donella H. Meadows *et al.*, *The Limits to Growth* (New York: Universe Books, 1972).

28. Keith Melville, "The Future Will Be," *The Sciences* 12, no. 10 (December 1972).

29. Wilbert E. Moore and Eleanor Bernert Sheldon, "Monitoring Social Change: A Conceptual and Programmatic Statement," *Proceedings of the Social Statistics Section, 1965* (Washington, D.C.: American Statistical Association, 1966), pp. 144–49; Bertram M. Gross, ed., *Social Intelligence for America's Future* (Boston: Allyn & Bacon, 1969).

30. Norman V. Petersen, "A New Ethic of Technology . . . A Crisis!" mimeod. 1969.

31. Wilbert E. Moore, "The Utility of Utopias," *American Sociological Review* 32, no. 6 (December 1966): 771.

32. *Footnotes to the Future* 3, no. 2 (February 1973).

33. Herbert J. Gans, "The Effect of a Community on Its Residents: Some Considerations for Sociological Theory and Planning Practice," in Gans, *People and Plans,* pp. 12–24.

34. Karl Menninger, talk delivered at Delos Seven, Athens Center of Ekistics, Athens, 1967.

35. Charles A. Beard, Introduction, in J. B. Bury, *The Idea of Progress* (New York: Dover, 1955), p. xx.

Theory and Research:
The Case of Studies in Medical Education

PATRICIA KENDALL

W HEN I was invited to contribute a chapter on medical sociology to this volume, I felt it an unusual opportunity to examine the interplay between Merton's theoretical concerns and empirical research in which he and I were engaged for some years.

This topic seemed particularly appropriate in view of Merton's well-known and long-standing interest in the reciprocal relations between theory and research. "Sociological Theory" (when this article was reprinted it was given a new title: "The Bearing of Sociological Theory on Empirical Research") and the complementary article, "The Bearing of Empirical Research upon the Development of Sociological Theory," were first published in 1945 and 1948, respectively.[1] As the titles of these articles suggest, on the one hand theoretical statements can lead to empirical investigation, and, on the other hand, research can prove crucial in the development of theory.

It will turn out, as our analysis proceeds, that there is a third way in which theory can be related to research. This is when both develop simultaneously, when, in other words, it is impossible to determine whether the theory preceded the research, or the other way around.

Rather than discuss the topic in the abstract, I shall use, for reference points, parts of an unpublished paper that I wrote in 1960, as the studies on medical education carried out by the Bureau of Applied Social Research,

Patricia Kendall is Professor of Sociology at Queens College and the Graduate School of the City University of New York.

301

under Merton's direction, were drawing to a close.[2] The original aims of this summary paper were threefold: (1) to indicate briefly why and to what ends the studies were undertaken, (2) to spell out some of their underlying theoretical and methodological principles, and (3) to describe several findings which had been developed since the publication of *The Student Physician* in 1957.[3]

For our purposes here, using this paper as a frame of reference has additional merits. Since it was written in *1960,* it represents the thinking of those working on the so-called Medical Project at that time. In addition, since it was *written* in 1960, it minimizes the possibility that lapses in memory distort the history of our studies. I shall quote the parts of this paper that contribute to an understanding of the interplay between theory and research in Merton's work.

The paper opened with a description of how the Medical Project came into being:

The Bureau of Applied Social Research of Columbia University began its studies into the sociology of medical education approximately eight years ago. The impetus for this research came from two sources. On the one hand, a group at Columbia had for several years been interested in studies of the professions, and particularly in the processes by which the uninitiated novice is transformed into a fully qualified practitioner of his profession. Speculation about the nature of these processes resulted in many hypotheses, but throughout the need for concrete data was keenly felt.

The University Seminar on the Professions in American Society, of which Merton was a member, included representatives from medicine, law, architecture, engineering, social work, the ministry, nursing, and education. That the sociology of the professions was to be a primary focus of the Bureau's studies in medical education is evident in the prominence it was given in a discussion of the "intellectual origins" of the research, as these were spelled out in the original proposal to the Commonwealth Fund:

Our interest in this study is a direct outgrowth of the work of the University Seminar on the Professions in American Society. . . .

In its deliberations, the Seminar concluded that the professional school represents the single most critical phase in the making of the professional man, since it is there that the outlook and attitudes, and not only the skills and knowledge, of practitioners are first shaped by the profession. Nevertheless, it was noted, systematic knowledge of the social and psychological environment constituted by schools in the various professions is virtually at an irreducible minimum; that is to say, it is almost entirely absent.

With its interest in developing a long-range program of research in the sociology of the professions, the Bureau of Applied Social Research came to the conclusion that the medical school, above all other professional schools, would best justify sociological study at this time. . . . We have reached the conclusion, which grows the more often it is examined, that the sociological analysis of the medical school would contribute most, both to the profession and to sociology.[4]

Thus, sociological interests constituted the first and also the primary reason for wanting to undertake studies of medical education. A second set of concerns, these originating with medical educators, soon provided additional impetus for the examination of medical schools. These latter interests were spelled out in some detail in the 1960 paper:

> At the same time, medical educators were beginning to inquire into the effects of innovations which had been introduced into the curricula of many, if not most, medical schools in the last decade or two. Some of these innovations were quite radical . . . ; others were more limited. . . . But, however extensive they were, these innovations shared a common objective: through them medical educators hoped that their students would develop an interest in and ability to provide comprehensive medical care. In the words of a slogan often used by these medical educators, their students were to view patients as "persons rather than as disease entities."
>
> The background and history of these innovations can be briefly told. At the turn of the century there were many medical schools in the United States that were little better than diploma mills. Prominent educators in the more reputable medical schools wanted the [low-quality] schools abolished; they wanted to raise standards of medical education, and more specifically to make sure that medical students received a firm grounding in science. These aims were realized shortly after the publication of the celebrated Flexner Report in 1910. Soon after the appearance of that document there was a wave of reform in American medical education. The medical schools developed a standardized curriculum in which the first two years were devoted to thorough study of the basic medical sciences such as anatomy, physiology, biochemistry, pharmacology, and so on. Under this curriculum medical students have substantial contact with patients only after they have received training in these basic medical sciences.

As an aside, the Flexner Report merits one brief comment here. Flexner's assignment to assess existing medical schools focused on the parlous state of the scientific training which most provided. In the course of his evaluation, he made passing reference to the research capabilities of the schools, but none to the aspect of service to the community. Although it is beyond the scope of this paper to answer the question, it would be interesting to find out whether his failure to mention service was an oversight on Flexner's part or whether the obligations of medical schools were expanded after 1910. If the latter is the case, it then would be equally interesting to find out when this change occurred and under what conditions. In any case, today medical schools are held to be responsible for training, research, and service to the community.

Another aside—this one, however, directly linked to Merton's writings—is suggested in the following segment from my paper:

> It was gradually felt that the reforms, necessary as they were, brought with them certain undesirable consequences. Foremost among these was what some medical educators described as the "dehumanization" of their students. In their opinion, strong emphasis on the scientific aspects of medicine led their students to lose whatever personal interest in patients they may have brought with them to medical school. They regretted these tendencies, not only because of their belief that

physicians should have a humanitarian view of their patients, but, more importantly, because of their conviction that the effective practice of medicine requires the physician to explore the entire life situation of the patient, and not only the specific complaint which brings him to the doctor's office.

One of Merton's earliest and best-known articles, that on the "Unanticipated Consequences of Purposive Social Action,"[5] is clearly reflected here. As the title of the article implies, social acts sometimes have unforeseen outcomes, and Merton takes it as his task to spell out some of the reasons for this. Before taking up his main problem, he elaborates two distinctions which are relevant in the present connection. First, he says that "undesired effects are not always undesirable."[6] In other words, it is instructive to distinguish between unanticipated consequences that are desirable (these might be called "windfalls") and equally unforeseen outcomes that are undesirable. Second, Merton states that "... it is not assumed that in fact social action always involves clear-cut, explicit purposes," and then goes on to say that the aim of action may be "nebulous or hazy."[7] On both points, medical educators are easily classified. The curriculum reforms which grew out of the Flexner Report were explicit; but, in the long run, they turned out to have undesirable side effects.

My paper continues with further details of how the Bureau became involved in studies of medical education and medical students.

To counteract these undesirable tendencies, and to enable their students to develop appropriate attitudes toward patients and toward medical practice, medical educators began to design the innovations mentioned earlier.... As these innovations were made, the medical educators responsible for them began to wonder whether or not they were producing the desired effects. They therefore began to express interest in having their new educational programs evaluated. The Commonwealth Fund, which has supported many of the innovations since their inception, was also interested in sociological studies of medical education; consequently, they were receptive to a proposal from the Bureau in the spring of 1952. ... At the same time, Dr. George G. Reader, director of the Comprehensive Care and Teaching Program which was then about to get under way at Cornell University Medical College, invited the Bureau to participate in an evaluation of his program. Shortly after this, Dr. T. Hale, Ham and his colleagues at Western Reserve University asked whether we might be able to include their medical school in our research.

It is clear from the above that medical educators had a concrete goal in mind when they came to us—and to other sociologists—for assistance: they wanted help in assessing the effectiveness of the new educational programs they had introduced. Such evaluation is in vogue today, largely because various agencies of the federal government require it in the grants and contracts they underwrite. But such evaluation studies have not always been so general, not even at the time when medical educators were interested in them. For example, there is no mention of evaluation in some of the major textbooks on methods of social research that were published fifteen or twenty years ago.[8] Several books on evaluation have since appeared.[9]

Ideally, an evaluation study is based on a "before-and-after" design, with the stimulus introduced in the interval between the pre- and the post-tests. Ideally, also, there should be a control group to rule out the influence of such factors as the maturation of the subjects or their exposure to outside events.[10] The complexities of evaluation studies undoubtedly discouraged some medical educators from authorizing or supporting them in their departments or programs. For example, the Executive Faculty of Cornell University Medical College was reluctant to have the fourth-year class divided at random into an experimental group, which would be exposed to the novel experiences provided by the Comprehensive Care and Teaching Program (CC&TP), and an exactly equivalent control group from which these experiences would be withheld. Similarly, the educators at Western Reserve University were not prepared to have half of each class study under the old curriculum, while only half were exposed to the new. For these reasons, evaluation making use of experimental techniques could not be carried out.

As it turned out, the curriculum design worked out by the directors of the CC&TP was close to what is called for in a classic evaluation study. The fourth-year class was divided in half, not at random but according to the preferences expressed by the students. (Luckily, however, there were no discernible differences between the two halves.) During the first semester, one half of the class studied medicine, pediatrics, and psychiatry in the CC&TP, while the other half studied surgery, obstetrics-gynecology, and an elective; at mid-year, the two halves exchanged places. It was thus possible to evaluate the effects of the CC&TP both in the middle and at the end of the fourth year.[11]

Having described separately the sociological and the educational concerns underlying our studies, the 1960 text went on to indicate that, from the beginning, the two were combined in the research:

> The Bureau agreed to undertake these studies with the proviso that they not be defined only as evaluations of educational programs. It was our belief, justified by later developments, that if the investigation were given a sufficiently broad base, it could satisfy our sociological interests as well as the more strictly pedagogical interests of medical educators.

This passage suggests the relation between basic and applied research, a topic to which considerable attention has been given in recent years. While Merton's writings have generally been concerned with the advancement of basic research and theory, he has not neglected problems of application. Thus, he has authored or co-authored several articles on the topic. For example, in an early article he spelled out some of the dimensions that affect public images of social science and thus help determine the extent to which the assistance of social scientists will be sought and used.[12] The dimensions Merton singled out are as follows:

objectivity—ranging from the view that social science is merely private opinion masquerading as science to the faith in its rigorously objective quality

adequacy—ranging from a belief in its unmitigated futility to belief in social science as the means of social salvation

political relevance—ranging from belief in its inherently "subversive" nature to belief that democracy can function adequately only if social science data are at hand

"costs"—ranging from the naive view that scientific results can be obtained with little expense (of time and funds) to the view that usable results are so costly as to be "uneconomic"

As I indicated in my 1960 paper, the Columbia studies of medical students were undertaken with both basic and applied objectives in mind. This is an unusual situation; more commonly, a study is undertaken with the hope that it will contribute to basic knowledge (although implications for action may later be culled from the data) *or* a different sort of study is carried out in order to find solutions to practical problems (although contributions to theoretical knowledge may later be extracted). In our case, both objectives were simultaneously incorporated into the research. As a result, the evaluation study at Cornell, which could have been limited to fourth-year students, was enriched by data about changes in attitude that took place during the first three years of medical school. And our broader study, which need not have examined so closely the experiences of fourth-year students, was similarly enriched by these details.

As a final note of introduction, the text emphasized once more the special relevance of carrying out studies in medical schools:

In fact, we welcomed the opportunity to carry out research in medical schools because, for a variety of reasons . . . , it seemed particularly appropriate to investigate processes of professionalization in those institutions.

There are two points to be made here. The first concerns the "variety of reasons" why medical schools provide a particularly strategic location for study; the second concerns the concept of "professionalization."

Regarding the first point, in the original proposal to the Commonwealth Fund, five reasons were advanced for considering medical schools especially suitable institutions in which to carry out sociological studies of the professions. These are (1) the high prestige of medical schools as contrasted with other professional schools; (2) the fact that medical students, in comparison with most other professional students, "must relate themselves to many and diverse groups," such as patients, nurses, social workers, and so on; (3) that, increasingly, modern medicine is "exploring the actual and potential connections between the medical and social sciences"; (4) that, especially in medicine, "the professional school is the fulcrum on which the advancement of the professional practice turns"; and (5) study of medical schools may make it possible to learn how they foster or hinder the developing expectations that the physician will "enter into many relations with the community, and not merely with his patients."[13]

The second point—that concerning the concept of "professionalization"—takes us farther back in Merton's intellectual biography. So far as I know, Merton does not use this term. When I introduced it in my paper, I had in mind a somewhat restricted version of the concept of "socialization." The latter is a concept to which Merton gave some attention in his introduction to *The Student Physician,* where he listed it as one of five sociological concerns contributing to the sociology of medical education.[14]

But the notions of "socialization," and, more especially, of "anticipatory socialization," are found in some of Merton's earlier writings. So far as I can determine, it first appeared in 1950, in a section on "functions of positive orientation to non-membership reference groups" in his essay on reference group behavior.[15] (When this article was later reprinted, the section was titled "Functions of positive orientation to non-membership groups: *anticipatory socialization.*"[16]) For his collected papers, Merton wrote a new essay on "Continuities in the Theory of Reference Groups and Social Structure," and this, too, contained discussion of anticipatory socialization.

There is a difference, however, in how the concept is treated in the two chapters. The earlier one was based on findings from *The American Soldier,* and as a consequence dealt almost exclusively with survey data concerning individual soldiers. In the section in question, Merton focused largely on the behavior and attitudes of soldiers who hoped to achieve a higher rank than the one they held. For them, anticipatory socialization was functional, acquainting them with the habits and attitudes of the group into which they wanted to move. But for their membership group, the group to which they belonged, the potential defection of the ambitious individual was dysfunctional, implying as it did a rejection of group norms and values. Merton goes on to speculate about the group pressures brought to bear on such aspirants. The soldier undergoing or experiencing anticipatory socialization is considered a deviant, and efforts are made to bring him back into line.[17]

When Merton takes up anticipatory socialization in his later chapter, it has a different cast. Here he treats the process as normal and virtually universal; it is involved in the acquisition of successive roles in the course of an individual's development. (He refers to "status-sequences" and "role-gradations.") About this second form of anticipatory socialization, Merton says:

> An explicit, deliberate, and often formal part of this process is of course what is meant by education and training. But much of this preparation is *implicit, unwitting,* and *informal,* and it is particularly to this that the notion of anticipatory socialization directs our attention.[18]

Clearly, this was the kind of "professionalization" with which our research was concerned. From didactic lectures and the behavior of more advanced students and faculty members, the student physicians who were the subjects of our investigation learned about the status toward which they were moving and the roles they would eventually assume. Later on in this chapter, we shall consider several findings, hitherto unpublished, which provide documentation for these processes.[19]

In my text, I then described the timing and locus of the studies:

Our studies began then in the spring of 1952, first at Cornell and somewhat later at Western Reserve. At the same time, we included the medical students at the University of Pennsylvania in our investigation because, while the faculty of that school was sympathetic to the principles of comprehensive medicine and had made some innovations to foster appropriate attitudes toward medical care, these had not been radical enough to modify the basic curriculum of the medical school. Collection of data from students at these three schools continued through the end of the 1957–1958 academic year. . . .

This brings to a close the introductory materials in my text. They were extensive because the theoretical and practical concerns underlying our studies were complex. Before moving on to selected findings, the paper took up some methodological questions:

The heavy emphasis of our studies on the notions of process and change has led us to rely mainly on the panel method. With the aid of a fairly standardized questionnaire, students have been followed through successive phases of their medical training. Because of the timing of our study, some classes filled out our questionnaire only during the later parts of their training; other classes provided data only during the early stages of their medical education; still other classes were followed for all four years. Chart 1, which is a somewhat stylized description of what was actually done, provides an overview of our procedures.

Chart 1. SCHEDULE OF ADMINISTRATION OF PANEL QUESTIONNAIRES

	Class of					
Stage of training	1954	1955	1956	1957	1958	1959
Beginning of first year				A	C	E
End of first year				B	D	F
End of second year			B	D	F	G
End of third year		B	D	F	G	
End of fourth year	B	D	F	G	H	

A: data collected in fall of 1953
B: data collected in spring of 1954
C: data collected in fall of 1954
D: data collected in spring of 1955
E: data collected in fall of 1955
F: data collected in spring of 1956
G: data collected in spring of 1957
H: data collected in spring of 1958

It is interesting that, in 1960, when some parts of the analysis had been completed and others were in process, I talked of the study as involving the panel method. In fact, it did not, for the most part. While repeated observations are necessary for a panel study, they do not automatically mean that panel analysis has been carried out. For this kind of analysis requires that the interaction of variables over time be examined.[20] It is not enough to study trends from one month to the next or from one class of students to the next. Instead, the internal changes, or turnover, must be analyzed. As our studies proceeded, we decided not to be so ambitious, except in a few cases. By and large, our analyses focused on the study of trends.

Another point of interest is that, although the medical school project is the only panel-type study that has been carried out under Merton's direction, many of the concepts central in his writings—anticipatory socialization, for example—presuppose panel data. (In pages to follow, we shall deal with other Mertonian concepts which have this character.)

Responses to the questionnaire were not the only data collected in our studies. My text goes on to describe other types of information that were obtained.

Responses to these panel questionnaires formed the core of the data for our studies. They were supplemented however by qualitative information systematically collected at Cornell and the University of Pennsylvania. At both of these medical schools, participant observers attended lectures, laboratory meetings and clinical sessions with the students, and took part in some of their informal activities. In addition, they trained a small number of students in each class to keep diaries of their experiences and of their reactions to these experiences and, as each week's journals were submitted, they interviewed the diarists intensively on what had been reported....

As a commentary on the importance of research traditions, it is interesting to contrast the methodological emphasis of our studies and that of *Boys in White*.[21] During the 1940s and 1950s especially, the tradition of the Bureau of Applied Social Research at Columbia was a quantitative one, and most empirical studies relied on survey techniques, the panel method, and the like. The tradition at the University of Chicago was quite different: it relied heavily on observation, the analysis of documentary materials, and other qualitative techniques. This dissimilarity in tradition is reflected in a corresponding dissimilarity in the methodological emphasis of the two studies. Ours, as has been noted, depended most heavily on panel-type techniques and only secondarily on qualitative methods. Just the reverse was true of *Boys in White*. Almost all of the findings reported in that volume were derived from observation or informal interviews; only as a sort of afterthought did the authors construct what might be called "quasi-tables."

Since I intended my paper to serve as an overview of our studies in medical education from their beginnings in 1952 up to the time of writing in 1960, I decided to devote more space to their theoretical and methodological background than might have been the case under other circumstances. At the same time, however, I wanted to present sample findings. Those that were chosen had several features in common: (1) they had not previously been published; (2) for the most part, they came from sections of the data that were still in the process of being analyzed; and, perhaps most importantly, (3) while each topic was independent of the others, there was an underlying theme that bound them together. It is to these findings that we now turn.

The role-set of the medical student*

The subject of our investigation, most broadly defined, was the professionalization of medical students, and the processes through which this is accomplished. First of all, then, we had to specify what is meant by professionalization.... Obviously, the most salient kind of professionalization which medical students undergo is their acquisition of the technical knowledge and skills of the physician.... However, we did not feel that we, as sociologists, were competent to study or evaluate the technical performance of medical students. This is not to say, of course, that we did not make use of whatever measures of performance—such as grades and ratings—were available to us. But for the purposes of our research, this technical professionalization was considered secondary to the complementary development of appropriate attitudes and orientations....

But it will be recalled that the specification of the dependent variables was only half of our task. Equally important, in terms of the assignment we set ourselves, was the identification of the processes *by which this professionalization comes about. Had we intended to be exhaustive in the specification of these processes, we would undoubtedly have dealt with many which were intentionally neglected. For example, we have given little attention to the kind of questions which would be of interest to an educational psychologist—whether one kind of teaching method is superior to another in creating a particular attitude. Instead, our orientation as sociologists led us to look for the interpersonal interactions in medical school which might be instrumental in bringing about attitude change. Medical students have been viewed as involved in a network of interpersonal relations with four significant groups in their environment: their parental families, their peers, the medical school faculty, and patients....*

* At several points in the 1960 paper, major themes were introduced by subtitles. This is one such instance.

Many items in our questionnaire dealt with different aspects of this network of relationships. Limitations of space prevent us from spelling out all that are relevant. We can, however, briefly summarize a few of them. (Others will be clarified in the substantive sections which follow.) Regarding their relations with their parents, we asked, for example, how important their mothers and fathers had been in their decision to study medicine. Among numerous questions we asked about the relationship of students with each other, there was a so-called sociometric item, which requested each student to name his three best friends and then to indicate where he had met them and how much time he spent with them. Regarding their relations with members of the medical school faculty, students were asked to indicate how much interest the faculty took in them and how many faculty members knew them by name. Finally, we asked many questions about students' relations with patients.

Among these was a query about how confident each student would feel in the face of a number of threatening situations.

The text then continued to set the stage for the substantive findings:

> *This conception of the role-set of a medical student has provided the organizing principle for much of our research. Each type of interaction has been made the object of special study, with two goals in mind. First of all, there has been an effort to characterize each kind of interaction. . . .*
>
> *Once the nature of these different kinds of interactions is clarified, then there is an effort to relate each to the development of attitudes toward medical practice and standards of medical care. That is, we have explored the extent to which each set of interactions is an agent in the professionalization of medical students. . . .*

There are several things to be said at this point. First, it is interesting that in 1960 I used the term "role-set," even though it had not existed when the studies I was summarizing were being carried out.[22] Not only was the phrase newsworthy, it also was evocative of the problems with which we had been dealing.

Although the term "role-set" was not a part of the sociological vocabulary at the time our studies were being planned, a precursor was. In the original proposal to the Commonwealth Fund, written in 1952, the term "matrix of social relations" was introduced as a basic concept. Again, it is interesting that, with one exception, the full implications of this earlier notion were not fully exploited in our research. To explore a matrix of relations means studying the interconnections between all elements. This was not done, and, given the fact that our investigation was exploratory and without precedent, perhaps it could not have been done.

It may be worthwhile, however, to consider other kinds of extensions that might have been made in our research. Our research plan called for examination of the way in which the student was separately related to each of the role partners that we had singled out for study. Almost without exception, what we did was examine the students' attitudes and evaluations of their partners, with special attention to how these varied over time. This analysis could have been expanded in at least two ways. In the first place, instead of only ascertaining students' attitudes toward patients, for example, we might also have interviewed patients regarding their assessments of the students' competency, considerateness, and so on.[23] This would have permitted us to see whether mutual perceptions and judgments were in close agreement. A second enlargement of what was actually done in our study—one that probably corresponds most closely to what Merton had in mind in his article—would examine how an individual responds to conflicting demands from two or more members of his role-set. Again, new kinds of data would be needed for this line of analysis. First of all, it would be necessary to find out if the individual were aware that conflicting demands were being made on him. If he were, one would then want to find out whether he felt that both sets of demands were equally legitimate, whether he was more inclined to meet the demands of one of the partners rather than the other, what consequences he thought might result from his failure to meet the two sets of demands, and so on. This, clearly, is a considerably more complex set of questions than we asked in our study. But they are the kinds of questions to which future studies of the role-set might be directed.

As we indicated before, we were concerned with students' relations to their parental families, to each other, to faculty members, and to patients. We now turn to selected findings in each of these areas. (It should be emphasized once more that none of these findings was reported in *The Student Physician* and that they were in process of being developed at the time I wrote the 1960 paper.) Each of the sections is introduced by an appropriate subtitle:

(1) The medical student and his family[24]

In any processual scheme, the student's relationships with his parental family precede the interactions which develop in medical school.

One way to learn about the influence of family background upon the attitudes, performance and career orientations of medical students is to focus on comparisons between students who are children of physicians and those coming from other types of occupational background. Do the sons of physicians start their medical training with a better picture of what this will involve, or do they bring with them an outmoded conception based on the experiences their fathers had a quarter of a century earlier? How do these anticipations affect their adaptation to the requirements of medical school?

Other characteristics of the family, and not only the fact that the father (or mother) is a physician, can have profound effects on the medical student. For example, the socioeconomic status of the family can influence the amount of financial support the student can expect during the course of his training. Thus, a student from a wealthy family can perhaps look forward to a long period of training without having to go into debt. And other characteristics, such as ethnic status, for example, can also be important. Nonetheless, in the preliminary analysis reported here, it seemed strategic to consider whether the student's father was a physician.

Not surprisingly, the sons of physicians are more likely than sons from other occupational backgrounds to value the professional advice of their parents. When they were already in medical school, all students were asked, "When it comes to making decisions regarding your future career in medicine, how much value do you attach to the advice and opinions of the following people?" On the average, nearly twice as many sons of physicians as sons from other social backgrounds reported that they valued the advice of their parents "a great deal" or "a fair amount"—78 percent as contrasted with 42 percent.

But even such apparently antecedent relations as those with one's parental family are not static. They too change during the course of medical school. And the pattern of their development is approximately the same for both the sons of physicians and those coming from other backgrounds.

Table 1. EXTENT TO WHICH SONS OF PHYSICIANS AND SONS FROM OTHER
OCCUPATIONAL BACKGROUNDS VALUE ADVICE OF PARENTS

| | *Percent valuing advice of parents* *"a great deal" or "a fair amount"* | |
Stage of training	Sons of physicians	Sons from other occupational backgrounds
End of first year	85	48
End of second year	81	44
End of third year	74	38
End of fourth year	73	35

*Table 1 indicates that, as students advance through medical school, the influence
of their parents steadily declines and is replaced with the influence of faculty
members, fellow students, and others met in the medical school environment.*[25]

(2) The medical student and his peers[26]

*As soon as they enter medical school, students begin to interact with each
other, and some of their contacts develop into friendships.*
*The role of student friendships can be evaluated by noting the extent to
which friends come to have similar professional values. But, since not all friendships are uniformly important, it becomes necessary to study types of friendships
in their bearing upon attitudes and values. For example, do students with friends
farther along in medical school acquire new attitudes earlier? Are friendships carried over from pre-medical school days a hindrance to attitudinal learning? The
symmetrical relation between friends at the same stage of training affords no a
priori grounds for assuming the direction which influence will take. Does the
academic standing or the relative popularity of the students determine which
member of the pair will be more likely to take over the attitudes and values of the
other?*

These are true processual questions of the kind discussed earlier. They
are the kind of queries for which the panel method is ideally suited. More
generally, these were the kinds of questions suggested by Merton in the article
he co-authored with Paul Lazarsfeld on "friendship as social process."[27] There
he introduced the terms "homophily," to stand for the phrase "a tendency for
friendships to form between those who are alike in some designated respect,"
and "heterophily," to encompass the phrase "a tendency for friendships to form
between those who differ in some designated respect." According to his analysis,
a number of processes are possible. For example, if two individuals hold
similar attitudes and express them, chance contacts may, in Merton's words,
be "mutually gratifying" and consequently may lead to further contacts; the
end result may therefore be close friendship. Or, to take a different case, close
bonds may have developed between two individuals long before either realizes
that they have divergent attitudes on some issue; the friendship may be main-

313

tained if one of the individuals accommodates his views to those of the other or if both refrain from discussing the topic on which they disagree.

Originally, Merton could only speculate about these processes because the data he used—those from his study of housing projects—were collected at one point in time and therefore did not lend themselves to true processual analysis. In the second part of their joint paper, however, Lazarsfeld recast Merton's propositions in formal terms and indicated the research methods and findings presupposed by each. Because this article was published in 1954 at a time when our field work was in full swing, we were able to incorporate relevant questions, such as the sociometric item alluded to earlier, and having this question were able to examine the formation and maintenance of friendships among medical students.[28]

Unexpectedly, however, the findings were negative.

> However intriguing these speculations, they can have only limited importance [in this instance]. For there is evidence in data collected at the University of Pennsylvania that, to a considerable extent, friendships are molded by external circumstances and change as these circumstances are altered. Thus, in the first and second years, student assignments in some, but not all, courses at the University of Pennsylvania are determined by position in the alphabetical listing of the class. In the third year, alphabetical listing is the sole determinant of divisions of the class into different student groups. But in the fourth year, alphabetical position is not used at all. As Table 2 indicates, friendship patterns follow these customary practices. In the first and second years, about a fifth of the friendship-pairs are separated by only one or two other students in the alphabetical listings of these classes; this percentage increases markedly during the third year, when alphabetical position assumes a more important role in class assignments; it declines again in the fourth year when alphabetical position is no longer a basis for the grouping of the students. . . .

Table 2. FRIENDSHIP CHOICES BETWEEN STUDENTS SEPARATED BY TWO OR LESS NAMES IN ALPHABETICAL LIST

Stage of training	Percent separated by two or less others in alphabetical list
End of first year	16
End of second year	20
End of third year	35
End of fourth year	20

Up to this point, we have been able to analyze with a fair degree of clarity how Merton's ideas were related, in time, to our studies of medical students. For example, we have no trouble in saying that the notion of anticipatory socialization antedated our research and helped determine its character.

The Lazarsfeld-Merton analysis of friendship is more problematic, however. A brief discussion of student-student relations was included in the original proposal for our study. It made no mention of the various processes discussed by Merton in the 1954 article on friendship. (It did, however, raise the possibility that friendships might be determined by "accidental" factors such as alphabetical position.) And yet almost the first efforts in studying student relationships were aimed at discovering whether or not homophily was present. In other words, questions necessary to study this phenomenon were not introduced until after the research was under way but, fortunately, not too late to yield relevant data.

As we indicated earlier, one section of the study, unlike the others, included reciprocal data on both the students' selections of esteemed faculty members and the faculty's designation of outstanding students. For the sake of brevity, only the students' choices of faculty members will be considered here.

(3) The medical student and faculty members[29]

Interactions with the faculty also begin as soon as the students enter medical school. Unlike relations with their peers, however, these interactions with instructors in the medical school are usually asymmetrical. That is, the teacher is more likely to influence his students than to be influenced by them.

Nonetheless, medical students have some control over the influence of the faculty if only in the sense that they select their role models. That is, they are not usually equally receptive to the influence of all instructors, but instead choose a few whom they try to emulate and after whom they pattern themselves. Because of this fact, the ways in which these selections are made and the changes in the selection process over time become interesting topics of inquiry.

The concept of role models did not originate with Merton, nor apparently does he find it particularly useful, as it is mentioned in only one brief section of *Social Theory and Social Structure*.[30] In that section, however, he introduces a useful distinction—that between reference individuals and role models. The former are individuals who are emulated in the totality of their multiple roles; the latter are models in a more restricted sense, with their behavior in only one or two roles serving as the ideal to be approximated. In his elaboration of this distinction, Merton makes a point which is of special relevance to the data we are considering here: he suggests that as individuals advance through different phases of their life cycles they may select different kinds of role models. The data of our study support this expectation:

There is evidence from Cornell Medical College that, in the early stages of medical school, students base their selections on relatively visible and stereotyped criteria. Thus, the less advanced the students, the more likely they are to choose as role models men who have achieved high rank on the faculty. Even more interesting, Table 3 shows that the less advanced the students, the more probable it is that they will select their role models from among the men who are older than average for their rank. In other words, the younger students tend to select the prominent "stars" on the faculty.

315

*Table 3.** THE RANK-SPECIFIC AGE OF ESTEEMED FACULTY MEMBERS
CHOSEN BY SOPHOMORES, JUNIORS, AND SENIORS

Rank-specific age	Sophomores	Juniors	Seniors
Younger than average	39%	46%	55%
Average	27	31	33
Older than average	34	23	12
Total cases	(86)	(123)	(216)

* Table 6.6 in David Caplovitz, "Student-Faculty Relations in Medical School: A
Study of Professional Socialization," unpublished Ph.D. dissertation, Columbia
University, 1960.

*As they progress through medical school, students seem to develop sensitivity
to professional merits of the faculty which are less easily visible. In order to measure this directly, of course, it would be necessary to have a test of professional
competence which could be administered to all faculty members; if the conclusion
were correct, we would expect that the more advanced students would more frequently single out as role models men who had achieved a high level of competence, regardless of rank. Lacking such direct indices of the faculty's merits, it is
necessary to rely on indirect measures. Table 4 reports a result in which promotion is taken as the index of merit. It shows that seniors were more likely than
juniors, and juniors more likely than sophomores, to choose as role models men
who subsequently received promotions to higher ranking positions on the faculty.*

*Although it cannot be established with any finality, this result suggests not
only that the more advanced students develop greater sensitivity to the professional merits of their instructors, but also that, as they move from one stage of
training to another, they become more fully indoctrinated into the value system
of the medical school. Thus, when asked which faculty members they especially
admire, the more advanced they are the more likely it is that students will indicate an instructor who has not yet, but who soon will receive public recognition
of the esteem in which he is held by his colleagues on the faculty. . . .*

*Table 4.** SUBSEQUENT PROMOTION OF FACULTY MEMBERS ESTEEMED
BY SOPHOMORES, JUNIORS, AND SENIORS

Stage of training	Percent of clinical choices subsequently promoted	Cases
Sophomores	31	(83)
Juniors	39	(119)
Seniors	44	(200)

* Table 6.7 in Caplovitz, "Student-Faculty Relations in Medical School."

Offhand, it is a simple enough matter to talk of role models; we therefore
would expect no difficulty in devising questions to single them out. But this

was not true in the present instance. A faculty member can be highly esteemed for any of a number of reasons; to ask a question about only one dimension would diminish his chances of being identified in our study as a student's role model. To avoid this undesirable possibility, a broad net was cast. Concretely, six separate questions were asked: (1) "Which faculty member do you admire for his ability as a physician?" (2) "Which faculty member, in your opinion, has made the greatest contribution to medical knowledge in his field?" (3) "Which faculty member do you most admire for his ability as a researcher?" (4) "Which faculty member, in your opinion, goes out of his way most often to help students?" (5) "Which faculty member do you admire most for his ability as a teacher?" (6) "Everything considered, which faculty member has had the greatest influence on your views regarding medicine?" If a student mentioned a particular faculty member in connection with any of these questions, he was classified as having selected that faculty member as a role model.

There is one other point worth noting. This section of the study dealt with role models, but more especially it dealt with socialization regarding the "proper" role models to be selected. For, as we have seen, the selection of role models was by no means fortuitous. Instead, as students progressed through medical school, they increasingly chose as role models the men who embodied the skills and values of the positions toward which they, the students, were advancing.

(4) Medical students and their patients[31]

One of the ultimate objectives of medical school is to teach students how to get along with their patients once they are in practice. But, of course, they have contacts with patients throughout the course of medical school, and these undoubtedly affect the patterns of attitudes and behavior which they finally develop.

To start with, the function of patient contacts seems to vary according to the stage of training at which the student finds himself. Our panel questionnaire included an item asking students what they derived from work with patients. Typically, second-year students reported that they viewed such contacts as an opportunity to acquire new medical knowledge. Fourth-year students, on the other hand, told us that they usually looked upon their contacts with patients as occasions to test their professional competence in making diagnoses, in performing technical procedures, and so on.

Then, too, attitudes toward patients can be importantly affected by almost accidental situations in which the student is placed. For example, the fact that a student-physician is assigned an uncooperative clinic patient can prevent or delay him from developing the types of attitudes and behavior in relation to patients which are judged normatively correct. Faced with the necessity of treating such a patient over a period of time, he may be tempted to give her orders, or to frighten her, rather than to help her understand the nature of her illness and the reasons for the regimen he has prescribed.

The uncooperative patient is not the only one who poses problems for the student-physician. There is also the patient known as a "crock," who presents a variety of complaints for which no medical explanation can be found. We did not deal with crocks in the paper because they are such a ubiquitous problem that processes of learning how to deal with them are not easily detected.

The preceding section of my paper also gives amusing evidence of the extent to which I, in 1960, had been socialized into the use of medical jargon. Because women, more than men, can "afford" to be ill, and because most hospital clinics are only open during the day time, the population of clinic patients is heavily female. Thus, when talking about clinic patients in the abstract, most hospital personnel—physicians, students, nurses, and so on—use the feminine gender.[32]

> But in spite of these variations which are due to stage of training or to accidental circumstance, in the end most students acquire the attitudes toward patients which are considered appropriate by medical educators. One of these is the ability to remain somewhat detached from one's patients.... That they do learn is attested by their answers to a wide variety of questions, of which we shall present one example here. Students were presented with a number of statements about their relationships with patients and were asked to indicate whether, in their actual or anticipated experience, these statements were true or false. One of them reads "There were times when I wanted to help my patients by buying things they needed." Table 5 shows a very pronounced decline in endorsements of this statement. At the end of their first year, two-thirds of the freshmen reported that they thought they would want to buy things for the patients they saw during their clinical years of training. This percentage declined to slightly more than half of the second-year students. By the end of the third year, less than a quarter of the students reported that this had been their experience. And among those approaching graduation from medical school, less than a fifth gave an affirmative answer.

Table 5. WANTING TO BUY THINGS FOR PATIENTS
ACCORDING TO STAGE OF TRAINING

Stage of training	Percent wanting to buy things
End of first year	67
End of second year	52
End of third year	23
End of fourth year	17

Here, in this final section, there is once more an interplay between Merton's theoretical writings and the Columbia research on medical education. In an article he wrote (with Elinor Barber) on sociological ambivalence,[33] there is a lengthy discussion of the structural factors that create ambivalence in the relationships between professionals and their clients. As part of this analysis, several references are made to the dilemma of the physician who must be compassionate toward his patient and yet sufficiently detached so that he can perform to the best of his capabilities.

In this instance, the research bears a different relation to the theory. Up to this point, we have seen that Merton's theories or concepts either antedated our studies and therefore helped to mold the form they took or were in the process of development as the research was being carried out. It would probably be too much to say that the analysis of sociological ambivalence derived exclusively, or even primarily, from our studies in medical education. But it is true that this research was part of the base from which Merton and Barber derived their important generalizations. For, not only are explicit references made to the Columbia investigation; in addition, the article makes use of concepts—notably, "detached concern"—that grew out of the research.[34]

In some important ways, this chapter can have no summary. That would imply an end to the weaving back and forth between Merton's theories and the research enterprise we worked on jointly. Hopefully, there will be no such end. It may very well be that, at some future time, Merton will return to the studies of medical education for data to confirm or enrich a theoretical problem he is developing. Conversely, it may happen that those of us interested in medical sociology will undertake research that once more will have the benefit of his systematic thinking. In either case, there will be a new sort of continuity.

NOTES

1. Robert K. Merton, "Sociological Theory," *American Journal of Sociology* 50 (1945): 462–73, and "The Bearing of Empirical Research upon the Development of Sociological Theory," *American Sociological Review* 13 (1948): 505–15. That Merton considers these two articles an important part of his work is indicated by his decision to include them in both the first and second editions of *Social Theory and Social Structure* (Glencoe, Ill.: Free Press, 1949, 1957) and in his more recent—and more selective—collection, *On Theoretical Sociology: Five Essays, Old and New* (New York: Free Press, 1967).

2. The paper was read at the 1960 annual meeting of the American Sociological Association.

3. Robert K. Merton, George G. Reader, and Patricia Kendall, eds., *The Student Physician* (Cambridge, Mass.: Harvard University Press, 1957).

4. Robert K. Merton, Patricia Kendall, and Mary Jean Huntington, "A Proposal for the Sociological Study of Medical Schools," Bureau of Applied Social Research, Columbia University, New York, 1952.

5. Robert K. Merton, "Unanticipated Consequences of Purposive Social Action," *American Sociological Review* 1 (1936): 894–904.

6. *Ibid.*, p. 895.

7. *Ibid.*, p. 896.

8. See, for example, William J. Goode and Paul K. Hatt, *Methods in Social Research* (New York: McGraw-Hill, 1952), or Claire Selltiz, Marie Jahoda, Morton Deutsch, and Stuart W. Cook, *Research Methods in Social Relations* (New York: Holt, 1959).

9. See, for example, Herbert H. Hyman, Charles R. Wright, and Terence K. Hopkins, *Applications of Methods of Evaluation* (Berkeley: University of California Press, 1962); Edward A. Suchman, *Evaluative Research* (New York: Russell Sage, 1967); and Francis G. Caro, ed., *Readings in Evaluation Research* (New York: Russell Sage, 1971).

10. For perhaps the most detailed analysis of the factors that can interfere with the proper interpretation of experimental results, see Donald T. Campbell and Julian C. Stanley, "Experimental and Quasi-Experimental Designs for Research on Teaching," in N. L. Gage, ed., *Handbook of Research on Teaching* (Chicago: Rand McNally, 1963). It should be noted that, while evaluation studies in the social sciences have been fairly infrequent, many have been carried out in connection with assessments of the relative effectiveness of different teaching techniques.

11. This is a somewhat oversimplified statement. For further details, see Patricia Kendall, "Evaluating an Experimental Program in Medical Education," in Matthew B. Miles, ed., *Innovation in Education* (New York: Teachers College Press, 1964), and Patricia Kendall and James Jones, "General Patient Care: Learning Aspects," in George G. Reader and Mary E. W. Goss, eds., *Comprehensive Medical Care and Teaching* (Ithaca, N.Y.: Cornell University Press, 1967).

12. Robert K. Merton, "The Application of Applied Social Science in the Formation of Policy: A Research Memorandum," *Philosophy of Science* 16 (1949): 161–81.

13. Merton, Kendall, and Huntington, "A Proposal for the Sociological Study of Medical Schools."

14. As a matter of fact, Merton, anticipating that some readers of the volume might be physicians, wanted to make certain that they did not equate the sociological concept with the similar sounding notion of "socialized medicine." To make sure of the distinction, he wrote an appendix to *The Student Physician* in which he spelled out exactly how "socialization" is used in sociology and psychology.

15. Robert K. Merton and Alice S. Kitt, "Contributions to the Theory of Reference Group Behavior," in Robert K. Merton and Paul F. Lazarsfeld, eds., *Continuities in Social Research* (Glencoe, Ill.: Free Press, 1950).

16. In Merton, *Social Theory and Social Structure,* rev. ed. (1957). (Italics added.)

17. *Ibid.,* pp. 265–71.

18. *Ibid.,* p. 385. See also pp. 384 and 386.

19. See especially the later section dealing with the relations between students and faculty members. See also, in Merton, Reader, and Kendall, eds., *The Student Physician,* the chapter by Renée Fox on "Training for Uncertainty" and that by Patricia Kendall and Hanan Selvin on "Tendencies Toward Specialization." It should be noted that a second major study of medical education was carried out pretty much simultaneously with ours and that it found little utility in the concept of socialization. See Howard S. Becker, Blanche Geer, Everett Hughes, and Anselm Strauss, *Boys in White* (Chicago: University of Chicago Press, 1961). It is not within the scope of this chapter to contrast the two investigations in any detail. Some useful comparisons are found in Samuel W. Bloom, "The Sociology of Medical Education," *The Milbank Memorial Fund Quarterly* 43 (1965): 143–84, and Daniel J. Levinson, "Medical Education and the Theory of Adult Socialization," *Journal of Health and Social Behavior* 8 (1967): 253–65.

20. Paul F. Lazarsfeld, "The Uses of Panels in Social Research," *Proceedings of the American Philosophical Society* 92 (1948): 405–10.

21. Becker *et al., Boys in White.*

22. Robert K. Merton, "The role-set: problems in sociological theory," *British Journal of Sociology* 8 (1957): 106–20; see also Merton, *Social Theory and Social Structure,* pp. 368–80.

23. One of the studies to be discussed below, that by David Caplovitz, did obtain complementary data from students and faculty members.

24. E. David Nasatir worked on this section of the study.

25. The data supporting the second part of this statement were not shown in my 1960 paper.

26. William Nicholls II worked on this section of the study.

27. Paul F. Lazarsfeld and Robert K. Merton, "Friendship as Social Process," in Monroe Berger, Theodore Abel, and Charles Page, eds., *Freedom and Control in Modern Society* (New York: Van Nostrand, 1954).

28. The simple analysis of sociometric choices is always complex; the analysis of sociometric choices over time—as is implied in such notions as the formation or maintenance of friendships—is even more complex. In simplest terms, what was done was as follows: (1) a friendship pair, as indicated by mutual selection in the sociometric question, was identified; (2) their agreement or disagreement on selected attitudes was ascertained; (3) after a period of time, it was determined whether those who initially were in agreement were more likely to maintain their friendship than were those who originally disagreed.

29. The following section is adapted from David Caplovitz, "Student-Faculty Relations in Medical School," unpublished Ph.D. dissertation, Columbia University, 1960.

30. Merton, *Social Theory and Social Structure,* pp. 302–03.

31. William Martin worked on this part of the study.

32. Correlatively, physicians are always referred to as "he."

33. Robert K. Merton and Elinor Barber, "Sociological Ambivalence," in Edward A. Tiryakian, ed., *Sociological Theory, Values and Sociocultural Change* (New York: Free Press, 1963).

34. See Renée C. Fox, "Training for Detached Concern in the Anatomy Laboratory," Bureau of Applied Social Research, publication A-253, 1957; Gene N. Levine, "The Good Physician: Some Observations on Physician-Patient Interaction," Bureau of Applied Social Research, working paper no. 3, Evaluation Studies of the Cornell Comprehensive Care and Teaching Program ,1957; and Harold I. Lief and Renée C. Fox, "Training for 'Detached Concern' in Medical Students," in Harold Lief, Victor Lief, and Nina Lief, eds., *The Psychological Basis of Medical Practice* (New York: Harper & Row, 1963).

Ironic Perspective and Sociological Thought

LOUIS SCHNEIDER

I T is the aim of this paper to support the view that irony is intimately bound up with a great deal of sociological thought and that ironic perspectives stimulate such thought profoundly. It would be quite absurd to go so far as to claim that thinking in ironic terms is the alpha and omega of the whole sociological enterprise. Thus, the most penetrating ironies, by themselves, could hardly yield a theory of social structure. But the sociological significance of ironic perspectives or terms is easily suggested, as we shall see, by efforts to specify the meaning of irony as soon as one gets away from a very limited conception of it as a figure of speech.

In a broad, general sense social life is rife with ironies. One might make considerable ironic play with what Sutherland called "'white-collar crime." The area of "race relations" is a most inviting one for the ironist. Modern technology in its social and cultural bearings is equally inviting and equally important. Bureaucracy is tried and true subject matter for irony.

Our reach, here at least, must be restricted. We shall be particularly concerned with irony as bearing first on structural-functional analysis (under the rubric, "Ironic Perspectives") and second on labeling theory. Consideration will then be given to the idea of iatrogenesis or medically generated disease, for its suggestiveness in relation to labeling theory and to some broader matters.

Louis Schneider is Professor of Sociology at the University of Texas at Austin.

There will follow comment on the ironic vulnerability of experts in general and on the limitations of the ironic perspective and a concluding word on irony and humanistic and scientific values.

Where there is irony,[1] there is a sense that things are not the way they are "supposed to be." Ironic outcomes of action involve an element of the unintended or unexpected. (Thus, "Irony is seen in a depiction of human action the consequences of which are opposite to what is intended by the participants." [2]) But irony also suggests a "knowing" or wry smile just because one witnesses the bafflement or mockery of the fitness of things, of their supposed-to-be character. This does not, however, preclude a certain affinity of the ironic with the tragic, coexistent with its affinity with the comic. There is certainly such a thing as tragic irony. Indeed, irony would appear to lend support to the contention of those students of laughter who claim that we laugh because if we didn't we would cry.

If irony suggests the existence of some persons who are capable of the "knowing" or wry smile because they were at least not taken completely by surprise by something that in fact was quite unintended and unexpected by others, and the former persons are "in the know," "wise," in on the secret, the latter, of course, are more innocent. Irony strongly hints also at a sense of incongruity going beyond nonexpectation or nonintention alone. The smile is "knowing" because one is, to be sure, "in" on things. It is, on the other hand, wry because one appreciates a special (incongruous) twist in the way things turn out. For instance, ostensibly powerful persons actually turn out to be weak; supposedly strengthless persons, strong. The effect of irony is in such cases enhanced when, say, the weakness of the powerful is traceable to some pretension of strength on their part or when the strength of the supposedly weak is achieved through the same qualities that were despised by others as the mark and confirmation of their weakness.[3]

For working out a minimum definition of irony as here conceived, one may propose the element of the unexpected or unintended in combination with the element of incongruity. Where an ironic sense prevails, let us say, one perceives in things the combination indicated. But the other elements indicated are also significant. Irony is emphatically not the same as cynicism or sarcasm or satire or a jaundiced view of the world. To allow a careless identification or coalescence of it with these things is to render it—and properly so—suspect for purposes of sociological analysis; and the present object is precisely to help rescue it for its uses for such analysis.

The element of the unintended or unexpected that irony happens to feature has caught the attention and challenged the reflection of numerous sociologists, including Robert K. Merton. The matter of different audiences or diversely socially located observers is bound to interest the sociologist. As well as incongruity, irony suggests ambiguity and paradox, which are indeed very close to it, and none but a simplistic sociology could fail to be alert to these things.[4] There is certainly enough here to intimate the sociological significance of irony. The effort will now be made to sustain in some detail the view stated in our opening sentence. The strategy we adopt is to build

324

the case for the view cumulatively and somewhat discursively as we inquire into the several matters that have already been designated as concerning us.

IRONIC PERSPECTIVES

"One of the basic results of [my] study," writes Merton in his main early work on science, "is the fact that the most significant influence of Puritanism upon science was largely *unintended* by the Puritan leaders. That Calvin himself deprecated science only enhances the paradox that from him stemmed a vigorous movement which furthered interest in this field." [5] There is a hint here that irony has played some role in Merton's sociological outlook. Despite our lack of concern with the detail of the relations of irony and paradox, since Merton does write "paradox" in the lines just quoted, it is worth noting an appropriate comment by another sociologist: "In the general meaning of paradox, something can be both paradox—a tenet contrary to received opinion —and irony—an outcome of events that mocks the fitness of things." [6]

This hint of irony in Merton's outlook is supported elsewhere in his work. In his paper on social structure and anomie, it would appear that a prime American virtue—ambition—curiously fosters a prime American vice—deviant behavior.[7] But there is rather more than this bare reference would suggest. It would also appear from Merton's paper that that "good thing"—democracy— generates a number of very uncomfortable consequences for many who under less democratic circumstances would be unhurt (at least, in some special, important ways). For the deviance in which Merton was interested, it will be recalled, arises in a context in which certain goals are widely shared by various classes in a democratic social structure, while it would have been less likely to occur where relevant goals *differed* by stratum or class. Less "democracy" would have generated less pain for a considerable part of the populace.[8]

The above perhaps already makes us receptive to the notion of strong affinity of structural-functional analysis with ironic perspective that Merton long ago suggested [9] and that Bruyn and Matza have rightly insisted upon in recent years. Bruyn writes that the effect of irony is "built into the theoretical pattern of functionalism" and draws particular attention to the matter of unintended consequences of social action; while Matza regards irony as "a central feature of functional analysis." [10] Matza reinforces his case by quoting Davis on prostitution, to the effect that "increased prostitution may reduce the sexual irregularities of respectable women. This, in fact, has been the ancient justification for tolerated prostitution—that it 'protected' the family and kept the wives and daughters of the respectable citizenry pure. . . . Such a view strikes us as paradoxical because in popular discourse an evil such as prostitution cannot cause a good such as feminine virtue, or vice versa." [11]

But something on the order of structural-functional analysis with an accompanying focus on unintended or unanticipated consequences and the concomitant suggestion of an ironic perspective long antedates formal and self-conscious structural-functional analysis in sociology. Merton on social structure and anomie ,and Davis on prostitution particularly may serve to remind us of the striking anticipations of the ironies likely to arise in a functionalist kind of orientation that are to be found in the work of Bernard Mandeville (a true "early sociologist," if ever there was one), as in his disquisitions on the social consequences of the ignorance of certain social classes, of prostitution (Mandeville's argument is "the ancient justification" that the unchastity of some women preserves the chastity of others—of course), of dueling.[12]

Not only is it true that Mandeville adumbrates present-day functionalist ironies, but in so doing he is constantly likely to confront us with his very suggestive views about how vice, in one or another form, leads to virtue in one or another form. It is conventional, in this connection, to refer to Mandeville's "paradoxes." But paradox here again has a general sense that at least brings it very close to irony. Economists have not forgotten Mandeville, and while sociologists do not remember him with quite the same sense for his relevance beyond his day, his mark within our discipline is nevertheless also traceable (even if not much attended to recently). The point here is to utilize Mandeville as a symbol for an ironic outlook that has even directly and with some frequency influenced sociologists.

Max Weber was well aware of Mandeville's ironic thought. He refers explicitly to *The Fable of the Bees*, cites the famous formula, "private vices, public benefits," and also refers aptly to *"jene Kraft die stets das Böse will und stets das Gute schafft."* [13] (In Priest's adroit Englishing of Goethe, we get "that power which would evil ever do and ever does the good.") We return to one Robert K. Merton, of whose knowledge of Mandeville's work there can be no doubt.[14] Merton turns the quotation regarding good and evil about, in a context of discussion of unlooked-for effects of the work of the Protestant reformers which damaged their original values. He refers to "the essential paradox of social action—the 'realization' of values may lead to their renunciation"; and he writes of *"die Kraft die stets das* Gute *will und stets das* Böse *schafft."* [15] The same Merton, many years later, reverted to the original form of Goethe's statement, observing that "evil intent *can* generate benign consequences." [16]

So vice can lead to virtue and virtue to vice. Evil can produce good and good, in turn, evil. Prostitution, it is argued, can sustain chastity. Ambition can help induce deviance. Religion can nourish a science that ultimately develops values and theses that challenge the religion that gave it strength. Such "paradoxes" may appear as part of the very ground on which functionalist ironies build, part of the foundation on which they are reared. To put it a bit differently, they need not be "additional" components in a functionalist and ironic position but rather an important portion thereof.

But it is hardly needful to confine one's self to structural-functional outlooks or adumbrations thereof in order to find significant ironic perspectives. Another position in sociology in which irony has played an important role is that of so-called labeling theory, which we turn to with a particular eye to its ironic component.[17]

LABELING THEORY AND IRONY [18]

Matza states what he calls "the neo-Chicagoan irony" succinctly as the irony that "systems of control and the agents that man them are implicated in the process by which others become deviant." [19] The general character of labeling theory is thus represented aptly enough. Labeling theory does stress the role of labelers or definers of deviance who act—fatefully, one might say—upon a deviance already existent. But they do act upon a deviance already existent.[20] Although there may be some confusion in the matter, there is certainly a saving awareness at least that not all deviant behavior is explicable as an outcome of labeling. Thus, Becker is careful to write that "it would be foolish to propose that stick-up men stick people up simply because someone has labeled them stick-up men or that everything a homosexual does results from someone having called him a homosexual." [21]

The notion of a deviance already existent on which more deviance is piled has been phrased in terms of a distinction between primary and secondary deviation. Lemert writes that "secondary deviation refers to a special class of socially defined responses which people make to problems created *by the societal reaction to their deviance*." [22] The distinction is an important one, for it would seem to allow easier avoidance of such absurdities as the notion that all crime is caused by policemen—an absurdity to which few would subscribe formally but one suggestive of excesses to which labeling theory is sometimes liable. It runs some danger, in its more careless representatives, of offering the vision of a radically mentalized universe in which phenomena like crime and mental illness have no reality *except* as they are superinduced by the very agents supposed to prevent or control or "cure" them or *except* as they are accorded a ghostly sort of existence because of the arbitrary labeling of persons who possess power,[23] with an element of the self-fulfilling prophecy suggested as some among the powerless tend to become that which the labelers say they are.[24]

This is said not because the writer fancies himself an expert on labeling theory (which he certainly is not) or feels called upon to pontificate about it. The point is rather, precisely, that there are instructive ironies involved in the labeling outlook which could only be destroyed or lose all force in a mentalistic travesty of social realities. Again, it seems that the distinction of primary and secondary can be helpful. Even Szasz, whose work on madness in mental institutions has so marked a labeling flavor, argues that there is such a thing as "contractual psychiatry," a psychiatry set in operation when persons who will often have had no deleterious influence exercised upon them by hospital personnel and who, therefore, in some sense have "emotional problems" antecedent to or independent of any institutionalization [25] make private arrangements with psychiatrists for treatment.[26] The point, of course, is the implied concession of the existence of some kind of "primary" mental illness.

When a certain rationality and realism are preserved in these matters, there is clear value in the stress that some sociologists have afforded on, say, the role that it is possible for psychiatrists to play in shaping the perception and self-perception of mental patients, without benefit to the latter or to their positive harm (and, some will also stress, without attention to the *initial* self-perception of the latter). "Rewards" such as approval may be forthcoming to patients once they accept the quite arbitrary diagnoses that psychiatrists may impose, which again do patients no good whatever.[27] Szasz has persuasively sustained an older physician's view that "barbarous" and "unphilosophical" treatment of "mental indispositions" in asylums will have the effect of inflating even originally small aberrations "into the full and frightful monstrosity of madness."[28] There is a measure of real power and cogency in such views: they do not rest on a wholly arbitrary reading of pertinent evidence. The ironies within this sphere become tragic and savage. The tinge of comedy so persistent in irony now disappears and the wry smile of the "knowing" observer now readily becomes an outright grimace.[29]

The case of mental illness in particular has been taken up in this context because of the inevitable suggestion of the "medical" which has been conventionally associated with such illness. Insofar as the psychiatrist intensifies the illness that he is supposed to cure or alleviate, through his professional ministrations (regarded as medical), we are confronted with the phenomenon of iatrogenesis. The whole matter of the ironies on which labeling theory has touched[30] calls for some consideration of iatrogenesis. There is, indeed, so much continuity between central labeling-theory concerns and the sphere of iatrogenesis that it would be ill advised for sociologists *not* to ponder their connections. But it will be remembered that the range of phenomena labeling theory touches on extends well beyond mental illness, taking in such various things as crime, delinquency, prostitution, drug addiction, homosexuality, and stuttering.

IATROGENESIS

Iatrogenic diseases are now recognized as very important.[31] Within the area of iatrogenesis, medical interest has been heavily concentrated on drugs. The authors of a comprehensive recent monograph on iatrogenic diseases write, "In correlating the data for this book, it has been apparent that two factors are the major contribution to the manifestation of iatrogenic disease. These are the abnormal patient reaction to a drug, and the development of unexpected toxicity when the several drugs are given in combination."[32] This sounds almost like a loose equating of iatrogenesis with drug-induced maladies (the drugs being medically prescribed, always), but, however large may be the role within iatrogenesis of drugs,[33] it is certain that current medical usage extends the meaning of iatrogenesis well beyond anything having to do with the medical administration of drugs.

The phenomena suggested by the term as currently used are very old. Medical dictionaries today will often define the term as meaning medical generation of illness or physician-induced illness (when the physician is working as a physician). In this general sense, the famous case of Ignaz Phillip Semmelweis (1818–65) and puerperal fever will clearly qualify as a case of iatrogenesis. It may be recalled that Semmelweis probed to the bottom of a Viennese hospital situation in which physicians, coming from the performance of autopsies to attend their patients in the last stages of pregnancy, would transmit lethal germs from the corpses to the living women.[34]

But if we include the transmission of disease as well as drug-induced illness under the rubric of iatrogenesis, we are still far from taking in the full reach of the term. Inspection of medical bibliographies indicates the publication, for example, of recent articles on "iatrogenic depression" and "iatrogenic anxiety" in journals such as *The Journal of the American Medical Association* and *The Psychiatric Quarterly*. "A Note on the Possible Iatrogenesis of Suicide" appeared in a recent issue of *Psychiatry*.[35] Wain's compilation on the origins of medical terms refers, under "iatrogenic," to "the production of a psychosomatic illness by overemphasis and exaggeration of the patient's true condition," aside from a standard mention of drugs.[36]

When the surgical blade slips and "the healing knife" destroys more tissue than it should, we also get cases plainly coming within the general meaning of iatrogenesis. The phenomena covered are various. There are evidently different types of iatrogenesis. The modes and mechanisms of iatrogenesis call for close inquiry, just as do modes and mechanisms of those secondary deviance-generating processes in which labeling theorists are interested. Yet the sheer scope or range of things fitting under the title of iatrogenesis suggests a certain comparability or parallelism with the scope of things that concern labeling theorists: on the one hand, a range of phenomena that includes crime, prostitution, mental illness, homosexuality, drug addiction, stuttering, among others; on the other, medical involvement and agency in disease transmission, generation of uncomfortable or parlous or suicidal mental states, unintended and unwanted effects of drugs, slips of the surgical knife. (There are certainly some possibilities of medical and sociological overlap of interest, as in the case of mental illness, notably.)

There is further suggestiveness in the juxtaposition of iatrogenesis and labeling perspective in that in both medicine and sociology it is quickly apparent that something like a distinction between primary and secondary "difficulty" is indispensable. If a drug is medically administered and intensifies the illness it is designed to treat or has unwanted side effects, obviously it does not follow that the drug generated the initial disease it was prescribed for. One of the dictionaries of medicine or nursing that the writer inspected under "iatrogenic" explicitly takes the term to refer to "a secondary condition arising from a treatment of a primary condition." [37]

It was remarked parenthetically, just above, that there are possibilities of medical and sociological overlap of interest. There are cases of iatrogenesis that strongly feature social situations that could easily come within the purview of the sociologist and presumably be analyzed with a fair degree of accuracy or penetration just in terms of his discipline. A case in point would be the social interaction between doctor and patient in which the doctor's conveying to the patient of his discovery that the latter has a mild hypertension that has had no significant damaging effect and is readily controlled by standard medication leaves the patient in an unnecessary panic. This is

329

clearly a matter of social relationships that simply happen to fall *within* a medical context. For certain sociological purposes, the particular medical context may not be important. There is hardly a question of medical "analogies" when both doctor and sociologist would be concerned with a problem in social intercourse. (Henderson noted several decades ago that physician and patient make a "social system." [38]) There is no deviance here and, accordingly, this sort of case has not interested labeling theorists. But this sort of case has entirely unmistakable continuity with the "social system" case presented by, say, interaction of psychiatrist and patient in a mental institution. Sociologists have not hesitated to discern a large "sociological" element here, and with evident justification, aside from the matter of special competences that psychiatrists may have.

Finally, the juxtaposition of labeling and iatrogenesis raises a point about the vulnerability of experts in general, within our society, which will be taken up in the next section. In the interim, given the dominant concern of this paper, it is appropriate to be insistent on the marked susceptibility of matters covered in both iatrogenesis and labeling theory to interpretation in ironic terms. Things are not as they are "supposed to be." They come out in ways unintended or unexpected, although there is also the suggestion that there are various audiences (often, indeed, more than just two) or observers privy to what is going on in varying degrees, some not "wise" at all. And ironies of interest for both labeling theory and iatrogenesis may well be intensified by the presence of flaws in those supposedly especially competent to "cure" or alleviate, while the flaws are both veiled by and involved in the qualities or features that are considered as the marks of competence itself.[39]

IATROGENESIS, LABELING, AND THE IRONIC VULNERABILITY OF EXPERTS IN GENERAL

What is "medical" and what is not? How seriously shall the idea of cure or of alleviation of illness be taken in certain contexts that are not indubitably "medical"? Should we decide in various cases that statements about "cure" are so barrenly rhetorical or so unequivocally intended for advertising uses that the statements simply cannot be taken seriously? Where if anywhere do medical "analogies" with situations encompassed in labeling theory warrant a more determined effort to establish continuities or strong affinities with the therapeutic and alleviative efforts of physicians? Where else may there be overlap, such as was suggested above, where there is no question of analogies at all and labeling theory and iatrogenesis converge on the same data?

Asking what is "medical" and what not, one is constrained to extend further the scope of inquiry into irony-laden situations that bear evident resemblances to those mentioned thus far. As has been noted, there are various types of iatrogenesis, as there are various ways in which labeling may get its effects. But we have stayed within certain limits. Suppose, however, we should consider the case of a middle-class teacher who inadvertently discourages lower-class students by the very exercise of skills and approaches that help her effectiveness among children of her own class background. Perhaps she has expectations about dress and comportment that make middle-class children comfortable with her but puzzle and disconcert those of lower-class background and impair their learning.

There are familiar presumptions about the job a teacher is supposed to do, and ironies lurk in the situation just described. But is it really worthwhile to try to assimilate it to medical categories such as iatrogenesis? One might well hesitate to do so, while recognizing points of resemblance. Modern society has, of course, witnessed the rise of a great variety of specialties in which there are requirements for considerable training and in which there is constant contact with a public supposed to be benefited by the specialists' services. A vast field for ironies has been opened up here. That is evident enough, whatever one may decide on the applicability of medical categories. There is a *pervasive* irony centering on the inadvertent (and sometimes arrogant) incompetence of competence. "You hurt where you are supposed to help, and you show some aptitude for doing so via the instrumentalities and skills that are supposed to be helpful." Internists, psychiatrists, youth counselors, teachers, and numerous others—all might at times be so addressed.

In this connection, it is worth remembering that the unwanted side effects of medically prescribed drugs have been referred to as "diseases of medical progress," as a part of the price that has to be paid for the achievement of improved medication. "In each prize, some sad germ of evil lies." [40] The ironies or difficulties that arise in connection with the incompetence of competence in areas ordinarily viewed as well removed from the medical sphere may be regarded as a price we must pay for the modern growth of expertness.

In the end, one must ask not only what is medical and what not but even what is ironic and what not. The term "ironic" can be extended in ways that are quite useless and silly. Fowler's *Modern English Usage*, toward the end of its article on irony, has this: "For practical purposes a protest is needed against the application of 'the irony of Fate,' or of 'irony' for short, *to every trivial oddity*." (Italics added.) There are areas of "expertness" in some sense (as, say, in hairdressing) where "simulation" of irony would very often presumably not be worth consideration.

LIMITATIONS ON THE IRONIC PERSPECTIVE

The point just stated suggests further cautions. Some dangers to which labeling theory is liable have already been noted. Those dangers, however, are not the only ones.

So-called common sense no doubt has its failings. And the sociologist always has an understandable desire to make a distinctive contribution to the analysis of social phenomena. He has an understandable desire to get away from the obvious, to penetrate deeper, to be analytically resourceful, to bring enlightenment. In his discussion of manifest and latent functions Merton wrote: "There is some evidence that it is precisely at the point where the research attention of sociologists has shifted from the plane of manifest to the plane

331

of latent functions that they have made their distinctive and major contributions." [41] Merton's own documentation of this assertion gives it good support, and, in general, the present writer has no real disposition to quarrel with it. Yet one has to recognize that, precisely because of desire to attain a more penetrating view of things, common sense may be unduly slighted and sociologists may reach for strained interpretations.

Some of the materials with which labeling theorists present us are hard to judge. Problems of sheer evidence loom large here. The writer lacks the space to handle them in any significant way nor is he well qualified to do so. Let us put things naively: Is *everything* that happens in prisons somehow confirmative of criminal ways? Is *everything* that occurs in mental hospitals destructive of the patient's emotional equilibrium? Put in this bald way, these questions can only evoke an offhand, "of course not" response, while they appear to leave labeling theory intact. But there is some force in what would appear the commonsense argument (bearing on the illustrative sphere of delinquency)—counter to the theme of secondary deviation—that "maintains that until the delinquent is caught, charged, and forced to face directly the fact of his delinquency, he will not be motivated to put an end to it." [42]

An important residue, a valuable contribution still remains in labeling theory. One merely seeks to preserve an essential sanity when one adds, simply, that there can be such a thing as irony-mongering or paradox-mongering, brought on by being excessively intrigued and finally bemused by the ironic perspective. With all the importance of iatrogenesis, doctors *do* cure people and alleviate their ailments. Teachers *do* teach numbers of children some things worth teaching. Policemen *do* do some of the work by way of public protection that TV has them doing practically exclusively. This may seem like undue agitation about the perfectly obvious. It does no harm, given certain unhappy potentials in the peculiar enthusiasms that sometimes arise in our field.

But the excesses suggested are not necessary. With appropriate restraints that disciplined sociologists should be able to exercise, ironic outlooks, we have argued and continue to argue, can be highly stimulating to sociological thought.

IRONY AND HUMANISTIC AND SCIENTIFIC VALUES

In one of the most gracefully stated arguments that we have for a humanistic bias in the field of sociology, Robert Bierstedt proposed that the field (whatever its status as science might actually be or should be) "owns a rightful place in the domain of humane letters and belongs, with literature, history, and philosophy, among the arts that liberate the human mind." [43] Irony has long been a potent component in works of literature, history, and philosophy. Its humanistic associations are obvious. No serious preoccupation with it on the part of a sociologist could possibly keep it free of such associations; nor is there any compelling reason that anyone should try this impossible thing.

At the same time, it is clear that the careful pursuit of the nuances, the twists and turns of irony in social life could well encourage detailed inquiry that moves toward the scientific kind of enterprise. It is not that men of letters, say, or philosophers must lack analytical rigor by comparison with sociologists. That is palpable nonsense. But the matter that has been gone over in the present paper may perhaps give a sufficient sense of the feasibility of undertakings of analysis—and of empirical investigation—that are in thorough harmony with the best the sociological tradition has to offer and that take advantage of and are stimulated by ironic outlooks. (Such undertakings have clearly already emerged, and one may hope that they will be carried further.) It may be suggested that the whole area of things here covered lends itself especially well to a blending of humanistic and scientific values in sociology. Unless I am badly mistaken, the work of the man in whose honor the present volume has been put together moves strongly in the direction of such blending.

NOTES

1. As we turn to the meaning of irony, it must be said there are some matters that it seems best to avoid on this occasion. There are, for instance, interesting problems having to do with irony as an outlook or stance on the part of an observer of things versus irony as somehow inherent in the nature of things observed, which will not be taken up. It would be too much of a distraction to try to alert the reader constantly to shifts from observer's perspective to quality of things observed. (The idea of a "double audience," referred to in note 3 below, it may be remarked, draws attention to irony as perspective or stance on the part of an observer.) It should also be understood that we shall not return faithfully and regularly to the detail of the specification of irony to be offered. The specification presents a set of convenient reference points for the reader.

2. Severyn T. Bruyn, *The Human Perspective in Sociology* (Englewood Cliffs, N.J.: Prentice-Hall, 1966), p. 151.

3. This view of irony draws on a number of sources. It is influenced by Bruyn, *The Human Perspective in Sociology*, pp. 150–57, and by David Matza, *Becoming Deviant* (Englewood Cliffs, N.J.: Prentice-Hall, 1969), *passim.* It receives support from the idea of a "double audience" (one "in" on things, one not, while the former is also aware of the latter's incomprehension) as set out in *Fowler's Modern English Usage,* 2nd ed. (New York: Oxford University Press, 1965), *s.v.* "irony." The exemplification of the powerful and the weak draws from a statement by Reinhold Niebuhr, *The Irony of American History* (New York: Scribner's, 1952), p. 154, as quoted in Matza, *Becoming Deviant,* pp. 69–70. There is, of course, much discussion of irony and its literary congeners by literary critics: see, for example, Northrop Frye, *Anatomy of Criticism* (Princeton, N.J.: Princeton University Press, 1957), *passim.* It is evident that irony is both a rich and occasionally somewhat elusive term. A strong sense—even too strong a one—of this richness and elusiveness is expressed in the Preface to A. E. Dyson, *The Crazy Fabric: Essays in Irony* (New York: St. Martin's Press, 1965).

4. The relation of irony to paradox, in particular, would be worth exploring. But the sense of the two terms does in fact often overlap, and for the purposes of this paper the writer is inclined toward a casual association of them, although there is a little incidental comment about the relations of the two in what follows.

5. Robert K. Merton, *Science, Technology, and Society in Seventeenth-Century England* (New York: Harper & Row, 1970), p. 58, n. 6. Max Weber, as everyone

knows, had stressed the same paradox in the field of religion-and-economy instead of religion-and-science—a most important precedence.

6. Matza, *Becoming Deviant*, p. 77.

7. Robert K. Merton, *Social Theory and Social Structure*, enl. ed. (New York: Free Press, 1968), chap. 6. (Hereinafter referred to as *STSS*.) Cf. Matza, *Becoming Deviant*, p. 77.

8. To interpret this as "opposition to democracy" would patently be nonsense. It is well known that Merton's work on social structure and anomie has been subjected to much criticism in recent years. One can only suggest here that it retains at the very least a measure of historical validity that has to do with the central irony about democracy that it rests upon. Thomas and Znaniecki, it may be observed, anticipated Merton's pertinent views in a limited but interesting way. They pointed out that Polish peasant girls immigrating to the United States who became sexually deviant here would not have been so tempted to deviance in their old-world situation, where the near impossibility of attainment of the marvels of "high life" —a class-conditioned near impossibility—would have been less upsetting to their tendency to be "good girls." It should be noted that this argument in no way rests on hostility toward a lower class or anything analogous thereto. See William I. Thomas and Florian Znaniecki, *The Polish Peasant in Europe and America* (New York: Dover, 1958), vol. 2, pp. 1820–21. (Thomas and Znaniecki's argument is a bit more complex than this would suggest, but it clearly incorporates the contention indicated.)

9. Merton, *STSS*, p. 122, where Merton himself writes of "paradox." The affinity of functionalist outlook and irony, it should, however, be added, is decidedly more evident in that variant of the outlook that has interested Merton than it is in the variant that has been developed by Parsons.

10. Bruyn, *The Human Perspective in Sociology*, pp. 151–52; Matza, *Becoming Deviant*, p. 77.

11. Kingsley Davis, "Prostitution," in Robert K. Merton and Robert A. Nisbet, *Contemporary Social Problems* (New York: Harcourt Brace Jovanovich, 1961), pp. 283–84, as quoted in Matza, *Becoming Deviant*, pp. 77–78. The "functions" of prostitution will shortly be alluded to again. It is worth noting that the supposed happy effects of prostitution in a larger social framework are apparently not altogether a matter of "latent functions." The reader may detect significant ironies in the circumstance that prostitutes themselves can verge on something like functionalist views of prostitution. Thus: "We girls see, like I guess you call them perverts of some sort, you know, little freaky people and if they didn't have girls to come to like us that are able to handle them and make it a nice thing, there would be so many rapes . . . "; or: "I could say that a prostitute has held more marriages together as part of their profession than any divorce counselor": (James H. Bryan, "Occupational Ideologies and Individual Attitudes of Call Girls," *Social Problems* 13 [Spring 1966]: 443, as cited by Edwin M. Schur, *Labeling Deviant Behavior* [New York: Harper & Row, 1971], p. 76).

12. See Bernard Mandeville's *The Fable of the Bees*, ed. F. B. Kaye (Oxford, Eng.: Clarendon Press, 1924), vol. 1, *passim*, for ignorance; vol. 1, pp. 95–100, for prostitution; vol. 1, pp. 219–22, vol. 2, p. 102, for dueling. On Mandeville's functionalist outlook generally, see Joseph Spengler, "Veblen and Mandeville Contrasted," *Weltwirtschaftliches Archiv* 82 (1959): 35–65, and Louis Schneider, "Mandeville as Forerunner of Modern Sociology," *Journal of the History of the Behavioral Sciences* 6 (1970): 219–30. Mandeville did incline to cynicism, and it is worth repeating that irony is *not* to be identified with that.

334

13. Max Weber, *Gesammelte Aufsätze zur Wissenschaftslehre* (Tübingen, Germany: Mohr, 1968), p. 33.

14. See Merton, *STSS*, pp. 20–21, 475.

15. Merton, *Science, Technology and Society in Seventeenth-Century England*, p. 101. (Italics added.)

16. Robert K. Merton, *On the Shoulders of Giants* (New York: Free Press, 1965), p. 14. Edward Shils writes that "although anomic actions are often pernicious in themselves and in their consequences there are some which may be pernicious and immoral in themselves and most beneficial in their consequences." This is classic Mandevillean doctrine. Shils adds to this statement the following one, in parentheses: "This was the view of Mandeville and Adam Smith, but it has not entered very centrally into modern sociology and particularly into the ethical-political outlook of modern sociologists" (Edward Shils, *Selected Essays* [Chicago: University of Chicago Department of Sociology, 1970], p. 61, note). One cannot be sure how justified Shils is in the first part of this latter parenthetical statement, regarding centrality, although he seems to be on strong ground in the portion of the statement relating to the ethical-political outlook of sociologists.

17. Structural-functional analysis has its limitations. If the writer did not think it had a residual value that goes beyond these, he would certainly not consider it worthwhile to trace the ironic strands in it. The same general statement holds for labeling theory.

18. The phrase "labeling theory" is used despite some evident discomfort over the too grandiose suggestions of the word "theory" in it. See Howard Becker, *Outsiders* (New York: Free Press, 1973), p. 178. The following outline of labeling theory is designedly most economical and inevitably made in the light of present interests.

19. Matza, *Becoming Deviant*, p. 80.

20. Here is one of the points on which this sketch is sketchy indeed. The question of what part norms play in labeling theory conceptions of deviance is not taken up. (We do not even consider the grounding of "primary" deviance.) The question is considered by Jack Gibbs, "Issues in Defining Deviant Behavior," in Robert E. Scott and Jack D. Douglas, eds., *Theoretical Perspectives on Deviance* (New York: Basic Books, 1972), chap. 2.

21. Becker, *Outsiders*, p. 179.

22. Edwin M. Lemert, *Human Deviance, Social Problems, and Social Control* (Englewood Cliffs, N.J.: Prentice-Hall, 1972), p. 63. (Italics added.)

23. Compare the aptly phrased strictures of Gerald D. Suttles, *The Social Construction of Communities* (Chicago: University of Chicago Press, 1972), p. 114.

24. There are also other reasons for reserve about labeling theory, as indicated below in the section on "Limitations on the Ironic Perspective."

25. No special view of mental illness is here being intimated or tacitly or insidiously supported. There is not even any bias against the possibility that ultimately it may prove sensible and scientifically justifiable not to regard such "illness" as illness at all. What is argued is simply that, whatever mental illness is, it is not to be considered as unreservedly and totally the product of the work of psychiatrists.

26. See Thomas S. Szasz, *The Manufacture of Madness* (New York: Harper & Row, 1970), Preface and p. 101.

27. See Thomas Scheff, *Being Mentally Ill* (Chicago: Aldine, 1966).

28. See Szasz, *The Manufacture of Madness*, pp. 127–28.

29. It is of interest that just as prostitutes appear to show some awareness of "functions" of prostitution, so it may be intimated in relevant literature that mental patients can get some inkling that it is possible that psychiatric personnel will

hurt them by their ministrations. Thus, Goffman comments that, in the patient outlook, "psychiatric staff are sometimes seen not as discovering whether you are sick, but as making you sick; and 'Don't bug me, man' can mean 'Don't pester me to the point where I'll get upset'" (Erving Goffman, *Asylums* [Garden City, N.Y.: Doubleday Anchor Books, 1961], p. 154, note).

30. Again, we have had to omit much. A fuller discussion of labeling would have taken into account the significant detail of stereotyping, retrospective interpretation and negotiation (see, for example, Schur, *Labeling Deviant Behavior,* chap. 3) and utilized such detail for the further exhibition of ironies.

31. The writer has made no effort to find recent studies of the incidence of iatrogenic illness. Barber reported in 1966 "a recent study" of the medical service of a university hospital, in connection with which "the house staff found that 20 per cent of all patients developed some iatrogenic trouble." See Bernard Barber, *Drugs and Society* (New York: Russell Sage, 1967), p. 182 and p. 182, note 52, for the source of Barber's information.

32. P. F. D'Arcy and J. P. Griffin, *Iatrogenic Diseases* (London: Oxford University Press, 1972), Preface, p. 5.

33. In the study Barber refers to (see note 31), more than half of the patients who were found to have iatrogenic troubles "suffered from iatrogenic complications originating in drugs that had been administered routinely" (Barber, *Drugs and Society,* p. 182). We should here at least mention explicitly the matter of inadvertently medically initiated drug addiction, following from legitimate medical use of drugs for analgesic or sedative purposes. There is evident reason for regarding this sort of thing as iatrogenic. But it is, to be sure, one of the iatrogenic phenomena of which there is thorough medical awareness.

34. A convenient, brief account of Semmelweis and his work is in Henry Sigerist, *The Great Doctors* (New York: Dover, 1971), pp. 354–59. There is irony in the hostile response from physicians that Semmelweis' epoch-making study of childbed fever evoked.

35. See "A Note on the Possible Iatrogenesis of Suicide," *Psychiatry* 36 (May 1973): 213–18.

36. Harry Wain, M.D., *The Story Behind the Word: Some Interesting Origins of Medical Terms* (Springfield, Ill.: Thomas, 1968).

37. Helen A. Duncan, R.N., *Duncan's Dictionary for Nurses* (New York: Springer, 1971). The particular language of two other dictionaries is also of interest in this light. *Dorland's Illustrated Medical Dictionary* (Philadelphia: Saunders, 1957), under "iatrogenic," refers to the generation of "additional problems" that result from the activity of physicians; while the *Encyclopedia and Dictionary of Medicine and Nursing,* ed. Benjamin F. Miller, M.D., and Claire B. Keene, R.N., B.S. (Philadelphia: Saunders, 1972), defines an iatrogenic disorder as one produced inadvertently in consequence of medical treatment "for some other disorder."

38. See L. J. Henderson, "Physician and Patient as a Social System" in Henderson's *On the Social System* (Chicago: University of Chicago Press, 1970), pp. 202–13.

39. At the end of this section on iatrogenesis, a word may be allowed on serendipity and iatrogenesis. The former term has been a favorite of Merton's, as all acquainted with his work know, and it is utilized with some frequency in *Social Theory and Social Structure* and in *On the Shoulders of Giants.* It will be recalled that serendipity, in scientific usage, refers to discovery of an unexpected or unanticipated but actually helpful datum which works toward modifying or initiating theory. Outside scientific investigation, the term refers to a happy faculty of inadvertently stumbling on good things. In both serendipity and iatrogenesis there is the element

of the unexpected or unanticipated, but, if serendipity refers to a faculty of stumbling on good things, much iatrogenesis may be said to involve the fact of stumbling on bad ones. (Intention in both cases may be taken to be unexceptionable.) A seriously conceived ironic outlook must take seriously the job of constructing types and families of ironies and of discriminating variants and neighbors thereof and deceptive resemblances thereto. In such an outlook, comparison of terms like serendipity and iatrogenesis may be considered to stimulate more than verbal play.

40. See the quoted matter from an article on drug toxicity in G. Zblinden, in the Preface to L. Meyler and A. H. Herkheimer, *Side Effects of Drugs: A Survey of Unwanted Effects of Drugs Reported in 1965–67* (Baltimore: Williams & Wilkins, 1968), p. 5, and the poetic lines quoted in Fielding H. Garrison, *Contributions to the History of Medicine* (New York: Harper's, 1966), p. 546. [I am indebted for the Meyler-Herkheimer reference to my friend Morton Ziskind, M.D., of the Tulane Medical School.]
41. Merton, *STSS,* p. 120.
42. Stanton Wheeler, "Deviant Behavior," in Neil J. Smelser, ed., *Sociology: An Introduction,* 2nd ed. (New York: Wiley, 1973), p. 681.
43. Robert Bierstedt, "Sociology and Humane Learning," *American Sociological Review* 25 (February 1960): 4.

On Formalizing Theory*

HANAN C. SELVIN

Most sociologists received their graduate education in departments that were dominated by a single person. They often describe their professional orientations by referring to this experience. They studied under Parsons, Hughes, or Park, they will say, and everyone knows what kind of sociologist each one is.

Those of us who were fortunate enough to have been graduate students at Columbia during the period from 1939 to 1970 had an altogether different experience. We were satellites, not of one sun, but of two, for Robert K. Merton and Paul F. Lazarsfeld so dominated sociology at Columbia during these three decades that no lesser figure of speech will suffice. Like a giant double star, each strengthened the other's radiance, and all of us basked in their combined illumination.

Dramatic as this metaphor is, it still does not do justice to the experience of being a graduate student under these two men. Many of us fell, sooner or later, into a regular orbit around either Merton or Lazarsfeld, with occasional showers of cosmic radiation from the other.

My career at Columbia was different. To retain the astronomical figure of speech, I spent three years in orbit around Merton, as his teaching assistant

*I wish to thank Christopher Bernert for exemplary help with this paper.

Hanan C. Selvin is Professor of Sociology at the State University of New York at Stony Brook.

and research assistant, then worked for a few months as Lazarsfeld's research assistant, and finally wrote my dissertation under a committee that included both of them.

This complex trajectory has given me close views of both men but also sufficient independence of each as to afford me intellectual distance from them. I am now much more identified with Lazarsfeld's style of work and intellectual interests than with Merton's, but I have also been sharply critical of certain aspects of Lazarsfeld's work.[1] Surely, my experience in working with Lazarsfeld has enabled me to take the same kind of detached and, I hope, constructive view of some of Merton's work as Lazarsfeld has done himself on occasion.

One such occasion serves as a model of what I hope to accomplish here. It is their joint essay, "Friendship as Social Process: A Substantive and Methodological Analysis," in the *festschrift* for Robert M. MacIver, edited by Berger, Abel, and Page.[2] I have a rueful admiration for this essay, especially for Lazarsfeld's methodological explication of Merton's *theory of homophily*, the extent to which people who are friends come to have similar values and vice versa. My admiration is rueful because Merton earlier had posed to me the same challenge that Lazarsfeld successfully met in his part of this article, and I had altogether failed to meet it.

My failure is worth a passing note because it did not stem from ignorance of the methodological tools that Lazarsfeld used. On the contrary, I was already well acquainted with his principal tool, his own "sixteen-fold table," which he had invented some years earlier to solve the problem: Which of two mutually interacting variables has the greater effect on the other?[3] The question that the sixteen-fold table helps to answer is: Which of these two effects is stronger?

When Merton first described to me his formulation of the theory of homophily, the adage that "birds of a feather -flock together" *and* the converse, almost Lamarkian, statement, perhaps now destined to become an adage, "birds that flock together tend to develop similar feathers," he asked me to find some device—graphical, statistical, or whatever—that would enable him to represent these two related phenomena. I had the right tool within my grasp, but I didn't know it! It is like the old joke about the man who is called in to repair a gigantic but malfunctioning piece of machinery that is emitting a *Thurberian pocketa-queep* instead of its normal *pocketa-pocketa*. He stands looking at the machine for a few minutes, asks that the machine be stopped, takes a screwdriver out of his pocket, and gives a small screw a quarter-turn. When the machine is restarted, it runs smoothly, *pocketa-pocketa*. The expert turns to his client and says calmly, "That will be $1,000." The client, outraged by such a high fee for what appears to be the work of a moment, asks for an itemized bill, which the expert promptly writes on a scrap of paper: "Knowing which screw to turn, $999; turning the right screw, $1.00; total, $1,000." Lazarsfeld knew which screw to turn; I didn't.

It isn't only Lazarsfeld's part of this essay that gives me a rueful feeling. When I reread Merton's Epilogue, some time after starting work on this paper, I realized that he had already said much of what I was planning to say about the benefits that sociological theorists might derive from such formal analyses or codifications.[4] I do not know now whether this is a case of independent discovery[5] or of my having read and internalized this passage and then having forgotten that I had done so. Whatever the source of this duplication, it has led me to raise the intellectual ante by looking at the value that a sociological theorist like Merton might derive from more explicitly mathematical and statistical formalizations than the virtually common-culture formalization that Lazarsfeld offered in the homophily article.

I do not mean to imply that the sixteen-fold table is in the common culture of everyday life. Instead, it was in the common culture of Columbia sociology at that period, and Merton was obviously able to grasp its full meaning, especially when there was a well-beaten, two-way path between his office and Lazarsfeld's. Moreover, Merton, the theorist, has always known a good deal more about statistics than most sociologists. His 1940 paper, "Fact and Factitiousness in Ethnic Opinionnaires," includes, I believe, the first use of tests of statistical significance to appear in the *American Sociological Review*[6] —years before the first textbook on statistical methods for sociologists.

I have chosen the two case studies of formalization described below from a larger set of possibilities. (Other writers have formalized different aspects of Merton's work; see Beauchamp[7] and Harary.[8]) The first, the matrix representation of sociograms, is of interest here because its use clarifies and operationalizes concepts that Merton was able to handle less incisively with his verbal theory; moreover, Merton was aware of this mode of representation at the time that he constructed his verbal theory,[9] and this example therefore shows how a more self-conscious mathematical orientation might have helped him. The second case study, numerical taxonomy, appeared on the intellectual scene only after Merton had demonstrated his need for it. It thus remains a viable option for Merton or one of his followers to pursue.

"THE INFLUENTIAL AND THE INFLUENCED"—APPLICATIONS OF MATRIX ANALYSIS

Chapter 10 of *Social Theory and Social Structure*[10] includes several problems in which the mathematical tool of a *matrix* both systematizes and extends Merton's analysis. More precisely, there are two distinct innovations juxtaposed here—the idea of representing a *sociogram* by a matrix and the idea of limiting the entries in this *sociomatrix* to 0's and 1's so as to make possible the algebraic manipulation of these matrices.

Ever since Moreno's invention of the sociogram to describe the patterns of interpersonal relations in a group,[11] social psychologists have been bothered by the chaos that the circles and lines of a sociogram may assume when there are more than a few individuals in the group.[12]

The first investigators to recognize that the spaghetti-like quality of such a sociogram can be organized into a meaningful structure by the use of a matrix were apparently Elaine Forsyth and Leo Katz,[13] but their matrix approach had only representational value. Unlike the later approach of Festinger,[14] the elements that Forsyth and Katz entered in their matrix did not lend themselves to mathematical manipulation. They used four symbols: an X to indicate a person choosing himself, a + to indicate a favorable choice ("likes" or "seeks advice from"), a − to indicate an unfavorable choice ("dislikes" or "would prefer not to associate with"), and a *0* to indicate no choice at all.

As nearly as I can reconstruct what happened next, Festinger[15] was puzzled by the problem of representing and analyzing sociograms in his housing data, and he enlisted the help of Luce and Perry, who were then graduate students in mathematics at MIT. Again, I do not know whether or not Luce and Perry were aware of the work of Forsyth and Katz, but they managed to conceptualize the sociogram as a matrix involving 1's and 0's, "1" standing for a choice on some criterion and "0" for no choice. By thus limiting themselves to "Boolean matrices," consisting only of 1's and 0's, they made it possible to use the mathematical methods that had been developed for such matrices; no such methods exist for the four-valued matrices of Forsyth and Katz.

To make these ideas more concrete, consider the following simple sociogram and its sociometric matrix (or "sociomatrix"):

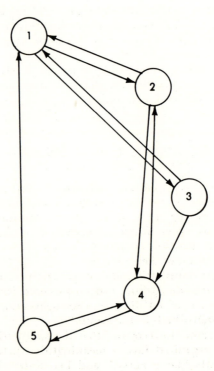

Figure 1. HYPOTHETICAL INFLUENCE STRUCTURE

Figure 1 represents five persons, each making two choices. Although the formalization presented here applies to any sociometric relation, it will be most useful to consider it as a hypothetical example of an "influence structure"; the arrows in Figure 1 thus stand for "seeks advice from"—person 1 seeks advice from 2 and 3 and so on. A glance at the sociogram shows persons 1 and 4 each influence three others, person 2 influences two others, and persons 3 and 5 each influence one other.

Table 1. SOCIOMATRIX CORRESPONDING TO FIGURE 1

				Chosen			
		1	2	3	4	5	*Total*
	1	0	1	1	0	0	2
	2	1	0	0	1	0	2
Chooser	3	1	0	0	1	0	2
	4	0	1	0	0	1	2
	5	1	0	0	1	0	2
	Total	3	2	1	3	1	

The sociomatrix shows exactly the same structure of influence. In the first row, the 0 in the first column indicates that person 1 does not seek advice from himself (such self-choices are usually forbidden). The "1's" in columns 2 and 3 of the first row show that person 1 seeks advice from each of these others, and the "0's" in columns 4 and 5 that person 1 does not seek advice from them. The orderly arrangement of the sociomatrix makes it easier to see the pattern of relations at a glance. The sum of the elements in each row is the number of persons from whom each chooser seeks advice (often, as in this example, the investigator limits the number of choices made by each chooser so that the total of each row is two). The sum of each column is the number of choices received by each person—that is, the number of persons advised. It is obviously easier to scan the sociomatrix and see that persons 1 and 4 receive three choices each than to follow the lines of the sociogram.

If this greater perspicuity of the sociomatrix were its only advantage over the relative chaos of the sociogram, that would be enough to justify its use, especially for larger structures than this simple example. However, as Luce and Perry demonstrated a quarter-century ago, representing the sociomatrix in this way makes it possible to use the operations of matrix algebra to unravel the complexities of the sociomatrix.[16]   The basic matrix operation in the Luce and Perry article is matrix multiplication.

Table 2.   A², SQUARE OF THE SOCIOMATRIX IN TABLE 1

Chosen

		1	2	3	4	5
	1	2	0	0	2	0
	2	0	2	1	0	1
Chooser	3	0	2	1	0	1
	4	2	0	0	2	0
	5	0	2	1	0	1
Total		4	6	3	4	3

A^2, the square of the sociomatrix in Table 1, appears in Table 2. Again, the choosers appear at the left and the chosen at the top. By comparing Table 2 with Figure 1 or Table 1, the reader can easily see that each entry in Table 2 is the number of two-link chains connecting each pair of chooser and chosen. Thus, the 2 in the first row and fourth column indicates that there are two two-linked chains, or 2-chains, connecting 1 and 4: 1 chooses 2 and 2 chooses 4; 1 chooses 3 and 3 chooses 4.

Although self-choices were defined as impossible in the original sociogram, it is possible for each person to choose someone who reciprocates his choice, thus forming a 2-chain from each person to himself. The number of such reciprocated choices appears in the major diagonal of the squared matrix, the line running from upper left to lower right. Thus, 1 is involved in two reciprocated choices, with 2 and 3; 2 is involved with 1 and 4; and 3 makes only one reciprocated choice with 1.

As in the original sociomatrix, the column sums highlight one aspect of each person's popularity as a source of advice, but this time as the giver of *mediated advice,* the end of a 2-chain. Note that person 2, who was chosen as a source of advice by only 2 persons in the original sociomatrix, is the most sought-after giver of mediated advice, being the terminal of six 2-chains, as indicated by the sum at the bottom of the second column of Table 2. Two of these chains are, of course, the reciprocated choices involving persons one and four, but the remaining four 2-chains involve mediation. Now how does it happen that person 2, chosen only moderately in the original sociomatrix, is so heavily chosen in these mediated choices? The answer lies in the sociometric position of the "mediators," the middle members of the 2-chains leading to 2. The four mediated 2-chains ending on person 2 go through persons 1 and 4, who are the most highly sought-after persons in the original sociomatrix. Thus, the comparison of the column sums of A and A^2 identifies person 2 as an "expert's expert," the person to whom the most consulted members of the group themselves turn for advice.

This is only the beginning of the insights that matrix methods can give. Three more applications of matrix methods exemplify their simplicity and power. Consider first Merton's proposition that those influentials most highly chosen by rank-and-file members of the community tend to "overchoose" each other. All that is necessary to test this proposition easily is to arrange the rows and columns of Table 1 in the order of choices received, so that the most-chosen persons come first and the least-chosen last, as in Table 3.

Table 3. REARRANGEMENT OF TABLE 1 IN ORDER OF CHOICES RECEIVED

		Chosen				
		1	4	2	3	5
	1	0	0	1	1	0
	4	0	0	1	0	1
Chooser	2	1	1	0	0	0
	3	1	1	0	0	0
	5	1	1	0	0	0

If Merton's hypothesis were correct, then the most-chosen influentials of this community, persons 1 and 4, should choose each other, which would put 1's in the upper left hand corner of the matrix, or, what is the same thing, should cluster their choices around the major diagonal of the matrix. In this hypo-thetical community, which may well be too small in any case for the kinds of social structure that Merton had in mind, Merton's hypothesis turns out to be false. The elite influentials avoid choosing each other. However, the validity of Merton's hypothesis is not at issue here; instead, the question is whether the sociomatrix provides a useful tool for testing that hypothesis on some real population. A glance at Table 3 is enough to show that the proposition is not confirmed.[17]

The sharp-eyed reader may have noticed that Tables 2 and 3 tell some-what different stories about the structure of influence in this hypothetical community. Although Merton's hypothesis did not hold for *direct* choices (Table 3), it does hold for *indirect* choices. Person 2, who receives the largest number of mediated choices, is directly chosen by the two members of the elite, persons 1 and 4. Again, the facts are not at issue. What the matrix for-malizations have accomplished here is to suggest that the structure of influence has more layers to it than Merton had assumed. Formal models, even when based entirely on hypothetical data, may thus have significant implications for substantive theory.

Two additional applications of matrix methods deserve mention here for their substantive importance. The first is a relatively simple advance over the idea of squaring the sociometric matrix. It was developed, I believe, by Duncan MacRae, Jr., and was brought to my attention by Alan B. Wilson. Instead of squaring the *sociomatrix A,* one multiplies the matrix by its *transpose, A',*[18]

345

the matrix derived by interchanging the rows and columns of A. Since matrix multiplication, unlike the multiplication of ordinary numbers, is not *commutative* (that is, the matrix product $AB \neq BA$), there are two such products, which may be denoted AA' and $A'A$. The elements of AA' are the number of times in which each pair of choosers agrees on its choices. The element in the second row and third column of the AA' matrix that can be derived from Table 1 would be 2, indicating that persons 2 and 3 agree on two of their choices (both choosing 1 and 4). Similarly, the product of the two matrices in the reverse order, $A'A$, yields another insight into the sociometric structure; here the cell entries are the number of times each possible pair of others is chosen (for example, we find a 3 in the fourth row and first column, indicating that the [1,4] pair is chosen by three different choosers—2, 3, 5). These two matrix operations, like those mentioned above, are standard routines in the program library of any modern computing center. Once the sociogram is transformed into the sociomatrix and entered into the computer, it would take only a few seconds to do the calculations and print out the results for a matrix of reasonable size.

One final application of matrix methods to the study of sociometric structures deserves mention here because it solves a problem that Luce and Perry had first posed a quarter-century ago, a problem that had eluded their efforts and those of other students of sociometric structures.[19] This is the problem of using matrix methods to isolate and identify the members of a sociometric *clique*. Looking at Richard Alba's solution to this problem, one can easily see that the problem confronting the earlier investigators was not only mathematical but also conceptual.[20] The definition of clique that Luce and Perry had set forth was plausible enough but empirically too difficult to work with in the complexities of real sociograms of moderate size. Once Alba perceived this, he was able to relax the definition of clique sufficiently to keep it meaningful and yet amenable to mathematical treatment.

NUMERICAL TAXONOMY AND THE SYSTEMATIC CLASSIFICATION OF GROUP PROPERTIES

The previous section rested on the application of a single mathematical idea, that of a matrix, to the representation and analysis of sociometric structures. Occasionally, the theorist who is willing to venture into deeper mathematical or statistical waters will encounter a full-bodied mathematical theory for some phenomenon of interest to him. This appears to be the case with *numerical taxonomy,* which answers Merton's implicit plea for a systematic approach to the classification of group properties:

> Taxonomy is far from being the whole of sociological theory. It is, however, an indispensable part. When we examine the current condition of sociological theory in the matter of conceptualizing and classifying types of groups, we must regret-

fully conclude that a sociological Linnaeus or Cuvier has yet to put in an appearance.[21]

No Swedish Linnaeus or French Cuvier has indeed appeared on the sociological scene, but they have perhaps been foreshadowed by two American sociologists, Selvin and Hagstrom,[22] and by British and American biologists, Sneath and Sokal.[23] In the light of the latter work, it now seems clear that Selvin and Hagstrom were looking for numerical taxonomy but did not know that they had found the first step toward that lofty edifice. Although nowhere mentioning sociology, even in their brief treatment of taxonomic problems in the social sciences, Sneath and Sokal provide the metatheory and procedures that Merton asked for in the passage quoted above.

The general orientation of numerical taxonomy appears succinctly in seven principles, which Sneath and Sokal trace back to Michel Adanson (1727–1806), a French botanist:

1. The greater the content of information in the *taxa* of a classification and the more characters on which it is based, the better a given classification will be:
2. A priori, every character is of equal weight in creating natural *taxa*.
3. Overall similarity between any two entities is a function of their individual similarities in each of the many characters in which they are being compared.
4. Distinct *taxa* can be recognized because correlations of characters differ in the groups of organisms under study.
5. Phylogenetic inferences can be made from the taxonomic structures of a group and from character correlations, given certain assumptions about evolutionary pathways and mechanisms.
6. Taxonomy is viewed and practiced as an empirical science.
7. Classifications are based on phenetic similarity.

This stark account may serve to whet the taxonomically inclined sociologist's interest in reading the entire work, an investment that ought to pay great dividends in the work of constructing a sociological taxonomy. Consider, for example, the implications of two of their principles.

First, consider Principle 2, that every character is of equal weight in creating natural *taxa* (the groupings or "boxes" of a taxonomic system). Like traditional taxonomists in biology, who believed that some properties of organisms were more important than others in devising a system of classification, Merton argues the opposite of Principle 2: "The decisive problem is, of course, that of identifying the theoretically strategic group properties which serve systematically to discriminate the operation of each resultant type of group from the others."[24]

The opposition between these two strategies could not be sharper. Elsewhere, Sneath and Sokal say that, far from being an ingredient in constructing a typology, differential weights or measures of theoretical importance will be an outcome of the numerical taxonomic procedures.[25] In other words, numerical taxonomists would argue that the kind of theoretical ground-clearing in which Merton was engaged in his "Continuities in the Theory of Reference Groups and Social Structure"[26] was unnecessary.

The distinction between important and unimportant characteristics should come, not from theoretical elaboration, but from the empirical relations of a large number of characteristics observed for a sizable number of groups. Selvin and Hagstrom observed some 65 characteristics of 67 groups, but even these numbers, large as they are in comparison with Merton's list of 26 group properties, are not large enough for the kind of analysis described by Sneath and Sokal. Moreover, Selvin and Hagstrom considered only *aggregative* group characteristics, those derived from properties of group members—for example, the proportion of Republicans, the mean income of fathers, and so on. Depending almost entirely on characteristics that could be aggregated from questionnaire data, they ignored the *integral* group properties, such as whether the group had a house mother (still common in those far-off days of 1959, but now largely vanished from the college scene), the nature of the group's living quarters, and so on. In retrospect, the method used by Selvin and Hagstrom seems consonant with the views of numerical taxonomists, but their choice of group characteristics was theoretically impoverished.

Another of the Sneath and Sokal principles that has an unexpected relevance to sociological taxonomy is their Principle 7: "Classifications are based on phenetic similarity." This means that one should look for the similarity of *currently observable* characteristics, not for the presumed phylogeny of biological organisms or for the histories of social groups.

I do not mean to erect an antihistorical canon on the basis of this principle, but merely to point out that, despite the current revival of interest in historical data and in an integration of historical data with quantitative procedures (witness the vogue for "historical demography"),[27] there are indeed social phenomena to which the histories of social units are largely irrelevant. One such phenomenon is the nature of social groups. In classifying types of groups, it does not matter whether the groups were initially formed around a charismatic leader, coalesced from unorganized aggregates of individuals, or were deliberately created as bureaucratic organizations. All that matters in constructing such a system of classification is the observable set of group properties at the moment of constructing the classification.[28]

WHAT IS TO BE DONE?

The claims set forth in this paper for the utility of mathematical and statistical ideas in the formulation of social theory have been relatively modest. Indeed, Merton's Epilogue to the Lazersfeld formalization of Merton's theory of homophily claims more for Lazarsfeld's argument than I have claimed for the relatively more advanced mathematical and statistical ideas in my other two examples. And, of course, it is possible to go much further in this direction, to argue that it is *only* with the aid of mathematics that a genuinely deductive theory, one permitting rigorous inferences from a small set of propositions, is even possible. Or, to take an even more extreme position, that the only worthwhile theory is a mathematically formulated theory.

348

This, I take it, was the position of the "Stanford theorists" during most of the 1960s.[29] The members of the Stanford group have already accomplished much of what they set out to do; they have developed several theories in mathematical form, most notably their theory of "status equilibration," and they have subjected these theories to stringent laboratory and field tests. Moreover, their students have now spread around the world, and their ideas are taking root in other departments of sociology. It is surely time, then, for a dispassionate review of their work, one that should seek to answer at least these two questions: (1) What has the Stanford group accomplished in the formulation of mathematical social theory that could not have been accomplished otherwise? (2) To what extent should the rest of us follow the Stanford lead?

My own position lies somewhere between the antimathematical and antiempirical position of Herbert Blumer[30] and the mathematical zealotry of the Stanford group. Sociologists ought to try to develop more mathematically formulated theories, even while recognizing that the time may never come when they can safely put all of their theoretical eggs into this basket.

In so severely limiting the goals I set for sociological theorists of the present and near future, I recognize that I may be labeling myself as a "retreatist,"[31] but I reject this label. Instead, I see myself as remaining squarely in the "conformist" category and trying to think of ways in which the social structure might be changed in order to give more sociologists access to the desired goals of mathematically formulated theories.

There are several ways in which sociologists who work mathematically with theory have acquired the necessary mathematical background. At the one extreme, there is a small minority who have come to sociology with a significant background in mathematics—for example, Paul F. Lazarsfeld, whose Vienna doctorate was in mathematics. Others, like James S. Coleman and Raymond Boudon, came to sociology from other fields that had a significant mathematical content; Coleman from chemical engineering and Boudon from econometrics. A third group, of which William N. McPhee[32] is an exemplar, recognized the value of mathematics only when they were already graduate students in sociology. McPhee had his first post-high school mathematics in an informal course that I taught one year at the Columbia University Bureau of Applied Social Research. A similar pattern is that of Robert McGinnis, who became a mathematical sociologist after attending a "summer institute" sponsored by the Social Science Research Council. Finally, there is that most remarkable category of all, the autodidact, or self-taught mathematical or statistical sociologist; my only example here is Alan B. Wilson, of the University of California, Berkeley, a statistical sociologist whose insight into linear statistical methods, such as factor analysis and regression analysis, is as dazzling as Lazarsfeld's into tabular analysis and scaling.

Clearly, then, many different means are available for achieving the subgoal of mathematical literacy.[33] This abundance of means for achieving mathematical literacy is all the more striking in view of the relatively small porportion of sociologists, be they graduate students or professionals, who are literate in mathematics.[34] It is now a full decade since Sibley's account of these deplorable facts, yet the general level of mathematical literacy among sociologists, especially among beginning graduate students, seems hardly to have risen at all.[35]

There is thus no lack of socially structured access to the means of mathematical literacy. I believe that the problem lies in the lack of attractiveness of the goal itself. More precisely, the goal of competence in mathematical and statistical sociology, whether at the level of original research or at the level of reading, does not yet seem legitimate to many sociologists. I offer here two suggestions for increasing that sense of legitimacy.

First, the Council of the American Sociological Association might suggest to the chairmen of all graduate departments of sociology that they state in their catalogs their intention of requiring a minimal level of literacy in mathematics, beginning at some date sufficiently far in the future as not to affect those students now "in the pipeline." I can envision some such chaste statement as this: "Beginning in 1980, the Department will require prospective graduate students to demonstrate their knowledge of elementary calculus and matrix algebra by either (1) presenting evidence of having satisfactorily completed such courses or (2) arranging to take an appropriate examination by mail." When I advocated such action by my own departments in the past, I was usually met with the objection that such a requirement would only drive students away toward other, apparently less demanding departments of sociology or to other fields, such as anthropology, where mathematical and statistical thinking is even less firmly established than in sociology. My suggestion that the Council of the ASA try to make such a requirement universal is intended to counter this objection. If such a requirement cost the field of sociology a few graduate students in the decades ahead, so be it!

"Ah, yes," the diehards will reply, "but such a requirement would have prevented Durkheim, Weber, or even Merton from becoming a sociologist. . . ." The question is, of course, moot. No one knows what Durkheim or Weber would have done, and I have not thought it necessary to ask Merton. Moreover, although I have been unable to verify this in published biographies, I believe that the kind of education that Durkheim and Weber received must have included some level of mathematics comparable to that advocated above. And, had such a requirement existed in 1931, when Merton began his graduate study at Harvard, I believe it altogether likely that he would have done whatever he had to do to become a sociologist. No two-semester course in undergraduate mathematics would have deterred a Merton, a Durkheim, or a Weber from becoming a sociologist!

My second suggestion for increasing the legitimacy of mathematics among sociologists derives from studies of the diffusion of intellectual innovations. Whether it be doctors contemplating a new drug,[36] poets adding new words to their poetic vocabularies,[37] or sociologists deciding on their analytic methods,[38] the spread of an intellectual innovation through such a field of inquiry or professional practice depends strongly on its advocacy or "certification" by the top elite. Even more important than mere verbal endorsement, when it is possible, is the actual adoption of the innovation by the members of such an elite; once the sociometric "star" of a clique of physicians adopts a new drug, its use diffuses rapidly through all those other physicians who look to him for advice or social support. It is this difference between verbal advocacy and overt behavior that makes me want to go beyond having the Council of the ASA simply recommend mathematical literacy.

What I have in mind here again involves the Council of the ASA, but this time in a program of planned social change. I would have it apply to a government agency or a private foundation for funds to train a small number of eminent social theorists—people now in their forties or fifties who do not use mathematical and statistical tools—to become competent in their use. If the Council were to approach this problem as a task of social organization, then it ought to be able to devise a program that would appeal to the funding agencies, attract the desired level of participants, and, most important of all, achieve its goals.

My own experience of some twenty-five years in avocationally teaching mathematics to sociologists suggests that something like the following program would achieve these goals:

> The program should be located at a comfortable, even luxurious spot relatively near to an established university but not in a densely settled urban area; it should thus appeal to sociologists with families as a comfortable place to spend a long summer but not one with a large number of potential distractions from the business at hand.[39] As a concrete example, the Center for Advanced Study in the Behavioral Sciences at Stanford would be ideal.

> The program would pay each participant for three months of summer work at his usual rate of pay, plus travel to and from the program's location for him and his immediate family.

> The program would recruit the best teachers and teaching assistants; it would assemble teaching aids, models, and audiovisual equipment of the highest quality. The program would organize its teaching activities in such a way as to make the experience maximally pleasant for each participant.

This last requirement deserves some elaboration. The participants should be able to get as much help as they need and to ask whatever questions they wish to ask, no matter how trivial, without embarrassing themselves. This means, for one thing, that all of the participants should be of approximately the same status in the field of sociology. It would not do, for example, to mix graduate students, young professionals, and older established professionals. This also means that, in addition to whatever lectures are delivered to plenary sessions of all participants, there should be daily opportunities for each participant to discuss his work with the instructors and assistants.

I have not thought it necessary to estimate the cost of such a program. It would be *very* expensive. Moreover, it would also require some sacrifice on the part of the staff and the students to be at all successful. In order that a significant amount of mathematics be learned in three months, I think it would be necessary for both the staff and the students to foreswear *all* other professional activities during the time spent at the program—no lecturing, no consultations, and, most of all, no writing!

One final requirement appears desirable: the program should emphasize to the students that there is no expectation of their becoming mathematical sociologists, of their trying to do research using mathematical tools, or of their teaching courses using such tools. The program's only aim is to create an elite of mathematically literate sociological theorists. Such a group of active theorists might well transform sociological theory in this century.

NOTES

1. Travis Hirschi and Hanan C. Selvin, *Principles of Survey Analysis* (New York: Free Press, 1973), chap. 10.
2. Robert K. Merton and Paul F. Lazarsfeld, "Friendship as Social Process: A Substantive and Methodological Analysis," in Morroe Berger, Theodore Abel, and Charles H. Page, eds., *Freedom and Control in Modern Society* (New York: Octagon Books, 1964), pp. 18–67.
3. Paul F. Lazarsfeld, "Mutual Effects of Statistical Variables," in Paul F. Lazarsfeld, Ann K. Pasanella, and Morris Rosenberg, eds., *Continuities in the Language of Social Research* (New York: Free Press, 1972), pp. 388–98.

    People who read the advertisements for Brand X are more likely to buy that brand than people who do not read such advertisements, but people who have already bought Brand X are also more likely to read its advertisements than people who have not bought it.
4. Merton and Lazarsfeld, "Friendship as Social Process," pp. 56–66.
5. Robert K. Merton, "Priorities in Scientific Discovery: A Chapter in the Sociology of Science," *American Sociological Review* 22 (December 1957): 635–59.
6. Robert K. Merton, "Fact and Factitiousness in Ethnic Opinionnaires," *American Sociological Review* 5 (February 1940): 13–28.
7. Murray A. Beauchamp, *Elements of Mathematical Sociology* (New York: Random House, 1970).
8. Frank Harary, "Merton Revisited: A New Classification for Deviant Behavior," *American Sociological Review* 31 (August 1966): 693–97.
9. In addition to the mathematical presentation by R. Duncan Luce and Albert D. Perry ("A Method of Matrix Analysis of Group Structure," *Psychometrika* 14 [June 1949]: 95–116), a layman's account of it appeared in Leon Festinger, Stanley Schachter, and Kurt Back, *Social Pressures in Informal Groups: A Study of Human Factors in Housing* (Palo Alto, Calif.: Stanford University Press, 1950), a book that overlaps Merton's own work on the social psychology of housing.
10. Robert K. Merton, *Social Theory and Social Structure*, rev. ed. (Glencoe, Ill.: Free Press, 1957).
11. L. J. Moreno, *Who Shall Survive?* (Washington, D.C.: Nervous and Mental Disease Monographs, 1934).
12. For groups as large as high school classes, the sociogram looks like the proverbial "bucket of worms"; see, for example, C. Wayne Gorden, *The Social System of the High School* (Glencoe, Ill.: Free Press, 1957), pp. 7–21.
13. Elaine Forsyth and Leo Katz, "A Matrix Approach to the Analysis of Sociometric Data: Preliminary Report," *Sociometry* 9 (1946): 340–47.

14. Leon Festinger, "The Analysis of Sociograms Using Matrix Algebra," *Human Relations* 2 (April 1949): 153–58.
15. *Ibid.*
16. Luce and Perry, "A Method of Matrix Analysis of Group Structure."
    Knowledge of elementary matrix algebra is now far more common among sociologists than it was in 1949. It is a good bet that the reader who needs help can get it from a student or a faculty member in a few minutes. For self-instruction, see Festinger, Schachter, and Back, *Social Pressures in Informal Groups,* chap. 8, or almost any standard text on linear algebra or finite mathematics.
17. For an application of this method to real data, see "The Growth of Scientific Knowledge: Theories of Deviance as a Case Study" by Stephen Cole elsewhere in this volume. Incidentally, Cole and I were unaware of our converging interests until after we had written first drafts of our papers.
18. Read "*A* prime."
19. Luce and Perry, "A Method of Matrix Analysis of Group Structure," and James S. Coleman and Duncan MacRae, Jr., "Electronic Processing of Sociometric Data for Groups up to 1,000 in Size," *American Sociological Review* 25 (October 1960): 722–27.
20. Richard D. Alba, "A Graph-Theoretic Definition of a Sociometric Clique," *Journal of Mathematical Sociology* 3 (1973): 113–26.
21. Merton, *Social Theory and Social Structure,* p. 308.
22. Hanan C. Selvin and Warren O. Hågstrom, "The Empirical Classification of Formal Groups," *American Sociological Review* 28 (June 1963): 400–11, reprinted in Theodore M. Newcomb and Everett K. Wilson, eds., *College Peer Groups,* NORC Monograph in Social Research no. 8 (Chicago: Aldine, 1966), with important criticisms and some afterthoughts by the authors.
23. Peter H. A. Sneath and Robert R. Sokal, *Principles of Numerical Taxonomy* (San Francisco: Freeman, 1973; first ed., 1963).
24. Merton, *Social Theory and Social Structure,* p. 309.
25. Sneath and Sokal, *Principles of Numerical Taxonomy,* p. 110.
26. Merton, *Social Theory and Social Structure,* chap. 9.
27. For example, John Knodel, "Law, Marriage and Illegitimacy in Nineteenth-Century Germany," *Population Studies* 20 (March 1967): 279–94, and "Infant Mortality and Fertility in Three Bavarian Villages: An Analysis of Family Histories from the Nineteenth Century," *Population Studies* 22 (November 1968): 297–318; and John Knodel and Etienne Van de Walle, "Breast Feeding, Fertility and Infant Mortality," *Population Studies* 21 (September 1967): 109–31.
28. One may speculate on how, if at all, Alfred C. Kinsey would have changed his procedures for studying sexual behavior if he had known of and agreed with the procedures of numerical taxonomy. Kinsey's approach was that of a classical taxonomist; he was deeply concerned with the sexual histories of his subjects and not merely with their sexual behavior at the time they were interviewed. See Alfred C. Kinsey *et al., Sexual Behavior in the Human Male* (Philadelphia: Saunders, 1948), and Edward M. Brecher, *The Sex Researchers* (Boston: Little, Brown, 1969).
29. For a selection of their papers on this subject, see Joseph Berger, Morris Zelditch, Jr., and Bo Anderson, eds., *Sociological Theories in Progress,* vol. 1 (Boston: Houghton Mifflin, 1966).
30. Herbert Blumer, "Sociological Analysis and the Variable," *American Sociological Review* 21 (December 1956): 683–90.
31. Merton, *Social Theory and Social Structure,* chap. 4.

32. William N. McPhee, *Formal Theories of Mass Behavior* (New York: Free Press, 1962).

33. What level of mathematical literacy is required for productive work in mathematical or statistical sociology? Of course, there is no upper limit to what is desirable here; the history of the physical sciences suggests that almost any branch of mathematics, however esoteric and abstract it may seem to be at the outset, will eventually yield applications to sociology. Thus, the sociologist who wants to do creative work with mathematical or statistical tools ought to acquire as many of them as he can and to continue acquiring them throughout his working life. It is perhaps more practical to ask for the minimum level of mathematical literacy that will enable a sociologist to *read* the work of such people as those listed in the preceding paragraph. My answer to this question is: a basic knowledge of the calculus and of matrix algebra. Many universities now offer sequences of courses in mathematics that provide this level of knowledge in one academic year. These courses are especially desirable when they are tailored to the needs of social scientists, draw their examples and problems from the social sciences, and attract high proportions of students from these fields.

34. Elbridge Sibley, *The Education of Sociologists in the United States* (New York: Russell Sage, 1963), and William M. Bates *et al.,* "Symposium on the Sibley Report," *American Sociologist* 2 (May 1967): 76–83.

35. This is my own impressionistic judgment, based on informal questioning of my own graduate students. The situation is surely better in departments with prominent mathematically oriented sociologists. Thus, Coleman had a steady supply of mathematically trained graduate students when he was at Johns Hopkins, and Otis Dudley Duncan will surely have a similar experience at Arizona. It will be particularly interesting to compare Coleman's experience at Chicago with Duncan's at Ann Arbor and Arizona. Coleman's attractiveness to mathematically trained graduate students may well be less in a large department of the first rank than Duncan's in a smaller and less prestigious department.

36. James S. Coleman, Elihu Katz, and Herbert Menzel, *Medical Innovation: A Diffusion Study* (Indianapolis: Bobbs-Merrill, 1966).

37. Josephine Miles, *Eras and Modes in English Poetry*, 2nd rev.. 3rd enl. ed. (Berkeley: University of California Press, 1964).

38. Hanan C. Selvin, "The Nondiffusion of an Intellectual Innovation," Presidential Address, delivered at the annual meeting of the Eastern Sociological Society, New York City, 1969.

39. Margaret Mead and Paul Byers, *The Small Conference: An Innovation in Communication* (The Hague: Mouton, 1968).

Relative Deprivation

ROBIN M. WILLIAMS, JR.

Nature has made men so equal in the faculties of the body and mind as that, though there be found one man sometimes manifestly stronger in body or of quicker mind than another, yet, when all is reckoned together, the difference between man and man is not so considerable as that one man can thereupon claim to himself any benefit to which another may not pretend as well as he. . . . *From this equality of ability arises equality of hope in the attaining of our ends.* And therefore if any two men desire the same thing, which nevertheless they cannot both enjoy, they become enemies; and in the way to their end, which is principally their own conservation, and sometimes their delectation only, endeavor to destroy or subdue one another.[1]

1. INTRODUCTION

THE basic concept of *relative deprivation* is deceptively simple: persons may feel that they are deprived of some desired state or thing, in comparison with some standard, or with the real or imagined condition of other people. The implications of this innocent-appearing statement are far from simple.

Many diverse examples demonstrate the reality of social comparisons, of evaluative judgments derived from such comparisons, and of both individual and collective responses to evaluated differences. Thus, the analyses in *The American Soldier*[2] showed that promotions in the air corps were rapid and widespread; in the military police, slow and scarce. But men in the air corps more often expressed dissatisfaction concerning promotions. In a second striking case, it was noted that racial discrimination was far more overt and pervasive in civilian life in the South than in the North, and Northern black soldiers stationed in the South were especially likely to express dissatisfaction

Robin M. Williams, Jr., is Henry Scarborough Professor of Social Science at Cornell University.

concerning discrimination. Yet preferences for Northern camps were not as great as might have been expected; many Southern blacks preferred to be stationed in the South, and Northern soldiers in Southern camps did not show any lowering of general adjustment to the army.

From these and a large number of other instances, Merton and Kitt developed their highly influential formulation of "relative deprivation theory."[3]

Since its initial formulation, the concept has been used to interpret findings concerning the effects upon task performance of noise and social stressors,[4] experiments on communications networks,[5] observations of vertical spatial positioning in social interaction,[6] studies of evaluative standards,[7] and social definitions of sickness or disease.[8] Conceptual developments have included analyses of the notions of deprivation,[9] injustice,[10] fair exchange, distributive justice, rewards, costs, and investments.[11]

Special interest has developed in the analysis of normative aspects of deprivation. Injustice may arise from an unfair rule, from the improper application of a norm, from the breach of a norm, or from a failure to properly consider a situation or a person. Thus relative deprivation may arise from comparisons involving conformity to procedural norms as well as from substantive inequalities.

To summarize, in somewhat oversimplified terms:

1. To receive less than one *wants* (desires, needs) results in a sense of *deprivation;*
2. to receive less than one *expects* results in feelings of *disappointment;*
3. to receive less than is *mandated* by accepted social rules and values (that to which one is entitled) results in a sense of *injustice.*

We would predict that, in general, a sense of injustice would be more potent than feelings of deprivation or disappointment as an antecedent to overt social behavior. A particularly strong effect would be expected when severe deprivations are regarded as arising from deceptive or coercive actions which violate high-ranking values.

2. CONCEPTUAL DEVELOPMENTS

Discussions of relative deprivation often deal at one and the same time with a complex cluster of related concepts.[12]

A first requirement is to make a sharp distinction among related notions, *viz.:* objective (or "absolute") deprivation, social comparison processes, and levels of aspiration or expectation.

Deprivation refers to a lack, dearth, absence, defect, want, deficiency. A lack is always defined by reference to something lacking. To speak of objective deprivation, then, we must mean only that something is present in one case and lacking to some degree in another case.

Relative deprivation *as a social condition* refers exclusively to the fact that one social unit *as compared with another* has "more" of some variable, for example, income, prestige, safety, piety. Since it is implied that deprivation refers to states defined as desirable by the relevant social actors, relative deprivation can be measured by reference to consensual norms of desirability. When such clear norms exist, collectivities are uniquely defined, and intergroup references are easily made.

When social norms are lacking, are ambiguous or vague, or are multiple and contradictory, social comparisons become highly variable and uncertain. Under these circumstances, sociopsychological factors play a greater part; that is, analysis must account for variations in perceptions and evaluations among individuals exposed to the same objective deprivations and to the same cultural and social referents for comparison.[13]

Now, since both aspirations and expectations are affected by social comparisons, "relative deprivation" could be defined simply as the condition of receiving less than one hopes for or expects to get. But this *intrapersonal* comparison clearly may differ in important respects from the comparison *between social units* that is implied by the ordinary use of the term "relative deprivation." For example, a primary response to a gap between personal aspiration and attainment is "frustration" or "disappointment," whereas the response to a gap between what one receives and what is received by reference individuals or groups is more likely to involve envy, resentment, and a sense of being unjustly treated.

Drawing on the work of Kurt Lewin and his associates on "level of aspiration,"[14] Festinger has proposed a sociopsychological theory of social comparison processes.[15] The scheme assumes that individuals are motivated to evaluate their opinions and abilities and that when "objective" (for example, physical) referents are not available these evaluations will be made by comparisons with other persons. In the absence of either a social or a physical point of reference for comparisons, evaluations are unstable. Referents will tend to be selected in such a way that significant comparisons are possible; specifically:

> Hypothesis III: The tendency to compare oneself with some other specific person decreases as the difference between his opinion or ability and one's own increases. . . .[16]

> Corollary III A: Given a range of possible persons for comparison, someone close to one's own ability or opinion will be chosen for comparison.[17]

The argument was that stable evaluations would develop when comparisons were made with similar others and that moderate differences between one's own opinions and abilities and those of the similar referent persons would result in change in the direction of those referents. However, to the extent that abilities are regarded as difficult to change because of nonsocial restraints,[18] Festinger argued, differences in opinion would be more threatening or otherwise unpleasant than differences in perceived abilities.[19] Although this presumption does not seem warranted as a universal rule, he correctly pointed to a tendency in competitive performances for individuals to focus upon a relatively narrow range for comparisons—excluding as irrelevant those "too good" or "too poor."[20] Experimental findings seemed consistent with the hypothesis that in competitive rankings, both high- and low-status individuals would seek to form segmental groupings of those of similar levels of performance.

Yet the experimental work had dealt with individuals—not with enduring collectivities, groups, or statuses—and only with opinions or performances, not with allocation of resources and rewards. The initial integration of sociological and psychological perspectives, so obviously needed, was sketched by Merton and Kitt. Among the permanent contributions of their analysis were the specifications of crucial areas requiring attention:[21] (1) multiple group affiliations, (2) multiple reference groups, (3) the dynamic processes of selection of reference groups, (4) the influence of social structure or situation upon these processes, (5) the processes that lead through comparisons to relative deprivation or relative satisfaction, and (6) the distinction between evaluations of group or institutional systems as against self-evaluations (for example, of personal achievement).

Building upon these central ideas, subsequent work revealed further essential distinctions[22]—and additional puzzles.[23] Kelley specified the difference between comparative and normative reference groups—the first serving as referents that supply standards for self-appraisal and the second as sources of one's own norms and values—but it is plain that a normative group may be also a comparative group. When the two types coincide, relative deprivation will be a matter of interindividual comparisons; if a comparison group that is not own's normative group is used, the comparison may be individual-to-referent-individual, individual-to-referent-group or group-to-group.

As Merton and Kitt pointed out, the analyses of *The American Soldier* had invoked three types of referents of comparisons: (1) actual associates in sustained social relations (friends, acquaintances, co-workers); (2) persons in the same status or social category (combat soldiers, captains); (3) persons in a different status or category. Relative deprivation or gratification may occur with reference to any attribute of these referents and may involve comparisons with higher, lower, equal, or unranked social positions.[24]

It thus gradually becomes apparent that relative deprivation can be treated formally as a subtype of a principle of *structural effects*—which, in turn, is part of a conception of *general consistency*.[25] The social condition of relative deprivation results from interpersonal (or intercollective) comparisons rather than from intrapersonal comparisons.[26] *It does not refer to levels of expectation or of aspiration except insofar as these involve comparisons among social units.* As the outcome of a social process, relative deprivation is a *consensually defined* condition and not merely a subjective *feeling-state of an individual.* The comparisons that result in feelings of relative deprivation, in other words, are *constrained comparisons* between definite social units or categories: married and single, officer and enlisted soldier, plumbers and professors, whites and blacks.

We recognize, of course, the ubiquity of a sense of deprivation or frustration arising from heightened expectations. For example, prior to 1930 doctors could do very little to cure disease,[27] but expectations and the physicians' performance were congruent. But with vastly improved capacity to actually cure, medical care is subject to expectations that outrun performance; hopes outrun expectations; and disappointment often is tinged with moral outrage concerning inequities in availability of help. Once more, in this sense, we see that "nothing fails like success." Note that it is not merely that aspirations and expectations have risen but that individuals are aware (or believe) that others have access to help that is not available to them.

Responses to the processes of social comparisons are affected by individuals' beliefs and perceptions concerning the "causes" or "loci of control" of their situation. Attributions of causality or control may be directed toward the self or ego, toward other individuals, toward social institutions and arrangements, or toward nonsocial factors.

Evidently, then, in analyzing phenomena of relative deprivation, it is essential to take into account at least the following categories or variables:

1. Attribute or dimension that is being evaluated
2. Other relevant attributes involved in comparison processes
3. Types of comparison units used as referents
4. Perceived loci of control or causation
5. Criteria accepted as legitimate for allocation of scarce values

Each of these aspects requires further explication. *Any* scarce value may become the object of processes of social comparison. It would be pointless to develop ad hoc listings. More useful will be illustrations of research findings. First, we will examine how *changes* affect both gratifications and the standards by which gratifications are defined and appraised.

3. RELATIONSHIPS AMONG CHANGES IN GRATIFICATIONS, EXPECTATIONS, AND ASPIRATIONS

In a classic study, Duesenberry argues that the ratio of savings to income is independent of the absolute level of income and, therefore, that over a long period of rising income the savings ratio would remain approximately constant.[28] On first glance, this hypothesis surely must seem contrary to common sense. As real income rises over time, it could be plausibly argued, the savings ratio will rise—unless offset by trend factors such as a shift from rural to urban living. But, in fact, detailed examination of a wide range of data showed that during "... periods of steadily rising income the aggregative savings ratio tends to be independent of income." In addition, moreover, there is a conclusion of special bearing on the concept of relative deprivation: "Over the trade cycle, the savings ratio is dependent on the ratio of current income to previous peak income."[29]

The analysis indicates that consumers establish a set of preferences for goods and services that are "interdependent and irreversible." And Duesenberry explicitly bases his theory on the assumption that consumption expenditures are strongly influenced by *comparisons* with other persons' consumption and, more generally, "... that the utility index is a function of relative rather than absolute consumption expenditures."[30]

More recent data[31] and analyses have supported these suppositions and have specified additional implications. Thus, expectations do change over time with changes in income, but at a given time expectations outweigh actual income change in effects on consumer behavior.[32] And the level of expressed satisfaction clearly is strongly dependent on relative economic position.[33]

Data relating income to reported happiness[34] have been collected in some thirty surveys in nineteen countries. A critical synthesis by Easterlin[35] arrives at the following conclusions:

> *In all societies, more money for the individuals typically means more individual happiness. However, raising the incomes of all does not increase the happiness of all.* The happiness-income relation provides a classic example of the logical fallacy of composition—*what is true for the individual is not true for society as a whole.*
> The resolution of this paradox lies in the relative nature of welfare judgments. Individuals assess their material well-being, not in terms of the absolute amount of goods they have, but relative to a social norm of what goods they ought to have.[36]

The international comparisons showed the following patterns:

1. Within a given country, at all time periods, the higher are individuals' incomes, the greater is the proportion reporting feelings of general satisfaction or happiness.
2. The proportions reporting happiness are not appreciably higher in the richer nations than in the poorer ones.
3. In the United States, where a series of samplings have been taken from 1946 to 1970, average happiness increased with increasing real income until 1957 and then dropped back to near its original level.[37]

Furthermore, increased objective levels of specified sources of gratification (income, housing, occupational rank, and so on) often are followed by increased dissatisfaction. Observe this example:

> About half of the nation's blacks remained dissatisfied with their housing throughout the 1960's. This situation contrasts sharply with white dissatisfaction with housing, which has steadily declined from 28 percent in 1949 to only 18 percent in 1969. Note, too, that black dissatisfaction with housing *increased* sharply between 1949 and 1963—from 32 percent to 54 percent—even though we know from considerable census data that black housing significantly improved in the aggregate throughout the 1950's.[38]

There seems to be adequate ground for thinking that expectancies and normative claims generally are adjusted rather promptly to large and continuing *increases* in real income. Although, as Durkheim long ago insisted, the "upward" process involves psychological strains and social dislocations, it is less difficult to raise standards of consumption than to lower them. Rapid decreases in reward are especially resisted. Thus, gradual reductions in gratifications, spread out over an extended period, are less likely to be experienced as severe deprivation than when the same total reduction occurs all at once or within a very short period. Feelings of relative deprivation occur when levels of gratification are falling in comparison to reference points that have remained constant or increased. Downwardly mobile workers under some conditions tend to retain both the aspirations and the "conservatism" typical of the stratum or group of origin rather than those of the lower-status stratum of destination.[39] Under other conditions, downwardly mobile persons manifest extreme discontent and often become politically radicalized.[40] What are the crucial differentiating conditions associated with strikingly different patterns of response?

The tendency of normative expectations and claims to rise to match increased opportunities, but to be maintained in the face of decreasing gratifications, has been called the "ratchet-effect." Why is there a ratchet-effect and under what circumstances will the ratchet give way?

Several major factors have been identified as important in maintaining or changing normative anchorages:

1. Higher aspirations are most likely to develop when and only when gains are attributed to one's own efforts or to the efforts of members of one's own group.[41]
2. Maintenance of standards in the face of objective decline is favored by:
   a. prior prolonged socialization into an ideology of open opportunity and individual success and responsibility;[42]
   b. functional proximity and frequent communication with persons who continue to hold the values and norms of the *status quo ante;* and
   c. a continuous trend of repeated substantial increments will have greater effects on aspirations, wants, norms of deservedness, and expectations than will either a single sudden sharp increase or increase reached through an erratic sequence of rising and falling episodes.

More generally, the following hypotheses are sufficiently well supported to warrant statement and further investigation:

1. When levels of real income received are rising for a majority of a population over a substantial period, there will be increases in expected levels, in aspirations, and in feelings that the achieved levels are appropriate and deserved (that is, an increase in levels of normative claim).
2. Of the three consequences, aspirations will increase most, expectations next, and normative levels (of claims or rights) will change least.
3. Increases in incomes and other rewards are more quickly accepted as normal and warranted than are decreases, and greater social opposition usually will be generated by rapid decreases.
4. Declines in rewards are least resisted when they are (a) slowly experienced over a long period and (b) do not initially bring the actual level

below a minimal normative level, for example, approximately the lowest experienced by adults in their working lifetime.

5. Decreases in rewards are most easily accepted when generally shared throughout a community or society, for example, deprivations in the Great Depression of the 1930s and those of the civilian population in World War II.

6. Aspirations will be affected most strongly when the increased (or decreased) gratifications follow upon acts *of the individual or his group* (decisions, rituals, petitions, threats, achievements, and so on) that are perceived as *bringing about a higher or lower level.*

7. Increased gratification perceived as accidental, fortuitious, bestowed, and the like is less likely to generate the expectation of recurrence or the aspiration to bring about such recurrence.

8. Changes in an individual's gratification level are most likely to lead to changes in both expectations and aspirations when *shared* with many others of similar position and circumstances.

9. Changes in claims to increased reward of some particular type can be produced by prior changes in some other category of right or privilege. Thus, in the United States, increased legal and political rights and increased educational levels were gained by ethnic and racial minorities during the 1950s and early 1960s, whereas relative income shares did not change greatly. Median annual income of nonwhite families as a percentage of income of white families was 51 in 1947 and 55 in 1965. (Since income [in constant 1971 dollars] was rising for both categories, the *absolute* gap actually widened from $2,784 in 1947 to $4,151 in 1965.)[43]

Indeed, a striking feature of social stratification in the United States since World War II has been the fixity of the income distribution from the late 1940s into the 1970s.[44] Furthermore, essentially the same rank ordering of occupational categories according to general prestige has persisted since the earliest studies in the 1920s.[45]

Given this stability of a highly unequal distribution of scarce values, during a long period of rising real incomes, it is understandable that relative deprivation remains important.

4. SELECTION OF SOCIAL COMPARISON UNITS: CAUSES AND CONSEQUENCES

We now turn to the *cross-sectional, or "locational,"* contexts that consist of the social units—whether statuses, categories, or collectivities—among which comparisons may be made.

Feelings of relative deprivation are encouraged by any social process that diminishes barriers to comparison and emulation between the advantaged and the less advantaged. Thus, in the United States over recent decades, political and legal rights, access to education, equal access to public facilities, and common exposure to mass media are all structural conditions encouraging black people to compare their income, jobs, and housing with those of white people. An inexact but serviceable generalization is: *The less the social distance between two unequally rewarded segments of a society, the more likely it is that comparisons will be made and that such comparisons will result in perception of relative deprivation or relative subordination or both.*[46]

Any differential in gratifications and deprivations as between any two social units, *A* and *B*, is the more likely to be noted and evaluated:

1. ... the greater the similarity between *A* and *B* in *generalized ascriptive or assigned statuses,* especially age, sex, kinship, marital status, ethnic collectivity, citizenship, or societal membership,

2. the more similar *A* and *B* are in *functional qualifications for rewarded performances,* for example, in technical training or education, experience, test performance;

3. the greater the similarity in rewards or gratifications in *most of a series* of items other than the one in which there is a marked differential,

4. *the more frequently each party receives information* about the gratifications and deprivations of the other party;[47]

5. the *higher the rank in a hierarchy of values* of the gratification being compared,

6. the *more rapid is any change* in a differential between *A* and *B;*

7. the more the differentials in levels of gratifications and deprivations *diverge from expectations* established prior to a given time (T_1),

8. the more the differentials diverge from *norms* of "right" or "appropriateness" established prior to a given time (T_1);

9. the larger the absolute size of the differentials,

10. the fewer the number of perceived distinct gradations among groups or categories, that is, the less continuous the differentials,

11. the more prevalent is anticipatory socialization for positively evaluated social positions and rewards that turn out to be extremely scarce, especially when scarcity is maintained by "arbitrary," categorical barriers.

12. "Fraternalistic" relative deprivation requires that Ego experience deprivations as due to membership in a category or collectivity sharing a common fate.[48] Such perceptions are especially likely when there are large differentials in control of scarce values as between members of highly visible social categories in a nominally universalistic occupational system.[49] When comparisons deal with groups or categories as such, the relative *gratification* of the individual becomes the relative *superiority* of a collectivity; the phenomenon is vividly illustrated in countless forms of invidious social distinctions.[50]

13. It is well established that, on the average, ambitions are *not* equally stimulated at all economic and social prestige levels. Inequality of education, income, and occupation in the parental generation is influential in producing differentials of aspiration and expectation among children and youths.[51]

Although empirical illustrations rarely correspond exactly to such analytical hypotheses, the above generalizations have been rendered plausible by data from widely scattered studies.

Many studies demonstrate that crucial comparisons tend to be directed toward nearby or similar social statuses or collectivities. Data for England and Wales, for example, show that the proportion of workers *who accept as "proper" an income near their own actual level* is higher for manual than for nonmanual workers at every income level. Relative satisfaction is especially high among manual workers whose actual income is in the higher brackets.[52] A reasonable inference is that manual workers tend to compare themselves with other manual workers, whereas persons in nonmanual occupations more often compare their incomes to those of higher-income business and professional strata.

Such comparisons rarely involve only a single aspect or attribute, such as income, but rather concern several bases of appraisal. For example, Patchen[53] found that in making specific comparisons of wages, oil refinery employees explain their satisfaction or dissatisfaction by the consonance or dissonance between pay differentials and "attributes relevant to pay." *Investments* or *qualifications* that are invoked to justify dissatisfaction with relative rewards include: education, skill, experience, responsibility, seniority, hard work, risk, and hardship.

When inequalities are stable, pervasive, ritualized, and strongly defended and enforced, the accompanying ideologies typically emphasize great social, cultural, or biological differences between the superordinate and the subordinate. But there is today, a "... general world-wide revolt against the 'premise of inequality.' "[54] Furthermore, urbanization and mobility juxtapose sharp and obvious inequalities that formerly were more nearly insulated by geographic and social barriers.[55]

Comparisons of the kinds that tend to produce feelings of relative deprivation are favored by emphasis on individual rights and responsibilities, on achievement, on universalism. To the degree that collective rights and responsibilities are emphasized, members of other collectivities are regarded as socially distant and "alien." If major rewards are defined as achieved rather than ascribed, any ascriptive bases for allocations tend to come into question. When *both* the norms of universalism-achievement and of ascription-particularism are simultaneously applied—as in systems of ethnic discrimination—the referents of comparison are likely to be ambiguous and situationally variable.

The more a society is organized in terms of universalistic norms, rather than rights and duties that hold only for particular relationships, the more likely it is that persons will compare their own gratifications and deprivations with those of other persons occupying a wide range of particular statuses.[56] Typically, there will be substantial inequalities in the distribution of scarce values among incumbents of these various statuses. Therefore, *the more universalistic the normative structure of a society (or other collectivity), the greater the likelihood of relative deprivation.* A specific implication is that the greater the number of legal provisions of equal rights for all members of a society, the more likely it is that remaining inequalities will be regarded by those less advantaged as deprivational or unjust or both.

Furthermore, to the extent that norms of performance rather than norms of ascription actually prevail, positions will be subject to relatively frequent change. Also, normative emphasis on achievement tends to link rewards closely to sense of personal worth. For both these reasons, *an achievement-oriented system tends to generate feelings of relative deprivation.*

But social comparisons are not always made. Hence, a comprehensive account of relative deprivation must deal with the conditions producing comparison or noncomparison. If comparisons are made, they may or may not result in perceptions or feelings of relative deprivation (gratification). If there are outcomes of relative deprivation (gratification), the further consequences, if any, must be elucidated.[57]

Selection of referents that involve relative deprivation or relative subordination seem to violate the principle of seeking comparisons favorable to self-regard. But such selections nevertheless often occur, because of one or several of the following conditions:

1. *Overwhelming salience:* The referent is so highly visible, powerful, intrusive, or otherwise immediately consequential that it cannot be ignored.
2. There is *expectation of locomotion* into the locus of the referent individual or collectivity, for example, age-grades, social rank, income strata, educational levels.
3. *Normative claims,* for example, norms of equality; norms of obligatory achievement striving; or consensually derived rules or obligations that direct comparisons with models, such as successful executives, saintly leaders, brilliant scholars, renowned scientists.
4. *Multiple dimensions of appraisal:* Comparisons may be made, and the implications accepted, because the referent individual or collectivity shares many attributes in common with Ego but excels in one or more other attributes. Similarity thus induces comparison, whereas relative deprivation is simply a correlated consequence. On the other hand, such comparisons do heighten relative deprivation, and dissatisfaction may be reduced by selecting a reference group having dissimilar characteristics that legitimize the inferior position of Ego.[58] Thus, when total similarity is great, comparisons on a specified attribute of ranking are likely to be confined to relatively small ranges, for example, workers of only slightly higher incomes.[59]

In a highly differentiated society of mass consumption, potentially invidious comparisons are very numerous. Conceivably the entire society could become "colloidal," with no enduring lines of clear or massive cleavage anywhere. Conceivably, on the contrary, the lines of comparison could become polarized and cumulative. What conditions are likely to lead toward one or the other of these outcomes?

A plausible set of predictions is that the conditions favoring the development of "class," or other massive collective, awareness of inequalities and relative deprivation include:

1. Massing; concentration of population; functional proximity of similarly situated persons
2. Differential interaction within-category and across-category (class, ethnic, racial, and so on):
   a. Amount: great within-category; moderate across-category
   b. Kind: fraternalistic within-category; competitive or coercive across-categories
3. Number of collectivities, categories, or strata: few
4. Continuous or discontinuous character of the categories, collectivities, or strata: clear boundaries, with little overlap of category memberships and referents
5. Social instability: a large amount of "uprooting" (rapid shifts in interaction patterns, referents, norms, and so on)
6. Degree of social mobility:
   a. intergenerational: high
   b. career: moderate
   c. short-term: low
7. Degree of "objective" inequalities: high
8. Variables in which inequalities exist (income, wealth, education, occupational prestige, authority, power, safety, lifestyle): differentials in power and income seem of primary importance but any of the main aspects may become crucial under some conditions. It is a safe generalization that conspicuous coincidence of several types of inequalities sharpens boundaries and tends to enhance collective awareness.

5. CONDITIONS AFFECTING LIKELIHOOD THAT SOCIAL COMPARISONS WILL BE FOLLOWED BY RESPONSES OF "RELATIVE DEPRIVATION"

Assuming that marked inequalities do exist and that social comparisons are indeed made, what additional factors may help us to understand why the outcome sometimes is indifference or neutrality, sometimes relative gratification, and sometimes relative deprivation?[60]

A first condition is the degree to which inequalities coincide with boundaries of social categories and collectivities. Thus, an "ingroup" will form when there is a combination of high similarity or interdependence within an interacting aggregate of persons and high dissimilarity as against another definable aggregate. The objective dissimilarity will be perceived as a basis for feelings of social distance, and the within-aggregate similarities will be perceived as a basis of closeness; these perceptions and evaluations will result in further accentuating the division of in- and out-groupings.

Given strong boundaries among collectivities, it is reasonable to predict that comparisons are most likely to be made, by any given Ego, with social objects that:

1. are highly visible: clearly definable and frequent objects of attention;
2. are functionally proximate: frequently encountered or otherwise consequential for Ego's interests and values;
3. are similar to Ego, in some master status that is a primary basis for allocation of rewards;
4. represent characteristics or social positions that are consensually defined as attainable by Ego;
5. represent values, interests, beliefs, or behavior patterns that are consensually defined in Ego's main membership groups as forbidden, inferior, immoral, or otherwise disvalued (negative comparison referent; "contrast conception").

Comparisons of the allocations of any scarce value among individuals or collectivities can focus either on current levels or on changes through time. The most cogent theories would predict that changes rather than static comparisons would be the more likely to produce marked positive or negative evaluations.

Very complex possibilities of comparisons are created when simultaneous consideration is given to present condition, change, expectation, type of scarce value, normative definitions, and multiple referents. But two of the most important referents of social comparisons in our society are income and occupational prestige. In aggregate evaluations, there is a consistent tendency to maintain a stable hierarchy of occupational rankings, in terms of both actual and normative, or recommended, incomes. Also, at different levels of absolute income the percentage differences separating major occupational groupings tend to be kept the same. Thus, Hayes finds in diverse samples from various Western countries that when persons are asked to estimate a just or fair income for each of ten well-known occupations, the recommended allocations:

1. follow the prestige ordering of occupations reported in numerous national studies;
2. are the more egalitarian, the more "Left" the raters are in political allegiance;
3. are essentially uncorrelated with the total amount of income allocated to the ten occupations;
4. with few exceptions, are consistently ranked across occupations whether the raters are egalitarian or nonegalitarian in general orientation;
5. give disproportionately large incomes to a few occupations, with wide gaps between these high-prestige occupations but with little spacing among other occupations.

Finally, although the data are not conclusive, it appears likely that the attributed income gaps between occupations are very similar in several different countries and among persons of widely divergent political orientations.[61] There is a perceptual-evaluative ordering that follows some pervasive implicit norms.[62] What some of these norms are is indicated by the tendency for higher ranks to be attributed to occupations representing high levels of responsibility, skill, training, and investment or sacrifice.

The following hypotheses are proposed as generally consistent with the available—although scanty—evidence, and accordingly as worthy of further specification and testing.

1. The comparisons that are likely to be most salient and consequential for feelings of relative deprivation involve social referents immediately above and below Ego's position.
2. A narrowing of differentials between Ego and those just below him are more salient and consequential than widening of differentials between Ego and those above his position.
3. Actual *reversals of rank order* will have greater stimulus value than changes in distance between ranks, as long as clearly perceptible, socially recognized differentials still obtain.
4. A widening differential with upper groupings or a narrowing differential with lower groupings will be less likely to produce a strong sense of relative deprivation when Ego's levels of returns are rising than when his levels are declining relative to the immediate past.
5. The greater the lifetime gain of Ego in relation to his generational or career starting level, the less likely is he to be strongly resentful of gains of those whose starting levels were higher.

Reactions of relative deprivation will have greatly different consequences depending on whether deprivation is conceived in *fraternalistic* (collective, "shared fate") or *egoistic* (individualistic) terms.[63] It is accordingly important to specify the circumstances most conducive to fraternalistic or egoistic orientations.

At the risk of leaving out many complexities, we will say that in general a fraternal rather than individualistic orientation is favored when similarity of condition prevails within a social category and a moderate (but not too large) difference in rewards and privileges separates its members from those of another collectivity within the same society. Fraternal responses are favored by ease of perceiving similarity. Hence, gross signalizing features common to members of a collectivity should—*ceteris paribus*—favor collective definitions of relative deprivation. Also, relative closure of intimate social interaction within the boundaries of a social category favors fraternalism.

Given similarity, visibility, and relative closure of interaction, the pressure toward fraternalism is vastly increased by strong barriers, of any kind, against social locomotion out of the category, as well as by "attachments" (for example, membership ties) within the collectivity.

A strong collective reaction of fraternal relative deprivation is to be expected, accordingly, when a close-knit social stratum of high homogeneity and visibility is suddenly reduced in wealth, income, power, prestige, safety, and so on, or is blocked from advancement while other "visible" social categories greatly increase their advantages. Predominantly egoistic responses, on the other hand, will characterize individuals in a situation of relatively rapid change in the positions of individuals between and among loose-knit and internally heterogeneous categories. Change in the positions of collectivities has effects both through differences in *sequences* and through *processes of comparison carried through time*.

Thus, the same objective "reward" (or "penalty") will have different effects in different sequences. A succession of rewards produces lowered incremental value of added units (for example, + + + +), whereas the same positive stimulus produces higher gratification when it follows a series of negative stimuli (for example, − − − +).[64]

Furthermore, changes in the relative positions of individuals and other social units always constitute social signals. Such signals not only indicate a current state of affairs but also affect expectations and aspirations. A special case of this signaling property is what Hirschman calls the "tunnel effect."[65] If two lines of automobiles are stopped in a tunnel and one finally begins to move, the initial reaction of drivers in the lane still stalled is not relative deprivation and resentment but relief and hope ("my turn will come soon"). Only if one's own movement is then inordinately delayed does the positive mood give way to frustration, irritation, moral outrage and so on. Hirschman suggests that poor people in developing countries initially accept vast inequalities in the belief that eventually they themselves also will benefit from economic development. But the tunnel effect is temporary. If hope is deferred time after time, while others move ahead, disillusionment is likely to be marked and the sense of relative deprivation especially strong.[66]

Actual historical social movements typically represent a complex interaction of the factors we have examined. Cases in point are numerous. An almost classic large-scale instance is that of "actual gains and psychological losses" among black Americans between 1945 and 1964.[67]

Open-class societies of increasing affluence tend also to experience an initial weakening of segmentary social structures[68] and of insulating barriers to emulation and invidious comparisons.[69] Responses of relative deprivation are minimized by: slow social change, low geographic mobility, low education, little exposure to mass media, sharp boundaries between strata and among ethnic groups and local communities, low rates of upward and downward social mobility, and primary importance of kinship as a basis of social organization. Individualized relative deprivation will be high under the opposite set of conditions.

A sense of relative subordination, or fraternal deprivation, is likely to be maximized when distinctive strata and ethnic collectivities are preserved in a society of much mobility and mass communication that is marked by great inequalities and rapid social change. Such a society combines rapid change and high aspirations with rigid structural barriers. Therefore, highly segmented societies provide extremely hazardous conditions for political stability if initial economic growth greatly widens and perpetuates inequalities among classes, regions, ethnic groupings, and the like.[70] Collective rather than only individual resistance, protest, or conflict will be the more likely, the greater the similarity of condition among those deprived and the sharper the contrast with some comparative segment of the society.[71] Hence, any society that strongly institutionalizes criteria of technical performance but categorically excludes or discriminates against ascribed-status categories is "asking for trouble."

The most striking latent regularity we seem to detect in the diverse data here reviewed is that a sense of *relative deprivation as a response to differentials in social positions is likely to be low when inequalities are stable, high when there are large and rapid changes.* "Adjustment" is the major type of response to large-scale, relatively constant inequalities which have existed over one or more generations. Resentment and protest are typical mass responses to large-scale inequalities under conditions of rapid change.

We suggest further that substantial *absolute* changes in societal levels of wealth, income, and power necessarily increase the prevalence of feelings of *relative* deprivation, except under some of the special circumstances of war and revolution. This result occurs because large and rapid changes almost never affect all main collectivities and statuses in the same way or equally. Therefore, relative position acquires high visibility, and those whose absolute or relative position is worsening will be aware of the differential rates of change. The effects will be greatest when relative worsening comes after enough stability that important segments of the society have built up firm expectations and claims.

6. RELATIVE DEPRIVATION AND COLLECTIVE ACTION

When we earlier examined relative deprivation as a condition to be accounted for, the primary question was: What antecedent and accompanying conditions are necessary or necessary and sufficient to produce the phenomena? When we now look upon relative deprivation as a hypothetical explanatory variable, either as temporarily prior or intervening between a causal factor and an outcome, the central query is: Given that relative deprivation exists to some degree, what consequences ensue in differing causal contexts?

The outcomes for which relative deprivation has been invoked as an explanatory variable include a diverse collection of psychological and social phenomena: social movements;[72] revolutions;[73] dissatisfaction with promotions, military draft, racial discrimination, overseas service, rewards of officers and enlisted men;[74] voting and voting preferences;[75] career decisions; civil disorders and rebellions.[76]

Efforts to find strong effects from status incongruity as a factor in relative deprivations have been inconclusive. But one important set of processes does seem to involve both incongruity and relative deprivation as effective explanatory conditions. The general effect of a high rate of individual economic advancement out of a low-status stratum is to reduce the likelihood of political mobilization of the disadvantaged segment as a solidary collectivity—especially if the upward economic mobility brings a substantial amount of social honor and is followed by social integration into the upper strata.[77] But, if upward economic or political mobility is accompanied by rejection of claims to acceptance, the rebuff is likely to drive the newly emerged middle- and upper-class individuals back into their (ethnic, racial, religious, regional) collectivity of origin. Such a combination of high economic or political position and of low social honor and acceptance favors "radicalization of leadership," that is, a collective-political attempt to change the existing system. An essential generalization in accounting for this outcome has been stated by Lopreato: "The likelihood of retaining political links with the class of origin (avoiding resocialization) increases with the degree of status discrepancies, namely, rejection."[78]

A qualification must be added. If the upwardly mobile segment is large and becomes both spatially and socially separate from the lower-class population of origin, a "passive rejection" by polite exclusion from the upper strata is insufficient to evoke a *collective* political response.[79] But sociopolitical arrangements that impel minority middle- and upper-class individuals to retain "ethnic" identity will facilitate politicization in any situation of crisis or polarization—possibly a main effect of segregation and discrimination against middle-class black people in the United States.[80]

We have seen that relative deprivation is one among many components affecting social behavior and that the status of relative deprivation as an intervening variable often has been indirect or inferential.[81] At the very least, adequate data for predictions of consequences must include direct indicators of relative deprivation and evidence of both the constraints on and the instrumentalities available to those who are deprived. Crawford and Naditch have contributed a useful typology combining relative deprivation-gratification with perceived locus of control over means of action. Their review of data on urban riot participation illustrates the usefulness of simultaneous consideration of discontent and of orientations concerning efficacy ("locus of control," or "fate control"). External fate is stressed by persons of low education, low economic position, and "traditional" (for example, rural, Southern) social background, whereas a sense of internal control and individual or collective efficacy is favored by relatively high education and by socialization in Northern urban settings. The crucial factor associated with a sense of powerlessness, however, is low income.[82]

The combination of characteristics that seems most likely to produce sustained militancy or protest would be: collective relative deprivation, strong sense of personal efficacy, and sense of collective lack of power.[83] Concretely, these conditions are likely to arise when a visible social category is severely deprived in income or political control relative to comparison groupings and when the members of the deprived collectivity have relatively high levels of education and political awareness.[84]

Two striking findings of the most carefully controlled analyses of ecological or community-level factors related to urban civil disturbances of the 1960s are

(1) that the sheer size of the black population was the best predictor of rioting, and (2) disorders were most likely to appear where the conditions of the black population were objectively least oppressive or deprivational. A plausible interpretation is that many black persons were responding to multiple deprivations and frustrations that were not local but national in salience.[85]

But discontent alone does not produce collective action.[86] Unorganized and dispersed masses of discontented people are not in a position to generate effective political pressure.[87] Only through communication and the subsequent emergence of leadership, authority, and division of functions—that is, organization—can discontent be mobilized and focused into collective dissent, protest, and structured opposition. Revolutions, for example, require not only rising expectations and massive sudden frustration (or massive threat to established interests), but the deprivation must be extended over a period long enough to activate organized protest and must strongly affect all or most of the main social formations supporting the political regime.[88] Furthermore, the main repressive forces of the regime (primarily, the army and the police) must not be overwhelmingly active and committed to quelling any protest—otherwise one will have "abortive" rebellion that will be decisively crushed.

As these few examples clearly imply, for predicting the consequences of relative deprivation three things are essential: (1) theoretical identification of a few crucial independent and dependent variables, (2) specification of major types of social contexts in which predictions are to be sought, and (3) multivariate analysis of antecedent-consequent relationships.

Our tentative suggestions for hypotheses answering to these difficult requirements include the following propositions.

1. The deprivations most likely to have the larger effects on subsequent attitudes and behavior involve *collective social comparisons* rather than only comparisons with *internalized standards of the individual.*
2. Relative deprivations prominently involving *power and prestige* are more consequential for collective action than those involving primarily other types of scarce values.
3. Major effects will be greatest when relative deprivations are (a) sudden and (b) involve widened *absolute* differences.
4. Essential distinctions among types of behavioral outcomes include: (a) individualized adjustments and strivings, (b) primarily expressive short-term collective protest or rebellion, and (c) sustained and organized collective action.
5. Differential likelihood of the outcomes listed in 4 (a, b, c) will be substantially affected by the relative resources and the degree of mobilization of dissenting and resisting collectivities and by perceived efficacy of control over means of action.
6. Discontented social elements are most likely to have a sense of high efficacy ("internal control") when (a) their objective resources have been increasing rapidly, (b) the opposing collectivities show weakness or

irresolution, (c) intragroup communication is intensive, and (d) intra-group consensus is high with regard to both grievances and locus of control.

It would follow from these hypotheses that sustained organized protest and pressure for change will be maximized under the following conditions:

1. a collective relative deprivation, especially in
2. prestige (or "social respect") and political power, which
3. occurs suddenly and results in an increased absolute gap between comparison referents, when
4. the deprived collectivity is large, commands substantial economic and political resources, has recently increased in relative power, is internally cohesive and is linked together by rapid and extensive communication, and when
5. the established regime and other control elements of the society have given signals of weakness, indecision, disunity, or actual encouragement of militant dissent.

NOTES

1. Thomas Hobbes, *The Leviathan: Parts I and II* (New York: Liberal Arts Press, 1958), pp. 104–5. (Italics added.)
2. Samuel A. Stouffer *et al.*, *The American Soldier: Adjustment During Army Life* (Princeton, N.J.: Princeton University Press, 1949), vol. I, pp. 250–58 and 550–66.
3. Robert K. Merton and Alice S. Kitt, "Contributions to the Theory of Reference Group Behavior," in Robert K. Merton and Paul F. Lazarsfeld, eds., *Continuities in Social Research: Studies in the Scope and Method of the American Soldier* (Glencoe, Ill.: Free Press, 1950).
4. David C. Glass and Jerome E. Singer, *Urban Stress: Experiments on Noise and Social Stressors* (New York: Academic Press, 1972).
5. James C. Moore, Jr., Eugene B. Johnson, and Martha S. C. Arnold, "Status Congruence and Equity in Restricted Communication Networks," *Sociometry* 35, no. 4 (December 1972): 519–37.
6. Donald W. Ball, *Microecology: Social Situations and Intimate Space* (Indianapolis: Bobbs-Merrill, 1973), pp. 24–25, and Herbert Spencer, *The Principles of Sociology*, part 4 (New York: Appleton and Co., 1898), vol. 2, p. 198.
7. Archibald O. Haller and Joseph Wallfel, "Significant Others and Their Expectations: Concepts and Instruments to Measure Interpersonal Influence on Status Aspirations," *Rural Sociology* 37, no. 4 (December 1972): 591–619, and Martin Patchen, "The Effect of Reference Group Standards on Job Satisfaction," in Herbert H. Hyman and Eleanor Singer, eds., *Readings in Reference Group Theory and Research* (New York: Free Press, 1968), p. 336.
8. Peter Sedgwick, "Mental Illness is Illness," *Salmagundi* 20 (Summer/Fall 1972): 212, a quarterly journal published by Skidmore College.
9. Robin M. Williams, Jr., *The Reduction of Intergroup Tensions*, Bulletin 57 (New York: Social Science Research Council, 1947), p. 53.

10. Edmond Cahn, "Justice," *International Encyclopedia of the Social Sciences* (New York: Free Press and Macmillan, 1968), vol. 8, p. 347.

11. Peter M. Blau, "Justice in Social Exchange," chapter 4 in Herman Turk and Richard L. Simpson, eds., *Institutions and Social Exchange: The Sociologies of Talcott Parsons & George C. Homans* (Indianapolis: Bobbs-Merrill, 1971), pp. 56–68, and George C. Homans, *Social Behavior: Its Elementary Forms* (New York: Harcourt Brace Jovanovich, 1961), p. 75. See Talcott Parsons: "Levels of Organization and the Mediation of Social Interaction," chapter 2 in Turk and Simpson, *Institutions and Social Exchange*, pp. 23–35.

12. Joseph R. Gusfield, "The Study of Social Movements." *International Encyclopedia of the Social Sciences* (New York: Crowell Collier and Macmillan, 1968), vol. 14, pp. 446–47.

13. James A. Davis, "A Formal Interpretation of the Theory of Relative Deprivation," *Sociometry* 22, no. 4 (December 1959): 282. See also J. E. Singer, "Social Comparison—Progress and Issues," *Journal of Experimental Social Psychology*, Supplement 1 (September 1966), pp. 103–12.

14. As Ryan points out, although discussions of experimental work have treated "level of aspiration" as a generally applicable concept, the actual research has dealt with individuals' "choice of level of success to be achieved in a single task" (Thomas Arthur Ryan, *Intentional Behavior: An Approach to Human Motivation* [New York: Ronald Press, 1970], p. 372).

15. Leon Festinger, "A Theory of Social Comparison Processes," Human Relations 7, no. 2 (1954): 117–40.

16. *Ibid.*, p. 120.

17. *Ibid.*, p. 121.

18. *Ibid.*, pp. 124–25.

19. *Ibid.*, p. 129.

20. *Ibid.*, p. 133.

21. Merton and Kitt, "Contributions to the Theory of Reference Group Behavior," esp. pp. 57–59.

22. Harold H. Kelley, "Two Functions of Reference Groups," in Guy E. Swanson, Theodore M. Newcomb, and Eugene L. Hartley, eds., *Readings in Social Psychology*, rev. ed. (New York: Holt, 1952), pp. 410–14; Kemper later distinguished the two additional types of (1) *informative* reference groups and (2) reference groups of *expected participation* (T. D. Kemper, "Reference Group, Socialization and Achievement," *American Sociological Review* 33, no. 1 [February 1, 1969]: 31–45).

23. The difficulty of predicting major social responses to collective relative deprivation is well illustrated by comparative study of two urban religious sectarian movements (Pentecostals and Seventh-day Adventists): although members of both apparently are "status deprived," both the religious ideologies and the behavior relevant to social mobility differ radically as between the two sects (Gary Schwartz, *Sect Ideologies and Social Status* [Chicago: University of Chicago Press, 1970]).

24. Merton and Kitt, "Contributions to the Theory of Reference Group Behavior," pp. 47–48.

25. See the analysis by J. A. Davis: "A Formal Interpretation of The Theory of Relative Deprivation," *Sociometry* 22, no. 4 (December 1959): 280–96.

26. Lester Thurow, "Toward a Definition of Economic Justice," *The Public Interest* 31 (Spring 1973), p. 69: "In economics textbooks, satisfaction springs only from a man's own income. *In the real world, relative incomes seem to dominate absolute incomes in terms of making people satisfied or dissatisfied. Preferences are inter-*

dependent rather than independent. Psychologists would label the same phenomenon envy." (Italics added.)

27. Eric J. Cassell, "Death and the Physician," *Commentary* (June 1969), p. 73.

28. James S. Duesenberry, *Income, Saving, and the Theory of Consumer Behavior* (New York: Oxford University Press, 1967; originally published 1949), p. 57.

29. *Ibid.*, p. 111.

30. *Ibid.*, p. 112.

31. *Social Security Bulletin* 36, no. 3 (March 1973): 72; Table M-31.

32. Institute for Social Research Newsletter, University of Michigan (Winter 1973), pp. 4–6.

33. *Ibid.*, p. 5.

34. Norman M. Bradburn, *The Structure of Psychological Well-Being* (Chicago: Aldine, 1969), and Norman M. Bradburn and David Caplovitz, *Reports on Happiness* (Chicago: Aldine, 1965).

35. Richard A. Easterlin, "Does Money Buy Happiness?" *The Public Interest* 30 (Winter 1973): 3–10.

36. *Ibid.*, p. 4.

37. Easterlin concludes: "By and large, the evidence indicates no relation—positive or negative—between happiness and national income. Whether the people in a particular time or place are comparatively happy is seemingly independent of the average level of income" (*ibid.*, p. 7). Two important cautions are in order: (1) the index of "happiness" perhaps could better be termed "reported satisfaction or adjustment", and (2) the range of societies sampled did not include the most poverty-stricken.

38. Thomas F. Pettigrew, "Attitudes on Race and Housing: A Social-Psychological View," in Amos H. Hawley and Vincent P. Rock, eds., *Economic Factors in Choice of Housing* (Washington, D.C.: National Academy of Sciences, 1973), p. 53.

39. Harold L. Wilensky and Hugh Edwards, "The Skidder: Ideological Adjustment of Downward Mobile Workers," *American Sociological Review* 24, no. 2 (April 1959): 215–31, and Harold L. Wilensky, "Measures and Effects of Social Mobility," in Neil J. Smelser and S. M. Lipset, eds., *Social Structure and Mobility in Economic Development* (Chicago: Aldine, 1966), pp. 98–140.

40. Joseph Lopreato and Janet Saltsman Chafetz, "The Political Orientation of Skidders," *American Sociological Review* 35, no. 3 (June 1970): 440–51.

41. R. W. Shomer, "*Effects of Chance and Skill Outcomes on Expectancy Recall, and Distributive Allocations,*" unpublished Ph.D. dissertation, University of California at Los Angeles, 1966; cited by Pettigrew, "Attitudes on Race and Housing," p. 162.

42. Presumably, the likelihood of a strong and prevalent ideology of this kind is, in turn, partially dependent on a societal history of considerable social mobility and economic development.

43. Current Population Reports, *Consumer Income: Money Income in 1971 of Families and Persons in the U.S.*, Series P-60, No. 85, December 1972, U.S. Department of Commerce, Bureau of Census, Washington, D.C., Table 9, p. 31.

44. Lester C. Thurow and Robert Lucas, *American Distribution of Incomes: Structural Problem,* Economic Joint Committee, 92nd Congress, 2d Session, March 17, 1972, p. 1. (pp. v–50.)

45. Robert W. Hodge, Paul M. Siegal, and Peter H. Rossi, "Occupational Prestige in the United States, 1925–1963," *American Journal of Sociology* 70, no. 3 (November 1964): 286.

46. In the Cornell Studies in Intergroup Relations, carried on prior to the main legal

and political changes of the 1950s and 1960s, it was striking to find that a higher proportion of black than of white people self-classified themselves as upper class —rather clearly by reference to position within a rigid, segregated subcommunity. See Robin M. Williams, Jr., *et al., Strangers Next Door:* Ethnic Relations in American Communities (Englewood Cliffs, N.J.: Prentice-Hall, 1964), p. 251.

47. Frequent communication of information is favored by spatial proximity, functional proximity, high rates of mass communication from diverse sources, high educational levels, substantial geographic mobility, and substantial amounts of leisure time.

48. Cf. W. G. Runciman, *Relative Deprivation and Social Justice* (London: Routledge & Kegan Paul, 1966), pp. 192–217. (Fraternalistic deprivation corresponds to "relative subordination" as used by James A. Davis.)

49. Note this summary from Thurow and Lucas, *American Distribution of Incomes,* p. 17: "From 1952 to 1968, the mean education of black male workers rose from 67 percent to 87 percent of white male workers, yet median wage and salary incomes only rose from 58 percent to 66 percent" (and most of the latter increase was due to movement from Southern to Northern locations rather than directly to increased education).

50. See the fascinating example in Robert A. Hall, Jr., "Thorstein Veblen and Linguistic Theory," *American Speech* 35, no. 2 (May 1960): 127.

51. Alan B. Wilson, "Residential Segregation of Social Classes and Aspirations of High School Boys," *American Sociological Review* 24, no. 6 (December 1969): 836–45.

52. Runciman, *Relative Deprivation and Social Justice,* pp. 203–05. At "high" income levels, the percentage expressing relative satisfaction is 43 among nonmanual but 56 among manual workers.

53. Martin Patchen, "A Conceptual Framework and Some Empirical Data Regarding Comparisons of Social Rewards," *Sociometry* 24, no. 2 (June 1961): 136–56.

54. Philip Mason, *Race Relations* (New York: Oxford University Press, 1970), p. 163.

55. Carl F. Grindstaff, "The Negro, Urbanization, and Relative Deprivation in the Deep South," *Social Problems* 15, no. 3 (Winter 1968): 325.

56. Denton E. Morrison and Allan D. Steeves, "Deprivation Discontent, and Social Movement Participation," *Rural Sociology* 32, no. 4 (December 1967): 414–34.

57. Cf. Judith Long Laws, "A Feminist Analysis of Relative Deprivation in Academic Women," *Journal of the Union of Radical Political Economics* (August 1972), pp. 1–28.

58. Herbert H. Hyman, "Reference Groups," *International Encyclopedia of the Social Sciences* (New York: Crowell Collier and Macmillan, 1968), vol. 13, p. 357. Cf. Martin Patchen, *The Choice of Wage Comparisons* (Englewood Cliffs, N.J.: Prentice-Hall, 1961).

59. This is a phenomenon of great practical importance in "wage contours"—relatively fixed historical differentials—that are crucial for the success of any program of wage controls. See Thurow, "Toward a Definition of Economic Justice."

60. Lewis A. Coser, "The Sociology of Poverty," *Social Problems* 13, no. 2 (Fall 1965): 140–48. Building upon Georg Simmel's suggestions, Coser shows that "poverty" is not sheer want or misery but rather is a socially recognized special status. Note further: "What may be felt to constitute unendurable deprivation in a society where the underprivileged compare their lot with that of others more favorably placed with regard to the distribution of income and wealth, may be accepted as legitimate in societies where no such comparisons are socially available or culturally sanctioned" (p. 140).

61. Donald P. Hayes, "Layman's Conception of Income Inequality," unpublished re-

search proposal, Cornell University, October 1972. (I am indebted to Professor Hayes both for permission to use his analysis of the cross-national data and for many stimulating discussions of basic theoretical problems.)

62. Cf. J. S. Adams, "Inequity in Social Exchange," in Leonard Berkowitz, ed., *Advances in Experimental Social Psychology* (New York: Academic Press, 1965), pp. 267–97.

63. The distinctions are Runciman's, in *Relative Deprivation and Social Justice*, pp. 31–35.

64. Kenneth J. Gergen, *The Psychology of Behavior Exchange* (Reading, Mass.: Addison Wesley, 1969), pp. 41–49. (The indicated effects hold within a given, relatively short, period.)

65. Albert O. Hirschman, "The Changing Tolerance for Income Inequality in the Course of Economic Development," *Discussion Paper Number 233*, rev. (Cambridge, Mass.: Harvard Institute of Economic Research, September 1972), esp. pp. 2–6.

66. See the discussion of the "inflationary spiral of demands." Thus created in some new nations, in Aristide R. Zolberg, "The Structure of Political Conflict in the New States of Tropical Africa," *American Political Science Review* 62, no. 1 (March 1968): 70–87.

67. Thomas Pettigrew, *A Profile of the Negro American* (Princeton, N.J.: Van Nostrand, 1964), p. 191.

68. See Duesenberry, *Income, Saving, and the Theory of Consumer Behavior*, pp. 25–32.

69. S. N. Eisenstadt, "Continuities and Changes in Systems of Stratification," in Bernard Barber and Alex Inkeles, eds., *Stability and Social Change* (Boston: Little, Brown, 1971), p. 79.

70. Compare Hirschman, "The Changing Tolerance for Income Inequality," pp. 14–18.

71. Compare the analysis of communalism in developing nations in Robert Melson and Howard Wolpe, "Modernization and the Politics of Communalism: A Theoretical Perspective," *American Political Science Review* 64, no. 4 (December 1970): 1112–30.

72. Joseph R. Gusfield, "Social Movements: The Study of Social Movements," *International Encyclopedia of the Social Sciences* (New York: Crowell Collier and Macmillan, 1968), vol. 14, pp. 445–52.

73. James C. Davies, "Towards a Theory of Revolution," *American Sociological Review* 27, no. 1 (February 1962): 5–19.

74. Stouffer *et al.*, *The American Soldier*, vol. 1, pp. 250–51, 125–26, 172, 181, 564.

75. Thomas Pettigrew, Robert T. Riley, and Reeve D. Vanneman, "George Wallace's Constituents," *Psychology Today* 5, no. 9 (February 1972): 47–49, 92.

76. Ivo Fierabend, Rosalind Fierabend, and Betty Nesvold, "Social Change and Political Violence: Cross National Patterns," in Hugh Davis Graham and Ted Robert Gurr, eds., *Violence in America*, vol. 2, pp. 499–500, and Ted Robert Gurr, *Why Men Rebel* (Princeton, N.J.: Princeton University Press, 1970).

77. Cf. Williams, *Strangers Next Door*, pp. 373–74.

78. Joseph Lopreato: "Upward Social Mobility and Political Orientation," *American Sociological Review* 32, no. 4 (August 1967): 592.

79. Donald R. Matthews and James W. Prothro, *Negroes and the New Southern Politics* (New York: Harcourt Brace Jovanovich, 1966), pp. 121 ff.

80. Dennis S. Ippolito, William S. Donaldson, and Lewis Bowman, "Political Orientations Among Negroes and Whites," *Social Science Quarterly* 49, no. 3 (December 1968): 549.

81. Thomas Crawford and Murray Naditch, "Relative Deprivation, Powerlessness and Militancy: The Psychology of Protest," *Psychiatry* 33, no. 2 (February 1970): 208–23, esp. p. 210, and Seymour Martin Lipset and Earl Raab, *The Politics of Unreason: Right-Wing Extremism in the United States, 1790–1970* (New York: Harper & Row, 1970), p. 444.

82. The data from a 1966 national NORC survey of black adults are analyzed by Murray P. Naditch in a forthcoming article, "Locus of Control, Relative Discontent and Competence: A Test of Means-Ends Theory."

83. See Melvin Seeman, "Alienation and Engagement," chap. 12 in Angus Campbell and Philip E. Converse, eds., *The Human Meaning of Social Change* (New York: Russell Sage, 1972), pp. 467–527.

84. For an analysis, as of 1964, that partially anticipated the urban violence of the later 1960s, compare Robin M. Williams, Jr., "Social Change and Social Conflict: Race Relations in the United States, 1944–1964," *Sociological Inquiry* 35, no. 1 (Winter 1965): esp. 15–24.

85. Seymour Spilerman, "The Causes of Racial Disturbances: A Comparison of Alternative Explanations," *American Sociological Review* 35, no. 4 (August 1970): 627–49; see also, Pierre van den Berghe, "The Benign Quota: Panacea or Pandora's Box," *The American Sociologist* 6, supplementary issue (June 1971): 43.

86. Income inequality is greatest among low-GNP nations and least in high-GNP nations. But domestic political violence tends to be highest in societies that combine moderate levels of per capita GNP and rapid social change with authoritarian political regimes. See Phillips Cutright, "Inequality: A Cross-National Analysis," *American Sociological Review* 32, no. 4 (August 1967): 562–78, and Betty A. Nesvold, "Scalogram Analysis of Political Violence," *Comparative Political Studies* 2, no. 2 (July 1969): 172–94.

87. Morris Janowitz, *Political Conflict: Essays in Political Sociology* (Chicago: Quadrangle Books, 1970), p. 830.

88. James C. Davies, "Toward a Theory of Revolution," *American Sociological Review* 27, no. 1 (February 1962): 60, and Crane Brinton, *Anatomy of Revolution* (New York: Vintage Books, 1957), pp. 264–75.

Social Structure and Mass Communications Behavior

Exploring Patterns through Constructional Analysis

CHARLES R. WRIGHT

T HE sociology of communications offers opportunities for the study of a wide spectrum of problems. This spectrum includes, but is not limited to, sociological analysis of audiences, communicators, communication processes, communications systems, messages and other content, and the effects of communications. Consideration of communications phenomena at the individual or personal level and at the level of socially organized mass communications introduces additional research opportunities and further complexity. Yet no matter which facet of this many-sided sociological field one turns up for inspection, there can be found Robert Merton's mark, indelible witness to the impact of a scholar who has been steadfast in tempering social theory with empirical research. Readers of this volume are well acquainted with Merton's significant contributions to the field of communications through his studies of mass persuasion, patterns of influence, content analyses of radio and film propaganda, and the social functions of the mass media. Less visible through direct mark, but nonetheless important to the development of the field, are Merton's many indirect contributions made through his influence on past and present colleagues, former students, their students, and *their* students (thereby the intergenerational continuity of science!).

Charles R. Wright is Professor of Communications and Sociology at the University of Pennsylvania.

The purpose here is not to review these many well-known contributions. Rather, we intend to explore, and to develop through examples based on research data, certain ideas about the study of social structure and mass media audiences—a topic that relates directly to an early insight by Merton that has not been given the subsequent prominence of research attention it deserves.

In *Social Theory and Social Structure,* Merton presented (in passing, almost as a throwaway clue) an important insight into why the sociologist interested in social structure should be attentive to findings from research on mass media audiences and suggests one way in which such research could be designed for even greater sociological relevance. He observed that even though commercial and other social needs, rather than sociological interests, have helped determine the major categories in terms of which the mass media audience is described or measured in America studies, these categories are nonetheless relevant to sociology ". . . since such categories as sex, age, education and income happen also to correspond to some of the chief statuses in the social structure. . . ."[1] Useful as these categories are, however, they do not exhaust the range of sociologically promising ways of classifying audiences, since

> a socially induced emphasis on particular intellectual problems may deflect research interest from other problems with as great or greater sociological interest, but with perceptibly little value for *immediate* market or military purposes. . . . Such dynamic categories with little direct bearing on commercial interests, as "false consciousness" . . . or various types of economically mobile individuals have as yet played little part in the description of audiences.[2]

False class consciousness and types of economic mobility are, of course, only two illustrations from the larger class of such dynamic sociological constructs which can and should be used to enrich the sociological yield of audience research. Exploration of the sociological utility of certain of these "new" ways of classifying audience data for purposes of relating communications behavior to social structure is the first theme to which this chapter is addressed, illustrated through secondary analysis of selected data from a national sample survey.[3] In developing this theme, we regard communications exposure as an important dependent variable and explore how it is related to the individual's positions within the social structure.

For our second theme, we treat communications behavior as an independent variable. In developing the theme, we demonstrate how the classification of people according to patterns in their mass media behavior provides important clues for the study of social structure and social processes.

SELECTING SIGNIFICANT STRUCTURAL VARIABLES FOR AUDIENCE RESEARCH

A typical finding in commercial audience research relates communications behavior to a single social characteristic of the audience. A correlation between magazine readership and income is a ready example. Sometimes, a characteristic of the respondent is treated as an independent variable with the result that we know the extent to which some form of media exposure varies according to sex, age, education, or other social category. At other times, the media behavior is treated as if it were an independent variable and then we are presented with profiles of an audience: what proportion are men or women, rich or poor, rural or urban, and so on. On occasion, two or three, seldom more, of these background variables are examined jointly, either to see how, for example, college-educated men differ from college-educated women in their exposure to television or to see what the demographic composition of that audience might be.

The typical demonstration of an empirical relationship between a single social characteristic of individuals and their mass communications behavior is, however, the lowest form of empirical datum. It is interesting, to be sure, since it refers to one status through which the individual is placed in the social structure, but of limited interest unless something more is presented. The addition of several statuses greatly increases the potential of such analyses, especially for purposes of sociological description. It is of value to know that magazine readership is correlated with income level and that the television exposure of college-educated men differs in some regular way from that of college-educated women. Given enough such items, one can go a long way toward construction of a statistical demographic portrait of the mass media audiences in a society. This has been the main thrust of past commercial, and some academic, audience surveys.[4]

With no intent to detract from the sociological value of prior audience analyses, even those that treat each social characteristic as if in isolation and especially those that go beyond this to provide information on jointly held characteristics, we wish to make a case for classifying audiences according to new combinations of social statuses. Their selection is informed by sociological theory, so that they relate the individual to the social structure in ways usually not considered in conventional audience research. This strategy does not necessarily require the use of a greater number of variables than has been used in conventional analysis (indeed, most of the illustrations to be presented involve only two independent statuses jointly considered). But it does call for construction of combinations not commonly found in audience surveys and for sociological imagination in their use.

The idea of classifying respondents by multiple social statuses is not a new idea, of course, and we make no claim for its originality. Students of social stratification, in particular, have long found it necessary to use combinations of social categories to describe the complexities of social structure with which they were concerned. In the field of group relations, a similar point was made by Milton Gordon some two decades ago. Commenting on the tendency for prior work in that area to have focused on one or two social categories, Gordon argues, "An adequate theory of social structure for modern complex societies must go far beyond age and sex categories to ascertain the broad social units within the national culture, each of which may allow for the unfolding of the life-cycle within its invisible but operationally functioning borders. . . . Such investigation, moreover, cannot afford to rest with one-category analysis."[5] The analytical utility of multidimensional classifications, as well as certain of their methodological characteristics, has been treated by Lazarsfeld and other methodologists.[6] But such classifications have not been widely used to theoretical advantage in the sociological analysis of mass media audiences; nor have such classifications been fully developed and discussed with respect to communications behavior and social structure.

In the study of the sociology of audiences to date (1975), we do not have theoretical or empirical guidance sufficient to suggest which major social statuses (if any) combine into types that are meaningful for understanding mass media exposure. What kinds of variables are we to choose from the countless numbers of ways in which individuals may be classified? In this essay, we focus upon those characteristics of individuals that reflect their social positions. We are not concerned here with psychological, physiological, or other nonsocial attributes. We are concerned with *social* categories and *social* statuses, that is, those characteristics that serve either to index the individual's position within the social structure or to point to the social roles that he is expected to play. A further restriction is imposed by considering only those social categories and/or social statuses for which one has theoretical or empirical reason to expect differences in media behavior. These expectations may be based either upon consideration of the differential lifestyles and opportunities for media use that accompany various positions in the social structure (for example, urban residence, higher wealth, membership in a more highly educated stratum) or upon consideration of the norms for communications behavior that are attached to a particular social status (for example, that children ought not to attend "sex" movies).

We shall direct our attention primarily to social categories of the first type, that is, those that index the individual's position within the social structure, placing him into social categories having different lifestyles, although these are not to be taken as lacking in normative implications as well.

Although the unit of behavioral analysis here is the individual, we urge that classification of individuals incorporate data putting them into relational context with others. As cases in point, we suggest that an individual's current position in the social structure (as indexed, for example, by his occupation) needs to be broadened to consider a longer time span, taking into account his social origins at least one generation into the past. Further, we are concerned less with idiosyncratic histories than with *patterns* of intergenerational combinations of histories that fix the individual within the social structure. It is some of these patterns that we examine below to see what difference, if any, they make for communications behavior.[7]

INTERGENERATIONAL OCCUPATIONAL MOBILITY AND COMMUNICATIONS BEHAVIOR

Let us follow through on one of the sociological classifications that Merton suggested as relevant to communications research: contrasting the media behavior of socially mobile and nonmobile individuals. An ideal approach would involve gathering data from a primary social survey. But lacking that resource, some initial headway may be made through reexamination, by secondary analysis, of survey data gathered for other purposes. We are fortunate in having available one such national survey which includes not only information about mobility but also a number of items about communications behavior. The survey selected is the best available for our purposes from fifty-four national surveys used by the author and his colleagues in a study of educational effects (see note 3). It is the best in the sense that it contains not only a variety of measures of intergenerational and current social statuses but also several good measures of communications exposure. The fact that it is rare to find a national survey combining both intergenerational mobility data and communications behavior data underscores Merton's point that such dynamic categories as "social mobility" seldom find their way into analysis of mass communications behavior.[8]

This survey contains data about the respondent's major occupation and the major occupation of his father. Using occupation as an index of socioeconomic position, then, we can compare the positions of sons with their fathers and thereby obtain a classification by intergenerational occupational (and hence social and perhaps economic) mobility. We limit our analysis here to males and to native-born white Americans, thereby eliminating complications attendant upon sex, race, and nationality; and we eliminate data from farmers and sons of farmers, because of the indeterminate ranking of farm occupations in social stratification and social mobility.

For purposes of the present analysis, specific occupations are grouped as either nonmanual or manual. Nonmanual occupations include professional, business executives, and white-collar jobs; manual occupations include all forms of blue-collar and service occupations. (Both categories exclude agricultural occupations, as noted.) Obviously, this crude classification overlooks the range of status differences within each occupational stratum, but the head-hands, nonmanual-manual dichotomy has been used on other occasions as a crude index of socioeconomic strata and, in turn, in studies of occupational and social mobility. In any case, we are limited by the number of respondents in the survey. (Additional analysis, not reported here, employed a greater number of narrower occupational strata, but the results neither contradicted nor greatly refined those obtained from use of the simple dichotomy.) Intergenerational social mobility refers to instances where a respondent is employed in a stratum different from that of his father; and stability refers to cases where both son and father were in the same broad stratum.

Seven measures of communications behavior are examined: reading a newspaper every day; reading one or more magazines regularly; reading a newsmagazine; watching television three or more hours a day (above the average for the total sample at the time of the study); watching televised news broadcasts daily; discussing local community problems at least once a week; and discussing politics at least once a week. As evident, these items include information on exposure to print and electronic mass media as well as engagement in face-to-face conversation about social issues. These are gross measures of communications activities, to be sure: reading newspapers, magazines, viewing television, and so on; and they by no means encompass the entire range of such activities (excluding, for example, movie-going). But some degree of refinement is introduced through our selection of responses to be considered: not just reading newspapers, but reading one every day; not just reading magazines, but reading one or more regularly; and reading a newsmagazine; not just viewing television, but watching it heavily—three hours or more a day; not just watching the televised news, but doing this every day; not just discussing local community problems and politics, but having such conversations at least once a week, sometimes more often. Data on a wider range of activities, more precise measures of quantity of use, and specific exposure to particular kinds of communications content are desirable. But analysis must begin somewhere, and the data available from this national survey provide a reasonable and satisfactory starting point. Regularities or lack of regularities discovered through analysis of these data can point the way for more refined data collection and more sociologically relevant analysis in the future.

How does social mobility, or lack of it, relate to communications behavior? Comparisons of communications behavior for stable and mobile individuals are presented in Table 1. The results are interesting, perhaps surprising. Certainly, they indicate that we are on the track of a sociological variable worthy of further consideration in communications research. But there are ambiguities as well. Clearly, individuals who have been mobile are more likely to use the common print media than are those whose intergenerational transition has not crossed the manual-nonmanual lines. But the two groups do not differ greatly in heavy television viewing, or some face-to-face discussions. Is there something about mobility that agitates toward a greater probability of using the print media? Perhaps, but to draw such a conclusion seems hasty and unwarranted. Social mobility itself is obviously a blanket concept that includes both upward and downward movement. Perhaps a clearer pattern will emerge if we compare the communications behavior of those who have moved up versus those who have moved down.

Table 1. COMMUNICATIONS BEHAVIOR OF SOCIALLY STABLE AND SOCIALLY MOBILE MEN*

Behavior (percent who:)	Stable (N = 392)	Mobile (N = 237)
Read a newspaper every day	73	91
Read magazines regularly	61	79
Read a newsmagazine	15	33
Watch TV 3 or more hrs. a day	40	34
Watch TV news broadcasts daily	68	73
Discuss local community problems at least once a wk.	47	46
Discuss politics at least once a wk.	56	64

* Native-born, urban, white males only.

It is a sign of our societal good fortune, but a taxing problem for the social researcher, that most of our intergenerational mobility has been upward. Only forty-eight men (among the white, native-born, nonfarm population) in this national survey were in manual jobs after having grown up in a family where the father did nonmanual work. Aware of the limitations to analysis posed by such a small number of downwardly mobiles, we can nevertheless examine their communications behavior with caution (see Table 2). Alas, the picture becomes murkier rather than clearer and a pattern eludes us. As examples, although upwardly mobile individuals are more likely than downwardly mobile ones to read a newspaper every day, they are not more likely to read magazines regularly. And the two groups differ inconsistently in the proportions engaged in other kinds of communications behavior.

Table 2. COMMUNICATIONS BEHAVIOR OF UPWARDLY
MOBILE AND DOWNWARDLY MOBILE MEN*

Behavior (percent who:)	Upward mobiles (N = 189)	Downward mobiles (N = 48)
Read a newspaper every day	92	75
Read magazines regularly	78	81
Read a newsmagazine	35	27
Watch TV 3 or more hrs. a day	33	38
Watch TV news broadcasts daily	72	77
Discuss local community problems at least once a wk.	48	40
Discuss politics at least once a wk.	72	54

* See Table 1.

Perhaps another refinement in conceptualization will aid our search for regularities in communications behavior. Stability itself masks two different kinds of experience: maintenance of two generations of nonmanual lifestyles or two generations of working-class experiences. Looked at in this way, the focus shifts from mobility (or lack of it) as the dynamic sociological concept and prompts consideration of a form of status sequence that spans two generations. The boy not only becomes the man but also moves from working-class status (albeit as a youth) to middle-class status in adulthood, or from middle-class to working-class; or he maintains the same middle-class or working-class status inherited from his family.

The four patterns of intergenerational social mobility and their associated communications behavior are presented in Table 3. The two central columns contain, of course, the upwardly and downwardly mobile individuals examined before. But now their behavior can be seen against the activities of those men who have experienced two generations (perhaps more) of middle-class or of working-class backgrounds. Given this perspective, the picture changes. Fairly sizable differences in the probability of various communications behavior appear between those individuals whose lives span two generations of middle-class experience and those whose lives combine the histories of two generations of working-class homes. For example, 86 percent of the second-generation middle-class men read a newspaper every day, in contrast with 70 percent of the second-generation workers. And the former are more likely than the latter to read magazines regularly, to read a newsmagazine, to discuss local community problems, and to discuss politics. They are less likely to be heavy viewers of television. Only watching television news seems unsystematically related to mobility patterns.

Table 3. PATTERNS OF INTERGENERATIONAL SOCIAL MOBILITY OR CONTINUITY AND COMMUNICATIONS BEHAVIOR (MEN ONLY)*

MOBILITY PATTERNS

Behavior (percent who:)	Two generations of middle class (N = 73)	New generation of middle class (N = 189)	New generation of working class (N = 48)	Two generations of working class (N = 319)
Read a newspaper every day	86	92	77	70
Read magazines regularly	85	78	81	56
Read a newsmagazine	38	35	27	9
Watch TV 3 or more hrs. a day	33	33	38	42
Watch TV news broadcasts daily	62	72	77	69
Discuss local community problems at least once a wk.	56	48	40	45
Discuss politics at least once a wk.	77	72	54	51

* See Table 1.

It is tempting to speculate about the relative impact of early childhood socialization versus the normative and situational demands of one's current social stratum, for the two mobile groups. Those men who are new to the middle class have been socialized in working-class families; and those new to the working class have grown up in middle-class homes. To the extent that adult communications habits are learned in the parents' home, one would expect that upwardly mobile individuals would behave more like the working class from which they came, and downwardly mobile individuals would continue to resemble individuals from their middle-class origins. To the extent that one's current socioeconomic position cultivates new behavior patterns, then one would expect each group to resemble the new stratum into which it has entered. Unfortunately for theory, the findings are mixed. But on balance, the new middle class behaves more like the old middle class than it does like its working-class origins, as exemplified by individuals who remained stable in their working-class origins. This finding lends itself to interpretation in terms of either new socialization into the new social stratum or response to the opportunities and demands of that new social status. And the new working class behaves somewhat like the old, with the exception of its greater propensity for reading, especially magazines, which might represent holdovers from the place accorded such printed materials in their childhood homes. But this is conjecture.

Conjecture aside, what emerges is a case for interpreting intergenerational mobility in terms of sociological dynamics other than mobility or stability per se. It directs attention to the patterns of intergenerational heritage and their attendant dynamics for influencing social and communications behavior. Whether these dynamics lie in the normative patterns to which children are socialized in middle-class or working-class families, to the more general life-styles that each setting involves, to the differential opportunities for communications exposure and expression that occur, or to some other dynamics is unknown.[9] It is still plausible, of course, that social mobility per se, with its attendant chances of anomie, anticipatory socialization, alienation, disappointment, and other consequences, remains an important explanatory factor in communications behavior. Our intent is not to dismiss this possibility, but to direct attention also to other aspects of social structure, giving emphasis to status continuity or discontinuity. To this purpose we turn now to another kind of pattern of intergenerational mobility: educational.

But before proceeding to the next line of analysis, it is necessary to elaborate upon the methodological strategy used in the preceding argument, viz. the manner in which two or more independent and test variables are introduced and interpreted in survey analysis. For many analytical purposes, the proper strategy of employment of a third variable in the interpretation of a relationship between two variables is well known.[10] The general strategies employed are designed to test, elaborate upon, or specify the relationship between two social characteristics—one treated as if it were an independent variable, the other the dependent variable. Were this our purpose, the proper sequence of analysis would be to present data on the relationship between the respondent's current occupational status (independent variable) and his communications behavior (dependent variable). Then we would introduce various third variables as test factors: in this instance, father's occupation. If the respondent's occupational level were found to be related to some communications behavior, for example, newspaper reading, then we would refine the analysis by determining whether or not this original relationship held once we controlled for the social origins of the respondent, as measured by his father's occupation. Our interest would be in learning whether or not (or the extent to which) present occupation continued to be related to communications behavior among individuals who had similar family origins. The purpose is to determine the *relative* importance of various characteristics as possible causes or contributory causes to the phenomenon under study, for example, newspaper reading. But that is not our strategy here. Rather, our concern is with demonstrating the combined consequences of several social structural factors, for example, father's occupational level and that of the son. We do not seek to find spurious, contingent, or hidden relationships. Rather, we look to see what social differences emerge when an individual combines the normative and objective features of several social characteristics and, more generally, what consequences are associated with different *patterns* of combinations of social status characteristics—a strategy for survey analysis that I call *constructional pattern analysis.*

INTERGENERATIONAL EDUCATIONAL MOBILITY

Having set the mode of analysis in the preceding section, we shall be brief about it here. Data are available about the highest level of schooling achieved by the respondent and by his or her father. (In this analysis, data are included for all respondents, regardless of sex, race, residence, or place of birth.) Respondents are classified into each of seven categories depending upon the combination of their education and their father's education. As examples, group *A* consists of men and women who have had college education and whose fathers also went to college—we label this the "two generations of college" group; group *B* consists of college-educated men and women whose fathers did not go to college—we label them the "first generation of college." They have been upwardly mobile through education, whereas the first group represents intergenerational continuity in educational status (leaving aside variations in range of education contained within each of the broad categories of college, high school, and elementary school achievement). We proceed with this classification down to the seventh group (*G*), which contains all persons whose highest formal education is in elementary school and whose fathers also went no further than that in school.

When the communications behavior of these seven groups is compared, important regularities appear (see Table 4). In general, with the major exception of television viewing, a larger proportion of individuals engage in communications behavior as one moves up the level of education for the respondent *and* as his educational experience builds upon that of the prior generation. Consider magazine readership as an example. When both the respondent and his or her father stopped their formal education at the elementary school level (*G*), only 38 percent read magazines regularly; but among those grammar school respondents whose fathers had a high school or college education (*F*), 50 percent read magazines. Sixty-three percent of the respondents whose high school education exceeded their father's (group *E*) read magazines; but 70 percent of those whose fathers also went to high school (*D*) read magazines, and 81 percent of them whose fathers went to college (*C*) read magazines. Among college-educated respondents whose fathers did not go to college (*B*), 86 percent read magazines, as do 90 percent of those whose fathers also were college educated (*A*). Similar regularities are obtained, with a few minor exceptions, for four of the other communications behaviors under study.

Table 4. PATTERNS OF INTERGENERATIONAL EDUCATIONAL MOBILITY OR CONTINUITY AND COMMUNICATIONS BEHAVIOR (MEN AND WOMEN, COMBINED)

Behavior (percent who:)	A 2 generations of college (N=129)	B 1st generation of college (up) (N=380)	C 1st generation of high school only (down) (N=80)	D 2 generations of high school (N=292)	E 1st generation of high school achieved (up) (N=682)	F 1st generation of elementary school only (down) (N=42)	G 2 generations of elementary school (N=440)
Read a newspaper every day	86	87	83	78	76	69	55
Read magazines regularly	90	86	81	70	63	50	38
Read a newsmagazine	50	37	22	17	12	7	4
Watch TV 3 or more hrs. per day	38	33	53	49	47	40	42
Watch TV news broadcasts daily	61	71	81	74	72	76	71
Discuss local community problems at least once a wk.	60	50	45	43	40	40	32
Discuss politics at least once a wk.	76	71	55	58	50	29	32

Current educational achievement makes a difference to be sure. Respondents, for example, who only attended elementary school but whose fathers had higher education sometimes behave more like their contemporaries who have experienced two generations of grade school instruction than like those who have benefited from two generations of high school education. Nevertheless, this first-generation elementary school group is more likely than the second-generation elementary school group to attend to newspapers and magazines, showing traces perhaps of earlier socialization in families where the father had more schooling.

These data suggest, then, that intergenerational educational status sequence is a useful concept for exploring regularities in communications behavior. The child who is the son or daughter of a college-educated man and who grows up to become a college-educated adult experiences a different status sequence from one who is the son or daughter of a grade school-educated father and who himself or herself has the same educational status as an adult. Some of the consequences of these different patterns are evident even in the gross measures of communications behavior at hand.

We have examined the impact on communications behavior of two patterns of continuity and discontinuity in lifestyles and opportunities: intergenerational occupational continuity or mobility and intergenerational educational continuity or mobility. Both appear to be related to subsequent adult communications behavior. As a third example of the value of such sociological concepts for research on audiences, we turn to a different kind of social continuity or discontinuity: that achieved through marriage, taking the educational achievement of both respondent and spouse as our focus.

MARITAL EDUCATIONAL STATUSES

The data report on the communications behavior of *individual* respondents, to be sure: newspaper reading, magazine reading, television viewing, conversations about public affairs, and others. But many of these activities are, or can be, centered in the home, where the style of life may reflect the educational impact of husband, of wife, or of both. We can regard the patterns of education combinations between husband and wife as grounds for a typology of families in terms of educational status homogeneity or heterogeneity; or we can classify families according to the highest amount of education received by either partner, with the view that the benefits of this schooling are shared by others in the family as a unit; or we can focus on individuals who have married "up" or "down" in terms of the educational background of their spouse. For purposes of our analysis, we classify all married respondents into six categories of family educational composition: marriages in which both the respondent and the spouse have been to college; only the respondent has been to college; only the spouse has been to college; both have been to high school only; either respondent or spouse has been to high school, but the other has not; and neither respondent nor spouse has gone to high school. Then we examined the data on communications behavior for each of these six combinations (see Table 5).

Table 5. PATTERNS OF MARITAL EDUCATIONAL COMPOSITION AND COMMUNICATIONS BEHAVIOR (MARRIED RESPONDENTS)

Marital educational composition

Behavior (*percent who:*)	A Both partners college-educated (N=278)	B Respondent college; spouse no college (N=220)	C Spouse college; respondent no college (N=229)	D Both partners high school-educated (N=836)	E Either partner high school; the other no high school (N=415)	F Neither partner high school-educated (N=385)
Read a newspaper every day	87	90	85	77	66	51
Read magazines regularly	93	83	76	66	52	35
Read a newsmagazine	51	31	22	12	7	4
Watcs TV 3 or more hrs. a day	31	39	43	48	51	43
Watch TV news broadcasts daily	66	74	76	72	78	69
Discuss local community problems at least once a wk.	54	49	38	41	34	30
Discuss politics at least once a wk.	74	68	55	52	38	27

The results provide the most consistent pattern of regularities and differences in communications behavior that we have encountered in our analysis thus far. Television news watching still follows no pattern. Otherwise, with only two minor exceptions, the educational impact on communications behavior appears to be additive for husbands and wives. That is, among college-educated respondents, those whose spouses also are college-educated are more likely than those whose spouses did not go to college to read magazines, to read newsmagazines, to discuss local community problems and politics; and less likely to view television heavily (column A versus B). Respondents who themselves did not go to college but who are married to someone with a college education behave differently from respondents in families where neither partner went to college. Respondents in families where both partners went to high school are more likely than respondents in families where only one partner went to high school to engage in reading of newspapers, magazines, newsmagazines, and to discuss community problems and politics. But the latter group is more likely to engage in such communications activities than are respondents in families where neither husband nor wife attended high school. Even the previously erratic data on television viewing now have the semblance of order, with an increase in the proportion of persons who view television heavily as one moves from families in which both partners went to college down toward families having less joint education (with the exception of a drop in percentage in the last column).[11]

The sociological import of our three sets of findings—on intergenerational occupational patterns, intergenerational educational patterns, and intramarital educational patterns—is now clear. Accounts of relationships between individual status characteristics, such as have been provided in past research, can be greatly enriched through examination of more complex social structural combinations of which they form only part of the pattern. It is still the case that communications behavior is correlated with one's occupation and one's education. But this association is a single bare sociological fact. Further illumination is provided by considering the structural context of such an association. One such perspective is given through consideration of the cumulative impact of prior statuses—in our examples, father's socioeconomic and educational statuses—which add continuity or discontinuity to the respondent's current statuses. Another perspective comes from considering the contextual modification of the impact of one's educational status through marriage to someone having greater, lesser, or equal education.

AGING AND COMMUNICATIONS BEHAVIOR

Recent years have seen an increase in the attention given to the sociological consequences of aging.[12] But even though various descriptions have been provided of the relations between age and communications behavior, few of these are relevant for the study of the effects of aging, since most such studies truncate the age distribution at the higher end or lump all individuals aged fifty (or sixty) and above.[13] An exception is presented by Schramm,[14] who reviews the available literature on the aged population as an audience. Even this extensive review, however, reveals only very limited national survey data on communications behavior for more refined categories of age above sixty-five. Only one such source is cited. In view of the patent sociological significance of age stratification in general and of the process of status sequencing represented by aging, and in light of the almost complete lack of data on the effects of aging on communications behavior, we selected this one social variable initially as an exception to our intention not merely to review communications behavior by single social statuses. The opportunity to explore this variable was too good to let pass by, since the national sample at hand permitted classification of respondents by precise age even up to the oldest person. Subsequently, as will be seen below, we found that understanding of the impact on communications behavior of this rarely documented social status can be enriched through construction of other concurrent social statuses.

Since our concern is with aging, not with age stratification, we do not compare communications behavior over the entire range from youth through old age. Rather, we focus on the critical years immediately preceding and during the transition from middle age to elderly. Therefore, we classify respondents into four age categories—individuals in their fifties, sixties, seventies, and eighty and above—and examine their communications behavior. A word of caution is ,in order. The national sample survey being used, as most such surveys, is based on a national area probability sample of persons living in private dwelling units. This means that it excluded those who are institutionalized. Since the aged who are institutionalized may differ in their communications behavior (and in other respects) from those who are still at home, it is unwise to generalize from the current findings to all the aged. What we do have are rare data on the effects of aging on communications behavior for those individuals who were not confined to institutions at the time of the survey. This is much better than nothing and considerably richer than previously published data on the topic.

The clearest conclusion that can be drawn about the negative effects of aging on the communications behavior under study is that there aren't many! (See Table 6.) The proportion of adults in their eighties who read a newspaper every day, read magazines, watch television heavily, and discuss community problems is not very different from the proportion of persons in their fifties who do such things. And there is no systematic, monotonic pattern of major decline in these communications activities with aging, except a drop in the proportion who engage in conversations about politics. (There is published evidence that other kinds of communications activities, especially those that require leaving the house, such as movie attendance, do decrease with age.)[15] Schramm's conclusion that "the use of television and newspapers remains fairly constant and may even increase in the years after middle age" is supported by our data if we interpret him to.mean that these activities do not decrease with aging.[16] The proportion of persons reading a newspaper every day remains constant over the years, while heavy television view-ing increases with aging until one reaches the eighties. Viewing of televised news broadcasts, common among people in their fifties, becomes even more likely among the aged.

Table 6. EFFECTS OF AGING ON COMMUNICATIONS BEHAVIOR

AGE STATUS

Behavior (percent who:)	Fifties (N=420)	Sixties (N=350)	Seventies (N=258)	Eighty and above (N=47)
Read a newspaper every day	77	77	75	75
Read magazines regularly	64	57	58	60
Read a newsmagazine	17	15	12	11
Watch TV 3 or more hrs. a day	35	46	50	38
Watch TV news broadcasts daily	72	78	81	83
Discuss local community problems at least once a wk.	37	38	32	32
Discuss politics at least once a wk.	48	44	30	23

One difficulty in interpreting data on the effects of aging on communica-tions behavior is that change in age status may have different consequences as it is combined with changes in other social statuses. This obvious social fact reminds us, of course, of the point raised earlier in this chapter: more valuable sociological analyses are to be had by considering complex combina-tions of social statuses rather than each status alone. One doesn't simply suffer physiological and social ravages of time as one grows old. Other statuses change, some forming common status sequences in our society: from married to widowed; from homeowner to renter, perhaps; from head of household to dependent—to mention but a few examples. Also, the consequences of ag-ing can differ if one is rich or poor, healthy or ill, man or woman, black or white. From these many modifying status changes that accompany aging, or that set its context, we select two for further examination: the transition from the status of employed to that of retired and becoming a widow or widower.

For purposes of the first analysis, we subdivide each of our four age cohorts into two subgroups of employed or retired (excluding housewives and a few individuals who are unemployed but not retired) and then examine their communications behavior. In this way, we combine aging with the status sequence from employment to retirement or the absence of such a sequence (see Table 7).

Limitations on the analysis are readily apparent. Even working from a national survey containing thousands of cases, one can find few individuals under age sixty-five who are retired and, conversely, few who are still em-

Table 7. COMBINED EFFECTS OF AGING AND RETIREMENT ON COMMUNICATIONS BEHAVIOR (MEN AND WOMEN COMBINED)

| | AGE STATUS | | | | | |
| | Fifties | | Early sixties | | Sixty-five and above | |
Behavior (percent who:)	Employed (N=264)	Retired (N=29)	Employed (N=95)	Retired (N=31)	Employed (N=55)	Retired (N=280)
Read a newspaper every day	78	66	81	68	82	75
Read magazines regularly	65	55	67	61	64	53
Read a newsmagazine	16	17	19	6	14	14
Watch TV 3 or more hrs. daily	28	48	31	58	33	51
Watch TV news broadcasts daily	70	66	74	87	78	82
Discuss local community problems at least once a wk.	42	45	47	48	40	36
Discuss politics at least once a wk.	51	59	56	42	49	37

ployed after the age of sixty-five. Therefore, the data must be interpreted with caution. They are instructive, nonetheless. The probability of engaging in various kinds of communications activities is not reduced very much by aging per se when it is not accompanied by a disjunction in employment status through retirement. By contrast, the status sequence from employment to retirement (assuming that those who have retired would have behaved like those in their age cohort who are still employed, if the former had not retired) is accompanied by a decrease in the percentage who read newspapers and magazines (but not newsmagazines) and an increase in the percentage who view television heavily. Retirement also decreases the probability of discussing politics (except among the early retirees), but it appears to have negligible consequences for the discussion of local community problems.

Once again, the addition of a simple, relevant, second social variable has enriched our understanding of the sociology of the audience. In this instance, in contrast to those presented earlier, the second variable (employed or retired) is not additive to the first (aging) in its impact on communications behavior. It does not even specify, in the formal logic of survey analysis, the conditions under which aging has an effect, for there is no systematic difference in the communications behavior among the retired as they grow older or among the employed. Rather, the analysis suggests that a status change commonly associated with aging (namely, retirement) is more significant than aging per se, having an impact on both relatively young as well as elderly individuals.

A second change in social status which unfortunately commonly accompanies aging occurs with the death of one's spouse. Not only does this circumstance leave the bereaved individual to face further aging alone, without the companionship of a spouse, but at any time in life the death of one's spouse places the survivor in the position of an involuntary and unplanned status sequence from married to widowed. Amid the many changes in lifestyle that accompany adjustment to this new status, it is not at all clear or predictable from prior theoretical or empirical data what, if any, changes occur in the regular communications habits of the individual; more particularly, we know little about how these habits change with the interaction of the joint changes in these two major social statuses: age and marital. Our concern, then, is to begin to illuminate these effects.

Our strategy here, as in our treatment of retirement, is to compare the communications behavior of all widowed respondents with all married respondents in the same age category and to compare the changes, if any, in communications behavior that accompany aging for persons who are widowed and those who are not (see Table 8). The data are most clear. There is no systematic way in which the communications behavior of widowed persons differs from that of married persons, nor are there differential changes between the two groups by aging, with the possible exceptions that married respondents are somewhat more likely to discuss politics regularly than are widows and widowers and to watch daily television news broadcasts.[17]

Table 8. COMBINED EFFECTS OF AGING AND LOSS OF MATE ON COMMUNICATIONS BEHAVIOR (MEN AND WOMEN COMBINED)

Behavior (percent who:)	Fifties		Sixties		Seventy and above	
Marital status:	Married (N=334)	Widow; widower (N=36)	Married (N=241)	Widow; widower (N=76)	Married (N=179)	Widow; widower (N=112)
Read a newspaper every day	78	83	78	75	77	73
Read a magazine regularly	66	61	57	53	59	61
Read a newsmagazine	17	22	16	13	12	12
Watch TV 3 or more hrs. a day	35	39	50	40	50	47
Watch TV news broadcasts daily	73	69	83	69	85	78
Discuss local community problems at least once a wk.	38	36	39	40	34	31
Discuss politics at least once a wk.	51	46	47	39	32	26

AGE STRATUM

Here, then, in contrast to the findings about the effects of retirement, we have an instance in which the introduction of a second variable to that of aging, a variable that informed theory and conventional wisdom would specify as a reasonable modifier of the aging process, has no major impact on communications behavior among the aged. We close this section of our exposition with this useful example demonstrating the imperative need for systematic research, rather than conventional assumptions, using multiple statuses.

COMMUNICATIONS BEHAVIOR OF THE URBAN POOR

Our final example of sociological variables useful in the study of communications audiences is a simple one and serves no immediate theoretical objective. It concerns a serendipitous set of findings that serves to illustrate the need for simple descriptive statistics on communications audiences not ordinarily found in published reports.

Recent social concern over the economically disadvantaged members of our society has not been without its impact upon the field of communications research. From this concern has come a number of published studies and a variety of claims about the communications behavior of the urban poor. A recent comprehensive review of the findings in this area has been provided by Dervin and Greenberg, who conclude, "The media research all converges: the poor are heavy users of television and radio and, in comparison with the nonpoor, low users of magazines and newspapers."[18] They also conclude, among other things, that low-income blacks watch more television, show more use of magazines, and make less use of daily newspapers than do low-income whites. The reviewers, quite candidly, draw these generalizations from a variety of studies mainly based on local (perhaps noncomparable) samples. Since urban poverty is, by definition, localized in urban places, it is plausible to argue that local surveys are more relevant than national data for discovering the correlates of poverty. Nevertheless, data based upon a nationwide survey would, at the least, provide a broader background against which to assess and interpret the local findings. Such studies are within the powers of secondary analysis, and, by way of illustration, we present the data from the national survey at hand.

The purpose of this illustration is descriptive; we are not concerned with comparisons between the communications behavior of the urban poor and that of the urban rich, the rural poor, or the general population. We seek to illustrate the value of the lowest level of simple descriptive data about the communications behavior of a special stratum in the social structure. But we refine this description one step by construction of comparative data for the urban poor-white population and the urban poor blacks.

One shortcoming of the national sample survey for our purposes is immediately apparent. A nationwide probability sample includes only a small number of cases who represent the urban poor. We include as urban all individuals who live in places classified as cities (whether small or large) or in a

398

large metropolitan core. This excludes persons living in areas classified as rural farm, rural nonfarm, towns, and nonmetropolitan suburbs. Our criterion for "poor" is reporting a total family income (before taxes) of less than $3,000. By these criteria we located in the sample 119 urban poor: 59 white and 60 black. The communications behavior of these 119 urban poor is reported in Table 9.[19]

Table 9. COMMUNICATIONS BEHAVIOR OF THE URBAN POOR (AND BY RACE)*

		Urban poor, by race	
	Urban poor	White	Black
Behavior (percent who:)	(N=119)	(N=59)	(N=60)
Read a newspaper every day	53	63	43
Read a magazine regularly	32	39	25
Read a newsmagazine	8	10	5
Watch TV 3 or more hrs. a day	46	51	42
Watch TV news broadcasts daily	70	73	67
Discuss local community problems at least once a wk.	31	29	32
Discuss politics at least once a wk.	29	29	30

* Urban includes all individuals living in places classified as cities (whether small or large) or in a large metropolitan core. Excluded are individuals living in areas classified as rural farm, rural nonfarm, towns, and suburbs. Poor includes all individuals reporting a total family income (before taxes) of less than $3,000 for 1966. Also see note 19.

What is the value of such descriptive findings? Not, as we have noted, to make comparisons with other, more "advantaged" segments of the population. We know full well that income is related to media use and therefore need not labor the relative differences in media behavior between the poor and the more well-to-do. What is of value is to illuminate the communications behavior of individuals locked into a particular segment of the social structure, a segment that has been characterized as potentially unreachable by ordinary communications means. Is this the case? To what extent do the urban poor consist of the hard-to-reach members of the society, somehow out of the mainstream of mass and personal communications?

Obviously, any interpretation of the findings reflects the expectations and perspectives of the analyst. One can dwell upon the fact, for example, that nearly two-thirds of the white urban poor read a newspaper every day and take this as an optimistic sign; while all of these people are economically poor, fully two-thirds have not dropped out of the audience for one of the nation's major channels of mass communications. Television news watching is an even more common daily activity, engaged in by 70 percent of the urban poor. A more pessimistic analyst can focus on the third of that population who do not read the newspaper daily. Both the social optimist and the pessimist have to reckon with the fact that being poor and black reduces the probability of being in touch, on a daily basis, with the press and also reduces somewhat the chances for being a regular or heavy user of such other mass media as magazines and television. On the other hand, face-to-face conversations about local community problems are regularly engaged in by about three out of every ten members of the urban poor, black or white, as are conversations about politics. These constitute, at the least, a core of poor people who are actively involved in social communications and who therefore, in that respect, are not dropouts from the social system of which they are an economically disadvantaged part.

The findings also bring perspective to various generalizations previously based primarily on metropolitan local samples. We do not find nationally, as an example, that low-income urban blacks are more likely than their white counterparts to watch television heavily or to show more use of magazines (generalizations presented by Dervin and Greenberg, 1972).[20] They are somewhat less likely than whites to read a newspaper every day; but they are about as likely as poor whites to engage in discussions about local community problems and about politics.

Obviously, more research is needed to flesh out these findings and to resolve as well as to raise questions about generalizations describing the communications behavior of the urban poor. Once a good sociological description is available, then we will be in a better posture to consider the relevance of these facts and to relate them to our understanding of the role of communications for persons variously situated in the social structure.

PATTERNS OF MASS COMMUNICATIONS EXPOSURE AS INDEPENDENT VARIABLES

We turn now to our second major theme, the value of attending to mass communications exposure as an important sociological independent variable for the analysis of society. Earlier sociological research in the field of mass communications behavior introduced the concept of "all or none" as a descriptive phrase. It was intended as a shorthand way of saying that the probability of an individual using all of the mass media of communications is greater if he uses even one than if he uses none. That is, people who are exposed to newspapers are also more likely to use radio, to attend movies, and to read magazines than are individuals who are not newspaper readers. The relationship is far from perfect, of course, and many individuals attend to one or another medium more than to others. Researchers sometimes referred to those who use many of the available channels of mass communications as "media-minded." Persons whose habits favor a particular medium were sometimes characterized by this specialty, for example, as "radio-minded." Such terms sound archaic today, especially in a society such as ours, which has nearly reached a saturation point in the availability of all media of mass communications to its members. Cost is no longer a serious deterrent to media use, and even the urban poor are known to make great use of television, formerly the most expensive of mass media in terms of initial capital investment by the consumer.

Yet there was something behind these earlier conceptualizations that should not be lost to sociology simply because of the high probability of "use" brought about by the current ubiquity of the mass media. Our vision remains clearer, perhaps, when we consider other societies in which the mass media are less developed and not so readily available to the total population. There we are likely to be sensitive to the potential role that such institutions of communications can play in the social and political processes of the society. Perhaps we have been too myopic in our view that within our own society the widespread opportunities for mass communications have minimized the social significance of differential use of these media by various segments of the population.

What is required to bring the problem back to the surface of attention is a raising of the threshold of the operational definition of "exposure." It is unlikely, given our technological and economic development, that many individuals in our society "never" read newspapers or magazines, or never view television, or never listen to the radio. To pose the question in these terms is specious. Raising the threshold even a slight notch, however, adds meaning. Who among our population can be said to be so integrated into the stream of social communications that they regularly, perhaps even on a daily basis, are members of the mass audience for not merely one but several of the major channels of information and entertainment in our society? And who, if any, fall outside of this main stream of communications flow? And what difference does it make if people are tuned in or tuned out of this daily transmission of the odds and ends, as well as the major components, of our common information and popular culture?

Such questions direct attention toward important and, as yet, hardly explored research problems in the sociology of mass communications. As a step toward exploring the area, we present data bearing on two matters: patterns in communications exposure within society, and the relation between patterns of mass media exposure and even such elementary involvement in the society as is indicated by familiarity with simple facts about the current political scene and face-to-face discussions about social and political problems.

SOME PATTERNS OF MASS MEDIA EXPOSURE

A brief personal digression here may serve to explain the patterns of media exposure selected for attention in this section. For unknown reasons, too deeply buried in idiosyncratic motives to warrant unearthing, I have long been interested in people who *don't*. Perhaps the Columbia tradition of concern with deviant cases, to which Robert Merton contributed, accounts for this fascination with the contrary. Whatever the cause, this has been a thread winding through much of my own research starting with a doctoral dissertation about sociology graduate students who don't become socialized as social scientists; subsequent research on graduate students who don't succeed in earning M.A.'s or Ph.D.'s; evaluation of planned social action programs, looking for ways in which they don't (as well as do) succeed; and, eventually, research about people who don't communicate, at least when expected to in certain situations. This last-mentioned project introduced the concept of "opinion avoiders" into the communications literature.[21] It referred simply to individuals who do not engage in an exchange of opinions about a topic in a social context within which most people do so. The term was meant to be, and empirically shown to be, topic-specific: people who avoided personal communications about foreign affairs, for example, might very well be active in communicating about some other topic. Furthermore, it was found that these opinion avoiders also made little use of available formal (including mass) media of communications about the topic which they rarely discussed with others. The concept was complemented by its counterpart, the "opinion seeker"—the individual who actively sought the views of others about some topic and who, it turned out empirically, made extensive use of available formal and mass communications dealing with the topic. The concepts bear obvious similarity to such terms as the "chronic know-nothing" on the one hand and the information seeker on the other.[22] A small extension led to consideration of the degree to which some segments of the society might be communications "dropouts," that is, not integrated into the mainstream of social communication, mass or personal, about some topic. Further extension leads to the logically prior consideration of whether there is a segment of society that is outside the mainstream of mass communications in general (regardless of topic) and another that is tightly tuned in to several, if not all, of the media. Thus, we return to the significance of looking for patterns of communications exposure within the population.

As noted above, the search for individuals completely isolated from the mass media in our society is not promising; conversely, almost everyone has some exposure to all of the mass media. Therefore, we set our threshold of exposure a bit higher. From the survey available, we classify respondents according to whether they read a newspaper every day and whether they view television heavily or hardly at all (more than three hours a day for the former, less than an hour a day for the latter). The results are presented in Table 10. (Since the data used do not sample the population in such a way as to proportionately represent individuals in larger metropolitan settings, the data are not to be projected to the actual distribution of these combinations of communications behavior within the national population of the time. Nevertheless, they give some indication of the feasibility of finding various combinations within a national sample survey, and they are adequate for our subsequent purpose of exploring the relation between patterns of communications exposure or avoidance and being informed about even the most elementary facts of the political system.)

Table 10. OVERLAPPING EXPOSURE TO NEWSPAPERS AND TELEVISION
AMONG A NATIONAL SAMPLE OF AMERICAN ADULTS, 1967*

| | *Amount of daily television viewing* | | | | |
Newspaper reading:	3 hours or more	1 or 2 hours	Less than 1 hour	Percent	Totals
Every day	32%	28%	13%	73	1859
Less than daily	12	9	7	27	689
Percent	44	37	20	100	
Totals	1122	930	496		2548

* Sampling design overrepresented smaller communities in relation to metropolitan centers, and therefore these data should not be interpreted as representative of the proportions of adults in the entire nation who engage in these combinations of communications behaviors.

Less than one person in ten for the sample appears to be outside the daily reach of newspapers and television. Even these persons may be among the audience for other mass media (about a third, in fact, read magazines regularly, but our concern is with accessibility of the audience to daily, immediate mass communications). About a third of the population in the survey not only are daily readers of the newspaper but also view television at least three hours a day, well above the average time for the total population under study. We regard these two types as low and high users of the mass media. In addition, we consider those individuals who read a newspaper daily but view television hardly at all (that is, less than an hour a day) as essentially "print-oriented"; and those who view television heavily (three or more hours a day) but fail to read a newspaper every day as "television-oriented."

These are the four communications exposure patterns with which we are concerned, and therefore we drop the other mixed and ambiguous combinations from further analysis.

PATTERNS OF COMMUNICATIONS EXPOSURE AND
POLITICAL INFORMATION AND CONVERSATIONS

Having classified respondents into four categories according to their patterns of mass communications exposure, we examine their knowledge about six simple facts on the political scene and their participation in face-to-face discussions about local community problems and politics (see Table 11).

Table 11. PATTERNS OF MASS COMMUNICATIONS EXPOSURE AND
POLITICAL INFORMATION AND DISCUSSION

	Patterns of exposure			
	High users, both newspapers and television	High users newspapers; low television use	High users television; low newspaper use	Low users of both newspapers and television
Information (percent who know:)	(N=821)	(N=330)	(N=301)	(N=166)
State capital	96	97	93	86
Voting age in state	96	95	94	88
Name of state's governor	91	92	82	74
Name of head of local government	70	72	51	55
Name of one or both U.S. senators	62	63	38	41
Name of local U.S. congressman	42	47	24	26
Behavior (percent who:)				
Discuss local community problems at least once a wk.	42	47	27	25
Discuss politics at least once a wk.	52	58	34	30

There is a clear relationship between exposure to mass media and simple political knowledge. Individuals who are daily users of newspapers and/or television are more likely than others to know the name of their state capital, the state's legal voting age, and the name of its governor. At the same time, there is differentiation between those who are print-oriented and those who are television-oriented. Regular readers of daily newspapers, who do not use television very much, are clearly more likely to be informed about four of the six items than are those who view television heavily but do not read a newspaper every day. And the latter are no more likely to know the names of their senators, congressman, or local government leader than are people who make little use of either newspapers or television.

Heavy users of newspapers, both those who do and those who do not also make heavy use of television, are more likely to be involved in face-to-face conversations about local community problems and about politics than are persons who are only television-oriented or who pay little attention to either medium.

It would appear on balance, then, that heavy use of the media, and especially of newspapers, is related to greater awareness of the political scene and to participation in additional communications about such social matters through regular discussion with other people.[23] We run the danger, however, of imputing more social significance to these relationships than they may warrant. After all, we know full well that media exposure is related to other social characteristics of the individual, especially his education, and that these latter qualities may be related to political and other knowledge, perhaps irrespective of media exposure. As a limited test of this possibility, we examine next the relation between patterns of media exposure and political knowledge and discussion among individuals having approximately the same amount of formal education, that is, grade school, high school, or college.[24] (We drop from further consideration the items about the state capitals and the legal voting age, both of which were known by nearly all respondents.) The results are presented in Table 12.

Table 12. PATTERNS OF MASS COMMUNICATIONS EXPOSURE AND POLITICAL INFORMATION AND DISCUSSION, CONTROLLING FOR EDUCATION OF RESPONDENT

	High users, both newspapers and television	High users newspapers; low television use	High users television; low newspaper use	Low users of both newspapers and television
		Grade school education		
Percent who:	(N=189)	(N=74)	(N=114)	(N=89)
Name state governor	87	88	76	62
Name community leader	72	78	51	54
Name one or both senators	46	42	24	29
Name congressman	36	30	15	15
Discuss community problems	40	41	23	22
Discuss politics	39	33	23	18
		High school education		
	(N=472)	(N=145)	(N=159)	(N=51)
Name state governor	91	91	84	82
Name community leader	67	64	52	53
Name one or both senators	63	63	44	47
Name congressman	40	47	28	37
Discuss community problems	39	45	29	26
Discuss politics	51	57	39	29
		College education		
	(N=159)	(N=111)	(N=28)	(N=26)
Name state governor	97	97	93	100
Name community leader	76	77	39	62
Name one or both senators	79	76	57	69
Name congressman	55	59	39	42
Discuss community problems	50	53	32	50
Discuss politics	70	77	50	76

The relation between patterns of mass communications and political knowledge and face-to-face discussions continues to hold regardless of the amount of formal schooling of the respondent. Whether we consider the responses of individuals who have gone to grade school, high school, or college, those respondents who are daily readers of newspapers (whether or not they also view television heavily) are more likely to be informed about elementary political facts and to discuss local problems and politics than are individuals who merely view television heavily or who are not heavy consumers of either television or newspapers. The only exceptions are found among the small number of college-educated respondents who are low users of both media, an interesting deviant subgroup about whom we would welcome additional information from a larger sample.

Another way to look at the same set of data is to consider the consequences of combined patterns of educational status and media usage. Thus, the combination of a college education and daily newspaper reading produces a higher proportion of informed individuals than the combination of grade school education and less than daily newspaper reading. In general, any combination of more formal schooling and daily newspaper readership results in higher proportions of informed individuals than a combination of lesser schooling and little newspaper readership.[25]

The data also demonstrate the importance of information about media usage as a social datum. We have deliberately chosen the traditional social status measure most likely to be associated with knowledge, *viz.* formal education. Nevertheless, in comparison with its impact, the significance of patterns of mass media exposure on the proportions of individuals who are informed is considerable. The gains in proportions of persons who are knowledgeable that are associated with the increment of schooling between grade school and high school are often no greater than (and sometimes less than) the gains associated with daily use of the newspaper versus failure to use it, among individuals of equivalent formal schooling. For example, the proportion of individuals who knew the name of their state's governor, among those who make little use of either newspapers or television, rose from 62 percent among the grade school stratum to 82 percent among those who had gone to high school; but among those in the grade school stratum alone, it rose from 62 percent among those who use neither medium to 87 percent among those who read newspapers daily and who view television heavily.

Our data bear upon knowledge held in only a limited sphere, politics, and therefore further research extending the range of subjects is obviously necessary before one can generalize. As Robinson, among others, has noted, there is a need for additional research that takes into consideration the *type* of information that media (and formal education) can convey.[26] Nonetheless, these findings are consistent with others in the literature. More to the point, they serve to demonstrate, albeit with limitations, the virtues and sociological relevance of building information about combinations or patterns of mass communications exposure and social status into sociological analyses of the social structure and its consequences.

CONCLUSION

We have attempted to demonstrate, within limitations imposed by the data at hand, the need to conduct analyses of mass communications audiences through construction of typologies of social position more complex than are ordinarily used in mass media research. And we have illustrated the value of including data on mass media exposure as a variable in the classification of individuals within the social structure. The demonstrations have been limited, on the one hand, by the absence of complex indicators of social structure in most available social surveys and, on the other hand, by the crude measures of media behavior which most such studies employ. Obvious refinements and more robust analyses depend upon a greater quantity and quality of data to be collected in future studies.

Consider first the dependent variable of mass communications exposure. We have limited our attention exclusively to broad indicators of mass media usage. Other criteria which are necessary to flesh out a more complete picture of audience behavior include, but are by no means limited to, consideration of more refined measures of exposure to a medium or to combinations of media or to numbers of media (multimedia exposure), the social context within which media exposure takes place (for example, alone or with others, in private or in a public place), and exposure to particular communications content (for example, type of content, particular topics, specific messages). The manner in which any one or all of these aspects of audience behavior are related to one's position in the social structure has yet to be mapped, let alone explained, from a sociological perspective.

Consider next the independent variable, position within the social structure. How is one to select in advance what kinds of information about social positions are to be profitably included in audience surveys of the future? We have suggested two criteria: that the datum should index an individual's position within social strata in the social structure that one has reason to believe limits or enhances the chances for use of the mass media, or some social status whose role enactment carries normative prescriptions for greater or lesser (or qualitatively different) usage of the media. This is a start—and a step beyond what we ordinarily do. Nevertheless, it is limited.

Consider briefly the richness and complexity introduced by attention to social roles. Future research can profit from a distinction in the types of accounts of social roles which Merton distinguished in an earlier essay: depictive, sociographic, and analytical.[27] Depictive accounts of social roles are portraits such as might be written by a novelist or other observer untrained or uninterested in sociological analysis. From these we might learn, for example, what seemed to be the television behavior of a typical blue-collar worker during the 1960s. Portraits of the typical worker would have the ring of verisimilitude without the annoying qualifiers of statistical accounts of frequency distribution, measures of central tendency, range, and other such restrictions. Such portraits are primarily used as parts of a story narrating the more complex web of social relationships, plot and drama. Sociographic accounts, by contrast, also classify social roles in categories drawn from everyday life (for example, professional or worker) but describe them in terms of certain verifiable attributes that catch the sociographer's eye. Thus, we may learn that men are more likely to view televised sports events than are women. But why? We may even go so far as to determine that the norms of a society prescribe that men should be interested in and witness sporting events (televised or communicated through some other form) while women are discouraged from or even forbidden to enjoy such pleasures. We thus arrive at a certain level of systematic and quantitative knowledge about the social demands of various roles within a society. Certainly this is a more sophisticated and complex body of knowledge than comes from fictional narratives, typical though the latter may be. "Such sociographic accounts," writes Merton, are "an indispensable phase in the movement toward the sociological analysis of social roles. Fairly concrete descriptions of the norms embodied in a social role are plainly required before they can be subjected to more abstract analysis."[28] This sociographic level is, as the reader is aware from our preceding discussion, all too rare in the current research literature on the sociology of mass media audiences. Hence, the main themes of our present paper.

But beyond depiction and sociography, writes Merton, "is the third way of examining social roles, the way of the sociological theorist. From the standpoint of theory, social roles are combinations of designated properties and compounds of designated components . . . [which] . . . do not make for immediate recognizability of the role."[29] Critical as such classifications of the properties and components of social roles may be to the development of sociological knowledge, they seem far removed from everyday "reality," Merton notes, and thus "laymen often find sociological analyses absurdly remote from the world of direct and untutored sense experience when they mistakenly assume that sociologists are trying to describe the social world photographically."[30] One might add that this may well be the reason why so many conventionally sponsored studies of mass media audiences fail to provide either the necessary data or theoretical insights for an analysis of audience behavior in terms of sociologically significant components of the social roles which the audience members hold, either within the larger social structure or as audience members per se.

Merton's essay specifies several formal components of social roles that have been suggested by the theories of Sorokin, Parsons, and himself. These include, to mention but a few, direction of the social relation (mutual or one-sided), extensity, intensity, duration, affectivity or neutrality, diffuseness or specificity, universalism or particularism, observability of role performance, size and complexity of role-sets, and degree of clarity or vagueness of role prescriptions.

It is beyond the scope of this chapter to develop the applicability of these concepts to mass media audiences. The examples provided thus far, however, are not without relevance. We have suggested that not merely social mobility (itself possibly an abstract sociological characterization of roles), but also the intergenerational class continuity or discontinuity of lifestyles indexed by such mobility, is a useful way of classifying individuals in order to study their communications behavior. We have seen how the social role of being married can be refined by considering the homogeneity or heterogeneity of the educational statuses of the two partners and, in turn, how this relates to mass media usage. And we have speculated on the normative features of such role combinations that might account for differences in communications behavior. We have, at points, suggested the utility of such concepts as role-sets and status-sequences for analyzing media behavior: the former aiding understanding of how an individual's communications habits may be altered by the characteristics of one role partner, a spouse; the latter through consideration of movements between generations, or aging and retirement.

All these are but scratches on the surface, however. Much needs to be done. Little is known, for example, about the role partners who are relevant within the social context of exposure to mass communications, be they television programs or movies. What differences, if any, does the public or social visibility of being an audience member make in communications exposure and response?[31] Are there role strains that are built into audience activities? Do these conflicting demands account, for example, for the ambivalent, even guilty or hostile, attitudes toward viewing television among persons holding certain social roles in our society?[32] Are there sources of ambivalence toward mass media users built into our social structure?

These and other pressing problems remain hardly touched by the history of some thirty-odd years of research on mass media audiences. It seems time that the massing of statistical demographic descriptions of audiences, which "make sense" to the sponsor and layman, is supplemented by sociological analyses in terms that may seem less photographic and less immediately practical but which, in the developing history of our science, will enrich and extend our sociological understanding of communications behavior in complex social structures. It is toward this long-range goal that the present paper is dedicated, as a modest step forward along guidelines seen years ago by the theorist and scientific investigator to whom this volume is a tribute.

NOTES

1. Robert K. Merton. *Social Theory and Social Structure* (Glencoe, Ill.: Free Press, 1949), p. 212. The passage is from Merton's introduction to his chapters on the sociology of knowledge and mass communications.

2. *Ibid.*

3. The current study derives from a larger set of secondary analyses (sponsored by the Spencer Foundation) on the enduring effects of education. For results of the larger study see Herbert H. Hyman, Charles R. Wright, and John Shelton Reed, *The Enduring Effects of Education* (Chicago: University of Chicago Press, forthcoming). Data employed in the current paper come from survey 4018 of the National Opinion Research Center. I am pleased to acknowledge indebtedness to Professors Sidney Verba and Norman H. Nie, who directed the original survey in 1967 and who generously made their data available to us for secondary analysis. Results of their primary analysis, as well as technical details about the survey and the sample employed, can be found in S. Verba and N. Nie, *Participation in America: Political Democracy and Social Equality* (New York: Harper & Row, 1972). The analyses in this paper are based on the unweighted portion of the national sample. I am also grateful to Mr. Patrick Bova, of NORC, for his assistance in furnishing the data and associated code books.

Much of the computer tabulation was made possible through financial assistance from the University of Pennsylvania's Computer Center, under project number 2200; I wish to express my gratitude to them and to The Annenberg School of Communications (University of Pennsylvania) for research assistance. I am pleased to acknowledge the able assistance of Linda Park, who carried out all of the computer tabulations in addition to being a generally helpful and willing research assistant. Special thanks are due to Herbert H. Hyman, who encouraged these analyses, and to him, Mary E. W. Goss, and John Shelton Reed for constructive criticisms of earlier drafts of the manuscript.

4. An earlier review of the sociological significance of commercial studies of mass communications and additional discussion of this matter are contained in Charles R. Wright, "Access to Social Science Data in Commercial Communications Reports," *Public Opinion Quarterly* 28 (Winter 1964): 573–83.

5. Milton Gordon, "Social Structure and Goals in Group Relations," chap. 5 in M. Berger, T. Abel, and C. Page, eds., *Freedom and Control in Modern Society* (New York: Van Nostrand, 1954), p. 142. Gordon suggests the term "subculture" as appropriate to "these internal structures, made up of a combination of social categories and usually providing for the unfolding of the life-cycle. . . ." For understanding group relations, he proposes a paradigm that divides social structure into smaller subcultural structures according to combinations of ethnic group (race, religion, or national origin), social class, region, and rural or urban residence; thus Negro, upper-class, Northeast, urban would be one possible subculture. Gordon's selection of these four dimensions upon which to build his subcultural divisions is informed by his concern with understanding group relations. The subcultural types that he proposes are more than combined statistical categories; they are real social divisions, contexts within which important social processes such as socialization and primary group relations occur. Individuals of an ethnic-social class-regional-residential combination similar to one's own are likely to be the kind of people one feels "at home" with, and in this sense that particular subculture becomes the group of "participational identification" (in contrast, perhaps, to the "historical identification" which is attached to a single important status, such as ethnic group membership).

6. See, for example, Paul F. Lazarsfeld, Ann Pasanella, and Morris Rosenberg, eds., *Continuities in the Language of Social Research* (New York: Free Press, 1972), esp. pp. 9–118.

7. In this emphasis, we differ from Gordon's implicit contrast between the subculture of origin (into which, he states, one is born) and the subculture of achievement which mobile individuals enter later in life. We join these two sets of statuses to investigate their *combined* impact upon the behavior of the adult respondent, whose current position in the structure is determined not only by his present status but by his heritage.

8. For a thorough exposition on the strategies and logic of secondary analysis, see Herbert H. Hyman, *Secondary Analysis of Sample Surveys* (New York: Wiley, 1972). For an earlier analysis of the relation between social mobility and television program preferences among residents of one Southern community, one of the rare exceptions to the general neglect of such sociological variables in communications research, see Leonard I. Pearlin, *The Social and Psychological Setting of Communications Behavior* (unpublished doctoral dissertation, Sociology, Columbia University, 1956), pp. 71–73.

9. For a persuasive discussion of the need to consider intergenerational factors in understanding current communications behavior on an individual level, see Ray L. Birdwhistell, *Kinesics and Context* (Philadelphia: University of Pennsylvania Press, 1972), esp. pp. 3–23.

10. See as examples the excellent treatments of this topic in Herbert H. Hyman, *Survey Design and Analysis* (Glencoe, Ill.: Free Press, 1955), Paul F. Lazarsfeld and

Patricia Kendall in Paul F. Lazarsfeld and Robert K. Merton, eds., *Continuities in Social Research* (Glencoe, Ill.: Free Press, 1950), and Morris Rosenberg, *The Logic of Survey Research* (New York: Basic Books, 1968).

11. The reader might wonder whether marital heterogeneity in educational status had the same impact upon communications behavior for men and women. This appears to be the case. As examples, among those college-educated respondents whose spouses had less than a college education, 88 percent of the men and 92 percent of the women read a newspaper daily. And among those respondents with less than a college education whose spouses were college-educated, 84 percent of the men and 85 percent of the women read a newspaper daily. Comparisons among male and female respondents with mixed marriages at the college level show similar differences within each sex for general magazine readership, newsmagazine readership, heavy television viewing, television news watching, discussion of community problems, and discussion of politics.

12. See Matilda Riley *et al.*, *Aging and Society*, vols. 1–3 (New York: Russell Sage, 1969–1972).

13. See Wright, "Access to Social Science Data in Commercial Communications Reports."

14. Wilbur Schramm, "Aging and Mass Communication," in Riley *et al.*, *Aging and Society*, vol. 2, chap. 12.

15. See, for example, Rolf Meyersohn, "A Critical Examination of Commercial Entertainment," in Robert Kleemeier, ed., *Aging and Leisure* (New York: Oxford University Press, 1961), pp. 243–72.

16. Schramm, "Aging and Mass Communication," p. 361.

17. It will have occurred to the reader that the sex of the respondent may make a difference in the impact of loss of spouse upon communications behavior. Unfortunately, for the sake of analysis, it is impossible to pursue this possibility empirically. The majority of widowed respondents from all three age strata were women, 92 percent of those in their fifties, 78 percent in their sixties, and 71 percent of those aged seventy or more.

18. Brenda Dervin and Bradley Greenberg, "The Communications Environment of the Urban Poor," in F. Gerald Kline and Paul Tichenor, eds., *Current Perspectives in Mass Communications Research* (Beverly Hills, Calif.: Sage, 1972), p. 200.

19. The sample at hand overrepresented smaller communities in relation to metropolitan centers, and therefore these data should not be interpreted as representative of adults in the entire nation.

20. Dervin and Greenberg, "The Communications Environment of the Urban Poor."

21. Charles R. Wright and Muriel Cantor, "The Opinion Seeker and Avoider: Steps Beyond the Opinion Leader Concept," *Pacific Sociological Review* 10, no. 1 (Spring 1967): 33–43.

22. For a discussion of the chronic know-nothing, see Herbert H. Hyman and Paul Sheatsley, "Some Reasons Why Information Campaigns Fail," *Public Opinion Quarterly* 11 (Fall 1947): 412–23.

23. That the kind of source of mass communications that an individual relies on for information makes a difference in the amount and accuracy of knowledge that he has is well demonstrated by Schramm and Wade for science information, health information, and (to a less clear extent) public affairs. (Wilbur Schramm and Serena Wade *et al.*, *Knowledge and the Public Mind*, Institute for Communications Research, Stanford University, Palo Alto, Calif., mimeod, 1967.) Secondary analysis of several social surveys leads these researchers to the conclusion that "so far as our evidence takes us, there is reason to believe that a person whose main

source of information in any of these fields is the print media is likely, other things being equal, to have more information and more complete information about the field than is a person whose main source is the broadcast media" (p. 92). It is of interest to note, however, that knowledge in the field of public affairs was related to use of the print media only among respondents who had not been to college. The researchers suggest that this qualification to the general relationship is due to the simple items of information requested during the interviews where "most of the questions merely inquired whether a person had 'heard of' so and so, and television can meet that need nearly as well as print in most cases" (p. 91). They do not explain why they believe that television can meet that need as well as the print media (if it does so) for the college-educated but not for those with high school or grade school education.

24. An exception to the usual lack of classification by multiple statuses, noted above, is found in the recent and informative work of John Robinson, "Mass Communication and Information Diffusion," in Kline and Tichenor, eds., *Current Perspectives in Mass Communications Research*. Robinson employs secondary analysis of national sample surveys, combining the background variables of education, income, (sometimes) occupation, and race in order to yield six groups within the United States which show large differences in information scores about the Far East; but he is unable to relate these groups to patterns of mass media usage with data from the same survey because no media usage questions had been asked in the original survey. Therefore, he utilizes a second national survey, containing media data, to examine the relation between his six types and communications exposure. He suggests that level of education is the major factor distinguishing the six groups in terms both of their information levels and their usage of the media.

25. It is pertinent to note here a major difference in analytical strategy, reflecting different purposes between our analysis and the excellent treatment of a similar topic by Robinson (*ibid.*, p. 81). Robinson's concern is with searching for the complex interactions between social characteristics and media behavior in order to determine how much of a difference is made by usage of each medium in explaining individual differences in information levels, once other background and media usage had been taken into account. To achieve his purpose, Robinson employs a Multiple Classification Analysis which shows the effects of single variables once the effects of all others are held constant. These other variables are sex, race, education, and usage of other media. By contrast, our concern is the effects of education together with patterns of media usage both leading to differential proportions of informed persons within the total population. Despite these differences in purpose and analytical procedures, however, Robinson's conclusions and ours are compatible. He concludes that print media usage is much more crucial in explaining differentials in information levels (measured at the individual level) than is broadcast media usage. We conclude that the proportions of individuals having even elementary political information are greater among daily newspaper readers than among heavy general television viewers among all educational strata.

26. *Ibid.*, p. 83. For a recent example of classification of items of knowledge during secondary analysis of national sample surveys, distinguishing among items that refer to popular culture, public affairs, and academic knowledge, see Herbert H. Hyman, Charles R. Wright, and John S. Reed, *The Enduring Effects of Education*.

27. Robert K. Merton and Elinor Barber, "Sociological Ambivalence," in Edward Tiryakian, ed., *Sociological Theory, Values, and Sociocultural Change* (Glencoe, Ill.: Free Press, 1963), pp. 91–120.

28. *Ibid.*, p. 101.
29. *Ibid.*
30. *Ibid.*, p. 102.
31. See, for example, the interesting ethnographic account of the attempts to hide social visibility among male patrons of urban pornographic bookstores, by David Karp, in "Hiding in Pornographic Bookstores," *Urban Life and Culture* 1, no. 4 (January 1973): 427–51.
32. For data on such feelings, see Gary Steiner, *The People Look at Television* (New York: Knopf, 1963). Also see Robert Bower, *Television and the Public* (New York: Holt, Rinehart and Winston, Inc., 1973).

IN THE SPIRIT
OF MERTON

Sociology and the
Everyday Life

ALVIN W. GOULDNER

H EREWITH, some notes on the notion of the everyday life in relation to
the concerns of sociology. Perhaps the first, most elemental consideration is this. The Everyday Life (EDL) makes references to (focalizes)
certain patterns or routines of social existence as a *constructed* order, as the
outcome and product of human work. The concept of the EDL thus resists
any idea of social patterns as givens but, rather, seeks to make explicit what
is involved in the making and doing, in the constructing, of social patterns.
Seen from this standpoint, the EDL is a conceptual effort consistently to ·de-
reify the reified concept of "culture," which sees it as something "inherited,"
on the one side, and as "transmitted," on the other; as if it were a kind of
brick that could exist by itself between and apart from transmitter and re-
ceiver. In one part, then, the notion of EDL may be seen as a tacit critique
of a conventional and reified notion of culture. But as I shall suggest shortly,
the concept of an EDL is not only a critique of a technical concept such as
"culture," but also has deeper roots in the critique of certain traditional
features of ordinary, everyday, Western culture.

The importance of this theme in modern social theory has been conveyed
to us most recently by Henri Lefebvre from the standpoint of his own
individuated neo-Marxism and also, of course, by ethnomethodologists such
as Harold Garfinkel, most profoundly by his teacher Alfred Schütz, as well
as by scholars including Aaron Cicourel, Harvey Sacks, David Sudnow, Jack

*Alvin W. Gouldner is Professor of Sociology at the University of Amsterdam,
and Max Weber Professor of Social Theory at Washington University.*

417

Douglas, and others. Which is not to say, of course, that the EDL to which a Lefebvre refers is identical with that of the ethnomethodologists. Quite clearly, Lefebvre's project is the *critique* of EDL, while the Ethnos' project is its description.

This difference in intellectual task is deeply connected with their different conceptions of what EDL is. Clearly, for example, Lefebvre's critique of EDL premises that he views it as having certain internal contradictions that require its transcendence. The more descriptive, ethnographic, and even positivistic focus of the ethnomethodologists, however, premises a conception of EDL as less contradictory, and perhaps even devoid of contradiction.

Another related problem: Lefebvre sees EDL as a creative realm with a potential for the extraordinary, while the Ethnos emphasize the importance of ordinary language (OL). Their emphasis on OL sometimes disposes certain Ethnos to deemphasize (and to devaluate) technical languages and technical concepts. As a result, EDL is not usually *problematic* for the Ethnos. It is a concept that they are more likely to take as given than to investigate and to reflect on theoretically and critically. Since we, for our part, do not share any tendency to confine ourselves to OL, we have no compunction about developing a critique of the notion of EDL and to make it problematic. EDL, after all, is not an ordinary concept but an extraordinary one; the *concept* of EDL was not concerted by "ordinary" men but by "extraordinary" men: intellectuals.

1

From a historical standpoint, one of the first concerns with EDL is to be found in Plato's criticism of the "upside-down existence." Here, the ordinary mode of human existence surfaces only as a foil to the philosophical life which, unlike the former, is a critically examined existence; as a life in which human ends no less than their means are brought before the bar of reason. EDL is here conceived of negatively. It is the sphere where men are caught up in the pursuit of things of lesser value—of wealth, of fame, of ordinary appetites and earthly loves, rather than manifesting more reflective and rational concerns. It is not too much to say that modern Western theoreticity begins with a critique of this EDL, seeing it as something from which one must detach oneself, if one is to live properly. If Socrates is the philosopher of the "marketplace," of EDL, nonetheless, he goes there largely to *disrupt* its thoughtless routines and to bring men back to an awareness of themselves. EDL is the sphere of the "Cave" where men are essentially sleepwalkers, not yet awakened to the good and true. It is a world of only *seeming* reality.

The transvaluation of EDL—which is to say, the acceptance and envaluing of EDL—is, in Greek antiquity, the project not of a philosopher but of an artist, the great dramatist Euripides. Formerly, EDL made its appearance in the Greek tragedy through the presence of the Chorus, many of which were composed of low-status, dependent—subordinate personages, old women or old men, slaves, suppliants, fallen gods, and nonindividuated persons. In Euripides this underworld of EDL now surfaces and subordinate

418

persons play a more frequent role as featured actors. Now, in Euripides, EDL and its ordinary folk make their appearance at the moment of a profound crisis in the heroic culture of antiquity and along with a biting critique of this elite, heroic culture. Euripides speaks for the antihero of EDL; he speaks against the traditional hero's compulsive striving, his competitivness, his quest for individual superiority, excellence, achievement; Euripides speaks against war, against killing, against the classical masculine quest for eminence and holds this to be a realm of empty vanity. In a way, Euripides speaks on behalf of the EDL that the *women* of antiquity had known. Calling on others to reject the quest for power, fame, and physical courage, he extols love, the love of children particularly. Fondle each day lovingly, says Euripides: "What the common people do, the things that simple men believe, I, too, believe and do."

Both Plato and Euripides each express the crisis of classical culture, but in different ways. Plato, by attempting to overcome the failures of achievement-oriented culture, by controlling its competitiveness, by renewing its contact with the sacred, by subordinating it to reason. In effect, Plato tries to purify or cleanse high, classical culture, to sublimate its heroic impulses, and thus he separates himself from EDL. Euripides, however, seeks to endow EDL with a new value. He contrasts it invidiously with the heroic life, he sees the meaning of the human as dwelling within the EDL, not in its transcendence. For Euripides EDL is associated with the life of "ordinary" people—those whom the armada left *behind* at home, on its way to Troy; those excluded from power and fame, the weak, the stigmatized, the lowly, who were unworthy or incapable of heroic pusuits. EDL is thus at first a residual world. It is that which is left over after the high and mighty have gone. It is in the world of the women, the children, the old, the slaves. The EDL world cannot become a repository of value except with the failure of the heroic value system. EDL and heroism emerge, then, as polar contrasts.

The subsequent history of the EDL in the West is importantly shaped by Christianity, at least until the Enlightenment. In one part, Christianity demeaned EDL as the sphere of the worldly, the fleshly, the appetites. In one way, EDL was for Christianity only a waiting-room, a moral gymnasium, a testing ground; EDL was the "this world" in which men waited and prepared their souls for eternity. EDL was thus a subordinate realm, a spiritual prelude. From this standpoint, what happened in EDL was trivial compared to the eternity that was to follow. From another, however, EDL was also a sphere in which men gave conformity to the highest Christian duties of love, charity, and brotherliness. Moreover, if it is man's soul that should matter most to him, and if it is the condition of this soul that counts, then a life devoid of greatness and achievement might still possess the highest value a man might seek: the welfare of his soul. On the one hand, then, the doctrine of an eternal soul led men beyond the ordinary EDL; on the other hand, the doctrine of the universality of souls allowed men to value ordinary existence apart from worldly achievement.

The significance of EDL for the Christian was further enhanced by the church's insistence that good works might affect the future of one's soul. Indeed, there was always an important side of Christianity in which it was held that a man's duty was not done simply if he loved *God*. A man also had an obligation to give testimony and substance to God's word by doing his duty to others, by brotherliness, by charitableness. EDL provided Christians with a pathway to eternity by transcending the egoism of ordinary existence in EDL and by enacting in EDL the extraordinary existence of love. This side of Christianity, which envalues the significance of EDL, is of course greatly fortified by Protestantism, as Max Weber has shown in his analysis of the meaning of ascetic, this-worldly religions. Here EDL is brought under the most disciplined control of sacred prescription and here EDL becomes a realm in which one's personal achievements and successes become "monuments" to the glory, the goodness, and the blessing of God. Here, in one's relation to EDL, one may discern the salvation (or damnation) of one's eternal soul. Protestantism thus produces many of its subsequent world-transforming consequences precisely because it greatly intensifies the significance that Christians attribute to EDL. Still, the significance that may be attributed to EDL within the framework of an operative Christianity remains severely limited by two factors: first, by the openness of Christianity to the extraordinary, in Catholicism God's miracles, and, more generally, to God himself; second, by the hierarchical metaphysics of Christianity within which the EDL remains subordinated to the sacred and whose value derives from its linkage to the sacred.

The Enlightenment began a new chapter in the history of the EDL insofar as its critique of religion as a failure of reason—as a superstition— began to attenuate Christianity's concept of the sacred, thus truncating that which was beyond the mundane EDL. The Enlightenment brings the masses with their urgent needs and new skills onto the historical stage; it proclaims the possibility of happiness in everyday life, increasingly making EDL the arena of the highest, indeed, of the only, sphere of fulfillment. Ernst Cassirer's appreciation of Voltaire's new philosophy of history provides a clear picture of the new role that the Enlightenment assigned to EDL: historians should cease, said Voltaire, to study only political events, the fate of kingdoms, or great battles. The center of gravity now moves from political to cultural history: "His attention is particularly attracted by sociological details. He would rather know and depict . . . the forms of family life, the kind and progress of the arts and crafts." "I do not like heroes," exclaims Voltaire, "they make too much noise in the world." Once again, the EDL defines itself by counterposing itself to the heroic.

We might suggest that the romanticism that announced itself self-consciously in the first part of the nineteenth century, but whose first great spokesman was Rousseau, insists that the very success of the Enlightenment's EDL contains a certain failure. The new EDL confronting the romantic has overthrown its old boundaries and is no longer limited by a subordination to the sacred; the new EDL claims that it is the only realm of *value* because it is the only realm. This claim flattens and prosaicizes existence, says romanticism. That this EDL with its ugliness, misery, and boredom—that this should be *all* there is—is a devastating and demoralizing prospect to romanticism.

The misery of EDL is no longer redeemed by a sacred significance; the ugliness and boredom is no longer made tolerable by the expectation of a future beyond. It was the task of romanticism to attempt to reenvalue EDL, the specific EDL that it had been bequeathed by the Enlightenment. Romanticism sought to transform this graceless EDL; it sought to redeem it, to raise it up, to enhance it, to restore a lost mystery to it—in short, romanticism sought to "romanticize" EDL. The romantics saw the world as peopled by persons who possessed extraordinary qualities, "genius," those who are characterized by special talents that give them access to the extraordinary. The romanticists sought to relieve the grayness and blandness of the new EDL and to make life colorful.

We might say that from the very beginnings of Western culture EDL was the object of a *struggle*, as well as the instrument of a struggle. The Enlightenment, for example, used EDL as a critique of ancient hierarchies of lineage and church. It was used as an honest foil, the realm of the good, simple, of the Jacques Bonhomme who was "what he ate," to cast discredit on the high flown with their traditional pretensions. There are no mysteries, there is only ignorance and superstition, proclaimed the Enlightenment, thus seeking to expunge the extraordinary.

The romantics, however, while open to the extraordinary, often tended to conceive it in an unearthly, partly sinister, frequently weird light: their world was peopled with werewolves, vampires, puppets-come-alive, by the grotesque and ominous. Romanticism failed to protect the extraordinary as a *secular*, this-worldly thing. At the same time, however, the romanticists' pantheism and, more generally, their resurrection of "nature" were often a redemption of what, from the religious standpoint, was once deemed lowly and base: the flesh.

Let me suggest a few of the more general and more analytic aspects of the EDL to which this skimpy note calls attention: I have suggested repeatedly that EDL is a *counter*concept, that it gives expression to a *critique* of a certain kind of life, specifically, the heroic, achieving, performance-centered existence. The EDL established itself as real by contrasting itself with the heroic life and by reason of the crisis of the heroic life.

EDL is, therefore, also a tacit critique of the *political*, because politics is conventionally conceived as an arena of struggle, competition, and as a conflict of parties and leaders. In one degree, then, EDL is the nonpolitical sphere of existence and is thus a sphere rather different from the *public* existence with which politics is concerned. Concerned with the recurrent or routine, EDL differs from the public political life which is constantly in crisis, undergoing dramatic struggles, debating new policies and policy-relevant events. No matter how democratic or revolutionary, modern politics is the historical heir of the sublimation of the heroism of elites.

EDL is thus much closer to the kind of lives that have been traditionally imposed upon women in most Western societies, having precisely the kinds of recurrences that fill a woman's day in its round of child-tending, feeding, and housekeeping. To use a distinction once suggested by Jack Seeley, EDL is exactly that—that is, it is the recurrences of life that occur during the *day*time, not during the *night*time when men come home and churn things up and when nonroutine things, such as visiting and sexual activities, pre-

421

sumably take place. EDL is the culture of the daytime rather than of the nighttime. EDL is thus a sphere of maintenance—where nourishment and sleep are to be had, where wounds are to be licked, where acceptance is not totally contingent on achievement. EDL is at the interface between culture and "nature" or individual need.

Implicit in the notion of EDL is a certain model of social *change*, a model in which change does not come about primarily through the initiatives of elites and heroes but by massive movement in the collective minutiae of existence. It is not simply that here in EDL the masses are vaunted or extolled, in contrast to elites and leaders. Rather than emphasizing either the wars controlled by elites or the revolutions made by masses, EDL attends, for example, to the common manner in which parents treat their children every day or to the manner in which men dominate women, every day. The EDL is the pedestrian and mundane life that is so commonly recurrent that its participants scarcely notice it. EDL is the seen-but-unnoticed life. It is the everyday, the mundane, the secular, the deserted-by-the-sacred, the god-emptied life. The model of social change implied by a concern with the EDL is one that "goes beyond" the political and seeks a broader, more diffuse variety of changes in life, in the things-at-hand and within the person's control. Implicit in the EDL is the quest for a broader "cultural" revival rather than a narrower political thrust. What is sought, and what is said to count, is a change in the entire texture of EDL, not simply in parliaments, parties, or even the apparatus of the state. And this change of EDL is experienced as being possible here and now, at once and without waiting, and indeed without great dependence upon others.

2

These, we might suggest, are some of the fundamental albeit tacit meanings of EDL. Most fundamental of all, however, and as Harold Garfinkel insists, is the "seen-but-unnoticed" nature of EDL and of the common rules and shared background assumptions that stabilize EDL, establishing it as the standard of what is "natural" or "normal."

Garfinkel also rightly indicates that these background assumptions constitute the "points of departure and return for every modification of the world of everyday life" whether these departures be dreams or theater. "The member of the society uses background expectancies as a scheme of interpretation." Normally, it is not these background expectancies that are problematic, although some (and, occasionally, many) become such. Rather, such backgrounds are the primordial standards with which men commonly begin to interpret and to understand departures from the expected.

It is precisely such departures from the expected that constitute the realm of the *historical*—or, at least, are necessary for admission to that realm. The historical is constituted by those individualized events of imputed significance to the group that depart from the expected. It is precisely the EDL of the group and its common background assumptions that constitute its standard of the normal and, thereby, of the more-than-normal, or extraordinary, which is history. History, then, as objects, events, and persons spoken about, is grounded in the nature of EDL itself. The historical is that which is *not* the everyday; the EDL is the "bank" along which the moving, churning river of history passes.

As a topic to be written, history in the West arises precisely with the detribalization of Greek life in antiquity, with its disruption of the most ancient routines of tribal existence, a disruption that culminates in the extended exhaustion of the Peloponnesian War that Thucydides chronicled. At first, written history is and, indeed, long remains the unique doings of elites and heroes and is thus obviously constituted by departures from EDL. Nonetheless, the newer or modern history beginning with the Enlightenment also remains boundaried by EDL. That is, when the focus moves from political to cultural history, to the recounting of the "spirit" that animates a nation, or of its crafts, arts, industries, sciences, and philosophies, the focus still remains on the cutting edge of the new, the emerging, the progressive, and the modern, not on the massive enclave of remnant tradition.

Here the scope of the historian's interest has dilated greatly. Nonetheless, it is still boundaried and limited by EDL, which however changed in content and scope remains the seen-but-unnoticed that is the tacit standard for the new and the noticed which is the historian's focal concern. In short, the noteworthy that is history remains grounded in the noticeable, and this has its limiting boundary in the realm of the seen-but-unnoticed that is EDL. Cultural history, social history, or the history of civilization—in a word, "modern" history— reflects a new EDL, an EDL with a new and for a while more delimited scope. For with the great revolution of 1789 and its Napoleonic reverberation throughout Europe, and with the industrial "revolution," EDL is itself subjected to a thoroughgoing, continuous, and visible transformation.

Much of the *Communist Manifesto* may be read precisely as a response to the dissolution of Europe's traditional EDL, of its older "Civil Society." The emergence of a new division of labor, of new ways to earn a livelihood and the loss of old ones, the growth of new modes of communication and transport and currencies and laws, of new living standards and expectations and the undermining of the old ones, of new family relations, of new roles for children and women—all this speaks of the revolutionary transformation of EDL, of the destruction of the old, traditional EDL. All this is the emergence of a new EDL which, because new, becomes more visible, as does the older EDL that was recently lost.

But it is not only the new visibility of the once unnoticed areas of life that allow it to become the focal object of the new cultural and social historians. It is, also, the new importance and value that are now attributable to the masses who dwell in this once unnoticed realm of EDL. With the shattering events of the revolution of 1789 and its overthrow of a great king, a gilded court, and an ancient religion, the masses now emerge from the unnoticed anonymity of their once enclaved existence in the old EDL and

423

they burst onto the scene of the nonroutine, noticeable sphere of the historical. In short, the masses "make history." One can now attribute to them an activity level, a degree of potency, and a measure of worth that was once attributable only to elites and heroes. It is this newly imputed heroic significance of the masses, and not only the sheer visibility of the newly changed EDL, that is reflected in the new social and cultural histories.

3

Viewed as a set of rough guidelines for understanding social theory and social theorists, these considerations suggest that much of a theorist's self-understanding of his social origins will be formulated by him in terms of history, and specifically historical events. For it is these that will be most visible to him, as to others in his society. These considerations also suggest that, for the social theorist as for others in his society, the historical and visible events of his world are interpreted by him in terms of the commonplaces and background assumptions of the EDL he shares with others and which are considerably less visible to and, indeed, comparatively unnoticed by him.

Both realms, then, may be and are here expected to shape social theory —the historical and the everyday. Yet while not at all neglecting the historical as a source of social theory, and thus without at all viewing the theorist's self-understanding as a mere "false consciousness," it is a reflexive sociologist's special task to attempt to focalize the significance of the EDL as a grounding of theory. This is so for several reasons, for the EDL is the source and the realm of those recurrent experiences and background assumptions that are the grounding of the historical and are, therefore, central to the theorist's self-understanding. Moreover, EDL as a disrupted existence is a source of the objects to which history gives its newly focalized attention. It does so partly as the background against which the unfamiliar now becomes visible and as an obsolescent *old* thing toward which one may also adopt the detachment of the stranger. With the disruption of the old EDL, it is not only the new but the *old* that becomes more visible.

Here, again, we need to keep perspective and remember two things. First, that the theorist's interpretations of history and EDL are not only shaped by the unnoticed background assumptions that he shares with ordinary members of his society but are also shaped by the noticed and problematic postulations of the specific, formal, and technical tradition of his extraordinary intellectual specialization and its special subculture. This technical tradition is involved in a complex interaction with the theorist's background assumptions, and both, individually and in their interaction, are consequential for his own explicit and special social theories.

A second point deserving reiteration is that while all these levels must be dealt with in an effort to understand social theories and theorists, I hold that theorists should operate in terms of a special operating code, a special set of analytic directives that impose an obligation to concentrate on making manifest those levels of life that are, under certain conditions, only latent; a code requiring theorists to focus on uncovering the covered-over; to speak what has normally been enclosed in silence. This, in turn, means that I accept a special obligation to clarify the theorist's involvement in the EDL of his society, to indicate the permeation by that EDL of his life and work, and to explicate the, for him, tacit knowing of the background assumptions that he shares with other ordinary members of his society, and to explicate their *consequences* for the theorist's interpretation of his society's history and his craft's technical tradition.

If the special task of a "reflexive sociology" is to ground theory in everyday life—as the boundary and frame of history—this is precisely because it is not EDL, but history, that normally will be focal to most participants in a human group. This, however, is not simply the special task of a sociology of knowledge that arises because social theorists are craftier than others, when it comes to disguising their own groundedness in everyday life. Indeed, we might entertain the opposite implication, namely, that if "even" theorists— the professional insomniacs who presumably never sleep and "see everything" —if even they easily neglect the impact of everyday life, at least *their* everyday and their own grounding in it, then we had best assume that "ordinary" men, nontheorists who like their night's sleep, are no less, indeed, probably more, unwittingly shaped by their own everyday life.

Correspondingly, if it is the function of a reflexive sociology to exhibit the manner in which theory is grounded in EDL, then this is simply a special case of any sociology's function, which is to exhibit the ordinary group's everyday life. In other words, sociology's distinct function is to liberate EDL from the neglect that is the fate of the commonplace. Which is to say, its task is to focalize the seen-but-unnoticed. Sociology's task, then, is to transform the common perspective on the common and, as a special case, to heighten the stable accessibility of the common: to make it visible. Sociology's task is thus to liberate subjugated reality, to emancipate underprivileged reality.

This formulation of the mission of sociology seems an appreciable distance from the common one in several ways. The common perspective speaks of sociology as "discovering" reality, as finding or constructing new social laws or regularities, whereas our emphasis here is not on the discovery of the new *but on the display of the already known*. That is, sociology's task here is *re*covery, not *dis*covery.

This implies a second way in which the view here of sociology's task is nonconventional, namely, that the "object" of knowledge here, men, is unlike other objects of knowledge, in that they can participate in, have, and share the knowledge developed. They not only provide "data," in whose interpretation they play no part, but are themselves interpreters of their own and of one another's behavior. Sociology is that special study that is about those who investigate their own behavior, who have their own theories about their own collective being and have substantial knowledge of this life of theirs. Sociology is the study of human beings who can construct and achieve a sociology and who continually do so as part of their own seen-but-unnoticed construction of EDL.

An essential difference, then, between the findings of, say, physicists and sociologists is that, ontologically, there is no significant difference between subjects and objects in sociology, while there is such a difference in physics. In effect, what we have in sociological work are two different groups of investigators, or two different communities of theorists, each simultaneously confronting the other with essentially the same interests. Or, to try again: the study of social life by sociologists generates a situation that is much more like the research of two competing (or different) groups of scientists than it is like the situation in which physicists study, say, high-speed particles. The people sociologists study are surely more nearly like physicists than they are like the "things" physicists study.

Sociologists and those they study constitute interacting, competitive, epistemological communities. To the extent that each operates with a distinct paradigm shaping the terms of his understanding (of what is going on), it is exceedingly difficult to demonstrate convincingly—to one another—the sure and convincing superiority of each one's special standpoint. I say difficult, not impossible. In other words, I do not assume an incommensurability of paradigms or a significant untranslatability of languages. But the point is that this is, indeed, a problem in social theory that does not exist in physics.

Why is this a problem that must be considered in sociology? Why not simply treat people "as if" they were like atoms, or atomic particles? In some part, because if you do so they will resist or sabotage you. People, in our time, do not take easily to the prospect of being treated as things. Moreover, if you do—if, that is, you study (or treat) people as if they were things—then you are aligning yourself with all those forces in the social world that already do that to men. You are then not simply engaged in studying the world but in changing it politically. To the extent that we treat men as things, and reward them for compliant thingification, we are not simply studying them in their "natural" state but, rather, reinforcing and *creating* in them—rather than "discovering"—the very thingified condition we have defined as "natural." A situation defined as real is real in its consequences, even when those defining it are sociologists. We are thus creating the very condition we will later claim to discover.

There is also a sampling problem. When we study people "as if" they were nonpeople—that is, "things" like any other—what we will learn about them applies truly to them only to the extent that they are thinglike entities whose own understanding and consent need not be consulted or sought. Such a social science, then, is at best a science of men-as-things but not a science of men who are both things *and* nonthings seeking to transcend their thinghood and succeeding in doing so to some degree. To a social science of men-as-things, explanations suffice. For "explanations" are readings of human situations intended primarily (or only) for those outsiders who do not care how those whom they have studied understand the results of these studies, or if they concur in the conclusions to which they come. "Explanation" in sociology is (1) an "outsider's" accounting that is offered to others defined as being outsiders like himself and is (2) indifferent to the judgment of those "insiders" who are not members of the investigator's own epistemological community.

In contrast, and when this standpoint is rejected, when the investigator accepts his likeness (not *identity*) with his objects, when he accepts his co-subjecthood with them, what he offers as an understanding of their behavior is presented not only to his own group of specialists but to all, in and out, to specialist and "layman" alike. When an accounting is offered for consideration, appraisal, co-judgment by those who were studied, it is no longer an "explanation" but an "interpretation." The failure of ordinary persons to find this accounting "interesting," their failure to find it "relevant," their failure to judge it true or reliable is a matter of moment and concern to the investigator who does not sharply and radically separate his own epistemological group from theirs.

This is not to deny that, at any given time, some investigators may well believe certain things to be true and important about laymen, even though the latter do not then share their beliefs. Such particularistic beliefs must be problematic to sociologists in ways that analytically comparable beliefs need never be problematic to physicists. Upon discerning the particularism of his epistemological group's beliefs, the sociologist (unlike the physicist) must make these beliefs problematic. Specifically, he must *account for* the disinterest and disbelief of group members in his accounting. If he cannot do so, then it would seem *prima facie* true that he does not understand the people of whose behavior he is offering an accounting. An investigating community has good reason to have grave doubts about its own understanding of another community if the latter does not share or will not accept that understanding or cannot over time be persuaded to do so. First, because, in general, it is questionable whether outsiders can properly believe something about another when those who (by definition) may be in a special position to know something about themselves refuse to consent to the profferred understanding. Without compelling evidence to the contrary, it is elitism and antiuniversalistic arrogance to suppose we know another's existence better than he does himself. The burden of proving that claim must and should be placed squarely upon those making it. Secondly, an investigating community's inability to secure consent from the other also exhibits a degree of ignorance about the latter that surely must legitimately strengthen our doubts about the adequacy of their knowledge.

From this standpoint, then, sociology is a study of everyday life whose object is not so much to discover but to *recover* the nature of that EDL— to help the "object" to become less of an object and more of a subject, to become more fully aware of and hence more fully in control of his EDL. Sociology's only choice is to study and relate to people's worlds either in that way or as if they were "things," thus reinforcing their thingification and making them ever more such. Essentially, then, sociology has no choice between studying the world "as it is" or intervening and changing it through its studies. The latter is inevitable. All that is in question is how it shall intervene in the world, to what end, and with what awareness, but not whether it shall do so.

427

4

Normal sociology, then, is the theory and the study of the ordinary *thing*. Of what everybody lives. Of the shared and common things among men. Of their regularities and structured being. And it is a search for the "laws" that govern them. But normal sociology cannot actually "study" the ordinary but must construct it, must work at constructing it, in a certain way. Normal sociology must, that is, specifically learn how to treat people as if they were something else. As if they were not people, as if being a person was of no consequence in the knowing of men. This is difficult. This takes hard work. It is not, in other words, a "natural" view or condition to which we come without effort. To study and to live an ordinary life, to make a life ordinary is an achievement. But this is the work of sociology. The task of normal sociology, as we have known it, is to help make social life ordinary—to construct, not simply discover, the ordinary social life.

But people resist. Indeed, it is fundamentally normal sociology's drive to make human life ordinary that generates much of the "resistance" to sociology. It is not only that ordinary people believe that sociologists are an elite striving to manipulate or control them that generates hostility toward sociology. It is also normal sociology's impulse to make the world ordinary. Note that the most familiar objection to sociology's findings is not that they constitute a potential danger—although this will increase—but, rather, that they are "obvious." Essentially, this objection—all too often a correct and valid one—means that normal sociology is the study of everyday life grounded in an effort to construct it as ordinary.

In other words, the reproach of "obviousness" does not arise simply from the study of EDL as such but from the perspective taken on it, the perspective of EDL as "ordinary." Every group member, faced with the sociologist's picture of his life—faced, that is, with the sociologist's portrait of his EDL as *ordinary*—experiences it as a tacit claim for the sociological "outsider's" special insight which, correspondingly, devalues the "insider's" rationality, competence, maturity. The sociologist is seen as claiming to know as much about the insider's life on the basis of a brief study that he, the group member, has required a lifetime to learn. This, of course, is seen as being a very big claim indeed, however tacit and unspoken. Often enough the group member is correct. That, indeed, is often the claim being made. To characterize the sociologist's findings as "obvious," then, is to reject his tacit claim that it is possible to know a group's life and history better than it itself does with only brief acquaintance. To characterize the sociologist's findings as "obvious," then, is to reject the sociologist's claim to a superior knowledge of everyday life, of the ordinary; it is to reject his claim to being a supramember, to having escaped the limits of the everyday; it is to reject the normal sociologist's paradoxical but tacit claim to be extraordinary.

Yet the problem of sociology as a study of EDL has, at least, two sides. It is not just a question of the flaws of sociology. For even if sociologists did nothing but help others to recover their lives, that would be no small accomplishment. And if people's lives have to be recovered, it must mean that they have somehow been lost. Shall we assume that those who lost (or lost track of) their lives are merely the innocent victims of a heartless system who were themselves not culpable for what had happened?

The theorist, being an ordinary man (as well as an extraordinary one), can look at his own work in some part from the standpoint of those whom he is studying, and he can take their role toward his own work. In short, he already fears that they are soon to tell him how ordinary *his* own work and life are and how "obvious" his results. In some part, he already knows this; their caustic judgment on his work is no new discovery but only a recovery that he resists. In short, ordinary persons are trying to bring the theorist to a remembrance—to remind him that he is one of them and no better than they are. Rather than accept this, however, the theorist often seeks to avoid it by accentuating his difference with those he speaks about. Indeed, rather than speaking to them, and being thus constrained to remember who he is, the theorist commonly chooses the safer course of speaking *about* them, or even for them. He is tempted to accentuate the originality of his merely marginal distinctions and conceptually to trumpet his modest *apperçus* into "discoveries." The social theorist, in short, is working hard at being different from, and superior to, the ordinary member. The greater the danger that he will remember this chastening similarity (between himself and the other), the more he may redouble his efforts to differentiate himself. The theorist is, therefore, constantly tempted to exaggerate his claims for his work-product and his work-role, to present them as extraordinary even though he seeks to define the world as ordinary, as disenchanted, as devoid of mystery, and secured to the understanding of men.

What does it mean to make the world ordinary? Better, what must be done to make it ordinary? For one thing, the everyday world's reality must be so established as to be taken as given, and not as problematic. Everyday life is constructed of things whose reality is not normally problematic, which is why it consists of things that are seen but unnoticed. It is this that constitutes the secured, hence *ordinary,* character of the world. In a secured world, one need take no notice. In a secured world, we may neither notice others nor be noticed by them.

To construct the social world as real, reality must be constructed in a special way; it must be constructed as a given and not be infused with problematicity; it must be constituted as something that can be finished rather than being established as a continuing construction, or as an unending work. In sociology, this means that society must be presented as an object-thing and as separate from the process of "making" it. Being external, or taken to be external, objects are used as points of orientation and hence constitute terms and frames in which the self may be defined. Both sociologists and the men to whom they make reference are object-making; and in part they both make objects for much the same reason: to constitute terms of reference that are security-enhancing. Objects constitute stable differentia in regions, thus constituting the terms in which the region may be defined. One "sees" the objects, rather than the enregioning space. Objects thus constitute the organizing structures of social worlds. Much of their orienting, stability-giving, hence world-constituting, function is made possible by the assumption that they are out there; that they are the not us; that they are "objective," not subjective.

The normal sociologist's reification of "culture" and of "society" as object-things is essentially the same kind of construction as the ordinary person's construction of an object-centered social world. Both defocalize the extent to which these objects are of their own making. In the world-construction of ordinary persons, such an effort has ambiguous consequences. It is, on the one side, as said above, a way of organizing the region in which living takes place and of constituting stable points of reference within it. One can "look back" at and one can "come back to" objects, for they are "there."

5

Objects *limit* movement and derandomize activity. In that very limit there is both security and frustration. An object world is a world in which some outcomes are more probable than others. But if an object world is stable, security-giving, hence, world-constituting, the very limits which on the one side constitute protections are, on the other side, prohibitions. Limits are boundaries which on the one side enable certain things and, on the other, disable us from doing other things. On one side of limits there are constraints; on the other, freedoms.

Without objects, then, there is the disorientation and instability of *anomie,* for without objects there is no out-there world, and all is possible as in a dream. But once a social world is organized around a set of out-there objects, it possesses the inherent possibility of becoming a constraint which, far from always giving us the satisfaction of knowing where and what we are, can at some point frustrate us precisely with its out-there character. Objects constitute the social world as something not-us, as beyond-us, and thus foster our sense of being in an alien place. The object world, constituted as a not-us to provide a secure and coherent place for "us," becomes at some point an alienating enclosure: prison.

If the normal sociologist constitutes "society" as an object-thing, he is selectively concerned to do so in order to view society as man's world, as constituting the grounding for men and the place in which they can be, and become, men. Society as object-thing is seen as that which exists apart from and hence can anchor men. But this is one-sided. For an anchor can also hobble. Its very stability is also a disabling constraint.

What is systematically missed in normal sociology, then, is the problem of alienation. What is systematically missed in normal Marxism, however, is that there is a degree to which alienation, or *some measure* of alienation, derives from the inevitable tasks of world constitution. What is missed is that there can be no secure world which, precisely because of its security, does not at some point contribute to the hobbling alienation of men. What is missed in normal Marxism is that—unless there are things not dependent on men, unless there are things that men see as alien, as not them, that exist apart from their wishes and without their permission—there can be no stable points of reference by which men can orient themselves and from which they can derive security. There can be no stable social world unless men can both rely on and submit to the reality of the Other. In brief, what the normal Marxist misses in the problem of *anomie*.

In the very act of making the world stable, men risk creating their own imprisonment. In the very act of freeing themselves from a world not-theirs, men risk depriving themselves of shelter.

If the reality of the social world is spoken about, especially if it is continually spoken of, and, most especially, if the character of the social world as an object is spoken about and affirmed repeatedly, then that reality and that objectivity are cast into doubt. They are no longer secured. To affirm that something is real and is objective, to say it, is simultaneously to make that reality-objectivity problematic; to say it is real simultaneously raises the possibility that it is *not* real. For every affirmation brings its own negation into view. For to affirm is to contend; it is to contend against the negation; it is to enter into a contention with the negation. To affirm, then, is to be contentious, and the contentious is that which is not secured. To affirm the objectivity and reality of a social world, then, is to cast a shadow of doubt upon that very reality.

How then may the objectivity and reality of a social world be spoken without affirming it? How may it be spoken without the ambiguity of affirmation? One must speak in a certain, very special way: one must speak "objectivistically." To speak objectivistically is to conceal the speaking-subject in the form of speech employed; it is to conceal that someone, some subject, is speaking the object; it is to conceal that the object spoken of is and must be an object *to* someone; it is to present objects in speech as if they existed apart from all speech, thereby constituting a world without speakers. To speak objectivistically is to conceal that it is men who are speaking about men. It is a fundamental function of a certain kind of scholarly rhetoric, the *im*personal treatise, to construct an objectivistic view of social worlds that serve tacitly to insinuate the reality of the social world without responsibly affirming it, and thereby all the more firmly establishing it as real.

More particularly, the impersonal scholarly treatise form of speech—the "objective" style of speech—is speech that, by defocalizing its own character as speech and by focalizing what it is a speech *about*, namely, a set of objects presumably existing apart from it—such speech further occludes the *non*monologic character of the speech; it further conceals that every speech is an answer to a question raised by someone else, that it is a "reply" inspired by what someone else had said before. Objectivism thus conceals that the speech is not only about a topic but is an *address* to persons, publics, or audiences; that it is therefore part of a dialogue, rather than being a monologue; that it must therefore be evaluated in terms of its position in and contribution to that dialogue; and that to evaluate speech is to evaluate it partly with respect to its dialogue-situation and not only in terms of the topic-object to which it makes explicit reference.

To evaluate the "work" of theorists and scientists, then, is to see it as dialogue-situated *speech*, speech addressed to, grounded in, and constituting a community of speakers; men sharing a special culture of rules for evaluating the truth of their claims, but not a culture that is only an object but is also a doing and continual redoing by its members who, addressing and hence having relations with one another (as well as with their "culture"), also *do* a total social structure constituting them as a "group." "Objectivism," then, is the ideology by which such scientific communities defocalize their speech and hence conceal the grounding of their speech in the full character of their community, and not only in the object-society about which they speak, thus defocalizing the complex and numerous contingencies on which their speech (and its claims) depends; hence diverting attention from the many ways their speech may be implicated in and shaped by the community of speakers and their needs, rather than in the character of the *objects* to which their speech makes reference.

Objectivism, then, is an ideology that hides the speaker behind his topic, thereby communicating the reality and objectivity of that to which his speech makes reference. Men thus seek and construct certainty of being, reality, by concealing or repressing the many things by which that certainty is denied or which are dissonant with the semblance of certainty.

Sociology has the problem of constituting the social world's reality, of constituting society as real, without making pointed affirmation of this and thereby speaking ambiguously about that reality. To do so, it speaks of society as an out-there world, as externalized and externally situated. To intimate the reality of society, sociologists defocalize the manner in which they along with other, nonsociologists, participate in the construction of that world and have not merely discovered it. It is thus that the social world is made solid, secured, ordinary.

Ordinariness and stability are the ontological requirements of security. Or, more properly, of the sense of security, and of passivity and acquiescence also. To construct a social world that is ordinary and solid is to quiet doubts and anxieties, to relax and tranquilize; it is to create a world in which one can be at home, or rather, at Home. Normal sociology's task, then, is to put men at their ease and to make the world homey. It is to populate it with those like ourselves, persons prepared to negotiate reasonable terms, so that each may continue to enjoy his familiar comforts. This has one small merit as a characterization of normal, academic sociology: it helps explain how it is possible to have a "science of man" that lived through continual catastrophes and people-devouring wars without speaking of war, of imperialism, of conflicts, tensions, poverty, of racism, of sexism, of hunger, of false promises, viciousness, and envy. These, after all, are scarcely the furnishings of a homey world.

The goal of normal sociology here is certainly not an improper one. Sociology's ambition is aimed correctly. The task is indeed to make men at home in the world. But it is only possible for *men* to be at home, not things. Things have a place, not a home. If normal sociology seeks to make the world a home, it must first allow men in it. It must first people it, rather than thingify it. What normal sociology does is to make the world homey by disguising man's critical condition, poised on the extra-ordinary.

432

Intellectual Types and
Political Roles*

SEYMOUR MARTIN LIPSET and ASOKE BASU

L ITERATURE on the role of the "intellectual" consists of a vast body of descriptive "linguistics"[1] which is not integrated into any coherent theoretical framework. The present analysis, centered on the political role of the intellectual, attempts a limited contribution to that objective, a "paradigm" based on independent, but crosscutting, dichotomies: intellect-intelligence and innovative-integrative. Our intent is to provide a heuristic though still largely descriptive model reflective of the complexity of politically relevant roles performed by the intellectual. Such a model hopefully may aid in future empirical endeavors to understand the intellectual's place in society. A note of caution must, however, be exercised. The term "paradigm" has formal, logical connotations. It is not our attempt to pigeonhole various roles intellectuals perform into a rigid logical framework. To do so would deny the fluidity of the societal process. Rather, we wish to stress the diverse manifestations of the role of the intellectual.

*This essay has been written as part of a comparative study of intellectuals undertaken at the Center for International Affairs of Harvard University under grants from the Ford Foundation and the National Endowment for the Humanities.

Seymour Martin Lipset is Professor of Political Science and Sociology and Senior Fellow of the Hoover Institution at Stanford University. Asoke Basu is Professor of Sociology at California State University at Hayward.

Before engaging in an analysis of the role of the intellectual, we present relevant comparative and historical literature documenting the generality of an inherent antipathy between intellectuals and the powers throughout modern history, particularly since the rise of the secular intellectual. Reference to factors inherent in the nature of the role of "intellectual" which gave rise to such phenomena will be discussed in subsequent sections of this paper.[2]

Much of the analytic literature dealing with intellectuals has emphasized their seemingly inherent tendency to criticize existing institutions from the vantage point of general conceptions of the desirable, ideal conceptions which are thought to be universally applicable. Thus, Joseph Schumpeter stressed that "one of the touches that distinguish [intellectuals] ... from other people ... is the critical attitude."[3] Raymond Aron argued that "the tendency to criticize the established order is, so to speak, the occupational disease of the intellectuals."[4] Richard Hofstadter noted: "The modern idea of the intellectual as constituting a class, as a separate social force, even the term *intellectual* itself, is identified with the idea of political and moral protest."[5] Lewis Coser in defining the term stated: "Intellectuals are men who never seem satisfied with things as they are.... They question the truth of the moment in terms of higher and wider truth...."[6]

These concerns are iterated by the fact that "intelligentsia" and "intellectuals," the two words most commonly used to describe those in occupations requiring trained or imaginative intelligence, were used first in the context of describing those engaged in oppositional activities. "Intelligentsia" first began to be used widely in Russia in the 1860s referring to the opposition by the educated strata to the system. It was generally defined as "a 'class' held together only by the bond of 'consciousness,' 'critical thought,' or moral passion."[7] "Intellectual" as a noun first secured wide usage in France during the Dreyfus case in 1898. A protest against Dreyfus' imprisonment signed by a variety of writers and professors was published as the "Manifesto of the Intellectuals." The anti-Dreyfusards then tried to satirize their opponents as the self-proclaimed "intellectuals."[8]

These generalizations about the characteristic moral and political stance of intellectuals have also been noted with respect to specific historical periods. Robert Waelder concludes that "since the last days of the Sophists, they have been in the habit of questioning and challenging values and the assumptions that were taken for granted in their societies."[9] Luther's revolt against the church found its initial support from the faculty and students of his University of Wittenberg and elsewhere in Germany.[10] Hobbes, writing of the causes of the English Revolution in *Behemoth,* concluded that the universities were the principal source of the rebellion. "The universities have been to this nation, as the wooden horse was to the Trojans.... The core of the rebellion, as you have seen by this, and read of other rebellions, are the universities; which nevertheless are not to be cast away, but to be better disciplined."[11]

Tocqueville, in an analysis of the next great European revolutionary wave, made reference to factors that affected the outlook of intellectuals and their influence on the *Body Politik* as major sources of revolutionary ardor. He argued that intellectuals built up in men's minds an imaginary ideal society in which all was simple, uniform, coherent, equitable, and rational in the full sense of the term. It was this vision of the perfect State that fired the imagination of the masses and little by little estranged them from the here-and-now. . . . When we closely study the French Revolution we find that it was conducted in precisely the same spirit as that which gave rise to so many books expounding theories of government in the abstract.[12]

Joseph DeMaistre, an even more conservative analyst of the Revolution, also emphasized that "many French intellectuals were instrumental in bringing about the Revolution." He complained at the beginning of the nineteenth century,

one sees nothing but *intellectuals;* it is a profession, a crowd, a nation; and among them the already unfortunate exception [of opposing religion and authority] has become the rule. On every side they have usurped a limitless influence. . . . The so-called philosophers have all a certain fierce and rebellious pride which does not compromise with anything; . . . they find fault in every authority. . . . If they are allowed, they will attack everything. . . .[13]

Congruent with Tocqueville's analysis, Namier saw the 1848 events as the "outcome of thirty-three creative years," in which intellectuals throughout the continent fostered, in Lamartine's words, "a moral idea, of reason, logic, sentiment, . . . a desire . . . for a better order in government and society."[14] A variety of other analyses of political developments in France, the German states, Italy, and Russia point to the role of intellectuals and students in undermining the legitimacy of existing regimes. Friedrich Engels credited the growth of social criticism in Germany in the 1840s, in part, to the writings of the literati, who were wont to include "political allusions" in their writings. "Poetry, novels, reviews, and drama, every literary production teemed with what was called 'tendency,' that is, with more or less timid exhibitions of an anti-governmental spirit."[15] In France, young intellectuals and Bohemians frequented the Left Bank expounding, according to Cesar Graña, "radical-sounding, erratic political ideas."[16]

Though the Marxist movements have made the leading role of the working class in the revolution a matter of dogma and have frequently treated intellectuals as predominantly members or allies of the dominant strata, they could not avoid recognizing their importance for the movement. Thus, Lenin tells us:

The teaching of Socialism . . . has grown out of the philosophical, historical, and economic theories that were worked out by the educated representatives of the propertied classes—the intelligentsia. The founders of modern scientific Socialism, Marx and Engels, themselves belonged by social status to the bourgeois intelligentsia. Similarly, the theoretical teaching of Social-Democracy emerged in Russia . . . as a natural and inevitable outcome of the development of thought among the revolutionary Socialist intelligentsia.[17]

Much more recently, Chou En-Lai advised a group of visiting young Americans: "According to our experience, it is always intellectuals who start out,

435

because it is easier for them to accept revolutionary theory, and revolutionary experience from books."[18]

The historical record in prerevolutionary Russia and China bears Lenin and Chou out, not only with respect to the role of intellectuals as formulators of radical ideology, but also as providing important groups of supporters. In Russia the various revolutionary movements were intellectual- and student-based until the Revolution of 1905. That revolt began with a student strike, which subsequently spread to the workers and sections of the peasantry.[19] The Chinese movements favoring modernization, which first led to the overthrow of the Manchu dynasty, and later to the massive protests which culminated in the formation of the Communist party, also were primarily based on the students and intellectuals.[20]

Historically, the American intellectual has been seen as a source of unrest. The abolitionist and later editor of the *New York Tribune,* Whitelaw Reid observed in 1873:

> Exceptional influence eliminated, the scholar is pretty sure to be opposed to the established.... While the prevailing parties in our country were progressive and radical, the temper of our colleges was to the last degree conservative. As our politics settled into the conservative track, a fresh wind began to blow about the college seats, and literary men, at last, furnished inspiration for the splendid movement that swept slavery from the statute book.... Wise unrest will always be their [the scholars] chief trait. We may set down ... the very foremost function of the scholar in politics, *To oppose the established.*[21]

Much more recently, Daniel Patrick Moynihan concluded that since about 1840 the cultural (intellectual) elite in large measure has rejected the societal norms.[22]

The reader may get the impression that intellectual and student involvement in protest is confined to left-wing or progressive movements. This is not true, as witnessed, for example, by the intellectuals and students who constituted a core segment of the activist support for the Fascist party of Mussolini, and of the National Socialist party of Hitler, before they took power, as well as among fascist and assorted anti-Semitic right-wing extreme groups in France and various countries in Eastern Europe up to World War II.[23]

As Wilhelm Röpke noted, "In Germany ... where the university professor has always had exceptional standing ... it was from the universities that most of the other intellectuals drew the disintegrating poison that they then distributed."[24] Fascism, like diverse forms of leftism, had many meanings for diverse groups of supporters. But "the Fascism of the intellectuals above all had its origins in sheer rebelliousness, in an anarchistic revolt directed against the established order."[25] It was a militant antibourgeois movement. The French fascists who took "the avowed socialism and anti-capitalism of fascist ideology more seriously than others ... were especially literary intellectuals ..., men who were violently opposed—emotionally, intellectually and morally —to bourgeois society and bourgeois values."[26]

The complacency of the despised, hard-working bourgeois was accompanied by a threat which struck the intelligentsia as equally distasteful and far more frightening—the threat of anonymity, due to the speed at which industry and mechanization were advancing and the progressive rise of masses who could at last participate in the administration of a world in which they had previously been voiceless. . . .

To this threat of anonymity Fascism seemed to offer a solution, for it reconciled the cult of the hero with a mass movement. It defied social transformation by its deliberate protection of traditional values and attempted to impose a social structure which, though aristocratic in form, was based on individual merit regardless of social origin.[27]

There is, of course, no reliable quantitative estimate of the distribution of political sentiments among Italian and German intellectuals before the triumph of fascism. In both countries, particularly in Germany, left-wingers were also prominent. Much of the literature concerning the Germans in the Weimar period deals with the role of various groups of left-wing intellectuals, many of whom were Jewish, who attacked German political, social, and economic institutions in bitter terms, exhibiting total contempt for the culture.

Looking back, as one who was for a time part of all this, Franz Werfel confessed:

. . . "There is no more consuming, impudent, mocking, more devil-possessed arrogance than that of the avant-garde artist and radical intellectual. . . . To the accompaniment of the amusedly indignant laughter of a few philistines we inconspicuously heated up the hell in which mankind is now frying." Keyed as they were to a mood of downfall and destruction, writers and intellectuals as a whole failed to see that the culture which they were slandering included everything upon which their existence as artists, writers and intellectuals rested. . . .[28]

Although, as the example of the Weimar intellectuals demonstrates, intellectual criticism may be "leftist" or "rightist," intellectuals are rarely defenders of the status quo. As Florian Znaniecki pointed out, radicals, or "novationists," as he called them, require serious "critical reflection," intellectual analyses, a formal ideology to develop an oppositional force, while those who seek to maintain the established base their position on traditional standards. Consequently, "conservatives are less 'intellectual' and rationalize their defense of the traditional order mainly in reaction to arguments of their opponents. This does not apply to 'reactionaries,'" that is, to critics of the society from the Right who base their position on a belief in the superior worth of a previous social order.[29] Thomas Molnar distinguished three types of intellectuals, the intellectual as "Marxist," as "progressive," and as "reactionary." As he noted, "conservatism" as an intellectual doctrine arose in response to the triumph of the Left, and has been dedicated to the "restoration of the old order," not to the preservation of any existing system. Conservative intellectuals have generally been at odds with the spirit of their age, have perceived themselves as a minority resisting the dominant Left, liberal, progressive, political or social mood. Usually identified with the values of religion and patriotism, the

437

state or nation, they, like the Left intellectuals, have been antibourgeois, anti-materialistic—hence, their vulnerability to fascist appeals.[30]

The disposition of intellectuals to find the dominant culture and institutions of their society in distress need not take a political or activist form. Indeed, as Max Weber has noted, the tension between intellectualdom and the imperfect, confused, messy social order often may take forms far removed from the political arena. His discussion of alternative reactions has obvious relevance to the contemporary scene.

> The salvation sought by the intellectual is always based on inner need, and hence it is at once more remote from life, more theoretical and more systematic than salvation from external distress, the quest for which is characteristic of nonprivileged classes.... It is the intellectual who transforms the concept of the world into the problem of meaning.... As a consequence, there is a growing demand that the world and the total pattern of life be subject to an order that is significant and meaningful.
>
> The conflict of this requirement of meaningfulness with the empirical realities of the world and its institutions, and with the possibilities of conducting one's life in the empirical world, are responsible for the intellectual's characteristic flights from the world. This may be an escape into absolute loneliness, or in its more modern form, e.g., in the case of Rousseau, to a nature unspoiled by human institutions. Again, it may be a world-fleeing romanticism like the flight to the people, untouched by social conventions, characteristic of the Russian *Narodnitschestvo*. It may be more contemplative, or more actively ascetic; it may primarily seek individual salvation or collective revolutionary transformation of the world in the direction of a more ethical status. All these doctrines are equally appropriate to apolitical intellectualism and may appear as religious doctrines of salvation, as on occasion they have actually appeared.[31]

To limit analyses of intellectuals to their roles expressing their alienation, however, would be a clear oversimplification of the complexities involved in the relationship of intellectuals to their society and polity over time, and in different countries. It would ignore their system integration and value elaboration function. As noted earlier by one of us, an exclusive emphasis on intellectuals as

> critics of society and necessarily detached from it ... avoids some of the knottiest problems about the place of the intellectual in modern society. If intellectuals are by definition alienated, then the problem of what happens when they assume other roles in organizations, or move directly into the political arena is simply dismissed.... Those who postulate the eternal isolation of the intellectuals do not see the powerful social forces pulling them towards commitment.[32]

Any attempt to understand the dimensions of the roles of the intellectual in the polity must also include a study of the *sources* of authority in the cultural system. Weber attempted to explain the critical dimension of power within a particular cultural system by delineating three concomitant forces of society—authority, material interest, and value orientation. The greater the monolithic direction of these forces, the greater the concentration of power.[38]

438

Weber identified the intellectuals as the group "predestined" to propagate the national value system, who form the "leadership of a 'culture community.'" He saw a necessary relationship between them and those who "wield power in the polity," since "there is a close connection between the prestige of culture and the prestige of power."[34] Following in this tradition, Eisenstadt states:

> Political authorities need the basic legitimation and support which can be provided mostly by intellectuals. . . . Hence the continuous tensions and ambivalence on the symbolic and structural levels alike, between the intellectuals and the holders of power or authority, focus around the respective nature, scope and relative autonomy of participation of the intellectuals and the political powers in the socio-political and cultural orders and is rooted in their continuous mutual interdependence.[35]

To examine the role of the intellectual in the various systems, it is necessary to account for the nature and the source of the allocation of authority between intellectualdom and polity. A basic structural requisite for the intellectual's positive adaptation to the broader cultural system is mechanisms to integrate these two communities.

A brief review of different historical-cultural systems will serve our point. Weber, in discussing the nature of Brahminical scholarship, noted that

> the concept of legitimacy was rather simply that the single prince was ritualistically correct when and to the extent to which his behavior, especially toward the Brahmins, conformed with the holy tradition . . . but no matter what power an Indian king might yield in matters of ritual he was never at the same time a priest . . . in contrast, the oldest tradition of the Chinese knows nothing of independent priests standing beside a strictly secular prince. Among the Indians the role of the prince has apparently grown out of strictly secular politics, . . . whereas in China it grew out of the role of supreme priest.[36]

Different configurations of political and theocratic power were equally consequential in the rise first of Christianity and later of the Protestant sects. Troeltsch emphasized:

> . . . by its own inherent energy the religious idea itself neutralized secular distinctions; and with this depreciation of political and economic value the barriers between races and classes and peoples were also removed. . . . It was also quite natural that Christianity [and Protestant sects] should primarily seek and find its disciples among those who were feeling the weight of this oppression most acutely . . . another quite obvious point . . . a religion which sets its adherents in absolute opposition to the State religion, and to the social and civic customs with which it is connected, can only now and again . . . win its adherents among those circles which, by their wealth and education, are most closely connected with these institutions.[31]

In the Western intellectual tradition, separated increasingly from church and state, intellectual activity has been more disposed to question the very source of authority. Particularly in the developed democracies of the United

States and Europe, the failure to provide ". . . support for a universalistic ethic of merit, of freedom, and of scientific and intellectual creativity and originality" has frequently resulted in tension between the intellectual and the state.[38] It is not surprising that Western educated leaders from Asia and Africa were among the first to call for freedom from the same countries where they studied.

Inherent in the structural changes which have been described as leading to a "postindustrial society" since World War II has been a growing interdependence between political authority and intellectualdom. Such socioeconomic systems are highly dependent on superior research and development resources, which mean better support for universities and research centers and a much larger component of persons who have passed through the higher education system, thus creating a mass, high-culture market which pays for the institutions and products of the artistic community. Governments are often the main sources of financing for both sectors of intellectualdom. Recognition and financial rewards from the polity conceivably should help to reduce the historic tensions and the intellectual's sense of being an outsider. A further trend pressing in this direction is the fact that the complexities involved in "running" an advanced industrial or postindustrial society forces laymen, both political and economic leaders, to seek advice in depth, to defer to the scholarly-scientific community. Many, therefore, have seen these trends as fostering the role of the intellectual as participant, as leading to the "interpenetration" of scholarship and policy.[39]

Such "integrative" trends have been questioned as undermining the capacity of intellectuals to act as social innovators. Thus, Nettl has suggested that the very processes that enhance the worth of scholars to the powers, the growth of needed arcane knowledge, have resulted in a variety of highly minute particularistic specialties, thus reducing their potential to behave as intellectuals in the political arena, to be concerned with structural rearrangements according to universalistic principles. And given such developments, a society with the "much-vaunted freedom of expression," such as the American, "is less conducive to intellectualism" than one like the Soviet Union, which by its very demand that intellectuals be totally committed presses them to criticize a more repressive society from the vantage point of universalistic principles.[40]

From a quite different political perspective, Kissinger has raised a comparable query to Nettl's concerning the capacity of the scholar to combine the roles of participant expert and spokesman for societal values. His cogent question signals a dilemma. Fifteen years ago he remarked that "the intellectual as expert is rarely given the opportunity to point out that a query delimits a range of possible solutions or that an issue is posed in irrelevant terms. He is asked to solve problems, not to contribute to the definition of goals."[41] Yet, as we note below, the actual behavior of western intellectuals in the past decade casts doubt on the thesis that greater interdependence will reduce alienation. The new "postmaterialist" protest movements of "postindustrial" society are largely led and based on the intellectuals and their fellow travelers among students and those in the communications and research and development worlds. Greater societal importance appears to have helped spread the adversary culture of the intellectuals more widely among the educated classes, who reappear on the political scene as a new intelligentsia in the sense in which that term was used in Czarist Russia.[42]

WHAT IS INTELLECTUAL?

Many attempts have been made to describe what is meant by the term "intellectual." These tend to depict the "intellectual" as a man of ideas who creates and symbolizes the broader function of the human mind. He harnesses the essential and critical values of the society. Thus, he is a creator, evaluator, and applicator of societal expositions on which culture takes form.[43]

Many of the efforts to define the stratum have included almost all those employed in occupations involving higher learning. One of the earliest, by Samuel Coleridge, described the "clerisy" as comprehending "the learned of all denominations, the sages and professors of the law and jurisprudence, of medicine and physiology, of music, of military and civil architecture, of the physical sciences, with the mathematical as the common organ of the preceding; in short all the so-called liberal arts and sciences, the possession and application of which constitute the civilization of a country, as well as the theological."[44] The most influential contemporary analyst of the behavior of intellectuals, Edward Shils, has offered a comparable comprehensive definition of the category:

> Intellectuals are the aggregate of persons in any society who employ in their communication and expression, and with relatively higher frequency than most other members of their society, symbols of general scope and abstract reference, concerning man, society, nature, and the cosmos. The high frequency of their use of such symbols may be a function of their own subjective propensity or of the obligations of an occupational role, the performance of which entails such use.[45]

Given the diffuse character of his definition, it is not surprising that Shils includes among intellectuals not only those engaged in the "production (creation) and consumption (reception) of works of science, scholarship, philosophy, theology, literature, and art," but those involved in "intellectual-executive roles," as well. Thus he urges:

> Large-scale engineering projects, irrigation schemes, military operations, and administrative and judicial organizations tend to utilize generalized knowledge. Even where the empirical element (i.e., the experience of the practitioner) dominates, the large scale of such operations evokes in those responsible for their execution a sense of need for some more general principles to govern their actions. These general principles are not merely theoretical legitimations of the undertaking but are integral to the executive actions through which the projects are realized. The techniques and skills in these executive actions rest on or involve the performance of intellectual actions.[46]

To fully grasp the variation in behavior of the broad classes of activities perceived as "intellectual," it is necessary to differentiate among the dichotomies, intellect-intelligence and innovative-integrative.

The distinction between intellect and intelligence in mental activities has been made by a number of writers. As Hofstadter noted:

> . . . intelligence is an excellence of mind that is employed within a fairly narrow, immediate, and predictable range; it is a manipulative, adjustive, unfailingly practical quality—one of the most eminent and endearing of the animal virtues. Intelligence works within the framework of limited, but clearly stated goals, and may be quick to shear away questions of thought that do not seem to help in reaching them. . . .
>
> Intellect, on the other hand, is the critical, creative, and contemplative side of mind. Whereas intelligence seeks to grasp, manipulate, re-order, adjust, intellect examines, ponders, wonders, theorizes, criticizes, imagines. Intelligence will seize the immediate meaning in a situation and evaluate it. Intellect evaluates evaluations, and looks for the meanings of situations as a whole.[47]

The link between the application of "intellect" or "intelligence" to political orientations has been put well by G. Eric Hansen:

> Both intelligence and intellect are involved in all cognition, yet there seems to be a relative ascendance of one or the other not only in individual cognitive acts, but in the total existence and self-affirmation of the individual person. Esthetic, normative and religious judgments are typically marked by the ascendance of intellect: abstracting, synthesizing, judging, wondering, and imagining. More objective, mechanical judgments, those broadly conceived as involving "economics" or "engineering" . . . tend to be marked by the ascendance of intelligence. While intelligence moves out toward a meeting of the world and reality, to treat with them [extroversion], intellect brings the world to the self, interiorizes it, and makes it part of the ontic processes of the self [introversion]. . . .
>
> The political styles of the two tendencies are thus fundamentally divergent and only marginally related to intelligence or levels of education. Engineers, though requiring high intelligence and superior education, have shown very conservative tendencies in politics. The other extroverted and manipulative professions, dentists, physicians, and lawyers, have also tended toward the right. The more detached, introverted, and abstract professions . . . have shown very marked liberal/radical tendencies. The more detached and introverted the person (and thus choice of occupation) the more strongly the intellectual component seems to manifest itself in liberal politics. ["As a tendency," these include "the poet, the artist, and the man of morals and letters . . ."] . . . . In the case of the scientist, natural or social, it is especially difficult to make distinctions. The fine blend of both intellect and intelligence needed in these fields reflects the tension between the objective world and the discrete methodologies used to explore it.[48]

Some of the authors cited earlier have suggested another fruitful dichotomy to account for the variation in political beliefs, the difference between those oriented toward innovation and those primarily concerned with integration, including the transmission of the traditional culture and skills. Prototypically, these may be seen in the variation in activities between the research scholar or creative artist and the teacher or preacher. It has been argued that those engaged in *creative* work in the area of ideas, art, and science are inherently disposed to also reject other aspects of the status quo, including politics. This capacity for criticism, for rejection of the status quo, is not simply a matter of preference by some critical intellectuals of this quality of mind. Rather, it is built into the very nature of their occupational roles. The distinction between the integrative and innovative roles traditionally implies that those involved in the former use ideas, findings, to carry out their jobs, while the latter's activities involve the creation of *new* knowledge, *new* ideas, *new* art. To a considerable extent, in scholarly and artistic endeavors, one is much more rewarded for being original than for being correct—an important fact, a crucial aspect of the role insofar as we consider the consequences of such intellectuals becoming more significant politically.[49]

This emphasis on creativity is central to many definitions of the intellectual, such as those of Robert Merton and Theodore Geiger, which stress that intellectuality defined as a concern for creativity is a role component, which may be found in varying occupations, as the most useful way to approach the subject. Thus Merton notes that " 'the intellectual' refers to a social role and not to a total person." Persons may be considered

> intellectuals *in so far* as they devote themselves to cultivating and formulating knowledge. . . . [I]t does not follow that every teacher or professor is an intellectual. He may or may not be, depending on the actual nature of his activities. The limiting case occurs when a teacher *merely* communicates the contents of a textbook. . . . In such cases, the teacher is no more an intellectual than a radio announcer.[50]

To stress the innovative aspect of various professional activities as "intellectual" does not deny that most intellectuals involved in such roles are also engaged in activities that involve reaffirming and transmitting aspects of existing culture. There are inherently relatively few *pure* innovators, that is, individuals who spend their entire vocational energies on efforts at creation. However, as one of the authors has noted elsewhere:

> The creative intellectuals are the most dynamic group within the broad intellectual stratum: because they are innovative, they are at the forefront in the development of culture. . . . The characteristic orientation of these "generalizing intellectuals" is a critically evaluative one, a tendency to appraise in terms of general conceptions of the desirable, ideal conceptions which are taught to be universally applicable.[51]

Here the creation of knowledge forms the foremost concern. To such innovators, rules and regulations often pose frustration. As guardians of ideas, they wish to search for the timeless origin of "truths." Yet they hopefully seek their final fulfillment in integrating these into the wider domain of the society. Such an effort may not result in a positive acceptance by the laity. Thus, alienation may ensue. However, as Shils has noted, all those involved in intellectual activities also serve *integrative* functions. It is clear that their creative skills may be used for the "presentation of orientations toward general symbols which reaffirm, continue, modify or reject the society's traditional inheritance of beliefs and standards. . . . They fulfill authoritative, power-exercising functions over concrete actions as well."[52]

MATERIALIST INTERPRETATIONS OF INTELLECTUAL PROTEST

The interpretations of the critical orientations of intellectuals which credit them to the inherent concerns of roles involving more emphasis on intellect as distinguished from intelligence or on innovation as distinct from integration are in conflict with those advanced by analysts who would explain the diverse products of the mind, solely or primarily in terms of existential determinants, as responses to interests and affiliations.

Marx and Engels, though denying any dominant thrust to the politics of intellectuals, found it necessary to discuss the factors related to varying forms of political involvements. In line with their emphases on materialist (interests) as distinct from idealist (values) explanations of behavior, the early Marxist fathers identified intellectual radicals as drawn from the deprived or unsuccessful members of their stratum, suggesting that protest politics reflected discontent with their inferior social position. This assumption produced invidious explanations such as proposed by Engels to account for their critical politics in the German states before 1848. He argued: "It became more and more the habit, particularly of the inferior sorts of literati, to make up for the want of cleverness in their productions by [anti-governmental] political allusions which were sure to attract attention."[53]

Bakunin, though more sympathetic to the revolutionary role of students and intellectuals, identified the radical elements among them as *"déclassés."*[54] Henri de Man, writing in the late 1920s, also believed that the *déclassés,*

> pseudoscientists . . . ; unsuccessful inventors; unpublished poets; painters overburdened with originality; the ragtag and bobtail of Bohemia [are more likely to be found in the ranks of] communism and fascist nationalism [which] are the refuge of the ultras, . . . movements of extremists, and are therefore more congenial to the destructive nihilism of these thwarted individualists.[55]

Kornhauser has offered a similar set of explanations in suggesting that "free-lance intellectuals are more receptive to political extremism than are other types of intellectuals," because, in part, "rewards are much less certain to be forthcoming . . ., the form of the reward less predictable, and the permanence of the recognition more tenuous."[56]

During the 1960s, the heavy participation of students and intellectuals in the New Left movements clearly necessitated some analysis of the sources of this "bourgeois-based" radical movement. Some Marxist writers have continued to explain intellectual radicalism in "materialist" terms. Thus, the Belgian Trotskyist Ernest Mandel has argued that the protest of intellectuals is related to "profound change in intellectual employment," that is, to the downgrading in status, opportunity, freedom of work, and reward inherent in the mass growth and consequent bureaucratization of the occupations sub-sumed in the stratum.[57] Communist literature on New Left activism often suggests the related thesis that students and intellectuals are a coerced, alien-ated stratum forced to carry out the tasks that the economy requires. In seeking to explain why 1968 was a year of widespread student and intellectual revolt through much of Europe, an article in the *World Marxist Review,* the organ of international (pro-Russian) Communism, stresses that the years 1967 and 1968 "have been marked by the rise of mass unemployment," that jobs were not available in sufficient quantity to keep up with the wave of expansion of universities. The article argued: "These contradictions affect the intellectual community in the same way as they affect workers. After all, are not 80 to 90 per cent of the intellectuals in the big capitalist countries wage-earners."[58] An analysis by a Chilean Communist of the prevalence of a radical anti-imperial-ist outlook among Latin American intellectuals suggests that it reflects their excessive exploitation inherent in the fact that few intellectuals can earn a living from creative activity, that "most of them can devote only their spare time for their vocation." Engaged in nonintellectual work, the Latin American intellectual

> has to spend the best part of his time and energy in activity distasteful to him . . . and, although realization of this wounds his pride, he is a semi-proletarian because of the way in which he earns his livelihood. He fully fits Engels' defini-tion of the proletariat . . . "reduced to selling their labor power in order to live."[59]

On the whole, efforts to account for intellectual revolt as reflecting the narrow self-interests or the resentments of the declassed intellectuals have declined. Rather, the growth in the numbers of revolutionary intellectuals is perceived by many radical writers as a consequence of the collapse of bour-geois institutions and values, a breakdown that intellectuals can see and react to more clearly than others. Except to identify intellectuals as a harbinger of radical change, the Marxist movement still lacks an explanation of intellectual radicalism. Any real effort to understand the sociology of protest must return to the concerns of Hobbes, Tocqueville, and others, namely, aspects inherent in the role of the intellectual that repeatedly place him in the alienated and revolutionary camp. Crucial to understanding the nature of such aspects is the distinction between intellectual as innovator and the integrative dimension of intellectual activity and between the emphasis on intellect and intelligence.

THE POLITICAL ROLES OF THE INTELLECTUAL

We have discussed two dichotomies—intellect-intelligence and innovator-inte-grator—as related to varying political roles. These dichotomies are cross-cutting though independent. While "intellect" tends to be "innovative" and "intelligence" tends to be "integrative," the correlation is far from unity. This distinction forms the basic focus of our specification of the political roles of the intellectual. Our attempt to circumscribe the activities of intellectuals from early times to the present to interpret their society and culture indicates they

445

fall primarily in four prototypical roles: (1) Gatekeeper, (2) Moralist, (3) Preserver, and (4) Caretaker.[60]

The following paradigm contains the logic of our typology.

	Intellect	Intelligence
Innovator	A (Gatekeeper)	B (Moralist)
Integrator	C (Preserver)	D (Caretaker)

Our discussion of these four types is designed largely to illustrate the typology rather than to demonstrate its utility as a research tool. The examples point up the complex interrelated aspects of the different roles and the difficulties involved in any effort to unravel their overlapping interconnections in the "real world." For the most part, we have sought to illustrate the types by discussing variations in behavior among those involved in high cultural institutions, rather than to take the easier path of contrasting the more obvious differences between those clearly involved in cultural and scholarly activities and those engaged totally in what Shils calls "intellectual-executive roles." If this paradigm has any utility, it should ultimately lend itself to an analytical understanding of the varying political behaviors of those engaged primarily in what may be called the "cultural-scholarly" roles.

TYPE A: GATEKEEPER

Since his appearance as a recognizable social type, the *creative* intellectual has frequently assumed the gatekeeper role, often becoming the innovative spokesman for contending tendencies, opening the gate of ideas. His *essais* concern the "whole" man.[61] He is an independent thinker whose Talmudic search is for universal historical meaning. His concern is with the "core values" of a given civilization.[62] Edward Shils, though stressing that a creative scholar or writer may actually be much more involved in roles that press him in a more conservative (preserver) direction than in those that involve him in being a tradition-breaking intellectual, also emphasized the gatekeeper role in suggesting that in

> all societies, even those in which the intellectuals are notable for their conservatism, the diverse paths of creativity, as well as inevitable tendency toward negativism, impel a partial rejection of the prevailing system of cultural values. The very process of elaboration and development involves a measure of rejection.[63]

As long as higher education was primarily in the hands of the churches, instruction by the faculty involved revealed traditional truth and basically sought to socialize new generations in the accepted system of values.

446

Colleges, therefore, were centers of conservatism. The secularization of the university with the associated emphasis on original research and creativity is a major factor associated with the university becoming a center of social unrest in modern times.

The difference between those who use intellect to create knowledge and those who apply intelligence to carry out the work of society has been used by C. P. Snow to account for the variations in political behavior of engineers and scientists.

> The engineers ... the people who made the hardware, who used existing knowledge to make some thing go, were, in nine cases out of ten, conservatives in politics, acceptant of any regime in which they found themselves, interested in making their machine work, indifferent to long-term social guesses.
>
> Whereas the physicists, whose whole life was spent in seeking new truths, found it uncongenial to stop seeking when they had a look at society. They were rebellious, protestant, curious for the future and unable to resist shaping it. The engineers buckled to their jobs and gave no trouble, in America, in Russia, in Germany, it was not from them, but from the scientists, that came heretics, forerunners, martyrs, traitors.[64]

Yet if the hypotheses discussed earlier which relate the critical politics of the intellectual to the emphasis on originality and creativity as the key aspect of the role are correct, then it should follow that *the most creative people are also among the most alienated politically*. The few systematic quantitative efforts to test these hypotheses seem to indicate such a relationship.[65] We should note that these results do not, of course, demonstrate that activities associated with intellectual creativity press men to take a more critical political position. They are congruent with the argument that the kind of mind or background that impels men to question society also makes for success in intellectual activities. This thesis has been suggested by various analysts. Thorstein Veblen indicated over half a century ago:

> The first requisite for constructive work in modern science and indeed for any work of inquiry that shall bring enduring results, is a skeptical frame of mind. The enterprising skeptic alone can be counted on to further the increase of knowledge in any substantial fashion. This will be found true both in the modern sciences and in the field of scholarship at large.... For the intellectually gifted ... the skepticism that goes to make him an effectual factor in the increase and diffusion of knowledge among men involved a loss of that peace of mind that is the birthright of the safe and sane quietist. He becomes a disturber of the intellectual peace....[66]

Outside the university, among the "free" intellectuals, such as the artistic ones (or scientists before they were absorbed by higher education), stress on originality and innovation, on creativity, on following up the logic of development in a field has been held responsible through much of modern history for the conflict between intellectuals and their patrons, the people who pay for what they do. Hence, the greater length of their record as gatekeepers. Conflict is endemic in the intellectuals' need for autonomy and freedom, in their

447

opposition to efforts at control of their product attempted by those for whom they work, a tendency which is magnified in authoritarian societies. In such systems the hostility of the intellectuals toward the dominant authorities of their societies is extremely strong, since in these countries it is clear that they are under dictation as to what they can and cannot do.[67] As politics intrudes on them, they become more oppositionalist. This was strikingly evident in Communist China before the crackdown. As Schwartz notes:

> The particular animus of the [Chinese] regime toward the intelligentsia [since 1957] ... reflects of course the shocking revelations of the "Hundred Flowers" episode of 1956–57 ... [T]he official slogan, "Let the one hundred flowers bloom, let the hundred schools contend," was meant to suggest to the intelligentsia that a certain undefined area of free discussion was now open to them. What emerged was highly revealing. Not only were the literary and cultural politics of the regime attacked; not only did professionals challenge the authority of the Party within their areas of competence; but there were even those who raised the dread question of power itself. The very grounds on which the Communist Party claimed political infallibility were challenged. In raising the question of political power, the "civism" of the Chinese intelligentsia went beyond anything that has occurred in the Soviet Union since the inauguration of the "Khrushchev era."[68]

In democratic societies many intellectuals also tend to be sharply critical of those who appear to have power over them, a criticism which takes on a variety of forms.[69] C. Wright Mills pointed to "the really impressive historical evidence ... of the cultural apparatus, the intellectuals—as a possible, immediate, radical agency of change."[70]

In recent years there has been an encroachment on the self-image of the intellectual as a person who can comment on whatever is going on in society. The technical expert increasingly argues that the areas in which he has expertise should not be open to intellectual debate or, for that matter, to popular argument. The growth of, or emphasis on, expertise, or specialization, threatens the general intellectual's self-esteem and is, therefore, resented and rejected by many of them. Thus, journalists Joseph Kraft and Max Ways have pointed to a steady decline in the influence of "outsider" intellectuals, including scientists, on U.S. policy from Roosevelt to Kennedy stemming from the fact that the numbers of intellectuals directly involved in full-time high-level government posts increased greatly.[71] Kenneth Galbraith in a 1963 talk regretfully noted that the growth in reliance on bureaucratic intellectuals meant that brilliant general intellectuals had much less influence, in part because there is much less "abrasive controversy within administrations, and much greater emphasis on order, discipline, and conformity."[72] Ironically, therefore, the factors making for greater reliance by government on some significant intellectuals as *experts* may have enhanced the sense of separation, of alienation from government, by the much larger number who remain outside and see themselves as more ignored by power than ever. This is strikingly evidenced by the fact that the presence of many academics in the Cabinet and other high positions under Presidents Nixon and Ford (Kissinger, Schlesinger, Schultz, Levi, Dunlop, Burns, and Moynihan) did not reduce the tension between intellectuals and power-holders.

In a sense, this process through which an increase in the influence of the intellectual class as a whole may be experienced by many of the politically concerned among them as a decline is paralleled by the way in which the enormous increase in support for all forms of intellectual activity, involving a massive growth in the numbers involved, has also served to heighten the possibilities for frustration and consequent political alienation among them.[73] Intellectual life is characterized by a marked emphasis on a relatively few winning recognition for significant achievements.[74] Hence, the large majority are "failures," as well as "outsiders," a fact they are disposed to blame on the "patron," the existing society, even though many more intellectuals than ever have great influence on public policy and there is much more support for cultural and scholarly activities, including much higher incomes. Even the "successful," at any given moment, probably feel much more insecure, and therefore frustrated, about their position, given the constant threat to their eminence from the ever increasing number of young competitors seeking to dethrone them.

Modern society is in a position of needing the university, needing intellectuals, needing students more than any other society ever has, and thereby has become more dependent on them, more influenced by them. Ironically, the increased status and consequent greater political influence of the intellectuals as a stratum form part of the source of the radical intellectual's rejection of American society.

The university, however, has gained influence over other social elites. More and more it has become the major source of all elites, who must be certified as competent by their passage through the university. Thus, the dominant tendencies, ideas, and moods of the university infiltrate into the summits of most other key institutions.

This process suggests a reversal of Tocqueville's description of nineteenth-century American intellectuals who, finding themselves at variance with the laity, withdrew into private circles, where they supported and consoled each other.[75] It is more in line with efforts such as those of Mills and Bottomore to identify intellectuals as a "class" which seeks to affect society. As the latter notes in discussing the rise of the "modern" intellectual, "The growth of the universities, associated with the spread of humanistic learning, made possible the formation of an intellectual class which was not a priestly caste, whose members were recruited from diverse social milieux, and which was in some measure detached from the ruling classes and ruling doctrines. . . ."[76]

The distinction to be emphasized here differentiates "aristocratic" versus "democratic" elite linkages rather than "class" power as such. It is in the West particularly that transformation of intellectuals from aristocratic to democratic elite linkages have occurred.

These shifts have affected many once integrative institutions, including both the Protestant and Catholic churches in recent years. Harvard theologian Harvey Cox in the early 1960s heralded the dawn of the secular era. "Secularization is the liberation of man from religions and metaphysical tutelage, the turning of his attention away from other worlds toward this one."[77] The changes in the churches reflect an identity transformation, along with adjustments in theology and ritual. One of the major sources of this shift results

449

from the fact that key theological figures in these churches have taken the leading secular intellectuals as their key reference group, and now include people who consider themselves as intellectuals. Increasingly, these leaders seek the approbation of the universities. Yet it is difficult to become linked to the university community with its emphasis on innovation and retain a concern for interpretation of traditional religious dogma. This modernization of the church reflects the extent to which theology has become a part of intellectual life generally. Thus, religion has become an institution pressing for social change, even for radicalization, a fact that has consequences for the general value system of the larger society.[78]

The mass media is another integrative institution showing signs of being affected by ties to the learned world. More and more people who write for the major papers, or are in charge of broadcasting, share similar values and political orientations with the critical intellectuals.[79]

TYPE B: MORALIST

We begin with Dostoevski's apostolic injunction from *The Brothers Karamazov:*

> Judge Thyself who was right—Thou or he who questioned Thee then? Remember the first question; its meaning, in other words, was this: "Thou wouldst go into the world, and art going with empty hands with some promise of freedom which men in their simplicity and their natural unruliness cannot even understand . . . for nothing has ever been more unsupportable for men and a human society than freedom.[80]

In this prototypical role, the intellectual is both the examiner and the evaluator. In preindustrial society, intellectuals assumed the "sacred" right to *interpret* their society. The "monopoly" of the early Mystics of the Middle Ages articulated alternative Christian values.[81] The moralist role in the West, the concern with rooting out heresy, often found in high secular places, is linked to the fact that in

> Christian Europe the intellectual class first appeared as clergy, a fact that still conditions the attitudes of intellectuals today—not least those of them who are irreligious. In today's criticism of political policies one can still find the explicit statement that it is the function of intellectuals to be "the conscience of society." Europe's clergy criticized "the world" from the view point of higher spiritual values.[82]

With increasing differentiation in the Western societies, the "organized stratum" began to dissolve. The "free" intellectuals began to undertake the task of *inspection.* In Europe this development was linked closely to the emergence of the "idea" of the Renaissance. As Robert Nisbet has stressed, the humanists of this period closely resemble the morally righteous intellectuals of earlier and later eras. Unlike the "gatekeepers," however, most of them were "not scholars, not scientists, not philosophers, and not genuine literary creators or artists."

450

What we do find in rich abundance [among them] is cleverness of thought and brilliance of style. If there is a single word that best describes the mentality of the Sophists, humanists, *philosophes*, and others, it is *brilliance:* manifest in the quick thrust or *riposte*, the use of paradox and of inversion of meaning, the derivation of iridescent qualities, overwhelming verbal, from the already known, and perhaps above all, the polemical style.[83]

This category of brilliant innovative critics who have used intelligence more than intellect has often focused on cultural and educational critique as distinct from a concern with actual institutional change. That is, the moralists hold up the society to scorn for failing to fulfill basic agreed-upon values. They challenge those running the society with the crime of heresy. As a group, however, they tend to be fascinated with power, exhibited, at times, in exaggerated fear of it when seemingly directed against them and, at other times, in adoration of the charismatic leader with whom they can identify.

In nations undergoing "modernization," the process has been often impeded by moralistic intellectuals from the Right, such as the *pensadores* in Latin America who denounce technological change for undermining the spiritual-cultural values of the society, and from the Left, who often object to the same changes in comparable terms as introducing "Western" or imperialist values.

It is difficult to operationalize the distinction between the "gatekeeper" and the "moralist," but it may be argued that in the twentieth-century United States politically involved intellectuals have been more prone to resemble the latter than the former, beginning with the pre-World War I intellectuals who backed the egalitarian, seemingly antibusiness, objectives of the Progressives and Socialists. The prototypical examples of this group were the "Young Intellectuals," drawn heavily from Ivy League backgrounds and "from secure upper-middle class families."[84] Their characteristic locale was Greenwich Village in salons maintained by wealthy precursors of the Manhattan-based radical chic of more recent time.[85] But this "movement" of radical cultural critics, who held fund-raising parties for poor Wobbly strikers and marched in women's suffrage parades, broke down when faced with the seduction of "intellectual power" in the form of Wilson's administration and the subsequent threat to socialist opponents of America's participation in World War I.[86]

From the twenties on, many of the most outspoken American intellectuals expressed renewed antagonism to the business class from which came "dullness, stupidity, aggressiveness in commerce, conformity to the remnants of traditional morality, and a moral opportunism linked with certain blind convictions about the economic status quo."[87] In most cases, their apocalyptic revulsion appeared to take the leftist form of reconstruction. In America adherence to Marxism largely served as a method of "cultural protest." In the early twenties an alarmed California millionaire, Edward L. Doheny, called his fellows to battle against "a majority of college professors in the United States [who] are teaching socialism and Bolshevism."[88] Contrary to Doheny's concern, the Marxist sociologist Tom Bottomore has argued that beyond its manifest function of "protest" Marxist "criticism" largely helped American scholars to withdraw from the wider social arena, which he related to the inability of the intellectual to bridge "political theory" to "political action." The lack of a "two-way intellectual traffic" as Bottomore notes, signaled the absence of an effective radical platform in North America.[89]

The breakdown of American capitalism manifested by the Great Depression of the 1930s provided a test case for Bottomore's hypothesis. Large segments of the intellectual and educated communities flocked to support of the Communist and Socialist parties. Yet, as in the earlier instance of Wilson's New Freedom, the appearance of a reform President of aristocratic origins, Franklin Roosevelt, who openly flattered intellectuals and incorporated some into his administration as experts, was able to win their enthusiastic support, particularly when they were able to combine interaction with "antibusiness" power in America with a pseudoradical love affair with the Soviet Union.[90]

As Nisbet notes in a different context, the behavior of the moralist critic reveals a "fascination with power; especially the kind of power to be found in the leader,... for in such power there is greater flexibility of use, less likelihood of its being rooted in and therefore hindered by ordinary social codes and conventions."[91]

Following World War II, the moralistic admiration for, contempt of, and fear of power, exhibited in the combination of involvement in radical-chic elites in Hollywood, New York, and Washington, while expressing a polemical disdain for American culture and a belief that the United States is a repressive society, led many to fear the consequences of continuing to question the functionings of the society, particularly during the McCarthy era. Leslie Fiedler, David Riesman, and Nathan Glazer derided the "loud fears of the intellectuals" and suggested that their exaggerated estimate of the strength of McCarthyism was linked to the "outlived illusions of the Left."[92] Cold War heightened the intellectual's anxiety. As Christopher Lasch wrote of the behavior of many "leftist" intellectuals of that time, they "...have not hesitated to criticize American popular culture or popular politics, but...they have [not] criticized the American government or any other aspect of the officially sanctioned order."[93]

Yet concern over McCarthyism was to provide the catalytic agent that helped to transfer the cultural critiques of the postwar era into the politicization of the sixties. For as Nisbet noted:

> No single figure, no single issue back in the 1930's had ever seized the minds of faculty members as did the person of Senator Joe McCarthy and the cause he represented in the 1950's. . . . Nothing that came out of the fierce disputes of the 1930's, not even the almost religious hatred of fascism among liberals and radicals, ever transferred itself so completely to the halls of the university, ever attached itself, so to speak, to the very roles of academics, as did the threat of McCarthyism, as this threat was almost universally perceived by university faculty.[94]

The politicization of intellectual life which flowed from McCarthyism was largely reflected in a strong identification with a relatively conservative political figure, Adlai Stevenson, a man who sought to deemphasize economic and minority group issues in favor of a stress on the decline of moral, cultural, and ecological standards in American society. "Himself something of a conservative in early views, the product of quasi-aristocratic lineage and breeding, Ivy League to the core, gifted in all the rhetorical and stylistic ways that are dear to intellectuals everywhere, Adlai Stevenson was the almost perfect polar opposite to Senator Joseph McCarthy," and it should also be noted to his more liberal "populist" opponent inside the Democratic party, Senator Estes Kefauver.[95]

The linkage of cultural-academic concerns to national politics in the fifties made possible the intense politicization of intellectualdom in the ensuing decade. But it is interesting to note that the subsequent cultural-political folk hero of that period, John F. Kennedy, was not popular among nonpolicy-involved intellectuals during his lifetime. Stevenson and, to a lesser extent, Hubert Humphrey were the preferred candidates of the politicized intellectuals who despaired of Kennedy, whose record revealed no great political passions and who had sat out the fight against McCarthy while other members of his family, including his brother Robert, had actively supported him. For many, the choice between Kennedy and Nixon meant no choice. "In looking over the now-ancient journals of 1960 we can see how bitter the intellectuals were over the choice of candidates and philosophies, how sure they were that the ages of McKinley, Coolidge, and Eisenhower had put their unequivocal stamp on the American culture."[96]

Recognizing his difficulties with this constituency, Kennedy deliberately emphasized the "public role of the intellectual" during and after his inauguration. And as Joseph Kraft indicated, this emphasis had "a political purpose—as plain as the appointment of a Negro judge or a Polish Postmaster General. It is aimed to be specific, at the egghead liberals within the Democratic party. . . ."[97] But during the thousand days of the administration, Kennedy continued to meet with considerable rebuffs. Nine months after the young President took office, James Reston wrote a column in the *New York Times* discussing the "discontented intellectuals." He noted that the new regime was being described as "the third Eisenhower administration," that the intellectuals were "disenchanted by the absence of new policies, the preoccupation with political results, the compromises over education and the techniques of appointing conservatives to put over liberal policies and liberals to carry out conservative policies."[98] And in an article published in November 1963, just before the assassination, Kraft reported that, in spite of the large number of academics who held important posts in the administration as "technical bureaucrats" and its use of cultural awards as "a form of patronage," there was considerable tension between the administration and the intellectuals. "Harsh criticisms have come from the novelists Norman Mailer and James Baldwin, the playwright Gore Vidal, and the political scientists Sidney Hyman and Louis Halle. 'Where,' the critic Alfred Kazin asked in a notable essay, 'is the meaningful relation of intellectuals to power.' "[99]

Ironically, the tragic death of the young President and his succession by Lyndon Johnson, who appeared to typify the "wheeler and dealer" politician, accomplished what Kennedy had been unable to do in life. This change was curiously prophesied before the 1960 election by James MacGregor Burns, who, after noting the lack of appeal of Kennedy's nonemotional pragmatic orientation, stated: "If he should die tomorrow in a plane crash, he would become at once a liberal martyr, for the liberal publicists of the land would rush to construct a hero."[100]

During the mid-1960s, American intellectuals once again appeared to take over the role of polemical "moralists" with respect to political criticism, denouncing the system for betraying its own basic democratic and anti-imperialist beliefs. Beginning with the faculty-initiated teach-ins against the Vietnam War in 1965, they played a major role in sustaining a mass antiwar movement out of which a number of radicals emerged. A variety of statistical data serves to validate Kenneth Galbraith's boast about their political effect.

> It was the universities—not the trade unions, nor the freelance intellectuals, nor the press, nor the businessmen . . .—which led the opposition to the Vietnam War, which forced the retirement of President Johnson, which are forcing the pace of our present withdrawal [1971] from Vietnam, which are leading the battle against the great corporations on the issue of pollution, and which at the last congressional elections retired a score or more of the more egregious time-servers, military sycophants and hawks.[101]

Yet with the decline in American military participation in the Vietnam War and the end of mass forms of political protest, the support for moralistic *political* perspectives also has been undermined. Working within a society, in which no left-wing third party has secured more than 2 percent of the vote since World War I, American intellectuals, like American students, have returned to an emphasis on cultural and educational criticism. Their most important policy-relevant critiques have dealt with the inequities of the educational system. Their principal spokesmen continue to challenge the society for preserving inequality, but largely from the vantage point of its failure to live up to traditional American ideals of equality of opportunity. Their predominant political issues are the ancient American progressive causes, the corruption of the environment and politics, which they again blame on American business, on the monopolies (*née* trusts), and on the inherent greed of commercial civilization.

In a larger sense, however, the emphasis on the "moralist" as distinct from the "gatekeeper" role among American intellectuals in recent times may reflect the fact that, unlike revolutionary intellectuals in other places, and other times, they have not known what they want. As Crane Brinton noted:

> [I]t is clear that the [American] intellectuals for the most part do not know the good arrangements, institutions, beliefs—not even the "ism"—they want in place of existing evil ones. . . .
> This lack of a firm positive program, even in politics, is surely a major reason why the alienation of American intellectuals today is not a "transfer of allegiance," not a symptom of possible revolutionary action in our society . . . ; and this lack is also a major reason . . . why the state of mind of our intellectuals in 1932 was no sign of a coming revolution, a coming which was hardly threatened, or promised, in the slightest in our perhaps all-too-stable American society.[102]

Hence, once more, we return to our earlier emphasis on the intellectuals' source of authority and their integration into the larger social milieu. The absence of large numbers of American intellectuals who have applied innovative intellect to politics has reflected the nation's professed philosophic "outlook," its liberal egalitarianism. However, the extent to which these people have been unable to adapt to the larger political system has been largely due to the conflicting "rights" in interpreting their authority as between "scholarship" and "art" or "ideas" and "politics." The "messiah" disavows his potential *following*. He becomes the "watchdog" for the social system. For him, the task of the Grand Inquisitor never ends.

TYPE C: PRESERVER

Aron has noted that behind all "doctrines" and all "parties" are intellectuals who translate "opinion or interests into theories."[103] In this role of preserver, he may often be a tradition-maker helping to frame the legitimation for authority, old or new. As Eisenstadt puts it: "They participate in the symbolic and institutional frameworks of such traditions, or as performing their functions as the conscience of society within the framework of existing traditions."[104]

In contributing to system maintenance, however, intellectuals become integrated themselves as part of the cultural system, often fostering what Weber called the "National Idea." In a highly differentiated society, this role becomes the "expression of a special craft."[105] They apply reason to the organized institutional framework of society. As Shils noted, "Alongside these institutions for the formation of skills, the guidance of dispositions, and the preliminary exercise of the capacity for judgment, there are also the institutions in which these skills, dispositions, capacities are to be brought into serious operation. . . ." This attitude is derived from world-historic cultural roots. Thus, Znaniecki rightly asserts that in order for intellectuals to perform this role they must be able to explicate the knowledge of past to present society.[106] Their power lies largely in their ability to narrate human destiny. They integrate the ethos of their society.

The articulative powers of Japanese intellectuals in helping to reconstruct their society during the Meiji Restoration illustrates the significance of this role. As Jun Etō remarked:

> No matter how radically they differed from one another in their literary or political opinions, Meiji writers shared in the dominant national mission of their time: the creation of a new civilization that would bring together the best features of East and West, while remaining Japanese at its core.[107]

Although the key Marxist intellectuals, as formulators of original concepts and strategies fostering fundamental change, properly fall under the category of those who have applied intellect as gatekeeping innovators, they also should be seen as the formulators of new traditions which have served to create a new legitimation for hierarchical relationships in postcapitalist society.[108] Various critics have even argued that Marxism emerged as an ideological expression of the "class interests" of the intellectuals who foresaw socialism as a social system dominated by them as the spokesmen for the incompetent masses. Jan Machajski, a Polish former Marxist, writing at the turn of the century, paralleled the interpretation that Marxists presented of the role of populist and egalitarian slogans of the American and French revolutions in legitimating bourgeois class rule in his analysis of the consequences of successful Socialist revolution. Like the anarchist theoretician Michael Bakunin, he argued that it would result in a society controlled by the mandarins. And he suggested, predating the similar thesis of Robert Michels, that concepts of participatory democracy, of control of the machinery of complex industrial society by the masses, in a system in which opposition politics and protest were ruled out, were utopian and would only serve to conceal the fact that such a society would be severely stratified with respect to power and privilege.[109]

As might be expected, Machajski's writings about the preservative functions of Marxist ideology have not been allowed to circulate in the Communist world, but there is some reason to believe that his analysis and predictions have bothered the leaders of the Soviet Union. Machajski and his teachings were subject to vitriolic attack in *Pravda* in 1926 when he died and again in 1938, when they were condemned as "outrageous, hooligan, and dangerous to the Soviet state."[110]

Views similar to Machajski's have been enunciated more recently by the senior Marxist in British Sociology, T. B. Bottomore, who argues that in the Soviet Union "the sentiment of equality is exploited by asserting the moral superiority of a 'classless' society in which privilege is no longer privilege but only a beneficent necessity on the road to perfect justice. This doctrine, which justifies the rule of an elite over the masses, is only the most recent version of an ancient, almost venerable hypocrisy." Bottomore sees more hope, therefore, for the furtherance of egalitarian objectives in western countries than in the Communist ones, because the masses can defend themselves in the former.

> We may expect, in the democratic countries, a continuing, gradual diminution of economic inequalities, and alongside this an expansion of educational and cultural opportunities for those large social groups which have, until recently, derived remarkably little advantage, in the way of a more satisfying, more civilised life, from the immense productivity of modern industry. In the Communist countries, on the other hand, we may expect a continued growth of inequality, an increase in the material and cultural advantages of the ruling elite. The causes of this divergence are plain. The dominance of a privileged class can only be ended where the mass of the unprivileged have political power, and where it is possible for rival elites to emerge which challenge and limit the power of the ruling elite. These conditions of political democracy are not independent of the economic structure of society but neither are they entirely determined by it. Where they are lacking, a privileged class is able to maintain and extend its privileges whether it "owns" the means of production or not.[111]

In recent years, a number of neo-Marxists have openly called for and supported the role-type of the intellectual formulator of revolutionary ideals, a position explicated in semidisguised form much earlier by Lenin in *What Is*

To Be Done?[112] Lefebvre has suggested that the "control of ideas ... is the only judge and supreme criterion of knowledge."[113] Marxist theorists have never faced up to the implications for communist society of entrusting such power of narration and preservation to intellectuals. Kostas Axelos, a Marxist analyst, has pointed to the need for "a critical examination of the Bolshevik theory of the role of the intellectual ... in formulating the class consciousness of the proletariat...."[114]

Marx himself, of course, rejected this role, though he can be cited as a prime example of an intellectual "tradition-maker." He criticized as bourgeois "utopians," those socialists who think that "the working class is incapable of its own emancipation ... [that] it must place itself under the leadership of educated ... bourgeois."[115] Hence, from such a point of view, every intellectual must be viewed with suspicion. This is precisely the source of Marxist anti-intellectualism.[116] Yet as Henri de Man noted, "It is not a little peculiar that Marxism, although ... it was conceived by intellectuals, should have no place for these in its description of society."[117]

The growing impact of postrevolutionary intellectuals and the university community on the body politik of various nations is a result of more than just an increased demand for trained talent. The intellectuals articulate "modernity." In the developing nations, they have been the "only initially available modern elite" whose assignment has been to establish a rationalistic argument between "protest and change."[118] The developed societies have equally provided a role for them as a "mirror of conscience."[119]

We have noted earlier arguments that endemic in the occupational role of "intellectual" is a strong preference for working *outside* the system. As Coser notes: "When intellect is harnessed to the pursuit of power it loses its essential character ...; to harness it to the chariot of power is to emasculate it."[120] Yet intellectuals also feel that they alone should be the "special custodian" of basic system values like reason and justice (which are related to the nature of their occupational role), striking out passionately when they fear the national identity is threatened by some gross abuse.[121]

Even though for the most part intellectuals see themselves in a world "they never made," they have been "bound" by an "unexpungible identity" with the nation, since it has been the *raison d'être* of the literary and scholarly intellectuals.

In their role as tradition-maker, intellectuals become participants. The critical intellectuals (both type A and B), though, continue to deny the possibility of participating in government, without betraying their ideals.[122] They view the "others" as conservationist and unholy. The growth in social importance of intellectual institutions and skills, for example, the university and science, has made it possible for the "caretaker" intellectuals to bring statements of their concerns to the attention of the public. The laity now read and take notice of intellectual products. From the point of view of the intellectuals, this gives them a chance to discuss and participate in a larger arena than was previously afforded. Such pragmatic attempts, interestingly enough, are often viewed by both the *Gatekeepers* and the *Moralists* as a source of anti-intellectualism. The "avant-garde" questions the "clerisy."[123] For in large part the fear expressed is perhaps that in becoming a spokesman the intellectual might forfeit the right to question the main assumptions of his society. This would deny his elitism. In fact, however, we must recognize that intellectuals have often assumed the role of spokesmen for the society. Both Dahrendorf in his study of the German society and Moddie in an analysis of development of Brahminical scholarship in India have noted this role as a "classical attitude" of the group. Here the intellectual ". . . becomes part of the existing order of authority."[124] Dahrendorf suggests that many Weimar ministers of state were of this type. Comparable roles are played by intellectuals in many of the "new" and developing nations, as occurred in the early United States.[125]

As a spokesman, the participant intellectual has become vulnerable to the charge of "sell out," a charge often made by other intellectuals. C. Wright Mills, in discussing the social role of the intellectual, suggested that

> the intellectual must constantly know his own social position. . . . If he forgets this, his thinking may exceed his sphere of strategy so far as to make impossible any translation of his thought into action. . . .
> Knowledge that is not communicated has a way of turning the mind sour. . . . The basis of our integrity can be gained or renewed only by activity. . . . It cannot be gained nor retained by selling what we believe to be ourselves. When you sell the lies of others you are also selling yourself. . . .[126]

How and when does an intellectual conform to his society? This dilemma has often posed serious philosophical debate. Should the intellectual remain aloof, lest he lose his objectivity? As noted, a conformist outlook has often been looked at as a sign of cowardice. For much of the ability of the "monk" to conform to his society largely depends on the extent to which he finds the social structure, including the polity, encouraging him to interact on an equal, full, and intimate basis with other sections of the elite, who show a regard for his opinions.

The answer in part, therefore, to the question of the varying patterns of "conformity" among intellectuals lies in the different positions of the intellectual in social systems of different times and places. Although consideration of these comparative factors goes beyond the limited scope of this discussion, it is important to point up the need to pay attention to the larger structural context in which intellectual activity takes place. From Tocqueville on, assorted commentators on the comparative role of intellectuals have suggested that British intellectuals, though given little formal role recognition—the very word is regarded as un-English—have long been accepted as part of the establishment, of that group of high-level "cousins" who attend the same schools, belong to the same clubs, and listen to each other, regardless of differences in opinion or roles. One who already belongs cannot "sell out."[127] In France, on the other hand, those intellectuals not directly involved in government have extremely high public status, are fawned on by the press, but have almost no direct influence on the governing elites. Insofar as the intellectuals can have a sense of full participation, it has been by cooperating with "counter-elites" of the Left currently, but in part of the Right in the past.

In the United States, on the whole, intellectuals have perceived themselves as doubly outsiders—unloved by the governing elites and "public opinion." Conversely, America has provided more comfortable incomes and more provision for employment in universities and other institutions. As a society without the kind of social establishment derivative from aristocratic norms, it has not given diffuse elite status to intellectuals (or anyone else) and has sharply differentiated between experts and intellectuals. British intellectuals, handled more "sensibly" than their compeers elsewhere, are better able to play the "preserver" role, to explicate the national tradition in a positive fashion. The American outsiders, as we have seen, tend to transpose into moral conflicts controversies which are far more concerned with means than with ends, while the French, who are even more frustrated by their structural position, are prone to take on an even more intense moralistic role, which, according to Aron, leads them "to ignore and very often to aggravate the real problem of the nation."[128]

TYPE D: CARETAKER

The critical understanding of this role can mainly be attributed to the advent of the Industrial Revolution. Society now needed functionaries who could maintain the scientific order, which began in the Western societies as early as 1500. It was an intellectual revolution, for man sought to explain the world differently. "The change," as Bronowski states, oriented men ". . . from a world of things ordered according to their ideal nature, to a world of events running in a steady mechanism of before and after."[129]

The ensuing attempt toward a pragmatic definition of scientific theory gave rise to industrial development. This "orderly" transformation was no mere coincidence of history. Intellectual conditions as early as the sixteenth century, notably in England and France, afforded a strong impetus to the emergence of industrial society. As evident in the American Revolution, Puritan understanding was more than an attempt at describing the mechanical functions of the universe.[130] The Paris Meetings by the "scientists"—Descartes, Desargues, Fermat, Pascal, and other noted social thinkers—began a *rational* dialogue in explaining social conditions. The Royal Society was established November 28, 1660, at a meeting in Gresham College, London. These men largely held Puritan sympathies.[131]

The interaction of the cultural elements and the civilization formed the cornerstone in Merton's discussion of the role of the Puritan intellectual in the development of the industrial society. As he noted, "the Puritan ethic, as an ideal-typical expression of the value-attitudes basic to ascetic Protestantism generally, so canalized the interests of seventeenth-century Englishmen as to constitute one important *element* in the enhanced cultivation of science."[132]

The Protestant ethic reflected the elementary belief that the social and economic conditions of rationality and opportunity would be met. Ascriptive hierarchy began to be replaced by achieved rights. This signaled the beginning of the modern state, which gave rise to the idea of objectivity—an institutional prerequisite to the development of legal-rational authority.[133] As Crozier suggests, it diminished "the uncertainty of social action."[134] The growth of the nation-state ushered in the rapid development of "public servants" now employed to administer the secular state.[135] An essential task was the development of a codified legal system. Bendix notes that "proper systematization was the work of university-trained judges . . . that gave a special impetus to the formal rationality of the law."[136] The traditional exegesis replaced the consideration of the individual *(Einzelindividuum).* Legal administrators now became the essential innovators of the political community, and, literally for the first time, intellectuals systematically began to share in the maintenance of the bureaucratic structure. In this social dualism, the intellectual became the *caretaker.* The "monk" had discovered the New World.

Bureaucratic authority separated the sphere of "public" and "private" domain. It further established an institutional hierarchy where competency was to be based on occupational merit.[137] It emphasized achievement. Increasingly, in the industrial societies, this meant that individuals would educate themselves for a career and that qualified officers could maintain and manage social services. Educators were now called upon to train civil servants to manage bureaucracies. The "felicific calculus," as Bentham called it, gave birth to the term "utility" in the maximization of pleasure and the minimization of pain. The critical function for the government was hence proclaimed to be contained in the "minimax" principle.[138] The intellectual as educator became a social functionary.

The pluralistic conditions were now manifested in the emphasis on universalism and achievement. Intellectuals as social planners called for an examination and reduction of aristocracy. As Schumpeter noted: "The state, its bureaucracy and the groups that man the political engine are quite promising prospects for the intellectual looking for his source of social power. As should be evident . . . they are likely to move in the desired direction with not less 'dialectical' necessity than the masses."[139]

Raymond Aron, commenting on the advanced industrial society, has noted the spread of distributive roles as *scribes,* those who make up the operational staff of public or private administrations, and *experts,* those who make their knowledge available to others.[140] These are then the accountants who manage the nerves of their society; they undertake the role of the custodian. In a technobureaucratic society, as noted earlier, the skills of these experts increasingly are called for in the implementation of policies. Shils points out:

> There must therefore be a body of persons capable of reproducing and transmitting this pattern of technical and specialized knowledge and skill. A body of persons different in the substantive content of their intellectual culture but having parallel functions, is not less necessary for providing the education requisite to administration and public discussion.[141]

The increasing participation of intellectuals in government is, as Merton indicates, a process linked in their minds to their earlier commitment to change their society. He observes that the choice originated with the intellectuals themselves.

Intellectuals who may have previously pledged their allegiance to political movements seeking to modify our economic and political structure have now in increasing numbers, it would seem, adopted the alternative of seeking to work these changes through constituted governmental authority. Insofar as the intellectual thus conceives the present place of government, he is likely to find himself thinking in terms of supplying the expert knowledge upon which are based executive decisions which move in new directions.[142]

These professionals in a major way have assumed a leadership role. Schumpeter pointed to the increased "direct relationship" between intellectuals and the bureaucracy.[143] This trend has been resisted by the business professionals, who, especially in America, have viewed themselves historically as a source of national leadership providing support for community values.[144] Not incorrectly, they see the bureaucratic intellectuals as maintaining strong ties with the more critical unattached ones outside of government, particularly in the university, who continue to act as "gatekeepers" or "moralists." Ironically, the intellectual in his role as "caretaker" often pays particular attention to these criticisms precisely because his fellow "free" intellectuals argue that in his abandonment of innovation and intellect he has given up his claim to be an "intellectual." Henry Kissinger was moved a decade and a half ago to a classic defense of the caretaker as intellectual in answer to such contentions.[145]

The increased power, status, and income of this technical elite have been the topic of an international seminar convened by Professors Bell and Dahrendorf. Their concern serves to highlight both the theoretical and practical significance of this prototypical role of the intellectual as caretaker. Bell's "axial principles"[146] of the postindustrial society emphasize the structural trends which have fostered these developments.

(a) In "The Post-Industrial Society," economy (as measured in terms of G.N.P. in the labor force) has shifted from the manufacturing to the services sector, which require a larger university trained group of professionals at the summits.[147]

(b) The increase in professional and mechanical class enhances "technocratic forms of decision-making."[148]

These trends which greatly benefit intellectualdom as a stratum are seen by some as reducing the historic tension between power and intellect.[149]

CONCLUDING REMARKS

Our attempt in this essay has been to develop the prototypical political roles of the intellectual. Attention in attempting such a paradigmatic analysis has been paid to discussing social conditions which contribute to the development of such roles.

The place of the intellectual in the society is neither inherently contradictory nor abusive. The fulfillment of the myriad of his roles lies in his capacity to assume responsibility and move away from interpreting the society from a particular ideological dogma. This is particularly true for the new nations. The extent to which intellectuals, and other elites of such nations, are able to define their authority on a legal-rational basis will foretell the future stability of these countries. Intellectuals define the content of legitimacy. Any discussion as to the oppositional role of the intellectuals must take into consideration the role of the nation in providing a creative and critical dimension of the intellectual's own legitimacy. In his narrative role, he may have to become both "monk" and "messiah."

Yet as John Ward has pointed out, the very nature of the intellectual role, even when perceived in conservative "preserver" terms, presses those who fulfill it to undermine social stability.

> But once you set a man to thinking, curious things are bound to happen. At this point an ironic consequence follows. In the very act that society assigns the intellectual, that is, in preserving and transmitting the values of the culture, in expressing and giving voice to the values that inform the culture, intellectuals are driven inevitably toward heresy. One needs to be careful here. By heresy I do not mean simply the out-of-hand rejection of, the mindless rebellion against, the values of the culture, but something much more complex. In the very act of formulating and articulating the values of the culture, the intellectual is driven to see tensions and even contradictions within the system of values that society knows and cherishes as tradition. . . . So, even as cleric, even as conservator of and embodiment of the tradition of the past, the intellectual is, in accepting that role, plunged deeply and inevitably into the battles of his own time.[150]

In advanced industrial or postindustrial society, we would argue that the growth in the size and influence of an academic research establishment, and free-lance intellectualdom, which insists on being critical, is undermining the capacity for "action intellectuals" to maintain social equilibrium. Daniel Bell, in presenting his analysis of postindustrial society, contends "the deepest tensions are those between the culture, whose axial direction is anti-institutional and antinomian, and the social structure, which is ruled by an economizing and technocratic mode. It is this tension which is ultimately the most fundamental problem of the post-industrial society."[151] As noted elsewhere:

> The basic tensions, the contradictions within the system, come increasingly from within the elite itself—from its own intellectual leaders supported by large segments of its student children. In Hegelian terms the contradiction of post-industrial society, whether Communist or non-Communist, may be its dependence on trained intelligence, on research and innovation, which requires it to bring together large numbers of intellectuals and students on great campuses and in a few intellectual communities located at the centers of communication and influence.[152]

Thus, we return at the end to Schumpeter's question: Can an advanced industrial society win the allegiance of its intellectuals by being successful in material terms? He concluded that it could not, that all its achievements would be as ashes in the writings produced by intellect, that intellect is inherently alienated. To gain the participation of the intellectuals, power must offer more than bread, it must allow access to a court of glory—Camelot?

NOTES

1. For an elaboration on the confusion, consult Lewis S. Feuer, "The Political Linguistics of 'Intellectual' 1898–1918," *Survey* 16 (Winter 1971): 156–83.

2. For earlier related efforts, see S. M. Lipset, "American Intellectuals: Their Politics and Status," *Daedalus* 88 (Summer 1959): 460–86, in revised form in Lipset, *Political Man* (Garden City, N.Y.: Doubleday Anchor Books, 1963), pp. 332–71; S. M. Lipset and Richard B. Dobson, "The Intellectual as Critic and Rebel: With Special Reference to the United States and the Soviet Union," *Daedalus* 101 (Summer 1972): 137–98; S. M. Lipset, "Academia and Politics in America," in T. J. Nossiter *et al.* eds., *Imagination and Precision in the Social Sciences* (London: Faber, 1972), pp. 211–89; and, more recently, E. C. Ladd, Jr., and S. M. Lipset, *The Divided Academy: Professors and Politics* (New York: McGraw-Hill, 1975).

3. Joseph Schumpeter, *Capitalism, Socialism and Democracy* (New York: Harper Torchbooks, 1950), p. 147.

4. Raymond Aron, *The Opium of the Intellectuals* (New York: Norton, 1962), p. 210.

5. Richard Hofstadter, *Anti-Intellectualism in American Life* (New York: Knopf, 1963), p. 38.

6. Lewis A. Coser, *Men of Ideas* (New York: Free Press, 1965), p. viii.

7. Martin Malia, "What Is the Intelligentsia?" in Richard Pipes, ed., *The Russian Intelligentsia* (New York: Columbia University Press, 1961), p. 5. The word itself was apparently coined in Germany in the 1840s.

8. Louis Bodin, *Les Intellectuels* (Paris: Presses Universitaires de France, 1962), pp. 6–9; Maurice Paléologue, *Journal de l'affaire Dreyfus* (Paris: Plon, 1955), pp. 90–91; Hofstadter, *Anti-Intellectualism in American Life*, pp. 38–39.

9. Robert Waelder, "Protest and Revolution Against Western Societies," in Morton A. Kaplan, ed., *The Revolution in World Politics* (New York: Wiley, 1962), p. 15.

10. Herbert Moller, "Youth as a Force in the Modern World," *Comparative Studies in Society and History* 10 (April 1966): 238.

11. Thomas Hobbes, *Behemoth: The History of the Causes of the Civil War of England* (London: Crooke, 1682; repr. ed., New York: Burt Franklin, n.d.), p. 74. See also Mark Curtis, "The Alienated Intellectuals of Early Stuart England," in Trevor Aston, ed., *Crisis in Europe, 1560–1660* (London: Routledge & Kegan Paul, 1965), pp. 295–316.

12. Alexis de Tocqueville, *The Old Regime and the French Revolution* (Garden City, N.Y.: Doubleday Anchor Books, 1955), pp. 146–47.

13. Jack Lively, ed., *The Works of Joseph DeMaistre* (New York: Macmillan, 1965), pp. 50, 269.

14. Lewis Namier, *1848: The Revolution of the Intellectuals* (Garden City, N.Y.: Doubleday Anchor Books, 1964), p. 2. The quote from Lamartine is from his *Histoire de la revolution de 1848* (1849), vol. 1, p. 3.

15. Friedrich Engels, *The German Revolutions* (Chicago: University of Chicago Press, Phoenix Edition, 1967), p. 134.

16. Cesar Graña, *Modernity and Its Discontents* (New York: Harper Torchbooks, 1964), p. 73.

17. V. I. Lenin, *What Is to Be Done?* (Oxford, Eng.: Clarendon Press, 1963), p. 63.

18. "Premier Chou En-Lai Discusses Nixon Trip with Americans," *The Guardian* 23 (September 8, 1971): 11.

19. Franco Venturi, *Roots of Revolution* (London: Weidenfeld & Nicolson, 1960); Bernard Pares, *Russia Between Reform and Revolution* (New York: Schocken

Books, 1962), pp. 161–282; Lewis S. Feuer, *The Conflict of Generations* (New York: Basic Books, 1969), pp. 88–172.

20. Y. C. Wang, *Chinese Intellectuals and the West* (Chapel Hill: University of North Carolina Press, 1966), esp. pp. 229–361; Chow Tse-Tsung, *The May Fourth Movement: Intellectual Revolution in China* (Cambridge, Mass.: Harvard University Press, 1960); Richard Walker, "Students, Intellectuals, and the Chinese Revolution," in Jeanne J. Kirkpatrick, ed., *The Strategy of Deception* (New York: Farrar, Straus & Giroux, 1963), pp. 87–108; John Israel, *Student Nationalism in China, 1927–1937* (Stanford: Stanford University Press, 1966); John Israel, "Reflections on the Modern Chinese Student Movement," in S. M. Lipset and P. Altbach, eds., *Students in Revolt* (Boston: Houghton Mifflin, 1969), pp. 310–33.

21. Whitelaw Reid, "The Scholar in Politics," *Scribner's Monthly* 6 (1873): 613–14.

22. "Text of a Pre-Inauguration Memo from Moynihan on Problems Nixon Would Face," *New York Times,* March 11, 1970.

23. The most comprehensive analysis of the involvement of intellectuals in fascist movements in different parts of Europe is Alastair Hamilton, *The Appeal of Fascism: A Study of Intellectuals and Fascism, 1919–1945* (London: Anthony Blond, 1971).

24. Wilhelm Röpke, "National Socialism and the Intellectuals," in George B. de Huszar, ed., *The Intellectuals* (New York: Free Press, 1960), pp. 346–47.

25. Hamilton, *The Appeal of Fascism,* p. xx.

26. Robert J. Soucy, "The Nature of Fascism in France," in Walter Laqueur and George Mosse, eds., *International Fascism 1920–1945* (New York: Harper Torchbooks, 1966), p. 41.

27. Hamilton, *The Appeal of Fascism,* pp. xx–xxi.

28. Joachim C. Fest, *The Face of the Third Reich* (London: Weidenfeld & Nicolson, 1970), p. 261. For more detailed analyses of the left-wing intellectuals of the Weimar, see George L. Mosse, *Germans and Jews* (New York: Fertig, 1970), pp. 171–225; Istvan Deak, *Weimar Germany's Left-Wing Intellectuals* (Berkeley: University of California Press, 1968); Harold L. Poor, *Kurt Tucholsky and the Ordeal of Germany 1914–1935* (New York: Scribner's, 1968); Peter Gay, *Weimar Culture, The Outsider as Insider* (New York: Harper & Row, 1968).

29. Florian Znaniecki, *The Social Role of the Man of Knowledge* (New York: Harper Torchbooks, 1968), pp. 70–71.

30. See Thomas Molnar, *The Decline of the Intellectual* (Cleveland: Meridian Books, 1961), esp. chap. 5, "The Intellectual as Reactionary," pp. 157–98.

31. Max Weber, *The Sociology of Religion,* trans. Ephraim Fischoff (Boston: Beacon Press, 1963), pp. 124–25.

32. Lipset, *Political Man,* p. 333.

33. Max Weber, *On Law in Economy and Society,* ed. and annotated Max Rheinstein, trans. Edward Shils and Max Rheinstein (New York: Simon & Schuster, 1954), p. 324; also, see the discussion by a leading Weberian scholar, Reinhard Bendix, *Max Weber: An Intellectual Portrait* (Garden City, N.Y.: Doubleday, 1960), pp. 286–97.

34. H. H. Gerth and C. Wright Mills, eds., *From Max Weber: Essays in Sociology* (New York: Oxford University Press, 1946), pp. 176, 448.

35. S. N. Eisenstadt, "Contemporary Student Rebellions—Intellectual Rebellion and Generational Conflict," *Acta Sociologica* 14, no. 3 (1971): 171.

36. Max Weber, *The Religion of India,* trans. and ed. Hans H. Gerth and Don Martindale (New York: Free Press, 1958), p. 141.

37. Ernst Troeltsch, *The Social Teaching of the Christian Churches,* trans. Olive Wyon (New York: Harper Torchbooks, 1960), vol. 1, pp. 49–50.

464

38. S. M. Lipset, "The Possible Political Effects of Student Activism," *Social Science Information* 8, no. 2 (April 1969): 15.
39. Bernard Cazes, "The Intellectuals: Between Expertise and Prophecy? and Concluding Remarks on the First Meeting (Paris, 1972)," seminar sponsored by The International Association for Cultural Freedom, Aspen, Colorado, July 6–9, 1973.
40. J. P. Nettl, "Ideas, Intellectuals, and Structures of Dissent," in Philip Rieff, ed., *On Intellectuals* (Garden City, N.Y.: Doubleday, 1969), pp. 80–82, 118–19; see also T. B. Bottomore, *Elites and Society* (London: Watts, 1964), pp. 70–71.
41. Henry Kissinger, "The Policymaker and the Intellectual," *The Reporter* 20 (March 5, 1959): 23.
42. For a detailed discussion of such developments see S. M. Lipset, "Social Structure and Social Change," in Peter Blau, ed., *Approaches to the Study of Social Structure* (New York: The Free Press, 1975), pp. 172–209.
43. For an elaboration, consult Everett Knight, *The Object Society* (New York: Braziller, 1960), p. 45; Coser, *Men of Ideas*, pp. viii, x; Jacques Barzun, *The House of Intellect* (New York: Harper Torchbooks, 1961), p. 3; Edward Shils, *The Intellectuals and the Powers and Other Essays* (Chicago: University of Chicago Press, 1972), p. 3; Aron, *The Opium of the Intellectuals*, p. 210; Paul A. Baran, "The Commitment of the Intellectual," *Monthly Review* 13 (May 1961): 17; Ralf Dahrendorf, *Society and Democracy in Germany* (Garden City, N.Y.: Doubleday Anchor Books, 1967), p. 268.
44. S. T. Coleridge, *On the Constitution of the Church and State,* as quoted in Crane Brinton, "Reflections on the Alienation of the Intellectuals," in Alexander V. Riasanovsky and Barnes Riznik, eds., *Generalizations in Historical Writing* (Philadelphia: University of Pennsylvania Press, 1963), p. 220.
45. Edward A. Shils, "Intellectuals," in David Sills, ed., *International Encyclopedia of the Social Sciences* (New York: Macmillan and Free Press, 1968), vol. 7, p. 399.
46. *Ibid.*, p. 400.
47. Hofstadter, *Anti-Intellectualism in American Life*, p. 25. See also Barzun, *The House of Intellect*, pp. 4–5, and Coser, *Men of Ideas*, p. viii.
48. G. Eric Hansen, "Intellect and Power: Some Notes on the Intellectual as a Political Type," *The Journal of Politics* 31 (May 1969): 312–14.
49. Daniel Mornet, *Les Origines intellectuelles de la revolution française, 1715–1787* (Paris: Collin, 1967).
50. Robert K. Merton, *Social Theory and Social Structure*, enl. ed. (New York: Free Press, 1968), pp. 263–64. See also Theodore Geiger, *Aufgaben und Stellung der Intelligenz in der Gesellschaft* (Stuttgart: Ferdinand Enke, 1949), pp. 2–3.
51. Lipset and Dobson, "The Intellectual as Critic and Rebel," p. 138.
52. Edward Shils, "The Intellectuals and the Powers: Some Perspectives for Comparative Analysis," in Rieff, ed., *On Intellectuals*, pp. 32–33; see also Shils, "Intellectuals," pp. 399–415; see also Talcott Parsons, "The Intellectual: A Social Role Category," in Rieff, ed., *On Intellectuals*, pp. 3–24.
53. Engels, *The German Revolutions*, p. 134.
54. Robert Michels, *Political Parties* (New York: Collier Books, 1962), p. 315.
55. Henri de Man, *The Psychology of Socialism* (New York: Holt, 1927), p. 226.
56. William Kornhauser, *The Politics of Mass Society* (New York: Free Press, 1959), pp. 186–87; see also Coser, *Men of Ideas*, pp. 263–74.
57. Ernest Mandel, "The New Vanguard," in Tariq Ali, ed., *The New Revolutionaries* (New York: Morrow, 1969), pp. 47–53.
58. "Upsurge of the Youth Movement in the Capitalist Countries," *World Marxist Review* 11 (July 1968): 6–7.

59. V. Teitelboim, "Problems Facing Latin American Intellectuals," *World Marxist Review* 11 (December 1968): 73–74.
60. The first two terms are derived from discussions by Coser, *Men of Ideas,* p. x, and Hofstadter, *Anti-Intellectualism in American Life,* pp. 28–29.
61. Montaigne, *The Complete Essays,* trans. Donald M. Frame (Stanford, Calif.: Stanford University Press, 1948).
62. Coser has explicated this function in his study *Men of Ideas.*
63. Shils, "The Intellectuals and the Powers," p. 30.
64. C. P. Snow, *The New Men* (New York: Scribner's, 1955), p. 176.
65. For summaries and discussions of these studies together with reference to the various extant surveys, see Lipset, "Academia and Politics in America," and Lipset and Dobson, "The Intellectual as Critic and Rebel." See also Ladd and Lipset, *The Divided Academy: Professors and Politics,* pp. 125–48.
66. Thorstein Veblen, "The Intellectual Pre-Eminence of Jews in Modern Europe," in his *Essays in Our Changing Order* (New York: Viking Press, 1934), pp. 226–27, and Paul F. Lazarsfeld and Wagner Thielens, Jr., *The Academic Mind* (New York: Free Press, 1958), pp. 161–63.
67. Conner Cruise O'Brien, "Thoughts on Commitment," *The Listener* 86 (December 1971): 834–36; Jascha Kessler, "The Censorship of Art and the Art of Censorship," *The Literary Review* 12 (Summer 1969): 410–31; Ferdinand Kolegar, "Literary Intellectuals and the Politics of Perfection," *Indian Sociological Review* 3 (October 1965): 79–90; Juan Onis, "Cubans' Ordeal Arouses Artists," *New York Times,* September 9, 1971, p. 18; A. I. Solzhenitsyn, "Letter to the Fourth All-Union Congress of Soviet Writers," *Bulletin of the Munich Institute* 15, no. 8 (August 1968): 39–43; S. S. Voronitsyn, "Intellectual Opposition to the Party Leadership," *Bulletin of the Munich Institute* 15, no. 12 (December 1968): 19–23; Edith B. Frankel, "Alexander Tvardovskii—The Loyal Rebel," *The Jerusalem Post Magazine,* December 31, 1971, p. 25; Kung Chun and Chao Hiu, "How to Look at Intellectuals Correctly," *Peking Review* 8 (February 1969): 5–6; Anthony Gittings, "Shift in Chinese Education Policy," *The Guardian,* September 26, 1971, p. 4; Alan Bouc, "Cultural Revolution Comes Full Cycle," *Le Monde,* October 7, 1970, p. 8; Solomon John Rawlin, "The Polish Intelligentsia and the Socialist Order: Elements of Ideological Compatibility," *Political Science Quarterly* 83 (September 1968): 353–77; Aleksander Matejko, "Status Incongruence in the Polish Intelligentsia," *Social Research* 33 (Winter 1966): 611–38.
68. Benjamin Schwartz, "The Intelligentsia in Communist China: A Tentative Comparison," in Pipes, ed., *The Russian Intelligentsia,* p. 180.
69. See Lipset and Dobson, "The Intellectual as Critic and Rebel," for a discussion of the United States and the Soviet Union.
70. C. Wright Mills, *Power, Politics and People, The Collected Essays of C. Wright Mills* (New York: Ballantine Books, 1963), p. 256.
71. Joseph Kraft, "Washington Insight: Kennedy and the Intellectuals," *Harper's* 227 (November 1963): 112–17, and Max Ways, "Intellectuals and the Presidency," *Fortune* 75 (April 1967): 147–49, 212–16.
72. As quoted in Kraft, "Washington Insight," p. 116; see also Ways, "Intellectuals and the Presidency," p. 212.
73. Geiger, *Aufgaben und Stellung der Intelligenz in der Gesellschaft,* pp. 118–19; see also Norman Birnbaum, "The Making of a Vanguard," *Partisan Review* 36, no. 2 (1969): 220–32.
74. Eric Hoffer, "Where the Real Rat Race Is," *San Francisco Examiner,* December 23, 1968, p. 14.

75. Alexis de Tocqueville, *Democracy in America* (New York: Vintage Books, 1956), vol. 2, p. 375.

76. Bottomore, *Elites and Society,* p. 65.

77. Harvey Cox, *The Secular City: Secularization and Urbanization in Theological Perspective* (New York: Macmillan, 1966), p. 15, and chap. 10, "The Church and the Secular University"; Ernest Werner, "Remodeling the Protestant Ministry," *American Scholar* 34 (Winter 1964–65): 31–49; James MacManns, "The Pressure on the Pulpit," *The Guardian,* May 5, 1973, p. 5.

78. James A. Pike and John W. Pyle, *The Church, Politics and Society: Dialogues on Current Problems* (New York: Morehouse-Gorham, 1955); James A. Pike, *If This Be Heresy* (New York: Harper & Row, 1967); Daniel Berrigan, *False Gods, Real Men* (New York: Macmillan, 1967); Daniel Berrigan, *The Trial of the Catonsville Nine* (Boston: Beacon Press, 1970); and R. H. Preston, ed., *Technology and Social Justice: An International Symposium on the Social and Economic Teaching of the World Council of Churches from Geneva 1966 to Uppsala 1968* (Valley Forge, Pa.: Judson Press, 1971).

79. See Lipset and Dobson, "The Intellectual as Critic and Rebel," pp. 180–81 and references thereto.

80. Fyodor Dostoevski, *The Grand Inquisitor on the Nature of Man,* trans. Constance Garnett (New York: Liberal Arts Press, 1948), p. 28.

81. Norman Cohn, *The Pursuit of the Millenium* (New York: Oxford University Press, 1971).

82. Ways, "Intellectuals and the Presidency," p. 149.

83. Robert Nisbet, "The Myth of the Renaissance," *Comparative Studies in Society and History* 15 (October 1973): 486–87.

84. Henry F. May, *The End of American Innocence: A Study of the First Years of Our Own Time* (Chicago: Quadrangle Books, 1964), p. 304.

85. See Coser, *Men of Ideas,* pp. 111–19, and S. M. Lipset, *Rebellion in the University* (Boston: Little, Brown, 1972), pp. 153–55.

86. Randolph Bourne, *The War and the Intellectuals* (New York: Harper Torchbooks, 1964), pp. 3–14.

87. See Lipset, *Rebellion in the University,* p. 161.

88. Cited in Arthur M. Schlesinger, Jr., *The Crisis of the Old Order, 1919–1933* (Boston: Houghton Mifflin, 1957), p. 49.

89. T. B. Bottomore, *Critics of Society: Radical Thought in North America* (New York: Pantheon Books, 1968), p. 39.

90. "Special circumstances, which cannot be recaptured, made possible the warm alliance between American intellectuals and the New Deal. Franklin Roosevelt cast himself as a champion of the underprivileged against the 'economic royalists,' seen as the holders of the real power, who could be blamed for not preventing the Depression. This David versus Goliath position was congenial to the intellectuals. They could support Roosevelt without aligning themselves with what is now called 'the Establishment' " (Ways, "Intellectuals and the Presidency," p. 212). For an analysis of the way in which American intellectuals related to the Roosevelt and subsequent administrations, see Edward Shils, "From Periphery to Center: The Changing Place of Intellectuals in American Society," in Bernard Barber and Alex Inkeles, eds., *Stability and Social Change* (Boston: Little, Brown, 1971), pp. 211–43, esp. pp. 220–27.

91. Nisbet, "The Myth of the Renaissance," p. 487.

92. Leslie Fiedler, "McCarthy," *Encounter* 3 (August 1954), pp. 10–21. See also David Riesman and Nathan Glazer, "The Intellectual and the Discontented

Classes," in Daniel Bell, ed., *The Radical Right* (Garden City, N.Y.: Doubleday, 1963), pp. 87–114.

93. Christopher Lasch, *The Agony of the American Left* (New York: Vintage Books, 1969), p. 73.

94. Robert Nisbet, *The Degradation of the Academic Dogma* (New York: Basic Books, 1971), pp. 143–44.

95. *Ibid.*, p. 144.

96. Ronald Berman, *America in the Sixties, an Intellectual History* (New York: Free Press, 1968), p. 4.

97. Kraft, "Washington Insight," p. 112.

98. James Reston, "Washington on Kennedy's Discontented Intellectuals," *New York Times*, October 8, 1961, p. 10E.

99. Kraft, "Washington Insight," pp. 114, 112.

100. James MacGregor Burns, "Candidate on the Eve: Liberalism Without Tears," *New Republic* 143 (October 31, 1960): 16.

101. For a detailed summary of evidence to this effect, see Everett Carll Ladd, Jr., and Seymour Martin Lipset, *Academics, Politics, and the 1972 Election* (Washington, D.C.: American Enterprise Institute for Public Policy Research, 1973), pp. 5–32, and *The Divided Academy: Professors and Politics*, pp. 31–34.

102. Brinton, "Reflections on the Alienation of Intellectuals," p. 235.

103. Aron, *The Opium of the Intellectuals*, p. 209. See also Kurt Wolff, ed., *From Karl Mannheim* (New York: Oxford University Press, 1971), pp. 110–15.

104. S. N. Eisenstadt, "Intellectuals and Tradition," *Daedalus* 101 (Spring 1972): 1.

105. Max Ascoli, *Intelligence in Politics* (New York: Norton, 1936), pp. 17–41.

106. Edward Shils, "Toward a Modern Intellectual Community," in Shils, *The Intellectuals and the Powers and Other Essays*, p. 336; Znaniecki, *The Social Role of the Man of Knowledge*, p. 39.

107. Jun Etō, "Natsume Soseki: A Japanese Meiji Intellectual," *American Scholar* 34 (Autumn 1965): 603. Further, Bellah provides a careful historical documentation on the reasons "skeptical" intellectual activities did not flourish in Japan (Robert N. Bellah, "Intellectual and Society in Japan," *Daedalus* 101 [Spring 1972]: 89–115).

108. Coser, *Men of Ideas*, pp. 141–42.

109. Unfortunately, little of Jan Machajski has been translated into English. For a brief sample from his book, *The Intellectual Worker*, see V. F. Calverton, ed., *The Making of Society* (New York: Random House, 1937), pp. 427–36. Max Nomad has been Machajski's main American disciple and has summarized and applied his teachings in *Aspects of Revolt* (New York: Noonday Press, 1961), pp. 96–117; *Dreamers, Dynamiters and Demagogues* (New York: Waldon Press, 1964), pp. 103–08, 201–06; and *Political Heretics* (Ann Arbor: University of Michigan Press, 1963), pp. 238–41. See also Paul Avrich, "What Is 'Machaevism'?" *Soviet Studies* 17 (July 1965): 66–75; Marshall Shatz, "Jan Waclaw Machajski: The 'Conspiracy' of the Intellectuals," *Survey* 62 (January 1967): 45–57; and Bottomore, *Elites and Society*, p. 66.

110. Shatz, "Jan Waclaw Machajski," p. 57; Nomad, *Aspects of Revolt*, p. 117; and Avrich, "What Is 'Machaevism'?"

111. T. B. Bottomore, *Classes in Modern Society* (London: Ampersand Ltd., 1955), pp. 48–49, 61–62.

112. See George Lukacs, *History and Class Consciousness* (London: Merlin Press, 1971), esp. pp. 299–329.

113. Henri Lefebvre, "S'agit-il de penser," *Le Monde*, January 29, 1964.

114. Kostas Axelos, "Des 'intellectuels révolutionnaires' à 'Arguments,'" *Praxis* 4, no. 3–4 (1968): 419.

115. Karl Marx and Friedrich Engels, *Selected Works II* (New York: International Publishers, 1968), pp. 626–33.

116. In the socialist movement, see Henri de Man, *The Psychology of Socialism* (New York: Holt, 1927), pp. 298–304, and John Spargo, "Anti-Intellectualism in the Socialist Movement: A Historical Survey," in his *Sidelights on Contemporary Socialism* (New York: Huebsch, 1911), pp. 67–106. Engels discusses anti-Marxist attacks on anarchists against "any schoolmaster, journalist, or any man generally who was not a manual worker as being an 'erudite' who was out to exploit them" (Friedrich Engels, "On the History of Early Christianity," in Karl Marx and Friedrich Engels, *On Religion* [Moscow: Foreign Languages Publishing House, 1957], p. 319).

117. De Man, *The Psychology of Socialism*, p. 195.

118. S. N. Eisenstadt, *Modernization: Protest and Change* (Englewood Cliffs, N.J.: Prentice-Hall, 1966), p. 158.

119. Ralf Dahrendorf, "Der Intellektuelle und die Gesellschaft," *Die Zeit* 13 (March 29, 1963): 20.

120. Coser, *Men of Ideas*, p. 185.

121. Hofstadter, *Anti-Intellectualism in American Life*, pp. 28–29.

122. For an evaluation and criticism of this orientation, see Kissinger, "The Policy-maker and the Intellectual."

123. Marcus Cunliffe, "The Intellectuals: The United States," *Encounter* 4 (May 1955): 23–33.

124. Dahrendorf, *Society and Democracy in Germany*, p. 269; A. D. Moddie, *The Brahminical Culture and Modernity* (New York: Asia Publishing House, 1968); also, for a provocative philosophical discussion on this intellectual attitude, see Martin Buber, *Between Man and Man* (Boston: Beacon Press, 1959), pp. 83–103.

125. S. M. Lipset, *The First New Nation* (Garden City, N.Y.: Doubleday Anchor Books, 1967), pp. 84–85.

126. Mills, *Power, Politics and People*, pp. 299–300; see also Noam Chomsky, "The Responsibility of Intellectuals," *New York Review of Books* 8 (February 1967): 16–26.

127. See Coser, *Men of Ideas*, pp. 350–53.

128. Aron, *The Opium of the Intellectuals*, pp. 248, 234.

129. As quoted in J. Bronowski and Bruce Mazlish, *The Western Intellectual Tradition* (London: Hutchinson, 1960), p. 108; see also Herbert Butterfield, *The Origins of Modern Science* (New York: Free Press, 1965).

130. Robert E. Butts and John W. Davis, eds., *The Methodological Heritage of Newton* (Oxford, Eng.: Blackwell & Mott, 1972).

131. Robert K. Merton, "Science, Technology, and Society in Seventeenth-Century England," *Osiris: Studies on the History and Philosophy of Science, and on the History of Learning and Culture* (Bruges, Belgium: St. Catherine Press, 1938), vol. 4 (no. 2), pp. 360–32. See also Sir Henry Lyons, *The Royal Society, 1660–1940: A History of Its Administration Under Its Charters,* (New York: Greenwood Press, 1968).

132. Merton, *Social Theory and Social Structure*, p. 628.

133. For a review of the causal *tour de force* of Weberian conceptualization, see Reinhard Bendix, "Max Weber's Interpretation of Conduct and History," *American Journal of Sociology* 51 (May 1946): 518–26.

134. Michel Crozier, *The Bureaucratic Phenomenon* (Chicago: University of Chicago Press, 1969), p. 204.
135. Ernest Barker, *The Development of Public Services in Western Europe* (London: Oxford University Press, 1944).
136. Bendix, *Max Weber*, p. 407.
137. Michael Young, *The Rise of the Meritocracy* (London: Thames & London, 1958); also Gerth and Mills, eds., *From Max Weber*, pp. 196–244.
138. Jeremy Bentham, *Introduction to the Principles of Morals and Legislation*, J. Lafleur, ed., *Hafner Library of Classics*, no. 6, 1948. See also Oskar Morgenstern, "Die Theorie der Spiele und des Wirtschaftlichen Verhaltens," part 1, *Jahrbuch für Sozialwissenschaft* 1 (1950): 113–39.
139. Schumpeter, *Capitalism, Socialism and Democracy*, pp. 310–11.
140. Aron, *The Opium of the Intellectuals*, p. 203.
141. Shils, *The Intellectuals and the Powers and Other Essays*, pp. 175–76.
142. Merton, *Social Theory and Social Structure*, p. 267.
143. Schumpeter, *Capitalism, Socialism and Democracy*, p. 155.
144. Daniel J. Boorstin, *The Americans: The National Experience* (New York: Vintage Books, 1967), pp. 115–23.
145. Kissinger, "The Policymaker and the Intellectual."
146. For an early elucidation of this thesis, consult Daniel Bell, "The Measurement of Knowledge and Technology," in Eleanor Sheldon and Wilbert Moore, eds., *Indicators of Social Change* (New York: Russell Sage, 1968), pp. 145–246; also consult Daniel Bell, "The Post-Industrial Society: The Evolution of an Idea," *Survey* 18 (Spring 1971): 102–68, and, more recently, Daniel Bell, *The Coming of Post-Industrial Society: A Venture in Social Forecasting* (New York: Basic Books, 1973).
147. Bell, *The Coming of Post-Industrial Society*, chap. 2.
148. Daniel Bell, "Technocracy and Politics," *Survey* 17 (Winter 1971): 1–24.
149. Gerhard Lenski, *Power and Privilege* (New York: McGraw-Hill, 1966).
150. John Ward, "Cleric or Critic? The Intellectual in the University," *The American Scholar* 35, no. 1 (1965–66): 105–06.
151. Bell, *The Coming of Post-Industrial Society*, p. 44.
152. Lipset and Dobson, "The Intellectual as Critic and Rebel," p. 184; see also Lipset, "Social Structure and Social Change."

The Myth of the Renaissance*

ROBERT NISBET

1

T HE Italian Renaissance of the fifteenth century is unique among ages of claimed cultural efflorescence, the so-called golden ages, in that it is largely the creation of a single man, Jacob Burckhardt. His *Die Kultur der Renaissance in Italien,* published in 1860, almost immediately established the Quattrocento in Italy as a major period of intellectual as well as artistic history, as the seedbed of modernity, and as the most resplendent avatar perhaps since the Athenian fifth century B.C. of the Muse's visits to this world. Beyond this, I think it can fairly be said that Burckhardt's book, while it did not actually create, lent immense reinforcement to a periodization of European history that is even today among the most cherished idols of the Western mind.

Whatever the defects of the book, and they are many, however much Burckhardt owed to others, especially Michelet whose own work on the Renaissance and its origins in the Italian humanist mind carried with it even the celebrated phrase "the discovery of the world and of man" that Burckhardt was to feature, no one will take from Burckhardt's book the impact upon almost all readers that bespeaks originality and literary power in high degree. Rare to this moment is the reader who does not come away from the book with emotions akin to those that seized Keats on reading Chapman's Homer. Burckhardt's book remains today what it was almost immediately declared to be at the time of its publication, one of superlative imagination and, for that

* This essay is an enlarged and revised version of a review-essay that appeared in *Comparative Studies in Society and History* (October 1973).

Robert Nisbet is Albert Schweitzer Professor of Humanities at Columbia University.

471

day, impressive scholarship. The stuff of charisma lies in the book, a point I shall come back to shortly in reference to the devoted scholarship of Renaissancists in our day.

To Burckhardt's book more than to any other is owing the ineradicable belief, among professional Renaissance scholars and educated laymen alike, that the Renaissance, with its core the Quattrocento of Burckhardt's imagination, is one of the truly great ages of thought and culture in world history, fit rival for the fifth century B.C. in Athens, the first century in Rome, the thirteenth and seventeenth in Western Europe. As we shall see, there is really very little to sustain this belief, but one can only stand in awe of the tenacity with which it is held and of the almost ritual devotion given it. Ask any moderately educated person today to name one great period in the history of mankind, and the answer almost certainly will be "the Renaissance." *The* Renaissance! There may be ignorance or doubt about ancient Athens and Rome, about the several centers of immense achievement in the histories of certain non-Western civilizations, but about the existence and intellectual opulence of the Italian Renaissance, and its unquestioned role of seedbed of all modernity, there is no doubt whatever. Burckhardt has seen to that!

So has he seen to the way we commonly, even to this moment, envisage the structure of cultural history in the West. What Everyman knows is that Western culture began, for all practical purposes, in Greece, from which it passed to Rome where it remained visible for several centuries, only to succumb to the combined impact of the barbarian invasions and the ascendancy of the Christian church. There followed the Dark Ages and the Middle Ages during both of which periods the lamp of learning burned feebly, the result of the suffocating influence of Christian theology and scholasticism which were concerned only with man's spiritual nature and, of course, with the supernatural. Individuality, reason, and the technological imagination all lay in fetters. A monolithically corporate society, dominated by Christianity, supplied the fetters.

Then, beginning with the fifteenth century in Italy, came the Renaissance —a period at once responsible for revival of ancient, especially Greek, learning, for sustained assaults upon Christian dogma and hierarchy, and for release of the individual from the many restraints clericalism and scholasticism had put upon him during the long medieval period. The major figures in the Italian Renaissance were the humanists who, all the while they were attacking medievalism, were, through learned commentary upon Greek and Latin texts rescued from monasteries and universities, setting in motion the intellectual forces that would lead eventually to the philosophic and scientific splendors of the late sixteenth and the seventeenth centuries. The hallmarks of humanism, in revolutionary contrast to those of the Middle Ages, were individualism, rationalism, secularism, and, not least, politics conceived as an art.

From Italy the Renaissance passed in the late fifteenth and early sixteenth centuries to France, the Low Countries, Germany, and eventually England. The qualities of mind and spirit which the Italian humanists had first released from medieval piety and corporatism became, *mutatis mutandis,* the stuff of Reformation, Age of Reason, and Enlightenment. With due apologies to

Alexander Pope on Newton, we may say, in honor of Burckhardt's view of modern European cultural history and its impact upon Everyman:

> "Europe and Europe's mind lay hid in night;
> God said, 'Renascence be!', and all was light."

For how many persons in our day must that not be the sovereign conception of Western European history?[1]

2

It is far from the sovereign view, though, of a large number of scholars in our day, including just about all medievalists, comparative historians, and experts in the histories of philosophy, science, and technology. Not for this imposing group the Burckhardtian view of history with its firm assumption that intellectual progress came to a complete stop in the Middle Ages, its picture of medieval society as one of corporatism and torpidity, individuality extinguished, and its conviction that the Italian fifteenth century is the unique seedbed of modernity where, for the first time in many centuries, an interest in the world and man flourished, thus generating the currents that were to flow into the seventeenth century. For this whole assemblage of scholars, in many special fields of study, the so-called Italian Renaissance turns out to be no renaissance at all if by this word there is reference to major, substantive areas of intellect and learning. Far from being a splendid age of culture, fit rival of the Athenian fifth century B.C., the Quattrocento is seen as hardly more than a small eddy in late medieval waters.

Turn to the comparative historians. Spengler's *Decline of the West,* Toynbee's *Study of History,* Kroeber's *Configurations of Culture Growth,* Petrie's *Revolutions of Civilization,* Sorokin's *Social and Cultural Dynamics,* Thorndike's *History of Civilization,* Rosenstock-Huessy's *Out of Revolution* will do for a start. All, without exception, see the Italian Renaissance as a nullity at best, a decline in excellence at worst. Spengler writes: "It produced no wholly great personality between Dante and Michaelangelo, each of whom had one foot outside its limits." Kroeber, writing of literature, says: "Precedent is all in favor of not accepting such a period," and he dismisses it utterly from philosophical and scientific importance. Toynbee refers to the Western concept of the Renaissance as an "egocentric illusion," Rosenstock-Huessy calls the period "one of the ugliest and darkest hours of the past." Flinders Petrie dismisses the Quattrocento as but "the resort of copying an earlier period . . . an artificial system which has no natural development or root in the mind. . . ." Sorokin treats the period as one of significant decline from earlier heights in the medieval West, and Thorndike, in a book that has its full measure of respect for earlier and later periods of efflorescence of culture, clearly has little besides disdain for the Italian Renaissance.

The really devastating attacks, though, have come from medievalists and from the historians of philosophy and of science. From the first group, the medievalists, revolt against the Burckhardtian conception of the Middle Ages and the flow of European history was almost immediate. There is no need here to go into the rich detail of medievalist assault on the concept of the Renaissance. It has been dealt with memorably in Wallace K. Ferguson, *The Renaissance in Historical Thought,*[2] an impressive work in intellectual history. Suffice it to say that medievalists of the stature of Duhem, Haskins, and Thorndike made rather short work of the Burckhardtian premise of the Middle Ages as a period when human consciousness "lay dreaming or half awake under a common veil," a veil "woven of faith, illusion, and childish prepossession," with individuality indistinct and man "conscious of himself only as member of a race, people, party, family, or corporation—only through some general category." The same short work has been made of the parallel notion of the Middle Ages as a period of economic torpidity and social immobility. In the face of a long succession of works by Coulton, Powers, Bloch, Pirenne, Thrupp, and others, only a rash soul would today argue seriously the thesis of either immobility or of submergence of individuality. The twelfth and thirteenth centuries form, as we know in rich detail, one of the most eruptive ages in human history—socially, economically, culturally, and intellectually. In the presence of an Innocent III, Abelard, or Roger Bacon, not to mention the merchants, artisans, and soldiers of the time, it is difficult indeed to sustain the still astonishingly prevalent conception of medieval torpidity, single-minded piety, and absence of individuality.

Equally devastating to the Burckhardtian perspective have been the works of historians of science and technology. Clearly, it is impossible to hold any longer to the view of the Middle Ages as a long interregnum in the history of these areas. If we are looking for the acorns from which sprang the great oaks of the sixteenth and seventeenth centuries, we can find these easily enough in the truly remarkable experimental and theoretical works of Robert Grosseteste and Roger Bacon, among others. Far from its being necessary to hypothesize an Italian (or other) Renaissance in the fifteenth century to account for the works of Copernicus and Galileo, it is increasingly clear, as Herbert Butterfield[3] has pointed out in a brilliant essay, that both Renaissance and Reformation—whatever their importance in other spheres of study—simply fade into oblivion so far as the history of science is concerned. And as Lynn White[4] has shown us in a series of impressive works, it was the thirteenth century, and not the fifteenth or sixteenth, that "produced the 'invention of invention,'" thus marking the true "moment of crisis in mankind's relation to the natural environment."

Nor has the Italian Renaissance fared better in studies of the history of philosophy. Again, we are obliged to say that it is the twelfth or thirteenth centuries, not the fifteenth, that truly mark the beginning of the "discovery of the world and of man." Etienne Gilson has laid to rest forever the Enlightenment-sprung picture of medieval philosophy so obsessed by the heavenly and so preoccupied by the insignificance of this world as to have had no room in it for metaphysics, ethics, esthetics, anthropology, and psychology. As Gilson has emphasized and demonstrated in a score of works, medieval acknowledg-

474

ment of God's kingdom enhanced, not diminished, appreciation of man's nature and his works.

To be sure, even stipulating medieval greatness in the philosophy of the world and man, a case might still be made out, all other things equal, for the Italian Renaissance along these lines. After all, what had been so buoyant and boundary-breaking in the philosophies of Abelard, Albertus Magnus, and Thomas Aquinas earlier had become, by the fifteenth century, increasingly formalized and didactic. That is the rather common fate of intellectual efflorescences in history. As Livingston Lowes showed us many years ago in poetry and as Thomas Kuhn has demonstrated more recently, creative spasms are very often followed by longer periods of what Lowes called "conventionalization" and Kuhn "routinization."

Did not, then, the Italian humanists, working from pagan texts in the atmosphere of lethargy that scholasticism had generated, restore buoyancy to Western philosophy, instill in it the creative insights which were to result in the towering systems of Descartes and Leibnitz a couple of centuries later? Alas, there is almost no evidence of this. On the basis of studies directly in the history of European philosophy, it is possible to say of it what Herbert Butterfield has said of European science: the Italian Renaissance is not needed. But rather than turn to scholars outside the Renaissance guild on this point, a few words from Paul Oskar Kristeller, himself a Renaissancist of stature, can be allowed to stand: "I should like to suggest that the Italian humanists on the whole were neither good philosophers nor bad philosophers, but no philosophers at all." And for those who think the humanists classical scholars: "The humanists were not classical scholars who for personal reasons had a craving for eloquence, but, vice versa, they were professional rhetoricians, heirs and successors of the medieval rhetoricians, who developed the belief, then new and modern, that the best way to achieve eloquence was to imitate classical models."[5]

3

But is this what the Italian Renaissance must be reduced to: an age of rhetoricians and copyists, more concerned with the manner than the substance of thought; an eddy among late medieval currents rather than a new and powerful current leading straight to Descartes and Leibnitz? If so, there is indeed a very wide gulf between the image of the period which continues to shine brightly and the actual content of the period as this may be found through systematic historical study. Far from being, as Voltaire and so many others have thought down to the present moment, one of the great ages of cultural history in the world, the Quattrocento would appear to be at best a very minor and indistinct period, at worst no period at all in cultural history, only a part of what Huizinga called the waning of the Middle Ages. Even putting great ages to one side, it is quite evidently no longer possible to sustain the Burckhardtian thesis of the Italian Renaissance as a prime mover or even catalyst in the cultural history of modern Europe.

In many ways, this last is the unkindest cut of all. For, even after the actual content of the age of Italian humanism had been cut down to size, the supposition persisted that it had nevertheless been responsible for liberating France and the rest of Europe from what Burckhardt had called "the countless bonds which elsewhere in Europe checked progress." Under this view France, which was the vital link in Burckhardtian philosophy of history, had been no more than an intellectual desert in the fifteenth century, the product of medieval scholasticism's desiccating effects. It was, so the argument went, the diffusion of Italian humanism in the late fifteenth century that made possible the intellectual recovery of France, with the age of Montaigne, Bodin, and Calvin the lineal result.

Alas, the intensive researches of Etienne Gilson, among others, made clear enough that fifteenth-century France was anything but an intellectual desert, that it was in fact a century of extraordinary literary activity and buoyancy, and that all of this could be seen proceeding directly and continuously from the medieval age in France. Franco Simone, himself Italian, professor of French Studies at Turin, summarized, interpreted, and substantially added to what Gilson and others had begun in his notable *Il Rinascimento Francese* in 1961: "Even a cursory survey of current trends in French Renaissance studies discloses that the theory cherished by Romantic historiography—that the cultural renewal of France in the sixteenth century was brought about in the last years of the fifteenth century immediately and exclusively through the influence of renewed cultural activity in Italy—is now quite discredited."[6]

So it is, and with the discrediting of the concept of the Italian Renaissance as the vital agent, the prime mover, in reclamation of the desert Michelet and Burckhardt had declared France and northern Europe to be in the fifteenth century, there went the collapse of the foundations of what has undoubtedly been the single most popular theory of history during the past century—with the possible exception of the Marxian class theory. In blunt truth, the Italian fifteenth century is *not* one of the illustrious ages of thought in world history, is *not* a resplendent period of literature, philosophy, or science, is *not* the funnel through which Greek antiquity poured into Europe, thus awakening the sleeping giant from medieval torpidity, and it is *not* the cause, either material or efficient, of what we call modernity.

Why, then, does the guild of Italian Renaissancists flourish as it so plainly does today? Why does the concept of the Renaissance hold seemingly ineradicable appeal? How do we account for the paradox of a field of scholarship that has had so much of its substance chipped and even dynamited away by extramural scholars yet continues to show undiminished prosperity within and luster from without? Unkind critics might suggest some variant of Parkinson's law, or argue that the bush never burns so brightly as when its roots have been cut, or, more literally, point out that for the Quattrocento to survive has meant elongating it in such a way as to take its beginnings back to the high Middle Ages and its termination up virtually into the seventeenth century.[7]

As I shall indicate toward the end of this essay, there are other, more fundamental causes to account for the persisting appeal of the idea of the Renaissance in the popular educated mind, but I would like to suggest here what seems to me to be the principal force at work in the guild itself. And that is what Max Weber called "charisma" and, then, "routinization of charisma." As I said at the beginning, there is no exact parallel in modern scholarship for the profound and lasting influence of Burckhardt in Renaissance historiography (though one will think of Marx and Freud perhaps in other areas of thought and belief), and I am convinced that in Burckhardt we are dealing with a genuinely charismatic figure, in *The Civilization of the Renaissance in Italy* with a work that has assumed sacred overtones, and in present-day Quattrocento research and analysis with something closely approximating Weber's routinization of charisma—a process that, as Weber noted, is in no sense antithetical to scholarship. Offhand, it is hard to think of any other sphere of scholarship, apart only from Marxism and Freudianism, in which routinization of charisma is as fundamental and vivid as it is in the study of the Italian Renaissance.

I am aware, of course, that no one in the professional guild of Renaissance scholars, not even the veriest apprentice, would be caught declaring unqualifiedly for Burckhardt, any more than a Christian theologian today would be found declaring for the literal text of the Synoptic Gospels. Always, in any given book or article on the Quattrocento, we find the disarming statement that "of course Burckhardt's theory cannot be accepted today in anything like the form in which he advanced it." Always, the accents of sophisticated skepticism surround the subject—up, at least, to a point. But if the reader will look up to the ramparts of the guild hall, he will nevertheless see the Burckhardtian banner waving, enblazoned on it the proud words: "The Development of the Individual," "The State as a Work of Art," and, in largest letters, "The Discovery of the World and of Man."

The point is, modern scholarship in medieval studies, in comparative history, and in the histories of philosophy and science, for all its devastating effect upon the myth of the Renaissance, for all its obliteration of the original ground on which the Burckhardtian thesis rested, has had no more impact on the prestige and prosperity of the Renaissance guild than modern scholarship has had on the prestige and prosperity of Christianity. If members of the guild can no longer cite the history of philosophy or science in support of their belief in the Italian Renaissance as the source of what is distinctive and essential in modernity, they can—and do—turn to ever more recondite, specialized, and even metaphoric bodies of material to uphold the myth of the Renaissance.[8]

Consider two recent, impressive works in the study of the Italian Renaissance, both superbly printed and bound, each a work of art as well as of scholarship. (Recent experience has taught me that American publishers are more likely to go all out in their handling of volumes on the Renaissance than on any other subject.) The first is *Renaissance Studies in Honor of Hans Baron;*[9] the second, Charles Trinkaus' *In Our Image and Likeness: Humanity and Divinity in Italian Humanist Thought.*[10]

It would be impossible to praise too highly these books as works of scholarship. They complement one another nicely. For where the first is largely concerned with the political character of the Italian Renaissance, which was one of Burckhardt's major emphases, the other, by Trinkaus, following another of Burckhardt's principal leads, deals with the subjectivist, ego-exploring, and reflexive character of the humanists' interest in man. In short, the two books express admirably the two poles of Renaissance scholarship at the present time, the first political, the second subjectivist, each bound to be of keenest interest to our own age.

In both books we find firm declaration of allegiance to Burckhardt's grand vision. In the Baron volume, Denys Hay, of the University of Edinburgh, in his introductory essay, quotes without demur Professor Baron's own observation in 1960, a full century after the publication of Burckhardt's book, that "the core of the Burckhardtian conception of the Renaissance . . . may still prove superior to the competing views about the nature of the transition to the modern age." Plainly, charisma dies hard! Denys Hay is fully up to the mark. He declares that "what happened in Florence in the decades around 1400 was to colour deeply the whole picture of Europe in the course of the sixteenth century." Such profound influence, we are told, "would have been impossible at the level of mere ratiocination or decoration." Such humanists as Salutati, Bruni, Brunelleschi, and Massaccio supplied "ethical, educational, and cultural motivation in the governing classes of virtually the whole continent. . . ."[11]

Now, as I have stressed above, this is precisely the assessment of the Quattrocento one does *not* acquire from historians working outside the guild of Renaissancists. Despite the fact that demonstrations of the humanists' contributions to European thought have had to become more and more specialized and antiquarian, often indeed to the point of preciosity, with justifications making their way through charming little paths across the European intellectual landscape quite hidden to other eyes, there is no want of Burckhardtian acclaim for the overall significance of the Quattrocento. Despite all the ritual disclaimers with respect to Burckhardt that one finds in ongoing Renaissance scholarship, the banner nevertheless is regularly brought out to fly proudly. There is little in Hay's words on the Quattrocento to separate him from Burckhardt.

Turn now to Charles Trinkaus' book, which is the one I want to stay with during the next few pages, for of all books I have had opportunity to read on the Italian Renaissance this one seems to me the most original in theme and subtle in argument. If I find myself unconvinced by the book's effort to establish the overall significance and the modernity of the humanists, this is in no way a reflection upon Trinkaus' knowledge, which is profound, or his scholarship, which is meticulous and readably set forth. The influence of Burckhardt is clear. "The central conclusion of this book is that the Italian Renaissance, conceived essentially along Burckhardtian lines, was accompanied by a powerful assertion of will by the leading representatives of Italian humanism and among philosophical circles influenced by them."[12] Elsewhere, Trinkaus writes: "The true significance of the Renaissance and the humanist movement . . . lies more in what Burckhardt and Michelet called 'The Discovery of the World and of Man' than in a poorly founded, premature vision of political democracy."[13] Trinkaus' final words would appear to have their aim somewhere near Hans Baron's thesis, argued in his *The Crisis of the Early Italian Renaissance* and having had great influence on younger, politically conscious Renaissance historians of our time, that the main effect of the humanists was that of liberalizing and humanizing political power. I shall come back to this argument later. What we must now do, having established sufficiently, I think, that Burckhardt lives, is turn to Trinkaus' fascinating and original study.

4

The first point to make about the book is its timeliness. It is the awakening of the spirit of subjectivism that Trinkaus finds to be the chief attribute of the Italian Renaissance—in contrast to the objectivism of so much medieval thought, especially scholasticism—and it has to be admitted that we are ourselves living in a more than usually subjectivist age of literature and philosophy. His book should, and almost certainly will, have great impact on the many in our day who are preoccupied by the self, its levels of consciousness and the veils of awareness which must be pierced.

Trinkaus' emphasis in his two volumes on humanist subjectivism is quite in keeping, I think it worth pointing out, with Burckhardt's view of the Quattrocento as being, at one and the same time, concerned with the state and its power and, forming the opposite side of the same coin, with a subjectivism that "gave the highest development to individuality, and then led the individual to the most zealous and thorough study of himself in all forms and under all conditions."[14] As Burckhardt realized clearly, and emphasized to the end of his life, the essence of modernity lies in concentration of power on the one hand and, on the other, a kind of insulating preoccupation with the atomized self, both consequences of the general weakening of those intermediate structures of community and authority that had been so profuse during the Middle Ages: city, guild, manor, monastery, and the varied other manifestations of associative instinct that is never so strong as when central power is weak and obsession with self nonexistent or subordinate.

The merit and originality of Trinkaus' work lie not simply in his exploration of humanist subjectivism nor in his imaginative treatment of themes such as "man between despair and grace," "the will triumphant," "man's dignity and his misery," and "the condition of man," all fascinatingly dealt with through citations from humanist texts sufficiently generous to give us the flavor of what he is writing about. The signal distinction of the book is, I think, his profound emphasis on St. Augustine and on the very evident influence of Augustine upon the humanists in their theological writings. If there is a hero in *In Our Image and Likeness*, it is surely the Bishop of Hippo, and with every good reason. I believe it can be fairly said that only Plato competes with Augustine in direct, demonstrable influence on Western thought down to the present moment, and, so far as post-Roman thought is concerned, we have much reason for substituting Augustine for Plato in Whitehead's celebrated remark that Western philosophy is a series of footnotes on Plato.

What Trinkaus argues—and this is, it seems to me, the core of his book— is that among other waters the humanists swam in were those of theology, in particular a revived theology of the early Christian fathers, one based upon conceptions of grace and salvation which the humanists could use to good advantage against the formalism and objectivism of the late-medieval Christianity around them.

> Beginning with Petrarch, the humanists broke free from the bonds of religious externalism and objectivism that resulted from the application of the dialectical procedures of scholastic philosophy and theology to ordinary Christian life. The humanist turned back to man as a living, feeling subject. He found him frightened and overwhelmed with despair at the impossibility of believing that such a finicky deity could have any interest in the salvation of such a disorganized, loosely behaving, though well-intentioned Christian.[15]

From this basically Augustine-rooted, highly subjective view of man, with its pre-Reformation thesis that grace can neither be given nor taken away by sacraments, laws, and other externalities, that through faith and belief, not idle obedience to priests and monks, lies man's best and truest approach to God, the humanists moved, according to Trinkaus, steadily and surely through the Quattrocento to a vision of "volitional and operational man" and thence, chiefly through Valla, to a "passional" view, one centered in the "dynamics and power of the affects, of the will, of the emotions in human nature. . . ." Man, for the humanists, thus became by the end of the Italian Renaissance essentially the being he would remain thenceforth in the modern world, "an emotional force, imbued with love and hate, fearless of the consequences in enacting his purposes, not completely blind, since he had the intellect at his disposal, but careless of the voice of the intellect when his passions were sufficiently powerful to sweep him beyond it."[16]

As I say, such a thesis is, in addition to being bold, timely. It is hard not to conclude that Trinkaus has been affected by currents of thought and feeling and reflexiveness in our own age. I offer that not as criticism. After all, how is it possible for a major work of interpretation, no matter how far back in time its subject, *not* to be so affected? Still, it is a point to be noted in passing. We are ourselves living in an age of thought that, much like the Quattrocento, is increasingly bifurcated between a growing politicization of mind on the one hand and, on the other, a constantly growing preoccupation with the affective nature of personality and with the recesses of individual consciousness. It would seem not at all unlikely that scholarship today on the Italian Renaissance would reflect this bifurcation, and the two opposite interpretations of Italian humanism we get from Hans Baron and Charles Trinkaus go a long way in this respect.

That the humanists were keenly interested in theological issues, were influenced by Augustine in some degree at least, and were profoundly alert to the ways in which at least one vein of Augustinianism could be used polemically against Christianity as it existed in their time, and also against what they knew of or thought they knew of scholasticism—all of this Trinkaus makes vivid to us. As I have said, this aspect alone of the book is sufficient to earn it lasting place in the upper reaches of Renaissance study.

It is in keeping, though, with the Burckhardtian spirit that never fails to inspire members of the Renaissance guild that no matter how badly burned others may have been in efforts to make something *philosophically* important of the Quattrocento, Trinkaus should also seek, this time through the *via theologica,* to demonstrate that the humanists, in addition to being rhetoricians and theological polemicists, were philosophers. Trinkaus concedes that "the one thing we can be sure about is that most of the humanists were likely to know the works of the thirteenth- and fourteenth-century scholastics by reputation only" and that "there is ground for doubting even this in the case of certain humanists."[17] He is fully aware of the powerful testimony of Paul Oskar Kristeller along this line, whatever may be his views of what the medievalists and most historians of philosophy have had to say. He admits too that the humanists in attacking the scholastics were not offering content of a philosophical nature but were in fact asserting the importance of their own disciplines, which were, of course, rhetoric, grammar, and poetry—that is, the style and form of thought. Nevertheless, even as the moth heads to the flame, Trinkaus heads, in characteristic Renaissancist fashion, to the view that the humanists were, after all, concerned with philosophy.

> The point, however, that now needs to be stressed is that the humanists as part of the rhetorical tradition, itself, were concerned with philosophy. They were not concerned with philosophy within the technical branches of the subject inside which medieval scholasticism and the modern academic discipline of philosophy insist it must confine its discussion. Perhaps "ethics" and "aesthetics" are the only branches which the humanists would or could recognize as legitimate.... Although they did not enter into formal discussions of epistemology and metaphysics, it is hard to see how they could have dispensed with the problems involved in these disciplines. As a matter of fact they ordinarily assumed without analysis a certain mode of knowing and an underlying structure of reality, and probably for this most of all they deserve the charge of not being philosophers. But they did have their positions with regard to the problems of epistemology and metaphysics (excluding, of course, the epistemological and metaphysical problems involved in natural philosophy, physics, medicine, etc., which they reviled, with a certain justification, as irrelevant).[18]

Now, that is not one of Professor Trinkaus' better paragraphs. In fact, it is a bad paragraph, and quite uncharacteristic of the two volumes. The reason it is bad is that it has nothing, really, to say; or rather it has something to say that it promptly cancels, then restates in modified degree, concluding on a note that makes any philosophical pretensions for the humanists somewhat absurd. That the humanists were in some degree "concerned with philosophy" goes without serious question. Who isn't? Paraphrasing M. Jourdain in Molière's play, we are all delighted on occasion to discover that we are thinking philosophy as we speak prose. The only reason I have quoted a bad paragraph from an extraordinarily fine work of scholarship is to indicate how seemingly undauntable is the desire among students of the Quattrocento to make something really important of the humanists' thought and writing, something that goes beyond rhetoric and ordinary dialectics. The fact is, if by philosophy we mean anything that approximates what Descartes, Leibnitz, Hume, and Kant were to be concerned with, what Abelard, Duns Scotus, and Aquinas had lectured and written about two or three centuries earlier, not to mention Plato and Aristotle long before that, the Italian humanists have no more claim to be declared "concerned with philosophy" than do the Sophists of ancient Athens, the *philosophes* of the French eighteenth century, or those who write reviews at the present time in *Partisan Review*.

Once again, it is useful to be reminded of the paradox of the Italian Renaissance. It is, and has been ever since Burckhardt wrote his great work more than a century ago, "one of the world's great ages." Everyone *knows* that. The problem, the plaguing, nagging, gnawing problem, however, is to shore up this vision, as much a part of the cultural scene, thanks to Burckhardtian charisma, as is the vision of the Middle Ages as being static, torpid, and anti-intellectual. That is, to shore up the vision, all the while keeping a wary eye out on the mass of scholarship accumulated since Burckhardt which tells us, in essence, that the Burckhardtian perspective was almost totally false, that no Italian Renaissance of the fifteenth century need be hypothesized to account for the great oaks of sixteenth- and seventeenth-century philosophy and science, that a sufficient number of acorns—if that is the word with which to refer to the age of Aquinas and Grosseteste—can be found, and have been found, in the twelfth and thirteenth centuries. Modifying cliché, we can say that if Burckhardt hadn't invented the Italian Renaissance it would *not* be necessary to invent it today. Or wouldn't it? I shall come back to that interesting point at the end of my essay.

5

Fundamental to the Burckhardtian vision of European history is the conception of the Quattrocento as *modern;* that is, not merely an eddy among currents of the late medieval age of thought, not a manifestation of decline from heights reached earlier in the West—as ages of pandemic rhetoric, polemic, and conscious imitation so often are—but *modern* in the sense that its dominant values and insights are prototypes of the values of insights of the seventeenth century and after. Given the assaults on the authenticity of the period which have come from areas of scholarship outside the guild, efforts to demonstrate the modernity of the Quattrocento, like efforts to demonstrate its cultural and intellectual greatness, have had to be more and more ingenious. Such efforts range from art and letters to politics and war.

Trinkaus doesn't declare the Quattrocento modern. It is, he writes, "an autonomous period of history and therefore should not be strictly medieval, nor modern, nor even a hybrid conception of a transition between the two, but something clearly and definitely its own."[19] Well and good. But it is nevertheless a substantial part of the book's thrust to show that the *tilt* of the period is modern. The humanists, we read, offered "a new affirmation of the possibility and value of human action" and also a "vision of man controlling and shaping his own life and the future course of his history, and they stressed a new conception of human nature. . . ."[20] In the Foreword, Trinkaus makes plain his agreement with Burckhardt's "assertion of an energetic, individualist drive for fulfillment as a major motif of Renaissance culture" and, in broad outline, with Cassirer's conception of the period as the dawn of modern enlightenment, stressing only that this humanist modernity was reached not through the channels identified by Burckhardt and by Cassirer but through those of a basically Augustinian theology.[21] In sum, for all the "autonomy" of the period and its claimed separation from medieval and modern alike, it is made by its learned and talented student in this book to point quite as directly toward modernity as ever it had been by Burckhardt, Symonds, Cassirer, or others working from different vantage points but to the same end. Burckhardt saw the birth of the new image of man as the issue of marriage between the "Italian spirit" and a revived paganism. Trinkaus sees this birth as instead the product of "pre-scholastic Christian sources"[22] brought to high intensity by the humanists in their war against scholasticism and corporate orthodoxy. However defined, it is still modernity.

How will readers of Trinkaus react to the tilt? My guess is that intellectual historians of the Middle Ages, of philosophy, of science and technology, and of comparative ages of cultural efflorescence will be no more convinced than they have been by other statements of the seminal modernity, or premodernity, of the Italian humanists. Renaissancists, on the other hand, with due qualifications, are likely to feel fortified. My own view is that on the evidence supplied us by Trinkaus in two deeply researched volumes the *Quattrocento* may well be an "autonomous period," but the tilt, if any, is backward, toward the Middle Ages, rather than forward toward modernity.

I have two main reasons for this belief, both rooted in the long passages Trinkaus cites in several places in support of his view that the humanists were, stimulated by Augustine, working within anthropological and psychological perspectives regarding man's knowledge and culture. Within these perspectives, it seems to me, there are two tests, two touchstones of modernity in contrast to the medieval view. The first is the idea of cumulative, necessary progress. The second is the idea of self-knowledge as the stepping stone to all knowledge without assistance of authority or revelation. Both ideas, as we know, came into full light and prominence in the seventeenth century, chiefly in France. The question that must be asked about the *Quattrocento* in Italy concerns the degree, if any, to which adumbrations of either of these keystones of the modern mind may be found in humanist writings. Not, to be sure, the fully formed ideas themselves, but at least unambiguous anticipations of these ideas in the form of statements that will separate the humanists from the scholastics and university scholars around them in the *Quattrocento,* as well as from those writers, philosophers, scientists, and others who had been for two centuries at least, despite still current myth to the contrary, also concerned with man, with nature, with indeed, *mutatis mutandis,* "the discovery of the world and of man," albeit in Christian-medieval context.

In several places, with long passages provided from the humanists, Trinkaus deals with the humanists' unquestionable admiration for man as man and for man's works on this earth. There is no question of Petrarch's,

Manetti's, and Ficino's belief in the dignity of man,[23] in the superiority of man to other earthly beings, and in the wonders of his works in Florence and elsewhere. I confess, though, I find it hard to separate the spirit behind these passages from the analogous spirit of man's dignity, superiority, and the wonders of his earthly works that we can find in not a little medieval writing, as revealed, say, by Etienne Gilson, and there seems to me moreover to be a kind of narcissistic, competitive, parochial patriotism in what the humanists have to say about Florence which falls rather clearly within the context of town rivalry that abounded in the Middle Ages. A "Quarrel of Ancients and Moderns" did indeed exist in the Quattrocento, a limited preview in certain respects of the better known and more productive "Quarrel" of the seventeenth century, but whereas the later one yielded us the modern idea of cumulative development of knowledge, with superiority of "moderns" over "ancients" resting on this proclaimed principle of growth of knowledge through time, it is hard to find much more than temporal parochialism or narcissism in what the humanists had to say on the matter. Certainly, in the generous citations Trinkaus gives us, there is not so much as a glimmer of an idea of progress or development through time so far as knowledge is concerned.

This is the more striking, and disappointing, in light of the humanists' evident knowledge of and admiration for Augustine's writings. For, had they looked carefully enough, or been motivated to do so, they could have found most of the essential elements of the principle of the growth of knowledge. In a famous metaphor, Augustine likened the development of mankind's knowledge through the ages to the education of a single mind, one to be conceived, Augustine tells us, as living through all the epochs of mankind's existence on earth. In the seventeenth century, Pascal, Fontenelle, and Perrault were to take precisely this metaphor, extending its implication into the indefinite future, as their stated base of the idea of progress for which they are famous.[24]

But there is much more to Augustine's conception of the development of knowledge than his celebrated metaphor. In Book XXII, Section 24, of *The City of God,* we are given a truly remarkable panorama of mankind's progress through the ages in the arts, sciences, technology, philosophy, and other secular realms, along with, it might be stressed here, a virtually pagan appreciation of the beauties of the human body and mind. Much indeed of what Trinkaus quotes from Petrarch, Manetti, and Ficino in these respects seems almost derivative from Augustine's magnificent paean to human progress, though if it is we are given no suggestion of it by Trinkaus. But while, as I say, humanist writing here might seem derivative, at no point does it equal, does it seem as "modern" as, what Augustine wrote on all the wonders of mankind's development of the arts and sciences, of mastery of the physical world, and also of the human body and mind.

Granted that Augustine, following more or less faithfully Christian adaptation of the Greek-sprung metaphor of the cycle of genesis and decay (though without the idea of recurrence that went with the Greek conception of cycles), saw in his own day signs of a degeneration of culture that would, he thought, culminate in the ending of this world forever, he yet gives us a synthesis of past and present, a genuinely developmental, even progressive, sense of man through time that the humanists, with far more motivation, one might think, lacked utterly. Even more remarkable, given their period and their reading of Augustine, is the humanists' failure, at least in the extensive passages given us by Trinkaus, to go as far as Augustine did in crediting human progress to man himself. One may feel certain that Augustine did not feel he was taking away from God when, at the beginning of the long tribute to man's progress of knowledge in earthly and human matters, he credited all of this to what he called "the genius of man," "exuberant invention," and "an inexhaustible wealth in nature which can invent, learn, or employ such arts." I find little, if any, of that in what Trinkaus gives us from the humanists.

I trust it will be understood that I am not condemning the humanists for being what they weren't; that is, for not being more "modern" than they were. It is Trinkaus who implies modernity of mind for the humanists, as did Burckhardt. I am only emphasizing my own view that on the evidence given us the humanists were more nearly an eddy of medieval waters than a modern current with respect to the idea of progress and, beyond this, that there was a great deal in Augustine they failed utterly to get which, if they had got it, would, it is amusing to reflect, have made them very modern indeed. But that was left to the seventeenth century.

So was the second of what I have called the two pillars of the modern age: the use of awareness of self from which to work toward certainty of knowledge in philosophical and scientific matters. As we know, it was Descartes' celebrated statement of this that became the virtual hallmark of modernity, that played an enormous role in the social and moral sciences of the late seventeenth, the eighteenth, and the nineteenth centuries. *Cogito ergo sum.* This is the very essence of modern individualism. Do we find, amid all the undeniable expressions of a subjectivist character among the passages Trinkaus gives us, any inkling of this psychology of knowledge, this epistemology? I am afraid I do not find it. And here, as with respect to the matter of the relation of modern to ancient works and knowledge, the humanists might have gotten more from their beloved St. Augustine than they did. Think only of the following passage in *The City of God* (it reverberates through the *Confessions* and other works, philosophical in character, of Augustine):

I am most certain that I am, and that I know and delight in this. In respect of these truths, I am not at all afraid of the arguments of the Academicians, who say, What if you are deceived; for if I am deceived, how am I deceived in believing that I am? For it is certain that I am if I am deceived.... And, consequently, neither am I deceived in knowing that I know. For, as I know that I am, so I know this also, that I know.[25]

The Jesuit-trained Descartes, who may or may not have remembered his Augustine specifically and textually but who could hardly have escaped being stimulated and influenced by Augustine, makes such reflections the very basis of his *Cogito ergo sum* and, thence, a whole structure of reasoning which led to a conclusion of the expendability of revelation and tradition, even if Descartes did not explicitly draw the conclusion. I have not, however, been able to find a hint, not even in the section on Ficino, master Platonist *and* Augustinian, of this epistemology, this psychology of awareness and knowledge, so plainly to be found in Augustine (irrespective of Augustine's own context for the remarkable statement I just quoted) and, obviously, so revolutionary in its possibilities toward the scholasticism that the humanists hated.

Again I say, the purpose here is not that of disparaging the humanists. They were men of their time, which is to say, with Huizinga, of the waning of the Middle Ages. And bear in mind that Trinkaus himself claims no more, explicitly, for the humanists than their formation of an autonomous period that is neither medieval nor modern. Still, as I suggested, not I think unfairly, Trinkaus cannot resist, in many places, implying nevertheless that the thrust of the humanists was modern, that their subconscious, if not conscious, was looking toward the seventeenth century. And this I find unsupported, basically, by two splendid volumes of research in the ideas of the humanists of the Quattrocento.

6

Let us turn now to the case for the political modernity of the Italian humanists. Is this case any greater in substance? If so, it is to be found primarily in the work of Hans Baron, whose *The Crisis of the Early Italian Renaissance* is unquestionably the foremost study in this general area and has been since its initial publication in 1955. As I noted above, the routinization of Burckhardt today falls into the two large categories, each directly descended from the master, of subjectivism and individualization of thought on the one hand —admirably reflected in Trinkaus' book—and, on the other, of politicization of thought, of acceptance of politics as both art and vocation, and the claimed roots of this politicization in the Italian Renaissance.

Tensions within the Renaissance guild rising from the existence of these two broad perspectives are plain to be seen. Those who are skeptical of claims for metaphysical or epistemological novelty for the Quattrocento, or of its importance in the history of the literary imagination, tend to look to politics, finding in such minds as Valla and Salutati the origins of the modern political imagination, or what Baron has called "civic humanism." Conversely, we find, as we might expect, in one of Charles Trinkaus' persuasion, skepticism, not to say hostility, for this asserted political humanism. "Modern political democracy," writes Trinkaus, "was born in seventeenth-century England and eighteenth-century France, not in Renaissance Italy."[26]

In fairness, though, to Baron, he does not claim for Salutati and other humanists anticipations of modern democracy, though I dare say he would not demur if these were claimed in his presence. What Hans Baron argues is the rise in the Quattrocento of what he calls "civic humanism" and, then, its long-run influence in shaping the political character of the European mind. Baron writes:

Humanism, as molded by the Florentine crisis, produced a pattern of conduct and thought which was not to remain limited to Florentine humanists. From that time on there would exist a kind of Humanism which endeavoured to educate a man as a member of his society and state.... Whereas such an approach had nowhere been found before 1400, it became virtually inseparable from the growth of Humanism during the Renaissance.[27]

Now, it is no disservice to the internal contribution of Baron to the Quattrocento, just as fascinating to the outsider as that of Charles Trinkaus, to say that when this statement is set up against the longer, larger history of political thought in Western Europe, its thesis is at the very least highly questionable. One can define "civic humanism" or anything else in a way that will make historical validation or invalidation exceedingly difficult. There may well be something distinctive about the political thinking of the humanists; I believe there is, and will come to it momentarily. But to anyone who has read the Carlyles on medieval political thought in all the rich detail we get there, or the much more recent *The King's Two Bodies* by the late Ernst H. Kantorowicz, the claim of innovation for the Quattrocento in any respect having seriously to do with the history of the political mind, call it what we will, is a hard one to assimilate.

I find no references in Baron's book to the universities, to law, or to Roman Law. Surely it would be impossible to deny to the teaching of Roman Law in such centers as Bologna, from the time it became a vital element of the curriculum in the medieval period, a substantial role in the development of what Baron calls "civic humanism." From Bologna and other universities in Europe issued forth literally thousands of vigorous and active minds eager to apply where possible the insights regarding power and polity that lay in the *Corpus Juris Civilis*. Roman law, as the great Maitland wrote, was "the main agent in the transmutation" at the end of the Middle Ages "in men's thoughts about groups of men."[28] No one today, giving even scant regard to Roman law principles of citizenship, location of sovereignty in the people, rationalization of administration, and other seminal ideas of political membership in the social order, can doubt that Roman law teachings and texts in the European universities of the twelfth and thirteenth centuries had a profound role in the production of political intellectuals keenly interested in what, with no distortion, can be called "civic humanism."

To say that the Roman and civil lawyers of the medieval period were under the domination of the Church and could not therefore have had any clear sense of *amor patriae* would be to miss utterly the effective contexts in which the medieval lawyers thought and worked. As Kantorowicz has shown us at length and in great detail, the sentiments of *amor patriae* and of *pro patria mori* were widespread among the whole class of those trained in the precepts of Roman law. And this class, Kantorowicz notes dryly, "did not revel in the idea of patriotic massacre as occasionally humanists did...."[29]

What medieval thought did not have, despite the essential raw materials lying around in the Roman law texts, was any real conception of the modern territorial state with its claimed sovereignty over all other forms of association, as well as individuals, and its monopolization and centralization of power. For all the popularity among lawyers of *amor patriae,* society tended to be conceived throughout the Middle Ages as a *communitas communitatum,* a hierarchical assemblage of corporate communities, each, as von Gierke and Maitland have told us, with its own claimed right, function, and authority. The idea of the king's superiority to the law was scarcely to be found, as was any idea of society composed of legally discrete atoms. Not until the late sixteenth century, in Bodin's *Commonwealth,* do we get for the first time a distinct view of sovereignty in the modern sense, and even there it is weakened by a still insistent medieval tradition in Bodin's thought that elevated the patriarchal household and the innumerable *collegia* forming the larger social structure in a way not wholly consistent with Bodin's claim for sovereignty as being "absolute and perpetual power over the subjects and citizens in a Commonweale." It is Hobbes, well into the seventeenth century, who gives us our first unqualified look at the modern, unified, absolute legal state.

Now, if we were able to find so much as a glimmering of any of these modern political conceptions in the writings of the Italian humanists, as these are presented by Baron, we should think these writings to be indeed on the road to modernity in political philosophy. But we don't—at least in any greater degree than what we are able to find in medieval thought and, in substantially less degree, I am inclined to think, than what lay at least subliminally in the minds of medieval lawyers familiar with the exciting, if unfulfillable, leads given in the *Corpus Juris Civilis.* Not even later, in the writings of Guiccardini and Machiavelli do we get any foretaste of the modern idea of the political state and, with it, of citizenship as the central role in the social order. As J. H. Hexter has made lastingly clear,[30] whatever else one may find about politics in the writings of Machiavelli, one finds no conception of *lo stato.* We *do* find this in France during the same century in which Machiavelli wrote, but, on the evidence, it is not necessary to look beyond the line of political thought that had begun in the medieval universities and that had Roman law texts as its vital substance.

In sum, we are obliged, it seems to me, to render the same verdict on Baron and his school that we have on Trinkaus: not proved. I am referring to ideas, themes, and perspectives, not to more general and diffuse states of feeling. Philosophically speaking, the claimed modernity of the Italian humanists did not lead them, as I have suggested here, to so much as an adumbration of the modern ideas of progress and of the self as the epistemological foundation of knowledge nor, *pace* Hans Baron, does it seem to have led them even to the equally modern idea of the state or political community.

7

And yet the fascination with Italian humanists and their age remains. Who can resist it? The spell of Burckhardt's book hardly diminishes after we have found, thanks to modern historical scholarship, the hollowness of his claim for the humanists and for the Quattrocento. Why? How do we explain the appeal of the age and of the chief actors?

I have suggested the role of Burckhardtian charisma and of the routinization of charisma, and I do not now withdraw this. But this has principal effect in the academy, most particularly in the guild of Renaissancists. Even allowing for the predictable impress of Burckhardt's book on every educated mind that reaches it, this would hardly explain, I think, the persisting interest of generation after generation in the humanists—even when, as is usually the case, the interested layman is hard put to name any individual humanist with the possible exception of Petrarch.

I am inclined to think that we shall get farther in answering our question regarding the ineradicable appeal of the Italian Renaissance if we turn to comparative history and treat the humanists as members of a class or type that is in no way restricted to fifteenth-century Italy but that may be found appearing recurrently in the West ever since the Sophists in ancient Athens. It is hard to find a good single word for this class. I can think of no other than *intellectuals*.[31] Not scholars, not scientists, not philosophers, and not genuine literary creators or artists. Intellectuals! The genus is well enough known in Western society, beginning, as I have suggested, with the Sophists (though I do not here claim they were the very first; merely the first known to us in any detail), including also the rhetoricians of the late Roman Republic who flocked in after Rome's defeat of Greece, the *philosophes* in eighteenth-century France and their progeny throughout the nineteenth century in European coffee houses, and, by no means least, those of our day who write regularly on all manner of subjects for *The New York Review of Books* and countless similar journals.

How do we define in positive terms this class of which, I am suggesting, the Italian humanists are members? I have stressed sufficiently that in this class we find no evidence of the profundity of the philosopher, the erudition of the scholar, the method of the scientist, or the creativity of the true artist. What we do find in rich abundance are cleverness of thought and brilliance of style. If there is a single word that best describes the mentality of the Sophists, humanists, *philosophes*, and others, it is *brilliance:* manifest in the quick thrust or *riposte,* the use of paradox and of inversion of meaning, the derivation of iridescent qualities, overwhelmingly verbal, from the already known, and, perhaps above all, the polemical stance.

The last, polemic, is vital. I do not say there is never an element of the polemical in the philosopher or scholar or even the scientist, but no one would make this essential or even very noticeable in the ranks of these groups. But polemic comes close to being the very nature of the class of intellectuals in Western history, for it goes with that assault on traditional values and authorities, especially those of the religious establishment, that has been the hallmark of the intellectual in the West since the time of the Sophists. What else, basically, were the humanists and then later the *philosophes* and still later the revolutionary intellectuals of the nineteenth century concerned with but attack on the authorities of traditional society: attack, attack, always attack, as we might use here the classic phrase in modern military strategy.

With assault on traditional authority—whether of church, guild, university, monastery, or community—goes characteristically a fascination with power; especially the kind of power to be found in the leader, the tribune, despot or tyrant, for in such power there is greater flexibility of use, less likelihood of its being rooted in and therefore hindered by ordinary social codes and conventions. It was this union of contempt for authority and adoration of power that Plato hated in the Sophists, that Burke found detestable in the *philosophes,* and that led, as we know, to Burckhardt's alienation from not only his discovered Italian humanists but from modernity generally in the latter part of his life.

Nor should we overlook another characteristic of not merely the humanists but of other principal representatives of the class of Western intellectuals: the extraordinary combination of rootlessness and upward thrust of personal fortune. Not all intellectuals in the West have done as well as Voltaire did—becoming through shrewd speculations a millionaire—but on the evidence supplied us, we are justified in concluding that a fair number of Sophists, rhetoricians in Republican Rome, humanists, and *philosophes,* not to mention intellectuals of our own day, have not only done good by their standards, they have also *done well* by anyone's standards. Intellectuals, as first Burke, then Tocqueville observed—with the *philosophes* in mind—have tended to associate themselves with fluid, commercial wealth where movement and turnover are rapid and where cunning is vital rather than with more stable types of institutionally based wealth. It is this aspect of the Italian humanists that has struck Leonardo Olschki in his *The Genius of Italy,* Charles Trinkaus in his *Adversity's Noblemen,* and Arnold Hauser in his *The Social History of Art.* From dependence on this type of uncertain wealth and on the traits of mind necessary to achieve it has come, it is argued, the social insecurity and psychological instability that so many students of the Quattrocento from Burckhardt on have found to be attributes of the humanist mind. Alfred von Martin has given this a good deal of prominence in his *Sociology of the Renaissance,* noting, as had Burckhardt, the built-in conflict between humanist and the established classes, upper and lower.[32]

It is no wonder, given their assault on tradition and conventional authority, their brilliance and cleverness, their general disdain for the people, or at least the rooted classes and communities of the people, their incessant elevation of self and ego, their attachments to men of power, and their notable fondness for fluid wealth, that intellectuals as a class have never been very popular with most members of society. They have been disturbers of the peace, so to speak, often arrogant and self-seeking, contemptuous of other views and of the conventional channels of knowledge, never loath to break icons and to advance themselves by whatever arts happened to be in passing public favor, dedicated ostensibly to man's happiness and welfare but far more interested, on the evidence, in destroying, diminishing, and rendering less credible the ordinary pursuits of happiness and welfare in the societies around them. It is this combination of qualities that can, in the beginning, give popularity or at least notoriety to intellectuals at any given time but that can later lead to extreme disfavor and even hatred in the people for these self-same glorifiers of the aloof, critical, and rootless mind of the intellectual class. Certainly, all we know of the fate of the Sophists, of the humanists in late fifteenth- and early sixteenth-century Italy, and of the *philosophes* and their progeny during and after the French Revolution suggests that this class has good reason for a certain insecurity of mind and instability of thrust.

I believe we can date—for modern European purposes—the signal division between intellectual and society from the time of the Quattrocento. As Alfred von Martin has emphasized, the humanist-intellectual made a virtual fetish of his lack of roots in the social classes, of his detached position morally, and of "the self-sufficiency of a purely intellectual attitude—even though it thus contributed to its own isolation and exile."[33] Gone now, at least in humanist assessment, was the older, basically medieval division of the population into the *kleros* and the *laos,* with the man of learning and intellect considered a craftsman among other craftsmen, his material historical and philosophical knowledge rather than bricks, wool, and silver but not made thereby of superior status in the social order. Conflicts between scholar and townsman there were indeed in the Middle Ages, as the history of the university makes evident. The function of mind and of learning was nevertheless conceived, it would appear, as social, as contributory to the intellectual, moral, and social structure of mankind. Any conviction of the inherent superiority of the philosopher or scholar to churchman, guildsman, merchant, or peasant is hard to find in medieval writing.

It is not hard to find in humanist writing. A certain arrogance of spirit, of contempt for other ranks of society, high or low, and of disdain for all pursuits that did not begin and end in preoccupation with the self, all of this shines through clearly in the humanists—as apparently it did with the Sophists and most certainly with the *philosophes.* It was precisely this disdain for the rest of society and its fabric of authorities drawn from tradition and convention and this centering of attention upon the self conceived as liberated from this fabric that led to such common affinity between humanist and the single man of power. For in extreme centralization of power in a community can lie protection from the intermediate authorities born of traditional religion, morality, and association. Seemingly, there are no exceptions of note to the principle that the class of intellectuals in the West, humanists included, has despised authority and loved power, seeing in the latter a unique means of liberation of the subjectivist, private, self-centered spirit from the exasperating restraints of popular morality and convention.

But whether the West has been in one of its spasms of love and fascination or of hatred and persecution, its awareness of and its preoccupation with the class of intellectuals continue. Evidently, there is something as appealing in the lives of those whose egoism, arrogance, and contempt for the *lares* and *penates* are revealed in tract or polemic as there is in those who display these same qualities in the robbing of trains, the stealing from the rich, the gunfighting of the Old West, or the cornering of some commodity on the stock exchange. One can be a disturber of the peace as easily in a book or essay as in one or other of the capers we associate with a Robin Hood or a Jesse James. And, for the most part, especially when time's distance lends enchantment, as with Robin Hood or the humanists of the Quattrocento, public enchantment can be counted on.

Generally, public indulgence is greater, at least at the time of the disturbance, for the intellectual than for the bandit or embezzler. But, on the evidence of history, ages of efflorescence of intellectuals (I am not referring to philosophers, scientists, and scholars) are commonly followed by ages of repression of intellectuals, or at very least sharp antagonism toward intellectuals. Such, as we know, was the case in late fifth-century B.C. Athens when even a Socrates could incur public hatred; such was the case too with the humanists by the late fifteenth century in Florence, an antagonism that lasted for quite a while; and such was the case with the *philosophes* during the Revolution when the Jacobin police could hunt down a Condorcet and after the Revolution in the age dominated by Napoleon and his dislike of "ideologues." Being an intellectual, in short, is not without its dangers, no matter what the excitements may be that go with disturbing the peace.

8

There is, however, one other aspect of the Italian Renaissance that tends to win our unfailing interest in the period and in the humanists. This is to be found at the etymological heart of the word "Renaissance": *rebirth*. Although, as we have seen, the best scholarship in the histories of philosophy, science, technology, and political ideas—and there are some to say the same of even the arts—denies utterly in these areas what Burckhardt and his followers have professed to see, that is, rebirth or reawakening of vital themes long dormant in the West, the magic of the myth of rebirth will not be put down. Nor is it likely to. I am inclined to think the myth of genesis-decay-rebirth to be one of the truly constitutive ideas of the West, very probably of most other areas of civilization as well, and as evocative today as it was in the time of Hesiod.

Among the Greeks, not only among prophets and poets but philosophers of the stature of Plato and Aristotle, this idea of ceaseless genesis and decay, working in rhythmic succession through all time, was profoundly held. It was no less popular among Romans—*vide* Lucretius, Seneca, and Ovid—and, in substantially modified form, it was taken over by the Christians, reaching magnificent expression in Augustine. There, of course, there was no idea of cyclical recurrence, but what else is the Christian epic but a grand vision of mankind's genesis, development through the ages, and eventual extinction, to be followed by the transhistorical eternity of salvation or damnation? For Augustine, any "rebirth" would be spiritual and for eternity, not, as the Greeks and Romans had believed, secular and ever subject to recurrence on earth.

Likening of human history to the processes of growth and decay in nature inevitably led to fixing of attention on "stages" or "ages" of growth, with some labeled youthful and buoyant, others mature, and still others senescent, facing degeneration and death. We find these stages or ages in Plato and Aristotle, in Seneca, Virgil, and Ovid, among others, and we find them also as cardinal elements of the Augustinian, single-cycle, unilinear presentation of mankind's history on earth. There was no more doubt in Augustine's mind than there had been in Plato's that what now exists on this earth is destined to die.[34]

492

So was the idea of rebirth a popular one during the Italian Renaissance, as we might expect to be the case. It was made to order for the humanists with their conviction of the sterility, desiccation, and imminent death of scholasticism, along with other representations of the hated medieval-Christian order, and their conviction too of their own role, symbolized by pagan rhetoric and fancy dress, of restorer to the world of a life that had been taken away by clerics and scholastics. Later on a good deal of the same symbolism would be found among the secular, Church-hating intellectuals of eighteenth-century France, and still later in the works of Michelet who claimed to have gotten the idea of cyclical rebirth from Vico. Hating, as Michelet did, the whole Church- and feudal-drawn culture of Europe which seemed to him the real source of the repressions in Europe of the revolutions that had flared up in 1848, it is hardly to be wondered at that not only would he have dreamed of rebirth in his own day but that he would have seen this historiographic concept as vital to any understanding of the beginnings of the modern age. How attractive, in the writing of the history of Europe, to declare the Middle Ages a period of death of mind and the age of the humanists in Italy the beginnings of life! It is no wonder, then, that when Burckhardt's genius took this vision, this myth, over, it became, as I observed at the beginning of my essay, one of the most deeply rooted convictions of the modern educated mind, a very pillar of modern historiography with its still ascendant division of Western history into the periods we know so well and, not least, an aspect of modern secular dogma.

The greater exponents of progress in the nineteenth century—Comte, Spencer, Buckle, Marx, *et al.*—saw nothing wrong in allowing for fluctuations, for short-run periods of decline and, then, of resurgence in their unilinear trajectories of inevitable progress for mankind. In any event, the philosophers of inevitable progress, and this includes Herbert Spencer foremost, were concerned with mankind as a whole, not with any given nation, culture, or people at any given time. It was entirely in keeping with the idea of progress in the nineteenth century that there should be periods of occasional torpor and sterility in man's history—as during the Middle Ages in this view—with, however, restorative periods of creativity and buoyancy following closely in time.

The historiographic concept of the Renaissance was, then, made to order for the general philosophy of progress. Progress may be declared the normal state of change, with man's underlying nature conducive to progress, but there are bound to be occasional periods when superstition, ignorance, intellectual tyranny, and philosophies like scholasticism take command. And then, so the idea of unilinear philosophy went, sterility and drought are the results. But such ages are followed by their opposites. The world's great age begins anew. Renascence occurs; there is rebirth of the truly vital qualities in man's mind and culture; the wheels of progress again turn. So thought the ancient Greek philosophers, the Roman poets and naturalists, and so too thought the Italian humanists, steeped in the rhetoric if not the substance of ancient learning, and, then, the exponents of the Moderns in the seventeenth-century Quarrel of the Ancients and Moderns, the *philosophes* in the eighteenth century, the Jacobin visionaries of the Year II, and, not least for purposes of this essay, Michelet and Burckhardt in the nineteenth century.

Myth is powerful, often, as I think in the case of this myth, ineradicable. Of what use to explain that Europe and Europe's mind did *not* lie in night during the Middle Ages, that that period—in philosophy, science, scholarship, art, and technology—is indeed demonstrably one of the authentically great, creative ages in world history. Of what use to show, as historians of incontestable stature have shown, that the asserted Italian Renaissance was no renaissance at all, save possibly in a few of the arts of rhetoric and adornment, and that no such period is required to explain the great works of philosophy and science of the late sixteenth and the seventeenth centuries, that the line of continuity is as clear as it possibly could be to these works from those of Abelard and Grosseteste, among so many others. Myth, I repeat, is powerful. And where there is myth, the history of religion and of charisma's routinization teaches us, there must be substance found endlessly for the myth. Belief cries out for such substance and also for incessant reaffirmation of myth. The Renaissance lives!

It would be strange today in the West, with its full share of belief in the corruptness, the sterility, and the imminent defeat of the modern establishment, a belief as widespread among intellectuals in our time as ever it was in the Quattrocento and its humanists, if fascination with the Italian Renaissance were not as great as it so evidently is. And, leaving our contemporary humanist-*philosophe* intellectuals to one side, it is hard to miss even among a large number of our middle class, at least as their sentiments are revealed by polls, a vague, amorphous, but floating and powerful conviction that our culture, our social order, our morality are perhaps showing signs of what, under the spell of the West's most seminal myth, can be called senescence and decay, with some new renaissance man's best hope.

NOTES

1. Nor are such persons laymen only. Thus, Professor Denys Hay of the University of Edinburgh refers to the Quattrocento as one of "a few rare and exciting moments" in history where social and political factors "may induce innovations in the moral and ideological pattern which in the long run can transform art, letters, and certain aspects of public life" (Denys Hay, "The Place of Hans Baron in Renaissance Historiography," in Anthony Molho and John A. Tedeschi, eds., *Renaissance Studies in Honor of Hans Baron* [DeKalb, Ill.: Northern Illinois University Press, 1971], p. xxviii). Vincent Cronin, *The Florentine Renaissance* (New York: Dutton, 1967), writes that the age is "one of the brilliant periods of not only European but world history." For utterances of identical nature, see Robert Schwoebel, *Renaissance Men and Ideas* (New York: St. Martin's Press, 1971). That the Quattrocento was in its way a resplendent century is not to be doubted. The trouble with most of these glittering assessments is the tunnel vision, the lack of any comparative perspective behind them, and far from least, their footings in conventional Europocentric, unilinear historiography.
2. See Sidney R. Packard, "A Medievalist Looks at the Renaissance," in *Smith College Studies in History* (1964) for an updating both learned and charming of Wallace Ferguson's notable chapter on the medievalist revolt.

3. See Herbert Butterfield, "History of Science and the Study of History" in *Harvard Library Bulletin* (1959).
4. Lynn White, Jr., "Cultural Climates and Technological Advance in the Middle Ages," in *Viator,* vol. 2 (1971).
5. Paul Oskar Kristeller, "Humanism and Scholasticism in the Italian Renaissance," in his *Studies in Renaissance Thought and Letters* (Rome: Edizioni de Storia e Letteratura, 1956), pp. 561, 560. In fairness to Kristeller, I must also cite his statement on pages 12–13: "The influence of humanism on science as well as on philosophy was indirect, but powerful." Let those who have never used the word "indirect" cast stones.
6. Franco Simone, *Il Rinascimento Francese,* trans. H. Gaston Hall (New York: Macmillan, 1969), p. 37.
7. Thus, Schwoebel, in the Introduction to *Renaissance Men and Ideas,* has the Renaissance beginning with Dante and ending with Shakespeare. At least, the Renaissance concept was a meaningful one in Michelet and Burckhardt, however erroneous. Such extension as Schwoebel's—and he is far from alone—tends to bury meaning in a time-mass of some four centuries.
8. Not to mention the bizarre and the occult. See Wayne Shumaker's fascinating and richly detailed *The Occult Sciences of the Renaissance: A Study in Intellectual Patterns* (Berkeley: University of California Press, 1972). Such material, to be sure, is not exactly what Michelet and Burckhardt had in mind when they presented the Renaissance to the modern mind.
9. Molho and Tedeschi, eds., *Renaissance Studies in Honor of Hans Baron.*
10. Charles Trinkaus, *In Our Image and Likeness: Humanity and Divinity in Italian Humanist Thought,* 2 vols. (Chicago: University of Chicago Press, 1970).
11. Hay, "The Place of Hans Baron in Renaissance Historiography," p. xxviii.
12. Trinkaus, *In Our Image and Likeness,* Foreword, vol. 1, p. xx.
13. *Ibid.,* vol. 1, p. 283.
14. Jacob Burckhardt, *Civilization of the Renaissance in Italy* (New York: Harper Torchbooks, 1966), vol. 2, p. 303.
15. Trinkaus, *In Our Image and Likeness,* vol. 2, p. 768.
16. *Ibid.,* pp. 770–71.
17. *Ibid.,* vol. 1, p. 23.
18. *Ibid.,* pp. 24–25.
19. *Ibid.,* vol. 2, p. 761.
20. *Ibid.,* p. 767.
21. *Ibid.,* Foreword, vol. 1, pp. xx, xxii.
22. *Ibid.,* p. xxi.
23. See especially the long passage from Ficino, and Trinkaus' commentary, *ibid.,* vol. 2, pp. 482–86; also, vol. 1, pp. 193 and 240 ff., where the subjects are Petrarch and Manetti.
24. I have dealt in some detail with modernist use and adaptation of the Augustinian metaphor in my *Social Change and History* (New York: Oxford University Press, 1969), chaps. 2 and 3. On Augustine's idea of progress, see the late Theodor E. Mommsen's fine essay in his *Medieval and Renaissance Studies* (Ithaca, N.Y.: Cornell University Press, 1959), pp. 265–98.
25. St. Augustine, *The City of God* (Dods translation), Book XI, Section 26.
26. Trinkaus, *In Our Image and Likeness,* vol. 1, p. 283.
27. Hans Baron, *The Crisis of the Early Italian Renaissance* (Princeton, N.J.: Princeton University Press, 1966), pp. 460–61.

28. F. W. Maitland, "Moral Personality and Legal Personality," in *Collected Papers* (Cambridge, Eng.: Cambridge University Press, 1911), vol. 3, p. 309.

29. Ernst H. Kantorowicz, *The King's Two Bodies* (Princeton, N.J.: Princeton University Press, 1957), p. 245. It would be impossible to praise too highly this study in medieval political thought. Kantorowicz offers us the following quotation from the humanist Salutati, one I do not find in Hans Baron's work: "Thou knowest not how sweet is the *amor patriae:* if such would be expedient for the fatherland's protection or enlargement [*sic!*], it would seem neither burdensome and difficult nor a crime to thrust the axe into one's father's head, to crush one's brothers, to deliver from the womb of one's wife the premature child with the sword." Kantorowicz acknowledges that this is the youthful Salutati in political passion.

30. See especially J. H. Hexter, "The Loom of Language and the Fabric of Imperatives: The Case of *Il Principe* and *Utopia*," *American Historical Review* (July 1964).

31. No one has done more than the sociologist-historian Edward Shils to give historical and comparative identity to this important class. See his just published *The Intellectuals and the Powers* (Chicago: University of Chicago Press, 1972), and Philip Rieff, ed., *On Intellectuals* (Garden City, N.Y.: Doubleday, 1969).

32. Lauro Martines, in his *The Social World of the Florentine Humanists* (Princeton, N.J.: Princeton University Press, 1963), has sought to show, with some success, I should say, that there is bias in this view; see especially his fascinating "profiles" of some forty-five Florentines connected with humanism. Even so, I think the essential truth of the view found in Olschki, Trinkaus, Hauser, von Martin and others remains.

33. Alfred von Martin, *Sociology of the Renaissance* (New York: Harper Torchbooks, 1963), p. 55.

34. Curiously, the late Erwin Panofsky, in his "The First Page of Giorgio Vasari's 'Libro,'" failed to grasp the Augustinian-Christian view. He declares that Tertullian and Augustine "refrain from extending the biological parallel beyond the stage of maturity." This is anything but the case. That Christ, for Augustine, represented the "maturity" of the world and that the elect would pass from this world to endless bliss in no way offsets Augustine's conviction of the decay, degeneration, and eventual death of culture and society in this world. Panofsky's error seems to stem from reliance on a book he himself terms "inadequate," and which assuredly is: J. A. Kleinsorge, *Beiträge zur Geschichte der Lehre von Parallelismus der Individual und Besamtentwickling* (Jens, 1900). Kleinsorge's book contains some snapshots, so to speak, of use of the biological analogy, but has little if any notion of sources, contexts, and lineal relations. It is nevertheless this work that Panofsky draws from in large part in his discussion of the idea of genesis and decay and of the concept of rebirth. It may be the source in part of Panofsky's equally mistaken view that Vasari and his contemporaries were unaware of the possibility of decline for the *età moderna* they hailed.

The Writings of
Robert K. Merton

A Bibliography

MARY WILSON MILES

This bibliography is divided into seven sections:

1. Books, symposia, collections
2. Compilations
3. Articles and their reprintings
4. Introductions and Forewords
5. Miscellaneous writings
6. Book reviews
7. Commentaries on Merton's work

The list of writings is fairly complete, but there are some gaps. It does not include about a hundred reprintings of extracts from books, mainly from *Social Theory and Social Structure,* and although the list of articles is probably complete, there are gaps of information about reprintings up to about the mid-1950s. Not all book reviews have been identified, and the list of published commentaries is quite incomplete.

The bibliography is based in part upon earlier compilations by Dorothy Edi-Ale, John D. Holmyard and Robert M. Marsh. I am greatly indebted to Richard A. Lewis and Wesley Fisher for assistance.

1. BOOKS AND SYMPOSIA

1938 *Science, Technology and Society in Seventeenth Century England.* In *OSIRIS: Studies on the History and Philosophy of Science, and on the History of Learning and Culture.* Ed. by George Sarton. Bruges, Belgium: The St. Catherine Press, 362–632.

Mary Wilson Miles is Research Secretary to Robert K. Merton

1970   *Reprinted:* New York: Howard Fertig, Inc. With new introduction.
New York: Harper & Row, paperback edition.
Translations: Italian, French, Spanish (in press).

1946 *Mass Persuasion* (with the assistance of Marjorie Fiske and Alberta Curtis).
New York: Harper & Brothers.
1971 *Reprinted:* Stamford, Conn.: Greenwood Press.

1949 *Social Theory and Social Structure.* New York: The Free Press.
1957 Revised and enlarged edition.
1968 Enlarged edition.
Translations: French, Italian, Japanese, Spanish, Hebrew, Portuguese, German,
Russian, Czech.

1950 *Continuities in Social Research: Studies in the Scope and Method of "The
American Soldier"* (edited with Paul F. Lazarsfeld). New York: The Free Press.
1974 *Reprinted:* New York: Arno Press.

1951 *Patterns of Social Life: Explorations in the Sociology of Housing* (with Patricia
S. West and Marie Jahoda). New York: Columbia University Bureau of Applied
Social Research. Mimeographed.

1951 *Social Policy and Social Research in Housing* (Issue editor with Patricia S. West,
Marie Jahoda and Hanan C. Selvin). New York: *The Journal of Social Issues* 8,
nos. 1, 2.

1952 *Reader in Bureaucracy* (edited with Ailsa P. Gray, Barbara Hockey and Hanan
C. Selvin). New York: The Free Press.
1967 *Reprinted:* New York: The Free Press, paperback edition.

1956 *The Focused Interview* (with Marjorie Fiske and Patricia L. Kendall). New
York: The Free Press.

1956 *The Role of Social Research in Business Administration: A Case Study Based
Primarily Upon the 1930–1949 Experience of the Opinion Research Section of
the Chief Statistician's Division of AT&T* (with E. C. Devereux, Jr.). 2 vols.
New York: Bureau of Applied Social Research, 1956.

1957 *The Student-Physician: Introductory Studies in the Sociology of Medical Education* (with George G. Reader, Patricia L. Kendall and others). Cambridge,
Mass.: Harvard University Press.

1957 *The Freedom to Read: Perspective and Program* (with Richard McKeon and
Walter Gellhorn). New York: R. R. Bowker Co.

1959 *Sociology Today: Problems and Prospects* (edited with Leonard Broom and
Leonard S. Cottrell, Jr.). New York: Basic Books.
1967 *Reprinted:* New York: Harper & Row, paperback edition.
Translations: Spanish, Romanian, Russian.

1961 *Contemporary Social Problems* (edited with Robert A. Nisbet). New York: Harcourt Brace Jovanovich.
1966 Second edition.
1971 Third edition.
1976 Fourth edition. In preparation.

1965 *On the Shoulders of Giants: A Shandean Postscript.* New York: The Free Press.
1967 *Reprinted:* Harcourt Brace Jovanovich, paperback edition.

1967 *On Theoretical Sociology: Five Essays, Old and New.* New York: The Free
Press.

1969 *Social Theory and Functional Analysis* (in Japanese). Trans. by Togo Mori,
Yoshio Mori, and Kanazawa Minoru. Tokyo, Japan: Aoki Shoten.

1973 *The Sociology of Science: Theoretical and Empirical Investigations.* Edited by
Norman Storer. Chicago: University of Chicago Press.

1975 *The Sociology of Science in Europe* (edited with Jerry Gaston and Adam Podgorecki). Carbondale, Ill.: University of Southern Illinois Press. In press.

1975 *Toward a Metric of Science: Thoughts Occasioned by the Advent of Science Indicators* (edited with Yehuda Elkana, Joshua Lederberg, Arnold Thackray and Harriet Zuckerman). New York: John Wiley. In press.

2. COMPILATIONS

1974 *Perspectives in Social Inquiry: Classics, Staples, and Precursors in Sociology* (compiler and advisory editor, with Aron Halberstam). 40 vols. New York: Arno Press.

1975 *History, Philosophy and Sociology of Science: Classics, Staples and Precursors* (compiler and advisory editor, with Yehuda Elkana, Arnold Thackray and Harriet Zuckerman). 60 vols. New York: Arno Press.

3. ARTICLES

1934 Recent French Sociology. *Social Forces* 12, 537–45.

1934 Durkheim's Division of Labor in Society. *American Journal of Sociology* 40, 319–28.
Reprinted:
1965 Robert Nisbet, *Emile Durkheim.* Englewood Cliffs, N.J.: Prentice-Hall, 105–12.

1935 The Course of Arabian Intellectual Development, 700–1300 A.D. (with Pitirim A. Sorokin). *ISIS* 22, 516–24.

1935 Fluctuations in the Rate of Industrial Invention. *Quarterly Journal of Economics* 49, 454–70.

1935 Science and Military Technique. *Scientific Monthly* 41, 542–45.

1936 Civilization and Culture. *Sociology and Social Research* 21, 103–13.

1936 Puritanism, Pietism and Science. *Sociological Review* 28, 1–30.
Reprinted:
The Bobbs-Merrill Reprint Series in the Social Sciences, S–192.
1962 Bernard Barber and Walter Hirsch, eds. *The Sociology of Science.* New York: The Free Press, 33–66.

1936 The Unanticipated Consequences of Purposive Social Action. *American Sociological Review* 1, 894–904.
Reprinted:
The Bobbs-Merrill Reprint Series in the Social Sciences, S–328.
1967 Die unvorhergesehenen Folgen zielgerichteter sozialer Handlung. In Hans Peter Dreitzel, ed. *Sozialer Wandel.* Berlin: Hermann Luchterhand Verlag, 169–83.

1937 Some Economic Factors in Seventeenth Century English Science. *Scientia: Revista di Scienza* 62, 31, 142–52.

1937 Science, Population and Society. *Scientific Monthly* 44, 165–71.

1937 Social Time: A Methodological and Functional Analysis (with Pitirim A. Sorokin). *American Journal of Sociology* 42, 615–29.
Reprinted:
The Bobbs-Merrill Reprint Series in the Social Sciences, S–275.

1937 Sociological Aspects of Invention, Discovery and Scientific Theories (with Pitirim A. Sorokin). In Pitirim A. Sorokin, *Social and Cultural Dynamics.* 4 vols. New York: American Book Co., 2, 125–80, 439–76.
Reprinted:
1962 Totowa, N.J.: Bedminster Press.

499

1937   The Sociology of Knowledge. *ISIS* 27, 493–503.
    Reprinted:
    The Bobbs-Merrill Reprint Series in History, H–146.
    1964   Irving L. Horowitz, ed. *Historia y Elementos de la Sociologia del Conoci-miento.* Trans. by Noemi Rosenblatt. Buenos Aires: University of Buenos Aires Press, 1, 65–74.

1938   Science and the Social Order. *Philosophy of Science* 5, 321–37.
    Reprinted:
    1962   Bernard Barber and Walter Hirsch, eds. *The Sociology of Science.* New York: The Free Press, 16–28.

1938   Social Structure and Anomie. *American Sociological Review* 3, 672–82.
    Reprinted:
    The Bobbs-Merrill Reprint Series in the Social Sciences, S–194.
    1949   Logan Wilson and W. L. Kolb, *Sociological Analysis.* New York: Harcourt Brace Jovanovich, 771–80.
    1949   Ruth Nanda Anshen, ed. *The Family: Its Functions and Destiny.* New York: Harper. 1958 rev. ed., 273–312.
    1949   Elizabeth B. Lee and Alfred M. Lee, eds. *Social Problems in America: A Source Book.* New York: Holt, 20. Extract.
    1953   Karl de Schweinitz and Kenneth W. Thompson, eds. *Man and Modern Society.* New York: Holt, 386–94.
    1957   Lewis A. Coser and Bernard Rosenberg, eds. *Sociological Theory: A Book of Readings.* New York: Macmillan, 490–99. 1964 2d ed., 548–58.
    1958   Herman D. Stein and Richard A. Cloward, eds. *Social Perspectives on Behavior.* New York: The Free Press, 517–29.
    1958   Eduardo Hamuy, ed. *Antología sobre Estratificación.* Santiago, Chile: Editorial Universitaria, 295–340.
    1960   *Cuadernos de la Facultad Latinoamericana de Ciencias Sociales.* Santiago, Chile: Andrés Bello, 51–95.
    1962   Johannes A. Ponsioen, ed. *The Analysis of Social Change Reconsidered.* The Hague: Mouton.
    1962   Marvin E. Wolfgang, Leonard Savitz, and Norman Johnston, eds. *The Sociology of Crime and Delinquency.* New York: John Wiley & Sons, 236–43. 1970 2d ed., 238–46.
    1963   Hendrick M. Ruitenbeek, ed. *Varieties of Modern Social Theory.* New York: E. P. Dutton & Co., 364–401.
    1964   Bernard Rosenberg, Israel Gerver, and F. W. Howton, eds. *Mass Society in Crisis.* New York: Macmillan, 122–30.
    1965   André Levy, ed. *Psychologie Sociale: Textes Fondamentaux Anglais et Américains.* Paris: Dunod Editeur, 393–421.
    1966   Rose Giallombardo, ed. *Juvenile Delinquency.* New York: John Wiley & Sons, 93–102.
    1966   Tom Murton, ed. *Law Enforcement and Dangerous Drug Abuse.* Berkeley: Regents of the University of California, vol. 1.
    1968   Mark Lefton, James K. Skipper, Jr., and Charles H. McCaghy, eds. *Approaches to Deviance: Theories, Concepts and Research Findings.* New York: Appleton-Century-Crofts, 32–43.
    1968   Sozialstruktur und Anomie. In F. Sack and R. König, eds. *Kriminalsoziologie.* Frankfurt: Akademische Verlagsgesellschaft, 283–313.
    1969   Donald R. Cressy and David A. Ward, eds. *Delinquency, Crime and Social Process.* New York: Harper & Row, 254–84.

1969   William A. Rushing, ed. *Deviant Behavior and Social Process*. Chicago: Rand McNally & Co., 79–86.

1969   Gresham M. Sykes and Thomas E. Drabek, eds. *Law and the Lawless*. New York: Random House, 208–20.

1969   Walter W. Wallace, ed. *Sociological Theory*. Chicago: Aldine Publishing Co., 162–83.

1970   Richard D. Knudten and Stephen Schafer, eds. *Juvenile Delinquency: A Reader*. New York: Random House, 75–81.

1970   Peter Worsley, ed. *Modern Sociology: Introductory Readings*. Baltimore: Penguin Books, 464–71.

1971   H. Taylor Buckner, ed. *Deviance, Reality, and Change*. New York: Random House, 55–61.

1972   R. Serge Denisoff, ed. *Theories in Conflict*. Belmont, Calif.: Wadsworth Publishing Co., 99–110.

1972   John A. Perry and Murray P. Seidler, eds. *Contemporary Society*. San Francisco: Canfield Press, 106–14.

1975   Ronald A. Farrell and Victoria L. Swigert, eds. *Social Deviance*. Philadelphia: J. B. Lippincott Co., 143–55.

1939   Science and the Economy of 17th Century England. *Science and Society* 3, 1 (Winter), 3–27.
       Reprinted:
       1962   Bernard Barber and Walter Hirsch, eds. *The Sociology of Science*. New York: The Free Press, 67–88.
       1967   Brian Tierney, Donald Kagan, and L. Pearce Williams, eds. *Great Issues in Western Civilization*. vol. 2. New York: Random House, 55–62.

1939   Bureaucratic Structure and Personality. *Social Forces* 18, 560–68.
       Reprinted:
       1948   Clyde Kluckhohn and Henry A. Murray, eds. *Personality in Nature, Society, and Culture*. New York: Knopf, 282–91. 1967 rev. ed., 376–85.
       1950   Alvin W. Gouldner, ed. *Studies in Leadership*. New York: Harper and Brothers, 67–79.
       1951   Robert Dubin, ed. *Human Relations in Administration*. New York: Prentice-Hall, 163–68. Also in 1961, 1968, and 1974 eds.
       1957   Lewis A. Coser and Bernard Rosenberg, eds. *Sociological Theory: A Book of Readings*. New York: Macmillan, 458–69. 1964 2d ed., 488–99.
       1958   Herman D. Stein and Richard A. Cloward, eds. *Social Perspectives on Behavior*. New York: The Free Press, 577–84.
       1959   W. Lloyd Warner and Norman H. Martin, eds. *Industrial Man: Businessmen and Business Organizations*. New York: Harper and Brothers, 63–77.
       1961   Amitai Etzioni, ed. *A Sociological Reader on Complex Organizations*. New York: Holt, Rinehart & Winston, 48–61. 1969 2d ed., 47–59.
       1962   Sigmund Nosow and William H. Form, eds. *Man, Work, and Society: A Reader in the Sociology of Occupations*. New York: Basic Books, 457–61.
       1962   Eric and Mary Josephson, eds. *Man Alone: Alienation in Modern Society*. New York: Dell Publishing Co., 123–32.
       1963   Neil Smelser and William T. Smelser, eds. *Personality and Social Systems*. New York: John Wiley and Sons, 255–64.
       1963   Hendrik Ruitenbeek, ed. *The Dilemma of Organizational Society*. New York: E. P. Dutton & Co., 119–31.

1964   Joseph A. Litterer, ed. *Organizations: Structure and Behavior.* New York: John Wiley and Sons, 373–80.

1965   André Levy, ed. *Psychologie Sociale: Textes Fondamentaux Anglais et Américaines.* Paris: Dunod Editeur, 23–35.

1966   Gerald D. Bell, ed. *Organizations and Human Behavior.* Englewood Cliffs, N.J.: Prentice-Hall, 199–207.

1968   Paul Wasserman and Mary Lee Bundy, eds. *Reader in Library Administration.* Washington, D.C.: NCR Microcard Editions, 56–62.

1968   Renate Mayntz, ed. *Burokratische Organisation.* Köln-Berlin: Kiepenheuer & Witsch, 265–76.

1968   Scott G. McNall, ed. *The Sociological Perspective.* Boston: Little, Brown & Co., 215–25.

1970   Eric A. Nordlinger, ed. *Politics and Society: Studies in Comparative Political Sociology.* Englewood Cliffs, N.J.: Prentice-Hall, 59–67.

1971   Dean L. Yarwood, ed. *The National Administrative System.* New York: John Wiley & Sons, 378–87.

1939   Crime and the Anthropologist (with M. F. Ashley Montagu). *American Anthropologist* 42, 384–408.
Reprinted:
    1964   Bernard Rosenberg, Israel Gerver, and F. W. Howton, eds. *Mass Society in Crisis.* New York: Macmillan, 16–30.
    1969   Gresham M. Sykes and Thomas E. Drabek, eds. *Law and the Lawless.* New York: Random House, 138–50.

1939   Fact and Factitiousness in Ethnic Opinionnaires. *American Sociological Review* 5, 1 (February 1940), 13–28.

1941   Intermarriage and the Social Structure: Fact and Theory. *Psychiatry* 4, 361–74.
Reprinted:
    1964   Rose L. Coser, ed. *The Family: Its Structure and Function.* New York: St. Martin's Press, 128–52.
    1964   William J. Goode, ed. *Readings on the Family and Society.* Englewood Cliffs, N.J.: Prentice-Hall, 56–64.
    1972   Milton L. Barron, ed. *The Blending American.* Chicago: Quadrangle Books, 12–34.

1941   Karl Mannheim and the Sociology of Knowledge. *Journal of Liberal Religion* 2, 125–47.

1941   Florian Znaniecki's *The Social Role of the Man of Knowledge:* a review essay. *American Sociological Review* 6, 111–15.
Reprinted:
    1957   Lewis A. Coser and Bernard Rosenberg, eds. *Sociological Theory: A Book of Readings.* New York: Macmillan, 351–55.

1941   Arnold Toynbee's *A Study of History:* a review essay. *American Journal of Sociology* 47, 2 (September), 205–13.

1942   The Family Encounters the Depression: A Reanalysis of Documents (with E. W. Burgess et al.). New York: Social Science Research Council. 127 pp. Mimeographed.

1942   A Note on Science and Democracy. *Journal of Legal and Political Sociology* 1, 115–26.
Reprinted:
    1972   Barry Barnes, ed. *Sociology of Science.* Middlesex, England: Penguin Books, 65–79.

1943   The Formation of Scales of Socioeconomic Status: A Comment (with Genevieve Knupfer). *Rural Sociology* 8, 236–39.

1943   Studies in Radio and Film Propaganda (with Paul F. Lazarsfeld). *Transactions, New York Academy of Sciences* ser. 2, 6, 58–79.

1944   The Boomerang Response (with Patricia L. Kendall). *Channels.* National Publicity Council for Health and Welfare Service, 21, 1–7.

1944   Paternal Status and Economic Adjustment of High School Graduates (with Bryce Ryan). *Social Forces* 22, 302–06.

1944   The Value of High School Scholarship on the Labor Market (with Bryce Ryan). *Journal of Educational Sociology* 17, 524–34.

1945   Role of the Intellectual in Public Bureaucracy. *Social Forces* 23, 405–15.
      Reprinted:
      1946   M. F. Ashley Montagu, ed. *Studies and Essays in the History of Science and Learning: Offered in Homage to George Sarton on the Occasion of His Sixtieth Birthday.* New York: Henry Schuman, 521–43.

1945   Sociology of Knowledge. In Georges Gurvitch and Wilbert E. Moore, eds. *Twentieth Century Sociology.* New York: Philosophical Library, 366–405.
      Reprinted:
      1955   Paul F. Lazarsfeld and Morris Rosenberg, eds. *The Language of Social Research.* New York: The Free Press, 498–510.
      1960   *Translation:* Arabic. *UNESCO.*

1945   Sociological Theory. *American Journal of Sociology* 50, 462–73.
      Reprinted:
      The Bobbs-Merrill Reprint Series in the Social Sciences, S–195.
      1959   Funciones de la Teoria Sociologica con respecto a la Investigacion Empirica. *Boletin del Instituto de Sociologia.* Universidad de Buenos Aires, 12, 5–25.
      1964   Hans Albert, ed. *Theorie und Realitat.* Tübingen: J. C. B. Mohr (Paul Siebeck), 119–36.
      1964   D. C. Miller, ed. *Handbook of Research Design and Social Measurement.* New York: David McKay Co., 9–13.
      1964   *Sociologia* 26, 2, 207–25.
      1968   May Brodbeck, ed. *Readings in the Philosophy of the Social Sciences.* New York: Macmillan, 465–83.

1946   The Focused Interview (with Patricia L. Kendall). *American Journal of Sociology* 51, 541–57.
      Reprinted:
      The Bobbs-Merrill Reprint Series in the Social Sciences, S–467.
      1955   Paul F. Lazarsfeld and Morris Rosenberg, eds. *The Language of Social Research.* New York: The Free Press, 476–89.
      1960   *Cuadernos del Boletin del Instituto de Sociologia.* Universidad de Buenos Aires, 13, 21, 168–86.

1947   The Machine, the Worker, and the Engineer. *Science* 105, 79–84.
      Reprinted:
      1947   *Chemical & Engineering News* 25, 362–65.
      1951   Robert Dubin, ed. *Human Relations in Administration: The Sociology of Organization.* New York: Prentice-Hall, 119–21. Also in 1961, 1968 and 1974 eds.
      1962   Sigmund Nosow and William H. Form, eds. *Man, Work and Society: A Reader in the Sociology of Occupations.* New York: Basic Books, 82–87.
      1962   Charles R. Walker, ed. *Modern Technology and Civilization.* New York: McGraw-Hill, 408–13.
      1965   Ernest Dale, ed. *Readings in Management: Landmarks and New Frontiers.* New York: McGraw-Hill, 204–05.

1968   Charles R. Walker, ed. *Technology, Industry and Man: The Age of Acceleration.* New York: McGraw-Hill, 89–94.

1970   Simon Marcson, ed. *Automation, Alienation and Anomie.* New York: Harper & Row, 394–400.

1947 Selected Problems of Field Work in the Planned Community. *American Sociological Review* 12, 304–12.

1947 The Expert and Research in Applied Social Science. New York: Columbia University Bureau of Applied Social Research. Mimeographed.

1948 The Bearing of Empirical Research upon the Development of Sociological Theory. *American Sociological Review* 13, 505–15.
Reprinted:

1951   Alfred McClung Lee, ed. *Readings in Sociology.* New York: Barnes & Noble, 47–62.

1959   *Boletin del Instituto de Sociologia.* Universidad de Buenos Aires, 12, 29–48.

1960   *Cuadernos de la Facultad Latinoamericana de Ciencias Sociales.* Santiago, Chile: Andrés Bello, 23–49.

1964   Delbert C. Miller, ed. *Handbook of Research Design and Social Measurement.* New York: David McKay Co., 7–8.

1964   *Sociologia* 26, 2, 227–43.

1964   Milton L. Barron, ed. *Contemporary Sociology: An Introductory Textbook of Readings.* New York: Dodd, Mead & Co., 533–46.

1966   Alex Inkeles, ed. *Readings on Modern Sociology.* Englewood Cliffs, N.J.: Prentice-Hall, 23–26.

1967   Peter I. Rose, ed. *The Study of Society: An Integrated Anthology.* New York: Random House, 35–47. 1970 2d ed., 31–43. 1973 3d ed., 42–53.

1968   May Brodbeck, ed. *Readings in the Philosophy of the Social Sciences.* New York: Macmillan, 483–96. •

1969   Leonard I. Krimerman, ed. *The Nature and Scope of Social Science.* New York: Appleton-Century-Crofts, 214–16.

1970   Louis D. Hayes and Ronald D. Hedlund, eds. *The Conduct of Political Inquiry.* Englewood Cliffs, N.J.: Prentice-Hall, 99–103.

1970   Dennis P. Forcese and Stephen Richer, eds. *Stages of Social Research: Contemporary Perspectives.* Englewood Cliffs, N.J.: Prentice-Hall, 14–27.

1948 Discrimination and the American Creed. In R. M. MacIver, ed. *Discrimination and National Welfare.* New York: Harper & Brothers, 99–126.
Reprinted:

1967   Peter I. Rose, ed. *The Study of Society: An Integrated Anthology.* New York: Random House, 480–98. 1970: 2d ed., 449–64. 1973: 3d ed., 366–81.

1948 A Note on Mass Persuasion. *International Journal of Opinion and Attitude Research* (Spring), 101–08.

1948 Mass Communication, Popular Taste, and Organized Social Action (with Paul F. Lazarsfeld). In Lyman Bryson, ed. *Communication of Ideas.* New York: Harper & Brothers, 95–118.
Reprinted:
The Bobbs-Merrill Reprint Series in the Social Sciences, S–163.

1957   Bernard Rosenberg and David M. White, eds. *Mass Culture: The Popular Arts in America.* New York: The Free Press, 457–73.

1962   Reo M. Christenson and Robert O. McWilliams, eds. *Voice of the People: Readings in Public Opinion and Propaganda.* New York: McGraw-Hill, 340–44.

1973 Massekommunikasjon, folks smak og organisert sosial handling. In Hans Fredrik Dahl, ed. *Massekommunikasjon: Ein Bok om Massemedienes Vekst og Virkninger.* Oslo: Gyldendal Norsk Forlag, 134–51.

1948 The Position of Sociological Theory. *American Sociological Review* 13, 164–68.

1948 The Self-Fulfilling Prophecy. *Antioch Review* (Summer), 193–210.

Reprinted:

    1951 Arnold M. Rose, ed. *Race Prejudice and Discrimination.* New York: Alfred A. Knopf, 510–22.

    1953 Paul Bixler, ed. *The Antioch Review Anthology.* Cleveland and New York: World Publishing Co., 295–310.

    1957 Ralph Ross and Ernest van den Haag, eds. *The Fabric of Society.* New York: Harcourt Brace Jovanovich, 240–56.

    1958 *Readings in the Social Sciences.* Cairo: Dar Al-Ma'aref Printing House, 2, 1 (Winter), 49–76.

    1960 *Cuadernos de la Facultad Latinoamericana de Ciencias Sociales.* Santiago, Chile: Andrés Bello, 97–122.

    1963 William Petersen and David Matza, eds. *Social Controversy.* Belmont, Calif.: Wadsworth Publishing Co., 157–65.

    1964 *Colleccion Derechos Humanos.* Buenos Aires: Ediciones D.A.I.A., 5–31.

    1964 Edward C. McDonagh and Jon E. Simpson, eds. *Social Problems: Persistent Challenges.* New York: Holt, Rinehart and Winston, 354–64.

    1967 Ephraim H. Mizruchi, ed. *The Substance of Sociology: Codes, Conduct & Consequences.* New York: Appleton-Century-Crofts, 225–39.

    1968 Nona Y. Glazer and Carol F. Creedon, eds. *Children and Poverty.* Chicago: Rand McNally & Co., 16–20.

    1972 Edwin P. Hollander and Raymond G. Hunt, eds. *Classic Contributions to Social Psychology.* New York: Oxford University Press, 260–66.

1948 Social Psychology of Housing. In Wayne Dennis, ed. *Current Trends in Social Psychology.* Pittsburgh: University of Pittsburgh Press, 163–217.

Reprinted:

    1966 William L. C. Wheaton, Grace Milgram, and Margy Ellin Myerson, eds. *Urban Housing.* New York: The Free Press, 20–29.

1949 Election Polling Forecasts and Public Images of Social Science (with Paul K. Hatt). *Public Opinion Quarterly* 13, 185–222.

1949 Social Structure and Anomie: Revisions and Extensions. In Ruth N. Anshen, ed. *The Family: Its Functions and Destiny.* New York: Harper & Brothers, 226–57.

1949 Patterns of Influence: A Study of Interpersonal Influence and Communications Behavior in a Local Community. In Paul F. Lazarsfeld and Frank Stanton, eds. *Communications in Research, 1948–49.* New York: Harper & Brothers, 180–219.

Reprinted:

    1961 Edward C. Banfield, ed. *Urban Government.* New York: The Free Press, 490–500.

    1963 Matilda W. Riley, ed. *Sociological Research.* New York: Harcourt Brace Jovanovich, 153–65.

    1966 Roland L. Warren, ed. *Perspectives on the American Community.* Chicago: Rand McNally & Co., 251–65. 1973: 2d ed., 188–202.

    1968 Herbert Hyman and Eleanor Singer, eds. *Readings in Reference Group Theory and Research.* New York: The Free Press, 278–96.

    1969 Robert Mills French, ed. *The Local and the Cosmopolitan in a Community.* Itasca, Ill.: F. E. Peacock Publishers, 311–24.

1949 The Role of Applied Social Science in the Formation of Policy. *Philosophy of Science* 16, 161–81.

1950 Contributions to the Theory of Reference Group Behavior (with Alice Kitt Rossi). In Robert K. Merton and Paul F. Lazarsfeld, eds. *Continuities in Social Research*. New York: The Free Press, 40–105.
Reprinted:
    1953 Reinhard Bendix and S. M. Lipset, eds. *Class, Status and Power: A Reader in Social Stratification*. New York: The Free Press, 403–10. 1966: 2d ed., 510–15.
    1964 Lewis A. Coser and Bernard Rosenberg, eds. *Sociological Theory: A Book of Readings*. New York: Macmillan, 264–72. 1964: 2d ed., 276–84.
    1965 André Levy, ed. *Psychologie Sociale: Textes Fondamentaux Anglais et Américains*. Paris: Dunod Editeur, 470–80.
    1968 Herbert Hyman and Eleanor Singer, eds. *Readings in Reference Group Theory and Research*. New York: The Free Press, 28–68.

1951 Social Scientists and Research Policy (with Daniel Lerner). In Daniel Lerner and H. D. Lasswell, eds. *The Policy Sciences*. Stanford: Stanford University Press, 282–307.
Reprinted:
    1951 H. D. Lasswell and Daniel Lerner, eds. *Les "Sciences de la Politique" Aux Etats-Unis: Domaines et Techniques*. Paris: Librairie Armand Colin, 243–305.
    1961 W. G. Bennis, K. B. Benne, and R. Chin, eds. *The Planning of Change*. New York: Holt, Rinehart and Winston, 53–69.

1951 Large-Scale Community Research in the Epidemiology of Essential Hypertension in Man. In *A Symposium on Essential Hypertension*. Boston: Commonwealth of Massachusetts Recess Commission on Hypertension, 327–34.

1951 The Research Budget. In Marie Jahoda, Morton Deutsch, and Stuart W. Cook, eds. *Research Methods in Social Relations*. New York: Dryden Press, 342–51.

1952 Brief Bibliography for the Sociology of Science (with Bernard Barber). *Proceedings, American Academy of Arts & Sciences* 80, 2, 140–54.

1954 Friendship as a Social Process: A Substantive and Methodological Analysis (with Paul Lazarsfeld). In Morroe Berger, Theodore Abel, and Charles Page, eds. *Freedom and Control in Modern Society*. New York: Van Nostrand, 18–66.
Reprinted:
    1963 Alvin W. Gouldner and Helen P. Gouldner, eds. *Modern Sociology: An Introduction to the Study of Human Interaction*. New York: Harcourt Brace Jovanovich, 338–42.
    1970 F. Chazel, Raymond Boudon, and Paul F. Lazarsfeld, eds. *L'Analyse des Processus Sociaux*. The Hague: Mouton, 249–66.

1955 The Socio-Cultural Environment and Anomie. In H. L. Witmer and R. Kotinsky, eds. *New Perspectives for Research on Juvenile Delinquency*. Washington, D.C.: U.S. Government Printing Office, 24–50.

1955 The Knowledge of Man. In Lewis Leary, ed. *The Unity of Knowledge*. New York: Doubleday & Co., 150–54.

1956 Studies in the Sociology of Medical Education (with Samuel Bloom and Natalie Rogoff Ramsøy). *Journal of Medical Education* 31, 552–65.

1957 Some Preliminaries to a Sociology of Medical Education. In Robert K. Merton, George G. Reader and Patricia L. Kendall, eds. *The Student-Physician*. Cambridge, Mass.: Harvard University Press, 3–79.

1957 The Role-Set: Problems in Sociological Theory. *British Journal of Sociology* 8, 2, 106–20.

Reprinted:
The Bobbs-Merrill Reprint Series in the Social Sciences, S–193.

1964   Lewis A. Coser and Bernard Rosenberg, eds. *Sociological Theory: A Book of Readings.* New York: Macmillan, 376–87.

1967   Der Rollen-Set: Probleme der soziologischen Theorie. In H. Hartmann, ed. *Moderne Amerikanische Soziologie: Neuere Beiträge zur soziologischen Theorie.* Stuttgart: Ferdinand Enke Verlag, 255–67. 1973: 2d ed., 316–33.

1968   Louis W. Stern, ed. *Distribution Channels: Behavioral Dimensions.* Boston: Houghton Mifflin Co., 63–72.

1970   Peter Worsley, ed. *Modern Sociology: Introductory Readings.* Baltimore: Penguin Books, 245–54.

1971   Richard R. MacDonald and James A. Schellenberg, eds. *Selected Readings and Projects in Social Psychology.* New York: Random House, 25–31.

1971   Nelson Graburn, ed. *Readings in Kinship and Social Structure.* New York: Harper & Row, 297–99.

1957   Priorities in Scientific Discovery: A Chapter in the Sociology of Science. *American Sociological Review* 22, 6, 635–59.

Reprinted:

1961   S. M. Lipset and N. Smelser, eds. *Sociology: The Progress of a Decade.* Englewood Cliffs, N.J.: Prentice-Hall, 166–92.

1962   Bernard Barber and Walter Hirsch, eds. *The Sociology of Science.* New York: The Free Press, 447–85.

1958   Procedures for the Sociological Study of the Value Climate of Medical Schools (with Richard Christie). In Helen H. Gee and Robert J. Glaser, eds. *The Ecology of the Medical Student.* Evanston, Ill.: Association of American Medical Colleges, 125–53.

Reprinted:

1963   Alvin W. Gouldner and Helen F. Gouldner, eds. *Modern Sociology: An Introduction to the Study of Human Interaction.* New York: Harcourt Brace Jovanovich, 123–35.

1958   Medical Education as a Social Process (with Patricia L. Kendall). In E. G. Jaco, ed. *Patients, Physicians and Illness.* New York: The Free Press, 321–50.

1958   The Functions of the Professional Association. *American Journal of Nursing* 58, 50–54.

Reprinted:

1958   *Feliciter.* Canadian Library Association, 3, 6 (February), 2–6.

1966   Bonnie and Vern Bullough, eds. *Issues in Nursing.* New York: Springer Publishing Co., 77–87.

1969   *American Journal of Hospital Pharmacy* 26 (November), 636–41.

1958   Issues in the Growth of a Profession. *Proceedings of the American Nurses' Association* (June 10), 2–12.

1959   Notes on Problem-Finding in Sociology. In Robert K. Merton, Leonard Broom, and Leonard S. Cottrell, Jr., eds. *Sociology Today.* New York: Basic Books, ix–xxxiv.

1959   Social Conformity, Deviation and Opportunity-Structures. *American Sociological Review* 24, 2, 177–89.

1959   The Scholar and the Craftsman. In Marshall Clagett, ed. *Critical Problems in the History of Science.* Madison: The University of Wisconsin Press, 24–29.

1960   "Recognition" and "Excellence": Instructive Ambiguities. In Adam Yarmolinsky, ed. *Recognition of Excellence.* New York: The Free Press, 297–328.

1960   The Search for Professional Status: Sources, Costs, and Consequences. *American Journal of Nursing* (May), 662–64.

1960   The Mosaic of the Behavioral Sciences. In Bernard Berelson, ed. *The Behavioral Sciences Today*. New York: Basic Books. 1963: new ed., 247–72. 1971: Harper & Row, paperback ed.
    Reprinted:
    1960   Moderne Wissenschaft von Menschen. *RIAS* 1 (December 21).
    1962   *Revista de Ciencias Sociales* 6 (March), 5–24.

1960   Some Thoughts on the Professions in American Society. *Brown University Papers* 37, 1–17.

1960   The Corporation: Its Coexistence with Men. In Melvin Anshen and George L. Bach, eds. *Management and Corporation 1985*. New York: McGraw-Hill, 57–61.

1960   The History of Quantification in the Sciences. *Items* 14 (March), 1–5.

1961   Social Problems and Sociological Theory. In Robert K. Merton and Robert A. Nisbet, eds. *Contemporary Social Problems*. New York: Harcourt Brace Jovanovich, 697–737. 1966: 2d ed., 775–823. 1971: 3d ed., 793–845.

1961   Social Conflict in Styles of Sociological Work. *Transactions, Fourth World Congress of Sociology* 3, 21–46.
    Reprinted:
    1961   *Revista de Ciencias Sociales* 5, 2, 105–32.
    1970   James E. Curtis and John W. Petras, eds. *The Sociology of Knowledge*. New York: Praeger, 507–30.
    1970   Larry and Janice Reynolds, eds. *Sociology of Sociology*. New York: David McKay Co., 172–97.

1961   The Role of Genius in Scientific Advance. *New Scientist* (November), 306–08.
    Reprinted:
    1970   Liam Hudson, ed. *The Ecology of Human Intelligence*. Middlesex, England: Penguin Books, 70–78.

1961   Now the Case for Sociology: The Canons of the Anti-Sociologist. *New York Times Magazine*, July 16.
    Reprinted:
    1962   *Newsletter, The Midwest Sociological Society* 2, 2 (March), pt. 2, pp. 1, 4–6.
    1963   Nelson W. Polsby, R. A. Dentler, and P. A. Smith, eds. *Politics and Social Life: An Introduction to Political Behavior*. Boston: Houghton Mifflin Co., 64–67.
    1964   Milton L. Barron, ed. *Contemporary Sociology: An Introductory Textbook of Readings*. New York: Dodd, Mead & Co., 35–40.
    1965   Thomas E. Lasswell, John H. Burma, and Sidney H. Aronson, eds. *Life in Society*. Chicago: Scott, Foresman & Co., 26–29.
    1972   R. Serge Denisoff, ed. *Theories in Conflict*. Belmont, Calif.: Wadsworth Publishing Co., 18–22.
    1974   George Ritzer, ed. *Social Realities: Dynamic Perspectives*. Boston: Allyn & Bacon, 14–18.

1962   Status Orientation in Nursing. *American Journal of Nursing* 62, 70–73.
    Reprinted:
    1965   James K. Skipper, Jr. and Robert C. Leonard, eds. *Social Interaction and Patient Care*. Philadelphia: J. P. Lippincott Co., 377–83.

1962   Notes on Sociology in the U.S.S.R. (with Henry Riecken). *Current Problems in Social-Behavioral Research*. Washington, D.C.: National Institute of Social and Behavioral Science, 7–14.

1962 The Role of the Nurse: Locals and Cosmopolitans. *NSNA News Letter* 9 (Fall), 3–6.

1963 Sociological Ambivalence (with Elinor Barber). In Edward A. Tiryakian, ed. *Sociological Theory, Values and Sociocultural Change.* New York: The Free Press, 91–120.

1963 The Ambivalence of Scientists. *Bulletin of the Johns Hopkins Hospital* (112), 77–97.
Reprinted:
1964 *Revista de Occidente.* Madrid, 2, 44–70.
1965 Norman Kaplan, ed. *Science and Society.* Chicago: Rand McNally & Co., 112–32.
1966 William J. Goode, ed. *The Dynamics of Modern Society.* New York: Atherton Press, 282–97.
1966 Die ambivalente Haltung des Wissenschaftlers. In Alphons Silbermann, ed. *Militanter Humanismus.* Frankfurt: S. Fischer Verlag, 330–55.

1963 Resistance to the Systematic Study of Multiple Discoveries in Science. *European Journal of Sociology* 4, 237–82.

1963 Sorokin's Formulations in the Sociology of Science (with Bernard Barber). In P. J. Allen, ed. *P. A. Sorokin in Review.* Durham, N.C.: Duke University Press, 332–68.
Reprinted:
1972 G. C. Hallen and Rajeshwar Prasad, eds. *Sorokin and Sociology: Essays in Honour of Professor Pitirim A. Sorokin.* Agra, India: Satish Book Enterprise, 85–124.

1963 Basic Research and Potentials of Relevance. *American Behavioral Scientist* 6, 86–90.

1964 Anomie, Anomia and Social Interaction: Contexts of Deviant Behavior. In Marshall Clinard, ed. *Anomie and Deviant Behavior.* New York: The Free Press, 213–42.

1964 Practical Problems and the Uses of Social Science (with Edward C. Devereux, Jr.). *Trans-Action* 1, 18–21.
Reprinted:
1970 Warren G. Bennis, ed. *American Bureaucracy.* Chicago: Aldine Publishing Co., 111–19.

1964 Sources of Stress in Society. *Journal of Neuropsychiatry* 5, 413–14.

1965 The Environment of the Innovating Organization. In Gary Steiner, ed. *The Creative Organization.* Chicago: University of Chicago Press, 50–65.

1966 Dilemmas of Democracy in the Voluntary Association. *American Journal of Nursing* (May), 1055–61.
Reprinted:
1966 *Association Management* 18, 8 (August), 6–16.

1967 On the History and Systematics of Sociological Theory, and On Sociological Theories of the Middle Range. Both in Robert K. Merton, *On Theoretical Sociology: Five Essays, Old and New.* New York: The Free Press, 1–38, 39–72.

1968 Observations on the Sociology of Science. *Japan-American Forum* 14, 4 (April), 18–28.

1968 The Matthew Effect in Science: the Reward and Communication Systems of Science are Considered. *Science* 199, 3810 (January 5), 55–63.
Reprinted:
1968 *New Society,* January 18, 80–83.
1970 *Sociologický Časopis.* Academia Nakladatelství Československé Akademie Věd, 2, 6, 121–32.

1968 Seminars without Constraints. *Columbia University Forum* 11, 1 (Winter), 38–39.

1969 Sociology, Jargon and Slanglish. *Subterranean Sociology Newsletter* 3, 2 and 3 (April).
Reprinted:
1972 R. Serge Denisoff, ed. *Theories in Conflict.* Belmont, Calif.: Wadsworth Publishing Co., 52–58.

1969 Behavior Patterns of Scientists. Co-published: *American Scientist* 57, 1 (Spring), 1–23, and *American Scholar* 38, 2 (Spring), 197–225.
Reprinted:
1970 *Leonardo* 3, 2 (April), 213–20.
1973 Nicholas M. Regush, ed. *Visibles and Invisibles.* Boston: Little, Brown & Co., 146–67.
1973 Bernice T. Eiduson and Linda Beckman, eds. *Science as a Career Choice.* New York: Russell Sage Foundation, 601–11.
1975 Paul Weiss, ed. *Knowledge in Search of Understanding: Essays by Members of the Frensham Group.* Mount Kisco, N.Y.: Futura Publishing Co. In press.

1969 The Social Nature of Leadership. *Congress Papers of the 14th Quadrennial Congress, International Council of Nurses.* Basel: S. Karger, 310–19.
Reprinted:
1969 *American Journal of Nursing* 12 (December), 2614–18.

1970 Sociology of Science: An Introduction. In Robert K. Merton, *Science, Technology and Society in Seventeenth Century England.* New York: Howard Fertig, Inc. New York: Harper & Row, paperback ed.

1970 The Ambivalence of Organizational Leaders. In James F. Oates, Jr., *The Contradictions of Leadership* (ed. by Burton C. Billings). New York: Appleton-Century-Crofts, 1–26.
Reprinted:
1969 *Boletin Uruguayo de Sociologia* 8, nos. 15, 16, 17 (December), 184–202.

.1971 Insiders and Outsiders: An Essay in the Sociology of Knowledge. In R. N. Saxena, ed. *Conspectus of Indian Society.* Agra, India: Satish Book Enterprise.
Reprinted:
1971 A. R. Desai, ed. *Essays on Modernization of Underdeveloped Countries.* Bombay, India: Thacker & Co., 1, 438–57.

1971 The Competitive Pressures: The Race for Priority (with Richard Lewis). *Impact of Science on Society* 21, 2, 151–61.
Reprinted:
1972 *Mercurio: Sintesi del Pensiero Economico e Sociale Contemporaneo* 15 (March), 39–44.

1971 Patterns of Evaluation in Science: Institutionalization, Structure, and Functions of the Referee System (with Harriet Zuckerman). *Minerva* 9, 1 (January), 66–100.
Reprinted:
1971 *Physics Today* 24, 7 (July), 28–33.
1972 *Zagadnienia Naukoznawstwa: Problems of the Science of Science.* Committee on the Science of Science of the Polish Academy of Sciences, January 29.
1973 Rolul Referentilor in Stiinta. In *Societati Prezente, Societati Viitoare.* Trans. by Michael Cernea. Bucharest: Editura Politica.

1971 The Precarious Foundations of Detachment in Sociology. In Edward A.

Tiryakian, ed. *The Phenomenon of Sociology.* New York: Appleton-Century-Crofts, 188–99.

1972 Age, Aging, and Age Structure in Science (with Harriet Zuckerman). In Matilda W. Riley, Marylin Johnson, and Ann Foner, eds. *A Theory of Age Stratification.* Vol. 3 of *Aging and Society.* New York: Russell Sage Foundation, 292–356.
Reprinted:
1973 Virsta Cercetatorilor. In Mircea Ioanid, ed. *Stiinta si Dezvoltare.* Trans. by R. Strausser. Bucharest: Centrual de Informare si Documentare in Stiintele Sociale si Politice.

1972 Insiders and Outsiders: A Chapter in the Sociology of Knowledge. Rev. ed. *American Journal of Sociology* (July), 9–47.
Reprinted:
1972 Robert K. Merton et al., *Varieties of Political Expression in Sociology.* Chicago: University of Chicago Press, 9–47.

1972 On Discipline Building: The Paradoxes of George Sarton (with Arnold Thackray). *ISIS* 63, 219, 473–95.

1972 A Professional School for Training in Social Research (with Paul F. Lazarsfeld). In Paul F. Lazarsfeld, ed. *Qualitative Analysis.* Boston: Allyn and Bacon, 361–91.

1975 Structural Analysis in Sociology. In Peter M. Blau, ed. *Approaches to the Study of Social Structure.* New York: The Free Press, 21–52.

1975 Thematic Analysis in Science: Notes on Holton's Concept. *Science,* 188 (April 25), 335–38.

1975 Social Knowledge and Public Policy. In Mirra Komarovsky, ed. *Sociology and Public Policy: The Case of Presidential Commissions.* New York: Elsevier Scientific Publishing Co. In press.

1975 George Sarton (with Arnold Thackray). In Charles Coulston Gillispie, editor-in-chief, *Dictionary of Scientific Biography.* New York: Charles Scribner's Sons. In press.

4. INTRODUCTIONS AND FOREWORDS

1949 Introduction to Logan Wilson and William L. Kolb, *Sociological Analysis.* New York: Harcourt Brace Jovanovich, xi–xiii.

1950 Foreword to George C. Homans, *The Human Group.* New York: Harcourt Brace Jovanovich, xvii–xxiii.

1952 Foreword to Bernard Barber, *Science and the Social Order.* New York: The Free Press, xi–xxiii.

1952 Introduction to Dallas Smythe, *New York Television 1951–1952.* Urbana, Illinois: National Association of Educational Broadcasters, iii–viii.

1953 Foreword to Hans Gerth and C. Wright Mills, *Character and Social Structure.* New York: Harcourt Brace Jovanovich, vii–ix.

1958 Foreword to Blaine Mercer, *The Study of Society.* New York: Harcourt Brace Jovanovich, v–vi.

1960 The Ambivalences of Le Bon's *The Crowd* (introduction to the Compass Edition of Gustave Le Bon, *The Crowd*). New York: Viking Press, v–xxxix.

1960 Foreword to Harry M. Johnson, *Sociology.* New York: Harcourt Brace Jovanovich, iii–v.

1963 Introduction to Allen Barton, *Social Organization Under Stress.* Washington, D.C.: National Academy of Sciences—National Research Council, xvii–xxxvi.

Reprinted:

1969 Allen H. Barton, *Communities in Disaster: A Sociological Analysis of Collective Stress Situations.* Garden City, N.Y.: Doubleday & Co., vii–xxxvii.

1963 Foreword to Hubert J. O'Gorman, *Lawyers and Matrimonial Cases: A Study of Informal Pressures in Private Professional Practice.* New York: The Free Press, vii–xiv.

1963 Foreword to Matilda White Riley, *Sociological Research.* 2 vols. New York: Harcourt Brace Jovanovich, xiii–xv.

1963 Foreword to Leila A. Sussmann, *Dear FDR: A Study of Political Letter-Writing.* Totowa, N.J.: The Bedminster Press, xiii–xxv.

1964 Introduction to Jacques Ellul. *The Technological Society.* New York: Alfred A. Knopf, v–viii.

1970 Introduction to Imogen Seger, *Knaurs Buch der Modernen Soziologie.* Munich and Berlin: Knaur, 7–10.
Translations: Italian, English, French.

1971 Foreword to Lewis A. Coser, *Masters of Sociological Thought.* New York: Harcourt Brace Jovanovich, vii–viii.

1975 Introduction to Julián Marías, *The Structure of Society.* University of Alabama Press. In press.

5. MISCELLANEOUS WRITINGS

1935 What Happens in the First Year After High School: Studies of the Graduating Classes since 1917 Show the Flux of Employment Conditions and the Trend in Higher Education. *Boston Evening Transcript Magazine,* July 20.

1936 Translation from the Italian: Corrado Gini. Real and Apparent Exceptions to the Uniformity of a Lower Natural Increase of the Upper Classes. *Rural Sociology* 1 (September), 257–80.

1936 Overview of German Journals of Sociology. *American Sociological Review* 1, 301.

1937 Translation from the Italian: Corrado Gini. Problems of the International Distribution of Population and Raw Materials. *Annals, American Academy of Political and Social Science* (January), 1–14.

1940 A Communication. *American Sociological Review* 5 (August), 647–48.

1941 Bibliography: Robert K. Merton. *Psychiatry* 4 (August), 503–04.

1946 The First Year's Work, 1945–6: An Interim Report of the Columbia-Lavanburg Researches on Human Relations in the Planned Community. June. Mimeographed.

1947 Should the Scientists Resist Military Intrusion? The Seven Propositions of Professor Ridenour. *American Scholar* (Summer), 356–57.

1948 What Do We Know about Prejudice? *University of Chicago Round Table,* no. 528, May 2.

1948 Why People Vote the Way They Do. *University of Chicago Round Table,* no. 551, 1–10.

1951 The American Soldier. *University of Chicago Round Table,* no. 692, July 1.

1952 An Horrific Caricature. *American Scholar* 21, 356–58.

1957 In Memory of Bernhard J. Stern. *Science and Society* 21, 1 (Winter), 7–9.

1967 A Mild Demurral. *American Sociological Review* 32 (August), 637.

1969 Foreword to a Preface for an Introduction to a Prolegomenon to a Discourse on a Certain Subject. *American Sociologist* 4 (May), 99.

1970 Thoughts on our Present Discontents. Commencement Address, Kalamazoo College, Michigan, June 14.

6. BOOK REVIEWS

1935   Collier, K. B. *Cosmogonies of Our Fathers. ISIS* 24, 167–68.

Homans, G. C. and C. P. Curtis. *An Introduction to Pareto. ISIS* 23, 295–96.

Huxley, Julian. *Science and Social Needs. ISIS* 24, 188–89.

Mead, G. H. *Mind, Self and Society, ISIS* 24, 189–91.

Usher, A. P. *A History of Mechanical Inventions. ISIS* 24, 177–80.

1936   Barnes, Harry Elmer. *The History of Western Civilization. ISIS* 25, 598–99.

Carritt, E. F. *Morals and Politics. ISIS* 25, 296–97.

Gilfillan, S. C. *The Sociology of Invention. ISIS* 25, 166–67.

Gini, Corrado. *Prime Linée di Patologia Economica. American Sociological Review* 1, 324–25.

Griffiths, O. M. *Religion and Learning. ISIS* 26, 237–39.

Gruenberg, B. C. *Science and the Public Mind. ISIS* 25, 273.

Jones, R. F. *Ancients and Moderns. ISIS* 26, 171–72.

Libby, M. S. *The Attitude of Voltaire to Magic and the Sciences. ISIS* 24, 442–44.

Lovejoy, Arthur O. and George Boas. *Primitivism and Related Ideas in Antiquity. American Sociological Review* 1, 156–57.

Marvin, F. S. *Old and New Thoughts on the Modern Study of History. ISIS* 25, 297.

Schuhl, Pierre-Maxime. *Essai sur la Formation de la Pensée Grecque. American Sociological Review* 1, 683–84.

Soddy, Frederick. *The Frustration of Science. ISIS* 25, 274.

Sonnabend, E. *Il Fattore Demografico nell'organizzazione Sociale dei Bantu. Rural Sociology* 1, 529–30.

1937   Cioli, Lionello. *Orientamenti e Svilluppi della Politica Economica. Rural Sociology* 2, 103–04.

Gini, Corrado. *Saggi di Demografia. Rural Sociology* 2, 107–09.

Revelli, Paolo. *La Densita della Popolazione nella Storia della Geografia. Rural Sociology* 2, 241–42.

1938   Bowman, Isaiah. *Limits of Land Settlement. ISIS* 29, 268.

Burn, A. R. *The World of Hesiod. American Sociological Review* 3, 304–05.

Clark, G. N. *Science and the Social Welfare in the Age of Newton. ISIS* 29, 119–21.

Factors Determining Human Behavior and *Authority and the Individual.* Harvard Tercentenary Vols. *ISIS* 28, 151–54.

George, W. H. *The Scientist in Action. ISIS* 29, 159.

Hellpach, Willy. *Einführung in die Völkerpsychologie. American Sociological Review* 3, 612.

Lynd, R. S. and H. M. Lynd. *Middletown in Transition. Rural Sociology* 3, 110–11.

Parsons, H. C. *A Puritan Outpost. Rural Sociology* 3, 110–11.

Schuhl, Pierre-Maxime. *Machinisme et Philosophie. ISIS* 29, 528.

Stern, B. J. *The Frustration of Technology. ISIS* 29, 567.

1939   Arnold, T. W. *The Folklore of Capitalism. ISIS* 30, 400–01.

Beloff, Max. *Public Order and Popular Disturbances. American Sociological Review* 4, 434.

Benson, Adolph B. and Naboth Hedin, eds. *Swedes in America. Rural Sociology* 4, 119.

Billington, R. A. *The Protestant Crusade 1800–1860. American Sociological Review* 4, 437.

Bready, J. Wesley. *England Before and After Wesley.* American Sociological Review 4, 437.

Brinkmann, Carl. *England seit 1815.* American Sociological Review 4, 433–34.

Coulton, C. G. *Social Life in Britain from the Conquest to the Reformation.* American Sociological Review 4, 434.

Dixon, R. A. and E. K. Eberhardt. *Economics and Cultural Change.* Annals, American Academy of Political and Social Science 201, 282.

Halbwachs, M., ed. *Annales Sociologiques, 1937.* American Sociological Review 4, 438.

Hall, Jerome. *Readings in Jurisprudence.* ISIS 31, 264.

Haller, William. *The Rise of Puritanism.* American Sociological Review 4, 436.

Hogben, Lancelot, ed. *Political Arithmetic.* ISIS 30, 555–57.

Katz, Daniel and R. L. Schanck. *Social Psychology.* ISIS 31, 265.

Kohn-Bramstedt, Ernest. *Aristocracy and the Middle Classes in Germany.* ISIS 30, 356.

Mayer-Daxlanden, Hans. *Immigrants: First Case-Story Book on Immigration and Naturalization.* Rural Sociology 4, 377.

Mumford, Lewis. *The Culture of Cities.* ISIS 30, 401.

Stonequist, Everett V. *The Marginal Man: A Study in Personality and Culture Conflict.* ISIS 30, 401.

Whitehead, T. N. *The Industrial Worker.* ISIS 30, 401.

Woodward, E. L. *The Age of Reform.* American Sociological Review 4, 433.

1940   Barnard, Chester I. *The Functions of the Executive.* ISIS 31, 584.

Bogardus, Emory S. *The Development of Social Thought.* American Journal of Sociology 46, 393–95.

Gini, Corrado et al. *I Contributi Italiani Progresso della Statistica.* ISIS 32, 469.

Hofstra, Sjoerd. *De Sociale Aspecten van Kennis en Wetenschap.* ISIS 31, 566.

Hooton, Ernest A. *Crime and the Man* and *The American Criminal: An Anthropological Study.* ISIS 32, 229–38.

Landis, Paul H. *Social Control.* American Journal of Sociology 45, 936.

Ludlum, David M. *Social Ferment in Vermont 1791–1850.* American Sociological Review 5, 272.

Lundberg, George A. *Foundations of Sociology.* ISIS 32, 481.

Mead, George H. *The Philosophy of the Act.* ISIS 31, 482–83.

Miller, Perry. *The New England Mind.* ISIS 32, 427, and American Sociological Review 5, 271.

Panunzio, Constantine M. *Major Social Institutions.* Annals, American Academy of Political and Social Science 208, 240–41.

Robbins, Lionel. *The Economic Basis of Class Conflict.* ISIS 32, 482.

Ross, E. J. *Fundamental Sociology.* American Journal of Sociology 45, 937.

Watson, David. *Scientists Are Human.* ISIS 31, 466–67.

1941   Barnes, Harry E., Howard Becker, and Frances B. Becker, eds. *Contemporary Social Theory.* American Sociological Review 6, 282–86.

Bernal, J. D. *The Social Function of Science.* American Journal of Sociology 46, 622–23.

Creedy, F. *Human Nature Writ Large.* American Journal of Sociology 47, 127.

Doob, Leonard W. *The Plans of Men.* ISIS 33, 413.

Haring, Douglas G. and Mary E. Johnson. *Order and Possibility in Social Life.* Annals, American Academy of Political and Social Science 214, 245–46.

Jung, Carl G. *The Integration of the Personality.* American Sociological Review 6, 289–90.

Smith, T. V. and Marjorie Grene. *From Descartes to Kant.* ISIS 33, 416.

Stern, B. J. *Society and Medical Progress. Science and Society* 5, 390–92.

Thompson, James W. *The Medieval Library. American Journal of Sociology* 46, 764.

Toynbee, Arnold J. *A Study of History. American Journal of Sociology* 47, 205–13.

Warner, W. L. and P. Lunt. *The Social Life of a Modern Community. Survey Graphic* 31, 438–39.

Wood, Ledger. *The Analysis of Knowledge. ISIS* 34, 73.

1943   Campbell, F. S. *Menace of the Herd. Political Science Quarterly* 59, 637–38.

Cargill, Oscar. *Intellectual America: Ideas on the March. American Sociological Review* 8, 227–28.

Meyer, Gladys. *Free Trade in Ideas. American Sociological Review* 8, 228–29.

Sington, D. and A. Weidenfeld. *The Goebbels Experiment. Journal of Legal and Political Sociology* 2, 173–74.

Warner, W. L. and P. S. Lunt. *The Status System of a Modern Community. Survey Midmonthly* 79, 191.

1945   Kardiner, Abram with Ralph Linton, Cora DuBois, and James West. *The Psychological Frontiers of Society. New York Times Book Review,* July 1, 4.

Kelsen, Hans. *Society and Nature: A Sociological Inquiry. Annals, American Academy of Political and Social Science* 239, 222–23.

Leighton, Alexander R. *The Governing of Men. New York Times Book Review,* July 22, 1, 14.

1946   Castiglioni, Arturo. *Adventures of the Mind. New York Times Book Review,* April 21, 6.

1948   Chapin, F. Stuart. *Experimental Designs in Sociological Research. United States Quarterly Book List* 4, 196.

Frank, Lawrence K. *Society as the Patient: Essays on Culture and Personality. United States Quarterly Book List* 4, 481–82.

Fromm, Erich. *Man for Himself. United States Quarterly Book List* 4, 194.

Rodnick, David. *Postwar Germans. United States Quarterly Book List* 4, 442–43.

Smith, B. L., H. D. Lasswell, and R. D. Casey. *Propaganda, Communication and Public Opinion. College and Research Libraries* 9, 372–73.

1949   Centers, Richard. *The Psychology of Social Classes: A Study of Class Consciousness. United States Quarterly Book List* 5, 238.

Stouffer, Samuel A. et al. *The American Soldier. United States Quarterly Book List* 5, 387–88.

1950   Hawley, Amos H. *Human Ecology: A Theory of Community Structure. United States Quarterly Book List* 6, 358–59.

Hovland, Carl I. et al. *Experiments on Mass Communication. United States Quarterly Book List* 6, 91–92.

Inkeles, Alex. *Public Opinion in Soviet Russia. United States Quarterly Book List* 6, 359–60.

Irion, Frederick C. *Public Opinion and Propaganda. United States Quarterly Book List* 6, 360.

1953   DeGrange, McQuilkin. *The Nature and Elements of Sociology. United States Quarterly Book List* 9, 463.

Wiener, Norbert. *Ex-Prodigy: My Childhood and Youth. United States Quarterly Book List* 9, 268–69.

1954   Festinger, Leon and Daniel Katz, eds. *Research Methods in the Behavioral Sciences. United States Quarterly Book List* 10, 102.

Riesman, David. *Individualism Reconsidered, and Other Essays. United States Quarterly Book List* 10, 557.

1955 Hyman, Herbert H. *Interviewing in Social Research*. United States Quarterly Book List 11, 250–51.

Towle, Charlotte. *The Learner in Education for the Professions*. United States Quarterly Book List 11, 374–75.

Usher, Abbott P. *A History of Mechanical Inventions*. rev. ed. United States Quarterly Book List 11, 149.

1956 Boek, W. E. and J. K. Boek. *Society and Health*. American Journal of Nursing 56, 720.

Park, Robert E. *Society*. United States Quarterly Book List 12, 86–87.

1959 Taton, R. *Reason and Change in Scientific Discovery*. American Sociological Review 24, 264.

1961 Marti-Ibanes, Felix, ed. *Henry E. Sigerist on the History of Medicine*. American Sociological Review 26, 287–88.

Roemer, M. I., ed. *Henry E. Sigerist on the Sociology of Medicine*. American Sociological Review 26, 287–88.

Winch, Peter. *The Idea of a Social Science and Its Relation to Philosophy*. ISIS 52, 596–99.

1968 Greenberg, Daniel S. *The Politics of Pure Science*. New York Times Book Review, October 6, 36.

Haskins, Caryl P. *The Search for Understanding*. Science 160, 640–41.

Watson, James D. *The Double Helix*. New York Times Book Review, February 25, 1.

1972 Hoffman, Banesh. *Albert Einstein: Creator and Rebel* (with Martin J. Klein). New York Times Book Review, November 5, pt. 1, 3, 39.

7. COMMENTARIES ON MERTON'S WORK

Abel, Theodore. *The Foundations of Sociological Theory*. New York: Random House, 1970, 170–72, 188–96.

Achim, Mihu. *Sociologia Americană a Grupurilor Mici*. Bucharest: Editura Politica, 1970, chap. 2.

Andreeva, Galina M. *Sovremnaia burzhuaznaia empiricheskaia sotsiologiia: kriticheskii ocherk* [Contemporary Bourgeois Empirical Sociology: A Critical Essay]. Moscow: Mysl', 1965.

Bakhitov, M.Sh. *Amerikanskaia funktsional'naia teoriia obshchestva* [American Functionalist Theory of Society]. Moscow: Znanie, 1962.

Barbano, Filippo. *Teoria e Ricerca nella Sociologia Contemporanea*. Milan: A. Giuffrè-Editore, 1955.

———. Teoria e metodo nell'indagine delle scienze sociali: introduzione a saggi di R. K. Merton e Talcott Parsons. In Angelo Pagani, ed. *Antologia di Scienze Sociali*. Vol. 1, *Teoria e Ricerca nelle Scienze Sociali*. Bologna: Società Editrice Il Mulino, 1960, chap. 1.

———. H. Marcuse, R. K. Merton et il Pensiero Critico: "Sociologia Negativa" e Sociologia Positiva. *Sociologia*, September 1967, 31–58.

———. Social Structures and Social Functions: the Emancipation of Structural Analysis in Sociology. *Inquiry* 11 (1968), 40–84.

———. L'Opera del Merton nella Sociologia Contemporanea (Introduction to R. K. Merton, *Teoria e Struttura Sociale*). Bologna: Il Mulino, 1959, ix–xxvi. R. K. Merton e la Analisi della Sociologia (Introduction to 2d ed., completely revised translation). 1966, vii–lviii. Le Teorie Sociologiche tra Storicità e Scienza (Introduction to 3d edition). 1971, vol. 1, vii–xxxiv.

Barnes, S. B. and R. G. A. Dolby. The Scientific Ethos: A Deviant Viewpoint. *European Journal of Sociology* 11 (1970), 1–25.

Berkhofer, Jr., Robert F. *A Behavioral Approach to Historical Analysis.* New York: Free Press, 1969, 193–98.

Bialyszewski, Henry. Functional Conception of Social Change. *Studia Socjologiczne* 37 (1970), 63–98.

Boskoff, Alvin. Functional Analysis as a Source of Theoretical Repertory and Research Tasks in the Study of Social Change. In G. K. Zollschan and W. Hirsch, eds. *Explorations in Social Change.* Boston: Houghton Mifflin Co., 1964, 213–43.

———. *Theory in American Sociology.* New York: Crowell, 1969.

Boudon, Raymond. Remarques sur la notion de fonction. *Revue Française de Sociologie* 8 (1967), 198–206.

———. Note sur la notion de theorie dans les sciences sociales. *Archives Européennes de Sociologie* 11 (1970), 201–51.

———. *The Uses of Structuralism.* London: Heinemann, 1971.

Buckley, Walter. Structural-Functional Analysis in Modern Sociology. In Howard Becker and Alvin Boskoff, eds. *Modern Sociological Theory.* New York: Dryden Press, 1967, 236–59.

Burstyn, Harold L. and Robert S. Hand. Puritanism and Science Reinterpreted. *Actes du 11ᵉ Congrès International d'Histoire des Sciences,* 139–43.

Carroll, James W. Merton's Thesis on English Science. *American Journal of Economics and Sociology* 13 (1954), 427–32.

Cernea, Stela. Noile Dimensiuni ale Functionalismului în Conceptia Sociologică a lui R. K. Merton. *Sinteze Sociologice: Structuralismul Functionalist în Sociologia Americană.* Bucharest: Editura Stiintifica, 1970, chap. 3, 137–95.

Clinard, Marshall B., ed. *Anomie and Deviant Behavior: A Discussion and Critique.* New York: The Free Press, 1964.

Cloward, Richard. Illegitimate Means, Anomie and Deviant Behavior. *American Sociological Review* 24 (1959), 164–76.

——— and Lloyd E. Ohlin. *Delinquency and Opportunity.* New York: The Free Press, 1960.

Cohen, Harry. Bureaucratic Flexibility: Some Comments on Robert Merton's "Bureaucratic Structure and Personality." *British Journal of Sociology* 21 (1970), 390–99

———. Pseudo-Gemeinschaft: A Problem of Modern Society. *Western Sociological Review* 5 (Summer 1974), 35–46.

Cohen, I. Bernard. Essay Review: *Science, Technology and Society in Seventeenth Century England. Scientific American* 228 (1973), 117–20.

Cole, Stephen. In Defense of the Sociology of Science: A Critique of A. R. Hall's "Merton Revisited." *G.S.S. Journal.* Columbia University Graduate Sociological Society, 1965, 30–38.

Crespi, Pietro. Robert K. Merton e la Sociologia Americana. *Il Pensiero Critico* 2 (1960), 1–11.

Crowther, J. G. *Science in Modern Society.* London: The Cresset Press, 1967, 290–99.

Current Biography. Robert K. Merton 26 (1965), 20–23.

Cuzzort, R. P. The Unanticipated Consequences of Human Actions: the Views of Robert King Merton. *Humanity and Modern Sociological Thought.* New York: Holt, Rinehart and Winston, 1969, chap. 4.

Demerath, Nicholas J. III. Synecdoche and Structural-Functionalism. In N. J. Demerath and R. A. Peterson, eds. *System, Change and Conflict.* New York: The Free Press, 1967, 501–18.

Deutsch, Morton and Robert M. Krauss. *Theories in Social Psychology.* New York: Basic Books, 1965, 174–76, 190–203.

Dolby, R. G. A. Sociology of Knowledge in Natural Science. *Science Studies* 1 (1971), 3–21.

Downey, K. J. Sociology and the Modern Scientific Revolution. *Sociological Quarterly* 8 (1967), 239–54.

Dubin, Robert. Deviant Behavior and Social Structure: Continuities in Social Theory. *American Sociological Review* 24 (1959), 147–64.

Elkins, Stanley and Eric McKitrick. *The Hofstadter Aegis*. New York: Alfred A. Knopf, 1974.

Ellemers, J. E. Enkele Kanttekeningen bij het Functiebegrip van Merton. *Sociologische Gids* 3 (1956), 168–73.

————. Misvattingen en Stereotypen over de Amerikaanse Sociologische Theorie. *Sociologische Gids* 8 (1961), 233–41.

————. Robert K. Merton. In L. Rademaker and E. Petersma, eds. *Hoofdfiguren uit de Sociologie: Modernen*. Utrecht-Antwerp: Het *Spectrum*, vol. 3, chap. 3, 39–61.

Fishbein, Martin. *A Perception of Outgroup Members: A Test of Merton's Reference Group Theory*. Urbana, Ill.: Dept. of Psychology, University of Illinois, Technical Report No. 17, August 1962.

Goddijn, H. P. M. Het Funktionalisme in de Sociologie. *Sociologische Gids* 8 (1961), 242–68.

————. *Het Funktionalisme in de Sociologie: Met Name in de Verenigde Staten*. Assen: Van Gorcum, 1963, chaps. 4, 5.

Hagstrom, Warren O. *The Scientific Community*. New York: Basic Books, 1965.

Hall, A. Rupert. Merton Revisited, or, Science and Society in the Seventeenth Century. *History of Science: An Annual Review*. Cambridge: W. Heffer, 1963, 2, 1–16.

Harary, Frank. Merton Revisited: A New Classification for Deviant Behavior. *American Sociological Review* 31 (1966), 693–97.

Herpin, Nicolas. *Théorie et Expérience chez Robert K. Merton*. Paris: Sorbonne, 1967. Unpublished dissertation.

Heyt, Frisco D. and Karl-Dieter Opp. Eine Integrations-strategie und ihre Andwendung auf die Anomietheorie. *Mens en Maatschappij* 43 (1968), 72–99.

Hill, Robert B. *Merton's Role Types and Paradigm of Deviance*. New York: Columbia University, 1969. Unpublished dissertation.

Hinkle, Roscoe C. and Gisela J. Hinkle. *The Development of Modern Sociology*. New York: Random House, 1954.

Horowitz, I. L. Fuentes y Componentes del Analisis Funcional en Sociologia. In I. L. Horowitz, ed. *Problemas Metodologicos del Funcionalismo en las Ciencias Sociales. Cuadernos del Boletin del Instituto de Sociologia*. Universidad de Buenos Aires, 12, 1959, 297–305.

————. *Professing Sociology*. Chicago: Aldine Publishing Co., 1968, 190–97.

Hunt, Morton M. How Does It Come to Be So? Profile of Robert K. Merton. *New Yorker* 36 (January 28, 1961), 39–63.

Isajiw, Wsevolod W. *Causation and Functionalism in Sociology*. London: Routledge & Kegan Paul, 1968, chap. 3.

Kanamaru, Yoshio. Anticipation, Action and Consequences on the Basis of Robert K. Merton's "Unanticipated Consequences. . . ." *Japanese Sociological Review* 21 (1970), 2–19.

Kearney, H. F. Merton Revisited. *Science Studies* 3 (1973), 72–78.

King, M. D. Reason, Tradition and the Progressiveness of Science. *History and Theory: Studies in the Philosophy of History* 10 (1971), 3–32.

Kling, Alain J. Homophilie des Valeurs ou Influence par Sympathie? Une Experimentation. *Revue Française de Sociologie* 8 (1967), 189–97.

Kuhn, Thomas S. The History of Science. *International Encyclopedia of the Social Sciences*. New York: Macmillan, 1968, vol. 14, 74–83 ("The Merton Thesis," 79–82).

Landau, Martin. On the Use of Functional Analysis in American Science. *Social Research* 35 (1968), 48–75.

———. *Political Theory and Political Science.* New York: Macmillan, 1972.

Lehman, Hugh. R. K. Merton's Concepts of Function and Functionalism. *Inquiry* 9 (1966), 274–83.

Lepenies, Wolf. Melancholie als Unordnung bei R. K. Merton. *Melancholie und Gesellschaft.* Frankfurt am Main: Suhrkamp Verlag, 1969.

Loomis, Charles P. and Zona K. Loomis. *Modern Social Theories.* 2d ed. New York: D. Van Nostrand, 1965, chap. 5, 246–326.

Madge, John. *The Origins of Scientific Sociology.* New York: The Free Press, 1962.

Maisonneuve, J. *Psycho-Sociologie des Affinités.* Paris: Presses Universitaires de France, 1966, 270–75, 282–87.

Manis, Jerome C. and Bernard N. Meltzer. Blumer and Merton: Social Roles and Sociological Theories. *Sociological Focus* 7 (1974), 1–14.

March, James G. and Herbert A. Simon. *Organizations.* New York: John Wiley & Sons, 1958, 37–47.

Martindale, Don. *Nature and Types of Sociological Theory.* Boston: Houghton Mifflin Co., 1960, 425–27, 471–76.

———. Limits of and Alternatives to Functionalism in Sociology. In Don Martindale, ed. *Functionalism in the Social Sciences.* Philadelphia: American Academy of Political and Social Science, monograph 5 (February 1965), 144–62.

Martínez-Ríos, Jorge. Análisis Functional de la "Guelaguetza Agricola": Una Prueba Empírica del Paradigma de Robert K. Merton. *Revista Mexicana de Sociologia* 26 (1964), 81–125.

Matza, David. *Becoming Deviant.* Englewood Cliffs, N.J.: Prentice-Hall, 1969, 57–62, 96–99.

McKitrick, Eric. Study of Corruption. *Political Science Quarterly* 72 (1957), 502–14.

Mitroff, Ian I. *The Subjective Side of Science.* New York: Elsevier, 1974.

———. Norms and Counter-Norms in a Select Group of the Apollo Moon Scientists: A Case Study of the Ambivalence of Scientists. *American Sociological Review* 39 (1974), 579–95.

Mizruchi, Ephraim H. Aspiration and Poverty: A Neglected Aspect of Merton's "Anomie." *Success and Opportunity: A Study of Anomie.* New York: The Free Press, 1964.

Mori, Yoshio. Merton to Mills: Shakaigaku no Hensei [Merton and Mills: Reflections on Sociology]. *Jinbun Kenkyu* 11 (1960), 1031–51.

Mouzelis, Nicos P. *Organisation and Bureaucracy: An Analysis of Modern Theories.* London: Routledge & Kegan Paul, 1967, chap. 3.

Mulkay, Michael. Some Aspects of Cultural Growth in the Natural Sciences, *Social Research* 36 (1969), 22–52.

Mulkay, M. J. *Functionalism, Exchange and Theoretical Strategy.* London: Routledge & Kegan Paul, 1971, chap. 5.

Nagel, Ernest. A Formalization of Functionalism. In *Logic Without Metaphysics.* New York: The Free Press, 1956, 247–83.

Naka, Hisao. Sociology Today in Japan. Presented to the Massachusetts Sociological Association, November 13, 1971.

Nelson, Benjamin. Review Essay: *Science, Technology and Society in Seventeenth Century England. American Journal of Sociology* 78 (1972), 223–31.

Novikov, Nikolai V. *Kritika Sovremennoi Burzhuaznoi "Nauki o Sotsial'nom Povedenii"* [A Critique of Contemporary Bourgeois "Science of Social Behavior"]. Moscow: Vysshaia shkola, 1966.

519

Opp, Karl-Dieter. Theories of the Middle Range as a Strategy of the Construction of a General Sociological Theory: A Critique of a Sociological Dogma. *Quality and Quantity,* 1970, bd. 4.

——. *Abweichendes Verhalten und Gesellschaftsstruktur.* Darmstadt: Hermann Luchterhand Verlag, 1974, 123–56.

Oromaner, Mark J. The Most Cited Sociologists: An Analysis of Introductory Text Citations. *American Sociologist* 3 (1968), 124–26.

——. Comparison of Influentials in Contemporary American and British Sociology. *British Journal of Sociology* 3 (1970), 324–32.

——. The Structure of Influence in Contemporary Academic Sociology. *American Sociologist* 7 (1972), 11–13.

Osipov, Gennadii V. *Sovremennaia Burzhuaznaia Sotsiologiia. Kriticheskii Ocherk* [Contemporary Bourgeois Sociology: A Critical Essay]. Moscow: Nauka, 1964.

Pagani, Angelo. Sulla Dinamica della Burocrazia Pubblica: Weber, Merton, Blau. *Notiziario di Sociologia* 2 (1959), 3–8.

Park, Peter. *Sociology Tomorrow: An Evaluation of Sociological Theories in Terms of Science.* New York: Pegasus, 1969, chap. 11.

Pedersen, Eigil and Kenneth Etheridge. Conformist and Deviant Behaviour in High School: The Merton Typology Adapted to an Educational Context. *Canadian Review of Sociology and Anthropology* 7 (1970), 70–82.

Phillips, Derek L. Epistemology and the Sociology of Knowledge: The Contributions of Mannheim, Mills and Merton. *Theory and Society* 1 (1974), 59–88.

Poviña, Alfredo. *Sociologia 70.* Cordoba, Argentina, 1971, chap. 7.

Ramsøy, Natalie Rogoff. Merton og Funksjonalismen. In N. R. Ramsøy, B. A. Sørensen, et al. *Sosiologiens Klassikere.* Oslo: J. W. Cappelens Forlage, 1971, 74–85.

Rodriguez, Garcia Fausto E. Notas Metodologicas sobre Merton. *Revista Mexicana de Sociologia* 29 (1967), 387–406.

Rogers, Everett M. and Dilip B. Bhowmik. Homophily-Heterophily: Relational Concept for Communication. *Public Opinion Quarterly* 34 (Winter 1970–71), 523–38.

Rose, Arnold M. On Merton's Neo-Functionalism. *Alpha Kappa Deltan: A Sociological Journal* (Spring 1960), 14–17.

Rose, Gordon. Anomie and Deviation: A Conceptual Framework for Empirical Studies. *British Journal of Sociology* 17 (1966), 29–45.

Rose, Jerry D. The Moderate Approach to Sociological Functionalism. *Acta Sociologica* 13 (1970), 127–31.

Santucci, Antonio. Il problema dell'Analisi Funzionale nella Teoria Sociologica di R. K. Merton. *Quaderni di Sociologia* 23 (Winter 1957), 3–21.

Schweiker, William. Status Consistency and Merton's Modes of Individual Adaptation. *Sociological Quarterly* 9 (1968), 531–39.

Scott, Marvin B. and Roy Turner. Weber and the Anomic Theory of Deviance. *Sociological Quarterly* 6 (1965), 233–40.

Semenov, Vadim S. Merton, Robert King. In F. V. Konstantinov et al., *Filosofskaia Entsiklopediia.* Moscow: Sovetskaia entsiklopediia, 1964, vol. 3, 398–99.

Silverman, David. *The Theory of Organisations.* New York: Basic Books, 1971.

Smith, Dusky Lee. Robert King Merton: From Middle Range to Middle Road. *Catalyst* 2 (1966), 11–40.

Solow, Robert M. Merton's *Science, Technology and Society in 17th Century England.* Harvard University, January 14, 1942. Unpublished manuscript.

Sorokin, P. A. *Sociological Theories of Today.* New York: Harper & Row, 1966, 445–56.

Sprott, W. J. H. *Science and Social Action*. New York: The Free Press, 1954. 113–22.

Statera, Gianni. La Sociologia della Scienza di Robert K. Merton. *La Critica Sociologica* 3 (1964), 19–33.

——. La Sociologia come Scienza Critica. *Problemi* 2 (1968), 315–22.

Storer, Norman. *The Social System of Science*. New York: Holt, Rinehart and Winston, 1966, chaps. 1, 5.

——. Chapter introductions to Robert K. Merton, *The Sociology of Science*. Chicago: The University of Chicago Press, 1973, pp. xi–xxxi, 3–6, 139–41, 223–27, 281–85, 415–18.

Swiggum, Shirley E. Toward an Extension of Merton's Anomie Theory. *Proceedings, Southwestern Sociological Association* 19 (1969), 55–59.

Sztompka, Piotr. Statczna: Dynamiczna wersja Funkcjonalizmu. *Studia Socjologiczne* 4 (1969), 157–91.

——. The Logic of Functional Analysis in Sociology and Social Anthropology. *Quality and Quantity* 5 (1971), 369–88.

——. *System and Function*. New York: Academic Press, 1974.

Tallman, Irving. Adaptation to Blocked Opportunity: An Experimental Study. *Sociometry* 29 (1966), 121–34.

——. Balance Principle and Normative Discrepancy. *Human Relations* 20 (1967), 341–55.

Taylor, Ian, Paul Walton, and Jock Young. *The New Criminology*. London: Routledge & Kegan Paul, 1973, 91–110.

Taylor, Laurie. *Deviance and Society*. London: Michael Joseph, 1971, 138–54.

Tenbruck, Friedrich H. Max Weber and the Sociology of Science: A Case Reopened. *Zeitschrift für Soziologie* 3 (1974), 312–20.

Thurlings, J. M. G. Merton, Gouldner, en de "net balance" hypothese. *Sociologische Gids* 8 (1961), 82–90.

Timms, Noel. *A Sociological Approach to Social Problems*. London: Routledge & Kegan Paul, 1967, 24–31.

Turner, Jonathan H. *The Structure of Sociological Theory*. Homewood, Ill.: Dorsey Press, 1974, chap. 4.

Ugrinovich, D. M. Marksizm, Strukturalizm, Funktsionalizm. *Vestnik Moskovskogo Universiteta* 8 (1970), Philosophy, 42–52.

Wallace, Walter L., ed. *Sociological Theory*. Chicago: Aldine Press, 1969.

Wanderer, Jules J. An Empirical Study in the Sociology of Knowledge. *Sociological Inquiry* 39 (1969), 19–26.

Wells, Alan. Cleavage Lines for Divergence in Sociology. *Human Mosaic* 4 (1969), 79–90.

Westie, Frank R. Academic Expectations for Professional Immortality: A Study of Legitimation. *American Sociologist* 8 (1973), 19–32.

Yoshida, Tamito. The GNIV Model of Human Groups: A Systemic-Functional Analysis. *Japanese Sociological Review* 14 (1963), 42–73.

Young, Jock. New Directions in Sub-Cultural Theory. In John Rex, ed. *Approaches to Sociology: An Introduction to Major Trends in British Sociology*. London: Routledge & Kegan Paul, 1974, 160–86.

Young, Robert. The Historiographic and Ideological Contexts of the Nineteenth-Century Debate on Man's Place in Nature. In Mikuláš Teich and Robert Young, eds. *Changing Perspectives in the History of Science: Essays in Honour of Joseph Needham*. London: Heinemann, 1973, 344–438.

Zamfir, Catălăn. *Metoda Normativă în Psihosociologia Organizării*. Bucharest: Editura Stiintifică, 1972.

Zamoshkin, Iurii A. *Krizis Burzhuaznogo Individualizma i Lichnost'* [The Crisis of Bourgeois Individualism and Personality]. Moscow: Znanie, 1966.

Zdrawomyslow, Andrej G. On the Critique of Functionalism. *Studia Socjologiczne* 37 (1970), 53–62.

Zvorykin, Anatolii A. V poiskakh obshchesotsiologicheskoi teorii: o ee kriteriiakh (kritika teorii R. Mertona i T. Parsonsa) [In Search of General Sociological Theory: Concerning Its Criteria (A Critique of the Theories of R. Merton and T. Parsons)]. In F. V. Konstantinov et al. *Marksistskaia i Burzhuaznaia Sotsiologiia Segodnia.* Moscow: Nauka, 1964, 327–40.

Index

INDEX

525

A 5
B 6
C 7
D 8
E 9
F 0
G 1
H 2
I 3
J 4